History of the
Southern Yacht Club

This watercolor of the first Southern Yacht Club was done by Selina E. Bres Gregory, mother of New Orleans's famed sculptress, Angela Gregory. Mrs. Gregory painted this picture while a student at Newcomb College in 1897. Photo by Rufus Alldredge, Jr.

History of the Southern Yacht Club

Flora K. Scheib

A FIREBIRD PRESS BOOK

Gretna 2000

Copyright © 1986
By Flora K. Scheib
All rights reserved

Manufactured in the United States of America

Published by Pelican Publishing Company, Inc.
1000 Burmaster Street, Gretna, Louisiana 70053

*I dedicate this book to
Jack, my late husband and skipper*

The old SYC had been enlarged over the years since it was erected in 1878, but the pilings had deteriorated and the building condemned in 1898.

Contents

Preface		xi
Chapter I	1849–1953	1
Chapter II	1854–1860	17
Chapter III	1860–1877	21
Chapter IV	1878–1884	25
Chapter V	1884–1894	37
Chapter VI	1895–1900	53
Chapter VII	1901–1904	61
Chapter VIII	1905–1909	87
Chapter IX	1910–1916	95
Chapter X	1917–1920	105
Chapter XI	1921–1925	129
Chapter XII	1926–1929	163
Chapter XIII	1930–1938	195
Chapter XIV	1939–1944	221
Chapter XV	1945–1949	235
Chapter XVI	1950–1955	249
Chapter XVII	1956–1961	271
Chapter XVIII	1962–1965	295
Chapter XIX	1966–1971	313
Chapter XX	1972–1977	349
Chapter XXI	1978–1981	369
Chapter XXII	1982–1986	385
Chapter XXIII	Yacht Clubs of Alabama	425
Chapter XXIV	Yacht Clubs of Florida	439
Chapter XXV	Yacht Clubs of Louisiana	453
Chapter XXVI	Yacht Clubs of Mississippi	461
Chapter XXVII	Yacht Clubs of Texas	493
Appendix		501
Index		507

This is a copy of the original minutes of the Southern Yacht Club's first meeting, held in Pass Christian, Mississippi, on July 21, 1849.

—— On motion of J.B. Walton the club adopted the name of "Southern Yacht Club".

—— On motion a committee of seven were appointed by the Prest. to draft laws, rules, regulations &c, for the governance of the club. The President appointed Messrs. H. Foseman, L. M. Herman, H. E. Lawrence, Thos Byrne, Geo. Engelhart, H. Rareshide & J.B. Walton.

—— On motion the President, Dr. Robb & Mortimer Turner were added to the Committee. On motion the above Committee were allowed thirty days to report in.

—— On motion Mr. H. R. W. Hill was unanimously elected an Honorary member of the club, & the Secy was instructed to notify him of his election.

—— The Secy was instructed to notify all those names had been placed on the list of members, requesting them to advise at an early day whether it was agreeable to them.

—— On motion adjourned to meet on Monday 23rd at 11 o'C. a.m.

Approved —
James H. Behan P.

T. O. Bifon
Secy

The West End is a scene from West End Park on Lake Pontchartrain showing hotels and restaurant (circa 1880).

The West End amusement park's roller coaster was positioned close to the entrance of the Southern Yacht Club (circa 1880).

Preface

The Southern Yacht Club on the south shore of Lake Pontchartrain in New Orleans, Louisiana is as traditional as the city's Mardi Gras. The club's site has been a landmark for as long as Mardi Gras has been an annual celebration there. *The History of the Southern Yacht Club* is an in-depth study that chronicles the life of this 137-year-old club, and the story also extends into the glorious past of the many other yacht clubs along the Gulf Coast from Texas to Florida. Nurturing these smaller neighboring clubs for nearly fourteen decades, the Southern Yacht Club became recognized as the patriarch of yachting in the South.

Founded in 1849 at a meeting held in the Montgomery Hotel at Pass Christian, Mississippi, the Southern Yacht Club (SYC) is the second oldest yacht club in the United States. It was organized four years after the New York Yacht Club's founding in 1844 (Encyclopedia Britannica, 1968, "Yachting," p. 589).

This book is a tribute to those yachtsmen who sacrificed their time and finances to keep yachting the "noblest of sports" despite insurmountable odds. During the Civil War years Admiral David Farragut ordered Lake Pontchartrain closed to all water traffic after the capture of New Orleans in 1862. In World Wars I and II yacht clubs and boats were confiscated by the government for military use. The SYC was converted into a hospital during the first world war, housing 2,555 returning convalescing soldiers, a remarkable service recording not one death. At the same time the SYC wives also contributed to the national cause by knitting socks and sweaters for servicemen and collecting donations for war bonds and the Belgian baby fund. In other years sailboat races were cancelled because of yellow fever and cholera epidemics, when thousands in this area lost their lives. Later, obstacles to the sport of sailing were the stock market crash and its ensuing Great Depression, which brought bankruptcy to the SYC and a drop in membership from 3,000 to 250. The patient, expert planning that solved many of these man-made and natural problems included several of the most skillful "tacks" in sailing history.

This history includes tales of many exciting races in "sandbaggers" and 21-footers and the Marine Marathon classic, as well as the tragic sinking of the *Nereus*. These events are vividly described by the "old salts" in the SYC monthly publication, the *Barometer*, which is freely quoted.

Long a regional social mecca, the Southern Yacht Club was the scene of many dances and parties of the "smart set" of New Orleans and of coastal families from as far away as Mobile, Alabama. Several great regatta parties are recalled, as they were popular affairs as early as the 1850s. Of particular interest was the "bloodless duel" on the grounds of the Grand Hotel in Point Clear, Alabama, fought in 1851 over the hand of a Southern belle at a regatta dance following the long-distance race from New Orleans to Mobile Bay.

An integral part in the life of the Southern Yacht Club has been its association with the other yacht clubs from Corpus Christi, Texas to Sarasota, Florida, all members of the Gulf Yachting Association which was formerly the Southern Gulf Coast Yachting Association organized in 1901. Competition among these clubs has produced many national, international, and world champions, two Olympic gold medal-winning teams, and crewmen in the America's Cup races. Combined with unique racing programs and ever-changing fleets of magnificent yachts, these yacht clubs have brought fame to the Gulf area, recognized today as one of the most outstanding yachting centers in the world.

Over the 137 years many devastating hurricanes and storms racked the coastline from Texas to Florida, furnishing tragic and frustrating chapters in this history. The 1969 hurricane, Camille, which was considered the worst ever to strike our shore, carried with it four yacht clubs, hundreds of lives, thousands of boats, and millions of dollars in property damage. "The South will rise again" has become an established slogan of the resident people along the southern rim of the United States. The battered and rebuilt coast has risen again and again to become the spawning ground for the many skillful champions that have been produced by the yacht clubs determined to continue sailboat racing.

Aside from historical facts about New Orleans and Lake Pontchartrain found in scores of books relating to the Crescent City, the history of the Southern Yacht Club was obtained from its own musty Minutes books which date from the first meeting held on July 21, 1849 and which have been continuously maintained to date. These original records, on sheets yellowed with age, were written in a beautiful

Spencerian style, a method sadly phased out by the advent of the typewriter. Other yacht clubs were born, died, and then were resurrected, as Southern survived with its original Minutes in its original location.

Many interesting stories for this book were found in the SYC's monthly publications, the *Barometer* and the *Tell-Tale*, as well as several nautical magazines. The editors and writers for the SYC were all recognized journalists of professional status.

I wish to thank the members of the Fourth Estate. Newspaper articles about sailboat races were very dramatically described when writers covered this new sport in the early years, actually a few years after *The Picayune* was founded. All Southern newspapers were given credit for the popularization of yachting, especially its revival three times after three wars had reduced the sport to a low ebb. Several sports writers were honored for their contributions. The Southern Yacht Club and the Gulf Yachting Association made them honorary members in appreciation of their coverage.

I am grateful to the many friends who loaned their scrapbooks and pictures. The well-known New Orleans sculptress, Angela Gregory, generously submitted one of the most valuable paintings of the Southern Yacht Club as it appeared in 1896, shortly before it was demolished. The work had been executed by Miss Gregory's mother, formerly Selina E. Bres of Newcomb College in New Orleans at that time. Also the family of Charles Byrne who reside in San Diego, California, have in their possession the oldest SYC trophy, which had been won by Thomas Byrne in the very first SYC regatta held in 1849. Another member of the Byrne family, Mrs. Kenneth Shelton of Galveston, Texas, owns the club's second oldest trophy, which had been won by Thomas Byrne in 1853. Stunning photographs of these treasures have been supplied by the Byrne family.

Of inestimable value was the counseling I received from the late Leonard Huber, the widely recognized historian, author, and co-author of many books and publications on the history of New Orleans. His was heartening encouragement, for he looked over my notes and praised the idea of a sailing history in the South as a unique and timely project. I cherish the recollection of a delightful afternoon spent with Mr. Huber when he joined me at Miss Gregory's home on Pine Street to identify her mother's painting, and to discuss some of my writing ideas. Former SYC Commodore Nathaniel C. Curtis was a fourth guest that day, enthusiastic also as one of New Orleans's history-oriented architects, and also noted as the commodore responsible for developing the club's effective displays of trophies and framed pictures of historical boats and memorabilia.

After my husband's death in 1980, it was very difficult to continue with my manuscript, which I had started some twenty years before when we had delved together into his massive collection of newspaper clippings, souvenir programs, and other interesting yachting memorabilia in order to cover the history of a club that was so dear to our hearts, the Southern Yacht Club.

One of my early professional contacts was with Lily Jackson around the year 1978. Lily is a popular feature writer for *The Times-Picayune/The States-Item* newspaper. Her encouragement helped me to venture into a field totally foreign to my limited experience of writing for local magazines and yacht club publications. Next, I spoke with Gordon Gsell, a member of the SYC and a good skipper who was also a journalist and a staff reporter for *The Times-Picayune/The States-Item.* Many of his articles have appeared in *Yachting* and other nautical magazines. His approval of my manuscript was of prime importance to me because he related to the times and races referred to in my book. He introduced me to John Korbel of John Korbel Video Enterprises, Inc., whose direction and consultation were very valuable.

To go forward, I was most fortunate to find Cora Payzant, a friend, a SYC member of long standing, and a skipperette. Her other qualifications made it complete, as she was a graduate of Tulane University, with a B. A. in Journalism, and she had been a reporter for the *New Orleans Item.* Cora has spent the past four years agonizing with me over sections of my manuscript. Without her support and patience and the understanding of her SYC skipper husband, Dr. Arthur Payzant, this book may have settled down in Davy Jones' locker.

Last but not least, I am grateful to my son and two daughters who were supportive at all times. They were the reason I had to complete the "labor of love" begun by their father and me long, long ago.

History of the
Southern Yacht Club

This historic silver pitcher was won by Thomas Byrne in Coralie in the first SYC regatta held on August 6, 1849, in Pass Christian, Mississippi, and is in the possession of the descendants of Thomas Byrne living in San Diego, California. Photo by Wanda Tritton Robin.

The first Gold Cup challenge race was won by John G. Robinson's Pilgrim on September 18, 1849. Only winners of previous races were allowed to participate.

CHAPTER I

1849–1853

PRESIDENTS	TERMS
J. W. Behan	1849
T. L. Dabney	1850–51
Harry W. Hill	1852
W. E. Leverich	1852–53

THE EARLY YEARS OF YACHTING

A nation that is today the dominant force in world affairs was but an infant republic still struggling for survival in 1849. And yet to those Americans who lived in the mid-nineteenth century, it was the age of miracles. Great things were brought into being. The telegraph, steam trains, steamboats, and steamships thrilled the imagination. The California gold rush was on; Indians and buffalo trod the trackless plains west of the Mississippi. Zachary Taylor, a Southerner, the twelfth president of the United States, had just been inaugurated as chief executive. Disagreements in Congress over the balance of free states and slave states were increasing; however, the impending conflict between the North and the South seemed to have little effect on life in New Orleans.

Steam vessels were beginning to appear on the Seven Seas in 1849, but "sails" were still supreme. Tall ships, staunch Yankee clippers, and American frigates were seen skimming over oceans, lakes and rivers.

The South was considered the wealthiest section of the country in the 1840s and 1850s. It was the time when cotton was king and New Orleans rivaled New York as a port and banking center. Money was plentiful and everyone was gainfully employed in commerce, industry or agriculture.

In the New York area, many types of boats were being built by the prominent yachtsman John C. Stevens and his brother, Edwin A. Stevens. It was aboard one of their yachts, *Gimcrack*, a 49-foot waterline schooner built in 1844, that the New York Yacht Club was organized on June 30, 1844.

New Orleans businessmen traveling back and forth from New York and Boston, carrying on the economic growth of the South, realized how increasingly popular yachting had become and that the recently organized New York Yacht Club was flourishing since its founding. They were aware that in addition to pleasure sailing, the growth and development of the South and particularly New Orleans, which was already the nation's second largest seaport, would be greatly enhanced with the promotion of a yachting center in this area. The prospects looked very good: New Orleans is blessed with one of the largest lakes in the United States, Lake Pontchartrain, 625 square miles, 40 miles long and 24 miles wide with an average depth of 12 to 15 feet, plus the waters of Mississippi Sound on the Gulf of Mexico, which nature had stocked with an abundant amount of fish.

Those infant, ante-bellum days of yachting were really the sport's hey-day in the South. Those were good old times when it is said there was plenty of money for everybody and it was considered the proper thing for young gentlemen to have a yacht, just as much as it was a matter of course for the young bloods of the time to have their horses, dogs, and guns.

Wealth, fashion, and the art of good living had made the Crescent City by far the most polished cosmopolitan center of the American continent. There were many racing yachts in the South. A regatta was reported held on the North shore of Lake Pontchartrain in the early 1840s. (The South shore was not conducive to racing because of the heavy traffic of commercial steamboats.) Along the Gulf Coast from Bay St. Louis, Mississippi to Mobile, Alabama sail boat races were held during the summer months. One regatta was reported in *The Daily Crescent* of July 23, 1849, p. 2, being held on July 21, 1849 at Pass Christian, Mississippi.

Because of the sizes and varieties of boats which had been brought down from the North, many controversies over race management had arisen and from this confusion surfaced the need for organizing a boat club. Of great assistance in the developing of a racing center were the suggestions from many fine young Southern gentlemen who were returning from schools in the North and from abroad with ideas they had obtained on their visits to the yachting centers of other places.

Many New Orleanians spent the hot summer months on the Gulf Coast with their families, and Pass Christian in Mississippi, just 65 miles out of New Orleans, was their favorite resort. It was during the summer season of 1849 that a group of vacationing yachtsmen from the Crescent City and other Gulf Coast areas met at the Montgomery Hotel in the Pass on July 21, 1849 and formed a boat club known as the Southern Yacht Club.

THE BIRTH OF THE SOUTHERN YACHT CLUB

An account of the first meeting of the Southern Yacht Club was found in an article written in 1892 by the Southern Yacht Club's Secretary, the journalist L. P. Sampsell:

"With all hands on board at the Montgomery Hotel in Pass Christian where the well-to-do citizens of New Orleans and other parts of the Gulf Coast gathered for fashionable entertainment, a group of businessmen associated with yachting in the Southland, held a meeting on the night of July 21, 1849 to form a 'boat club'.

"That evening sixty or more Southern gentlemen of the good old aristocratic and chivalrous school, bless them, sat down to dinner and over their cigars, 'the walnuts and the wine,' formed the 'Southern Yacht Club'. Many a brimming glass was quaffed that night by those jolly spirits of the long ago to 'Yachting, the noblest of sports'."

Following are the minutes of that historic meeting:

Pass Christian, Miss.
July 21, 1849

A meeting of gentlemen interested in boating on the lakeshore was called at Montgomery's Hotel, Pass Christian, for the purpose of organizing a boat club.

President: J. W. Behan, Thos. Kershaw, J. O. Nixon, Mortimer Turner, E. Jones McCall, J. B. Walton, L. S. Levy, M. Farrell, H. Fassman, A. B. Commack, H. E. Lawrence, J. B. Rathborne, John Hiddleston, S. F. Hermann, B. F. Simms, Jno. G. Robinson, R. H. Montgomery, H. Rareshide (Pres. Stingaree Club) and J. S. Dabney.

The names of the following gentlemen were added to the list of members by the parties whose names are attached:

Jas. Campbell of
   E. Pascagoula   by S. F. Hermann
Thos. Byrne of Biloxi   by J. O. Nixon

Jas. Robb of Pass Christian	by J. O. Nixon
Jno. U. Bell of Pass Christian	by J. W. Behan
Jno. Egerton of Pass Christian	by T. Kershaw
W. B. McCutcheon of Pass Christian	by H. E. Lawrence
Jno. W. Woodruffe of Pass Christian	by H. E. Lawrence
W. L. Balfour of Miss. City	by S. F. Hermann
Geo. Urquhart of Bay St. Louis	by S. F. Hermann

Mr. J. W. Behan of Pass Christian was duly elected President. Thos. Kershaw of Pass Christian, W. L. Balfour of Miss. City, Thos. Byrne of Biloxi, Jas. Campbell of E. Pascagoula, Geo. Urquhart of Bay St. Louis were duly elected Vice-Presidents.

Mr. J. O. Nixon of Pass Christian was duly elected Secretary.

On motion of J. B. Walton, the club adopted the name of *Southern Yacht Club*.

J. O. Nixon, Secretary

The name "Southern" was chosen because the club claimed members from a wide territory, including a great number of Southern cities.

The "objects of the association" were specified:

1. To improve the construction and speed of our boats.
2. To promote a good feeling among the members by friendly rivalry.
3. To secure a rational amusement during the summer months for ourselves and the residents of the shores of the Gulf.
4. To offer appropriate prizes to those who, by skill in sailing and construction of their boats, are able to excel.
5. To provide a fund by subscription from the members, and by the entrance fees to secure the above objects.

Membership dues were fixed at $10.00 per annum.

James W. Behan, the first president of the Southern Yacht Club, was a wealthy New Orleanian whose summer home was located in Pass Christian, Mississippi. Research in New Orleans directories and business publications of the time the Southern Yacht Club was founded indicates the vast majority of those responsible for the creation of this fine institution were men actively and prominently identified with the business life of the Southern metropolis. They were wealthy coffee merchants, coal merchants, cotton brokers, commission merchants, stockbrokers and bankers.

Many have wondered why a New Orleans yacht club should have been organized in a village on the Gulf Coast beyond the confines of the State of Louisiana. The explanation is now history.

In 1849, and for many years thereafter, New Orleans was not generally a healthful place during the hot summer months. The ships that came into New Orleans from the tropics brought along with their cargos a special kind of mosquito, a germ-bearer that created havoc through tragic yellow fever epidemics with mortality statistics too high to ascertain. It is easy to understand why the city's summertime action had for years occurred "across the lake." Thus it was that the lowly mosquito helped set the stage for the Southern Yacht Club's birth on the Gulf Coast shore, where boats were anchored ready for regattas.

To travel from New Orleans to Pass Christian in the year 1849, long before bridges or trestles spanned the Rigolets and Lake Pontchartrain, one had to board the only means of transportation eastward, lake steamers. The Great Mobile & New Orleans Mail, operating a line of packets between New Orleans and Mobile, stopped en route at Pass Christian, Bay St. Louis and other "watering holes" and handled much of the mail and passenger traffic between the Crescent City and New York. The greater part of a day was often required to make the trip.

During this period, a trip to New York was pointedly advertised by the stage coach company as being "safe and healthful" because the public knew that coach drivers who carried passengers through Alabama and Georgia stayed north of Florida as a safety precaution against warlike Seminoles ever on the lookout for unwary palefaces. Such were the pitfalls of vacation travel northward in 1849. Thus the prospect of frequenting nearby water resorts to watch colorful sailboat races was an appealing alternative welcomed by boating enthusiasts along the Mississippi Gulf Coast, as well as by pleasure-loving New Orleanians.

THE FIRST SYC ANNUAL REGATTA

The first annual regatta under the auspices of the Southern Yacht Club was held on August 6, 1849 off the pier in front of the Montgomery Hotel at Pass Christian, Mississippi. When word reached the news media about the regatta, *The Picayune* reported: "All eyes from Mobile to New Orleans are turned toward the Southern Yacht Club. The noble sport of yachting can be as successfully cultivated in our waters as in those of New York, Massachusetts and Narrangansett Bay. We have all the enterprise, all the wealth, all the gentlemanly feeling necessary.

"The first boat to arrive for the big event was the beautiful yacht 'Eliza Riddle' owned by H. Rareshide, the president of the Stingaree Club located in Mandeville on the north shore of Lake Pontchartrain. Moored at the wharf in front of the hotel, with his suite on board, President Rareshide was received by the venerable officers of his club. After an introduction to the masters, at which sundry bottles of Heidseich, Southside and Dickey Jones were discussed, the President returned to shore under the salute from the Long Tom of the yacht."

The style of today's sports writing is far different from its flowery beginnings. Sailboat racing, like journalism, was in its infancy when *The Picayune* reported:

> It was a gala day at the Pass. The race was watched with breathless interest and attended with a good deal of incident. The quiet harbor was thronged with boats, gay with streamers, and manned by athletic crews neatly attired in their simple uniforms and the Hotel had its full capacity of guests, among whom were a brilliant gathering of the fair sex from New Orleans and Mobile.
>
> The fleet was swelled by volunteer craft, which had not entered for the prize or were excluded by the rules. As they closed together in the sweep on passing the flag boat, stringing after each other with strained sheets and flowing sail, urged together at their utmost speed like fiery coursers rushing to the goal, the spectacle was extremely beautiful. Beyond that point, the scene assumed a different aspect and a new beauty.
>
> Dark clouds came up suddenly — the sky was overcast, a heavy squall struck the gay fleet, scattered it abroad, and summoned the combatants to an unexpected strife with the angry elements. Reefs were taken in but some in their eagerness to press on were overtaken before they had

made all secure, caught in the squall, lay broadside over. One was so long in righting that some of her companions, alarmed, were about running down wind to her relief, just as the buoyant craft rose from the immersion and pushed on bravely in the race. The gale scattered the boats widely.

The course was described: "Starting from the wharf of the Hotel to and around a Flag boat to be stationed one mile N.W. of the Cat Island Light House, thence around the Light Ship to the South mark — thence, Home, coming in from the West and between the Fishing Pier Head to Wharf of the Hotel, distance about 18 miles. The boats started at 37 min. past 12 o'clock."

All boats raced together, but handicaps were awarded on the basis of forty-five seconds per foot keel length. It was another anchor start as were all races in the old days, with not less than eighteen feet of cable out.

The official report of the Judges of the First Southern Yacht Club Regatta reads:

Rig	Name	Keel	Entered by	Hours	Place
Sloop	Undine	23.10	R. A. Heirn	4.01	1
"	Eliz. Riddle (Stingaree Club)	28.4	H. Rareshide	4.13	2
"	Coralie	25.2	Thos. Byrne	4.18	3
"	Pilgrim	24	J. G. Robinson	4.21	4
"	I. L. Titus	36	J. O. Nixon	4.23	5
"	Anna	30	M. Farrell	4.30	6
"	I. Mitchell	26	F. A. Lunsden	4.55	7
"	Rigoletto	20	Thos. Kershaw	4.36	8
"	Laura	20	G. A. Pynchon	4.43	9
"	R. Morris	-	W. B. Porter	4.46	10
Schooner	Eugenie	30	H. Fassman	4.47	11
Sloop	Harry Hill	19	J. O. Nixon	5.07	12
"	Rebecca	16	W. B. McCutcheon	5.09	13
"	Mary Baker	12.6	J. G. Robinson	5.21	14
Schooner	LaGonalouse	28	Sidney Story	-	15
Sloop	Virginia	-	J. G. Robinson	-	16
"	Cora	15	J. O. Nixon	-	17
"	Mary Ann	29	R. H. Montgomery	Dis.	18

The sloop *Undine* is listed as having crossed the finish line in first place. However, the *Coralie*, owned by Thomas Byrne, won the Hotel Pitcher on corrected time. This prized possession belongs to the great-grandson of Thomas Byrne, Charles A. Byrne of San Diego, California, who submitted the picture of this trophy, expertly photographed by Wanda Tritten Robin of San Diego, California.

Skippers were tough barnacles in those days, using a triangular course of eighteen miles for an afternoon of racing. They had no time limit and raced until midnight, if necessary. However, the race course was positioned between lighthouses and beacons.

FIRST SYC REGATTA PARTY AT PASS CHRISTIAN

Reported *The Daily Crescent*, August 8, 1849, p. 2, "Following the regatta, the spacious ballroom of the Montgomery Hotel was the scene of fashionable entertainment attracting the leading belles and beaux of New Orleans, Mobile and intermediate points. Chaperones were everywhere. The most formal introductions were necessary before a couple could even dance. A social dinner was held where there was, of course, wine, wit, mirth and music."

When dealing with parties, newspapers had to proceed with extreme caution. It was quite "au fait" to publish the glories of the ballroom, "to dilate upon the wistful looks and the pure, unalloyed loveliness of Southern femininity," but that was as far as an editor dared go. Even though she be the belle of the ball, it was not considered good form to put the name of an unmarried female in public print. And the cad who did so would have had at least one duel on his hands. One example of such reporting appeared in *The Picayune* when it went about as far as the law allowed in reporting a Pass Christian regatta dance in the manner of a crossword puzzle:

> Mobile was ably represented by Miss A_____N, a most charming young lady. Our city might well have been proud of her fair representatives, among them being: Miss G_____T, Miss M_____S, Miss L_____W, Miss D_____E, Miss Y_____R and several others.

Such were the social restrictions when the Southern Yacht Club and other yacht clubs entered the century's second half. Southern womanhood, in the days prior to the War between the States, occupied such a high pedestal as to make one wonder how mere man ever had enough temerity to hold a fair hand or propose marriage.

The novelty of the regatta was over, but such events took a fixed place among amusements on the coast. Hardly a week passed without one, and they were announced as the regular sports of the season at Pass Christian. "To SYC members we are indebted for the naturalization of these manly and healthful exercises," reported *The Daily Cres-*

cent of August 17, 1849.

THE LADIES OF PASS CHRISTIAN TROPHY

The excitement of the first Southern Yacht Club regatta prompted the ladies of Pass Christian to dedicate a silver pitcher to the Southern Yacht Club, to be known as the Ladies of Pass Christian Trophy and to be awarded to the winner of the second regatta, which was held on August 20, 1849. The first boat of the First Class (all boats over 26 ft. keel) would win the Ladies prize. The first boat of the Second Class (all boats from 20 to 26 ft. keel) would be entitled to the Hotel Pitcher, and the first boat of the Third Class (all boats under 20 ft. keel) would be entitled to the club prize. No boat was to receive more than one prize. Winning the Ladies of Pass Christian Trophy was the *John Pierce* owned by Mr. A. L. Saunders.

At a SYC meeting held the following day, August 21, 1849, it was ordered that the names of all the Pass Christian ladies be inscribed on their trophy as well as the name of the winning boat, *John Pierce*. Following is a list of those ladies:

Miss Marguerite Burthe
Mrs. V. Burthe
Mrs. Mary M. Hart
Mrs. H. R. W. Hill
Mrs. W. B. Knox
Mrs. A. Levy
Mrs. E. A. Levy
Mrs. A. G. Mayers
Mrs. E. A. McNeil

Miss M. Montgomery
Mrs. R. H. Montgomery
Mrs. E. Munroe
Miss Sarah Munroe
Mrs. J. O. Nixon
Mrs. H. D. Ogden
Mrs. L. D. Partee
Miss Ada Pierce
Miss C. Pierce

Miss Caroline Pierce
Miss Cora Pierce
Mrs. Thos. Randall
Mrs. A. L. Saunders
Mrs. C. Seviler
Mrs. Amenaide Simms
Mrs. M. K. Simms
Mrs. Julia Stewart
Mrs. A. W. Walker
Mrs. C. C. Warfield

An interesting story is told about this beautiful silver pitcher. It was lost and presumed to have been the victim of "Silver Spoon" Butler's passion for collecting silver during the Civil War days. (General Benjamin J. Butler is reported to have collected much of the silver left in homes in New Orleans after they were invaded or deserted, earning the title of "Silver Spoon" Butler.) The trophy was found in a New York pawn shop in the early thirties by a friend of

Commodore Garner H. Tullis of the Southern Yacht Club and sent to him as a gift. The Tullis family generously donated the pitcher to the SYC.

There were several SYC meetings held in the Montgomery Hotel during the racing season at which many resolutions were passed; for example, it was "Resolved that persons running boats be prohibited from betting on results. The club will do all it can to discontinue gambling among its members." Also, it was "Resolved that any boat belonging to a member of SYC shall be entitled to make a wreath in a corner of the club signal for every prize she takes."

A committee was appointed to draft a constitution for the Southern Yacht Club. The members were: J. A. Ameling of Bay St. Louis, Thomas Byrne of Biloxi, W. Foster of Pass Christian, J. O. Nixon of Southern and J. B. Todd of Mobile. Capt. Winslow Foster of Pass Christian was elected unanimously as the first Honorary member. It was voted that the next meeting be held in New Orleans in January 1850 and that all future meetings during the winter months be held in the Crescent city.

THE FIRST GOLD CUP CHALLENGE RACE

The final SYC regatta of that year was held on the Gulf Coast on September 18, 1849. The four entries were A. L. Saunders' *Undine*, Thomas Byrne's *Coralie*, J. A. Ameling's *Picayune*, and J. G. Robinson's *Pilgrim*. The trophy for this event was a gold cup beautifully engraved, which was won by the *Pilgrim*. The cup is known as the SYC Gold Challenge Cup. Only the winner of a race was permitted to sail for this trophy.

Louisiana History, the journal of the Louisiana Historical Society, recorded the advent of sailing sponsored by the newly created Southern Yacht Club: "Sailing became the passion of the 1849 season along the Gulf Coast. Ten regattas were held at Pass Christian, Biloxi, Bay St. Louis, and Mobile between August 6 and September 14. A lively rivalry arose between New Orleans boats like *Eliza Riddle, Coralie, Undine* (formerly a Mobile boat) and such Mobile and Pass Christian yachts as *Mary Ann, Hiern, Pilgrim,* and *Lama*." (Winter 1962 Vol. III, No. 1.)

THE FIRST SYC REGATTA
ON LAKE PONTCHARTRAIN

Continued *The Journal*:

> Naturally, the question arose, "Shall New Orleans have a regatta?" It was Dan Hickok of the Franklin House at West End who finally sponsored the first Southern Yacht Club regatta on Lake Pontchartrain. Offering the prizes himself, Hickok opened the race to every rig...from a man-of-war down to a sailing skiff.
>
> Held on September 21, 1849, Hickok's first regatta was the hit of New Orleans' summer season. The lakeshore was jammed hours before race time. The host of the Franklin served oysters, fish and crabs with champagne sauce to the spectators, while gentlemen in 'Turkish trousers,' white shirts, and straw hats thronged the bar to enjoy a mint julep or a sherry cobbler. Ladies rocked on the wide verandas or remained in the airy parlor, sipping iced lemonade or sangaree. Candidates were on hand to add a little spice to the mixture. A second race is reported to have been held on Lake Pontchartrain in October 1849.
>
> Excursion boats from the Mississippi resorts and from Lake Pontchartrain hotels followed the races, and large numbers of visitors attended the victory balls and soirees held in the evenings. Results of the races were closely followed by New Orleans newsmen, especially "Aquatic" of *The Daily Crescent*.

After the organization of the Southern Yacht Club, its members proceeded to improve the size of its fleet and quality of boats. Many large and famous schooners and sloops were purchased in Boston and New York and brought to these waters. Yachting continued to flourish and the fleet of yachts became quite large up to the time of the Civil War.

PRESIDENT T. L. DABNEY—1850-51

At the first Southern Yacht Club meeting to be held in New Orleans, in January 1850, T. L. Dabney of Pass Christian, one of the founders of the SYC, was elected the second president. Serving with him were Vice-Presidents James I. Day of New Orleans, J. B. Todd of Mobile, Alabama, and J. O. Nixon of Pass Christian, who was re-elected Secretary. At a later meeting it was resolved that the office of Secretary be combined with that of the Treasurer.

These early meetings were held in the Varieties Club or the Verandah Hotel on St. Charles Street in Parlors 5 and 7. In the latter building was founded the oldest carnival organization in New Orleans, the Mystic Krewe of Comus, in 1857. Another frequent gathering place was in the parlors of the old St. Charles Hotel, that grand old landmark which enjoyed worldwide recognition as the resort of planters and politicians, river men and sporting gentry before the war.

Again, *Louisiana History* records the early days of the SYC:

> Regattas held under Southern Yacht Club's rules were strictly amateur contests. Prizes were donated by the club out of membership funds and entrance fees or by hotel proprietors like Hickok or Montgomery. Silver plate was the usual trophy, ranging from $20 cups to pitchers and salvers valued over $200. Occasionally disputed contests in the regattas led to private challenges between owners, and the resulting races, run for high cash stakes, were always well attended.
>
> One of the objectives of the SYC had been to improve the construction of sailing craft. Many of the early "yachts" were merely glorified "fishing smacks." The first Pontchartrain regattas were "for anything that carries sail," but soon this was restricted to vessels under 15 tons, carrying fore and aft sails, but not luggers and steamboats.
>
> Except for an occasional open race, entrants were usually grouped in three classes, first class, 28 feet or more; second class, 22 to 28 feet; and third class, 15 to 22 feet. *Eliza Riddle*, *Coralie*, and *Undine*, all typical first class boats, were of ten tons displacement and the champions of many early regattas.
>
> By 1850 there was "an evident improvement in the style of the craft" and there was "more of a uniformity displayed in the dress of the crew of the different vessels." Yachting on the lake was becoming more refined. In 1850, regattas at Pontchartrain, Pass Christian, Mobile and Point Clear drew thousands of spectators and the best of competitors. Many yachts were locally built in Algiers, New Orleans or Mobile, Alabama, and a lively competition developed between the latter two.

THE FIRST LONG-DISTANCE RACE TO THE COAST

The new racing interest that had developed from the first regatta held on Lake Pontchartrain in September of 1849 carried over into the 1850 sailing season. This high spirit among skippers was evident when on July 4 the SYC fleet departed from West End on Lake Pontchartrain and raced to Pass Christian on the Gulf Coast, initiating what has become the oldest continuous yachting event in this hemisphere, the "race to the coast."

The Southern Yacht Club's minutes had this to say about the historic race: "At a meeting held on July 2, 1850 in Parlor 5 of the St. Charles Hotel, the sailing master of each yacht was notified to meet the judges in the Front Room of the Hickok Hotel at West End on the morning of the 4th of July.

"Mr. Hickok was authorized to charter the Lugger *Duke* to serve as a stake boat and to follow the regatta to the Pass, provided the *Duke* can be obtained for $25.00." Everything was ship-shape for the firing of the starting gun at 9 o'clock on the morning of July 4, 1850.

Conditions were not good for the start of such a race until the long wharf was completed at the mouth of the New Basin Canal at West End, where a good start would be possible. Another factor involved the finishing of a long pier by the Montgomery Hotel in Pass Christian where the race would terminate. With the completion of both of these projects, the race got under way.

The fleet consisted of the finest quality sloops and schooners of the day. The race was won by *Crocodile*. In second and third places were *Roger Stewart* and *Mischief*, respectively. There were twelve entries. The distance covered was 65 nautical miles in six hours and fifty minutes. Three more races were reportedly sponsored by Captain Hickok and held on Lake Pontchartrain in 1850.

SAILING AND ROWING
ON LAKE PONTCHARTRAIN

Organized rowing in New Orleans began at the lake long before organized yachting. As published by the Louisiana Historical Association in the book *Louisiana History*, records show that organized rowing began with the Wave Boat Club in the mid-1830s.

> The *Wave* which was a boat owned by the Wave Boat Club, was a clumsy six-oared craft forty feet in length, its sides flared out, the whole shell scraped thin to save weight. Rowing parties, accompanied by soft-cushioned ladies' barges, were often held by the club, but organized racing seems to have been secondary.
>
> A more competitive rowing group was organized in later years. In 1836 the Lady of the Lyon Boat Club was formed. By 1839 more clubs were founded citywide: The Algerine, Knickerbocker, Locofoco, Edwin Forrest, Washington and Creole Clubs. All were amateur clubs made up of young men of the 'upper class.' Their races were held on Lake Pontchartrain, Bayou St. John, Madisonville and in the Mississippi River between New Orleans and Algiers on the river's west bank.
>
> Disaster struck at the height of this boating craze when a Mississippi River flood in May 1844 destroyed most of the boat houses, carrying away boats, prizes and trophies. For the next eighteen years yachting was to hold the public fancy.

The Daily Crescent in 1850 reported that "of all the spectator sports popular in New Orleans, none save horse racing attracted as many viewers as the rowing and sailing regattas at the lake."

Transportation to these events was afforded by means of the New Basin Canal which extended for a distance of six miles from the lake through the upper part of the city, the town of Carrollton, and ended where is now located the Amtrak station. Passengers were carried by means of barges. This service began in 1840. These mule-drawn barges provided a leisurely ride to the lakefront from the Halfway House, which was a station located halfway to the lake, at the end of City Park Avenue near the cemeteries. The ride on these awning-covered barges cost 20¢; they were "commodious and desirable...pleasant cushioned seats." The hour's ride was made three times daily and six times on Sunday.

Another means of transportation came with the completion of the railroad line. The Jefferson & Lake Pontchartrain Railway Company in 1840 was chartered to build a line from the City of Carrollton to the lake. This project was started in 1851. The company was sold later to the New Orleans & Carrollton Railway Company and the line was completed in 1853. Powered by steam engine, horse and mule prior to electrification in 1898, this is the oldest continuous operating street railway line in the world. Today it is known as the St. Charles Streetcar Line.

There was also the old Pontchartrain Railroad, the terminus of which was at Milneburg, reported to be the first summer resort to be established on the lakefront. It is said that whenever the feeble engine of the locomotive Smokey Mary that ran on the tracks would break down, the crew would hoist sails and bring the little train gliding into 'port,' its sails flapping in the breeze.

ANTEBELLUM DAYS ON THE LAKEFRONT

The Pontchartrain lakefront became a very popular antebellum resort area after the building of the railroad between the city and the lake. The restaurants with their distinctive cuisine were popular places to dine and many visiting celebrities have written about their famous food. Jenny Lind, the famous opera singer, who in 1850 was a guest of the Baroness Pontalba, who commissioned the Pontalba apartments on Jackson Square, was enthralled with the cuisine at Boudro's, as was William Makepeace Thackeray, who immortalized Boudro's in *A Miss Bubble*: "At which comfortable tavern on Pontchartrain we had a bouillabaisse than which a better was never eaten at Marseilles...."

Resorts of almost equal popularity developed concurrently 24 miles across Lake Pontchartrain along the northern shore of the lake, centered mostly in the towns of Mandeville and Madisonville, where regattas were held in the 1840s.

The racing season of 1851 on Lake Pontchartrain witnessed more boats participating in regattas under the leadership of President T. L. Dabney who was reelected for the year 1851 with a few new officers: Vice-Presidents, Edmund McIlhenny of New Orleans, C. C. Williams of Pass Christian, Thomas Byrne from Biloxi and H. Rareshide of Mandeville, Secretary-Treasurer.

PRESIDENT HARRY W. HILL—1852 (Died in office)
PRESIDENT W. E. LEVERICH—1852-1853

When the Southern Yacht Club returned to its annual meeting in 1852, elected to office as president was Harry W. Hill. Unfortunately, the new president was stricken ill a few months after his election and died. Vice-president W. E. Leverich was unanimously elected to replace Hill for the year 1852. Replacing Leverich was Edmund McIlhenny. Also reelected as vice-presidents were Thomas Byrne of Biloxi and J. B. Todd of Mobile. After one year's absence, J. O. Nixon returned as secretary-treasurer.

There was much action on Lake Pontchartrain and along the Gulf Coast during the racing season of 1852. The third annual long distance race from West End to Pass Christian was extended to Point Clear on Mobile Bay in Alabama. There were many entries in this popular event, which was not without incident. As the boats entered Mobile Bay heading for the finish line at Battles Creek Wharf at Point Clear, a storm slammed the coast and tragedy struck when a boom from one of the yachts knocked a crewman into the water. Before help could reach him, the young man drowned.

A DUEL AT DAWN FOLLOWS
REGATTA PARTY AT GRAND HOTEL

Another incident occurred which was potentially as tragic. A New Orleans gallant and his Mobile rival became embroiled in an "affair of honor" at the dance in the Grand Hotel following the race. Reported *The Picayune*:

An unpleasant affair between two gentlemen occurred at the hotel, which, it is said, will lead to a duel with pistols at dawn. The two gentlemen were escorting a young lady to the tea table when one of them, apparently out-rivaling the other, was told that he was acting impertinently. A slap in the face by the New Orleans gentleman immediately followed.

It later developed that the matter was settled, bloodlessly, at the required fifteen paces. The Mobilian's pistol snapped and failed to fire. The Orleanian fired but missed. Their seconds then intervened, both sides freely admitting that their honor had been fully and completely satisfied.

At dinner that evening at the Point Clear Hotel, interspersed with much vintage champagne, an entente cordiale prompted a toast and a promise to meet again at the regatta next year.

And that's how it was with gentlemen sailors in the old South—formal, maybe, but never dull.

YELLOW FEVER EPIDEMIC CANCELS RACES

At the SYC annual meeting of 1853, the entire board of directors and flag officers was reelected. The sailing season was marred by another yellow fever epidemic. However, before the outbreak, the long distance race was held in July and was won by Thomas Byrne in his new craft *Edith*. See the picture showing the silver cup that was won by the *Edith* presented by the Ocean Springs Yacht Club for this race in 1853. This photograph was submitted by a great-granddaughter of Thomas Byrne, Mrs. Kenneth Shelton, who resides in Galveston, Texas and is the owner of this trophy.

Thousands of inhabitants perished in the 1853 yellow fever epidemic which was considered the most severe in the history of New Orleans. Intermittently, until 1905, yellow fever epidemics continued to plague the local community, but none matched the staggering statistics of 1853 when it was reported that there were approximately 8,000 deaths. Naturally, a severe toll was taken on the sport of yachting because of this health hazard, but the club continued to operate.

CHAPTER II

1854–1860

COMMODORES	TERMS
Thomas Kershaw	1854–55
Sidney Story	1856–57
John G. Robinson	1858
Richard Milliken	1859
Ignatius Szymanske	1860

TITLE OF "PRESIDENT" CHANGED TO "COMMODORE" THOMAS KERSHAW—1854–1855

At the annual meeting held in 1854, Thomas Kershaw, one of the founders and one of the club's first vice-presidents, had the distinction of receiving the title of commodore. Until that time, commodore was strictly used in naval ranks. Commodore Kershaw's flagship was the racing sloop *Rigoletto*, which had sailed in the first Southern Yacht Club regatta held in 1849. His officers elected with him were vice-commodores Richard Milliken, C. M. Waterman, and Edmund McIlhenny. W. E. Leverich was made an Honorary Member.

It was reported by *The Daily Crescent* that only hotel-keepers on the lakefront were able to promote a Fourth of July race during the 1854 sailing season, because of the lack of interest. Gradually, spirits were lifted and the epidemic's survivors found waterfront activity a morale booster.

When Commodore Thomas Kershaw was reelected to office in 1855, his first vice-commodore was Sidney Story, his second vice-commodore was Edmund McIlhenny, his third vice-commodore was George May, secretary was H. Rareshide of Mandeville, and treasurer was J. O. Nixon. Judges were E. A. Fish and Charles Callahan.

COMMODORE SIDNEY STORY—1856-57

The new commodore for the year 1856 was Sidney Story. Serving with him were First Vice-Commodore George May, Second Vice-Commodore John G. Robinson, Third Vice-Commodore Thomas Byrne, Secretary Benjamin Story, and Treasurer J. O. Nixon. Judges were Alfred McIlhenny, Captain Whann, I. H. Bass, and W. G. Mullen.

Commodore Story was one of the most famous yachtsmen the South ever produced. His flagship was the well-known schooner *Lagonaluse*, which also sailed in the first SYC regatta in 1849.

It was recorded in the minutes of the 1856 annual meeting that "the opening regatta was forced to be postponed for want of stake boats. All of the craft used for buoys were out fishing."

The year 1857 brought the reelection of Commodore Sidney Story. Thomas Byrne was elected first vice-commodore; Louis Pident, second vice-commodore; R. G. Musgrove, third vice-commodore; Benjamin Story, Secretary; and J. O. Nixon, Treasurer. Members of the Board were as follows:

J. W. Balfour	P. B. Leeds
F. B. Brand	Thomas Lowell
W. B. Clarkson	S. McC. Montgomery
A. Commack	B. M. Pond
A. G. Green	J. W. Price
P. I. Hebert	Edward Pugh
Henry Huntington	W. Quintel
J. Lawton	Sidney Symanski
	George Whittemore

COMMODORE JOHN G. ROBINSON—1858

Commodore John G. Robinson, one of the original founders of the club, was elected to lead the SYC in 1858. He was an Englishman and ranked with the best sailors in this country. His flagship was the famous *Pilgrim*. The other flag officers were: Richard Milliken, first vice-commodore; H. McNeil Vance, second vice-commodore; Edmund McIlhenny, third vice-commodore; James McCloskey, secretary; and J. O. Nixon, treasurer. Members of the board were as follows:

George Binder	John McDonnell
R. H. Dix	G. S. Mandeville
St. Leon Dupre	R. Nixon
Robert Fish	Daniel Peters
Adam Giffen	

THE FIRST JUNIOR DIVISION OF SYC

Before he left office in 1858, Commodore Robinson inaugurated the first Junior Division of the Southern Yacht Club. These young men were permitted to sail boats 23 feet and under. During the first year twelve boats raced. This movement has proven to be the lifeblood of the Southern Yacht Club throughout the many years of its existence.

COMMODORE RICHARD MILLIKEN

A native New Orleanian and a prominent philanthropist, Richard Milliken, was elected commodore of the Southern Yacht Club for the year 1859. His reputation as a yachtsman was outstanding in his sloop and flagship, *Ripple*. The officers elected to serve with Commodore Milliken were first vice-president, John G. Robinson; second vice-commodore, Sidney Story; A. G. Green, treasurer, and J. O. Nixon, secretary. Members of the Board were as follows:

W. R. Adams	N. B. Keene
J. S. Anderson	D. D. Logan
J. C. Barelli	T. McClellan
C. C. Cammack	J. E. McClure
R. C. Camp	G. W. Parker
Joseph Collins	E. T. Parker
J. W. Dabney	H. St. Paul
E. H. Ellis	W. H. Peters
J. Ferguson	G. M. Simpson
George Foster	T. Thayer
H. H. Joachim	E. A. Tyler
	J. G. Worner

COMMODORE IGNATIUS SZYMANSKE—1860

Elected to serve as commodore for the year 1860 at the July 18, 1860 meeting was Ignatius Szymanske. Other flag officers were past-commodore Sidney Story, A. G. Green, J. W. Balfour as vice-presidents, J. O. Nixon, secretary, and Andrew Haynes, treasurer. Past Commodore Milliken and Thomas Byrne were appointed a committee to revise the laws of the club, to report some time the next winter. The Civil War intervened and that next meeting was held in 1878.

THE ANTEBELLUM REGATTA—1860

Because of the unrest created by talk of a Civil War, very little interest was displayed in sailing in 1860. One race was scheduled and held in the Fourth of July regatta. Four boats entered. They were H. Minor's *J. W. Balfour*, which finished the 15-mile course in five hours and forty-six minutes, followed by C. Braisted's *Adena*, J. Moloney's *Benecia Boy*, and D. Peters' *Phantom*.

The size of this 1860 race was perhaps a weathervane for the immediate future, as 1860 was the last of New Orleans' prosperous years for a very long time. Tragically, like the city itself, the spirit of sailing was to weather a storm equalled by no hurricane in the city's history.

The year 1860 was comparable to the bright Sunday afternoon before "the winds began to pick up" foreboding the 1856 hurricane. The port of New Orleans had just completed its most profitable year ever. The magnificent French Opera House was less than a year old and was considered a hallmark of cultural progress. The city's opera and theatres, Mardi Gras, and the famous Metairie race course attracted important visitors from throughout the United States. Stars of the European dramatic and operatic stage, renowned figures such as Jenny Lind, Danny Elssler and Adelina Patti, considered it a privilege to appear before a discriminating New Orleans audience.

New Orleans had expanded by incorporating villages once considered beyond city limits, and not only was the city known as the nation's wealthiest but now she ranked third in population.

The coast shipping trade ceased its extensive use of the port facilities because of the war, but the Lake Pontchartrain Railway Company continued operating until 1864, when it was abandoned. In 1865 the Union Army built a short-lived railway along the west bank of the New Basin Canal to West End in order to handle cotton deliveries.

"REGISTERED ENEMIES OF THE U.S." DEPORTED FROM WEST END

With the approach of the Civil War, all activities ended at West End. Rowing and yacht clubs disbanded, not to form again until the 1870s; the hotels became overcrowded with war refugees and soon fell into disrepair. An 1863 drawing in *Harper's Weekly* shows "registered enemies of the United States" being deported from West End.

CHAPTER III

1860–1877

Civil War and Reconstruction Period

LAKE PONTCHARTRAIN DURING THE CIVIL WAR

Yachting was suspended on Lake Pontchartrain during the War between the States (1861–1865), when Admiral David Farragut and the Union Fleet took possession of New Orleans early in the conflict. Many of the club members joined the Confederacy, quite a few performing yeoman service on vessels of an extemporized navy. Their yachts were utilized during the war, some as blockade runners, and others pressed into service as supply carriers, etc.

The following is taken from the book *Lake Pontchartrain* by W. Adolphe Roberts; it serves as a synopsis of Lake Pontchartrain's fate during the Civil War: "Far from fearing that secession would have a destructive effect, the majority of the merchants as well as politicians argued that by becoming the chief seaport of an independent republic, New Orleans stood to gain enormously.

"The mass of the South's foreign business must pass this way, while the upper Mississippi Valley would still be forced to use the river route for many products . . . . " Then the outbreak of hostilities climaxed a series of political events too well known to call for repetition here.

THE RECONSTRUCTION PERIOD

The Civil War and the Reconstruction covered a period of seventeen years, May 1, 1860 to April 24, 1877. Although devastated, the spirit of the people of New Orleans proved indestructible as they set about repairing a metropolis crushed by war.

Canal Street and Esplanade Avenue were alive with the gay color of promenaders. The French Opera House and the St. Charles Theatre played to large audiences. The carnival balls were held as scheduled. On January 6, 1870 the Twelfth Night Revelers came into being with a parade of eighteen floats, accompanied by a cavalcade of mounted maskers. The theme of the parade was "Twelfth Night Revel." The Revelers held their initial ball at the French Opera House. Their ball marks the beginning of the carnival season.

Also popular during the 1870s were the steamboat races that have become legendary. The most notable of these was the famous July 1870 race between the *Natchez* and the *Robert E. Lee* from New Orleans to St. Louis, Missouri. The *Robert E. Lee* was declared the winner when it arrived in St. Louis 3 days, 18 hours, 14 minutes after departing the Crescent City. (The writer's grandfather, Captain Peter Peppers, was first mate on the *Robert E. Lee* in this memorable race. Several years later he captained the *Robert E. Lee* as well as many other famous steamboats of the time.)

A popular Sunday outing for many New Orleanians was an excursion to Lake Pontchartrain on the Pontchartrain Railroad, or perhaps an overnighter to Mandeville on the north shore of the lake, or to the Mississippi Gulf Coast by steamboat. After October 29, 1870 one could travel from New Orleans to Mobile by train, on the new Louisville and Nashville Railway.

On September 13, 1870 *The Picayune* reported, "The closing regatta of the Southern Yacht Club was held on Lake Pontchartrain. The rival yachts were the *Protos*, *Limas*, and *Mathilda*. The *Protos* came in one minute and 18 seconds ahead of the *Limas*. The *Protos* was entered by Charles T. Howard and sailed by J. Clements. Attendance at the lake was quite large."

PROSPERITY AND MERRIMENT RETURN TO NEW ORLEANS

In an effort to restore New Orleans to the gay and prosperous city it had been before the war, a group of businessmen persuaded Governor Henry Clay Warmoth of Louisiana to grant them a permit for the Fairgrounds race track, which was opened in 1872. There had been racing in the city since 1837, but the Civil War had intervened.

Then came a new monarch, Rex, to reign over Mardi Gras. Numbered among those who organized this legendary group were several members of the Southern Yacht Club. One of the members, Charles T. Howard, was responsible for the legislation passed into law on April 4, 1872, making Mardi Gras a legal holiday in Louisiana. Howard, who reigned as Rex in 1877, was later elected commodore of the SYC in 1884.

THE FIRST REX PARADE

The April 4, 1872 isue of *The Daniel* (a daily publication issued by Daniel H. Holmes, an SYC member and president and founder of D. H. Holmes) has an exciting account of the first Rex parade:

> "As in the ante bellum times, each Carnival season was an era replete with breathless splendor, so yesterday brought New Orleans once more to its all but vanished repute as the gayest city in America, for instead of wandering at random about the city's streets, our merry makers were gathered into a procession under a new monarch, Rex, King of Carnival, whose mysteries proclamations and edicts through the past ten days calling upon his loyal subjects to meet him for celebration at the Henry Clay statue (foot of Canal Street) have aroused the interest of all in the community."

THE END OF THE CARPETBAGGERS

Reconstruction was a period of many changes and much discontent, until the withdrawal of Federal troops in April 1877. The struggle for political power was terrific during this period. There were military governors within the Union lines, military governors within the Confederate lines, impeached governors, acting governors, and *de facto* governors, for a total of twelve governors in the seventeen years from 1860 to 1877.

In another article appearing in *The Daniel*, the ousting of the carpetbaggers was related: "This movement came about after President Hayes received a letter signed by Archbishop Porche of the Catholic clergy, also T. Hugh Miller Thompson, rector of Trinity Church, Dr. B. M. Palmer of the First Presbyterian Church and by businessmen Hugh McClosky, Daniel H. Holmes, John H. Clarke, A. B. Griswold, T. Danziger, Leon Godchaux, Antoine Alciatore and countless others." Most of these gentlemen were members of the SYC.

President T. L. Dabney
1850, 1851

Commodore Sidney Story
1856, 1857

Commodore Richard Milliken
1859

Commodore Emile J. O'Brien
1878, 1879, 1880, 1884, 1885,
1886, 1887

Commodore Arthur A. Maginnis
1881, 1882, 1883

Commodore Robert S. Day
1888, 1889, 1890, 1891

CHAPTER IV

1878–1884

COMMODORES | TERMS
Emile J. O'Brien | 1878-79-80
Arthur Ambrose Maginnis | 1881-82-83

COMMODORE EMILE J. O'BRIEN—1878-80

A highly spirited group of Southern Yacht Club members met on June 3, 1878 to plan the reactivation of the sport of yachting and to build a yacht club on Lake Pontchartrain. Permission from the U.S. Government had been granted for the building in 1867, and plans and specifications were prepared now for a clubhouse at the mouth of the New Basin Canal.

It was due to the tenacity and dedication of Emile J. O'Brien, who was ably assisted by Commodore John G. Robinson, that a group of old salts and their sons, some 300 of them, assembled at this momentous post-war meeting. O'Brien was unanimously elected commodore. He was to serve in this capacity during the club's second life from 1878 to 1880 and again from 1884 to 1887. Commodore O'Brien was deservedly given the title "Father of the Southern Yacht Club."

Like so many other Southern Yacht Club commodores, Commodore O'Brien had his roots on the Mississippi Coast. His were planted on the dividing point between Bay St. Louis and Waveland, set back from the beach drive amidst a cluster of magnolia trees. Commodore O'Brien was a successful New Orleans cotton broker and also an avid fisherman. His wife, Kate Musket, was the niece of the Scottish inventor, Robert Musket, who developed the modern steel-making process which became the basis for the Andrew Carnegie fortune. Miss Musket made her debut in New Orleans at the Twelfth Night Ball.

In addition to Emile J. O'Brien as commodore, the other elected officers were H. Rareshide of Mandeville, first commodore; E. L. Israel, second commodore; O. F. Jamison, secretary; and J. B. McConnell, treasurer.

Approval of plans for the erection of the first Southern Yacht Clubhouse was given, and several innovations were introduced to the 300 members present that would pertain to the general welfare of the organization. Annual dues were fixed at $12.00. Much care would be exercised in admitting new members, the idea being to build up an organization of men actually interested in the sport of yachting. House Rule #3 stated that "All persons residing twenty miles or more from the City of New Orleans shall be deemed strangers. Drinks shall be served by the house-keeper from the sideboard on members' orders only, and the bar shall be closed on the departure of the last train." By foot, the trek from the club to the city was six miles.

FIRST POST-WAR ANNUAL SYC REGATTA

When the SYC was reorganized in 1878, its 300 members owned a fleet of nationally prominent yachts. Fifteen answered the gun for the starting of the first post-war Southern Yacht Club annual regatta on the morning of June 23, 1878. The entries were:

Cydnus	*Linwood*
Gov. Claiborne	*Loulou*
Germaine	*Pluck and Luck*
Juanita	*Restless*
LaBelle	*Susie B*
Lady Emma	*Xiphias*
Lemnus	*Zephine*
	Zoe

"Yachtsmen from all the clubs along the Gulf Coast were present. A 12-pounder brass cannon, property of the Washington Artillery, and which had seen action at the battle of Gettysburg, was used to summon the yachts. New Orleans was on the 'qui vive.'

"Presentation of trophies was made at the St. John Boat Clubhouse on Bayou St. John as the Southern Yacht Club's home was not completed. A beautiful piece of silverware from Tiffany's New York was presented to the winner, Colonel R. G. Ogden of the Southern Yacht Club. Dancing followed, the music being furnished by the band of the Louisiana Field Artillery," reported the *Barometer*, the SYC monthly publication.

Transportation to the lakefront was greatly improved when on April 20, 1876 the New Orleans City and Lake Railroad started running its "dummy" engine—a locomotive with its boiler and running gear completely enclosed, with open-sided trailer cars—from the Halfway House to West End, extending out into the lake on jetties. The service was later extended down Canal Street to Carondelet Street in June 1876. The line was eventually electrified in 1898.

It was Commodore O'Brien who nourished the membership of the Southern Yacht Club. With his flagship *Zoe* he staged regattas with beautiful new boats and club-owned craft. "Two regattas were held in 1878 on Lake Pontchartrain, weathering the blight of reconstruction," reported *The Picayune*.

A resolution was passed at the 1879 meeting stating that "no salute on Sunday shall be permitted and only flag officers and new vessels should receive the salute."

It was announced that the club was incorporated on May 13, 1879 "to encourage athletic and other exercises... and to foster and encourage social intercourse among its members." A report stated that in the first year of the club's rejuvenation, over $4,000 in dues had been received and the total membership was 404—393 active members, 3 honorary members, and 18 new members.

Before the meeting adjourned, congratulations were extended to two SYC members who had reigned as Rex: Albert Baldwin in 1876, and Charles T. Howard in 1877.

MEDICAL MANUAL FOR SKIPPERS

Each member was handed a manual titled *Notes on the Treatment of Medical and Surgical Emergencies on Yachts*, which was compiled by Fleet Surgeon J. West Roosevelt of the Seawanhaka Corinthian Yacht Club. The book "suggested treatment for burns, sunstroke, cholera and delirium tremens, 15 grams of chloral hydrate and 30 grains of potash. If there is much depression, an occasional dose of whiskey can be given." A member felt disposed to comment that in view of the generally abstemious disposition of the rank and file of the membership, it is doubtful that an occasion was ever needed for this prescription. Also noted was a newspaper advertisement at that time, reading, "Try Parker's Sarsaparilla for blood trouble."

One hundred years from now, maybe the 1985 "Suggested Medications for Cruising" recently published will sound just as amusing.

NAUTICAL DRESS UNIFORMS APPROVED

A report from the committee on uniforms appointed by the commodore was read. A letter received from the Mannings Yacht Agency of New York stated that the necessary nautical attire for officers and members consisted of the following:

Full Dress Uniform: A double-breasted Sack Coat of Navy Blue flannel with two rows of large size gilt buttons, four in number on each side. Pants of Navy Blue flannel same as coat. Vest of White Drilling single-breasted to button nearly to the throat with five small gilt buttons. Neckerchief of black silk. Buttons, U.S. Navy, Cap, Navy Blue cloth with ribbed silk bank 1¼ inches wide not more than 3¼ inches high, circular top - visor to be crescent shape 1½ inches wide at widest part.

Designation of Rank: Commodore - Cap ornaments - a foul anchor 1½ inches in length placed horizontally embroidered in gold with a silver star ½ inches in diameter at each end, and one above the anchor with a space of 3/16 of an inch between anchor and stars.

First Vice-Commodore: Same as Commodore, substituting a star below the anchor in place of one at each end.

Second Vice-Commodore: Same as Commodore, omitting stars at each end of anchor.

Captains: Two crossed foul anchors 1½ inches
Secretary: Foul anchor with letter "S" above.
Treasurer: Foul anchor with letter "T" above.
Members: Foul anchor.

Coat Ornaments:
Commodore: 5 stripes gold lace 1/8 of an inch wide, the first below and joining the cuff seam, and the others above 1/8 of an inch apart.
First Vice-Commodore: 4 stripes as above.
Second Vice-Commodore: 3 stripes as above.
Captains, Secretary and Treasurer: 2 stripes as above.
Members: 1 stripe as above.

Service Dress:
Shirts: Navy blue flannel, wide collar open trimmed with white—S.Y.C. on breast.
Pants: Same material as shirt.
Caps: White drilling without visor with name of yacht club, when forming part of a crew, in gilt letters round the band.
Slippers: White canvas.

Rank may be designated by embroidery in white on shirt above S.Y.C. on left arm.

The club button selected was a pilot wheel with SYC in the center. The club's first burgee design, adopted in 1849, was a double tail with blue background and white letters *SYC* in the center. (This burgee was replaced in 1896 with a flag with one flowing point, and blue background with white letters *SYC* in the center.)

DEDICATION OF THE FIRST SYC HOME

It came to pass. The Southern Yacht Club was now located in its first clubhouse, a two-story frame structure dominated by a large portico and surmounted by a cupola, on piers off the west canal jetty. The opening was fittingly celebrated on June 5, 1879 by Commodore Emile J. O'Brien, who gave an elaborate dinner in honor of the members of the Southern Yacht Club and many visiting yachtsmen from the Gulf Coast.

As decreed at the annual meeting in 1879, all officers were dressed in full uniform. Proper yachting attire was mandatory at all events. So they all came dressed in double-breasted sack coats of navy blue flannel with two rows of large gilted size buttons, pants of navy blue flannel, vest of white drilling to button nearly to the throat, neckerchief of black silk, all worn with white canvas slippers!

"Commodore O'Brien personally donated $100 toward the music, refreshments and Chinese lanterns for the proposed Promenade Concert to be held on the evening of the opening regatta," recorded the minutes.

When the opening regatta was held celebrating this historic occasion, quite a large fleet of sailing yachts were on the lake. Reported the *Picayune*, "There were large crowds that assembled at the club to witness the races, and the spacious galleries of the Southern Yacht Club were crowded with lady friends.

"Commodore O'Brien viewed the event with much excitement on his flagship *Zoe*.

"The club burgee flew from the flagpole on the clubhouse while there was dancing inside to the music furnished by the band of the Louisiana Field Artillery."

Boat owners were delighted when in 1880 the City of New Orleans, after the new club's quarters were completed, deeded to the club an area behind the lake levee for the creation of a yacht harbor, where boats could be kept in protected waters and boathouses built.

Previously, boats were anchored in Bayou St. John or on the Gulf Coast.

SYC ADDS TO DEVELOPMENT OF WEST END PARK

With the Southern Yacht Club's stately new house came more development of recreational and social activities along the lakefront. In 1871, the steam "dummy" trains which travelled along the east side of the New Basin Canal from the Halfway House to the lake had become a key link in the bedazzling real estate expansion, and their operation kept the pleasure resort popular and lively. The area's name was changed from New Lake End to West End in 1880.

In time, a splendid shell road ran along the New Basin Canal from the city to the lake on the west side. The city built a drawbridge over the New Basin Canal which brought many visitors to view the beautiful gardens, restaurants, and amusement park located on the revetment with a large platform extending into the lake. One of these restaurants, Bruning's, built in 1849, is still operating in the same location at West End.

There were two hotels, the rebuilt Pontchartrain Hotel, which hosted royalty, and a railroad belvedere, and now there was also the beautiful Southern Yacht Club. All of these glamorous sites magically transformed the shoreline into a mini-Riviera.

Inside the park, the New Orleans Railway Company installed ornamental cast iron posts with a single round white glass globe atop. Metairie Ridge Nursery installed $9,000 worth of trees and shrubs. W. A. Dilzell was awarded the contract to install "the largest prismatic fountain in the world" at a cost of $24,000. This fountain, with multihued dancing waterspouts, made a colorful backdrop and the perfect complement for the Sunday evening ballet dancers who performed in their sequined tulle skirts in the pavilion.

Openair concerts were very popular. Military bands such as the Eighth Mexican Cavalry Band and the West End Military Orchestra were frequently featured during the 1880s and 1890s. The West End Opera Company also performed. The leader of the Eighth Mexican Cavalry Band called himself Vascaro. His ninety musicians were the hit of the 1884 Cotton Centennial Exposition, where they performed daily at noon. One of their specialty numbers, which sold thousands of copies, was "Sobre las Olas," known by jazz bands generations later as "Over the Waves." The song "West End Blues" immortalized the area and its jazz origin.

Movies made their New Orleans debut at West End on June 28, 1896. Electrical engineer Allen B. Blakemoore of the New Orleans City and Lake Railroad set up Edison's "Wonderful Vitascope." From a small booth, short subject films were hand-cranked for openair projection onto a canvas screen in front of the bandstand, for which eventually current was borrowed from the nearby trolley line electrified at the end of the century.

Located in the amusement park were a busy merry-go-round, a Ferris wheel, a carousel, and a large roller coaster. Today it is difficult to picture the Victorian SYC edifice side by side with its noisy, squeal-rousing neighbor. The clanging roller coaster was positioned close to the yacht club's entrance, with lake water beneath the tracks and the existing dark "tunnel of love" at the ride's end.

Over the years, hotels, restaurants, and bath houses spread along the lake's shoreline as far as Spanish Fort. The lakefront became a recreational center. Several jazz greats, Louis Armstrong, Ormand J. Piron, Oscar "Papa" Celestin and others performed on platforms and in pavilions there.

Music historians Al Rose and Edmond Souchon of New Orleans asserted that West End, along with other Lake Pontchartrain resorts, was the birthplace of jazz, not Storyville. They point out that jazz was formulated well before Storyville was established and that relatively few jazz musicians ever played in Storyville.

GENERAL GRANT IS GUEST OF SYC

With New Orleans healing from its Civil War wounds, the diplomatic Commodore O'Brien invited General Ulysses S. Grant to be a guest of the Southern Yacht Club in 1880. The war was of a bygone era, and the former Commander-in-Chief of the Union Army was on a world tour. He was following his second term as eighteenth president of the United States with extensive travel in Europe, the Far East, and parts of this country.

Upon his arrival at the Southern Yacht Club, Grant was given a formal 21-gun salute by the Club's cannon. For his signature in the Club's registration book a whole page has been devoted, one of the Club's many autographs of famous visitors.

General Grant's day spent with Commodore O'Brien on the shores of Lake Pontchartrain in the luxurious yacht *Zoo* must have been one of the happiest in the general's remaining years, for shortly after that summer of 1880, he was destined for bankruptcy, having placed his finances in unscrupulous hands. However, through the assistance of Mark Twain, who became the publisher of the memoirs on which Grant spent many months, the former President regained a sizeable income, sufficient to finance the lingering illness of his last years.

THE STORY OF THE SYC'S BRASS CANNON

The brass cannon referred to in the account of General Grant's visit to the Southern Yacht Club was used to salute many dignitaries who visited the club. It had a colorful and fascinating past, having been one of the guns aboard the schooner of the filibustering Captain William Walker of New Orleans, who was sometimes referred to as "the Grey-eyed Man of Destiny."

The story is told that Captain Walker was a soldier and sailor of fortune. When he fitted out his Nicaraguan expedition in 1855, a number of young Orleanians interested in adventure were persuaded to go along. One of the youths was put in charge of cleaning the cannon daily, and he was proud of his work. But when the Civil War started, Walker had the cannon removed from the schooner and gave it to the youth for safekeeping. In the great game of "bury the spoon," which took place in the city when General Benjamin T. Butler, commander of the military force at Ship Island, took over the city during the Civil War, the boy's family buried the cannon in the back yard of their old mansion on Coliseum Square. After the war it was returned by the lady of the mansion to the Southern Yacht Club. This story was taken from the *Barometer* and written by R. Lee Edwards.

For years this cannon stood with its nose pointed toward the fort of Bucktown until vandals stole it. It has never been found.

FAMOUS YACHTS

Old SYC race records and newspaper accounts were studded with the heroic deeds and exploits of outstanding yachtsmen and their yachts, and the dramatic and thrilling descriptions of famous races.

Commodore Emile J. O'Brien's *Zoe*, the prizewinning sloop of the time and the two boats *Pilgrim* and *Coquette*, ably handled by the Englishman John G. Robinson, dominated racing during the club's first decade, along with Thomas Kershaw's *Rigoletto*. These three boats got the winner's salute more often than any of their rivals.

Dr. R. A. Murphy's *Toutsy*, a little sloop that compiled a nice record during the last half of the eighteenth century, was formerly the cat-rigged *Undine* which had sailed in the club's inaugural regatta. *Toutsy* was 19 feet, 11 inches on the water line but carried the largest spread of canvas of any boat in her class. *Toutsy* was the first boat in the South to use hollow spars, then new in the yachting game.

Since organized racing had been established in 1849, the Southern Yacht Club had witnessed an interesting evolution of racing boats on Lake Pontchartrain and the nearby Gulf Coast. First there were the schooners and big sloops that had been popular a half-century ago. Then came the picturesque "sandbaggers," which carried a tremendous yardage of canvas and required stalwart crews to handle them. These boats were called "sandbaggers" because they actually carried sand bags as ballast. The crew, some twelve to thirteen men, had to be strong and coordinated, as they first had to shift two 50-pound bags of sand (60 when wet) to the high side before each tack.

The yachts in the 1880s were built to last for more than a generation, with solid oak booms and bowsprits made from one tree trunk. The boats of those days were grotesque in appearance compared with the sleek, graceful craft of these times. They carried bowsprits almost twice as along as the hull and a boom which projected many feet beyond the stern. How they carried such tremendous expanses of canvas as they did is a wonder. In addition to a huge mainsail, these boats hoisted high-reaching club topsails and several jibs.

FIRST INTERSTATE REGATTA IN "SANDBAGGERS"

With its affairs in such good shape, the club decided to have a grand Interstate Regatta for the season of 1880. The object was to keep the club in its rightful place as one of the leading proponents of boat racing and, if possible, to attract Northern and Western yachtsmen to the South's splendid yachting waters, with a focus on New Orleans as an outstanding yachting center.

Shifting-ballast boats were the only kind used for racing in the smaller classes, and New York and New Orleans had a monopoly on the sport, there being great rivalry between the two cities. It was a question as to which would claim the championship of the "sandbaggers." To settle the question, the Southern Yacht Club issued a showdown in planning the Interstate Regatta, thereby affording an exciting opportunity to settle the question.

The minutes of the Southern Yacht Club state, "The club advertised a prize of $1,200 if two boats started, and if three or more started the prize would be increased to $1,500, a princely prize indeed, and one which seldom had been equaled during that period."

The race was sailed on June 20, 1880 and attracted the attention of the sporting fraternity all over the country. The crack Northern boat *Silence* was sent down to represent New York, with Captain Ira Smith of that city in charge of her. He had an excellent crew and no time or money was spared in putting *Silence* in peak condition for the contest. The boats from SYC which participated were J. B. McConnell's *Pluck and Luck*, Alex Brewster's *Albertine*, E. Harris' *Cydnus*, H. Israel's *Lady Emma*, and R. L. Robertson's *Daisy*.

The event was won by H. Israel's *Lady Emma*. *Silence* was never taken back to New York, as it was purchased by a New Orleans yachtsman. She had been the fastest boat around New York. New Orleans now had the double distinction of having two champions, and, of course, was conceded to be the place to go for speedy "sandbag" sloops.

"In perusing the records of a truly noble organization, one cannot refrain from praising the deeds of those men who sailed sand-ballasted yachts under storm conditions, venturing out on the treacherous bosom of Lake Pontchartrain in gales that would have deterred more than one professional sailor. They knew no fear. They truly were 'iron men in wooden ships' loaded with sandbags besides," recorded R. Lee Edwards in the *Barometer*.

FIRST CLUB-OWNED BOATS

Before he left office in 1880, Commodore O'Brien recognized the advantages of having club-owned boats for the promotion of sailing by those members who could not afford to purchase a vessel. Through private subscriptions, the commodore was able to acquire the first club-owned boat of the Southern Yacht Club, a schooner, for $750.00.

Here was pioneer yachting wisdom at its sharpest. Wary of the ambience of luxury that surrounded yachting, Commodore O'Brien realized after a decade that it was time to develop a program which included skilled sailors personally unable to afford a big slick winner. This was good for the Southern Yacht Club and for those yacht clubs that followed Southern's movement—all benefitted from such a prudent investment. It improved the structure of racing for many years, and it is the basis for the success of the present day Gulf Yachting Association.

COMMODORE ARTHUR A. MAGINNIS—
1881-82-83

Succeeding Commodore O'Brien in office for the year 1881 was Arthur Ambrose Maginnis. Commodore Maginnis had reigned as Rex in 1880. His family had founded the enormous Maginnis Cotton Mills in New Orleans in 1854. (Cotton had been king, and the mill manufactured special fabrics indispensible to the nineteenth century housewife, such as sheeting, shirting, osnaburg, yarn, batting, and duck.)

Commodore Maginnis was an enthusiastic yachtsman and the owner of several yachts in addition to his flagship *Pickwick*, built by local boat builders. He also owned the *Gypsy* and the *Agnes*. The latter won the 1881 championship with expert crewmen Charles Thorn, Harry Pond, Mercer Patton, Allen Mehle, William Maginnis, and F. B. Craig. Peter E. Hellwege was the captain.

Serving with the commodore as flag officers were Edwin Harris, 1st vice-commodore; Harry T. Howard, 2nd vice-commodore; H. Harris, secretary; and James B. McConnell, treasurer.

At the April 20, 1881 meeting, the Southern Yacht Club was duly authorized to purchase from the U. S. Canal and Banking Company a certain piece of property lying north of the Bruning tract at West End. Mr. Fremaux was the land surveyor, at a fee of $25.00.

The Challenge Cup was presented to the club by one of its outstanding members, Charles T. Howard. Also it was reported that in the year 1880 there were 433 members in good standing and that seven regattas were held during the season.

Success again attended the efforts of the members of the SYC on the occasion of the opening regatta, May 24, 1881. *The Picayune* reported:

> Alex Brewster again demonstrated his skill at the tiller, bringing *Albertine* over the finish line first, covering the 15 mile course in 2 hours and 50 minutes. *Lady Emma* sailed by John Cornay finished second in 2 hours and 53 minutes. Samuel Heaslip, John Glynn, Jr. and R. L. Macmurdo presided as judges. On the second day of the regatta *Juanita* owned by J. R. deBuys and sailed by John Cornay won in his class. *Gypsy* owned by A. A. Maginnis and sailed by Sam Gauthier won

a handsome silver cup in the 4th class.

Dancing under the electric lights followed the regatta. When night set in upon the waters of Lake Pontchartrain, the electric lights were lit and the fresh young faces with their color heightened by the excitement of the evening looked even more beautiful. The scene was one upon which the eye loved to linger, and called forth the admiration of all who were fortunate enough to be present.

Commodore Maginnis was reelected at the annual meeting to serve for the year 1882. It was announced by the House Committee that arrangements had been made for a promenade concert. The opening regatta was marred by bad weather. Only one yacht, *Zoe*, entered by Henry Denegre, sailed through the gale to finish the 15-mile course.

The bad weather did not deter the dance following the regatta. The society editor of *The Picayune* again romanticizes the SYC party where, she reported, "many of society's beautiful favorites visited and joined the gallant yachtsmen in tripping the light fantastic. The graceful evolutions were kept up until the merry party was summoned into town by the shrill whistle of the last train."

There was much excitement awaiting Commodore Maginnis when he entered his third term in office in 1883. A number of match races indulged in by yachtsmen from the East, New York and Boston, who had sent their boats all the way to New Orleans, proved to be real thrillers. They competed against the vessels of Ed. Israel and John Lallande.

The SYC fleet was quite large that got under way for Point Clear, Alabama in July. As was the custom at the time, with scores of Orleanians owning homes on Mississippi Sound, the remainder of the summer would be spent at regattas along the coast.

CHAPTER V

1884–1894

COMMODORES	TERMS
Charles T. Howard	1884
Emile J. O'Brien	1884-85-86-87
Robert S. Day	1888-89-90-91
W. A. Gordon	1892
Thomas Sully	1893-94

COMMODORE CHARLES T. HOWARD—1884

At the annual meeting held in April 1884, Commodore Maginnis was applauded and thanked for his service to the club for three long years. A new slate of officers was submitted by ex-Commodore Emile J. O'Brien, nominating Charles T. Howard, Esq. commodore. "There being no other nominations, Charles T. Howard, Esq. was elected Commodore by acclamation," stated the minutes. Elected to serve with Howard were Emile J. O'Brien, 1st vice-commodore; Alex Brewster, 2nd vice-commodore; J. B. McConnell, treasurer; and H. P. Hopkins, secretary.

Commodore Howard was a prominent New Orleanian and a reputable yachtsman. In 1887 he had reigned as Rex. His many yachts were noted in the New York advertiser published in 1893, *The Boatswain's Log*. This is what it had to say about Commodore Howard:

> From 1865 to 1870 Mr. Charles T. Howard was one of the South's most enthusiastic yachtsmen. He owned several of the fastest sloops of their class in Southern waters. Pat McGeighan built two of them at Pamapo, N.J., where he is still located. These two boats were carried to New Orleans on the deck of a steamship. The first was the *Domino* which Mr. Howard bought from Gunther, the fur dealer. The other was the *Mattie*, and many a man living in and about New York today will call to mind the fact that she beat every small sloop in these waters

before leaving for the South.

The *Mattie*'s victories in Southern waters were no less than those in this, a breezier clime. She cleaned up everything in the shape of a yacht that lay claim to being speedy from Lake Pontchartrain to Mobile Bay. Southern yachtsmen got tired of having Howard win all the races, so a syndicate was formed, among which was the late Mayor of New Orleans, Joseph A. Shakespeare and Governor of Louisiana, Hon. Louis A. Wiltz, for the purpose of purchasing a boat called the *Meteor* that was at the time making a name for herself in New York waters. A bargain was consummated, and the *Meteor*, after arriving South, beat the *Mattie* three straight races.

COMMODORE O'BRIEN REPLACES COMMODORE HOWARD—1884

Commodore Howard resigned after two months in office, and Vice-Commodore Emile J. O'Brien replaced him to assume the leadership of the club for another term. It was reported that Commodore Howard was in very poor health.

"Every winter during the Carnival season, it is customary to see one or more of the large Northern yachts anchored at the Southern Yacht Club—the clubhouse is one of the show points to which visitors are first taken, and it continues to be a favorite landmark for tourists. Among the many boats that stopped in New Orleans was the renowned British auxiliary steamboat 'Sunbeam' with Lord and Lady Brassey, who stopped on their famous cruise around the world in 1884," reported the *Barometer*.

From December 1884 to March 1886 the World's Cotton Exposition was held in the City of New Orleans in the area that later developed into Audubon Park, on the uptown side of Canal Street. During this period many palatial steam yachts arrived from the North and were given anchorage in the Southern Yacht Club's harbor.

THE NEW SOUTHERN YACHT CLUB CHARTER

In 1884, the Louisiana State Legislature passed a new law which required the signing of a new charter by the Southern Yacht Club. A special meeting was called on June 13, 1884 at which the original Southern Yacht Club was dissolved. However, another meeting was called immediately thereafter, and the club was reorganized under the new charter, which was adopted for a period of ninety-nine years. The old officers were reelected, with Commodore Emile J. O'Brien remaining as commodore. Following are the names which appear on the new charter:

Francis W. Baker
H. O. Benedict
Jno. S. Boland
H. Bonnabel
M. S. Bringier, Jr.
Hugh W. Brown
P. B. Caufield
J. C. Denis
A. J. Ferran
Frank M. Hall
Jno. Hawkins
Andrew Hero, Jr. (Notary)
Richard Herrick
H. D. Hopkins
H. P. Hopkins
E. L. Israel
Frank Kennedy
W. M. Lynd, Jr.
A. A. Maginnis
A. P. Mason
J. B. McConnell
J. O. Nixon, Jr.
Emile J. O'Brien
R. L. Robertson, Jr.

W. Sanchez
Chas. A. Smith
Geo. Smith
V. Tanner
Jno. J. Ward

Honorary Members:

H. W. Hopkins
Emile J. O'Brien

Life Members:

Peter Blaise
C. F. Buck
S. Delgado
E. J. Demarest
E. S. Douglas
John Hawkins
Dave Jackson
Wm. Kern
Branch M. King
W. B. Kingrose
P. B. O'Brien
J. A. Walker

COMMODORE EMILE J. O'BRIEN—1884-85-86-87

Commodore O'Brien was again called upon to reactivate the sport of sailing. He was reelected commodore for the year 1885. Assisting him were Alex Brewster, vice-commodore; Charles D. Schmidt, rear commodore; J. B. McConnell, treasurer; and H. P. Hopkins, secretary. There was a revival of interest, as reported by the *Picayune* of June 13:

> The Southern Yacht Club does not propose to remain dormant this season. It has prestige for fine sport and hospitality to maintain, and proposes to give a grand regatta on Lake Pontchartrain to maintain its reputation.
>
> Since the days of the *Albertine, Silence* and other famous yachts, the sport is supposed to have lost some of its interest, however, the members as usual came to the front in time. The regatta was held on June 13th and after the race got under way, a squall came up which damaged many of the boats. *Mephisto* won the Challenge Cup race handled by Alex Brewster. *Annie M* entered by J. Morencovitch won a silver service. *Viola* entered by L. C. Fallon and sailed by Sam Heaslip won a bronze statuette barometer. The regatta proved beyond question that

yachting in New Orleans was anything but dead.

Alex Brewster owned the *Albertine* and the *Mephisto*. The latter won the Charles T. Howard Challenge Cup three years straight, to gain permanent possession of it.

FAMOUS YACHTS BROUGHT DOWN THE MISSISSIPPI RIVER

The years 1885 through 1891 were popular for the cabin sloop class. The 45-foot cabin sloop *Nepenthe* was sailed down the coast to her new home, New Orleans, in 1885. She was designed by Edward Burgess for Charles P. Richardson of New Orleans. The builder was George Lawley & Son of Boston.

Nepenthe became another famous yacht to carry the SYC burgee. Vice-Commodore Alex Brewster sailed her up East one summer in the 1890s, and she held her own in races on Long Island Sound and at Marblehead. That same year she beat the *Annie B.* of Mobile for the championship of the South in a celebrated match race in the open Gulf of Mexico outside Mobile Bay. She also beat the *Montauk* in a high stakes match race on Lake Pontchartrain.

Many yachts owned by Southern yachtsmen were brought down the Mississippi River by steamboats. It is recorded in the archives of the New York Yacht Club in Volume I, *The Yachts and Yachtsmen of America*, "One of the most luxurious steam yachts, *Montauk*, was brought down from New York on the deck of a steamer for Peter Labouisse, a prominent businessman of New Orleans. She was a centerboard cutter formerly called *George C.* Designed and built by William G. M. Reed of Brooklyn, New York and launched in 1887, the *Montauk* measured over-all 45 feet in length and she won many races along the Gulf Coast." The *Montauk* had a fine reputation around New York before being brought South, where she continued to spread her fame. The 45-foot sloop drew only 2 feet, 11 inches, a prime requisite along the shallow shores of the Gulf.

Foremost among the club's famous yachts was *Susie B.*, a 32-foot cabin sloop which reigned supreme for almost thirty years. Built in 1870 in Keyport, L. I., as *LaBelle*, she was brought to New Orleans in 1881 by A. McCutchen and owned successively by Buckner Ogden, C. Hargis, Alex Brewster, and Charles P. and William P. Richardson before she came into the hands of A. M. Cooke, who sailed her to many victories. Under Cooke's skillful handling, *Susie B.* was unbeatable. In 1889 she won five trophies in one day at Pass Christian. *Susie B.* was still champion of her class in 1902 and again in 1904 when she beat the new boats *Calipso, Chewink II,* and *Invader.*

The schooners *Nereus* and *Gertie* were added to the fleet. The *Lady Sarah* was sold and renamed *Nyanza,* continuing her former triumphs. Owned by A. S. Ranlett and J. W. Stone, *Nyanza* won eighteen races out of twenty-four starts.

For the fourth consecutive year Emile J. O'Brien was returned to office as commodore in 1887. Reelected with him was Alex Brewster, vice-commodore. The new officers were C. P. Richardson, rear commodore; H. W. Brown, Treasurer; and F. M. Hall, Secretary. At this annual meeting the "Ladies" were voted to be admitted to "all parts of the clubhouse."

COMMODORE ROBERT SLACK DAY—
1888-89-90-91

The year 1888 brought the passing of the commodoreship from the steady hands of Commodore Emile J. O'Brien to Robert Slack Day, another very prominent citizen and a prosperous cotton merchant of New Orleans. Commodore Day served for the years 1888 through 1891. (In 1892 he reigned as Rex.) Commodore Day's flagship was the steam launch *Idler.* He also owned the *Folly*, the handsome 57-foot centerboard schooner which is recorded in *The Yachts and Yachtsmen of America.* She was designed and built by W. Cogan of New Orleans.

At the 1888 annual meeting, Commodore Emile J. O'Brien was elected a life honorary member "without dues but with all fringes of an active member." Also at this meeting it was reported that the club-owned boat *Frolic* was sold for $500.

The opening regatta was held on June 5, 1888. The secretary of the SYC, L. P. Sampsell, wrote this account for a yachting magazine:

> With one of the largest crowds in years coming out to West End, fifteen boats answered the starting gun. *Susie B.*, 32', entered by Charles Richardson and masterly handled by Sam Gautier, won in the cabin sloop class over *Viola,* 37'8", entered by John Barkley and sailed by Sam Heaslip.
>
> Other boats entered were: *Hope* entered and sailed by Alex Brewster won the schooner race; *Stella* entered by J. Cuneo and sailed by Emile J. O'Brien won the second cabin sloop event and the open sloop race was captured by *Lady Sarah* entered by Larry O'Donnell and sailed

by Sam Gautier, also in the second race. Capt. A. K. Miller, Capt. Richard Francis and Major A. P. Williams presided as judges. In addition to the club prize, Mr. Lawrence Wiltz of the West End Hotel presented the successful boat in the first race with a handsome silk flag. The pennant is a beauty and bears the inscription "Champions-SYC-1889" and is a worthy gift from our young friend.

Following the race there was a regatta dance. Those serving on the Reception Committee were:

Geo. W. Booth	Judge A. Gastnell	H. R. Lewis
P. B. Caulfield	Jos. J. Hooper	George Lynd
E. Chassaignac	N. S. Hoskins	F. Moreno
J. H. Duggan	C. J. Ingalls	J. T. Scott
Geo. H. Dwyer	Blain Jamison	R. D. Scriven
F. C. Ford	Thos. A. Kelley	F. N. Volckman
	J. H. Lafaye	Charles Yenni

COMMODORE W. A. GORDON—1892

At the 1892 annual meeting of the Southern Yacht Club, held on April 11, W. A. Gordon was elected commodore, Vice-Commodore Alex Brewster was reelected, former Commodore Robert S. Day was made rear commodore, W. H. Brown became treasurer, and F. M. Hall was elected secretary. It was reported at the meeting that Mobile and Pensacola Yacht Clubs were invited to race at the Southern Yacht Club.

Commodore Gordon was very popular among the yachtsmen, and much of the club's progress is attributable to him and his fine executive officers. The schooner *Adrienne*, the commodore's flagship, was owned and skippered by him. She was listed in *The Yachts and Yachtsmen of America* as "a 63-foot centerboard schooner, designed and built by Stewart & Binney for W. A. Gordon and Westley E. Lawrence of New Orleans, La. She was launched in 1892 at Essex, Mass. and sailed down to New Orleans where she received a warm welcome." Some fine races were sailed among the *Adrienne*, the *Hope*, *Viola*, *Nereus*, *Gertie*, *Gerdes Bros.* and the *Folly*. She made many cruises, the farthest being to Havana, Cuba and back.

During Commodore Gordon's incumbency, many reforms were instituted and yachting was kept up to date. Massachusetts Bay 21-footers, Seawanahkas, and Sound Inter-clubs were introduced. In 1892, the Southern Yacht Club's fleet consisted of fifty craft, including several steam yachts.

THE SINKING OF THE *NEREUS*

Unfortunately, during the 1892 opening regatta a destructive storm hit the fleet as it was rounding the last stake on an otherwise pleasant race on Lake Pontchartrain. The *Barometer* relates the exciting story about the sinking of the *Nereus* on June 7, 1892:

> A light breeze was sweeping over Lake Pontchartrain at the start of the race, everything pointing to a most enjoyable afternoon. However, on the second round, ominous-looking dark clouds began to gather and the wind began to freshen.
>
> It was just about 6 o'clock when the full force of the blow struck the fleet. *Nepenthe*, a fine seagoing sloop owned by Charles P. Richardson and sailed by Alex Brewster, met the squall just as she turned the eastern stake, going over her beam end. Regardless of this, her skipper sent her plowing through the water, coming in a mile ahead of the balance of the fleet under almost full sail. She was greeted with a roar of applause by the big crowd huddled on the club gallery. The balance of the fleet came in under small sail, many of the sixteen entries running with bare masts.
>
> With the force of the wind continuing to increase, unable to make the entrance to the New Basin Canal, the big sloops *Nepenthe*, *Nereus* and *Nyanza* dropped anchors and prepared to ride out the storm. Despite two heavy anchors, *Nereus* soon began drifting in shore, struck the head of the club pier and after an hour's pounding broke up and went down, her crew managing to scramble up on the pier. Fearful that two anchors would not be sufficient to hold *Nyanza* in place, Sidney Ranlett, one of the owners, put out in a whale boat with an additional anchor. He succeeded in getting aboard after a hard battle with the waves, and was about to throw out the extra anchor when one that already was put out parted its line. Drifting helplessly in the seas, *Nyanza* now was hurled against the wreck of *Nereus*.
>
> Another dramatic touch was added when Frank Leovy, standing on the pier and seeing the danger his friend Ranlett was in, jumped off and swam to the yacht to assist him. But the waves were so high Leovy became utterly exhausted before he could reach his destination, being saved from drowning only by the timely action of his friend, Ranlett. He was brought back to shore in an unconscious condition, a whole hour being required to revive him.

The *Picayune* described the scene ashore.

> Meanwhile, the tempest rages. There was a band to furnish music for the 'light fantastic' but no one seemed in the mood to dance. The high wind broke panes, drove rain into the clubhouse, soon covering the dancing surface with water, destroying all the decorations. But, the lovely ladies sat about the clubhouse and on the sofas and amused themselves by listening to sweet music and eating dainty refreshments."

Yesterday's yacht club wife presents a sharp contrast to her modern counterpart. Given that same soggy situation, the 1980s wife would heap her glad rags on a bench in the ladies' locker room, don deck shoes and foul weather gear, then hit the dock with her man to help secure "their" boat. Somehow, she would stuff an acre of wet sails in the cabin, then split a manicured fingernail or two against the straining dock lines. But before she did any of this, surely she would save from ruin those party decorations she had worked all week to make.

THE ADVANCEMENT OF BOAT BUILDERS

After the decade 1840–50 when steam began to replace sail in commercial vessels, this type of power, and later the internal-combustion engine, was increasingly used in pleasure vessels. Large power yachts were developed, and long-distance cruising became a favorite pasttime of the rich.

In December 1866, it is noted that the first transatlantic yacht race (from Sandy Hook, New Jersey to England) took place among three American schooners. Contestants were the *Henrietta*, *Fleetwing*, and *Vesta*. The *Henrietta*, owned by James Gordon Bennett, Jr., won; her time, 13 days, 21 hours and 45 minutes.

It was not until 1870 that A. Cary Smith laid down the lines of the cutter *Vindex* on paper. This was the first American yacht to be designed from a drawing rather than a model.

In 1885, Edward Burgess became the most popular United States designer, because of the success of his compromise cutter, *Puritan*, which defended the America's Cup against the Watson-designed *Genesta*. The Burgess hull soon became the accepted United States standard. He subsequently designed two more successful America's Cup defenders, *Volunteer* and *Mayflower*. The *Mayflower* (1897) of 2,690 tons was purchased by the U. S. Navy in 1898 and was made the official yacht of the President of the United States until 1929. It saw active service during World War II.

The yachts of the '80s and '90s were graceful, elegant, and majestic, decorated below deck with the best furnishings and carpentry in a grand Victorian style. Their canvas was of the finest Egyptian cotton, and the area of sail was colossal. Their spars (masts, booms) were made of whole trees, their main booms trespassing far over the stern with great coils of manila sheeting, all handled without winches. To be invited on these boats was an honor.

The huge private yacht *Valhalla*, launched in 1894, amazed the entire yachting world by her size. She was a fully rigged steam auxiliary 245 feet overall with a crew of 100. She raced against the best boats of her time and was later used for world exploration and as a cold storage vessel.

NEW TYPES OF BOATS—
FIN-KEEL AND CATAMARANS

"In 1893," reported the *Barometer*, "the yachting world was exercised over the appearance of a new style of craft which was to fairly outsail the wind. The new model was the 'Catamaran,' or twin-hull vessel. Three were built in this part of the South. The *Nip and Tuck*, the *Ullman* and the *Boardman*. They were popular for a time and unquestionably very fast, but they were also unwieldy and soon dropped out of favor. They had nothing much to recommend them as racers, and particularly not as cruisers, for they featured no cruising accommodations and were not 'yachty' in any way. However, it was said that Nathanael Herreshoff designed and built one of these curious craft which attracted considerable attention in Northern waters."

J. W. Boone, Jr., one of the proprietors of the New Orleans Stencil Works on Natchez Alley, built at odd moments of spare time the first fin-keel sloop on these waters, named *Trilby*, from the lines of the *Scarecrow*, designed by W. P. Stephens of Forest and Stream. *Trilby* was built in a novel shipyard — the third floor of a business block in downtown New Orleans in 1893. She was not all that small — 25 feet overall, with an 18 feet water line and a 5½ feet beam.

COMMODORE THOMAS SULLY—1893-94

Thomas Sully, one of the greatest Southern architects, was elected commodore in 1893. His flagship was the yacht *Helen*. He also owned a naphtha launch, *Reckless*. The commodore was a lover of water and boats. He built championship boats on the shores of the Tchefuncte River.

When associated with Albert Toledano, Sully designed the first city skyscraper in downtown New Orleans, the Maritime building, which is ten stories high. His masterpiece was the St. Charles Hotel building of 1896. In addition to his many buildings, Thomas Sully designed some sixty-odd palatial mansions on St. Charles Avenue.

Elected to serve with Commodore Sully were Alex Brewster, vice-commodore; Lawrence O'Donnell, rear commodore; H. W. Brown, treasurer; and F. W. Hall, secretary.

A Measurement Committee was appointed to consist only of boat owners from each class. The clubs represented were Southern, Bay-Waveland, Pass Christian, Mississippi City, Biloxi and Ocean Springs. Southern was represented by Peter Labouisse, Lawrence O'Donnell, W. A. Gordon, and Sidney Story; Bay-Waveland by Lauphier Clausen; Pass Christian by Samuel Heaslip; Mississippi City by R. deBuys; Biloxi by L. Penrose; and Ocean Springs by W. dePass.

The Deed of Gift for the Sully Cup was accepted at the meeting and plans were made for the evening of the regatta to hold a promenade concert. Commodore Sully also donated $100 for music, refreshments, and Chinese lanterns.

Another cup was received, the Brewster Cup, donated by Alex Brewster. With the first race for this cup, the regatta committee evoked favorable comment when it stated that "all yachts will be required to carry numbers on their mainsails, making it easier to distinguish the various craft. This ruling met with especial approval on the part of landlubbers, enabling them to at least distinguish between a catboat and a schooner."

Many handsome trophies were donated by patrons of the SYC during the years 1888–1891. One was the Walker Cup, donated by Joseph A. Walker for competition among members of the Southern, Mobile, and Pensacola Yacht Clubs. The first Walker Cup race was sailed on June 7, 1893.

It was moved at the annual meeting that boats from the North be extended an invitation from the club to sail on Lake Pontchartrain during the winter months, and that an invitation also be extended to the Mobile Yacht Club.

An important decision was made at the meeting on recommendations that the club do away with sandbags on boats by reversing the sailing rules for open boats. This move was prompted by an incident in the Brewster Cup race when the *Agnes*, owned by W. B. Henry and sailed by George Dudley, which had gone out without her sandbags, nearly capsized.

THE DEMISE OF SANDBAGGERS AND THE REVIVAL OF ALL CLASSES

Sailing rules for open boats were revised in 1893, and sandbagging was eliminated. Naphtha or gasoline launches were now becoming quite popular, and the SYC had a small fleet of them enrolled by this time.

There was a great revival of all classes in 1893, and the outstanding vessels were the *Agnes*, *Florence* and *Presto*. The last, *Presto*, owned by SYC members Albert C. Marchall and R. J. Osborne, was the celebrated New York cruising yawl designed and formerly owned by Commodore Ralph Munroe of the Biscayne Bay Yacht Club of Florida. He was a leading yachtsman in America, who designed and owned ten yachts of this type — the only American-built yawl in these waters.

Pluck and Luck was owned by Albert Mackie. *Albertine* was owned and skippered by the well known Alex Brewster, who was vice-commodore in 1886. E. Harris was the owner of *Cydune*. Paul de Fuenter owned the *No Name* and R. L. Robertson owned *Daisy*. Following are the naphtha engine, open, and canopy-typed launches:

R. L. Bowling	— *Vision*
H. T. Cottam	— *Idylle*
Arthur Duvic	— *Carmita*
W. P. Kirschoff	— *Bijou*
George Mallard	— *Cupid*
Eugene May	— *Yvonne*
E. G. Schleider	— *Fred Fehr*
Jeff C. Wenck	— *Diane*

"General Order No. I" was sent out by the SYC fleet captain, C. P. Richardson, for the annual cruise to the coast to be held on June 18, 1893. The course will be recognized by today's SYC skippers as it is the same route as in today's "Race to the Coast":

> All yachts will assemble in front of the clubhouse at 3 o'clock P.M. preparatory to a start in a race to Waveland, at which point on July 4 a regatta will be given under the auspices of the Bay St. Louis and Waveland Regatta Association.
>
> The first gun will be fired from the clubhouse at 4:30 o'clock p.m. and starting at 5 o'clock p.m. sharp. The time allowance will be governed by the new racing rules. The course will be the regular run, except all yachts must pass to the southward of the old St. Joseph Lighthouse. The home stake will be opposite Nicholson Avenue, Waveland.
>
> All yachts must cross an imaginary line between the stakeboat and the shore. The stakeboat will be known by having a white, red and green light above each other as named. The course is estimated at forty-six miles. The first prize will be a handsome clock presented by M. Scooler;

the second prize a set of colors furnished by the Southern Yacht Club.

The captains of the yachts are ordered to attend a meeting on board of the flagship *Zoe* on July 3, at Waveland. On the morning of Tuesday, July 5th the fleet will sail for the islands, and such points as selected at the meeting of yacht captains referred to in above paragraph.

By order of the Commodore

C. P. Richardson, Fleet Captain.

The boats entered in this race were:

- *Silence*, 33'8"—owned by Peter Labouisse, sailed by Preston Herndon
- *Lady Emma*, 33'8"—owned and sailed by Emile Baumgarden
- *Mephisto*, 30'7"—owned by W. A. Brunet, sailed by Emile O'Brien
- *Lufki Humma*, 26'6"—owned by the Glenny Bros., sailed by Walter Glenny
- *Nyanza*, 26'6"—owned by Stone, Ranlett & Co., sailed by Sam Gautier
- *Toutsy*, 24'3"—owned and sailed by Dr. R. Murphy
- *Barton B.*, 23'1"—owned by H. O. Benedict, sailed by Peter Cooke
- *Agnes*, 26'6"—owned by W. B. Henry, sailed by George Dudley

THE HURRICANE OF 1893

It was called "The Angry Sea of 1893," the hurricane that struck along the Mississippi Gulf Coast in the summer of 1893. It was difficult for anyone to believe that another monstrous storm, the equal of 1856, was possible. Its destruction is vividly described by Dale Greenwood in a March/April 1969 issue of *Down South*, a Louisiana magazine:

> Boats of two, three and four masts that were built to brave the rough waters of the Seven Seas were finally defeated in the Mississippi Sound. Fifteen vessels remain under the sand between the islands (Ship Island and Cat Island) and the mainland, vessels on which those sailors had sat on the decks playing cards and telling tales of the sea on that fateful Sunday morning in 1893 just before a hurricane hit the shore of the Mississippi Gulf Coast 100 years ago.
>
> No names were given to hurricanes in those years. If there were a name to be given them it would be proper to call this one the 'Apocalypse' for surely the four horsemen rode that night.

The principal industry on the Gulf Coast in the 1890s was the shipping of yellow pine and other timber to foreign ports. The timber came from all over South Mississippi via river log rafts, barges, oxen, rail and schooners. After processing through the saw mills, these products were exported via ocean routes that began at Ship Island.

Ship Island had all the facilities of a port, and had a hospital, quarantine station, small shops and warehouses. At the end of the island was located Fort Massachusetts. Nearby was Chandleur Island with a quarantine station, beach houses and quarters for military men stationed there.

It began to come in with a cool breeze from the southeast that beautiful Sunday in early autumn. Large schooners and barges loaded with lumber bound for foreign ports filled the harbor. Hospital patients with the windows open were enjoying the cool breezes. Young lovers were strolling along the sandy beaches and also through the old Fort Massachusetts. The cattle on the farms on Cat Island were grazing leisurely.

That night the winds changed to the east-southeast, the sky began to darken and the clouds began to move with haste over the tall masts. By the time the winds began to howl, the seas began to roar, the sailors began to realize it was a hurricane and frantically hastened to batten down their ships.

By midnight the tides were high and the storm struck with all its force early the next morning with winds of 150 miles an hour. The huge four-masted *Simeon* from Norway cut its mast to avoid capsizing, as the *Remus* from Pascagoula crossed her anchor chains, sinking with no chance of assistance. The captain of the *Remus* tried to leap to the anchor chain on the *Simeon* but a wave tore him away. He disappeared into the sea with his ship.

The *Rozella Smith* of three masts, swept past the *Antilla*, both ships from Nova Scotia, tearing the front of the vessel off and taking part of the *Antilla*'s rigging before turning bottoms-up in the sea. Her entire crew was lost. The Austrian Bark *Annie E. B.* turned on its side, then went over and all but two of its crew perished. The two men floated on a log to Cat Island.

The *Augie L. Green* which had been bound for Galveston, Texas, from its home port at Pennsylvania, was wrecked at sea but was towed into Pensacola for salvage purposes. Only four of the large vessels remained but they were wrecked. Not one of the schooners survived.

The wreckage of the ships was swept to shore, many were found bottoms-up in the swamps and marshes. Bodies were strewn along the beaches like dead fish. Many were never found. Over 200 bodies were counted floating in the water near Cat Island. Two thousand were lost in other coastal areas.

The hospital and warehouses at Ship Island were gone. The northwest part of the island had been washed away several hundred yards. Nothing was standing on the island. To the south only a sand bar remained of

Chandleur Island. The islands would never again regain their popularity or beauty. Occasionally an anchor is picked up by a fisherman's boat and some can be found on display in their yards. Most are rusting away — their tragic stories lost in the soil around them.

At the 1894 annual meeting Commodore Thomas Sully was reelected. To serve with him were Alex Brewster, vice-commodore; Lawrence O'Donnell, rear commodore; J. Watson Glenny, secretary; and H. T. Howard, treasurer.

A smoker was proposed by the board to be held the following month. On account of a fire at West End, the annual regatta was postponed from May 20 to June 9th. Also approved was the change of the annual cruise to the Gulf Coast from July 4 to July 26, leaving the SYC in time to take part in the Waveland Regatta on July 28, 1894.

A club button was approved for the front of the cap and for the lapel. The design was a pilot wheel with a yacht in motion and the SYC monogram in the center of the wheel, which was to have a gold front and plated back. These buttons cost $1.50 each.

The last year of Commodore Sully's term in office continued to be very active, and the year found many fine boats in the SYC harbor. Among the total of 76 vessels were 11 schooners, 14 cabin sloops, 21 open sloops, 8 catboats, and 9 steam and 13 motor yachts. There were 370 members listed on the roster.

BIG BOATS IN SYC HARBOR—1894

The new schooner of the year was the *Meteor*, owned by Andre Fourchy and built by his company, Fourchy Bros. of New Orleans. She was a 50-foot overall yacht built of Louisiana cypress. She had an iron keel weighing 3,000 pounds and a steel plate centerboard of 1,000 pounds. She carried 1,500 pounds of cast iron fitted over her timbers—four large berths, a ladies' stateroom, and sailors' quarters.

The *Elaine* was built for W. A. Brunet by Peter Grubel after designs from Waterhouse & Cheesebrough of Boston. She was 55 feet overall, and in appearance she looked more like an English or Northern boat and may have been likened to a miniature *Defender* or *Valkyrie*, America's Cup yachts. In fact, she was the only boat of this type in the South, having no centerboard but relying on a deep and heavily weighted keel to carry her to windward.

The *Nepenthe* was now owned by George P. Agar, a cotton merchant, and W. S. Dudley. They cruised to New York in the *Nepenthe* and made a fine showing with the yachts of the New York Yacht Club on Long Island Sound. She followed the international races for the America's Cup and then returned to the Southern Yacht Club.

Captain P. S. Anderson had the only yacht in the Southern Yacht Club that ever crossed the Atlantic and "now flies the African elephant as a pennant," reported the *Barometer*. The *Tormentor* was the name of this 50-foot yacht.

Other members of the fleet were N. Emile Baumgarden, a prominent New Orleans real estate man, who owned the *Lady Emma*. She was an open sandbagger. After establishing a long string of victories during the 1890s and not having any more competitors, Baumgarden was obliged to dismantle and lay up the famous old sloop. F. F. Hansell, a member of the large firm of book publishers, F. F. Hansell & Bros., owned the steam launch *Hattie*.

The owner of the large catboat *Hero* was Edward Barq of the firm of Barq & Hughes. The *Barometer* reported that this firm manufactured "that delicious, sparkling and refreshing beverage 'Orangine' which is carried in many of the yachts' lockers as part of necessary stores for a cruise."

Charles F. Buck was often seen cruising on the lake in his large cabin cruiser. Mr. Buck was city attorney from 1880 to 1884. He was also a representative to U. S. Congress in 1894. Mr. Buck was president of the German Protestant Orphan Asylum and well known for his charitable and social work in New Orleans.

Semper Idem, the flagship of Commodore Albert Baldwin, was a large ocean-going steam yacht on which he entertained in the grand old manner.

The second Southern Yacht Club was dedicated in 1900. Added to the new structure, which was erected in the same location on Lake Pontchartrain, were two cisterns. This picture was submitted by Mrs. Charles L. Eshleman, Jr.

CHAPTER VI

1895–1900

COMMODORES	TERMS
Lawrence O'Donnell	1895–96
J. Walton Glenny	1897–98
Albert Baldwin	1899–1900

COMMODORE LAWRENCE O'DONNELL—1895–96

Elected commodore for the year 1895 was Lawrence O'Donnell, who was a highly respected Federal judge in the city of New Orleans. To serve with the commodore were the other elected flag officers: Alex Brewster, vice-commodore; Samuel F. Heaslip, rear commodore; L. D. Sampsell, secretary; and James Buckley, treasurer. (Mr. Buckley was a paroled Confederate from Mobile. After being a resident of New Orleans for thirty years, he became one of the well-known stationers in the city on Carondelet Street.)

The Commodore's flagship was the *Florence*, which was designed by him. O'Donnell was known as one of the best amateur boat designers in New Orleans. The 55-foot *Florence* was one of the most beautifully outfitted craft of her size in the United States. Her entire interior was done in white and gold trimmings. Red plush stuffed cushions and silk draperies adorned her cabin. And the Commodore's reputation as a host made *Florence* one of the most popular vessels ever to sail on Lake Pontchartrain.

THE AMERICA'S CUP RACES—1895

Traveling in 1895 was enhanced when the *Sunset Limited* resumed its route to Los Angeles and San Francisco from New Orleans. Reported the New Orleans *The Daniel* of September 26, 1895: "Each train is to have a special room fitted up for ladies, with library, the latest magazines and periodicals, reclining couches and other needed comfort. These cars will be 69 feet in length and will have seven boudoir sleeping berths, a wash-stand and the necessary lavatory fittings. Instead of being compelled to sit up all day in the 'Cubby' seat of a sleeper, while the liege lords may perambulate the train and gather in a special compartment to talk, smoke, etc."

All railroads were working toward making their train cars more comfortable and luxurious. This was no doubt the reason for several SYC members' taking off for New York and the America's Cup races of 1895. It was the year that the United States' entry *Defender* successfully defended the America's Cup against the Earl of Dunraven, who had returned with another *Valkyrie, Valkyrie III.*

At the 1896 annual meeting Commodore O'Donnell was elected to serve a second term. He was ably assisted by an excellent governing board:

A. M. Aucoin	H. T. Cottam	W. A. Gordon
Albert Baldwin	W. W. Crane	Peter Labouisse
N. E. Baumgarden	C. L. DeFuentes	W. B. Leonard
Charles F. Buck	J. B. Elliott, M.D.	Robert Lynd
H. L. Burton	J. D. Farrell	T. R. Richardson
T. W. Campbell	A. Fourchy	George Smith
A. M. Cooke	W. A. Gordon	J. W. Stone
E. L. Cope	F. F. Hansell	Thomas Sully
		A. Gordon Shepherd

There was much discussion at the annual meeting concerning the removal of the clubhouse "closer to the band stand at West End Park so that its galleries be constructed to overlook more closely the portion of the resort frequented by visitors, which would benefit the club." The cost of repairing the piling under the club was examined and found to be so high that it hastened the approval of replacing the old clubhouse. The total membership was 327, and the balance in the bank of $859.94 was announced by the treasurer. Approval was given to change the club burgee "from a swallow tail design to one with a flowing point."

Many new sloops and one new schooner joined the Southern Yacht Club fleet during Commodore O'Donnell's administration. Among the sloops were the *Tawanta* and the *Naiada*. The *Tawanta*, built by W. N. Johnson of Biloxi, proved to be a revelation, and it took only a few races to demonstrate that "the coming model had come," stated the *Barometer*. She was a jib and mainsail sloop and there was no comparing her with the old style sloops of her size, such as the *Zoe* and the *Susie B*. The *Nydia* was also built in 1896 by Johnson. She proved to be the fastest 30-footer in her class.

COMMODORE J. WALTON GLENNY—1897-98

A prominent New Orleans cotton broker and owner of several noted prize-winning vessels, J. Walton Glenny, was elected commodore of the Southern Yacht Club in 1897. Elected with Commodore Glenny at the 1897 annual meeting, which was held at an office in the New Orleans Stock Exchange, were: N. E. Baumgarden, vice commodore; George P. Agar, rear commodore; L. P. Sampsell, secretary; James Buckley, treasurer; A. M. Cooke, fleet measurer; Dr. J. G. Finney, fleet surgeon; and F. F. Hansell, fleet captain.

After Commodore Glenny was escorted to his chair, he presented a handsome silver trophy as an interclub challenge cup for Half-Raters. Deeds of Gift were approved for other fine trophies which Commodore Glenny donated to the club, namely, the Sully Cup for sloops, the Tranchina-Oliviera Cup for round bottom catboats, and the Scooler Cup for square-knuckle catboats.

Also at the annual meeting a new honorary office was voted on, that of harbormaster, and Mr. J. R. Behrens was appointed by the commodore to this position.

THE ADVENT OF THE NAPHTHA-POWERED BOATS

It was during Commodore Glenny's reign that naphtha-powered vessels brought about a great change in the type of boats being built. These motor boats were slow to catch on, but eventually, with advanced engineering ideas and improved internal-combustion engines fired by gasoline, they became quite numerous—so much so that the club found it necessary to form special rules and regulations to cover them and stage a fleet review and regatta for their benefit in 1904 and another regatta in 1905.

These naphtha-powered boats were not well received by yachtsmen. "The advent of the dangerous, stinking, unreliable naphtha engine in the early 1890s brought out a new breed of yachtsmen—motor boat men," was the statement made by yachtsmen to the *Barometer*.

Among the first SYC owners of these craft were:

H. T. Cottam—*Ideylle*
Arthur Duvic—*Carmita*
Lawrence Fabacher—*Marie*
F. F. Hansell—*Hattie*
W. P. Kirchoff—*Bijou*

George Mallard—*Cupid*
Eugene May—*Yvonne*
Col. R.C. Robertson—*Vision*
Edward G. Schleider—
    Fred Fehr
Jeff J. Wenck—*Diana*

NEW YACHT CLUBS ORGANIZE FROM TEXAS TO FLORIDA

At the turn of the century, more yacht clubs began to spring up along the Gulf Coast from Texas to Florida. In an article which appeared in a yachting magazine in 1892, SYC Secretary and journalist L. D. Sampsell stated, "New Orleans has become a popular winter resort for Northern people and many yacht clubs have been organized in the South.

"In addition to the Southern Yacht Club in New Orleans, other clubs formed are Mandeville on Lake Pontchartrain, Bay-Waveland in Mississippi, Mobile in Alabama, Pensacola, Jacksonville, Biscayne Bay and St. Augustine in Florida and Galveston in Texas." Mr. Sampsell further mentioned the activity on Galveston Bay and the Southern Yacht Club's participation in interstate regattas there.

On August 1, 1891 the *Picayune* reported that "the residents of Bay St. Louis, Mississippi will hold a regatta at Martin's Wharf on August 7th." In 1892 a Bay St. Louis and Waveland Regatta Association was formed by those close Gulf Coast neighbors. *The Times-Picayune* reported, "The Bay St. Louis and Waveland Regatta Association had sponsored the annual cruise of the Southern Yacht Club to Waveland on July 2, 1892. The estimated course was 46 miles. The first prize was a handsome clock presented by M. Scooler. The second prize was a set of colors furnished by the SYC."

Finally, the yachtsmen and civic leaders at the Bay sent a telegram to *The Times-Picayune* in August of 1898 announcing that the mayor and aldermen had met in Waveland and had unanimously passed a motion to grant a 99-year charter to the Gulf Coast Yacht Club (Bay-Waveland) with no corporation taxes necessary. The progressive group estimated that 200 subscribers at $25.00 each would total the $5,000 necessary to construct and equip a fine building, which was erected in 1898. The prospective members had as their objectives "annual regattas with a fine band of music to give concerts once or twice a week, as well as grand balls, etc. The rules of the respected Southern

Yacht Club of New Orleans are to be adopted with amendments suitable to the Gulf environs.

"The new clubhouse is located over the romantic waters of the Bay. It is connected to the shore by an 1100 feet wharf. The wharf begins at the foot of Washington Street, near the center of the town of Bay St. Louis. It is the handsomest equipped and prettiest of the clubhouses in the South," reported the *Picayune*.

The year 1898 held possibilities of another devastating war, this one with Spain. Fortunately, however, the war lasted only from April 21, 1898 to February 16, 1899, but it had created anxiety over the threat it posed to the progress yachting had made in the past few years.

THE OLD CLUBHOUSE OF THE SYC CONDEMNED

The forty-ninth annual meeting in 1898 ended with mixed feelings. Plans for the celebration of the fiftieth anniversary of the Southern Yacht Club were made with sad emotions as a letter received from the city engineer, A. C. Bell, was read, condemning the yacht club building and stating that immediate action should be taken.

Every effort had been made to save the Southern Yacht Club's first home. Mr. Fritz Jahncke of Jahncke Service was contacted to pump shells under the club's foundation; funds were being sought through subscriptions for new piling—all in vain. Orders were given for the demolition of the structure to take place following the fiftieth anniversary activities to be held in June 1899.

COMMODORE ALBERT BALDWIN—1899-1909

As the "Gay Nineties" drew to a close, Albert Baldwin, a man of great wealth, socially prominent and highly respected in the community, was chosen to lead the Southern Yacht Club in 1899. He had been Rex in 1876. Commodore Baldwin was president of the family-owned building materials company, A Baldwin & Co., and he was also president of the New Orleans National Bank. He was the son of a great capitalist and philanthropist. His flagship was a large ocean-going steam yacht, *Semper Idem*, on which he often entertained in the grand old manner.

Elected to serve with Commodore Baldwin were H.P. Richardson, vice commodore; John Soria, rear commodore; L. D. Sampsell, secretary; and James Buckley, treasurer.

An enthusiastic yachtsman, though not a windjammer, Baldwin accomplished much during his term of office. He sponsored more social activities and races, worked for the construction of a new and larger clubhouse, and fostered formation of the first organization banding yacht clubs of the Gulf Coast together in the Southern Gulf Coast Yachting Association, of which he was the first president.

During Commodore Baldwin's reign the race course was shortened from five miles to three miles so that spectators could better view the races. He selected the building committee for the erection of the clubhouse that was to replace the first home of SYC. G. Aletrino was appointed chairman of the committee with members George L. Lyons, H. A. Hamilton, John M. Huger, Chapman Hyams, Jr., Lawrence O'Donnell, J. W. Glenny, W. A. Gordon, F. F. Hansell, and George Smith. All were prominent and successful businessmen.

The fiftieth annual regatta races took place on June 3, 1899, but because of the unsafe condition of the building, there was no regatta dance or gathering of a large number of people for the occasion.

The ceremony of driving the corner pile of the new Southern Yacht Club house took place Saturday, October 21, 1899. Shortly thereafter the old building was torn down and the new structure started. Completed in 1900, it was designed by Hayward L. Burton of Burton & Frankel, architects. Hayward Burton was a talented architect and a real yachtsman, who also designed the beautiful Bay-Waveland Yacht Club at Bay St. Louis, Mississippi in 1898. Former SYC Commodore Thomas Sully was the consulting architect for the SYC Board of Governors on this project.

The bidders for this new edifice were Walter J. Carey & Bros., John McNally, Charles H. Charleston, Charles A. Sicard, A. Downey and C. W. Pohlman. All these bids were rejected, as the lowest from C. W. Pohlman was $11,245.00. In the new bidding, the office of Muir & Fromherz entered its bid of $10,000, but another bid by C. W. Pohlman of $8,314.00 was accepted. With furnishings, the total cost was $12,000.

In order to pay for this new building, subscriptions were issued in the form of certificates for the sum of $25.00 and upwards, bearing six percent interest, the loan to be in the amount of $7,500. All of the certificates necessary were issued and subscribed to very quickly in order that the bidding could proceed.

The new clubhouse was a two-story structure. "On the roof is a cupola whence with lorgnette or the naked eye a wide exposure of water may be seen—it is from this high perch the judges judge, and the reporters report and the timers time the big races," reported *The Times-Picayune*, "and the barnacle-encrusted pilings reflect like regal colonnades." The building was in the same location at the mouth of the New Basin Canal opposite the lighthouse, but closer to shore. "Built like the 'rock of Gibralter,' " said the *Barometer*.

DEDICATION OF THE SECOND SYC HOME

With great pomp and ceremony, the second Southern Yacht Club house was opened May 26, 1900. Master of the new quarters, Commodore Albert Baldwin graciously greeted the many members and their guests. Congratulatory messages were received from all over the country. *The Picayune* reported, "All West End was en fete, flags and bunting greeting the eye in every direction. Leading City and State officials lent their presence." Adorning the walls of the SYC were two beautiful oil paintings of the yachts *Nepenthe* and *Lady Emma*, proudly donated by ex-Vice Commodore N. Baumgarden.

Twenty-three yachts, the largest fleet in years, took part in the regatta celebrating this historic event. The winning skippers and their yachts were N. R. Bailey in *Dream*, J. Behrens in *Nymphe*, Alex Brewster in *Mephesto*, A. M. "Peter" Cooke in *Susie B.*, G. O. Herndon in *Montauk*, M. Moorman in *Louise W.* and John A. Rawlins in *Nydia*. Riding the waves and using their luxurious yachts for ladies to view the races, in addition to Commodore Baldwin's flagship, *Semper Idem*, were Theodore Grunewald's *Josephine*, ex-Commodore J. Walton Glenny's yacht, *Tawanta*, and Fritz Jahncke's commodious houseboat, *Aunt Dinah*.

At the ball held in conjunction with the activities, "The ladies of New Orleans, Mobile and the Gulf Coast were well represented. The southern belles enjoyed the champagne supper and dancing kept up to a late hour," reported the *Barometer*.

For posterity, following are the names of members who served on the Reception Committee for this historic event:

J. H. Abraham	E. W. Deming	Eustace Leche
George P. Ager	George H. Dunbar	Henry Lehman
B. W. Allen	Dr. John T. Elliott	P. A. LeLong
A. Baldwin, Jr	John T. Gibbons	G. A. Letrino
D. G. Baldwin	Charles Godchaux	A. Luria
Charles Ballejo	H. A. Hamilton	A. A. Maginnis

Dr. J. D. Bloom	E. Hernandez	John Mather, Jr.
C. F. Bodley	R. K. Hireman	Bernard McCloskey
George W. Booth	D. H. Holmes	A. K. Miller
A. G. Brice	Frank T. Howard	B. J. Montgomery
Hugh W. Brown	Ernest Huberg	N. H. Moody
E. C. Canning	John M. Huger	Charles Palfrey
Hewett Chapman	W. F. Huger	Charles G. Peters
H. T. Cottam	Fritz Jahncke	George Plant
James deBuys	Charles Janvier	James Rea
C. L. DeGuentes	Pembroke Jones	T. J. Woodward
J. H. DeGrange	Branch M. King	E. D. Wyman
Isaac Delgado	W. E. Lawrence	Victor Young

One sad note was added to the festivities—H. L. Rareshide, one of the oldest charter members of the SYC, who was very popular, passed away in April 5, 1900. He lived long enough to see the club in its fifty-first year.

YACHTING IN THE SOUTH ENDS FIFTY YEARS OF SURVIVAL

The first fifty years in the life of the Southern Yacht Club and all yacht clubs along the Gulf Coast from Texas to Florida were filled with more tragic events than could be found in any historical novel: the devastating hurricanes of 1856 and 1893, the Civil War and Reconstruction period, and the many yellow fever epidemics that plagued the South until 1905 were just some of the handicaps that were faced by our yachtsmen, better known as survivors. These men had great faith and dedication to a sport that they felt was good not only for the social life of our communities, which had been greatly demoralized by the Civil War, but more importantly to the economic growth of a downtrodden South.

CHAPTER VII

1901–1904

COMMODORE
Albert Baldwin

TERM
1901–02–03–04

BIG BOATS IN SYC'S HARBOR IN THE '80s AND '90s

In the 1880s and the 1890s the big cabin sloops were popular and extremely active. W. P. Richardson's *Susie B.* was the top brass then, having compiled a phenomenal string of victories. The other big contenders were:

Agnes	—	owned by Mather Conrad, John Upton, Abe Leverich, Jim Rainey, and Alfred Clement
Scamp	—	owned by H. O. Johnson and J. W. Luther with Davis Wuescher as skipper
Sea Em	—	owned by John Soria
Tawanta	—	owned by J. H. Duggan and A. B. Hunt. Later owned by J. Walton Glenny
Volante	—	owned by Andre Fourchy
Elaine	—	owned by W. A. Brunet
Edith L. Brown	—	owned by Peter Labouisse
Susie B.	—	owned by W. P. Richardson. Later owned by Wm. T. Burns, S. S. Levy, J. B. Sinnott, Jr., and A. M. "Peter" Cooke

Built during the winter of 1901–1902 by Messrs H. P. Johnson, J. W. Luther, and Davis Wuescher, *Scamp* was designed by Charles D. Mower of New York, one of the leading designers of small racing craft at that time. She was the first of the flat, scow speed models to be seen on Lake Pontchartrain. In the class, those under 33 feet in length by racing rule, was the leader of the fleet, the *Nydia*. *Scamp* was built for the express purpose of lowering the *Nydia* colors.

In the annual regatta of 1902, the flat bottom shovel-nosed sloop with Davis Wuescher at the tiller beat *Nydia* by one minute, seven seconds in a stunning upset. *Scamp* went on to win nine races in nine starts that year. She was proclaimed the "Champion of the Southern Gulf Coast Yachting Association and the Southern Yacht Club" and won $210 in cash prizes. Because of her radical design and speed, *Scamp* was broken up after she was ruled ineligible to race further in any of the established classes at the SYC.

During the '80s and '90s and as late as the teens, only two regattas for all classes of boats were held during a season. These were the opening or spring regatta in May and the fall or closing regatta on the last Saturday in August. Around the middle of June the boats raced to some point on the Gulf Coast where most of the boat owners stayed during the summer months, usually Pass Christian, and did not return until August. On weekends there were regattas at various points, Point Clear, Alabama and Bay St. Louis, Pass Christian, Gulfport, and Pascagoula in Mississippi. Sometimes there was a race to Mandeville on the north shore of Lake Pontchartrain and back in September.

The local races would start as soon as possible after the arrival at West End of the train from town. They were long contests sailed over 15-mile courses. The regattas were well attended. "The club held open house and anyone who received an invitation was there. The fair sex turned out in great numbers to see their favorite sailors," reported the *Barometer*.

There was considerable gambling on club races both before and after the Civil War. Members readily backed their favorite with cash. Betting on the outcome of races was extremely lively both before and during the course of the 15-mile contests. According to old newspaper accounts, pool selling on races was quite frenetic, especially while the yachts were making their first turn.

Individual boat owners made wages among themselves, and there were a number of match races for side bets of substantial sums. At the turn of the century this practice had just about vanished. Whether gambling had been frowned upon by club officials or whether it had lost its former appeal is not known, and there are no old timers of that era still around to tell us. Another practice that has long been gone was that of awarding of cash prizes in regattas. It was discontinued during the teen years.

These were the days when yachtsmen owned two and sometimes three luxurious yachts and Lake Pontchartrain was a sporting place to spend a weekend, as spectators often did, at the West End Park, where they could view this beautiful spectacle against the picturesque sunset on Lake Pontchartrain, "Owata," as the Indians named it.

NEW ORLEANS AT THE TURN OF THE CENTURY

At the turn of the century, New Orleans was still the South's largest city, boasting a population of more than 216,000. In the transition period from the strife-ridden Reconstruction period to the twentieth century, New Orleans benefitted from a resurgent economy and a conscious air of boosterism. Palatial mansions began springing up along the major avenues, while the old American Section began taking the form of the new modern American city. The nation had just emerged victorious from its war with Spain. These were the beginning years for many of the city's cultural, entertainment, and educational institutions. One of the most prominent institutions to rise during this first decade was the new Southern Yacht Club on Lake Pontchartrain.

The new and handsome clubhouse brought more enthusiasm and higher spirits among the SYC members. Commodore Baldwin was reelected in 1901 for a third term. His officers were Theodore Grunewald, vice-commodore; A. M. "Peter" Cooke, rear commodore; L. D. Sampsell, secretary; James Buckley, treasurer; Dr. R. L. Riley, fleet surgeon; Holmes Harrison, measurer; and Lawrence O'Donnell, fleet captain. The members of the Governing Committee were:

A. M. Aucoin
H. L. Burton
J. B. Campbell
P. F. Donnes, Jr.
Charles W. Drown, Jr.
W. S. Douglass
C. W. Gruber
H. A. Hamilton
Fritz Jahncke
Charles Janvier

P. G. Merrett
Emile J. O'Brien
P. S. Schneidau
Dudley Selph
C. W. Smith
T. G. Stahle
William Stout
Thomas Sully
M. C. Vaughan

At the 1901 annual meeting, Commodore N. E. Baumgarden was unanimously elected an honorary life member because of his long and valuable service to the club. James Buckley, who had held office for eight years, declined reelection as treasurer and was made an honorary member on motion by N. E. Baumgarden, seconded by J. S. Watters.

When the regular annual meeting of the SYC was held in 1902, there was a change in flag officers, other than that of commodore. Albert Baldwin was reelected; A. M. Cooke was elected vice commodore; J. M. Fornaris, rear commodore; J. J. Hooper, treasurer; and L. D. Sampsell, secretary.

At this meeting it was reported that another old-timer, past Commodore A. A. Maginnis had died. Eugene May and F. M. Ziegler, two prominent SYC members, passed away also. Extensive plans for the improvement of the pen were made by J. T. Coleman of the firm of Coleman and Malochee. The SYC flag emblem was made official, and A. M. Hill, jeweler, was authorized to make a "Burgee pin." Unanimously approved was the money necessary to purchase benches to be placed on the walkway entrance to the clubhouse. Also it was agreed that a safe should be bought for valuables of the club. (This safe still remains a part of the yacht club's office.) The board approved funds for replacing moss pillows with feather pillows. In addition, the amount of $50.00 was allotted for the screening of the galleries (porches) surrounding the new clubhouse for which the newly founded "Rocking Chair Fleet" expressed its gratitude.

This group of old-timers had seen their day of racing in the old schooners on Lake Pontchartrain and now spent their weekends reminiscing about the "good ole days" while relaxing in their tall caneback rocking chairs on the galleries of the yacht club. Now they could rock to their heart's content, unmolested by the gnats and mosquitoes.

THE "ROCKING CHAIR FLEET" OF THE SYC

In *The Times Picayune* of April 3, 1902, there was an article on the newly organized fleet at the Southern Yacht Club. The news leaked out after the annual meeting held in April.

> *The Rocking Chair Fleet Announces Ticket* One of the most unique and interesting features of the Southern Yacht Club election is the Rocking Chair Fleet ticket announced for prominence before the club, headed: For Front Commodore, George W. Booth. The balance of the ticket is

composed of yachtsmen of the old school and trainingship *Santa Maria*. They are all old sea-faring barnacles retired from service, fearless and brave, having rendered many a heroic act upon the waters of Lake Pontchartrain. A beautiful 'tablet' dedicated to them has been planted upon the famous shell pile where the old clubhouse used to stand.

Their entertainments for the summer months are looked forward to with pleasure, and invitations are at a premium. They will be held upon the Club's famous roof garden. Their illuminating aspects are obtained from West End's electrical power and the 'moon'.

Their regattas have a world-wide reputation and their fleet of boats (rocking chairs) are some of the speediest and most complete known to the waters of the dangerous lake.

They have laid out to the naked eye a most beautiful rectangular course of 15 miles, with the winds from all points of the compass, around the club's gallery, and their home stake to be off the 'bar'.

Their election is most assured, a large attendance and a full vote promised. The ticket is as follows: Front Commodore of the 'Rocking Chair Fleet,' George W. Booth; Swift Captain, William P. Richardson.

Steering Committee: Bar Pilot H. W. Brown; Chairman, Rock Pilot, W. J. O'Reardon; Rye Pilot M. C. Joyner; Sky Pilot, T. W. Campbell.

Weather Committee : Prophet on nor'easterns, James Rea, Chief Prophet; Prophet on sou'westers, A. Graffagnia, Prophet on sou'easters, L. Foster; Prophet on sea gulls and Mother Cary's chickens, Charles Ballejo; Prophet on fogs, mists, rain and hail, Frank Hackemuller; Prophet on Irish hurricanes, Dudley Salph; Prophet on moonshine, H. A. Hamilton; Prophet on aurora borealis, sun spots and heavenly disturbance station crow's nest on top of clubhouse, Emile J. O'Brien.

House Committee: Chief of Tramps' Gallery, H. Maspero, Chairman: Chief of Fire Brigade, R. D. Scriven; Chief of Life Saving apparatus, George Redersholmer; Chief of Indian Policy, J. H. Littleton; Chief of Dormitory, N. E. Baumgarden.

Committee of Sailor Talk: Past Master of nautical cuss words, J. S. Watters, Chairman; Instructor in Reefing anchors, Terry Tranchina; Instructor in spitting to windward, Herman Loeb; Instructor in tacking to leeward, Henry Shaw; Instructor in slicing mainbrace, C. W. Smith; Instructor in use of long glass, Patrick McCloskey; Instructor in use of starboard foret' gallant stuns'l boom, tricing line, block straping thimble-seizing, P. S. Anderson. Secretary of the Interior, 'John' the keeper. John Rawlins for Rear Commodore, (owner of many speedy yachts).

There is no doubt that these old barnacles were just as peppy and as feisty in the new yacht club as "rocking chair" sailors on the gallery of the clubhouse, as they had been spirited and competitive as skippers on the lake in days gone by.

FOUNDING OF THE SOUTHERN GULF COAST YACHTING ASSOCIATION

For a long time it had been evident that a union of the yacht clubs between New Orleans and Mobile would be mutually advantageous as there were numerous regattas being held up and down the coast and on Lake Pontchartrain. With consolidation in mind, the Southern Gulf Coast Yachting Association (SGCYA) was formed in 1901. The SGCYA was the forerunner of the present day Gulf Yachting Association (GYA), which was organized after World War I in 1920. In the SGCYA circuit races, each member yacht club entered its club-owned boat; the operation was similar to that of the GYA.

The first to initiate the idea were Commodore Emile J. O'Brien, who was a past master at giving transfusions in yachting circles when necessary, Sam Gautier, Duval Armstrong, L. D. Sampsell, Baron von Schneidau of Southern and Dr. D. A. Nash of Biloxi.

A silver loving cup called the Association Cup was presented by members of the Southern Gulf Coast Yachting Association for the winner of the SGCYA circuit.

The Southern Gulf Coast Yachting Association's booklet of 1903 tells the history of the beginning of this lusty body of yachtsmen:

> The Southern Gulf Coast Yachting Association was organized in the City of New Orleans in 1901, the date being April 28th. The latter is mentioned in the interest of posterity for there is no doubt that the yachtsmen of fifty years hence will point back to the day with pride somewhat akin to the way the members of the Southern Yacht Club feel when they think of the day that organization was formed half a hundred years ago and more.
>
> "The Association is such a lusty body in its salad days that it is pleasant to think about what a grand body it may become and what an influence it is destined to wield in the decades to come. There is no reason why, from a purely local union of the six yacht clubs situated on this corner of the Gulf, it should not expand and embrace all the yacht clubs from Galveston to the Southern most tip of the peninsula of Florida....
>
> "The racing rules of the Association are patterned after those of the Southern Yacht Club. Last year the Association put up a silver cup for the 18 to 22 foot open sloop championship, to be determined by the yacht winning the most races during the six Association regattas. The first winner of this cup was the *Urania* of the Biloxi Yacht Club. In addition to the cup there was a cock-of-the-walk flag to go to the yacht having the best record in every class recognized by the Association.
>
> "Speaking of cups brings to mind the fact that we here in the South are not as keen in that respect as are our Northern brethren of the craft,

for up there every Commodore of a club or a President of an Association is expected to give a trophy every year....

"The objects of the Association are of course to bring the yachtsmen of the section more closely together, to devise uniform rules and classes and to reap what other benefit there is in the old adage of 'in unity there is strength'....

"The Association was organized with five clubs enrolled viz: Bay-Waveland, Biloxi, Mobile, Pass Christian and Southern. A little later the East Pascagoula Yacht Club was admitted to membership, making six clubs on the roll for the first year.

"At a testimonial banquet given the night the Association organized, Commodore Emile J. O'Brien was presented with a handsome watch fob and charm from the commodores of the six clubs forming the Southern Gulf Coast Yachting Association by the president of the Association, Commodore Albert Baldwin. In addition to the title 'Father of the Southern Yacht Club,' Commodore O'Brien was given another more prestigious one 'Father of Yachting in the South"!

In an article he had written for a yachting magazine, L. D. Sampsell praised Commodore O'Brien

"as the father of later day yachting in the South, having started a revival of the sport about 1879 and in 1900 he was largely instrumental in organizing the Association which is so splendidly swaying the destinies of the noble pastime in this section.

Commodore O'Brien serves as SYC Regatta Chairman and officiated as judge for all association regattas. During more than 25 years he has not missed a single season either as a participant in contests or officiating in some capacity looking to the sport and enjoyment of others. Yachtsmen of the South cannot too highly honor and compliment this beloved guide, philosopher and friend."

The first board of officers of the SGCYA was elected at a meeting held on April 28, 1901 in New Orleans at the Southern Yacht Club: Albert Baldwin, president; L. D. Sampsell of the Southern Yacht Club, secretary-treasurer; and vice-presidents were Commodore E. J. Bowers of Bay-Waveland, Commodore J. C. Bush of Mobile, Commodore T. P. Dulion of Biloxi, Commodore Walter Gautier of Pascagoula, and Commodore J. H. Menge, Jr. of Pass Christian.

From the year 1901 newer and faster boats appeared on the waters of Lake Pontchartrain to challenge the "pet of the fleet," *Susie B.*

THE STORY OF *SUSIE B.*

One of the most successful racing yachts of the Southern Yacht Club, *Susie B.*, was built at Keyport, New Jersey in 1870 and was successfully raced there under her original name, *LaBelle*. She was reported to have won every race she entered for eleven years until the death of her owner in 1881, and this is where *Susie B's* tragic story begins.

Spurred by the love of the same lady, W. T. Force, Esq., the owners of *Susie B.* and her rival, a similar craft, sailed a match race for a $1,000 prize and the hand of the lady. The race was held on a sultry summer day—ten miles to windward and return. The wind was flukey, at times dead calm, and the boats hung close together. Mr. Force was observed sculling his boat out of a calm spot with a faint streak of breeze. A protest was entered and the race declared no contest.

Bitterness was accentuated when Force and the lady became engaged. Five weeks after the race, the two yachtsmen met on the street and Force was fatally wounded in a duel that occurred on the spot. It was rumored that the lady became a nun, but it is a fact that *Susie B.* was sold to Mr. McCutchon, a New Orleans coffee importer.

Mr. McCutchon raced the boat on Lake Pontchartrain in 1881 and for several seasons thereafter. *Susie B.* changed hands a number of times, being owned by men by the names of Buckner, Ogden, Hagie, and Charles P. Richardson, who later sold the boat to his brother, Walter P. Richardson. The latter sailed her hard for a few summers then laid her up, where she deteriorated badly for several years before being given to a syndicate composed of Vice-Commodore A. M. Cooke, William T. Burns, S. S. Levy, and J. B. Sinott, Jr. The understanding was that the syndicate would place her in proper condition.

By 1900, *Susie B.* was thirty years old and she was sailed in the First Class of cabin sloops of thirty-three foot length and over by A. M. Cooke, her sailing master. Under him she was to enjoy a phenomenal record.

The first five years the new challengers were:

Picayune	—	owned by Leonard and Yorke Nicholson
Nydia	—	owned by John A. Rawlins. Later bought by A. Baldwin Wood
Calypso	—	owned by Samuel F. Heaslip
Invader	—	Built by Peter Donnes, Jr. Later purchased by Eben and William Hardie and J. Walton Glenny
Chewink III	—	owned by SYC Vice-Commodore John A. Rawlins
Cricket	—	owned by John A. Rawlins (named for his wife's nickname)

Much was written about the "Big Three"— *Calypso, Invader* and *Chewink III*. The *Calypso* was designed and built by Charles C. Henley of Quincy, Massachusetts in 1901 for A. W. Chesterton of Massachusetts. She was 42 feet 6 inches overall, 25 feet on the waterline, with 12 foot 4 inch beam and 2 foot 6 inch draft. *Calypso* twice captured the championship of the 25 foot class in the yacht racing association of Massachusetts. Leading boat builders pronounced her the best example of centerboard sloops ever built and adapted for shallow waters. She was sold for $4,700 to Samuel F. Heaslip of the SYC in 1903. Before being shipped on deck of the Morgan Liner *El Aba* in 1903, *Calypso* was in winter quarters at East Boston. The *Invader* was designed by Burgess & Packard of Boston. *Invader* was built by Peter F. Donnes, Jr. in 1904 under a guarantee to beat *Susie B.* for a syndicate composed of F. Clay Viguerie, Robert Palestine, Maurice Heath, Joseph Tranchina and Harry Mitchel. *Invader* measured 40 feet length overall, 24 feet on the waterline, with 11 foot beam and 3½ foot draft. She had hollow spars and carried 1,145 square feet of sail. She was later purchased by Eben and William Hardy and J. Walton Glenny of SYC. *Chewink III* was built by Fenton for Vice-Commodore John A. Rawlins of SYC. The celebrated Boston racing sloop designed by Burgess & Packard was 49¼ feet long on deck, 25 feet on the waterline with 11 foot beam.

Cricket was built near Boston for John A. Rawlins in 1905. She was designed by Burgess & Packard who put up an $800 guarantee that she would beat any boat in the South under fifty feet in length. Named for the nickname of Mrs. Rawlins, this flat, wide scowlike boat with a weighted centerboard and self-draining cockpit measured 49 feet 9 inches length overall on deck, 40 feet on the waterline, with 14 foot beam and only 15 inches draft. She carried 1,290 square feet of sail (1,393 square feet of spinnaker and 1,000 square feet of balloon jib). *Cricket* was sailed from Boston to New York, then shipped to New Orleans via Morgan Line Steamer in time for the opening regatta of May 25, 1905. She proved to be a fast boat on the reaches but lost going to windward and was beaten by *Cadillac*. *Cricket* won her first race later in 1905 at Gulfport by twenty-six seconds over *Chewink* followed by *Cadillac*. In the Biloxi regatta *Cricket* won decisively and was hailed "Queen of the SYC Fleet." She cleaned up for the rest of that year, winning one race in a forty-seven knot gale and being crowned "Champion of the Season."

THE STORY OF THE *PICAYUNE*

In 1900, the brothers Yorke and Leonard Nicholson ordered *Picayune*. She was designed and built by William Johnson at Biloxi, Mississippi for one purpose, to beat *Susie B*. *Picayune* measured 44 feet length overall, 34 feet on the waterline, with a beam of 13 feet 6 inches. Lloyd Blake was her sailing master.

Susie B. and *Picayune* met for the first time on May 25, 1901 in the fiftieth annual regatta of SYC. *Susie B.* won the race in a driving head storm and never lost a race on Lake Pontchartrain or the Gulf Coast that summer. In the 1902 annual regatta, *Susie B.* again was victorious over *Picayune*. She also conquered the boats from Mobile, Biloxi, Pass Christian, and Bay-Waveland in the final regatta when a fleet of thirty-six boats competed.

In the 1903 annual regatta, *Picayune* finally found success with a new suit of lowcut sails—she beat *Susie B.* by one minute and twenty seconds. *Picayune* won again that year and these are the only two recorded defeats ever suffered by *Susie B*. As if to vindicate herself for these setbacks, *Susie B.* celebrated her thirty-third birthday on July 4, 1903 at Bay St. Louis by winning five prizes: $60 and the Gelpi Cup for first in her class; the Mexican Gulf Hotel Cup for first on corrected time and four gallons of champagne and half a case of fine liquor for first to finish. She again won the final regatta on the Gulf Coast in 1903.

Desperately trying to improve the speed of their boat, the owners of *Picayune* in 1904 cut two feet off *Picayune's* centerboard, moved her mast further aft, cut down her headsail and cast half of her inside ballast into a shoe on her keel, but by this time the fast northern sloops *Calypso*, *Invader*, *Chewink*, and *Cricket* were beating not only *Picayune* but also *Susie B*. This broke up the old rivalry and both boats were sold. *Susie B.*'s name was changed to *Rex*, while *Picayune* was sold to the U. S. and Columbia Trading Company and was taken to South America. *Picayune* met her death on a beach on the Columbian Coast when she was pounded to pieces on January 15, 1905; her remains were carried away by pirates.

(Leonard and Yorke Nicholson were brothers who owned the sloop *Picayune*. Their mother, after their father George Nicholson died, became the business manager of the local newspaper *Picayune* and after her death her two sons took over. Leonard Nicholson served as a member of the SYC board of governors for several years and was very active on committees until his death.)

THE STORY OF *NYDIA*

Built by William Johnson of Biloxi, Mississippi for John A. Rawlins, *Nydia* competed in the second class of Cabin Sloops (under 33 feet) in the late 1800s and early 1900s. She won the annual regatta of 1900 and 1901. She was beaten by *Scamp*, owned by Wuescher Bros & Johnson with Davis Wuescher sailing master in 1902. In 1904 *Nydia* was sold to A. Baldwin Wood. He skippered her to victory over the *Invader, Proteus, Lois, Rogue,* and *Dolphin* from 1905 through 1910.

Mr. Wood was the superintendent of the New Orleans Sewerage & Water Board, a position he held until his retirement in 1950. He was world-renowned for masterminding the complex drainage system in New Orleans by designing the world's largest network of low level canals and underground drains from the city of New Orleans into Lake Pontchartrain. The Wood Screw Pump, invented in 1913, was later used to drain the Zuider Zee in the Netherlands.

Wood's kinship with his boat never ceased. *Nydia* could be seen anchored beside the Biloxi channel near his summer home always in the glare of a permanent spotlight during darkness. After his retirement to his Biloxi home, each day would find him board his boat to set sail for a cruise of the blue water of the Gulf, with his dog by his side.

On May 10, 1956, *Nydia*, her skipper, and his dog, sailing out of the Sound toward Horn Island, were seen by a friend, the captain of a shrimp boat anchored at the dock, to whom he had waved his usual greetings. A short distance out, the captain noticed that his friend had dropped over on bended knees by the tiller of his boat and that the sails were fluttering in the wind. Quickly maneuvering alongside the *Nydia*, the captain realized that her skipper had been struck by a fatal heart attack.

In his will, Mr. Wood left to Tulane University over a million dollars stating: "It is hereby an obligation and provision of this will that my boat, the *Nydia* and her spars shall be carefully preserved by Tulane University for at least 99 years." It is a beautiful sight to see the glass-encased *Nydia* in the sunlit patio of the Tulane Student Center today, the faithful companion that carried a Viking into Valhalla.

At the dedication ceremony, J. Gilbert Scheib, a friend and colleague of Mr. Wood, who also worked with him on many city projects including the construction of underground drainage in the lakefront development, represented the Southern Yacht Club in paying tribute to this great skipper. Representing Tulane University Sailing Club of 1960, Frank K. Riess appropriately stated, "A tree has a body, but when it is fashioned into a beautiful boat, its timber then takes on a soul. This was Mr. Wood's love of the animate for the inanimate."

CLUB-OWNED BOATS FEATURE IN SGCYA CIRCUIT RACES

When the Southern Gulf Coast Yachting Association circuit was initiated, each club entered its club-owned sloop. These boats provided the feature race on the circuit. Following are the club-owned vessels:

Urania	—	Biloxi. Skipper, M. Billingsly
Red Skin	—	Southern. Skipper, John Dunn. Later replaced by *Kayoshk* with Peter Labouisse, skipper
Joker	—	Gulfport
Mr. Bub	—	Mobile. Skipper, William Johnson. Later replaced by *Vesper Belle*
Irma	—	Bay-Waveland. Skipper, Sam Gautier. Later replaced by *Virgin*
Moki	—	East Pascagoula
Flirt	—	Pass Christian. Skipper, J. W. Terrell. Later replaced by *Gladiola*

It was Samuel F. Heaslip of SYC who brought the speedy sloop *Gladiola* down fom the North and presented it to the Pass Christian Yacht Club in 1903, the year Heaslip was elected commodore of the Pass Christian Yacht Club. Formerly the *Galaten* of Canada, *Gladiola* was built to defend the International Cup by the Racine Boat Building Company of Racine, Wisconsin and won thirty out of forty races under the Inland Lake Yachting Association rules.

Built with double planking of cedar, the *Gladiola*'s interior bracing was light bicycle tubing. She carried 500 square foot of sail in her mainsail and jib, and her centerboard was a metal one. She measured 32 feet long on deck, 18½ feet on the waterline and was considered a queen among model-built yachts. In workmanship, the only boat that compared with her was the *El Herrie* of Mobile.

At the second SGCYA annual meeting held in 1902, the following officers were elected: J. C. Bush, commodore; L. C. Dorgan, secretary treasurer (both members of the Mobile Yacht Club), and vice-presidents were Dr. D. A. Nash, commodore of the Biloxi Yacht Club, E. J. Bowers, commodore of the Bay-Waveland Yacht Club, R. R. Krebs from the Pascagoula Yacht Club, and G. B. Penrose of the Pass Christian Yacht Club.

Plans were made for the 1902 SGCYA summer circuit to start on Mobile Bay from the Battle Creek wharf at Point Clear on July 3-4, and the program would work westward along the Coast with the final regatta to be held in New Orleans at the Southern Yacht Club on August 9.

When the boats left the Southern Yacht Club for Mobile, many spectators went over by sail and steam boats. The *Winona*, a revenue cutter, was gayly decorated. Southern, Bay-Waveland, Pass Christian, Biloxi, and Mobile Yacht Clubs were all represented in the featured race. It was a very successful season.

One of the races on the circuit was held on July 12, 1902 at the Pascagoula Yacht Club on Pascagoula Bay in Mississippi. Officiating at the regatta were Commodore Walter Gautier, Vincent Ros, R. A. Farnsworth, George W. Ladnier, and R. R. Krebs. Reported the daily newspaper: "Boats—*Adelaide* of Scranton and *Fanchon* of Biloxi, *Native 2*, *Dawn*, and *Bessie* owned by H. Dantzler of Scranton, *Eva*, *Mary* and the naphtha launch *Louise* of Moss Point were present with full compliments of interested spectators, among whom were many ladies, the crowd afloat and ashore numbering fully 1,000.

"*Adelaide* of Scranton was defeated by *Fanchon* and *Urania*. After the regatta, a well-attended and well-conducted ball was given at the pavilion under the management of the committeemen: Neo Ros, A. R. Miller, W. W. Woodman and J. A. Pelham."

Before the 1903 SGCYA racing circuit started, the Southern Yacht Club held its annual opening regatta. The *Lillian C*, owned by Rear Commodore Joseph V. Dunbar of the Bay-Waveland Yacht Club, was brought over as a special honor to the Southern Yacht Club and admired as one of the largest and most stately boats in the leisure fleet.

The SYC fleet left N. O. for the Bay-Waveland Yacht Club, where a series of races was held. Then on to Mobile Bay, the next stop on the SGCYA schedule. *The Times-Picayune* reported, "While the crowd was slim and the fleet slimmer, each of the Bay excursion boats brought crowds to Point Clear. It was distinctly a gay holiday crowd.

"The fleet on Mobile Bay was a decidedly more representative gathering than had been seen in these waters for many years. The accommodations ashore were far superior to anything the yachtsmen had had the pleasure of knowing in that quarter."

A JUBILEE! JUBILEE!
ON MOBILE BAY SHORES

After the races, a regatta party was held at the Grand Hotel. About midnight, mingled with the melodious sounds of the orchestra, came voices from the beach shouting, "JUBILEE! JUBILEE!" Everyone scrambled to grab pails, buckets, and nets and hastened to the beach to witness a phenomenon that occurs in no other place in this world.

Along the eastern shore of Mobile Bay for twenty-two miles, from Point Clear to Daphne, thousands of live fish and crustaceans come to the surface of the water. They appear stunned for a very short period of time, and as the tide changes, they dart away from the nets toward deep water—the jubilee is over. The seafood is edible because it is all alive.

The *Picayune* reported:

> The schedule called for a regatta at Pascagoula the week following the Point Clear races, but unfortunately the people of that historic and once most fashionable watering place did not awaken to the situation and the few interested men were compelled to abandon the enterprise.
>
> Once upon a time before the Civil War, Pascagoula was the most aristocratic point on the coast, but all the aristocratic feeling has gone, and in the place of the famous watering place, with its grand old colonial hotel, there has taken its place a quiet little fishing village, which does not wish to be disturbed by the progressive present....
>
> The yachtsmen had a week's holiday and then came the regatta at Biloxi, which ended most satisfactorily because the management had kept pace with the improvements brought about by the association of yacht clubs.

At the SGCYA third annual meeting held in Mobile in 1903, the following officers were elected: J. J. Kennedy, president; E. L. Suter, secretary-treasurer (both from Biloxi); the vice-presidents were: Commodores J. V. Dunbar, Bay-Waveland; LeBaron Lyons, Mobile; Dr. R. Duke, Pascagoula; E. C. Carroll, Pass Christian; and ex-Commodore Emile J. O'Brien of Southern. Mr. Gilbert Marshall of Bay-Waveland was elected official measurer, a new office created by the Association. The executive committee was composed of the president and the vice-presidents of the organization.

After the boats left Point Clear, they headed for the Biloxi Yacht Club to continue racing. The visitors and skippers were welcomed by the new officers and committeemen of the Biloxi Yacht Club for

1903: I Heidenheim, president; J. P. Hogan, vice-president; U. Desport, commodore; E. Dukate, secretary; R. R. Bragg, fleet surgeon; R. J. Lowry, measurer; and T. P. Dulion, regatta chairman.

CALYPSO AND CHEWINK III

Of particular interest was the meeting of the new vessels *Calypso* and *Chewink III* for the first time. A large crowd and plenty of entries made the regatta interesting and exciting, especially when *Chewink III* beat *Calypso*. *Chewink III*, sailed by the veteran skipper Samuel Gautier, had brought all of her Boston speed with her. She beat the *Calypso*, which was sailed by her owner, Samuel F. Heaslip, by 4 minutes and 40 seconds.

In the races at Biloxi a battle also took place between the *Urania* of Biloxi and *Gladiola* of Pass Christian. The *Picayune* reported:

> Before *Gladiola* reached Biloxi on its way back from Point Clear, there was a world of *Urania* money about, and the Biloxi sportsmen were willing to bet it. When the *Gladiola* did not hear the gun, started late and finished second, any chance for a killing on the *Gladiola* in the future was spoiled. Already the odds were up to 8 to 5, the *Gladiola* against the fleet and the chances were that it would be 2 to 1 at the Gulfport races, the next stop on the circuit.

THE FIRST GULFPORT YACHT CLUB REGATTA— 1903

The fourth regatta in the series of six like events of the racing and cruising circuit of the Southern Gulf Coast Yachting Association along the Gulf Coast in the summer of 1903 took place at Gulfport, Mississippi. The moment was special because it marked the entrance into the Association of the seventh club enrolled in the first three years of the organization—the Gulfport Yacht Club.

The officers of the Association and all member yacht clubs made a big effort to help the newcomer. The Southern Yacht Club lent to Commodore Jones of the Gulfport Yacht Club ex-Commodore Emile J. O'Brien and L. Burton of its regatta committee to look after the technical details of the races.

The program of the first regatta of the Gulfport Yacht Club was sailed under the rules of the SGCYA. The 18- to 22-feet open sloop class included the competitors for the Association Cup. In this race each of the clubs composing the Association was represented by a special boat. The first race was confined to schooners and catboats. The following day was devoted to races for cabin and open sloops, racing machines, and launches.

At the first meeting of the Gulfport Yacht Club in 1903, the following were elected to office and to committees: J. T. Jones, commodore; James C. Kennedy, vice-commodore; J. R. Pratt, rear-commodore; R. W. Shipp, secretary; George P. Hewes, treasurer; A. J. Catchot, fleet captain; Thomas Favre, measurer; Dr. J. B. Kilgore, fleet surgeon. Committee chairmen were:

J. W. Bozeman	A. McAlpin
Frank Foster	S. P. Mooreman
S. S. Henry	G. E. Northrop
H. Hadlow	F. V. Osborne
F. B. Hewes	W. T. Stewart
H. Hewes	J. T. Stopp
H. A. Jackson	Frank Taylor
E. C. Lucas	J. T. Walker
L. Martin	

These Southern gentlemen, dressed in their yachting attire, warmly welcomed their first Southern Gulf Coast Yachting Association regatta guests.

Covering the event, *The Picayune* had this to say:

> Great interest was shown in the regatta as many spectators were present. The steam yacht *Semper Idem* from New Orleans belonging to Commodore Albert Baldwin of the Southern Yacht Club was there with a party. Harry Howard sent from Biloxi his houseboat in tow of his launch *Sea Toy* and Walton Glenny's power yacht *Chewink III* with a party of friends aboard was also a visitor.
>
> The presence of these fine yachts with the Louisiana Naval Reserve ship *Stranger* laying off the pier, added an attraction to the scene. The spacious galleries and reception rooms of the headquarters of the yachtsmen, the magnificent new Great Southern Hotel, were thronged with fair visitors many of whom wore the colors or badges of their favorite craft.
>
> When the clubhouse at the end of the pier, which was being built by the Great Southern Hotel as an annex, is finished, one entire floor will be allotted to the yacht club for its sole use and benefit. This handsome gift will place the yacht club in possession of premises unsurpassed on the coast. Next year when the clubhouse is finished, the reunion at Gulfport will be eagerly anticipated by every yachtsman on the coast.

An excellent description of the Gulfport Yacht Club was given in the *Barometer*.

> The Gulfport Yacht Club is a handsome and substantial frame two-story building 125x100 feet, resting on a foundation of heavy wooden

piling. It is provided with a 20 foot gallery, extending along the entire length and overlooking the sea.

The first story is an immense cafe or casino covering the entire ground floor and walled in with glass on the south, east and west sides. The upper floor is fitted up as a large and handsome ballroom and gymnasium, the west end being occupied with dressing rooms, toilettes and baths for ladies, while the east end is similarly fitted up for gentlemen with the addition of lockers.

The upper floor of the gallery affords a good view of the yacht races, the western portion, as well as a portion of the gentlemen's club quarters being set apart for the use of the judges, timers and reporters.

The largest crowd of the season witnessed the regatta of the Gulf Coast Yacht Club. *Calypso* beat *Chewink III* to make the score even. A feature race was held for the Great Southern Hotel Cup. Mr. Gage Clark, manager of the hotel, presented the cup to *Kayoshk* the winner over *Moki* and *Virgin*.

It was the largest crowd that had gathered at any one point on the coast. Although the electric cars were not in operation, the Gulf and Ship Island Road operated a train from the depot to the end of the wharf all day, making the trips every fifteen minutes and last night the trains ran all night to the clubhouse. It is not unlikely that Commodore Jones will bring down a vessel for the *Calypso* and *Chewink* class. Gulfport is rapidly becoming second to New Orleans in yachting enthusiasm.

The next weekend the fleet was welcomed by the commodore of the Pass Christian Yacht Club, E. F. Carroll, who was also the proprietor of the Mexican Gulf Hotel.

"Last year," reported the *Barometer,*

the Pass Christian Yacht Club gave the people ashore a great surprise. Oscar Wilson, one of the committeemen, planned to have printed a programme of entries, and these were distributed along the shore showing the number carried by every yacht in the race. From the bathhouses and summerhouses, the residents could follow the race with ease. The undertaking was such a complete success that it will be duplicated this year.

Three big schooners were chartered by the Pass Christian Yacht Club to entertain the relatives and friends of the members and these crafts will follow the races throughout.

Every time there is a regatta at the Pass, the absolute necessity for a clubhouse becomes most pronounced. The Pass was the most fashionable and representative point on the coast and its residents were better able to construct what was needed than a good many other points which already had comfortable clubhouses. The club itself had planned a home for next summer and would shortly circulate a subscription list.

It was fully believed it would have no difficulty in raising the necessary stock to build. A committee on subscriptions and those who wish to get in on the ground floor, or on the piling, so to speak, could call upon them; Messrs N. E. Bailey, Commodore E. F. Carroll, S. F. Heaslip, John Menge, Jr., John M. Parker, Dr. A. R. Robertson and Oscar Wilson.

When the Southern Gulf Coast Yachting Association regatta got under way, Pass Christian was looking its best, crowded with holiday visitors, while its snowy white shelled roadways and the luxurious fringe of foliage in which its shored residents are embowered, contrasted brilliantly in the softened afternoon sunlight.

There must have been 200 spectator boats. Trains from both directions brought crowds of enthusiastic people. There were 99 boats entered. The big schooner, *Robin Hood*, had been anchored well out in the water opposite the long pier of the Mexican Gulf Hotel, and away up and down the shallows east and west of the starting line were strung out long lines of pleasure boats of all descriptions from the big revenue cutter *Winona*, and nearby quite a score of stately schooners loaded with regatta visitors, steam and motor yachts, large and small, cruising sloops, catboats, skiffs, and on down to the dainty canoes that were bobbing up and down on the big waves like tiny corks.

The *Seminole* from Mobile came over with the fleet and had a party on board. The *Chilian* with a large party of ladies from Bay St. Louis arrived. Walton Glenny of SYC got in with the *Pandora* with a number of ladies. Also, the *Josephine* with Captain Grunewald and party came. *Jennie* with Tom Sully and a party of friends, and the *Marie* with Lawrence Fabacher and a big crowd of friends were over. The *Security* with a big crowd, while Commodore Overall of the Mobile Yacht Club was on hand with the *Scimitar* and Commodore Bush and a large party of Mobile yachtsmen were aboard the big schooner *Falcon*. Ralph Smith arrived early with the *Lady May* and a large party of Mobilians aboard.

All yacht clubs belonging to the Association were well represented at Pass Christian, especially a large group from the newly formed Gulfport Yacht Club who were particularly noticeable from the fact that every one of its visiting members was in full yacht club uniform.

There is no doubt that this meeting on Southern waters will arouse lively interest. Not since the sailing of *Nepenthe* of Biloxi and *Annie* of Mobile off Fort Morgan some dozen years ago has there been such enthusiasm.

Previous to the holding of the SGCYA regatta, the Pass Christian Yacht Club held its 1904 annual meeting. The following officers were elected: Samuel F. Heaslip, commodore; E. F. Carroll, vice-commodore; Oscar Wilson, rear commodore; Dr. J. J. Washington, fleet surgeon. The Regatta Committee consisted of N. E. Bailey, E. Martin, Jr., John H. Menge, Jr., J. K. Norman, and Elmer Northrop.

"A special meeting was held later consisting of residents of the Pass and interested yachtsmen to provide ways and means toward securing a permanent organized yacht club here. A charter had already been secured and at this meeting over $1,600 was subscribed and the organizing of a club to be known as the Pass Christian Yacht Club with a handsome clubhouse is promised in the near future," reported the *Picayune*.

Local and honorary Regatta Committeemen of Pass Christian Yacht Club were:

A. J. Adams	J. C. Jury	Dr. N. J. Pinault
F. Anderson	J. H. Knost	Dr. George K.
N. R. Bailey, Jr.	J. H. Lang	Pratt
A. H. Bancroft	G. W. Logan	E. P. Ross
William Barkley	John MacDonald	S. J. Saucier
George P. Brandt	J. T. MacDonald	T. F. Sholars
Locke Breaux	Joseph Macheca	George Soule
Archie Buckner	E. P. McGee	L. P. Sperier
P. A. Capdau	E. Martin	Major A. H.
C. L. Chapotel	Frank Martin	Swanson
T. V. Courtenay	George B.	Walter Stauffer
J. F. Curtis	Matthews	A. G. Tebo
Rathborne deBuys	Captain M. L.	J. M. Terrell
C. J. Delacroix	May	W. A. Terrell
J. F. Del Corral	M. A.	R. B. Thornton, Jr.
M. Dinkelspeil	McClaugherty	Edward Toby
James Donlin	William McGinnis	W. Van
J. A. Fallon	J. M. McGlathery	Benthuysen
L. C. Fallon	E. H. Merrick	Paul Waddell
Prof. Ferrell	W. J. Montgomery	B. M. Walmsley
A. D. Geoghegan	John M. Parker	S. P. Walmsley
Oscar Gerin	R. B. Parker	George Weigand
J. W. Glenny	C. A. Pardue	T. J. Witherspoon
L Edward Hanson	F. L. Patenotte	F. Zeigler
Lawrence F.	Alfred Penn	
Heaslip	P. F. Pescud	

The *Barometer* reported:

After this last regatta was sailed on the Gulf Coast for the 1903 summer season, all boats headed for home (New Orleans). The *Pandora* with Commodore Glenny and party left for New Orleans, while the *Marie* which carried Mr. Lawrence Fabacher and several friends aboard will touch at Ship Island for a day's fishing before returning to New Orleans. The motor yacht *Josephine* owned by Ex-Vice-Commodore Theodore Grunewald, sailed about noon for Spanish Fort.

The *Chilian*, a big motor vessel owned by Thiel and Douglass was another of the power crafts to leave. She towed the catboat *Chiliktah* as far as Bay St. Louis where it will spend the summer at the Bay. Commodore Soria with Pat Foley on the yawl *Sea Em* will lay over until morning before starting out for the westward and home, Mobile. The *Picayune* with her crew aboard the yawl started for Nicholson Avenue at Waveland, her home port.

The big schooner *Falcon* with Commodore Bush of Mobile aboard was the first to weigh anchor at the Pass. She will go from this port to Horn Island for a few days of deep-sea fishing. Following the *Falcon* was Eugene Bush's *El Herrie* which raced in the recent International Challenge Cup.

This has been the departing day for the yachtsmen. Since shortly after midnight yachts have been getting under way for their home ports. Last night as far down as one could see, the anchor lights were scattered like street lamps of a city. Tonight the Bay looks like the scattered lamp lights of a village.

To end the 1903 season of circuit racing at Southern Yacht Club, under the auspices of the Southern Gulf Coast Yachting Association, the many entries in this final regatta were as follows: Pass Christian's *Gladiola*, Biloxi's *Urania*, Gulfport's *Joker*, Mobile's *Vesper Belle*, Southern's *Red Skin*, Bay-Waveland's *Irma*, East Pascagoula's *Moki* and two coast boats *Nina* and *Silence*.

Mr. Eugene Bush of the Mobile Yacht Club brought his handsome schooner the *Falcon* with a large party aboard, among them were Lyman Dorgan, Ed. Huger, Charles Hall, Percy Pettus and others. Pass Christian was represented by Dr. A. R. Robinson, O. L. Wilson, John Menge and Commodore E. F. Carroll, whose ball at the Mexican Gulf Hotel was one of the successes of the season.

Commodore J. T. Jones, the multimillionaire "daddy of Gulfport" sent his speedy power launch, the natty 'Grace' to take part in the motor launch race with Capt. A. J. Catchot, H. H. Minor, Capt. Walter Blount and others. Mr. John Legier of SYC offered his handsome launch, the *Henrietta* for the use of the Regatta Committee. Prizes were offered for schooners—$50.00; cabin sloops—$50, 40, 30; open sloops model $30.00; open sloops $30.00; special $30, 20; catboats $25.00.

The *Gladiola* was the champion of the 1903 season and the winner of the Association Cup. She also won the Gelpi Cup offered by Paul Gelpi & Sons for winning the greatest number of races in an open sloop. This Pass Christian champion received the cash prize for model open sloops and the case of beer offered by the New Orleans Brewing Association, thus wresting the championship of the SGCYA from Biloxi.

Money prizes were given and a basket of champagne was donated by Montgomery, Parker & Co.; A. Gerdes & Bros. donated a 30-foot pennant and an American yacht ensign to be given to the cabin sloop making the fastest corrected time.

Susie B. sailed by A. M. "Peter" Cooke, besides her cash prize, won a box of cigars offered by C. Doyle & Co., and also a case of beer from the N. O. Brewing Association. The visiting yachtsmen were entertained at a dinner, an elaborate affair, in the West End Hotel.

FIRE STRIKES SYC PEN

A couple of months after the closing of the 1903 sailing season, a disastrous fire struck the SYC pen, damaging twenty-nine boats and many boathouses to the extent of $40,000. As usual after a disaster, the Southern Yacht Club members rebuilt the fleet, and by the opening of the 1904 sailing season there were 125 steam yachts, launches, schooners, yawls, sloops, and cat rigs.

The Southern Yacht Club celebrated its 55th annual regatta in May 1904 with a large number of entries. Racing for the first time in the opening regatta was a new class which had gained considerable popularity. The machine open sloops called *Skates* were shallow draft and wide beamed with twin centerboard and rudders. They were 35 to 40 feet long and carried an enormous amount of sail to drive them at speed up to 18 to 20 miles an hour. Frequently, in heavy weather, it was necessary to carry large crews of 20 to 25 men.

For more than a decade these boats provided members with interesting races. In their initial race, V. J. Virgin's *Virgin* was the winner with John Dunn at the tiller. J. B. Campbell's *Kayoshk* was second, and S. F. Heaslip's *Gladiola* was third. Under the name of *Caroline*, *Virgin* had won the Inland Lakes Yachting Association Class A championship in 1901.

After the regatta there was a stag party. The Entertainment Committee provided an excellent programme of vocal and instrumental music. Among those who contributed to the evening's pleasure were: Percy Cahill, a black face comedian; "Romeo" the whistler, Joseph Costello; Ed. McCarthy, an Irish comedian; and Temple Black, tenor. The director was L. Pico.

The Race to the Coast for the Fourth of July week 1904 ended at the Bay-Waveland Yacht Club and was won by *Kayoshk* ably handled by Jack Campbell, Lloyd Blake, Peter Labouisse, and the Buckner boys.

The new 1904 Bay-Waveland Yacht Club officers welcomed the fleet. They were John A. Rawlins, commodore; L. H. Fairchild, vice-commodore; James V. Dunbar, rear commodore; Emile J. O'Brien, secretary; Richard Mendes, treasurer; W. J. Chapman, fleet captain; Carl Marshall, measurer; and Dr. R. J. Turner, fleet surgeon. The big clubhouse and its broad galleries were crowded with spectators long before the prep gun fired, the crowd being about equally divided between the male sex and the fair sex, all clad in yachting holiday attire.

A large party of ladies was invited aboard the Revenue Cutter *Winona*. At noon the little ship, dressed for the nation's holiday, opened up the national salute of twenty-one guns. All the yachts in the harbor fired off cannon crackers, and for a few moments it sounded like a real Fourth of July. In a stiff breeze, thirty-three vessels sailed in the second Gulf Coast race held at the Bay.

The Bay-Waveland Yacht Club was also the setting for the 1904 SGCYA meeting. The delegates present were: Emile J. O'Brien of Southern; E. A. Breath, Ed. Pinac, and T. L. Evans of Bay-Waveland; John J. Kennedy and W. L. Via of Biloxi; and ex-Commodore Lawrence O'Donnell of Pass Christian. The newly elected officers of the SGCYA for the year 1904 were: Commodore John A. Rawlins of Bay-Waveland, president; J. K. Glennon of Mobile, James E. Kennedy of Gulfport, Samuel F. Heaslip of Pass Christian, Richard Mendes of Bay-Waveland, Walter Gautier of Pascagoula and L. Via of Biloxi, vice-presidents; and Emile J. O'Brien also of Bay-Waveland, secretary. Gilbert Marshall was appointed the official measurer.

SYC PET CHAMPION *SUSIE B.* MEETS DEFEAT

In the final regatta held in August 1904 at the Southern Yacht Club, the leading event on the program was the race in which *Calypso* defeated *Chewink III* and *Susie B.*; *Nydia* defeated the *Invader*.

For her race, *Susie B.* was converted into what was practically a sandbagger, except that she was carrying live ballast instead of sandbags. 2,000 pounds of ballast had been taken out of her, leaving her stripped of the last pound, but in lieu of this, she carried a crew of 18 able-bodied men instead of six or seven, which would have been ample force to handle her. In fact, Vice-Commodore Cooke had made up a crew of twenty-one but three of them remained ashore.

Reported the *Barometer*, "The good old *Susie B.*, the Southern Yacht Club's pet champion, went down in defeat by the new boat *Calypso*. It was conclusive proof that *Susie B.* because of the newcomers, the *Calypso*, *Invader* and other new boats, is now to be regarded as a treasured old memento of a glorious past.

Chewink III had a crew of fourteen and *Calypso* had her usual seven. *Nydia* was also carrying a big crew for a small boat, not less than eight, while all other boats appeared normally manned as far as one could see from the judges' perch in the cupola of the clubhouse. The *Invader* had ten men on board.

The SYC's *Kayoshk*, cleverly sailed by Peter Labouisse, won the Association Cup. He led *Moki*, sailed by Commodore Walter Gautier of Pascagoula. The Bay-Waveland's *Virgin* was dismantled. The *Urania* of Biloxi was disabled, and the *Gladiola* of Pass Christian sprang a leak and withdrew.

Continued the *Barometer*:

> Captain Walter Jahncke's splendid model catboat the *Chilktah* was literally running away (as usual) from her competitors. Even the much vaunted speed of the Biloxi craft was not a match for her.
>
> Among the visitors for the event were Eugene 'Gene' and Curtis Bush, owners of the 'Falcon' who arrived by rail from Mobile. Commodore Jones of Gulfport and Bernard Chotard of Mobile also attended.
>
> At the banquet following the regatta, Commodore O'Brien in his usual humorous speeches created a great deal of fun. A feature of the banquet was the presentation to Commodore O'Brien "the daddy of yachting in the South" and the prime mover and instigator and worker for the promotion of the Southern Gulf Coast Yachting Association, of another magnificent gold watch and fob, a gift from the Commodores of the Mobile, Biloxi, Gulfport, Pass Christian, Bay-Waveland and Southern yacht clubs, as a token of their appreciation of his untiring efforts in the interest of yachting. The timepiece was presented by John A. Rawlins, President of the SGCYA. Commodore O'Brien was deeply touched and surprised and made one of the most heartfelt responses he has ever made. Thus ended the last regatta of the season of 1904.
>
> After the presentation of trophies, the visiting yachtsmen were entertained at dinner by the skippers of the *Chewink*, *Calypso* and the *Invader* at the West End Hotel. A delicious repast was served including choice wines and cigars. Near the end of the feast speeches were made.
>
> After a discussion at the dinner party concerning the closeness of the three boats over the season, it was decided to have a "race for fun," the Regatta Committee of SYC offering a copper cup to the winner, in order to make the results of the race a record. The race was held and the winner of the cup was *Chewink III* over second place *Calypso* with *Invader* third. *Calypso* was later sold to Vice-Commodore A. M. "Peter" Cooke for the sum of $4,700.

FIRST ALL-GIRL REGATTA—1904

Commodore Emile J. O'Brien had opened the door for the females in 1897 before he left office. He had initiated a resolution, which was adopted by the board, "to permit ladies to all parts of the clubhouse." Another more daring move was made when on September 3, 1904 the first "all-girl race," as it was referred to by the club, was sailed. The races were held in the Knockabout Class boats and were conducted around the same triangular course as that of regular races, much to the dismay of the "rocking chair sailors" who thought it was scandalous.

The winner of this first race was Miss Carrie Wuescher, sister of Davis Wuescher, a popular sailor of the time. She sailed in her brother's boat the *Sinner* with Edna Byrnes and Miss Aggie Roach as crew. In second place, on *Juanita*, was Miss Stella Hyman as skipperette and Miss Eleanor Frith and Mrs. E. Harper as crew. Third place finisher was Miss Hattie Dunn, skipperette, with Misses Mabel Clark and Lucie Whitcomb as crew, on *Siren*. The fourth place boat was *Rascal* with Miss Maude Bowe, skipperette and Mrs. J. J. Clark and Mrs. Ethel Bowe as crew.

Ladies had already entered the field as crewmen in America's Cup races. Harold K. Vanderbilt's wife ("Gertie" to her shipmates) was one of seven women to partake in Cup competition and the second of two American ladies who joined the afterguard. The other, Mrs. Oliver Iselin, sailed with her husband in 1895 and 1899 on *Defender* and *Columbia*. The most striking of their English counterparts was Mrs. William Henn, whose husband raced *Galatea* here in 1886 while she served tea below in a plush facsimile of a Victorian drawing room, complete with several dogs, a cat and a pet monkey.

WINTER VISITORS ARRIVE AT SYC

There was much activity on Lake Pontchartrain during the summer months of 1904 and into the winter season with the arrival of many boats from the North. A news feature from *The Times-Democrat* of November 25, 1904 reported:

> *Numerous Pleasure Yachts Arrive for the Winter Season.* This is the season of the year for the motor yacht fleet to be coming down the river bearing owners and friends seeking the waters of a milder climate. The number to come down this season will be larger than ever owing to the fact that the St. Louis Exposition has attracted a large fleet of yachts to the city during the last few months.
>
> The advance guard has already arrived, four large yachts having passed the city yesterday and gone down to Lake Borgne Canal locks enroute to Lake Pontchartrain and West End. Among those steam yachts are the *Zeta II*, a large gasoline motor cabin yacht which made the voyage from here up the river and across the Great Lakes to New York and thence down the Atlantic and across the Gulf back to this city about two years ago, the trip being a total of 6,000 miles.

The other Deming boat is a large houseboat, equipped with a gasoline engine. This cabin yacht *Cora II* is owned by H. U. Hayden of Chicago. The other fine cruising yacht *Everglades* is headed for Florida.

THE HISTORY OF THE SYC GOLD CHALLENGE CUP

The famous Gold Challenge Cup, which had disappeared before the Civil War, reappeared one day at the Southern Yacht Club in 1904, after an absence of some forty-odd years. Commodore John G. Robinson of the SYC was the first winner of the trophy in September 1849. He won it again in 1857, 1858, and 1859. These three consecutive victories enabled Robinson to retain the cup permanently.

"When the tocsin of war was sounded in 1861 and sons of the blue and gray deserted the pleasures for a more serious business, the Gold Cup disappeared," reported the *Barometer*. "Some forty years later the Cup was found in the possession of the family of descendants of slaves who worked for Captain Robinson. It was immediately returned to the Robinson family when a relative of the faithful servants of the captain discovered its owner."

In the minutes of the SYC dated May 12, 1904, it is stated, "A gold cup which had been won in a yacht race the year the club was organized, 1849, was presented to the club by Mr. Clark Nixon. On motion of Mr. Samuel F. Heaslip it was resolved to receive the cup and a card of thanks was voted Mr. Nixon."

After the recovery of the Gold Challenge Cup, the next winner of the trophy was *Cricket*, sailed by Alfred Ducourge in 1905. E. H. Wharton-Davies won it in 1909 and in 1910 with *Cadillac*. Then the winner was Alfred F. Landry's *Chewink* for two straight years, 1911 and 1912. J. F. del Corral's *Metawee* was first in the race in 1913. Winners of the cup during the following eight years are unknown, perhaps because of World War I and the lack of interest in sailing. The motorboat was just then coming into its own and many club members were into powerboating. Edwin G. Pinac's *Robin Hood II* won the cup in 1921 and in 1922. Blaise S. D'Antoni's *Sorceress* won in 1923 and his *Sorceress II* was listed in 1926. The other winners were: Stanton Jahncke's *Cinderella* in 1924 and Leslie P. Beard and J. Ben Ravannack's *Robin Hood IV* in 1925, 1927 and 1928. Evidently, because of the stock market crash, followed by the Depression of the thirties, there were no winners shown for 1929 through 1939. In 1940, the *Invader* of Robert B. Todd is inscribed and in 1941 Tom Brennan's *East Wind*. The cup was retired before World War II, never to leave its place in the trophy room of the Southern Yacht Club.

CHAPTER VIII

1905–1909

COMMODORE
Albert Baldwin

TERMS
1905–1909

THE YEAR OF THE FOUR BIG Cs
CALYPSO, CHEWINK III,
CRICKET AND CADILLAC

A parade of 200 boats went out on Lake Pontchartrain in the 56th annual regatta in May 1905. Quite a number of big power vessels with large parties of friends aboard was seen on the lake. The big schooner *Falcon* from Mobile, with the owners Eugene and Curtis Bush aboard, was present with George Dunbar's big schooner *Olga* from Pass Christian and the *Marie*, with a party of friends of Mr. Lawrence Fabacher. Commodore Baldwin's big flagship *Semper Idem* was handled by J. Walton Glenny with an excellent crew of Ashton Lawrence, Clem Penrose, and Baron P. Sefton von Schneidau, who were among the fourteen yachtsmen who made *Susie B.* famous. (*Susie B.* was now named *Rex.*)

In the regatta, the crowd centered its interest on the big four, *Cadillac*, *Calypso*, *Chewink III*, and *Cricket*. *Cadillac* was the winner in a very close contest and won the handsome silver cup offered by the SYC.

The *Calypso* and *Chewink III* were already located at the SYC when the *Cricket* arrived in New Orleans from New York via Galveston in December of 1904. She was brought down by Commodore John A. Rawlins, who was a long-time member of the SYC and at that time also commodore of the Bay-Waveland Yacht Club. *Cricket* measured 49' 6" overall, with 40' waterline, 14' beam, and 3' draft. The mainsail contained 1,340 square feet of canvas and the jib 274 square feet; the total working sail was about 1,615 square feet. This was a new boat built by Burgess & Packard of Boston.

After his *Calypso* had been beaten a few times in its first season, Samuel Heaslip sold her to A. M. "Peter" Cooke and then purchased the 1901 Canada's Cup champion *Cadillac* in November 1904.

The *Cadillac* was built at about the same time as the *Calypso*, in 1901, by Manley Construction Co. at Quincy Point, Massachusetts. She was known as the *Queen of the Great Lakes* and measured 48' 1½" overall, 28' 7" on the waterline, with 11' 5" beam. Her frame and keel were of oak and her trimmings of mahogany. Double planked, with waterproof material between the planking, she was as tight as a cork. Her complete inventory included eight large waterproof cushions of imitation leather, velvet Brussels carpet, oil cook stove, cooking utensils, dishes, silverware, and charts. She was purchased from a syndicate of Detroit yachtsmen.

The Times-Democrat reported, "The large cabin sloop yacht *Cadillac* recently purchased at Detroit, Michigan by Commodore Samuel F. Heaslip, President of the Southern Gulf Coast Yachting Association, was towed by J. B. Campbell's gasoline motor yacht *Seminole* from the river to West End. This was only one of many well-known yachts from the East and West coasts that Commodore Heaslip brought to Southern waters."

The *Cadillac* was the fastest 40-footer ever built. She raced continually for three seasons from the Straits of Mackinaw to the St. Lawrence River and had only been defeated four times since the original Canada's Cup races for which she was built. During 1903 when she went to Lake Ontario, she defeated every boat started against her.

THE STORY OF *CADILLAC*— QUEEN OF THE GREAT LAKES

The Times-Picayune of November 25, 1904 repeated an article written in *The Detroit Free Press* about the *Cadillac*. "Goodbye to the *Cadillac*! With tears in our eyes some of us watched her taking a land journey up Woodward Avenue behind a team of horses on a truck. One could not help a bit of sentiment. Many a time she has turned just the same way, but her nose was buried into the water, and there was a stake with a flag on it to mark her course. But it was probably her last journey in this section of the country. Hereafter, she will sail under the colors of the Southern Yacht Club. Well, here's good luck, *Cadillac*, and may you cause as much joy in the hearts of your new friends as you gave to those who loved you here."

Another interesting event held in conjunction with the 1905 opening regatta was the skipperette race, with Mrs. John A. Rawlins on *Cricket* coming first in the cabin sloops over 29 feet class; Mrs. C. E. Reine won on *Proteus*, a cabin sloop under 29 feet, and Miss Hattie Dunn was first in *Rascal* in the Knockabout class. The ladies raced on Saturday before the big race on Sunday.

YELLOW FEVER EPIDEMIC CANCELS RACE AT THE PASS

This was to be the last regatta to be held during the summer of 1905. *The New Orleans States* of July 23, 1905 out of Pass Christian reported: "The 11th annual regatta played in hard luck at Pass Christian. The yellow fever quarantine scare kept many away from the regatta. The Board of Health stated Pass Christian would be quarantined to all persons from New Orleans if they were not ill."

END OF YELLOW FEVER EPIDEMICS

Fortunately, 1905 was the year of a major discovery. Dr. Walter Reed, head of the U. S. Army Yellow Fever Board, identified the culprit responsible for the many yellow fever epidemics since the first, which had occurred in 1793. Dr. Reed demonstrated the carrier role of the mosquito, which had been brought into New Orleans from freighters whose cargoes were shipped from Africa. Controls were effectively undertaken, which reduced the possibility of these insects reproducing in areas of stagnant waters.

The many epidemics of yellow fever and the death toll of native New Orleanians from such attacks will forever remain a very bleak and horrible part in the history of our beautiful city.

SYC ENTERS FIRST INTERNATIONAL YACHT RACE

The Southern Yacht Club's first venture into international yacht racing occurred in 1906 when an invitation was extended to send a crew for the trial races in the Sonderklasse eliminations for the Roosevelt Cup at Marblehead, Massachusetts. The winner of this series would represent the United States against Germany in an international series of races at the Imperial Yacht Club in Kiel, Germany.

Upon receiving the invitation, Vice-Commodore Samuel F. Heaslip endorsed the idea of building a boat for these races and personally subscribed $1,000 toward its cost. A subscription was started among the club's 800 members to raise the $3,500 believed needed to build a new boat to the class specifications (20 feet waterline, 30 feet on deck, 7-foot beam, 5-foot draft, and 550 square feet of sail). A committee was appointed to handle the transaction. It consisted of a group of prominent members: Ernest Lee Jahncke, Judge Lawrence O'Donnell, Samuel F. Heaslip, Emile J. O'Brien, W. A. Gordon, and J. Walton Glenny. The boat was built and christened *New Orleans*. The team captain was ex-Commodore Emile J. O'Brien.

A Boston newspaper article of July 6, 1906 read:

> The *New Orleans* built by Small Bros. is to compete in the trial races to meet the three German sloops being sent over to represent Emperor William's nation in an international contest.
>
> President Theodore Roosevelt has offered a cup to the winner of these trial races and the Southern Yacht Club of New Orleans has contracted with Small Bros. of Boston for the construction of the fastest vessel they can build of the type arranged for which is called the Sonderklasse.
>
> The *New Orleans* was sailed by Commodore S. Heaslip in Boston in the Sonderklasse race of the Quincy Yacht Club annual regatta off Hough's Neck.

Heaslip was the skipper selected to represent the SYC in this race; however, when it was discovered by the Federal Government that Commodore Heaslip was not a naturalized citizen of the U. S., he was disqualified and Davis Wuescher sailed in his place, with crewmen C. Lawrence and John W. Luther. As soon as this oversight was brought to his attention, Heaslip immediately had the matter rectified. The Commodore had come from England at the age of three, and his family had settled in Pass Christian, Mississippi.

A broken mast in the second race forced Wuescher to withdraw from the contest after having won the first race. He finished seventh in a class of nine "Sonderklasse racers." A New York boat, *Vim*, was the winner with Charles Francis Adams, the great skipper who later piloted two boats to the America's Cup triumph over Sir Thomas J. Lipton's *Shamrocks*. The winner of the Marblehead event went on to Germany in 1907 to race for the Emperor William's cup offered by the Kaiser.

Sailing for a very long time was cancelled on Galveston Bay when in the summer of 1906 a vicious hurricane swept the island and with it took 6,000 lives. This is believed to be the greatest number of deaths from a hurricane in history.

The 1907 SYC annual regatta opened with the main attraction centered on the races of the three big *Cs. Calypso* was now owned by Vice-Commodore A. M. "Peter" Cooke, *Cadillac*'s owner was Commodore Samuel F. Heaslip and *Cricket* belonged to Commodore John A. Rawlins.

An exciting race in the 1907 annual regatta was the contest of the machine sloop *Seawanhaka* of Commodore Heaslip against Vice-Commodore Ernest Lee Jahncke's *Wahkita*. This famous racing yacht *Seawanhaka*, originally named *Manchester*, was designed by E. A. Boardman, one of the most successful yacht designers of the day and built by J. L. Bemer of the Manchester Yacht Club for the purpose of a challenge for the Seawanhaka International Challenge Cup in 1905. This cup race sponsored by the Seawanhaka Corinthian Yacht Club was initially held in 1895 and was dedicated for match racing between foreign yachts. It had been captured by Canada in the second match race in 1896 and successfully defended for eight successive years.

The challenge match, the eleventh match for the Seawanhaka Challenge Cup, was held on Lake St. Louis, July 20 to 24, 1905 and was won by *Manchester* against *Alexandra* of the Royal St. Lawrence Yacht Club of Canada. It was the most important yachting event of the year, particularly since America had at last regained the prize.

When *Manchester* was purchased the next year by Commodore Samuel Heaslip of Southern Yacht Club, there were headlines in the New Orleans *The Times-Democrat* with an article which described the purchase as "plainly destined to make the yachting season of 1907 one of the most sensational this section of the yachting world has known in many years." The boat was renamed *Seawanhaka* because "she was only the second United States-built and sailed craft that ever lifted the celebrated Canadian Cup of that name," stated the *Barometer*.

The *Seawanhaka*'s new owner became SYC's Edward H. Keep when Samuel Heaslip joined with J. M. Kinabrew, F. G. Otis, Henri T. Howard, and John Legier in buying the *Massachusetts*, champion of Northern waters and a successful defender of the Canada Cup previously won by *Seawanhaka*.

The *Massachusetts* was very similar in construction to *Seawanhaka*, both boats having been designed and built by Edward Boardman of Boston. The *Massachusetts*, however, was a trifle larger than *Seawanhaka* in beam and in total sail carried. *Seawanhaka* hoisted 520 square yards of canvas to *Massachusetts*'s 550 square yards.

In 1908 *Seawanhaka* was declared "Champion of the Southern Waters" and Ed. Keep, who was the skipper in all of the races, became one of the famous sailors of the Southern Yacht Club. A few years later, Keep sold *Seawanhaka* to C. B. Maginnis, who had owned *Senorita*. Ed Keep bought *Target*, another cabin sloop in which he won many victories.

HOUSTON YACHT CLUB HOSTS INTERSTATE RACE

Before the 1908 season was over, the Houston Yacht Club was host to an interstate race held on Galveston Bay. A crew of expert SYC skippers won the three-race series.

Then things began to happen to yachting. Interest lagged. Some blamed it on the increasing popularity of the automobile. New Orleans, as well as the rest of the nation, suffered from a general economic depression for the next few years.

Sailing activity on Lake Pontchartrain was very disappointing during the depressed years of 1907, 1908, and 1909. But lack of spirit in sailing did not diminish love for dancing, and every weekend found the would-be skippers swinging their ladies to the tune of jazz bands instead of the sound of sails whistling in the winds.

Regattas were festive occasions. Commodore Baldwin was a keen lover of yachting in all its phases and he entertained lavishly on board his flagship, *Semper Idem*, which was reported to be the most famous of yachts on our waters.

The officials for the opening regatta and dance of 1909, which would be the last for Albert Baldwin as commodore were:

Commodore, Albert Baldwin
Vice-Commodore, Ernest Lee Jahncke
Rear Commodore, G. M. Conrad, Jr.

J. R. Behrens	H. P. Johnson
A. R. Burt	A. J. Leverich
A. M. Cooke	T. D. Miller

F. S. Decker, Jr.
P. F. Donnes, Jr.
L. C. Glenny
J. W. Glenny
D. H. Holmes

W. T. Nolan
Lawrence O'Donnell
Walter Parker
Dr. R. L. Riley
L. D. Sampsell
J. R. Upton, Jr.

One high spot of the 1909 sailing season was Harry Howard, Jr.'s new boat *Xiphias*, a revolutionary machine cat-boat which was making her first appearance on Lake Pontchartrain. A decided departure from other vessels in her class, *Xiphias* was the only cat-boat in the fleet to have hollow spars, bilge boards, and double rudders. But she excelled, winning easily under Dave Wuescher's handling.

THE SOUTHERN YACHT CLUB WALTZ

One of Commodore Baldwin's many admirers, Miss Regina Morphy, "respectfully dedicated" to him "The Southern Yacht Club Waltz"—the sheet music for the piano was found in a collection of the Jazz Museum in New Orleans and donated to the archives of the SYC.

The machine sloop Seawanhaka was the champion of Southern waters in 1908 under the skillful hand of Edward Keep of the SYC.

CHAPTER IX

1910–1916

COMMODORES	TERMS
Louis H. Fairchild	1910–1911
Samuel F. Heaslip	1912–1913
Ernest Lee Jahncke	1914–15–16

COMMODORE LOUIS H. FAIRCHILD—1910-11

At the 1910 annual meeting and election of officers, Louis H. Fairchild was selected to serve as commodore and A. M. Cooke as vice-commodore, with E. H. Wharton Davies as rear commodore. Board members were: J. M. Kinabrew, J. W. Porch, and A. W. McLellan.

Commodore Albert Baldwin was praised highly for his dedication and service during his ten years as commodore of one of the largest yacht clubs in the United States, the SYC.

Commodore Fairchild was the senior partner in a brokerage house with John B. Hobson. Fairchild and Hobson was the largest brokerage business in the Southwest. At the turn of the century this well-known firm was the first to advertise "connections to New York and Chicago by private wires."

The commodore's summer home was in Waveland, Mississippi, where he served as mayor for ten years. His flagship was the beautiful yacht *Sweetheart*.

The first time the Grunewald Cup was sailed for was July 1, 1910. Challenging for this trophy were the *Cadillac, Sinner, Chewink III, Calypso* and the *Agnes* in a race of 140 miles from New Orleans to Mobile. The *Cadillac* won in remarkable time of 23 hours, 57 minutes and 23 seconds.

Sluggish business conditions in New Orleans and a continued lack of interest in sailing rendered the seasons of 1910 and 1911 uneventful. However, through his capable leadership, Commodore Fairchild was able to keep the club afloat.

COMMODORE SAMUEL F. HEASLIP—1912-13

The SYC's next helmsman for the years 1912 and 1913 was the prominent sportsman and financier, Samuel F. Heaslip, another famous yachtsman of days gone by who reigned with the leaders for over thirty years. He made his mark in the history of yachting by the many luxurious yachts he brought to the SYC fleet.

Elected with Commodore Heaslip were: J. C. LeBourgeois, vice-commodore; Lawrence Fabacher, rear commodore; W. H. Parham, secretary-treasurer; Dr. C. A. Dorrestein, fleet surgeon; and Herbert P. Johnston, measurer. Governing Board members were: William Allen, Charles E. Cormier, T. R. Falvy, F. E. Farrell, John Legier, Jr., and C. Lee McMillan.

The commodore was president of the Crescent Forwarding and Transportation Company, which operated the entire drayage business for the American Sugar Refining Company. He was one of the founders of the New Orleans Jockey Club, of which he was elected the first president in 1904. (The Jockey Club was organized a few years after the closing of the Metairie Race Track and until 1908 was a very popular place of entertainment and social dinner parties.) The Commodore's summer residence was in Pass Christian, where he had considerable investments and had been the commodore of the Pass Christian Yacht Club in 1904.

In 1912 the machine sloop class was brought to the forefront and the number of entries in that particular field was materially increasing. The so-called 1912 sailing season of SYC brought out more speedboats than sailboats.

A big surprise awaited all in attendance at the 1912 opening regatta when Leonard K. Nicholson, owner of that famous sailboat *Picayune*, appeared at the wheel of a power boat, the *Belladonna*. His winning ways remained with him, as he won the 20-mile contest. It was reported in the news media that Mr. Nicholson also was a champion "automobilist." This unique sailing season's participants, all former sailors, were:

Blue Wing II— a large craft owned by Farwell and Jahncke

Black Hawk—	another flyer owned by F. W. Salmen of Slidell
Kitsey—	owned by Gallagher and Ferran
Vim—	owned by J. Sabathe
Osprey—	owned by Arthur J. Moran, a cabin boat
Belladonna—	owned by Leonard K. Nicholson

THE FIRST SOUTHERN MARINE MARATHON

The first Southern Marine Marathon for power cruisers was run in 1912 from West End to Pensacola, Florida, a distance of approximately 200 miles. For many years it was recognized as the longest power cruiser race staged in salt water in the United States. Big fleets competed in this race annually until 1922, when it was abandoned.

While the machine sloops were grabbing all of the headlines, there was quite a fleet of dories that did some hard racing for several years. These included J. P. O'Leary's *Alabama*, Frank G. Otis' *Smoke*, Stirling Parkerson's *St. John*, L. H. Fairchild's *Little Sister*, George C. Rand's *Squab*, and E. A. Leonhardt's *Laset*. There were also James L. Rea's *Traveller*, Wm. A. Porteous, Jr.'s *Indian*, and E. H. Keep's *Bookmaker*.

The closing regatta of the SYC held on August 24, 1912 brought from the Gulf Coast a fleet of vessels. Mobile and Pensacola sent several boats for the races as did the Pass Christian and Biloxi Yacht Clubs.

Activity on Lake Pontchartrain during the 1913 season picked up considerably. The syndicate of J. M. Kinabrew, F. G. Otis, Henri T. Howard, and John Legier, headed by Samuel Heaslip, bought the *Massachusetts*, champion of Northern waters and a successful defender by the Americans of the *Seawanhaka* Cup against the Canadians in 1911. The new boat was bought for the 1913 sailing season as there was no race in 1912.

The noted naval architect, Edward A. Boardman of Boston, designed the *Massachusetts* (formerly *Manchester II*). He also designed *Stranger*, which was brought down by Heaslip from Winnebago, Wisconsin.

The *Massachusetts* was very similar in construction to *Seawanhaka*, both boats having been designed and built by Boardman. The measurements of the *Seawanhaka* were: length overall 34'11", waterline 24'8½", beam 8'4", draft 5½'. The *Massachusetts*, however, was a trifle larger than *Seawanhaka* in beam and in total sail carried. *Seawanhaka* hoisted 520 square yards of canvas to *Massachusetts'* 550 square yards.

At Pass Christian, on the final day of the 1913 regatta given under the auspices of the Southern Gulf Coast Yachting Association, after which there was a big ball held in the ballroom of the Mexican Gulf Hotel, Ed. Keep's *Seawanhaka* won over Samuel F. Heaslip skippering *Stranger*, and C. B. Maginnis' *Senorita*. Also sailing were the *Cricket*, which came over from Mobile, commanded by Capt. James R. Hagan, superintendent of wharves at Mobile, which was the winner over *Queen of the Fleet*, owned by C. MacDonald of Bay-Waveland, *Cadillac*, owned by Commander E. H. Wharton Davies, sailed by Johnny Dunn, and *Chewink III*, owned by A. F. Landry & Co. The *Seawanhaka* and the *Stranger* were later sold to the Mobile and Pensacola yacht clubs.

PRESIDENT AND MRS. WOODROW WILSON GUESTS AT THE PASS

President and Mrs. Woodrow Wilson spent their 1913 summer vacation at their favorite "peaceful haven," Pass Christian, referred to in *The Times Democrat* of June 23, 1913 as "The Newport of the South" along the Gulf Coast, "The Riviera of America." "Among those seeking refuge in this 'little haven' on the Gulf Coast are the President of the United States and Mrs. Woodrow Wilson. They are guests of an old friend, Miss Alice Herndon of Pass Christian at the Dixie White House."

Built in 1851, the Dixie White House has hosted six of our presidents: Andrew Jackson, Zachary Taylor, Ulysses S. Grant, Theodore Roosevelt, and Harry S. Truman, in addition to Woodrow Wilson, who was responsible for the name when he spent an extended winter vacation in 1913.

COMMODORE ERNEST LEE JAHNCKE—1914-16

When Ernest Lee Jahncke was elected commodore of the Southern Yacht Club in 1914, his term in office began under the stressing circumstances of a possible world war. Serving with Commodore Jahncke were: Chandler C. Luzenberg, vice-commodore; Abe Leverich, rear commodore; C. B. Fox, treasurer; W. H. Parham, secretary; Dr. A. A. Pray, fleet surgeon; Clarence G. Ferguson, fleet measurer. Board members were Rathborne deBuys, John Legier, Jr.,

Elmer E. Wood, Paul O. Fallon, and F. G. Otis.

Commodore Jahncke was a member of the family firm of Jahncke Service, Inc., the largest building materials company in the South. He reigned as Rex in 1913. The commodore was active in the racing machine class and as a power-boat enthusiast. He owned such speedsters as *Blue Wing I and II* and *Humpty Dumpty*. He also skippered several fine yachts—the *Reverie, Spitfire, Fiddlesticks, Quicksilver* and *Glendoveer*. The latter was Commodore Jahncke's flagship. The *Reverie* was one of the finest steam yachts in the country. The *Quicksilver* and the *Glendoveer* were in the government service during World War I.

When the opening regatta of 1914 was held, the commodore was faced with a group of sailors, jittery because of the drums of war. One bright spot at the regatta ceremony was the dedication of a flagmast to the club by Commodore Jahncke. His young daughter, Miss Adele Townsend Jahncke, christened the new flagmast by unfurling the club burgee and raising it to the peak of the mast.

The machine sloop class was brought to the forefront in 1914 with Commodore Samuel Heaslip in *Massachusetts* leading the competition again. The other boats were the *Target, Kyboshk,* and *Stranger*. These boats provided yachting fans with some good races.

The news of the cancellation of the America's Cup races in 1914 because of impending war came as a shock to Commodore Jahncke as well as the whole nation. As a member of the New York Yacht Club, the commodore was a favorite spectator at America's Cup races. The race was not resumed until 1922.

In 1915 Commodore Victor G. Mendoza, president of the Havana Yacht Club, visited New Orleans. The president was a welcomed guest aboard Commodore Jahncke's flagship *Glendoveer*.

PRESIDENT THEODORE ROOSEVELT
VISITS THE PASS

There was another prominent visitor to that "little haven" on the Gulf Coast, Pass Christian, in 1915—President Theodore Roosevelt. He was studying the bird life of the area and wrote an article about it in *Harper's Bazaar* that same year. The president was a guest of friends who lived in the Pass, Mr. and Mrs. John M. Parker. (Mr. Parker was elected governor of Louisiana in 1920 and served for four years.) Long after President Roosevelt's departure from the coast, people would come to see where "Teddy" Roosevelt had slept.

It was fortunate that the president returned to his home when he did, as a few days later the worst hurricane to strike New Orleans and the Gulf Coast in many years hit on September 29, 1915.

THE HURRICANE OF 1915

The SYC *Barometer*'s description of the 1915 hurricane follows:

> The yacht club pen had been filled with large and small sloops, rigged dories, cat boats, craft of all designs and sizes, when the storm slammed down and damaged at least 25 percent of the fleet. Yachts docked along the New Basin Canal had their upper decks battered by wind and waves. A collapsed boathouse crushed the *Elizabeth*, Albert Mackie's handsome power cruiser. Boats broke their moorings and crashed together. Shipyards, shops, docks and yachts at anchor were severely damaged.
>
> When the wind died down Commodore Ernest Lee Jahncke immediately stocked the Jahncke Service tug *Claribel* with food and fresh water and headed out to relieve people stranded in the Rigolets and on the Gulf Coast. The flagship *Glendoveer* soon followed with supplies for Chef Menteur and Pass Christian. Three more Jahncke tugs took off in all directions, bringing relief to victims of the storm, the *Aunt Dinah* leading the way. Bayou St. John was completely demolished. Along the Gulf Coast, the Biloxi Yacht Club was washed from its foundations and dumped in a heap two blocks away. Fortunately, with the ever increasing membership in the club, plans were immediately prepared by Byrd Enochs and Chris. Thompson of Biloxi for the erection of a new building of modern design, cost to be $2,500 to $3,000.

The last boat that Commodore Heaslip purchased before his death in 1916 was the machine sloop *America* which had a racing record in the New England area, being a champion on Marblehead waters. He owned *America* in a syndicate composed of Henri Howard, J. M. Kinabrew, and John Legier, Jr. The sloop was later sold after his death to another syndicate consisting of C. A. Sporl, George Plant, Raymond F. Harris, and Bainbridge Logan.

When Commodore Heaslip died, the Southern Yacht Club lost one of its most valuable and outstanding yachtsmen. He had improved the SYC fleet tremendously by bringing to Southern waters championship yachts from the North. Commodore Heaslip was also a popular sportsman and civic-minded New Orleanian whose interests extended to that "little haven" on the Gulf Coast, Pass Christian, where he was instrumental in the growth of that town.

When the SYC annual meeting was held in 1916, Commodore Jahncke was returned to office for a third term. It was announced at the meeting that Commodore and Mrs. Jahncke and Vice-

Commodore and Mrs. Harry L. Howard were the guests of the New York Yacht Club's Commodore E. C. Benedict on board his palatial yacht *Oneida*, which was visiting New Orleans.

The year 1916 was one of deep suspense. The country's threatened participation in global conflict turned the thoughts of young men from pleasure sailing boats to battleships and submarines.

Well aware of the lack of interest in yachting for the past four years, Commodore Jahncke also realized that there were many large craft resting in the SYC harbor waiting for some brave soul to tow them out into the open waters of the lake and the Gulf. He summoned their owners to a meeting in 1916 to discuss plans for the long distance race to Pensacola. This move was heartily received by all present. Those who answered the call were:

> *Grijaldo*—Captain G. Abunza's big cruiser
> *Nathalie*—owned by Dr. W. Milton Miller
> *Spitfire III*—owned by Captain J. Eugene Pearce
> *Waif*—owned by Captain Robert C. McClure
> *Violet*—Captain Percy S. Benedict's big cruiser
> The auxiliary yawl-rigged sloops were:
> *Seaweed*—owned by Sidney Menge
> *Jassax*—owned by A. R. "Babe" Roberts
> *Elizabeth*—Albert Mackie's palatial yacht
> *Quicksilver*—captained by Paul F. Jahncke
> *Glendoveer*—captained by Commodore Ernest Lee Jahncke

THE HURRICANE OF 1916

It was inconceivable that another hurricane could strike the coast following the 1915 monster, and such a thought was far from the minds of the eager yachtsmen who answered the gun on the starting line at 11 a.m. on the balmy morning of July 2, 1916 for the annual race to Pensacola, Florida.

Taking the lead was the Commodore Jahncke's Flagship *Glendoveer*. The parade of boats headed for the Rigolets then into the Mississippi Sound. But here to tell you about his harrowing experience in the hurricane of 1916 that struck the Gulf Coast is Harry L. Howard, who wrote the following article for the SYC *Barometer*:

> Many a New Orleans yachtsman now knows what two red flags with black centers displayed one above the other, which the government hung out from Pensacola to Biloxi, mean. When the race started from New Orleans at daylight on the morning of July 2nd, the weather was murky. However, the fleet arrived at Fort Morgan before sundown, where they

spent the night. At 5 o'clock the next morning, when the guns fired, each boat was off to Pensacola, sixty miles away on the last leg of the race.

The arrival of the fleet at Pensacola at 8 a.m. was orderly and impressive. Battleships saluted, Naval flags were dipped, Hydro-aeroplanes conveyed the yachts in. Unfortunately, Capt. Paul Jahncke with his yacht *Quicksilver* had to return to New Orleans by train owing to the serious illness of his little daughter. This, together with the rumors of the disturbance in the Gulf and the fact that Mrs. Ernest Lee Jahncke with a party of guests and children were aboard the *Aunt Dinah* in Biloxi without her regular crew, decided that the Commodore should get back as soon as possible, placing Capt. Joe Behrens in charge of the *Glendoveer* and the writer in charge of the *Quicksilver*.

The 4th of July found the little city alive with a patriotic preparedness parade, besides a yacht race and a bunch of New Orleans "Yachting Indians" all on its hands at the same time. However, due to the seriousness of matters at home, both the *Quicksilver* and the *Glendoveer* left for Biloxi.

At the banquet that night at the Pensacola Yacht Club, the wireless operator from the battle cruiser *North Carolina* advised the yachtsmen of an approaching disturbance and warned all small craft to remain in the harbor.

Early the next morning, Mobile wired that a hurricane was on the way. The fleet in Biloxi harbor got ready. The *Aunt Dinah* was moved up close to the Biloxi shore and the ladies and children sent ashore. Half an hour later, the hurricane burst in all its fury. The crews of the various boats in the harbor fought the storm all day and night.

Next morning the Biloxi harbor presented a scene of wreckage. Many boats were bottoms up, many others were ashore. Rescue work began at once. All wires and communications had been destroyed. Commodore Jahncke ordered the *Glendoveer* to sail for New Orleans with a big bag of Biloxi mail and more than one hundred messages to anxious relatives and friends to be delivered by telephone and special messenger. A message was received from the Florida City by wireless saying all crews and boats were safe.

For the second consecutive year, Commodore Jahncke had helped boats in distress by a storm. Afterwards, Biloxi residents were indebted to the Jahncke owned boats and tugs for hauling schooners and yachts off Deer Island and the Biloxi shore. One of the casualties was the *Quicksilver* which was washed ashore. The Biloxi harbor was literally strewn with broken masts and sunken boats with their sails floating in the wreckage.

"When daylight flashed its welcomed brightness on the waters, the *Aunt Dinah*, one of the Jahncke Service huge houseboats was in her same old place in the middle of the Biloxi harbor. It had weathered the storm with no damage," continued Howard's account.

The Picayune II, owned by Leonard and Yorke Nicholson of the SYC, was a champion of Southern waters for many years.

In 1904 the first all-girl regatta held by the SYC was won by Carrie Wuescher in her brother Dave's boat Sinner, with Edna Byrnes and Aggie Roach as crew.

The Aunt Dinah and the Porte Bonheur, shown in this picture, were the two most versatile yachts in the SYC. The Aunt Dinah was the mother ship of the Jahncke Service, Inc., fleet of beautiful yachts. She was a construction houseboat and an institution on the waters of Lake Pontchartrain and the Gulf Coast.

THE HISTORY OF THE *AUNT DINAH*

Many are those living today who may recall the *Aunt Dinah*. She was an institution on the waters of Lake Pontchartrain and the Gulf Coast, home away from home for so many sailors, in particular the skippers of the Star Class fleet who were towed to the coast for their races in those waters and who filled the dormitory of the *Aunt Dinah* for sleeping quarters. The *Aunt Dinah* was a huge construction houseboat belonging to the Jahncke Service, Inc. Its living room was twenty-six by sixteen feet, finished in dark cypress with buff-colored walls and panels between the beams of the ceiling and large French windows; it was furnished with a built-in bookcase on one wall, a piano player, a Victrola, a piano lamp, and comfortable chairs and lounges, with beautiful oil paintings, etchings, and a Rockwood landscape on the walls.

There were two brick fireplaces situated in an alcove at one end of the boat. The dining room, also twenty-six by sixteen feet, a large kitchen, two large bedrooms, and a bath completed the lower deck. The upper deck was a large dormitory with ten single iron beds. Many celebrities who visited New Orleans were entertained on board the *Aunt Dinah*.

The last few weeks of the 1916 sailing season were dispirited. Before the season closed, there was one last race among the 21-footers. This class of boat was brought down South in 1915 but was not active as a fleet until after World War I.

Again, Commodore Heaslip was a leader when he brought to the SYC fleet another machine sloop, the *America*, which he owned in addition to the *Seawanhaka*. He won over the other fine boats, Eddie Keep's *Target*, Davis Wuescher's *Stranger*, and Peter Cooke's *Susie B*. The *America* was formerly the *Massachusetts* and had a racing record in the New England area, being a champion on Marblehead waters.

Commodore W. A. Gordon
1892

Commodore Thomas Sully
1893, 1894

Commodore Lawrence O'Donnell
1895, 1896

Commodore J. Walton Glenny
1897, 1898

Commodore Albert Baldwin
1899–1909

Commodore Louis H. Fairchild
1910, 1911

CHAPTER X

1917-1920

COMMODORES	TERM
Chandler C. Luzenberg	1917
Percy S. Benedict	1918-19-20

COMMODORE CHANDLER C. LUZENBERG—1917

The conditions that faced Chandler C. Luzenberg when he was elected commodore of the Southern Yacht Club at the 1917 annual meeting were very dismal. With the tocsins of war near at hand, club members were tense and anxious. Since the summer of 1914, the European war had been getting closer and closer to the shores of the United States. With German submarines exacting a frightful toll, most Americans anticipated our immediate entrance into war. The United States broke off diplomatic relations with Germany on April 2, 1917, and President Woodrow Wilson delivered his war message to Congress. Two days later the United States was at war with Germany. Reported the *Barometer*:"Over 150 of the SYC's gallant lads answered the call to arms so that the honor of America might be preserved and that Old Glory might continue to wave triumphant at the masthead over the land of the free and the home of the brave."

Commodore Luzenberg was a prominent lawyer in the city of New Orleans. He owned the crack yacht *Mettawee*, one of the fastest in the fleet. His first proclamation was that all those who were in Uncle Sam's service be exempt from the payment of dues.

Despite low morale and coast-to-coast tension, the commodore was successful in mustering together a number of yachtsmen to hold the opening regatta. There was gloom everywhere, but the club was patriotically decorated with the Stars and Stripes. All yachts participating in the races, as well as those taking parties out to view the regatta, showed the national colors. "The Star-Spangled Banner" opened and closed the musical programs for each event.

The boats that participated in the SYC races were the *Sis*, owned by Lawrence Fabacher; *Hiawatha*, owned and sailed by Captain C. C. Furr (she beat the *Sis* which was sailed by Alfred Farrell), and the *Mettawee*, sailed by Chandler Luzenberg, Jr. The big cruiser *Grijalda* of Captain G. Abunza won over Dr. W. Milton Miller's *Nathalie* and J. Eugene Pearce's *Spitfire*. Captain Robert C. McClure's *Waif* defeated Captain P. S. Benedict's sturdy *Violet*. The race for auxiliary yawl-rigged sloops was won by Billy Fetterly's *Boomerang* over William Young's *Tomahawk*.

The commodore entered all regattas enthusiastically, promoted one-design boats, and helped to create the Junior membership, which offered recognition to the club's youngest sailors and kept the momentum going for those unable to serve their country.

In 1917 there were 1200 members in the club, but not a representative group showed much active interest "in spite of the three dances twice a week," reported the *Barometer*. The financial condition of the club was sound, and the final payment was made on the $5,000 loan to erect the bulkhead to the club. This work made the driveway to the clubhouse door an actuality.

On the lighter side of life, the social atmosphere at the club was enhanced when the board permitted the ladies of members to hold luncheons each Friday. The first "ladies' day luncheon" was held on March 23, 1917. These luncheons remain a popular monthly event today.

"To these mid-day parties, one arrives with colorful knitting bags, brim full of sober and very war-like wool to attest one's patriotism, at the same time soothing the last scruple of an over sensitive conscience implacably refusing all diversion that has not to do with the war. But what better setting if you please, while your nimble fingers evolve sox, could be more inspiring—nay conducive to war work than the broad expanse of good old Pontchartrain with its opalescent horizon?" reported the *Barometer*.

"For the first time in the history of the Southern Yacht Club, its club rooms were used for a subscription dance on August 20, 1917, the suspension of the House Committee's rules being for a most worthy cause. The proceeds derived from the entertainment went to a fund for the purchase of knitted sweaters and helmets," continued the *Barometer*.

An important notice was posted in the club the night of the dance, which read: "The practice of smoking by some ladies at the clubhouse, only recently revived, is considered by the Governing Committee as beneath the dignity of the club. The fact that such practice is obtained elsewhere is a matter with which we have no concern, and unless this practice ceases at once notice is hereby given that smoking in the clubhouse will be entirely prohibited."

The chaperones included Mr. and Mrs. Chandler Luzenberg, Colonel and Mrs. Allison Owen, Lieutenant Colonel and Mrs. Bryan Black, Major and Mrs. James Edmonds and Major and Mrs. Schaumburg McGehee. Also noted, as he usually attends all social functions, was Richie Holbrook accompanied by his "tin Lizzie."

Another one of the enjoyable affairs was the subscription dance given at the club by the Second Troop Cavalry, U.S.A., stationed at Camp Nicholls. The dance was largely attended by the members and military men, a neat sum being realized for the boys' mess fund.

Everyone who was able responded with subscriptions to the Liberty Loan, which was one of the steps necessary to obliterate for all time the "shadow of Kaiserism." Many of our yacht club boys had joined Louisiana's eighty thousand soldiers encamped at West End on the lakefront, at the City Park race track, on Tulane University campus and, of course, the buzzing Algiers Naval Station across the Mississippi River from New Orleans.

REBUILT BILOXI YACHT CLUB OPENS

Early in 1917 the Biloxi Yacht Club announced that its four-thousand dollar facelift was completed, as well as plans to stay open the year 'round, with handsome new furniture, pool and billiard tables, and a piano. Although the club had accepted resignations from its members called to Army service, a new executive group was ready to serve consisting of Commodore Douglas Watson, Rear Commodore Andrew Swanzy, and Vice-Commodore John F. Eistetter, assisted by Fergus Bohn and W. J. Wiltz.

They looked forward to the Fourth of July when the big long distance race for the William Garic Cup headed from West End toward Biloxi. With an attractive new building summoning the regatta participants, the Biloxi Yacht Club also announced: "This year

COMMODORE PERCY S. BENEDICT—1918-19-20

When Commodore Percy S. Benedict was elected to succeed Commodore Chandler C. Luzenberg in 1918, war clouds continued to hang over the world and the United States was still actively engaged in war with the Central Powers.

Elected to serve with Commodore Benedict were: C. B. Fox, vice-commodore; F. J. Foxley, rear commodore; and W. H. Parham, secretary-treasurer. Members of the Board were: Albert Mackie, fleet captain; Dr. A. A. Pray, fleet surgeon; G. H. Chapman, measurer; John R. Perez; and Howard N. Moody.

Commodore Benedict was a prominent attorney in New Orleans, and with his knowledge and administrative ability he was able to renew the spirit and build up morale of the yachtsmen.

When the 1918 opening regatta was held on May 5, a martial note was predominant in all arrangements. There was a record-breaking crowd on hand for the races. The commodore entertained many visiting yachtsmen from the Gulf Coast on his flagship *Violet*. He also owned another yacht, *Bunny*. Both boats were contestants in all of the SYC races to Old Landing at Madisonville and back. Later, in 1922, the *Violet* won the Southern Marine Marathon.

A regatta party was held after the races, which was handled by a committee composed of ex-commodore Ernest Lee Jahncke as chairman and Crawford Ellis and Frank B. Hayne as vice-chairmen. The daily *The Times Picayune* reporting on the social event stated,"There was dancing to jazz music, a form of melody which seems to be growing in favor in New Orleans, the place of its birth."

SYC CONVERTS TO HOSPITAL DURING WORLD WAR I

While the Southern Yacht Club supported each of the campaigns for war funds, perhaps the most beneficial assistance rendered was that of converting the clubhouse into a convalescent hospital during the influenza epidemic which threatened the lives of hundreds of boys in khaki. Cheerfully and unselfishly the SYC abandoned its palatial clubhouse and gave up its dances and favorite sport in order to play the role of Good Samaritan.

During the ravages of the disease, Manager George Mitchell was in charge of the club's service. The records show that the number of patients for the thirty-five days in 1918 that the convalescent hospital was open numbered 2,555, an average of 73 per day, and not one loss of life was reported. "Undoubtably, these remarkable statistics were due at least partially to the exciting visit paid to the convalescent ward by movie siren Theda Bara—a favorite movie star of the time," reported the *Barometer*.

In a letter to Commodore Benedict, Mr. Warren Kearney, who had charge of the Red Cross work, expressed appreciation for the splendid service rendered by the Southern Yacht Club. Also a letter of commendation was received from Newton D. Baker, the secretary of war. During the war years, handsome contributions were given by the SYC to the Red Cross, the United War Work Society, War Camp Community Relief, the Naval Relief Society, and the Belgian Babies Fund. The club sold $6,000 in liberty bonds and 1,000 war saving stamps.

WAR IS OVER—ARMISTICE IS SIGNED

November 11, 1918, Armistice Day, brought to an end World War I. Although the end came for Germany on this date, the Armistice was not signed until March 4, 1919. However, the Southern Yacht Club lost no time in summoning the members in order to revive the lost membership.

When the January 1919 meeting was held, it opened the seventieth anniversary year of the founding of the Southern Yacht Club. At the meeting, plans were inaugurated for a new clubhouse expansion program. A special committee was named by Commodore Benedict as an all-important part of this progressive step. The seven members of this team were recognized and able financiers of the South: John Legier, Jr., John E. Bouden, Jr., L. M. Poole, Dr. Paul H. Saunders, A. B. Wheeler, Hugh McCloskey, and George J. Glover, a local contractor and builder placed in charge of making the decisions in connection with the plans for this massive undertaking. The clubhouse was to be a blend of the architecture of southern Spain and Venice.

Other members of the House and Finance committees of this memorable year were:

Percy S. Benedict, chairman	Charles McLellan
Ben Beekman	Howard N. Moody

SOUTHERN YACHT CLUB

G. H. Chapman
D. D. R. Charbonnet
W. J. Church
W. K. DePass
W. H. Hendren
R. G. Irby
Adam Lorch, Jr.

Aubrey Murray
Leonard K. Nicholson
J. W. Pearce
W. H. Parham
John R. Perez
A. R. Roberts
Walton B. Smith

At the January 1919 meeting, honorary life memberships were extended to C. H. Hyams, Sr., Peter F. Pescud, and A. Graffanigia.

Commodore Benedict displayed a beautiful plaque at the meeting which was presented to the yacht club listing the names of those 150 SYC members who had participated in various branches of the service during World War I.

No greater gift could have been given to the cause than the sacrifice of the 150 SYC members who answered the call of Uncle Sam. "Three were called to the side of the Captain of us all during the mighty conflict," reads the wording on the plaque. The gallant men who gave their lives were Corporal Thomas A. Gragard, M. C., killed in action in the Bois de Belleau on June 6, 1918; First Sergeant Thomas I. Foley, Jr., who died in service from pneumonia and scarlet fever on March 26, 1918, aged 21 years; and Sergeant G. Leon Soniat, who died of spinal meningitis at Issoudan, France while in the service of his country.

SOME SYC MEMBERS WHO SERVED IN WORLD WAR I

E. L. Aschaffenberg
Leslie P. Beard
Stanley Behrman
Bryan Black
Reginald H. Carter, Jr.
D.B.H. Chaffe, Jr.
O. V. Claiborne
L. S. Clarke, Jr.
Harold Colton
T. B. Denegre
F. O. Denny
Geo. A. Diassellies
John Devlin
Geo. E. Dicks

Louis S. Goldstein
Tom Gragard
Frank Groves
F. F. Hansell, Jr.
Morris E. Hansell, II
C. J. Holland
Henri Howard
Chas. Karst, Jr.
Farwell Legendre
Lucien Lessene
John P. Longmire
Chandler C. Luzenberg, Jr.
Lucien E. Lyons, Jr.

Theo. L. Perrier
Jules Randon
W. T. Ritter
George Robert
G. W. Rowbotham
Dr. T. R. Rudolf
Otto Schwartz
Dr. John Smith
R. F. Spangenberg, Jr.
Harold H. Stream
Gus Tolson
George Troendle
Pierre Villere
Hugh Vincent
John Weckerling

John D. Ewing	Perle Mackie	Emmett White
Dr. E. D. Fenner	A. J. Marion, Jr.	J. M. White
Tuttle Flaspoller	Harold P. Nathan	Nelson Whitney
L. C. Frantz, Jr.	Charles Neely	Cuthbert Williams
John J. Gillespie	Peter O'Donnell	E. E. Wood, Jr.
Dr. Addley Gladden	Lowrie O'Donnell	Nelson S. Wooddy
	Sherman Pardue	
	W. E. Penick	
	Geo. B. Penrose	

There was a more cheerful and hopeful approach to the coming sailing season, although the boys were not all back from the war. Those that were had no spirit for returning to the boats, but their joy was expressed on the dance floor of the club.

The social calendar was filled with many parties. As mentioned previously, jazz seemed to be coming into style, and, within its own home, the SYC had a very interesting jazz band composed of friends who "played for fun." This group of musicians was known as the "Six and Seven-eighths" string band. Formed in 1911, it got its name because one of its seven members was so much shorter than the others. The band remained in existence until the sixties.

Dr. Edmond Souchon, a prominent New Orleans physician, organized the "Six and Seven-eighths" band when he was in his teens. He was a gifted musician on the banjo and guitar, and he sang along with the other business and professional men, who were Howard McCaleb, a young attorney who later became a judge on the Court of Appeal, Charles Hardy, Hilton "Midget" Harrison, Bob Reynolds, Bill Gibbens, and Commodore Ernest Lee Jahncke. They were especially fond of playing on the top of the *Aunt Dinah*, where the home-grown jazzmen always livened the cruises of Commodore Jahncke.

Powerboats had taken over the race course at the 1919 opening regatta. The decline in the number of sailing vessels and interest in that phase of yachting had been ominous since 1912, and this stagnation led some to believe that a grand old sport was about to perish.

Bemoaning the lack of interest in sailboats, ex-vice commodore N. E. Baumgarden, while rocking in his favorite cane-back chair on the club's porch, had this to say to the editor of the *Barometer*: "Gone are the days of the *Mattie*, sailed by Alex Brewster and his star crew of sandbag rustlers. Also, the *Lady Emma* owned by John B. Lallande, the *Mephisto* and the *Quarantina* and with them the exhilarating feeling to watch them dip their noses into the tiny waves that splashed against their sides.

"There is no sport than sailing that can give one a feeling of peace, a detachment from the office, sunbaked streets and the quivering heat—ahead, only the cool breezes and the changing waters of distant shores. Beneath you, a lovely thing of wood and snowy canvas racing through the waters as a fresh breeze whistles out of an indigo sky into the bellying sails."

He recalled the interesting background of one of the finest sailors of all times, Alex Brewster, who was a vice-commodore of SYC in 1880, and how in his *Susie B.* he beat Ira Smith from the North in the Interstate race held that year on Lake Pontchartrain. Commodore Brewster was well known in the East where he journeyed each year to witness the International Cup races. Among the other boats that he owned were *Domino, Hope, Mephisto,* and the *Meteor.*

Adding to ex-Vice-Commodore Baumgarden's comments, R. Lee Edwards had this to say: "During its 70 years of existence, the club has seen the evolution in yachting which brought forth the winged messengers of the sea seemingly impelled by Mercury with a wave of his caduceus. And these fleet machine sloops have been superseded by the express cruiser and the hydro-aeroplane so that now the sport of yachting almost rivals in celerity light and electricity themselves."

IN THE DAYS OF THE SANDBAGGERS
by Capt. R. Lee Edwards

In the early nineties when I sailed a sandbagger, it was hard work to sail a race. The crews raced "for blood". In those times, the crew, more than the boat, was the determining factor.

The sand-bagger was composed of sails, sand in bags, and crew—the hull was largely an adjunct. Such were the *Lady Emma* owned and sailed by former vice-commodore N. Emile Baumgarden, and *Zoe*, the fast sloop in which former vice-commodore Emile J. O'Brien won so many races, as well as *Mephisto*, a long champion in her class, owned and skippered by the late commodore Alex Brewster, all of the Southern Yacht Club.

When the sand-bagger was in her prime, there was no such thing as a "fin-keel" boat in southern waters. The shallow depth in most of the courses over which sailing craft were raced made light draft a prime necessity in all the boats. This meant centerboard types; indeed, the fin-keel had not then come into use, even where the depths of water warranted it, and the sailor-men of the yacht clubs knew only centerboard boats, from the largest of the sloops down to the smallest of the catboats. The hull of the sand-bagger of those days was built merely with a view to floating and sustaining the maximum of sails, sandbags and crew, with due regard to the essential maximum of speed lines possible.

One of the fastest of these old-time, plumbowed racers, was *Lady Emma*. Her beam was one-third of her length; her draft equal to the whole of the freeboard minus the centerboard reach. This was the usual proportion of the sand-bagger hull, but there was a tremendously long bowsprit and a generous jib, a very tall stick, the boom reaching far beyond the stern transom and the reach of the peak of the big mainsail. A club topsail of equally generous proportions, completed the rig.

Many wondered how the *Lady Emma* and the others of her type kept from spilling the wind out of their sails, to say nothing of turning over every time she came about. The answer to that was sand-bags, hard work, and skill as sailors.

In the weather work, the sand-bags had to be kept up to the high side, in such numbers, and whenever the skipper ordered them moved. More than this, they had to be shifted darned quick when the skipper shouted:"High side! Bags over!" Then Heaven alone could help the lubber who was slow on the job. And we slung them high, wide and handsome, with the big canvas spread popping overhead in the stiff wind as the skipper put her about on another tack. Of course, all the bags did not have to be shifted every time, and the skipper was as quick to order to cease heaving as he was to start us shifting them, whenever he had sufficient ballast on the high side to bring her properly about on the tack.

The sandbags carried varied in weight, according to the size of the ship and the amount of sail carried, but the designers and builders of the sandbaggers of the nineties had no set rules for figuring out their equations, either in algebraic quantities or otherwise, such as modern designers have. They "guessed" at it first—and they were mighty good guessers at that—and then they took the sand-bagger out and regulated matters by wind tests, in actual sailing in all kinds of weather.

Each sandbag weighed from 20 to 40 pounds. On the free-sheet run, before the wind, they were divided equally, half stowed on each side of the centerboard case. This case ranged from five to ten feet in length, and from two to nearly four feet in height, depending on the size of the boat, and the personal idiosyncracies of her owner and builder. The bags had to be heaved over this case, whatever its height, in the briefest possible time. When the skipper barked the "ready-about" order, and followed it with "Bags over!" you may imagine that there was more activity for the next minute or two on the sandbagger that there is under almost any circumstances on any sailing craft of today. Also, there was more real hard work for the crew.

As nearly as I can remember, after all these years, *Lady Emma* raced with 24 sandbags of 30 pounds each—twelve on each side of the centerboard when she was running free-sheet, before the wind. That meant that the crew had to shift up and over the centerboard case, every time the ship was put about on a new tack, about seven hundred pounds of ballast. And they had to do it in a mighty big hurry, particularly when two or more craft were splitting tacks in jockeying down the course. Hard as we were, and well-accustomed to the job, I cannot recall a race after which we were not well pumped out, and willing to call it a day. Indeed, in my opinion, the old time sand-bagger racing called for the hardest work ever performed by the crew of any pleasure craft in the world.

SOUTHERN YACHT CLUB'S SEVENTIETH ANNIVERSARY

When the Southern Yacht Club celebrated its seventieth anniversary in 1919, officers were reelected:

Commodore—Percy S. Benedict
Vice-Commodore—C. B. Fox
Rear Commodore—F. J. Foxley
Secretary-Treasurer—W. H. Parham
Fleet Surgeon—Dr. A. A. Pray
Fleet Measurer—L. H. Chapman

Board Members:
Gus B. Baldwin
W. H. Hendren
Chandler C. Luzenberg
John R. Perez
Dr. W. E. Winship

The gala celebration was held with a regatta of a large fleet of entries. The opening powerboat racing found many boats on the lake. Dr. W. M. Miller's *Nathalie* won over Commodore Benedict's *Violet*, flagship of the SYC fleet, and Sidney L. Menge's *Seaweed*. Others entered were Vice-Commodore Fox's *Brenda II*, *Chiliktah*, owned by C. A. Sporl and E. Plant, and *Naomo*, owned by H. N. Moody.

One of the latest and largest additions to the fleet of seagoing pleasure cruisers was *Elmasada II*, brought down from New York by Samuel Zemurray, a prominent local fruit importer. *Elmasada II* was the largest gasoline yacht in the club's fleet. She measured 110 feet in length overall, with 15 foot beam, and drew 4 feet 4 inches of water.

Another racing craft was the contender *Kitsey*, whose owners were Charles Ferran and William Gallagher. "Her trim jackfish hull will be hanging to the davits of the French steamship *Honduras* when she sails for Le Havre, France where she will be a participant in French waters," reported the *Barometer*.

Included in the fleet was the 40-foot *Quananche*, named for an Indian fish. "It was a proud moment," said the *Barometer*, "to introduce the *Quananche* with her 22 mph cruising speed, a product of a West End boatyard. Christening the boat, dressed in white from head to toe in a five-tier dress, white stockings and white shoes and a wide-brimmed straw hat as she broke champagne over the cruiser's bow, was Miss Coralie Aschaffenberg, grand-daughter of Albert Aschaffenberg, co-owner of *Quananche* with Dr. G. A. MacDiarmid." Mr. Aschaffenberg's son, Albert Jr., is the owner of New Orleans' famous luxury hotel the Pontchartrain.

Representing the new craft's competition were ex-Rear Commodore G. Mather Conrad's *Alga*, a handsome yacht which he had recently purchased from W. E. Penick, Albert Mackie's palatial yacht *Elizabeth*, C. B. Fox's *Brenda*, C. C. Furr's *Hiawatha*, Robert C. McClure's *Waif*, and Percy S. Benedict's *Violet*.

In the motorboat class were G. Abunza's big cruiser *Grijalda*, J. Eugene Pearce's *Spitfire III*, Dr. W. Milton Miller's *Nathalie*, Lawrence Fabacher's *Sis*, Charles C. Luzenberg, Jr.'s *Mettawee*, and Ralston S. Cole's *Mavoureen*.

An open handicap trophy was offered by Julius Werner and a handicap prize by Capt. Percy Benedict, to boats making ten miles per hour and under. Capt. Peter Sapton Schneidau offered a "slow boat" class trophy.

"Some 500 persons attended the regatta and there was a large dance held in conjunction with the celebration which featured the well known SYC jazz orchestra until a late hour." (The "Six and Seven-eighths" band?)

In addition to the racing of boats there were sailing canoe races, tilting matches, and swimming.

Many congratulatory messages were received from congressmen, senators, and thirty-five commodores of yacht clubs throughout the country. Among the well-wishers was the secretary of war, Newton D. Baker, who stated, "The patriotism evinced by your membership during the recent war with Germany is indeed one of the bright pages in your history that will live forever."

Governor R. G. Pleasant of Louisiana wrote, "This organization is something more than a club. It is an institution. During the long years of existence it has contributed much to the happiness of the citizens of New Orleans."

Secretary of the Navy, Josephus Daniels, sent congratulations "upon the tremendous expansion of your organization."

Sir Thomas J. Lipton wrote from England, "Being recalled to England on important business prevents my being with you upon the memorable occasion that you are about to celebrate.

"The 70th anniversary of the Southern Yacht Club is indeed an epoch-making event in history of the grandest of sports in your great country. That I cannot visit New Orleans, the city of my happy boyhood days, is another cause of regret, and upon my return to America it is my sincere hope to have the pleasure of once more meeting all my good New Orleans friends. In the meantime, let me assure you that I very highly appreciate the invitation of the club and send to the members my greetings." (Sir Thomas did return to America later in 1919 and was a guest at SYC.)

Mayor of New Orleans, Martin Behrman, said in his congratulatory letter, "Seventy years of generous rivalry of enviable reputation, of unswerving loyalty to home and country and of invaluable service to the youth of New Orleans constitutes the history of this splendid organization.

"During all these years, years of strife and vicissitude as well as of memorable achievement, the SYC has grown in strength, popularity, influence and usefulness. Today it is perhaps not only the oldest social organization in New Orleans, but is indissolubly associated no less with its aspirations for the future than with the fame of the past.

"As a friend, a sympathizer and brother as well as chief executive of this city, I am happy to extend to the Southern Yacht Club and to its members, congratulations and greetings on this memorable day fraught with so many pleasant and endearing memories." (Mayor Behrman was an honorary member of the Southern Yacht Club.)

GENERAL JOHN J. PERSHING VISITS SYC

In the early part of the SYC's anniversary year, 1919, another prominent personage was a guest of the club, General John J. Pershing, commander-in-chief of the United States Army in Europe. The members of the SYC turned out en masse to honor the General.

On the waters, the SYC had many notable visitors at its docks. Harold Vanderbilt arrived with his palatial yacht *Versable*. He stopped en route from upriver to Florida. Dudley Sharp brought his 71-foot yawl *Gulf Stream* from Houston, Texas. She had logged thousands of West Indian and Bahamian miles under her keel. Visiting our Southern waters on the Gulf Coast was R. S. McLaughlin's

113-foot, three masted *Azara*. She wore the Royal Standard when Edward, Prince of Wales, was entertained on board.

"The Friday 'Ladies Day Luncheons' which were inaugurated in 1917, continued to be popular in 1919 and were luscious food-conserving affairs, which have, under the skillful management of the catering department, found the point between Mr. Hoover's frugal recipes and Lucullus' palate-tickling ones and are becoming more and more in vogue as the season advances. Also, attendance at the dinner parties has picked up greatly during the summer months. There were crowds of stately matrons and pretty misses dancing with their sailor friends," announced the *Barometer's* editor, R. Lee Edwards.

Many New Orleanians and Gulf Coast residents will recall the elaborate luncheons and parties given in the old Southern Yacht Club. One of these was that of Mrs. George L. Gibbons, for bridge and lunch. Those ladies present were:

Mrs. William Gaines Blasdel
Mrs. C. E. Broderick
Mrs. John Bryan
Mrs. George A. Camors
Mrs. B. C. Casanas
Mrs. Auguste Claverie
Mrs. Albert Clerc
Mrs. Homer Dupuy
Mrs. William T. Jay
Mrs. Felix Larue
Mrs. Charles W. Mackie, Jr.
Mrs. C. A. McFarland
Mrs. Richard Pitard
Mrs. J. B. Sullivan
Mrs. P. J. Sullivan
Mrs. Walter W. Thomas
Mrs. A. Vizard

Also, a large luncheon was given by Mr. and Mrs. William Garic. Their guests were to honor the lovely young daughter of the Garics, Clara May. They were:

Charlotte and Beatrice Adams
Emily Cook
Louise Fenner
Edith Gorman
Elise Janin
Claire Joubert
Gladys and Olga Legier
Berthe Lockett
Elsa Manson
Amelie May
Lucille McFarland
Polly and Leila McIlhenny
Ethel and Lucille Mooney
Ethel and Mathile Ross
Peggy Mason-Smith
Marion Souchen
Edna and Marguerite Sullivan
Winnifred Waddell
Meriam Walmsley
Louise Wright

The club hosted many sorority and fraternity parties and judging from the account of one sorority dance reported in the *Barometer* times have changed, as you will see.

Doors were opened wide and the entire club mobilized into service for the delegation of the entire Tau Sigma sorority, a school girl club and their guests. The members and their trusty young escorts arrived at the witching hour—chaperons having been hurried along energetically by urging young daughters that not one minute of the precious 'up to midnight' time be wasted. Chaperoning the dance were Mr. and Mrs. Henry Flaspoller, Mr. and Mrs. John May, Mr. and Mrs. George Ferrier, Mr. and Mrs. C. B. Fox, Mr. and Mrs. Swan Sullivan and a few others. Among the young people there that evening were:

Elanor Allen
Kingsley Black
Ione Brady
Lillian Christ
Virginia Claiborne
Emily Cook
Lucy Dickson
Margaret Ferrier
Estelle Flaspoller
Ethel, Maud and Peggy Fox
Clara May Garic
Edith Gorman
Rai and Dorothy Graner
Anne Hardie
Marjore Hay
Frances Hupman
Claire Joubert
Nell Kearney
Berthe Lathrop
Gladys and Olga Legier
Katherine Luzenberg

Amelie May
Lucille McFarland
Polly and Leila McIlhenny
Dixie Milling
Lucille and Ethel Mooney
Dorothy Orr
Claire Parkhouse
Rebecca Perkins
Lydia Roberts
Juanita Rocquet
Peggy Mason-Smith
Marion Souchon
Katherine Stewart
Edna and Marguerite Sullivan
Elizabeth Van de Veer
Burdette Terrette Waldo
Betty Wall
Miriam Walmsley
Elizabeth White
Anna Wogan
Althea Wuerpel

Hardie Barkley
John Barkley
Durel Black
Grant Black
William Brierre
Bennie Brown
Frank Brown
Junior Burke
Walter Carroll
Frederick Clapp
John F. Clark
Gordon Clay
Irving Cope
Earle Crumb
Hughes de la Vergne
Willo Fox
Walter Hamlin
Ellis Moore
Harry Rainold
Williard Roberts

"One of the smartest luncheons given there recently was a pre-nuptial affair, Miss Mable Bouden entertaining in honor of the lovely young bride of Mr. Lucien Lyons, then in the last week of her Mildred Crumb days. The merry party included besides Miss Bouden and Miss Crumb, Mrs. T. H. Lyons, Mrs. L. E. Lyons and Mrs. E. H. Pennell of New Rochelle, New York."

MOTOR BOAT CRUISES RETURNED AT SYC

"Motor boat cruising was returned to the racing schedule for the 1919 season by Commodore Benedict as an appropriate Armistice celebration. It seemed that gracious, care-free old times were restored with the newly inaugurated series of five annual cruises. The first cruise got under way in the early part of the summer." It was appealingly described in the *Barometer*.

> A magnificent boat parade followed the *Violet*, the Commodore's flagship, as Commodore Benedict brought the fleet in squadron-fashion from West End to the Tchefuncte River, thence eight miles up the river to Wolverine Heights and to the spacious country home of F. Burguieres who turned the whole plantation over to the cruisers.
> Manager Mitchell of the Southern Yacht Club transported his staff to serve meals as well as a barbecue for all three days the cruisers remained on the plantations. On the return trip, the cruise took the form of a duck hunting and fishing excursion through the inland waterway to the west of New Orleans.
> The second trip soon followed and all participants, after their arrival in Bay St. Louis to picnic along the shores of the Jordan River, had supper under the pines.
> Saturday morning there will be the gathering of berries before breakfast and some fishing. In mid-day, after a light lunch, there will be a water carnival with masked bathers in costume. At supper time, there will be barbecue and a Kangaroo Court after which dancing will prevail in the woods. On Sunday morning divine services will be held on Cat Island, after which there will be surf bathing and shell gathering before the fleet returns to West End.

BIRTH OF THE FISH CLASS FLEET—1919

The loss of interest in sailing since the end of World War I was most distressing but well understood. Those men who had returned from the war were without the necessary funds to purchase a boat. However, one SYC member decided to do something about it, J. Rathborne de Buys, the club's race committee chairman. He addressed the decline theoretically, proposing to the SYC board a one-design craft of comparatively inexpensive construction be built, with several models owned by the club so that beginners as well as experts could learn to sail them.

Chairman deBuys contended that the club was not only dominated by power-boats but the other deadly enemies were "automobiles, with jelly-beans and flappers." To the jelly-beans and flappers Mr. deBuys' comment may have sounded Victorian, but his foresight was pure magic for the sport of sailing.

A committee composed of Mr. deBuys, Adam Lorch, A. R. "Babe" Roberts, Clarence Ferguson, Gordon Chapman, and Peter Donnes, yachtsmen all, studied plans of other one-design classes and came up with a design which incorporated features of the New England sharpie and the wide beam and low freeboard of the cat. To this was added the V-bottom or easy entrance and smooth wake with little suction—no curved forms—all board construction with chine and balanced rudder, using a gaff-rig sail.

The builder of the boats, Emil Hermann, placed the plans in the hands of Thomas D. Bowes, the prominent naval architect of Philadelphia, who checked them over in a thoroughly scientific manner and found them practical and correct.

These one-design sloops were made of cypress boards—the spars were adapted because of the necessity of prompt replacement in case of accidents and also because of saving in cost and difficulty in securing spruce.

The entire plan was warmly accepted by the SYC board and supported by ex-Commodore Ernest Lee Jahncke. Rathborne de Buys was commissioned to have six of the new boats built at a cost of $750.00 each. The class was given the title of *Fish Class* and all yachts were given names of the fishes of our Southern waters. The first six yachts of the fleet were named *Minnow, Tarpon, Pompano, Mackerel, Shark,* and *Porpoise.* Later the names were omitted and numerals used on the sails over the emblem of a fish. For a nominal fee anyone could sail these boats. This was especially popular among those members who had just returned from the war.

The Fish Class was the first original racing class introduced inside the Southern Yacht Club since its organization. All other boats had been brought down from the East and North.

When the first three of the six sloops were completed, the officers and governing board members of SYC sailed the first race on June 28, 1919, which was won by Leslie P. Beard, who defeated C. A. Sporl by just 35 seconds.

After the completion of the six Fish Class sloops, a race was held with SYC members participating. Cal F. Hadden won the series over J. B. Witherspoon, Earl Blouin, H. B. Hammett, Thomas Regan, Leslie P. Beard, and J. M. Kinabrew.

SIR THOMAS J. LIPTON VISITS U.S. AND SYC

It was reported out of Marblehead, Massachusetts on March 22, 1919, that Sir Thomas J. Lipton, sailing on the *Aquitania* on a trip to the U.S., had sent a cablegram to the Corinthian Yacht Club stating he would arrive in the States on March 26, where he would confer with American yachtsmen about the resumption of international yacht racing. Lipton's enthusiasm for yachting was boundless.

Sir Thomas had offered a cup for class P yachts at the Corinthian Yacht Club. He had also contacted the New York Yacht Club (NYYC) for another challenge for the America's Cup, but the NYYC replied that it prefered to wait until 1922 to resume international competition. (The war had prevented this race from being held in 1914 when Lipton had *Shamrock IV* ready. The boat was put in dry dock in Brooklyn until the America's Cup race was held in 1922, when Lipton was again defeated.)

In November, 1919, Sir Thomas was a visitor to New Orleans. He was the luncheon guest of Commodore Percy S. Benedict of the Southern Yacht Club. When he was introduced to the new fleet of Fish Class sloops in the SYC harbor, Sir Thomas, motivated by the great possibility for the advancement of sailing in interclub competition these boats could promote, promised to donate a trophy to the club with the proviso that it be contended for in the Fish Class sloops in interclub racing.

THE ROARING TWENTIES

The twenties roared into history, but there was a lot more substance to this era than knee dresses and hip flasks. For New Orleans, it was a decade of progress—a cosmetic facelift, including a $250,000.00 remodeled yacht club to add to a remarkable lakefront development, and the opening of the Industrial Canal, which introduced Lake Pontchartrain to the Mississippi River.

Also, the popularity of the SYC was reflected in the increasing reservations for fraternity parties, dinner dances, and the lively weekly lunches to which the ladies all wore pretty hats. However, omitted from the social schedule of events was the enjoyable "Southern Yacht Club Night" at the Strand Theatre, which featured on several occasions various sailing regattas held on Lake Pontchartrain; this program was discontinued.

SOUTHERN YACHT CLUB
$250,000 BOND ISSUE AND BOND HOLDERS

At the 1920 SYC annual meeting, Commodore Percy S. Benedict was elected to serve a third term. Because of the prosperity of the club, which was free of any indebtedness at that time, the members of the board were successful in their negotiations with the Whitney and Hibernia banks of New Orleans in securing a $250,000 bond issue for the complete remodeling and additions to the clubhouse, which was subscribed to in record-breaking time. The remodeling contractors were Riess and Moody, with Rathborne deBuys as architect and Henry Moses as interior decorator. They were assisted by the illustrious architect Thomas Sully, who had designed the original clubhouse in 1899.

Following is a list of *some* of the bond holders published in the *Barometer*:

Coleman E. Adler	A.D. Geoghegan (2)	T. T. Parker
N. Bellamore	Will J. Gibbens	Leon Pieffer
A. E. Berdon (2)	C. H. Hamilton	Jules A. Randon
B. C. Casanas	P. P. Hardie	W. S. Rembert
Oliver Clarke	J. G. Hauser	H. J. Robbert
M. F. Cook, Jr.	Wm Henderson	Jos. F. Scheurmann
B. S. D'Antoni	L. L. Hirsch	E. G. Schlieder
L. J. Dantzler	Leonard B. Keiffer	J. T. Segari
H. C. Davidson	J. D. Kenney	Chas. E. Smith
J. H. Davidson	Lee Krauss	Robert Spearing
E. A. Dunbar	A. Krower	C. A. Sporl
James P. Dunbar	Frank J. Matthew	Dr. Chas. F. Summer
Arthur Duvic Sons	Allen Mehle	B. J. Walle
Lawrence Fabacher, Sr.(2)	J. A. Mermilliod	Chas. A. Weiss
Lawrence B. Fabacher	Dr. W. Milton Miller	Wilson Williams
John Fabacher	F. J. Monteleone	Albert Tujague
Joseph Fabacher	Edgar Newman	Leon Tujague
Richard R. Foster	C. C. Olney	L. Viccaro
A. J. Gelpi	Ole K. Olsen	

It was announced at the annual meeting that Sir Thomas J. Lipton's gift had arrived from England, a magnificent silver trophy handcrafted by silversmiths in England, whereupon a resolution was adopted and Sir Thomas was sent an honorary membership extraordinary in appreciation for his generosity. Following is a copy of his letter of thanks.

City Road
London, E. C. 1st December 1920

Lipton's Offices
Telephone No. Clerkenwell 2019

My dear Commodore,
    I duly received the very handsome and beautifully illuminated copy of the resolution electing me an Honorary Member Extraordinary of the Southern Yacht Club and I am very greatly obliged to the members for the honour they have done me. I can assure you that I very highly appreciate their kind thought and I would ask you to convey to the officers and members of the Club my warmest and most heartfelt thanks.
    I am also greatly obliged for the interesting photographs and the very nicely bound copy of the "Barometer" for June, contents of which I have read with very much interest and pleasure.
    The kindness shown me by the members of the Southern Yacht Club I value very highly and shall always remember, all the more so that its headquarters are in the city with which my early days were so pleasantly identified.
    With renewed thanks and best wishes for the success and prosperity of the Club and its members,

(SGD) Yours Sincerely
Thomas J. Lipton

Commodore Benedict
Southern Yacht Club
New Orleans, La.

So that all New Orleanians could view this masterpiece of design, the Sir Thomas J. Lipton trophy, D. H. Holmes, the oldest and one of the most exclusive department stores in the South, through the courtesy of its president, F. W. Evans, who was a member of the SYC, prominently displayed the trophy for many months. Daniel H. Holmes, founder of D. H. Holmes, was one of the SYC's early members in 1850.

THE FIRST RACE IN THE NEW FISH CLASS SLOOPS

The first race in the six newly built Fish Class sloops was sailed in the early part of the 1920 summer season. Those privileged to be the skippers were Cal F. Hadden, who won the series, J. B. Witherspoon, Earl Blouin, H. B. Hammett, Thomas Regan, Leslie P. Beard, and J. M. Kinabrew.

THE FIRST SIR THOMAS J. LIPTON TROPHY REGATTA

With a fleet of new boats and a beautiful silver trophy to be awarded as a prize, Commodore Benedict invited the Pensacola Yacht Club to a team race in August 1920. The Florida yachtsmen graciously accepted the invitation and sent their top skippers to the event: Capt. Dave Witherill, Capt. Dan Sheppard, William Walthers, W. A. Curtiss, Peter Altrink, W. L. Mitchell, Oscar Sheppard, and Thomas H. Johnson. They won the series with three firsts sailed by William "Willie" Walthers. The expert skippers and crews who gave their best representing Southern were: Leslie P. Beard, Edward H. Keep, A. R. "Babe" Roberts, William A. Porteous, Jr., Finley Mitchell, Reginald H. Carter, and William B. Edgar, Jr.

Many visitors from the Gulf Coast witnessed this first race for the Lipton Cup and were impressed with the new Fish Class sloops. "The Pensacola Yacht Club's Commodore immediately purchased three of the original six boats from the SYC before returning home," reported the *Barometer*.

Capt. James C. Watson, chairman of the regatta committee of the Pensacola Yacht Club, and Commodore John H. Cross arrived at the head of the Pensacola delegation on the yacht *Mercathades*. Commodore E. B. Overton of the Eastern Shore Yacht Club of Mobile arrived to spectate with a representative group from Mobile, Walter Mitchell, Jr., R. J. Hermann, Norman Altice, and C. E. Burgess. When they returned to Fairhope, the home town of the Eastern Shore Yacht Club, plans were immediately initiated for the building of three Fish Class sloops to be ready for competition in the 1921 Lipton Cup event to be sailed at Pensacola, Florida.

FOUNDING OF THE GULF YACHTING ASSOCIATION

At a banquet given by Commodore Percy Benedict honoring the winners of the regatta, the Pensacola Yacht Club, the commodore presented a proposal for the forming of a yachting association of all yacht clubs on the Gulf Coast along with the same principles laid down by the Southern Gulf Coast Yachting Association, the parent organization organized in 1901, which had ceased to function before World War I. The idea was received with much enthusiasm.

Not since the founding of the Southern Yacht Club had there been

The Fish Class sloop was the first original racing class sloop introduced by the SYC. All other boats had been brought down from the East and North. It was a club-owned sloop and became the heart of the most popular fleet on Lake Pontchartrain and the Gulf Coast for fifty years.

Sir Thomas J. Lipton of England and of America's Cup fame presented the first of two Lipton trophies to the SYC in 1920 for interclub competiton in the club-owned Fish Class sloops.

Commodore Samuel F. Heaslip
1912, 1913

Commodore Ernest Lee Jahncke
1914, 1915, 1916

Commodore Chandler C.
Luzenberg
1917

Commodore W. Milton Miller,
M.D.
1924, 1925

Commodore Harry T. Howard
1921, 1922, 1923

Commodore Percy S. Benedict
1918, 1919, 1920

greater stimulus to the sport of yachting along the Southern rim of the United States than the coming of the Fish Class and the founding of the Gulf Yachting Association. Commodore Benedict's proposal had sensational appeal. A meeting was called in Mobile on November 13, 1920 with Commodore Ed. Overton of the Eastern Shore Yacht Club as host at the famous old Battle House hotel. Invitations were extended to the Houston, Southern, Biloxi, Eastern Shore, and Pensacola Yacht Clubs, and these were enthusiastically received.

The Battle House was such a popular Southern hotel in the beginning of this century that it is worthy of its own chapter in any Gulf Coast history.

THE BATTLE HOUSE IN MOBILE, ALABAMA

The following article was taken from the *Binocular*, a monthly publication of the Eastern Shore Yacht Club:

> The historic old Battle House, the first to be built and opened on November 1852, was a 240-room hotel which stood on the site of the old Waverly Hotel and Franklin House. The spot already had historic significance as Andrew Jackson once headquartered in the Waverly where he planned the gallant but unneeded victory at New Orleans. The first lessee of the hotel, Paran Stevens, whose wife was a leader in society in New York and one of the 400, became the originator of what is now known as the American plan in hotel management.
>
> "Other notables from around the world were among the guests, such as Sir Charles Lydell, Henry Clay, W. L. Yancy, Jefferson Davis, Generals Bragg, Beauregard and Taylor, also Admiral Semmes and other noted Confederates. Later came General Grant, Millard Fillmore, Woodrow Wilson and such famous theatrical names as Booth, Barrett, Forrest, McCullough, O'Neill, Janauschek and Bernhardt.

It was in this historic hotel that the first regular meeting of the Association was held on November 13 and 14 since its organization at the Southern Yacht Club in New Orleans on October 16, 1920.

At the initial meeting, in Fairhope, the Constitution and By-Laws drawn by Rathborne deBuys of SYC were adopted and the name of the organization, the "Gulf Yachting Association" (GYA), was approved. The represented yacht clubs at the meeting, Southern, Houston, Biloxi, Eastern Shore and Pensacola, were made charter members of the GYA.

> About fifty enthusiastic young men were present at the banquet. A talk was made by Commodore Percy S. Benedict of the Southern Yacht

Club on the reason for this meeting and the necessity of having a yachting association.

Short talks were also made by Commodore John H. Cross of the Pensacola Yacht Club, Mr. W. O. Woods, Secretary of the Houston Launch Club of Houston, Texas, Mr. F. W. Elmer, Secretary of the Biloxi Yacht Club, Mr. J. C. Watson, Ex-Commodore of the Pensacola Yacht Club and Mr. Wm. H. Parham, Secretary of the Southern Yacht Club. After the banquet, the delegates were taken to the dansante in the Battle House, where they had an enjoyable evening dancing.

The next morning the visitors were given a launch ride on the *Firefly*. This handsome yacht is owned by Mr. Louis Lorio. Mr. G. V. Rogers who piloted the launch and who has cruised with a good many of the delegates, showed them the river front and Chickasaw. They were taken to the Gulf Fishing and Hunting Club on Dog River where they were given a reception and barbecue. Chaperoning the barbecue were Mr. and Mrs. Lloyd Warner. The reception committeemen were Harry Drysdale, Chairman, Henry Sossman, C. E. Burgess, D. S. M. Unger and William Cooney. The young ladies of the hospitality committee were:

Eleanor Burgett
Gordon Burgett, Mrs.
Helen Courtright
Irene Gordon
Regina Hermann
Teelan Landauer of
    New York
Marion Overton

Esther Reynolds
Dorothy Ramsey
Catherine VanAntwerp
Grace Van Heuvel
Mrs. Lloyd Warner
Mrs. Bailey Westbrook
Eulalie Wheyland

A welcomed visitor to the Southern Yacht Club's fleet in 1920 was the first club-owned Patrol Boat, which was sorely needed for patroling races on Lake Pontchartrain and on the Gulf Coast. This purchase was made during the administrations of Commodores Luzenberg and Benedict, who were also responsible for approving the $10,000 purchase of a square of ground behind West End Park called the Pen, which was used to house the many yachts. There are still a few around today who remember the great boathouse parties in the old pen.

SYC POWER BOAT SQUADRON DIVISION

The Power Boat Squadron in New Orleans played a very active and important role on the waters of Lake Pontchartrain during World War I. With more than 300 powerboats in the SYC harbor in 1920, Commodore Benedict and his board approved the formation of a Power Boat Division within the club. Thus all yachting interests—

both power and sailing—were kept under control. The Power Boat Division operated under the rules of the SYC, Gulf Yachting Association, and the American Power Boat Association of which the SYC became a member in 1915.

"The public was obsessed with speed," reported the *Barometer*. "The nautical tournaments awakened interest and animated the public that congregated along the seawall, everyone eager to watch the developments and incidents in this interesting sport. Veritable aces in motor boating took part in these races. A new six-boat, one-design Combustion Engine Class, 21 ft. long, with speed up to 20 mph, spotlighted Southern."

"MISS NEW ORLEANS" RACES FOR HARMSWORTH TROPHY

The Southern Yacht Club, along with the city of New Orleans, was invited by the American Power Boat Association to participate in the Gold Cup races in 1920. In spite of the rumor that New Orleans would not have an entry, "all doubt was dispelled in a dynamite-like fashion when a meeting was held by the SYC committee appointed to consider ways and means for the building of such a craft," said the *Barometer*.

> Ever since H. N. Moody presented the 'build a winner' idea at the annual meeting of SYC in January, there has been activity along the desired lines. Boat builders of national fame have been in touch with the club and quick action which will enable our entry to be ready and tuned up for the big race in the Detroit River on September 6, 1920 is under way.
>
> The committee decided to pay Glenn H. Curtiss the sum of $10,000 to provide a two-man boat making a minimum of 70 miles per hour, 24 feet in length, single stem hydroplane, equipped with a 430-horse power Curtiss-Liberty motor. To do this a *Miss New Orleans* club was organized then and there and the membership lists were opened at once with Gus Baldwin having the distinction of being the first member by subscribing the sum of $100.00 towards the enterprise. The total of $15,000 was collected.
>
> Of the $15,000 it was decided to expend $10,000 on the boat, and $5,000 on the two races in which she will take part this season. The boat will be presented by the *Miss New Orleans* Club to the Southern Yacht Club after the races this year, and will be kept in permanent condition for these races, which are held each year.
>
> Mr. Curtiss in his report to the SYC board stated that the fastest speed in any of the previous races for the Gold Challenge Cup had been 63 to 64 miles an hour, so that he was giving the SYC considerable leeway

in the matter of speed, a sustained speed of 70 miles an hour. He also agreed to build no other contender this year for this trophy. He further stated that *Miss New Orleans* would be the equal of the *Miss America* which is to race for the Harmsworth International Trophy in England this summer.

Miss New Orleans finished out of the money in Detroit. However, *Miss America* did go on to win in Cowes, England the Harmsworth International trophy, the coveted British award in speedboat racing. The victory by *Algonac*, Michigan's Gar Wood, at 61.51 mph, brought this prestigious cup to the United States and Detroit, where it was sailed for in 1921.

Although an unsuccessful attempt was made by a New Orleanian in 1920 to win the Harmsworth trophy, a second attempt in 1982 was successful when another New Orleanian, Alvin C. Copeland, the nephew of SYC's 1932 Olympic gold medal winner, Gilbert T. Gray, won the Harmsworth trophy, which was presented to him at the Isle of Wight by King Constantine II of Greece. Copeland was driving a 38-foot Scarab named *Popeye*, powered by a 2-650 horsepower Mercury Marine engine, 482 cubic inches with Electronic Fuel Injection, at a speed of 104 m.p.h. To build *Popeye* the cost was $600,000, compared to the $10,000 spent for *Miss New Orleans* in 1920. The SYC venture was a one-time trial.

COAST GUARD STATION ESTABLISHED

The Southern Yacht Club played a major role in securing the U.S. Coast Guard station in the lighthouse at the mouth of the New Basin Canal directly opposite the SYC. There was a battle between the City of New Orleans and the U. S. Government seeking a sorely needed Life Guard station, and after many years of letter-writing an political confrontation, the government approved the measure on June 22, 1920.

CHAPTER XI

1921–1925

COMMODORES	TERM
Harry T. Howard	1921-22-23
W. Milton Miller, M.D.	1924-1925

COMMODORE HARRY T. HOWARD—1921-22-23

After a very successful three-year term in office, Commodore Benedict turned the gavel over to Harry T. Howard, a prominent local businessman, who was elected commodore. Commodore Howard had reigned as Rex in 1888. His officers were: Gus B. Baldwin, vice-commodore; A. D. Geoghagan, rear commodore; Dr. J. E. Landry, fleet surgeon; and Clarence J. Ferguson, measurer. The governing board members were ex-Commodore Percy S. Benedict, W. K. DePass, William H. Douglas, F. J. Foxley, and W. E. Winship. Howard's flagship was the *Loiterer*.

The SYC membership grew to gigantic proportions when the membership increased from 2,000 to 2,500. This was during the "jazz age" when dancing was popular—the ballroom was always filled, and dinner dances were held twice weekly.

With the $250,000 expansion program underway, it was agreed to raise the dues from $18.00 to $24.00 per year. At the annual meeting ex-Rear Commodore John A. Rawlins was elected to honorary life membership for his contribution to yachting for many years. Also, one of SYC's skippers extraordinary, T. Hoffman Olsen of Denmark, the New Orleans Danish Consul, was congratulated on his recent achievements, having won the Royal Danish Yacht Club's race of the year in Denmark in his big open sloop *Seawanhaka* and also the town of Peheleveg's honor in 1921.

At the 1921 Gulf Yachting Association's annual meeting held in Biloxi, Mississippi, Commodore Byrd Enochs of the Biloxi Yacht Club was elected president. The by-laws of the GYA were changed so that each club be named the domicile in alphabetical order, with the commodore of that club to be named president.

NEW ORLEANS PRESS REPORTERS HONORED BY SYC

At the 1921 annual meeting of the SYC accolades were extended to members of the press who were praised for their generous publicity of yachting activities at the SYC in their effort to revitalize sailing after the war years. Resolutions were adopted commending the two popular newsmen Wm. B. Keefe of *The Item* and Will R. Hamilton of the *Times-Picayune*. Both had been made honorary members of the SYC in 1918 for their contribution to the sport of sailing at that time.

At the meeting, approval was given to have built three more Fish Class sloops to replace those purchased by the Pensacola Yacht Club in 1920.

Commodore Howard made a wise appointment when former commodore Percy S. Benedict, the "human dynamo," accepted chairmanship of the Southern Marine Marathon. Run on the outside course the annual event was now the longest long-distance race then staged by any yacht club, since the Bermuda power cruiser races had been discontinued by the New York Yacht Club. The race covered 200 miles from New Orleans to Pensacola, Florida.

Another motor cruiser race was inaugurated from New Orleans to Mobile, Alabama in 1921, 140 miles to the Eastern Shore Yacht Club located on Mobile Bay, 20 miles from the open Gulf of Mexico. The picturesque Sand Island light marked the bar and entrance to the Bay. Then on to Pensacola, Florida.

Following the 1921 regatta party held at the Pensacola Yacht Club over the Fourth of July holiday, the entire fleet cruised back to Mobile Bay, where the armada from the Eastern Shore Yacht Club greeted and escorted them to Magnolia Beach for overnight hosting by Mobile yachtsmen. Then the Werner Cup contest began, with sights set for Biloxi, Mississippi.

Scene at the mouth of the New Basin Canal with the pleasure steamer Camellia in the forefront, the Southern Yacht Club at the left rear, and the old canal lighthouse on the right.

The Southern Yacht Club, remodeled in 1921 at a cost of $250,000, shows the added wings that gave it the city's largest dance floor and made it the most popular club for the social set in New Orleans.

The Pontchartrain Rowing Club on the New Basin Canal was a popular club to which many SYC members belonged.

The 1922 SYC Lipton Cup team tied with the Pensacola Yacht Club for first place in the Labor Day Sir Thomas J. Lipton Trophy Regatta. The SYC was unsuccessful in the first and second Lipton Cup races sailed in 1920 and 1921. Front row: William Porteous, James Haywood, Edward Estoup, Edward Pinas, John Luther. Back row: unknown; Peter Donnes, Menge Dixey, J. Ben Ravannack, Frank Ferrer, and John Longmire.

THE OPENING OF THE NEWLY REMODELED CLUBHOUSE

A very proud group of officers and members of the Southern Yacht Club greeted the opening of the long-awaited newly remodeled clubhouse in 1921. It was the consensus that the inconvenience was well worth it. Welcoming the guests as they arrived for the formal opening were the officers and governing committee members of the SYC.

"The tremendous growth of the membership," related the *Barometer*, "the club's absolute freedom from indebtedness, the new building are all the dreams from out of the Arabian Nights. The Aladdin's lamp, however, has been organization and work along constructive lines and with these fundamentals there is but one word which can properly describe the club's course, and that word is 'Success'.

"So, let all of us celebrate this success at the club's formal opening on May 7, 1921. An afternoon sport will be presented by the yachtsmen and in the evening Terpsichore will revel in all his latest creations. The Southern Yacht Club is the second oldest yacht club in the U.S. but the first over water and is preparing to be the largest."

At the banquet, Commodore Harry T. Howard presented ex-Commodore Benedict with a handsome solid silver service, consisting of six massive pieces, for his effort and leadership in the major job of remodeling the Southern Yacht Club. It was noted that 3,184 members and guests were present and 914 dinners were served. "The opening was celebrated with much éclat," said the *Barometer*.

The committeemen who served for this auspicious occasion were listed as a part of the souvenir program as follows:

RECEPTION COMMITTEE
C. B. Fox, Chairman

Gonzalo Abunza
J. A. Badger
E. V. Benjamin
A. W. Berdon
Edward S. Butler
John F. Clark
J. H. DeGrange
James Dinkins
W. P. Flower
W. B. Gillican

Stonewall Jackson
W. E. Jervy
John Legier, Jr.
Dr. R. C. Lynch
Paul H. Maloney, Sr.
H. B. Myles
J. D. O'Keefe
W. S. Penick
Jas. B. Ross
John S. Seymour

SOUTHERN YACHT CLUB

Frank B. Hayne
J. D. Hayward

W. P. Simpson
Frank B. Williams
Samuel Zemurray

FLOOR COMMITTEE
Judge Rufus E. Foster, Chairman

John H. Baldwin
Ben Beekman
L. E. Blanchard
W. H. Cowley
J. V. Dugan
F. W. Ellsworth
Louis C. Frantz
A. B. Freeman
H. L. Garic
H. E. Garic
J. M. Kinabrew
Harry N. Moore
Paul Maloney, Jr.

L. K. Nicholson
C. C. Olney
T. Hoffmann Olsen
R. J. Palfrey
Waldo M. Pitkin
J. Ben Ravannack
A. M. Savage
J. C. Shafer
J. W. Sherrouse
D. Sivewright
Ruben E. Tipton
Pierre A. Villere

SPECIAL FLOOR COMMITTEE FOR SEASON

J. W. Barkdull, Jr.
E. L. Betzer
David Bernhardt
E. R. Bernhardt
E. C. Brown
R. H. Carter, Jr.
Louis Coiron
Earl Crumb
John Devlin
Arthur Duvic, Jr.
Frank Ferrer
Harry Ferrer
Edward Finley
Morris Hansell II

L. C. Heilbronner
J. G. Hogan
P. W. Hogan
Charles Karst, Jr.
E. R. Montgomery
Felix Perrilliat
George L. Purves
J. Ben Ravannack
Leo Reilly
Roland Rexach
George Robert
Lester Smith
J. S. Stouse
C. O. Witte

The publicity committee, headed by W. H. Parham, assisted by Ben Beekman, L. S. Sampsell, Leonard K. Nicholson, Lawrence Deckbar, and Aubrey Murray, published a special edition of the *Barometer* which contained some very interesting data.

The dimensions of the newly remodeled clubhouse measured 250 feet by 150 feet with a dance floor of 126 feet by 58 feet. There was an alcove on the north side of the floor for a bandstand. Ceilings were 20 feet high. Galleries and dining space approximately 180 feet long were enclosed with French glass doors. The interior represented the cabin of a steamship with a frieze around the entire room and the four pillars in the foyer, with one end of the ballroom being done in anchors, sails, and intertwined rope.

Hatches were made in the ceiling along with chandeliers, which were life preservers with hanging lights. I remember well at a Saturday night "shipwreck" party one happy sailor had the bright idea of opening a hatch from the dormitory above and pouring a pail of water on the table of guests below. Having ruined the black taffeta evening gown of a lady guest, the highly inebriated young man was immediately removed from the building.

The foyer, or ladies lounge, was attractively furnished with large ivory wicker furniture, colorfully finished with cretonne cushions. The lights in the foyer and around the walls of the ballroom were regulation boat lanterns of heavy corrugated glass with steel tops and bottoms, which hung low and were very attractive.

The writer clearly remembers that standing in the corner of this foyer were three beautiful and shiny "one arm bandits" and an "iron claw" machine. They not only provided amusement for the members but were a great source of revenue for the club, that is until the law intervened and slot machines were banned in the Parish of Orleans. As the clubhouse was on the border-line of Jefferson Parish, where gambling was permitted, for as long as it was possible the Southern Yacht Club claimed residence in the Parish of Jefferson.

"Not the least among the attractions of the clubhouse," recorded the *Barometer*,

> in the lobby kept in cabinets were beautiful trophies, one of the most pleasing to a woman's eye being an immense silver bowl heavily embossed with water lilies, the leaves, the full bloom and the bud, which was the gift of Mrs. Deborah A. Milliken in memory of her husband, who was commodore in 1859. Another bowl with deer-heads for handles bears the date 1854. The beautifully hand-crafted silver Sir Thomas J. Lipton trophy standing over three feet high occupied the central position in the cabinet. There was also a miniature of the America's Cup which was competed for internationally at intervals ever since 1851.
>
> On the second floor, the dormitory and extensions to the east and west were subdivided into a lounge, with stairs to the cupola on the roof, ten private bedrooms; new toilets and new screened galleries were added to the dormitory for outdoor sleeping. A modern heating system was provided and modern electric lighting and fans for the various large rooms and small rooms installed. An 18 foot flag staff was erected on the roof.
>
> The porches were screened where the "Rocking Chair Fleet" and the old-timers who like to sit back in their easy chair puffing rings of smoke

and recounting reminiscences of bygone days, will find a likely place in the lounging room that has been provided, and the younger element, who don their yachting togs on with almost no provocation, will find in the dormitory everything their hearts could wish.

The details of the exterior and interior were designed to suggest the use of the building, for instance, the carving of the projecting beams into figureheads of famous vessels and yachts. The panels had moulds, replicas of the club yachts, such as the *Lady Emma, Nepenthe, Adrienne* and others. Also, the railings of rope netting used on large yachts, etc. For the interior the rooms were finished in detail suggestive of handsome cabins, saloons, etc. of famous yachts and vessels in nautical history. The kitchen was enlarged with three huge iron stoves to serve the large membership.

There were two piers leading from the clubhouse, the one on the east side of the club was built solidly of earth and concrete, forming a breakwater for the canal. On the pier proper extending from the clubhouse into the lake there was located a small race committee house. It was known as the 'judges' stand' where all races were started and finished. Along the pier one could find lovers strolling in the moonlight during a break in the dancing program.

The *Picayune* also referred eloquently to the opening of the yacht club:

> The Southern Yacht Club was always considered the social mecca of New Orleans and the newly renovated quarters with modern wicker furniture and a highly polished dance floor soon became fashionable for parties. Many formal openings of the Southern Yacht Club have come and gone year after year, but none was more brilliant than the celebration of the newly remodeled clubhouse.
>
> The Southern Yacht Club has been an historic building and the scene of many merry meetings about which so much yachting history has been written and in which the growth of the world's biggest yacht club was made possible. Fortunately, the work done did not necessitate the demolishing of the present building built in 1900 because the new edifice was built around the old structure with its stately verandas and towering cupola.

Many New Orleanians and Gulf Coast residents remember the parties at the Southern Yacht Club. They were festive occasions and it was quite the thing to receive an invitation to their great dances, such as the "shipwreck" costume dance, Halloween and New Year's Eve celebrations. The annual Opening Regatta and "Welcome Home to the Fleet" affairs were faithfully attended by skippers and crews. It was at one of these parties that I met my spouse, Jack, and there are many living couples today who were likewise introduced to their mates. These were happy times which were soon to be erased with the stock market crash of 1929.

At these fabulous parties, we danced to the tune of the jazz bands of such as Oscar "Papa" Celestin, Al Streiman, Johnnie DeDroit, and the ever popular René Louapre orchestra, which continues to be the most outstanding music for social events.

Before the opening of the club, the SYC board of directors met and approved a number of rules needed for the proper conduct of the dances. These rules were published by the *Picayune*. "Several new rules were invoked by the SYC governing board, since now the Southern Yacht Club has become a mecca for the 'smart set.' Because of the large number of stags at the parties, the governing committee passed a rule stating, 'Breaking in on the first dance will not be permitted, and the rule will be strictly enforced. Breaking in will only be allowed on an encore. Members not dancing will not be permitted to stand around on the main floor obstructing the dancers.

"Smoking will be positively prohibited in the Assembly Hall on dance nights." House rule #22 "Automobiles" under "Socials" was expressly adopted for this occasion: "Automobiles will not be permitted to park immediately in front of the club, nor will refreshments be served to individuals while in automobiles. The parking of cars with chauffeurs in the circle in front of the club will not be permitted on entertainment nights, the circle being reserved for cars of members without chauffeurs."

A BRIEF HISTORY OF THE NEW BASIN CANAL

A brief history of the New Basin Canal is in order because it is mentioned in many areas of this book and because the Southern Yacht Club is located at the mouth of this historic canal.

Truly a great engineering feat, the digging of this canal was accomplished in 1832. The cost was estimated to be $1,119,000. It took six years to complete the project because of the swamp land through which the canal was dug, which was dense with cypress tree stumps. The area was infested with mosquitos, which caused 8,000 workers to lose their lives—some historians say as many as 10,000 Irish and German immigrants were the victims of yellow fever caused by the insects, and cholera was another culprit. The bodies of these foreigners were buried where they fell.

The New Basin Canal was built to serve the "uptown" section or "American" sector when the city expanded on the upper part of Canal Street, the main street in the city. (The lower side of Canal Street is known as "downtown.")

Along the shores of the New Basin Canal many shipyards were located, the most prominent being the Jahncke Service, Inc. Fritz Jahncke, the owner, was a member of the Southern Yacht Club. He is credited with developing this canal as a commercial waterway. Jahncke Service was the largest and principal user of the canal, so much so that it has been referred to as "Jahncke's Ditch."

Prior to 1880, the only aggregate materials used in New Orleans and vicinity for the manufacture of concrete were shells transported by means of schooners from the shell bank bordering on the north shore of Lake Pontchartrain, and the sand from the Gulf Coast which was used for buildings. These materials were brought through the New Basin Canal by means of tugboats. The method was so laborious and expensive that Mr. Jahncke took the step of acquiring a hydraulic dredge, by going to St. Louis and leasing for $5,000 the first steam-driven hydraulic suction dredge used in the vicinity of New Orleans. Fritz Jahncke also went to Chicago and purchased a small tugboat which had been used in the first Chicago World's Fair as an excursion boat on Lake Michigan. This tugboat, *Claribel*, became an institution in the Jahncke business and was known as the flagship and pride of the fleet after several other tugboats were purchased.

Subsequently, Fritz Jahncke acquired a small shipyard on the north shore of Lake Pontchartrain at Madisonville on the Tchefuncte River, where he built many barges and tugboats to transport shells, gravel, and sand to New Orleans. He no longer brought the sand from the Gulf Coast, as he found the sand he needed in the bed of the Tchefuncte River. The *Meta*, *Fox* and *Carrie Currens* and a number of barges soon brought about an evolution in the handling of sand, gravel, and shell and other building material in New Orleans for the construction of many large buildings and paving of streets and sidewalks in the city. Fritz Jahncke was the first to install paved sidewalks, (they previously had been made of brick,) and also paved streets, which had heretofore been paved with Belgian blocks, cobblestones, or flatboat wood. He also brought about the formation of the Sewerage & Water Board.

The fleet of schooners that at one time carried this material into the city soon became obsolete and began to disappear as tugs and barges took their place, which in addition to building materials, carried charcoal, watermelons, and oysters.

A familiar sight for many years at the mouth of the New Basin

Canal were the pleasure boats *Camellia*, *Susquehana*, and *Southdown*, which carried passengers to picnic grounds across Lake Pontchartrain at Mandeville and Madisonville on the north shore. They afforded a very popular and happy pastime on moonlight nights with rides around the lake and dancing to the tune of famous jazz bands.

A popular spectacle on the canal over weekends were the speedboat races held between two prominent boat builders, Duvic Bros. and Higgins Industries. Their run started at the Black Bridge by Metairie Cemetery and ended at the mouth of the canal.

ROWING CONTESTS IN THE CANAL

Many Southern Yacht Club members were also active members in the Pontchartrain and St. John rowing clubs located on the levee of the New Basin Canal. J. Benjamin Ravannack who was secretary-treasurer of SYC for many years, was also the president of the Pontchartrain Rowing Club in 1921 and in 1939. He served with another SYC member, Herbert G. Jahncke, secretary-treasurer of the rowing club. During their regime, the Houston Yacht Club requested the Southern Yacht Club to ask Mr. Ravannack if he would promote a three-cornered meet between the canoe division of Houston Yacht Club and the University of Texas. Southern's role as genial mediary was self-rewarding.

The first regatta of the Pontchartrain Rowing Club was held in May 1914. During its first year it won the Southern Amateur Rowing championship. The club sponsored many sculling events in the canal, competing against the Bayou St. John Rowing Club. During the Sugar Bowl spectacular in New Orleans, rowing was an adjunct sport and proved to be very popular for a few years. Spectators would line the levees for several miles. Some would ride the West End streetcars as they frolicked along the tracks following the races.

PONTCHARTRAIN ROWING CLUB AND SYC
PLAY FOOTBALL FOR FUND

In 1921, the Southern Yacht Club and the Pontchartrain Rowing Club entered into a benefit football game in the Tulane University stadium for the annual *Times-Picayune* Doll and Toy Fund. Tulane University's famous football coach, Clark Shaughnessy, coached the Southern Yacht Club to victory and was rewarded with an SYC honorary life membership at the banquet held to honor the teams.

A BRIEF HISTORY OF BAYOU ST. JOHN

Not to be omitted from the history of Lake Pontchartrain is the historic natural stream of water that leaves the lake and enters the City of New Orleans, Bayou St. John. It has been noted many times in this book as the harbor for boats in the 1840s and 1850s. Along its shores were beautiful plantation homes, some of which remain today. Bayou St. John was discovered in 1699, when Iberville was seeking a shorter route to the Mississippi River. This bayou led to an Indian portage, later selected by Bienville for the location of the Crescent City, New Orleans.

Healthy competitive spirit was the race course mood during the summer sailing season of 1921 when the *Robin Hood II* owned by Ravannack, Pinac, and Ravannack and sailed by Edward Pinac, won the Gold Cup race. The cup in question was one of the oldest in American yachting, having been first contested for on Lake Pontchartrain in ante-bellum days.

The long distance race from West End to Pensacola in 1921 was won by Theodore Grunewald's swift express cruiser *Creole Sue*, which smashed all records for the 188 statute miles, covering the course in nine hours and thirteen minutes—twelve minutes better than the record established the previous year by *Brenda*, C. B. Fox's cruiser.

SYC SKIPPERETTES SAIL FIRST RACE IN FISH CLASS SLOOPS

The skipperettes appeared on the lake in the new Fish Class sloops to try their skill at the tiller of the new boats. Reported the *Barometer*, "The ladies decided to prove their superiority in the new sloops and on June 5, 1921 Miss Mildred Poole defeated Misses Estelle Carter, Alma Barriere, Estelle Danner and Mesdames Gordon H. Chapman and C. M. Dixey, receiving a big ovation as she came home in front in the first of many races that were sailed during the summer of 1921."

The first Lipton Cup classic sailed in the Fish Class sloops in 1920 was a shot in the arm for the sport. Word spread along the coast about the new club-owned boats, and several yacht clubs became interested in the purchase of a fleet for their club. Sir Thomas' gift had accomplished its purpose—to foster interclub competition.

One of the most famous 21-footers in the SYC fleet was Robin Hood IV, a champion for thirty years. She was owned by J. Ben Ravannack and Leslie P. Beard. Beard was the skipper.

Robin Hood II leads the way in the 21-footer race on the Gulf Coast with the Quakeress and the Sorceress in second and third place, respectively.

Garner H. Tullis's Windjammer finishing the first St. Petersburg-to-Havana race in 1930 to win the trophy in Class A.

The winning schooner and champion of the fleet, I. Heidenheim, followed by the Julia Delacruz in a Biloxi schooner race at Biloxi Yacht Club in Biloxi, Mississippi, in 1926.

LIPTON SENDS CONGRATULATIONS

In addition to Pensacola and Southern, there were two new entries for the second Lipton Cup series, Houston Launch Club of Houston, Texas and the Eastern Shore Yacht Club on Mobile Bay in Alabama. The latter club was the winner. When the news reached Sir Thomas in England, he went a message to the commodore of the Eastern Shore Yacht Club, Ed. Overton, congratulating him on the victory of his club in the new Fish Class sloops. This surprise letter overwhelmed the members of the Gulf Yachting Association and was an inspiration for more racing.

For posterity, the 1921 teams are listed: Eastern Shore, Commodore E. B. Overton, Irvin Jackson, L. H. "Dutch" Gaynor. In second place was the Houston Launch Club, Capt. Chas. Manniere, Frank Simone, A. W. Humphreville, and Frank Ives. Southern had the same skippers and crew that had sailed in the first series in 1920, Leslie P. Beard, A. R. "Babe" Roberts, Ed. H. Keep, Wm. A. Porteous, Jr., Finley Mitchell, Reginald H. Carter, Wm. B. Edgar, and Pieter Altink. Pensacola's crew consisted of the same members as the previous year, Wm. Walthers, Dave Witherill, Dan Sheppard, W. A. Curtiss, and Chas. Cottrell.

SYC AWAKENS YACHT CLUBS IN WEST LOUISIANA

The following is from the *Barometer* of July 1922:

> Lake Charles to have a Yacht Club. Due in a large manner to the instrumentality of the Southern Yacht Club, which has fairly set the pot boiling throughout this section of the country since its entry into the Mississippi Valley Power Boat Association, our sister city of Lake Charles has re-awakened its yachting fervor and in the immediate future a yacht club will be organized at that hustling Calcasieu city.
>
> Yachting spirit is on the upward trend throughout the Southern states just now and one of the most recent 'joiners' of the Mississippi Valley Power Boat Association is the Lake Arthur Boat Club of Lake Arthur, Louisiana. This hustling club, which is located in the very heart of "The Sportsman's Paradise," is but a few miles south of Lake Charles and with the entry of the latter city into the yachting game a great series of regattas is to be anticipated.
>
> Secretary-Treasurer W. H. Parham of the SYC was in Lake Charles during the past month and while there assisted in laying tentative plans for the organization of the Lake Charles club. The Lake Charles Association of Commerce is actively engaged in backing the movement together

with the Lake Charles "Daily American Press" which is ever working for the advancement of things which have to do with the making of a bigger and better Lake Charles.

Those owning boats in Lake Charles and Vinton, La.:

Paul Barbe
R. L. Cline
J. W. Gardiner
Henry Gray, Vinton, La.
J. L. Hennings
E. R. Henry
Robert Leake
Edgar Miller

C. O. Noble
Edw. E. Richards
Charles A. Richardson
    Vinton, La.
Hugo See
Elmer Shutts
Harry Shutts
A. D. Spooner
and others

MARSHAL FOCH OF FRANCE VISITS SYC

Another highlight of the year 1922 was the visit by Marshal Ferdinand Foch of France, who was extended an invitation to the SYC by his New Orleans friend, Charles deB. Claiborne. The announcement of his visit came through a committee of Franco-Louisianians, Louis Boucheix, Chancellor of the French consulate in New Orleans, and André Lafargue, member of the French Legion, of which Charles deB. Claiborne, scion of one of Louisiana's most distinguished families and descendant of the first French Governor of Old Louisiana, was chairman. Marshal Foch was known as the "Hero of the Marne." He had masterminded the counter-offensive and all-out drive which crushed the German army in 1918, obliging their representatives to join him in his private railroad car on a siding near Campiegne, France for the signing of the Armistice.

Impressed with the Southern hospitality shown him, Marshal Foch in appreciation expressed a desire to present personally a perpetual trophy to the Southern Yacht Club to be sailed for by all clubs affiliated with the Gulf Yachting Association. The trophy was received and dedicated to the newly formed 21-footer class at a banquet given in honor of Marshal Foch before he left the city. "In appreciation of his generosity, the members of Southern Yacht Club elected the Marshal an honorary life member and a specially prepared certificate of membership was directed sent to him at his home in France," stated the *Barometer*. "B. S. D'Antoni of the SYC was thanked for placing his Packard car and chauffeur at the disposal of the club for Marshal Foch."

When sailing resumed during the 1922 season, first on the schedule was the race from the West End to "Old Landing" on the Tchefuncte River, which ex-vice Commodore Theodore Grunewald in *Creole Sue* won on the thirty-eight mile run over T. J. McMahon's express cruiser *Lurline II* and Capt. E. B. Benjamin's swift *Indra*, ex-Commodore Percy S. Benedict's cruisette *Bunny*, Dr. W. Milton Miller's handsome new cruiser *Natasha*, and Hugh M. Wilkinson's *Wanderer* for the Thomas Sully Cup.

THE LAST SOUTHERN MARINE MARATHON RACE

For many years the Southern Marine Marathon was recognized as the longest power cruising race staged in salt water in the U. S. south of Philadelphia, since the New York Yacht Club abandoned its power cruising race to the Bermuda Islands as previously mentioned. It was a supreme test of boat and crew. Big fleets competed in it until 1922. The summer of 1922 witnessed the last of the great Southern motor cruiser classic races, which had been inaugurated in 1912.

The first to finish the race from West End to Pensacola was SYC Capt. A. W. McLellan in *Alden*, second was *Mac* owned by Rox Cowley of Pensacola. The three to finish were *Mercathades*, owned by Paul P. Stewart of Pensacola, SYC ex-Commodore Percy S. Benedict in *Bunny* and Russell Clark's *Visin* of SYC. SYC Hugh Wilkinson's cruiser *Wanderer* became disabled and had to abandon the race. A special race committee at Pensacola appointed to finish the race was composed of Commodore J. H. Cross, chairman, Captains Oscar Sheppard, Charles Cottrell, and Wallace Lamar.

The fleet left Pensacola to sail on to the Eastern Shore Yacht Club on Mobile Bay. The third race on the GYC circuit was to Biloxi, then on to the Bay-Waveland Yacht Club after a week of rest.

The final race was won by Cyprian A. Sporl with his crew of Callendar F. Hadden and William B. Edgar in the swift motor cruiser *Quicksilver*. They brought the ten-year-old trophy home for good. The massive bronze Marathon Shield adorns the walls of the Southern Yacht Club.

Following is a list of those boats that entered the last Southern Marine Marathon race:

Alden	—	A. W. McLellan, Southern
Au Revoir	—	Walter Boyer Gillican, Southern

Bunny	—	Commodore Percy S. Benedict, Southern
Creole Sue	—	Theodore Grunewald, Southern
Quicksilver	—	Capt. Cyprian A. Sporl, Southern
Rosalie	—	Capt. Manuel Duvic, Southern
Sue	—	Capt. Lawrence Fabacher, J.F.& B.S. D'Antoni, Southern
Visin	—	Russell Clark, Southern
Wanderer	—	Hugh M. Wilkinson, Southern
Ganther	—	Capt. H. Pickard, Pensacola
Grethen	—	Commodore Clarence Hutchinson, Pensacola
Mac	—	Rox Cowley, Pensacola
Martha	—	Capt. Dan Sheppard, Pensacola
Mercathades	—	Paul P. Stewart, Pensacola
Never Ready	—	Francis Taylor, Pensacola
Pal-O-Mine	—	Capt. C. J. Allen, Pensacola
Peep-O-Day	—	Dick Bingham, Pensacola
Annie W.	—	Capt. Jim Watson, Eastern Shore

These races were conducted each year and were most successful, except for the war years of 1917-18, when the races terminated in Biloxi, for during those years the harbor at Pensacola was planted with mines. At one time there were as many as forty boats entered in this race. One of the outstanding ones was *Sue*, owned by Capt. Lawrence Fabacher and the D'Antoni brothers, J. F. and B. S. She was the last of her kind in Maryland waters. She was built in connection with the events of the Jamestown Exposition for Pierre S. DuPont of Delaware, the Textile magnate, a prince of sportsmen.

Now, in addition to lack of interest after the war, difficulty in handicapping the craft, the hazards encountered on the rough waters of the Gulf of Mexico on the 188 statute miles from West End to Pensacola, the long trek to the Eastern Shore Yacht Club on Mobile Bay in Alabama that was added to the run in 1922 was more than the members could endure. Besides, they were still fuming over the price of gasoline, which had skyrocketed to twenty-seven cents a gallon.

In addition to its membership in the American Power Boat Association, the Southern Yacht Club joined the Mississippi Valley Power Boat Association in 1922 as the result of a visit here of Commodore Sheldon Clark of the Chicago Yacht Club. In February of 1923 and 1924 the Mississippi Valley Power Boat Association brought its midwinter championship races to Lake Pontchartrain, with the SYC as host. All of the real speedsters of that time competed here, including Commodore Sheldon Clark in his own *Miss Chicago*.

AMERICA'S CUP RACES RETURN IN 1922

The world of yachting was ecstatic with the return of the America's Cup races in 1922. Sir Thomas J. Lipton, hoping to win the cup this time around, challenged the United States with his fourth *Shamrock*, which had been in mothballs since 1914 when the great race was postponed because of World War I.

Sir Thomas' hopes were shattered again when Charles Francis Adams on the *Resolute* viewed the situation in a different light. He did not want to be the first U. S. contender to lose, which came very close to happening when the *Resolute* lost two races in the hardest match for the cup that this country had had to face.

Along the Gulf Coast waters, it was that time of the year, Labor Day weekend, to hold the Sir Thomas J. Lipton cup races with interclub participation by yacht clubs of the Gulf Yachting Association. The Eastern Shore Yacht Club had won the trophy in 1921 at Pensacola. The Mobilians were so enthusiastic over their club's winning the Lipton Cup that they planned an open campaign to double their membership for the 1922 Lipton cup races. The event was held over at Magnolia Beach on Mobile Bay.

In the campaign for more members, A. E. Reynolds of the Eastern Shore Yacht Club was general chairman, the members being divided into two teams. The "Sales" with Irvin Jackson as captain and the "Land Lubbers" with Robert Spotswood as skipper were the two competing teams. It was agreed that the losing team should banquet the winners at the close of the campaign, which lasted thirty days.

The old adage "nothing succeeds like success" was the motto of the Eastern Shore Yacht Club when they used the same expert sailors who had won the Lipton Cup the previous year. The skippers were Ed. Overton, Walter Mitchell, D. S. M. Unger, H. Hall, Jr., Irvin Jackson, and L. H. Gaynor. Added this year were Joe E. Baker, Dr. J. E. Brown, Stuart Cobb, Wilbur Devan, Joe L. Hermann, Sheldon Lord, Blake McNeely, D. Prichard, H. C. Staton, Frank Terrell, H. Todd, and Jerome Vanliew. The Houston Launch Club sent their skippers: Hubby Dancy, Roy Dancy, Henry Falk, Bob Killson, Milby Irama, and Jim Mannierre. Southern and Pensacola carried the same skippers that had sailed in the 1921 event. A large group of champions from Biloxi Yacht Club were sent to the regatta by their commodore, J. P. Moore, Jr.:

| J.A.Aoperson | E. C. Gay | Lorenzo McCaleb |

E. S. Beale	F. R. Gifford	J. B. Reynoir
Louis Braun	E. H. Gower	H. H. Roof
Ernest Desporte, Sr.	J. M. Grady	W. H. Rosing
	W. J. Grant	Dr. A. Russ
Ernest Desporte, Jr.	C. P. Huggins	M. B. Spotswood
	W. H. Joyner	
W. O. Clark	W. P. Kennedy	Dr. C. B. Warner
E. E. Elmer	Prof. W. Leach	
Byrd Enochs	Carl Matthes	Dr. Geo Wallace
F. W. Elmer, Jr.		
H. O. Flanders		D. C. Weir

The heated battle was a tie between Southern Yacht Club and the Pensacola Yacht Club. Southern won the right to hold the Lipton Regatta in 1923 as Pensacola had held this event in 1921.

The Pensacola Yacht Club was disappointed that it would be denied holding the Lipton Regatta in its new home. In 1922 the Pensacola Yacht Club had purchased the army concrete steamer *General Wilson* for a clubhouse. This steamer, which cost the government $300,000 to build, made but one trip and that was when the steamer first came from New York to Pensacola to enter the local quartermaster service. It was anchored in a special dredged basin. High consumption of gasoline made it unprofitable for the government to operate it, so the steamer was tied up. The price that the Pensacola Yacht Club paid for their novel clubhouse was less than $10,000.

Members of the Southern Yacht Club's 1922 Lipton team in picture are:

Front row:	Back row:
William Porteous	Peter Donnes
James Haywood	Menge Dixey
Edward Estoup	J. Ben Ravannck
Ed. Pinas	Frank Ferrer
Johnny Luther	John Longmire

In conjunction with the Lipton Regatta, a skipperette race was held and the Eastern Shore Yacht Club won with its expert ladies Misses Marion Overton and Emma Tamm. Skippering for the Biloxi Yacht Club were Misses Marguerite, Elma, and Evelyn Desporte. For Southern was the little twelve-year old daughter of ex-Commodore

Ernest Lee Jahncke, Adele Townsend Jahncke. She received the trophy for the outstanding skipperette in the regatta. The trophy was presented to her by Capt. Dave Witherill of the Pensacola Yacht Club.

At the 1923 annual meeting, Harry T. Howard was reelected commodore for a third term. A moment of silent prayer was offered for President Warren G. Harding, who had passed away during the week. The opening regatta was postponed in respect until the following weekend.

A letter was read by the commodore from Congressman James O'Connor of Washington, D. C. asking if the club would consider leasing Fort Pike. With visions of this area making an ideal hunting and fishing spot, the club agreed to place its bid of $5,000. The plan never materialized as the U. S. government withdrew its offer.

Fred J. Foxley was congratulated on winning the Chicago-to-Machinac race. As *The Times-Picayune* reported: "There have been those yachts that have had one shot of glory, Fred Foxley's cabin sloop *Helen* that went up to the Middle West in 1923 and won the Chicago-to-Machinac race."

When the SYC hosted the Gulf Yachting Association's annual meeting in 1923 it looked like old times. Members of the Gulf Coast yacht clubs arrived from Mobile, Pascagoula, Biloxi, Gulfport, Pensacola, St. Petersburg, Bay St. Louis, Houston, and Corpus Christi, Texas. It was a splendid regatta and the champions of the event were from the St. Petersburg Yacht Club.

DEDICATION OF INNER HARBOR NAVIGATIONAL CANAL

A great development on Lake Pontchartrain in 1923 was a part of the facelift referred to previously. It was the opening of the Inner Harbor Navigational Canal, or Industrial Canal, the waterway to commerce which was linked later to the Gulf of Mexico with the opening of the $100 million, 76-mile long Mississippi River-Gulf outlet. This canal is the only outlet that connects Lake Pontchartrain with the Mississippi River.

On February 6, 1923, the tugboat *Samson* chugged through the lock of the Industrial Canal to mark the opening of this new waterway. The Dock Board's boat steamed twenty minutes down river from the landing at the foot of Canal Street and swung into the canal lock. The water level in the lock was lowered six feet from the level of the river to that of Lake Pontchartrain in ten minutes, and the lock gates swung open to allow the *Samson* to pass into the inner harbor.

The *Samson* then churned lakeward in the canal as far as the Louisville & Nashville railroad bridge, which was not opened for the testing of the lock. Governor John M. Parker, Mayor Andrew J. McShane, and Dock Board officials rode aboard the *Samson* on the trip.

In the days following, the first of thousands of commercial vessels made the trip through the five-and-a-half-mile long canal. The canal took five years and $20 million to build. It is 650 feet long, 75 feet wide and 31½ feet over the sill at low water in the Mississippi River.

HALF MOON YACHT EXPLODES AT INDUSTRIAL CANAL CEREMONY

The official opening day of the Industrial Canal was celebrated on May 5, 1923. Many yachts gaily decorated with colorful bunting loudly proclaimed the event with fog horns tootin' and wavin' of flags. Among the numerous boats attending was the beautiful 40-foot power yacht *Half Moon*, which was owned by SYC member Walter Boyer Gillican. Having won the Express Cruiser Race of 1920, the *Half Moon* was to experience her last voyage on Lake Pontchatrain, one that quickly turned pleasure into disaster. A gasoline explosion in the engine room sent the *Half Moon* to the bottom of the lake, "taking with her everything we had on board, including some irreplaceable family silver," lamented Margaret Gillican Chamberlain, daughter of the owner who submitted this story.

Margaret, Mrs. Donald Chamberlain, whose husband is also a SYC member, was on board the *Half Moon* with her parents, sister and their neighbors, Buckner Chipley, Mrs. Chipley and their child, when Mr. Gillican hurriedly called "We're on fire—abandon ship." Splitting the canvas covering the dinghy, which was hanging on stanchions on the port side of the boat, with his pocket knife, Mr. Gillican ordered everyone into the careening dinghy. Mr. Sturges, the engineer on the boat, extricated the oars from beneath the split canvas and "my father pulled away from the *Half Moon* in seas that were higher than our heads," said Margaret.

When the boat was about fifty yards away from their dinghy, there was an explosion in the engine room. A woosh of orange flame shot out of the hatch, accompanied by a large billow of black smoke, and after a loud crackling noise the fire consumed the canvas covering the after deck. A second explosion engulfed the whole aft section of the *Half Moon* in a raging fire which brought her to her watery grave.

A heavy schooner tried in vain to reach the skiff. However, they were rescued by the launch *BooBoo*, owned by Milton Adler. Others on board were Mrs. Adler, Miss Louise Burton, and Harry Farrer. *The Times-Picayune*, describing the incident, reported, "While hundreds on the pier of the Southern Yacht Club watched in awe, they saw the *Half Moon* burn to its water level and sink into Lake Pontchartrain. The *Half Moon*, one of the costly and palatial yachts in the harbor, had recently been overhauled and redecorated, this was her first trip of the season."

Mr. Gillican had replaced *Half Moon* with another family yacht, sixty-feet overall, the *Au Revoir*, which was also a champion boat. His first yacht was the *Sweetheart*, and later with Bush LeBourgeois he acquired the *Iola*. One of Mr. Gillican's possessions was a three-masted derelict barque, the *Avenger*. This story also was related to the writer by Margaret Chamberlain.

Near the beginning of World War I, when every available ship was sorely needed, Mr. Walter B. Gillican had made a contract with Bisso Marine Company of New Orleans to salvage a three-master derelict barque the *Avenger*, lying on the seaward beach of Chandeleur Island in Mississippi Sound. The Bisso Company dug canals and hauled with tugs to try to float the ship, but were unable to do so before the time limit of their contract expired. A few days later, before another contract could be made, a mighty storm entered the Gulf. Apparently, the high winds and water combined to inundate the island. During the storm, the barque was freed from the beach, and was found on the landward side. This unusual happening made Ripley's "Believe It or Not" column.

COMMODORE W. MILTON MILLER, M.D.—
1924-25

At the 1924 SYC annual meeting, Commodore Harry T. Howard was succeeded by Dr. W. Milton Miller, a prominent local dentist. He served as commodore for two terms, 1924 and 1925. His activities in powerboating extended back to 1909. Commodore Miller's flagship was the beautiful *Natasha*, which was often seen in harbors along the Gulf Coast, for he cruised extensively and was a regular participant in club races, winning quite a few. His craft finished first in the 1924 West End to Pensacola race.

Aside from the elaborate plans that were discussed for the anniversary party to take place in September, a letter was read at the meeting from F. C. Billard, rear admiral and U. S. Coast Guard commandant, requesting through the commodore, the help and cooperation of all boat owners in the active operation of the Coast Guard in upholding the law by:

a) Strictly keeping away from rum-running vessels lying off the coast.
b) Having nothing whatever to do with rum-running tugs and motorcraft.
c) Giving due heed to Coast Guard vessels if requested to stop when signaled to do so by hail, and when necessary warning shots. The Coast Guard was charged with the duty of preventing the smuggling of liquor into the U.S. from the sea and from off the coast of the Gulf of Mexico. (This has a familiar ring today, the only difference is they are dope smugglers instead of rum-runners.)

The entire membership agreed to conform with the requests of the Coast Guard in its efforts to catch the smugglers.

The racing season of 1924 was very active. In the spring, at the invitation of the St. Tammany Yacht Club, the Southern Yacht Club made a long-distance race to Mandeville. A total of twenty boats covered the twenty-two mile trip from West End. There were five long distance races in the year with twenty-one different yachts participating, for a total of sixty-one entries in these races.

In the long distance race from New Orleans to Biloxi in 1924, a near disaster marred the return home of the fleet. *Reverie*, a Jahncke-owned yacht, was a contender in the long race; on her return trip a storm hit while she was coming through the North draw. The Jahncke boys, Stanton and Ernest Lee, Jr., sons of Commodore Ernest Lee Jahncke, narrowly escaped drowning when the boat sank.

THE HISTORY OF THE 21-FOOTERS

As previously mentioned, the 21-footer raceabout cabin sloops were brought down South in 1915. It was after World War I that Commodore Jahncke reactivated this class of boats. In order to promote interest, the commodore offered the handsome *Maid Marion* cup for the prize. The season's champion was the Commodore's son, Stanton, who won in the Marconi-rigged sloop *Maid Marion*. This was quite a feat as he won over such outstanding 21-footers as the *Robin Hood II*, *Quakeress*, *Sorceress*, and the *Circe*.

The 21-footers were sturdy craft that stood up to severe tests and strain. In 1922, in a race from Pass Christian to West End, this class withstood head winds which varied from twenty to forty knots. The two winners, *Quakeress III* in the Marconi-rigged class and *Sis* in the gaff division, had to be beached after they finished. At times in the race both boats had over two feet of water above the floorboards, yet they continued with all sails to beat every other class by over two hours.

Blaise S. D'Antoni's two 21-foot cabin sloops of the same name, *Sorceress*, a gaff-rigged sloop and *Sorceress II*, a Marconi-rigged sloop, were both highly regarded racing boats in the early '20s. Together, the two boats won sixty out of sixty-two races with D'Antoni at the helm. One of his crew was Capt. Frank Payne who was a partner in the internationally known firm of naval architects, Burgess, Swayze & Payne, the designers of the D'Antoni craft.

There were frequent changes in ownership and often names were changed so that it is difficult to tell which original boat was which in later years. After *Sorceress I* was purchased by Garner H. Tullis and had her name changed to *Mallegar*, she continued to win races for Tullis and James B. Heaslip, as did *Sorceress II* when owned and sailed by William T. Hardie. It is also known that *Pretty Quick* became *Spindrift* when completely rebuilt by Ed. Thomas and Richard Morse.

In May 1924 Commodore Ernest Lee Jahncke's new 21-footer *Cinderella* arrived in New Orleans from New York. She was designed by naval architect Fred Hoyt of New York and built by Nevins, Inc., City Island, New York. Her measurements were 30 feet 10 inch length overall, with a 21 foot length waterline, 8 foot 08 inch beam, 4 foot 10 inch draft, 6 feet 6 inch draft with centerboard down, and keel centerboard 3500 lbs lead on keel. She was unloaded and towed to West End, where her mast was stepped and rigged by Percy McCutchon and Walle Ravannack.

At the same time Blaise D'Antoni was having a 21-footer, another *Sorceress*, built in Long Island, New York to compete against Jahncke's *Cinderella*.

During the 1924 sailing season, *Cinderella* won nearly every race that she sailed. In the early fall she was sold, as the commodore's son, Stanton, had received an appointment to the Naval Academy and would not be around to sail her. The commodore sold *Cinderella* to Blaise D'Antoni and he renamed her *Princess*. D'Antoni now owned both the *Sorceress* and the *Princess*. Believing that his *Sorceress* was faster than the *Princess*, D'Antoni sailed her in a match race against the *Princess*, whose crew was that of *Robin Hood II*, skippered by Leslie P. Beard. The *Sorceress* won, and the *Princess* was sold to J. Ben Ravannack of SYC, who renamed her *Robin Hood IV*. A month later, Ravannack sold half interest in the boat to Leslie P. Beard.

A *ROBIN HOOD IV* STORY

One of the most famous of the 21-foot yachts in SYC history was the *Robin Hood IV*, nee *Cinderella*, which for more than thirty years showed her stern wake consistently to all rivals. She compiled an enviable record on Lake Pontchartrain under the guidance successively of Leslie P. Beard, J. Ben Ravannack, Robert Spotswood, Edward B. Overton, William Crane and Clarence Bonnett.

The regular crew for all the big races when *Robin Hood IV* was owned by Ravannack and Beard, was Walle Ravannack, the nephew of Ben Ravannack, who is responsible for this history of the 21-foot class of sloops. Here are excerpts from an exciting experience by Walle when he was crewing during a very important race:

> Under the skillful handling of skipper Beard and a well-trained crew of J. Ben Ravannack on the mainsail, Albert Sanchez on the jib and backstays, Walle J. Ravannack on light sails, Adrian (Red) Aitkend on light sails and also "Pic" Avengo, *Robin Hood IV* had a successful year in 1925, winning 11 out of 13 races, including the long distance race to Mobile, Alabama. In the following four years, *Robin Hood IV* raced with equal success and was recognized among sailors at SYC and along the Gulf Coast as the fastest sailboat in Southern waters.
>
> In 1929 on the long-distance race to Biloxi, at 12:30 a.m. just passing Pass Marianne light, with the wind and sea on her starboard quarter and carrying a spinnaker and huge balloon jib, the wind suddenly freshened, a white squall just ahead. Before the light sails could be doused, the mast carried away just below the spreaders, with upper part of the mast, rigging, light sails and part of the mainsail going over the side. It was quite a mess! 25 minutes after the *Robin Hood IV* was disabled, the *Sorceress* passed them, followed by *Quakeress* of J. M. Kinabrew, three minutes later.
>
> At about 2:00 a.m. the SYC patrol boat, seeing our distress flare, came up and took our towline and towed *Robin Hood IV* into Biloxi, arriving just after daylight. Albert Sanchez and Walle Ravannack took the first train out of Biloxi for New Orleans to get the spare mast and rigging. Arrangements were made to have it hauled to the L & N railroad station by truck and placed aboard a baggage car. We arrived in Biloxi with the spare mast the same day, July 2nd, and the next morning it

was stepped in the *Robin Hood IV*. She was ready to race again when the SYC fleet arrived in Biloxi from Mobile on the race back to New Orleans, which believe it or not we won.

Because of lack of competition, Ravannack and Beard sold the *Robin Hood IV* in September 1929 to Robert Spotswood of the Eastern Shore Yacht Club of Mobile, who in turn sold the boat to Ed Overton of ESYC. In the same year the *Sorceress II* was acquired by the Fay Brothers of Houston, Texas. Later the boat was bought by William T. Hardie of SYC, who brought the *Sorceress II* back from Texas. The new owners breathed new life into the class and they continued sailing them until the 1940s. Overhauled by Clarence Bonnett in 1964, *Robin Hood IV* continued her winning ways by capturing first place in the 1964 race to the coast in elapsed time and corrected time, followed by a victory in the handicap class of the 1966 Sugar Bowl regatta.

On a wall in the old clubhouse of the Southern Yacht Club hung a chart of the Gulf Coast waters from Terrebonne Bay to Mobile Bay. Attached was the following inscription:

This Composite Chart of Some of the
Finest Cruising Waters in These United States
is Given in Memory of the Grand Old 21-Footers

Robin Hood IV	Invader
Sorceress II	Mallegar
Quakeress III	Circe
Pretty Quick	Robin Hood II
Maid Marion	Sis
Balthasar	

"We led the fleet"

Following is a list of the boats in the 1924 fleet:

Machine Sloops:
Target—Ed. H. Keep
America—C. A. Sporl
Seawanhaka—T. H. Olsen

Cabin Cruiser Class:
Hiawatha—W. T. Lotz Syndicate
Agnes—Abe Leverich
Cadillac—Wm. A. Porteous, Jr. Synd.
Pretty Quick—Joe Duvic

Motor Boat Division:
Brenda II—Wm. Henderson
Quicksilver—Sporl & Plant
Haoma—H. N. Moody
Au Revoir—W. B. Gillican
Nathalie—Dr. Miller's flagship
Violet—Commodore Benedict's flagship
Elizabeth—Sidney Odenheimer
Toyship—J. B. Simmons

Sorceress—B. S. D'Antoni
Quakeress—J. M. Kinabrew
Catboats:
Cinq—Wallis-Pitard Synd.
Xiphias—Henri Howard
Sea Duck—E. H. Keep
Dory Class:
Indian—James L. Rea
St. John—James Heaslip
Traveler—L. M. Lessene

Loiterer—Commodore Howard
Gwendolyn—Rear Com. Gus B. Baldwin
Auxiliary Class:
Tomahawk—Wm. Young
Boomerang—Wm. Fetterly
Thistle—C. G. Ferguson
Alga—G. Mather Conrad
Speed Boats:
Kitsey—Chas. Ferran
Creole Sue—Theo Grunewald

SYC'S DIAMOND JUBILEE CELEBRATION

The $250,000 remodeling and redecorating job of the Southern Yacht Club was completed in time for the celebration of the seventy-fifth anniversary of the founding of the SYC. The date of the opening was planned to coincide with that of the first organizational meeting—July 21, 1849.

A club that had survived the many epidemics that ravaged the city of New Orleans during the early years of its existence and numerous hurricanes, storms, fires, and wars, was justified in having a great party in its honor. Invitations were extended, and acknowledgments with good wishes were received from editors of yachting magazines, powerboat association presidents, yacht club commodores, local and state officials, including Louisiana Governor Henry L. Fuqua, Senators Joseph E. Randall and Edwin S. Broussard, and Mayor Andrew J. McShane of New Orleans. A special edition of the SYC monthly publication the *Barometer* was produced with many glowing articles concerning the SYC. Some excerpts follow:

> The clubhouse was beautifully decorated with flags and bunting for this momentous event which took place on Saturday, September 27th with a grand review of the fleet in the afternoon and a banquet that night, limited to members and ladies of members' families only. There was a wonderful repast, a splendid vaudeville performance and a grand ball. More than 5,000 members and visitors paid tribute to the excellence of the accomplishments.
>
> Commodore Miller and Secretary Parham and their staff of amateur sailors are bent on making this anniversary jubilee a sparkling, iridescent and precious gem—the very Kohinoor of Diamonds in the club's long list of notable anniversary celebrations.
>
> With the unprecedented large roster of members, 3,000, and about 350 boats in its fleet, from the little catboat of one sail to the palatial ocean-going yacht, the Southern Yacht Club was considered the largest

yacht club in the United States.

The club is in splendid financial condition. Over $5,000 was spent in building a fleet of 12 one-design sloops called the "Fish Class" which have proven a delight to the members generally. These boats were named for some of the fish in Southern waters—*Blue Fish, Cat Fish, Flying Fish, Jack Fish, King Fish, Lady Fish, Moon Fish, Needle Fish, Pin Fish, Red Fish, Sword Fish,* and *White Fish.* Enrolled in the club's fleet are motor and sail boats of all types.

The Jubilee Committee:

Percy S. Benedict, Chairman
Crawford H. Ellis, Vice-Chairman

Claiborne Andrews	W. W. Butterworth	John M. Kinabrew
Henry H. Baker	Blaise S. D'Antoni	John P. Longmire
Gus B. Baldwin	F. W. Evans	C.C. Luzenberg
T. T. Barr	Robert Ewing	Dr. R. C. Lynch
N. Emile Baumgarden	Clarence G. Ferguson	W. H. McFadden W. Milton Miller
Leslie P. Beard	C. B. Fox	Leonard K. Nicholson
Henry V. Beer	A. D. Geoghegan	
Joseph R. Behrens	J. Walton Glenny	W. H. Parham
Wm. J. Bentley	Grady Harrell	William Pfaff
E. V. Benjamin	J. D. Hayward, Sr.	William A. Porteous
W. C. Boschert		
A. Brittin	William Henderson	L. D. Sampsell
Henry Dickson Bruns	W. H. Hendren	Charles E. Smith Thomas Sully
Thomas Burns	Harry T. Howard	Garner H. Tullis
Louis F. Buck, Jr.	W. R. Irby	Samuel Zemurray
Edward S. Butler	Leon Irwin	
	Walter Cooke Keenan	

RECEPTION COMMITTEE
Crawford H. Ellis, Chairman
J. Benjamin Ravannack, Vice-Chairman

C. H. Alker	Harry T. Howard	A. K. Miller
J. R. Behrens	Arthur S. Huey	J. Blanc Monroe
Percy S. Benedict	J. L. Hyde	H. N. Moody
Edward S. Butler	Leon Irwin	H. N. Moore
B. C. Casanas	Ernest Lee Jahncke	Y. P. Nicholson
W. J. Church		L. K. Nicholson
T. Bayne Denegre	Walter C. Keenan	James O'Connor
W. K. DePass	N. M. Leach	J. L. Onorato
James Dinkins	Harold Lejeune	Thomas T. Parker
Edgar R. DuMont	Lucian Lesserie	F. C. Pendleton

R. G. Fitzgerald
Richard R. Foster
L. C. Frantz
Chauncy French
A. D. Geoghegan
J. Walton Glenny
J. V. Gresham
Franz Hinderman

John P. Longmire
Chandler C. Luzenberg
I. L. Lyons, Jr.
George A. Mahe
Paul H. Maloney
Paul H. Maloney, Jr.
J. J. Mason
Ray W. McWilliams
Roy Mendes

Wm. Pfaff
J. C. Pierson
R. D. Reeves
I. T. Rhea
W. L. Richeson
J. Zach Spearing
Pierre Villere
W. E. Winship
E. E. Wood

The present clubhouse had cost $250,000 in 1921, and the fittings and furnishings upwards of $50,000. The total operation in 1924 represented about five million dollars.

The attractive new clubhouse enhanced the spirit among the yachtsmen, which encouraged them to enter more boats in the opening regatta than had been in competition for some time. (The club had had yachtsmen but the sailboat fleet had been small.)

Commodore Miller was ably asisted by a large group of governing board members whose number was increased because of the coming celebration of the club's seventy-fifth anniversary. Those elected to office were:

N. E. Baumgarden
Jos. R. Behrens
W. C. Boschert
A. M. Cooke
B. S. D'Antoni
C. Menge Dixey
W. B. Edgar
Crawford H. Ellis
Clarence E. Ferguson

C. M. Fetterly
Leon Irwin
Charles Karst, Jr.
Walter Cooke Keenan
John P. Longmire
George A. Mahe
Paul H. Maloney
J. A. Mermilliod
E. G. Pinac

John A. Rawlins
J. Ben Ravannack
F. D. Reilly
L. D. Sampsell
Charles E. Smith
John Vaccaro
Lawrence Wadsworth
Hugh M. Wilkinson
Percy S. Wilson

THE BIRTH OF THE SYC STAR CLASS FLEET

On a visit to New York in 1924, former commodore Ernest Lee Jahncke witnessed the second championship races of the Star Class Internationals sailed on Long Island Sound. He was impressed with this type of boat, which was a two-man 22-foot keel vessel with a 315-square foot sail area, suitable for sailing on the waters of Lake Pontchartrain.

1921-1925

Filled with enthusiasm over the possibility of developing a fleet of Stars at the Southern Yacht Club, Commodore Jahncke gathered a group of SYC members in the dining room aboard the *Aunt Dinah*. James D. Hayward, Jr. was elected fleet captain, William A. Porteous, Jr., lieutenant, Prentice E. Edrington, Jr., secretary, and Stanton Jahncke, treasurer. Other active members were N. Emile Baumgarden, William B. Edgar, Henry Menge, Jr., Paul Jahncke, Sr., Henry L. "Pic" Avegno, Clarence O. Ferguson, C. M. McMillan, William H. Parham, and R. Lee Edwards.

The International Star Class Association granted a charter dated November 7, 1924 which read: "To its New Orleans-Gulf Star Class Fleet with territory and jurisdiction limited to the waters of Lake Pontchartrain, Mississippi Sound and the Gulf of Mexico in the vicinity of New Orleans, La. in the United States of America. Charter members of this fleet: Ernest Lee Jahncke, J. D. Hayward, Stanton Jahncke, Prentice E. Edrington, Jr."

The Star was an open sloop designed by Wm. Gardner, a noted naval architect of New York. Work was started at once on twelve of these sloops in the shipyard of the Jahncke Dry Dock plant. The Star boats were built on the same mold, a strictly one-design class. Length overall from the original 23 feet to 22 feet 7½ inches, with 5-foot beam, 8½ foot draft, to the bottom of the 850 pounds of semi-fin keel ballast 3 feet 5 inches. They were Marconi-rigged, carrying a total sail area of 282 square feet, of which approximately 200 sqaure feet were in the mainsail and 82 square feet in the jib.

The Star Class International championship was scheduled to be held in New York in August of 1925. Eager to have an SYC entry, Commodore Jahncke agreed to be responsible financially for the building of a fleet of twelve of these one-design sloops, which ultimately would be privately owned. However, it was unnecessary to accept the commodore's generosity, for when the plan was presented to the members at a meeting, the boats were sold within ten minutes.

The boats were launched by derricks into the Mississippi River at the Jahncke Dry Docks on April 4, 1925, formed into a tow and taken through the new Industrial Canal locks by the SYC patrol boat in the charge of Capt. Dave Young. Jahncke towed six boats by *Fiddlestick*. The fleet was given a thunderous welcome as it arrived at West End, the yacht club's cannon and the gun on the 'Tern' booming salute after salute while every available siren from half-lung-power foghorns to mechanical gas-attack wailers shrieked, blared, howled and roared," reported the *Barometer*.

The rules of the Association required that when a sloop was enrolled, in addition to its name, it would be given a number which it had to maintain. The Southern Yacht Club's twelve boats registered had numbers from 254 to 265. It was suggested by one of the members that the boats be named after stars, so many of them were called after sparklers in the skies. Following is a list of the twelve Stars:

254 — *Spika*, Stanton Jahncke
255 — *Ochtend Star*, Paul Jahncke, Jr.
256 — *Pentacle*, Hermann P. Deutsch & A. R. Robert
257 — *Gemini*, John J. Voelkel
258 — *Blue Star*, Miss Evelyn Jahncke
259 — *Scutum*, Leslie P. Beard & Franz Hinderman
260 — *Jane*, James D. Hayward, Jr.
261 — *Fairplay*, Wm. A. Porteous, Jr. & Cal Fisher
262 — *Electra*, Fred Foxley
263 — *Kitalpha*, Harry D. Hardin & Ed. Pinac
264 — *Talita*, Earl Blouin & Eberhardt P. Deutsch
265 — *Sparkler*, Prentice D. Edrington, Jr.

The personal efforts of Commodore Jahncke to promote the new class were well rewarded when his son Stanton, age seventeen, with his crew, Henry Menge, was the victor in the first Star class race sailed on April 27, 1925.

Many had expressed anxiety for the safety of the crews of such tiny boats while sailing on the deep waters of the Gulf of Mexico. In order to allay such fears, on July 4, 1925, at 7 a.m. five Stars faced the starting line at the Southern Yacht Club's pier and were off on their ninety-mile run to Biloxi with the rest of the fleet on the race to the coast. The five boats finished within eight minutes of each other. The success of the cruise to Biloxi and back satisfied the most skeptical about the seaworthiness and safety of the Star Class boats.

With the Star Class Internationals just a few months away in New

York, the SYC race committee realized that any team challenging those that would be in the contest must be the best. The most reputable skipper of the Southern Yacht Club entered into a series of bitterly fought races. When the results from the five races were tabulated, Earl Blouin aboard the *Talita* with J. Eblen Rau as crew won the right to become the first SYC team to represent the club in international competition in the Star Class. In second place was A. R. Roberts with crew Johnny Luther on *Pentacle*, which was owned by Roberts and Hermann P. Deutsch, the noted columnist of *The States-Item* newspaper. The other participants were:

Prentice E. Edrington, Jr.	Stanton Jahncke
F. J. Foxley	Paul F. Jahncke
James D. Hayward	Edwin G. Pinac
Franz "Fritz" Hinderman	Wm. A. Porteous
	J. J. Voelkel

The headline of *The Times-Picayune* sports edition of August 9, 1925 read, "The Best Sailor in Dixie—Earl Blouin." The article continued:

> The crack crew of the New Orleans-Gulf Star Class Fleet, Captain Blouin and his able crew J. Eblen Rau, will leave via the L & N Railroad on Saturday morning August 22nd for New York, where they will take part in the series of races of the International Star Class Yacht Racing Association sailing against the best crews of the Star fleets from Canada, England, France, Belgium, Spain, Italy, Norway, Sweden, Denmark, Australia, Hawaii, Bermuda, Cuba, South and Central American Republics and possibly even distant Japan.
>
> In order to raise the necessary funds of upwards of $1,200.00 to send on to New York the Star Class sloop, skipper and crew, the local Star Class members will give a monster ball and vaudeville entertainment in the big ball room of the Southern Yacht Club at West End on August 4th.
>
> A royal good time is promised all who attend, having engaged the well-known Tuxedo Band to furnish the music. Also, eight of the best vaudeville acts now appearing at the Orpheum Theatre will be spread in between the dances.

A happy group of Star class enthusiasts boarded the L & N train on August 22, 1925 for New York. The only disappointed member was J. Eblen Rau, who was unable to make the trip as crew for Blouin. Eberhardt P. Deutsch was his substitute. Accompanying the team were Capt. Paul F. Jahncke, Sr. and Prentice Edrington, Jr. The Star boat was shipped aboard the Morgan Line Steamer *El Capitain* to New York. The stage was now set for the Internationals.

The SYC crew finished a respectable fourth in a field of fifteen entries in this third International Star Class championship sailed in 1925. The winner was Adrien Islen, III of the U. S. in his Star boat *Ace*. "Mr. Islen's charming wife is a native of New Orleans," reported *The Times-Picayune*. When the team returned to its home town, former Commodore Ernest Lee Jahncke gave a large banquet at La Louisiane Restaurant in downtown New Orleans.

SYC WINS LIPTON CUP FOR THE FIRST TIME

In a highly spirited event on Labor Day weekend in 1925, the Southern Yacht Club finally won the prestigious Sir Thomas J. Lipton cup. It had eluded the boys ever since its inception in 1920. Southern had tied with Pensacola in 1922; however, this time around the trophy belonged to SYC alone. The winning crewmen were Henry J. Avegno, Leslie P. Beard, William B. Edgar, Jr., James D. Hayward, Franz Hinderman, Edwin G. Pinac, William A. Porteous, Jr., and Albert Sanchez. The captains and crewmen received a right royal reception at West End upon their return from Pensacola aboard the yacht *Elmasada II*, of Samuel Zemurray.

At a party honoring the SYC champions of the 1925 Lipton cup races, all members of the crew were presented little gold knives. J. D. Hayward, Jr. received the Fish Class Good Sport trophy for 1925. Other SYC champions recognized for their accomplishments during the 1925 racing season were presented flags: *Invader*, owned by William B. Edgar, Jr. and Cal Hadden; *Sorceress II*, owned by B. S. D'Antoni; *Sis* owned by J. Pitard and J. Eblen Rau; and the *Robin Hood IV*, owned by J. Ben Ravannack and Leslie P. Beard.

At the semi-annual meeting of the Gulf Yachting Association held in conjunction with the Lipton cup races, SYC Commodore Dr. W. Milton Miller was elected president. All commodores of GYA yacht clubs were vice-presidents. It was announced by GYA Commodore Miller that the Southern Power Boat Association was born, "taking in every club on the Gulf of Mexico from Key West, Florida to Corpus Christi, Texas. The time had arrived for the South to have such an organization as there was one such association in the North and East, Middle West and Pacific Coast," according to the *Barometer*.

Approved at the GYA meeting was the use on the Fish Class sloops of the patent marconi back-stay sliding tackle, which greatly facilitated the handling of the back-stays. Also the rule requiring skippers to draw lots for the boats at least one hour before the first race was approved.

SYC SCHOONER STOLEN BY SMUGGLERS

The summer of 1925 will never be forgotten by one SYC yachtsman, Dr. Robert W. Gaston, whose newly built 56-foot yacht *Ida Q* found herself the victim of rum-running pirates who took her to Mexico.

When a schooner is stolen and sailed away into the great void which is the sea, there would seem to be little hope for recovery. *Ida Q* was stolen and—but read the yarn for yourself, as written for *The Rudder* in 1925 by Dr. Robert W. Gaston, owner of *Ida Q*:

> One would think "Pirates" were a thing of the past, and something not likely to be encountered in this modern time, but they operate even today as evidenced by the theft of the schooner yacht *Ida Q* on the night of August 18, 1925.
>
> *Ida Q* was a comparatively new schooner which had been built for me only two years before, her dimensions being fifty-six feet overall, thirty-eight feet on the water line, and six and one-half feet draught, designed by J. Murray Watts. Her ballast consisted of an iron keel of three and one-half tons and about five tons of iron inside.
>
> During the summer of 1925, I spent a good deal of time cruising along the Mississippi Gulf Coast, using as an anchorage the harbor of Gulfport in which city we had our family home. I commuted daily back and forth to New Orleans where I operated my business. It was late one afternoon after returning from the city that I walked down to the harbor to see the boat—it was not there. I thought she might have been moved by the harbor master to make room for another vessel, but this was not the case. After many inquiries of other boat owners along the dock, I then notified the authorities.
>
> By the next morning everyone seemed to know of the loss and several of my friends joined in the search. The Coast Guard located in Biloxi felt the thieves were rum-runners and as the yacht was fast and capable of going in any Gulf waters, were using it for rum-running operations. After cruising many hours along the various small islands in the region with no success, the service of a seaplane was sought. Through the assistance of the Secretary, W. H. Parham of the Southern Yacht Club, of which I am a member, government seaplanes were secured from the air station in Pensacola, Florida.
>
> For forty-eight hours no stone was left unturned and every island was thoroughly checked. Finally, when the light-keeper on Chandelier Island was contacted, he reported the *Ida Q* had passed early the previous morning just at daylight, making good time, and headed Southeast. He also reported there were four men on deck. It was evident that the thieves made their plans well and had everything in readiness on the night of August 18—a dark night with no moon and the cook who usually stayed

on board had taken the night off to visit his wife on shore.

I repeat, no stone was left unturned. The State Department in Washington notified the American Consuls at the various ports at which there was any probability of her entering. Time passed heavily. About the fourth day, I was notified that one of the United Fruit Company's steamers had reported passing her in the Gulf, heading Southeast, probably to Cuba. I wish to state here that Mr. Crawford Ellis head of the United Fruit Company was very kind in having his ships look out for her.

Two weeks passed when one morning, after arriving at my office, the telephone rang. It was long distance. Mr. Fly, Senator Pat Harrison's secretary, was on the telephone. The American Consul at Frontera, Mexico, had notified him the yacht had been found. There was a great deal of satisfaction in knowing where my yacht was. The next problem now, was to get her back home. The piratical crew skipped before the authorities could get hold of them.

After writing a full report of the case to Washington, the American Consul at Frontera took charge of the yacht. Those of you who have never had occasion to have any dealings with this branch of our government service, may wonder sometimes what they have to do, but you will certainly have reason to appreciate the value of this service when such an occasion as this arises.

The Consul not only took complete charge of the yacht, but took every precaution to see that she was properly protected against the stress of weather and took every step necessary to provide for the vessel's safety.

I considered the difficulties of sending a crew to bring her yacht home, and at first thought it might be advisable to sell her down there, if anything like a satisfactory sale could be made. But, after the exchange of numberless telegrams and other correspondence I decided to bring her home.

It was September in the very midst of the hurricane season, so I felt it would be advisable to wait until the latter part of October. After securing the services of an old friend, Captain Murdock, and a fellow member of the Southern Yacht Club, Wm. Porteous, the rest of the crew was found in Frontera, and having spent considerable time passing through the necessary formalities, we boarded the steamer for Mexico. It was two weeks before the *Ida Q* was ready for the return trip. So, on the day after Thanksgiving, after having secured two other men as additions to the crew, we were ready to set sail.

Just off Galveston we began to feel we were near home. Another blow, a small gale struck just as we hit the entrance of Galveston. We ran down the coast a few miles hoping to find an easy opening through which we could run in behind the islands, when suddenly we discovered a Coast Guard boat on our trail. We then heaved-to to permit him to come as near as possible.

He had been notified by the look-out, at the Coast Guard station ashore, that there was a suspicious looking schooner evidently trying to get inside. When we told the commander who we were and where we were from, he said, "Oh, yes, I remember all about you now." He then offered to take us in tow, for which we were very grateful, and after some difficulty, for it was still blowing heavily, we managed to get a line to him, and he towed us into the harbor. The commander gave us every assistance possible.

We arrived at 6:00 P.M., December 7th, having been eleven days on the return trip to the States and having encountered one northwest storm, and two small gales. All together, the voyage was most interesting, though we suffered some discomfort, the fact of accomplishing the trip across the Gulf in mid-Winter, added proof to what has often been said by marine authorities, that a comparatively small vessel, properly designed and well-built, may be just as safe as a larger one.

STAR CLASS BABY INTERNATIONALS IN CUBA

The Tropical Mid-Winter Star Class championship held in Havana, Cuba in March 1926 was the result of a casual suggestion by a New Orleans Star Class sailor, Prentice Edrington, while attending the last International races on Long Island Sound. At first it was to be a match race between the champion of the New Orleans-Gulf Star fleet and the champion of the Havana fleet. But the moment President George Elder of the Star Class heard of it, his thoughts of blizzards and zero-degree weather in New York in January urged him to suggest that it be made an open affair to all fleets of the Star Class. When permission to hold the event was granted by the International Star Class Executive Committee, it was provided that each fleet could enter one boat, and Havana was selected as the place.

Present in Havana for the Mid-Winters were:

Com. George A. Corry, "Daddy of the Stars" from Port Washington, L. I.
Com. George W. Elder, president of the Star Class of New York
Capt. Prentice E. Edrington, Jr., vice-president of New Orleans Star Class

Skippers and crews:

James D. Hayward, Jr., Pierre Donnes, New Orleans, *Jane*
Ernest Ratsey, with his father George Ratsey as crew, *Irex III*
Bill Enslee, Artee Webb, Gravesend, R. I.

F. F. Bedford, D. Starring, Central Long Island, *Maia III*
Al. Buckley, Gordon Curry, Port Washington, L. I., *Old Coon*
Pons of Havana with Alamilla as crew, *Siboney*, champion of Havana fleet.
Silva of Cienfuegas, Cuba, *Guincho*, with Villapole as crew.

The Southern Yacht Club's crew with James D. Hayward, Jr., skipper and Pierre F. Donnes, Jr. crew, came first in three races, but this was not sufficient as E. Ratsey and G. Ratsey in *Irex* won over the SYC entry *Jane*.

After their return home, Edrington related in the *Barometer* the escapades experienced by the boys at this most interesting and profitable event.

The first night in Cuba was celebrated by Captain Hayward and Donnes in pre Volsteadian fashion added and abetted by Commodore Peter Morales of the Havana Yacht Club whose only English was "Let's have another one." When Edrington returned at 11 p.m. from a trip to a sugar plantation, he was smothered by caresses from the *Jane's* skipper and crew who in unison cried "Oh! Prentice you missed it old boy! They gave us the yacht club tonight. It's ours to do with as we like." "Yes," said Prentice, "and tomorrow when you're sober they'll take it away from you."

On Saturday night the Havana Star fleet entertained the officers of the Star Fleet Association, the skippers and crews to a wonderful dinner at the Vedado Tennis Club when the prizes were given. Ratsey with four firsts came off with the lion's share. Three watches, a sterling silver cocktail tray, a sterling silver cigarette box, and other second and third place prizes, as well as the Mid-Winter Tropical Championship Cup.

To the boys of the States who finished second, went the handsome Bacardi Cup and four pairs of binoculars. James D. Hayward received a platinum and pearl watch chain, a sterling silver and gold cigarette case, a hammered silver flask (full) and a pair of Swiss binoculars. The Cubans were marvelous hosts. All Star Class men were quartered at the Havana Yacht Club, the most luxurious in the world. Its Commodore Peter Morales and its Vice-Commodore Rafael Posso did everything possible for the visiting yachtsmen.

Before the fleet departed, another race was held with the Americans sailing the Cuban boats and the Cubans sailing the American boats. Hayward of the New Orleans fleet led the fleet home an easy winner. The Cubans not to be outdone offered a bottle of Bacardi rum to the U. S. skipper finishing last. Some said Artie Webb, crewing for Bill Enslee, had a bucket overboard for he finished far behind and thereby assured himself of a drink of the wonderful Cuban rum. A Cuban skipper became so much enamoured of *Jane* that he prevailed upon her owner to leave her down there and in consequence Jimmy came back laden with cash, Spanish shawls and perfume.

CHAPTER XII
1926-1929

COMMODORES	TERMS
John M. Kinabrew	1926-27-28-29
Charles J. Tessier	1930-31-32-33
	(died in office)

COMMODORE JOHN M. KINABREW—1926-1929

A sailing man, John Monroe Kinabrew, took over the helm of the SYC in 1926 for the first year of a four-year term, during which his flagship *Quakeress III* proved stiff competition for the swift *Robin Hood IV* in the Marconi-rigged 21-foot class. In earlier seasons, Commodore Kinabrew had sailed the knockabout sloop *Sinner* with marked success, winning the long-distance race to Mobile in 1912. He was also a contestant in the first Fish Class sloop race in 1920.

The 1926 opening regatta was the most auspicious inaugural yachting event in many years. The weather was splendid, there was spirited racing and a large crowd of spectators. The motor craft of the club's big fleet streamed out of the West End harbor to view the races, all in gala attire of flags, pennants, and other bunting, and as each winner in a class raced across the finish line, it was greeted by a great din with whistles, fog horns and sirens. Bartlett's Concert Band entertained the guests.

There were fifty-three crafts participating, four big schooner yachts, eight powerful, swift cabin sloops, twelve Fish Class open sloops, five craft in mixed class of cabin sloops, two dory open sloops, five craft in mixed class open sloops, and five speedy catboats, 21-footers, and Stars.

In the Fish Class race Douglas Porteous won over James Heaslip, followed by Miss Adele Jahncke, I. Janssen, George Mahe, H. M. Lasage, Sam Tennant, J. C. Drake, A. I. Leverich, and K. M. King. Blaise S. D'Antoni in *Packard VIII* won in the 21-foot class; Garner

H. Tullis's schooner *Dolphin* won over Robert Moore's *Mallard* in the first schooner race held on Lake Pontchartrain in a long time. *Indian*, owned and skippered by James Rea, won in the dory open sloop race over L. V. Rand's *Chafilka*.

Every vantage point was well crowded with holiday groups. Bartlett's concert band entertained the crowds with lively music, playing first on the big pier, then on the broad lakefront gallery of the clubhouse. "They had to respond to numerous encores," said the *Barometer*.

NORTH AMERICAN YACHT RACING UNION REACTIVATED

It is interesting to note that up to about the year 1900 regulations affecting yacht racing and measurement rules had been in the hands of individual yacht clubs or local yacht-racing associations composed of clubs in the same locality. Thus they lacked uniformity in different sections of the country.

At the time of the agitation for a new measurement rule to supersede the length-and-sail-area rule, the New York Yacht Club called a conference of yachting organizations of the Atlantic Coast and the Great Lakes to bring about uniformity by persuading the other sections to adopt the Universal Rule then being formulated.

There still was no real governing body for yachting affairs in the United States until local yacht-racing associations and yacht clubs reactivated the North American Yacht Racing Union (NAYRU) in 1925. NAYRU had been founded in 1897. This was the first permanent legislative and governing body of national scope in the U.S.A., and through it both the racing and measurement rules were standardized and an appeals board for members was formed.

In 1927, delegates from this union met with delegates of the International Yacht Racing Union in London to bring about closer international cooperation. Realizing the value to the sport of international racing, the union recognized (in addition to the Universal rule) the International Rule used in European countries.

CLIFFORD D. MALLORY VISITS SYC

A distinguished yachtsman of the New York Yacht Club and the first President of the North American Yacht Racing Union reorganization in 1925, Clifford D. Mallory, was a guest of the Southern Yacht Club in the summer of 1926 at the invitation of former SYC commodore Ernest Lee Jahncke, also a member of the New York Yacht Club and recently elected to the NAYRU's executive committee.

President Mallory was invited to speak before the SYC membership in an effort to "spread the word" concerning the purpose of the North American Yacht Racing Union (NAYRU) to revive the spirit of sailing. Following are excerpts from his message, which was printed in the *Barometer*:

> "The real purpose of the North American Yacht Racing Union, into the honor of being the head of which I was, you might say, shanghaied by yachtsmen, is to bring about a more stable condition of affairs, generally, as pertains to the only, real, scientific branch of the sport of yachting, sail-racing. Anybody can take the wheel and steer a motor craft, if he knows anything at all about handling a boat; but it requires real brains, and skill, born of years of study and practice, to say nothing of inherent talent, to handle a sail craft skillfully in a race, or even on a cruise, or pleasure sail, ofttimes.
>
> "It's the greatest, cleanest gentleman's sport up to date, just as it was a century ago. While, of course, such will never be, I do not believe that even if it were commercialized, as baseball and other sports now are, it could ever be other than what it is, because the very nature of it makes most men honest, whether or not they are in other pursuits inclined to be so.
>
> "What the North American Yacht Racing Union has in view," he continued to say, "is the purpose of making all things equal, as nearly as may be possible, in the sail-racing sport. Most particularly the Union desires to arrive at building rules which will get away from the freakish type, and back to a wholesome type of sail craft which will combine the maximum of utility with the maximum of speed. The tendency today is toward nothing more nor less than racing freaks—narrow beam, deep draft, and utmost possible over-all length with shortest possible water-line length.
>
> "What we want to bring about is a wholesome type of craft, not a toothpick with a fake cabin-house on it, a craft that is fit only for racing, with a dog house for a cabin, a house that you have to get down and crawl into and then haven't even as much as an eight-inch shelf to stretch out on, to say nothing of ordinary bunk accommodations."
>
> President Mallory declared it as his opinion that a grace mistake has been made in going from centerboard—our original Southern type — to finkeel, or deep draft boats, in strict classification. Deep-draft, finkeel craft may be perfectly all right in certain waters of the United States where there is an abundance of draft of water, but such craft cannot be used in many other waters of this and other countries. The waterline length is what governs in most instances—in most classes—but there also is a deep proviso which makes such craft utterly impracticable in other sections of the country where there are only shallow waters.
>
> President Mallory further stated: "It is the aim of the North American Yacht Racing Union to adjust such matters so that New Orleans boats,

or Galveston boats, or Florida boats, can go into the deeper waters of the East and the lakes of the Middle West, and the waters of the Pacific coast, and race, on water-line length, and equal terms with the boats in those other deeper waters of the country, and boats from those deeper waters come down into the shallower waters and race, on equal terms, by reason of similar design and construction."

"In other words," President Mallory said, "it is the purpose of the NAYRU to bring about, first, a set of uniform building construction rules to apply to every section of the United States, with uniform racing rules, and second, to have European countries adopt the same building and racing rules, so that, eventually, they will become international.

"The New York Yacht Club has, so far, dictated much in this direction. But, while it holds the distinctive position it does, and deserves it by seniority, it should not, now, undertake to dictate as to universal classifications and building requirements. It is not right that any section, or group of sections, of the country should have absolute control of such matters. It is the purpose of the North American Yacht Racing Union to divide the yachting world of the United States into sections, each section to have representation in the organization, and each section to have a certain number of votes on all questions at issue. It must not, and will not, be a question of any one section, or group of sections, having control; it must be solely the question of whether the contention at issue is 'right,' the purpose of the organization being to have all things right and equal for all sections."

After declaring that he needed no coaxing to stop over in New Orleans, because he had done a great deal of sailing in Gulf waters, and that he is as much a Southern yachtsman as an Eastern one, having married a Galveston lady, President Mallory related how he has been sailing since he was twelve years of age, his earlier training had been in craft of the centerboard type, a type which he still believes is the best possible taken all-around, in the smaller craft, even in some types of the larger ones.

President Mallory left to spend the Christmas holidays with his wife and her family in Galveston.

Commodore Jahncke was instrumental in having the Gulf Yachting Association elected a charter member of NAYRU. He served for many years on the NAYRU executive committee. Replacing the commodore was Commodore J. Gilbert Scheib of the Gulf Yachting Association, who remained on the committee for eleven years. Commodore G. Shelby Friedrichs was elected for the next eleven years. His son, G. Shelby Friedrichs, Jr., replaced his father until the change in the organization was made to the United States Yacht Racing Union.

BILOXI SCHOONER RACES

Along the Gulf Coast a favorite in racing circles was the Biloxi schooner races. These majestic-looking vessels with their handsome white sails were a sight to behold on the waters of Mississippi Sound. The races were very popular events. In 1926 *The Rudder* yachting magazine sent one of its prominent journalists, reporter of America's Cup races Gerald Taylor White, to cover the Biloxi Schooner races. His exciting experience on board one of the schooners, *Mary Foster*, follows:

> Until a few days ago, the name Biloxi meant nothing beyond the idea that it was a Gulf Coast city and the scene of the annual Fishing Schooner Championship races. Today, we are wiser and happier, for we have experienced true Southern hospitality and have witnessed regattas here which stand head and shoulders over the usual affairs.
>
> In the first place, Biloxi is not the little fishing city we imagine. It is a clean, cool little burg which is a summer resort of the best people of many of the Southern states.
>
> The Biloxi schooners are not grubby craft but handsome white vessels about 70 feet overall and more often than not fitted with clean, cream-colored sails which would grace any yacht.
>
> It was due to the kindness of Byrd Enochs and John Meunier who got the permission of Captain Martin Fountain, Jr. that I was able to be on board the *Mary Foster*. The complete entry list was:
>
> | | |
> |---|---|
> | *Julia Delacruz* | *Sarah Ford* |
> | *I. Heidenheim* | *Curtis Fountain* |
> | *Captain Amos Ross* | *Lillian Holley* |
> | *Captain Frank Perez* | *Mamie Foster* |
> | *H. E. Grumble* | *L. Goldman* |
> | *Anna Eve* | *Mary Foster* |
>
> The last named schooner was the one which I boarded.
>
> When the gun went off, sang Captain Fountain, "Everybody forward and down to windward" and I fell prone just inside the windward rail. I sat up and tried to take a picture. "Down, down, damn you, get down" rang in my ears. I laid flat and a wiry native whispered "You must nevair put your head up. It spills the wind." I never sailed in a craft her size with so much life. Eventually, a figure crawled toward me and said the skipper wanted to see me. I expected to be thrown to the sharks and looked with yearning eyes at the Coast Guard boat some yards away. Captain Fountain, smilingly, said, "sit in the companion and you will be out of the way."
>
> Most of the fleet stood off while two of them started their own scrap, which ended in one of the schooners poking her bowsprit through the mainsail of the other.
>
> We discussed the fouls as we rushed along and I expressed my opinion only to discover that Biloxi Fishermen neither know or care anything about rules. If a boat is in your way, you sail over her or through her

at your own discretion. That was refreshing information and brought back to my mind weary nights arguing whether Bill Jones had squared away on the starboard tack when the two boats gently touched in the last race back home. What a wonderful thing it would be if rules were all as simple as they are at Biloxi!

At the last buoy, we were several seconds away from the winner *I. Heidenheim*, Champion of the Fleet.

These schooners are centerboarders, built locally and used for shrimp and oystering over some of the most prolific grounds in the world. Owing to the State law, they are not equipped with power of any sort. During the fishing season, the crews are composed of ten men or so, but when the race is on, the crew may number 40 keen-eyed expert sailormen of the old school. We have never seen a keener rivalry nor a better brand of sportsmanship. For seamanship and snappy sail handling, we enter the Biloxi fishermen for world honors.

The Biloxi Yacht Club is composed of a goodly number of expert yachtsmen and much credit goes to the management by such fine men as Commodore Elmer, Vice-Commodore Detweiler, Rear Commodore Russ, Captain Edmunds, Dr. Wallace, Andrew Swanzy, Albert Mallard, Ernest Desporte, J., R. H. Chinn, Sparks Vignes, A. V. Ragusin, L. C. McCaleb, E. H. Gower and Mayor John J. Kennedy. All prominent businessmen in the city of Biloxi.

"A BILOXI REGATTA"
by Gerald Taylor White

While the schooner race was the feature event of the two-day regatta at the Biloxi Yacht Club, the sailing yachts and a few power boats showed some remarkable racing.

The Gulf Yachting Association is composed of real seadogs and they carry sail until something breaks. A good part of the Star boat fleet of the Southern Yacht Club of New Orleans was wrecked en route from that city to the Biloxi Regatta because the boys insisted upon sailing these comparatively unseaworthy boats over the 80-odd mile open course between the two cities.

In most sections of the country, the boats would have been shipped by train or at least towed to the course. But, not for the Southern Yacht Club men, they carried on day and night until they either tore the canvas or spars out of the yachts or reached their objective.

In addition to the schooners darting through the maze of yachts, shot tiny outboard racers, Margaret-type hydroplanes, express cruisers, Dodge Watercars, Belle Isle Bearcats and the Gold Cup runabout Super Packard. In the Fish Class, Paul Fairley of Biloxi won.

Another featured race was between the fast Coast Guard express boats *Bullet* and *West Wind*, property of the Monteleone brothers of New Orleans [owners of the Monteleone Hotel on Royal Street]. *Bullet*, a heavy working boat, she once ran rum before they captured her, could not beat the pair of six cylinder Hall-Scott mariners in *West Wind*. *West Wind* later won the Southern Marine Marathon as *Creole Sue*.

In the 21-footer class, Southern Yacht Club's entry *Sis*, owned by Ray and Pitard, sailed by J. Eblen Rau; was the winner. Star Class sloop *Oschtend Star* owned by Paul Jahncke, Jr. won over *Electra* sailed by Robert Kuhn of SYC.

Another class peculiar to the Gulf Coast is sailing skiffs. These boats have earmarks of the old sandbaggers. *Jack Dempsey* won over *Gene Tunney*. This idea of naming yachts after prize fighters is new in yachting nomenclature.

In the small open machine sloops, J. A. Breath of Bay St. Louis was the winner in his *Interference* beating *Interruptin'*. *Toppan Tots* always put up fine racing on the Gulf and the two famous boats owned by Commodore Ernest Lee Jahncke were on hand as usual. *Minnie Meow* sailed by Ernest Lee Jahncke, Jr. won over *Kalico Kat*, sailed by his sister whose mainsail split.

SYC ENTERS INTERNATIONAL STAR CLASS CHAMPIONSHIP

During the summer of 1926, the Star Class fleet sailed its eliminations for the International Star Class championship, which would be held in September at Port Washington, Long Island. Earl Blouin with W. O. Humphreys as crew won the right to represent the New Orleans-Gulf Star Class fleet in the finals. Accompanying the team to Long Island was Prentice Edrington, Jr., who had been elected vice-president of the International Star Class Association. At the last moment, British Columbia and Eastern Long Island announced their inability to enter the races, and as a result there were only sixteen starters. Reported Edrington after his return home:

> When we arrived at Port Washington, Long Island, on Wednesday, August 25th, Manhasset Bay was anything but inviting to a yachtsman. It was raining and foggy. This condition, except for intermittent sunshine, continued into Sunday, August 29th, and when the first day of the series broke bright and cheerful with a brisk northwest wind blowing, the spirits of the contestants arose.
>
> The first race was held by the Bayside Yacht Club. The start was marred by the starting gun being fired one minute too soon due to an error by the committee. *Iscyra* defending Western Long Island, got off first followed by *Rhody* and *Sonny II*. Before the first mark was rounded *Rhody* took the lead and kept it to the finish over *Movie Star*. The New Orleans entry *Talita* cleverly sailed by Earl Blouin, finished fourth.
>
> That night, the Star men were guests of the Bayside Club, the feature being the vaudeville show presented by Ned Wayburn, when the future Broadway stars, the best talent of his wonderful dancing school, showed us everything terpsichorean from the "Black Bottom" up.

The second race was held off Larchmont breakwater under the auspices of the Larchmont Yacht Club. The third race was sponsored by the Port Washington Yacht Club. That night the Port Washington Club staff supper was a great success. Humphreys, Blouin's crew, introduced the famous "Ojen" cocktail—as made in the Southern Yacht Club pen under Fat Daly's famous formula, and Star men from all over the world got on the outside of the 'Pink Shimmy' (Pink Lady Cocktail) cocktail. The recipe for this famous SYC drink was submitted by the SYC Assostant Manager, Armond Schroeder:

PINK LADY COCKTAIL (Pink Shimmy)

1 egg white
1 tsp. grenadine
1 tsp. sweet cream
1½ oz. gin

Shake well with ice—strain into cocktail glass

Again as in the second race *Talita* had the chance to travel along with *Rhody* but Blouin chose a long tack over to Larchmont, one of the "God Help Me" tacks he so often took, and in so doing got out of sight of the turning mark. With an ebbing tide lee bowing him he greatly overlaid his stake and had to set his whiskerpole running free for the windward mark and finally ended the race in last position.

The fourth race was under the auspices of the New York Yacht Club. This famous and aristocratic organization had never before sponsored class racing as a class, and in such small boats, and we felt honored that they should agree to hold one of our races.

When the hour arrived for the tows to get under way, an east wind was blowing thirty miles and upwards and it was raining hard. Com. W. A. W. Stewart of the Seawanhaka Corinthian Yacht Club of Oyster Bay had loaned his fine one-design schooner *Nokomis*, as the committee boat. Oil skins and boots were the order of the day.

The mark boats, two *Wee Scotts*, were tied behind and a start made for Execution Light. The wind and head sea was too much for the small auxiliary power motor in the *Nokomis* and she had to be relieved by her tows. Finally, after battling with the wind and sea, she anchored at the starting line only to drag anchor. The skipper was rewarded for his hard work on the second attempt when she held.

Some idea of the severity of the wind and sea can be gained from the following: The *Nokomis*, a Seawanhaka schooner, 60 ft. over all, was tossed around like a cork. Her 9 ft. of draft did not help much. The regatta committee had to remain in the cockpit in all the rain to keep from being seasick. In fact, Chairman Davis and Tim Parkman gave an exhibition of spring (the return of the swallows). The Vice-President of the Star Class (Edrington) on this committee was the only salty one aboard, remaining below and eating up everything in sight.

The Coast Guard boats, husky 80 ft. sea crafts, rolled their rails under when in the trough and when heading into it took big green ones aboard. The wind at intervals blew forty-five miles an hour from the record of an areometer pressed in service. *Crapper's* jib was torn to shreds and cook on one of the Coast Guard boats was desperately sea sick. And through it all these tiny boats sailed six miles and were none the worse for their experience except that the crews were worn out by the bailing operations which alone kept them afloat.

At one time Inslee was knee deep in water inside his boat. If only Gerald Taylor White (writer for *Rudder* magazine) could have seen these Stars, the same Stars he characterised as "little unseaworthy boats" in his fine story covering the Biloxi Regatta in 1926! The race was cancelled.

The fifth race was run under the auspices of the Manhasset Bay Yacht Club. The wind came in at the start like a lion and suddenly went out like a lamb. *Rhody* well handled by Ben Comstock again won. It was on the second leeward leg *Talita* pulled up to shake out a reef, Blouin had left the tiller and the boom gybed suddenly, knocking the Frenchman overboard. Humphreys threw him a life preserver after his hold on his skipper's sweater tore away—lucky for him as Blouin could not swim. Rounding to *Talita* he picked up her skipper who, except for the shock from the cold water of the Sound, was good as ever. As a result of the delay *Talita* finished twelfth.

On Saturday night at the Manhasset Bay Yacht Club, the final dinnerdance was given and the prizes awarded. In number and value the prizes equalled those given in Cuba. Every participant in the series, whether skipper, crew or official, received a souvenir of the occasion.

Edrington reported that he was convinced our fleet had no chance in the series with our heavy mahogany boats. "Plans are on foot for the construction of a challenger in the east for the next series so that we can be on an even footing with the Eastern boats. Cedar boat or no cedar boat, the fact remains that we were up against the best of the Star boat sailors of the world, sailing in tidal waters unknown to our skipper."

At the Star Class Association's meeting in 1926, it was reported that the membership had increased to thirty-six in the Southern Yacht Club-Gulf Star Class fleet. It was also announced that a charter had been granted to the St. Andrews Bay Yacht Club of Panama City, Florida, by the International Star Class Association and that plans were being made for the building of fifteen of the new sloops.

An announcement of interest appeared in the 1926 *Barometer* stating, "Again the Bermuda race has been sailed over 660 miles of water ranging from calm to stormy, and again Bob Beavier has been the first to cross the finish line off St. David's Head. And once more John Alden with the latest in Malabar creations has won in his class. *Dragoon* was the name of the ketch sailed by Capt. Robert N. Bavier and his navigator was G. N. Wallace. The *Dragoon* was 66 feet overall and designed by Ford & Payne." More will be said about Bob Bavier in later chapters.

In a highly competitive field of champions in the 1926 Sir Thomas

J. Lipton trophy races, Eastern Shore Yacht Club tied with the St. Petersburg Yacht Club for the cup. Those sailing for Southern were Edward G. Pinac, William A. Porteous, Jr., and Leslie P. Beard. For Pensacola were the old faithful's Dave Witherill, William Walthers, and Thomas H. Johnson. Others were Capt. Paul Reese and A. B. Fogarty for St. Petersburg, Capt. Julian Spotswood of Biloxi, Ed. Overton of Eastern Shore, and Capt. Samuel Streetman of the Houston Launch Club in Laporte, Texas.

The semi-annual meeting of the Gulf Yachting Association was held and presided over by the Commodore A. L. Gandy of the St. Petersburg Yacht Club. Other clubs present and their representatives were Commodores Rex Cowley, Pensacola; Ed Overton, Eastern Shore; E. E. Elmer, Biloxi; and W. Milton Miller, Southern. The commodores of the Houston and Corpus Christi Yacht Clubs did not arrive, having missed their trains. At this meeting Bay-Waveland and Corpus Christi Yacht Clubs were elected members of the Gulf Yachting Association. They were represented by W. H. Parham of SYC.

The recommendation of the Fish Class Committee was approved to include a fourth race to be held on Labor Day. A new rule was adopted "prohibiting tampering with boats below the waterline after the dawn of the day of the first race. This comes of complaints that some of the racing sloops had been cleaned and slicked-up with vaseline after the first race of the series." With these revisions, the GYA meeting and the Lipton Regatta were very successful.

During the first year of Commodore John M. Kinabrew's term of office in 1926, there were many parties. It was claimed that the average attendance at the Wednesday and Saturday night affairs was 950 members and guests. The Halloween party in October was described as a supper dance with vaudeville attractions. "The ballroom and foyer, the galleries and pier all were decorated for the occasion with weird lighting effects adding atmosphere. Favors were distributed and there was an augmented orchestra costumed for the Halloween mood. Stunts arranged included a witch fortune teller, a Russian dancer, a Samoan dancer and an Egyptian dancer. The affair was one of fancy dress represented by the celebrities of early pirate tales, as well as witches, ghosts and black cats," reported the *Barometer*.

SYC WINS STAR CLASS MID-WINTERS IN CUBA

It was a great day for the New Orleans-Gulf Star Class Fleet when Southern Yacht Club's twosome, Prentice Edrington, Jr. as skipper and Gilbert T. Gray as crew, won the 1927 Mid-Winter Star Class series in Havana, Cuba in March in the boat *Sparkler II*. The long-sought-after trophy, the Bacardi cup, was finally in the possession of the SYC fleet.

"SIR THOMAS J. LIPTON IN NEW ORLEANS FOR YULE VISIT"

That was the headline of *The Times-Picayune* of December 24, 1927 (page 9, column 1). The report went: "When Sir Thomas left his drawing room on the Crescent Limited of the Louisville & Nashville Railroad, the famous Britisher was greeted by a special committee from the Southern Yacht Club and unnumbered individual admirers. Members of the yacht club committee included Commodore John M. Kinabrew, W. H. Parham and R. Lee Edwards."

The paper reported Sir Thomas J. Lipton's return to New Orleans on January 16, 1928 (page 17, columns 6-8): "I'M HOME AGAIN IN NEW ORLEANS," says Sir Thomas. "He will be the honor guest at a luncheon to be given at noon today by the Southern Yacht Club at their West End clubhouse." It was at this luncheon that Sir Thomas agreed to donate a cup for Star Class yacht racers of the Southern Yacht Club. A rising vote of thanks was given the famous sportsman for his generosity. Commodore Kinabrew presented to Sir Thomas J. Lipton an engraved gold card of honorary membership. More than a hundred members attended the luncheon.

At the 1928 annual meeting of the GYA held during the Lipton Cup Regatta at the St. Petersburg Yacht Club, Ed. Overton of the Eastern Shore Yacht Club was elected president. At this meeting two new yacht clubs became members of the GYA, Sarasota, of Sarasota, Florida and the St. Tammany, of Mandeville, Louisiana.

The St. Petersburg Yacht Club had two Fish Class boats on hand that would not be used, and being anxious to see all the boats in the races, the GYA board of governors requested that all entrance requirements be waived and that they endeavor to have Tarpon Springs Yacht Club join the association and sail in the series. This was done and the largest fleet to sail in a Lipton Regatta to date met on the starting line—sixteen boats.

It became evident that racing arrangements would have to be

altered in the GYA Lipton Regatta series with the large number of members participating in this event each year. It was decided that from 1928 on it would become a four-race series instead of three, with only one boat competing from each club instead of two.

An interesting story was told to the writer by J. Ben Ravannack, who was the secretary-treasurer of the SYC for many years and the owner of the famous *Robin Hood IV*. He recalled his meeting with Sir Thomas on his visit to New Orleans in 1928 in his suite at the St. Charles Hotel, where Mr. Ravannack was introduced to and welcomed by the Briton.

In the midst of a conversation, a little old lady arrived and was ushered into the parlor, where Sir Thomas introduced her as the owner of the boardinghouse where he had lived during his boyhood days while working in New Orleans at the streetcar barn in Carrollton uptown.

Lipton recalled with delight the "good pancakes and grits" that she served, and presented her with a basket of fruit which also contained an envelope. Inside she found a check for $10,000. Ecstatic, the sweet old lady kissed his hand with tears in her eyes and Ravannack admitted there wasn't a dry eye in that hotel suite among those privileged to witness human kindness at its purest.

Sir Thomas J. Lipton was a humanitarian and philanthropist. Although he made a fortune by parlaying his first earnings as a merchant grocer into a vast export empire, the Lipton Tea Co., he was always considerate of the poor. At his death in 1931, Sir Thomas left approximately a fifth of his fortune "to the poor mothers of Glasgow and their children." He was born in Glasgow, Scotland on May 10, 1850 of poor parents.

This second Lipton trophy was dedicated to the young fleet of Star boats. The first Lipton trophy had been presented to the Fish Class sloops in 1919. The Star Class champion, Prentice Edrington, was the first winner of Sir Thomas J. Lipton's newest gift to the SYC. He won the series in the new Star *Sparkler III*, which was brought down from Brooklyn, New York for the Star Class Internationals to be held in Newport Harbor, California in September 1928.

The sailing season of 1928 was a clear indication that economic conditions were worsening, for the spirit for sailboat racing was affected. This was evident when the gun fired for the opening regatta and only a small number of boats appeared on the starting line.

Not many boats answered the gun when the 1928 race to the coast got under way for the Fourth of July race week at Biloxi. However, in her usual winning way, the *Quakeress*, skippered by Commodore

Winning the SYC's first international trophy were Prentice Edrington, Jr., as skipper and Gilbert Gray as crew. This team won the International Star Class Championship in Los Angeles in 1928.

Presenting the Olympic gold medals to the winners (Gilbert Gray, skipper; Andrew Libano, crew) of the 1932 Olympic sailing event in the Star Class is SYC Commodore and Olympic committee member Ernest Lee Jahncke at the Los Angeles Coliseum.

Kinabrew, won the Cal Hadden trophy for crossing the finish line in first place. She won over the *Doris,* ably handled by Miss Doris Zemurray. In third place was the late ex-commodore Samuel Heaslip's son, James Heaslip, sailing the *Malegar. Bide-a-Wee,* owned by John Dane, won in the motorboat class. Elizabeth S. Odenheimer's entry, *Kingfisher,* and the *Crest,* owned by Alfred Tharp, were also winners.

FIRST ALL-GIRL CREW IN LONG-DISTANCE RACE TO COAST

Appearing for the first time in the history of the series of long-distance races to the coast was the all-girl crew from the Southern Yacht Club, sailing on the *Doris* that had finished second in the 1928 race to the coast. "Never before had a boat guided by feminine hands undertaken such a task. Crewing for Miss Doris Zemurray who skippered the big yawl schooner *Doris,* owned by her father, Samuel Zemurray, were Misses Maude Hoefeld, Julia Hoefeld, Rose Feingold and Josephine Fry. They surprised everyone and received so much applause as they arrived at the finish line in Biloxi, one would have assumed they had won the race," reported *The Times-Picayune.*

There was a large crowd of spectators on the coast for the race. Many had driven over just to ride on the new wooden bridge that spanned the Bay, which was opened on March 26, 1928.

SYC WINS INTERNATIONAL STAR CLASS CHAMPIONSHIP

The success of the new *Sparkler III* proved to be a good omen. Prentice Edrington, Jr., with his crew Gilbert T. Gray, won the coveted 1928 International Star Class championship in California. A total of seventeen boats was entered and sailing them were the finest skippers in the world. Serving on the International Star Class race committee for the championship races was Earl Blouin of SYC, who had sailed unsuccessfully in this event the two previous years.

The thrill of the victory was short-lived, however, as the clouds of financial doom hung heavily over the club. A special meeting was called on December 18, 1928 in the DeSoto Hotel in downtown New Orleans, at which time it was announced that because of the lack of sufficient funds to operate the club, the doors would be closed from January 3 to April 15, 1929, the date of the next annual meeting.

The SYC membership reassured Commodore Kinabrew and his flag officers, Vice-Commodore A. W. McLellan and Rear Commodore Leslie P. Beard, by electing them to a fourth term in office at the 1929 annual meeting. They were ably assisted by an outstanding group of local businessmen:

E. B. Briggs	Cal F. Hadden
W. B. Edgar, Jr.	C. A. Hartwell
Crawford H. Ellis	R. G. Irby
F. F. Farrell	John R. Juden, Jr.
R. W. Ferguson	Adam Lorch
F. X. Foxley	Dr. W. Milton Miller
	Charles A. Tessier

The Houston Yacht Club in Laporte, Texas played host to the GYA Lipton Cup teams in 1929. Only seven clubs participated in the event—Biloxi, Houston, Mobile, Pensacola, St. Petersburg, Sarasota, and Southern. Pensacola Yacht Club members were the winners of this prestigious trophy, which had become a prized possession of the Pensacola Yacht Club, having won the cup seven out of the nine years it was in competition (two of the years were ties with the Southern Yacht Club). The new method used of the Fish Class sloops carrying various colored flags on the peak of the mainsail to designate the club made it very convenient to identify one's team: Houston, green; Mobile, orange; Pensacola, red; St. Petersburg, white; Sarasota, red and white; Southern, blue.

Although times were difficult financially for all clubs, the gracious hospitality of the Houston Yacht Club's Commodore John S. Bonner and his board members, Dr. W. E. Bertner, H. H. Burghard, H. G. Comfort, W. E. Hamilton, C.S.E. Holland, George F. Howard, W. E. Humphreville, Jr., and J. Collier Hurley, was well extended to all visiting yachtsmen.

The docket of the eightieth SYC meeting was loaded with business, financing being the top priority on the agenda. Commodore Kinabrew graciously accepted a beautiful marine painting from ex-Vice Commodore Baumgarden on behalf of the family of the late Commodore Lawrence O'Donnell for the yacht club. An announcement was made by Commodore Kinabrew that the SYC had received an invitation to participate in the inaugural Ocean Race from St. Petersburg Yacht Club to Havana, Cuba, to be held in 1930. The invitation was immediately accepted by Garner H. Tullis, who agreed to represent the SYC with his 60-foot schooner *Windjammer*.

SYC HOSTS STAR CLASS INTERNATIONALS

Despite the financial crunch, the Southern Yacht Club in its usual role as host, officiated on Lake Pontchartrain at the 1929 Star Class International championship races. This prestigious contest had been won the previous year in California by SYC skipper Prentice Edrington, Jr. To state that this was a crucial time to hold the series was putting it mildly. The International Star Class races were held on October 20, 1929 and the stock market crashed nine days later on October 29, 1929.

In good neighborly fashion, many social clubs and hotels assisted in the entertainment programs for the out-of-town visitors here for the races. The New Orleans Country Club sponsored a dinner for the fleet one night during the week, as did the Metairie Golf Club on another evening. The Young Men's Gymnastic Club had a smoker for the men, while the New Orleans Country Club entertained the ladies at a luncheon. The Jung Hotel, where many dances were held when the club was closed, graciously held a night of entertainment for all the visitors, with its unique, newly built roof garden and ballroom with roll-back roof and disappearing windows.

Evidently the approaching years of the Depression had little effect on the skippers. Many leading yacht clubs in the United States were represented as well as those from Cuba, Hawaii, Barbados, and the Philippine Islands, for a total of twenty boats. There were several spectator yachts for the races and a large crowd was in attendance.

Prentice Edrington, Jr. was the defending champion, but having won all the honors there were to win in Star Class competition, he let his crew, Gilbert Gray, take the helm of *Sparkler III* and he acted as crew, to compete in the 1929 International Star Class championship to be held at the SYC. Gray and Edrington qualified for the finals but were not fortunate in their quest for the trophy. Gray finished a close second to the Johnson brothers in *Eel* from the Chesapeake Bay area who were the victors.

Aware of the importance of this championship event, Commodore Kinabrew arranged to have every detail ably handled by his committeemen:

Commodore	— John M. Kinabrew
Vice-Com.	— Ashael E. McClellan
Rear Com.	— Leslie P. Beard
Sec. Treas.	— William H. Parham

Percy S. Benedict	Gilbert T. Gray	J. Benjamin Ravannack
Earl Blouin	George R. Hammett	Edgar Rae, Jr.
Hart Brundige	Edward B. Jahncke	A. R. "Babe" Roberts
Auguste Capdevielle	Robert Kuhn	Alfred F. Page, Jr.
James H. Collins	John Longmire	Eblen J. Rau
W. A. Coker	Edward Montgomery	William Stuart
Joseph Deynoodt	E. F. Mire, Jr.	Harold D. Sporl
R. R. de los Reyes, Sr.	Silar Oviatt	L. D. Sampsell
Prentice E. Edrington, Jr.	William F. Pitard	Bryan Wayne
Clarence Ferguson	Gus Pitard	Davis S. Wuescher
		Clyde W. Wagner

This was Edrington's last race for SYC. He later became a judge and travelled on to the Philippine Islands, where he resided until his death in 1965. Prentice willed his collection of trophies to the Southern Yacht Club.

Shortly after the Star Class event on October 26, 1929, a special meeting was called by Commodore Kinabrew, who announced that the club was forced to close its doors, not to be reopened until May 1, 1930. From a total of 3,000 members in 1924, there was a drop to 608 in 1929, and by 1932 there were only 250 names on the roster.

At the meeting, which was held at the Roosevelt Hotel in downtown New Orleans, a special finance committee was appointed with Crawford H. Ellis, president of the United Fruit Steamship Company, the Pan American Life Insurance Company, and also the New Orleans Country Club, as the Chairman, and Callender F. Hadden, a prominent businessman; Charles J. Tessier, a top realtor in the South; and Garner H. Tullis, a successful cottonbroker.

After many meetings, the Whitney Bank agreed to forgive the SYC's indebtedness to the bank. The Hibernia Bank, in liquidation, was forced to foreclose. However, in cooperation with the presidents of both banks, the doors of the SYC remained open and financial matters were settled.

TULLIS WINS FIRST
ST. PETERSBURG TO HAVANA RACE

The morale of the SYC members in 1930 was quickly aroused when the news reached New Orleans that Garner H. Tullis had sailed his *Windjammer* over the finish line in Havana, Cuba to win the first St. Petersburg to Havana ocean race in Class A. The schooner yacht *Halligonian* of Houston Wall was the first to finish. She also won in Class B.

Although cruiser-type sailboats with auxiliary propellers were allowed in the races, only their sails were allowed to be used, the motors having been detached or sealed beforehand. The motor could be used only in case of emergency, and yachts being disqualified if they were forced to this extreme.

The distance of this race was 284 nautical miles, the greater part lying on the Gulf of Mexico. The first year of these races, the winning boat required less than two days to make the trip, but in 1933 the first yacht to reach Havana took five days and six hours. Eleven vessels took part in the first year, and as a matter of history it is reported that the speed record was established for the 284 miles separating St. Petersburg from Havana of forty-one hours, twelve minutes and twenty seconds. This event became a very popular ocean race until the Cuban revolution in 1958.

In the second St. Petersburg to Havana race in 1931, Garner H. Tullis returned to finish second in Class A. There were eight starters, with *Sunshine*, owned by H. S. Denniston of Mobile, finishing first and first in Class A. In Class B first place was won by Wm. B. Allen in *Game Cock*.

Samuel Zemurray's Elmasada II, the largest gasoline yacht in the club's fleet. She measured 110 feet in length overall and had 15-foot beam, and drew 4 feet, 4 inches of water.

COMMODORE CHARLES A. TESSIER—1930-33

The eighty-first annual meeting was held in May 1930 with a new commodore elected to office, Charles A. Tessier, a prominent realtor.

A standing ovation was given outgoing Commodore Kinabrew, the youngest commodore to hold office, for the superb job he had performed during four trying years under most difficult circumstances.

The stock market had crashed the previous year, 1929, and the nation was headed into a devastating depression. The club, like many other businesses and institutions, was heavily in debt; low in cash and faced with foreclosure on its clubhouse. Tessier put his shoulders to the wheel with a competent board: A. W. McLellan, vice-commodore; Robert Moore, Jr., rear commodore; Dr. W. A. Wagner, fleet surgeon; and Clarence O. Ferguson, fleet measurer. The board was coupled with a fantastic braintrust of fellow members, namely:

H. L. Avegno	Cal F. Hadden	J. Eblen Rau
Leslie P. Beard	William Henderson	J. Benjamin
Phillip G. Benedict	Walter F. Jahncke	Ravannack
E. B. Biggs	Robert Kuhn	A. R. Roberts
Auguste Capdevielle	A. L. Larmann	A. B. Paterson
	J. A. Mermilloid	J. A. Rawlins
Crawford H. Ellis	Louis V. Rand	Wallis Pitard
Gilbert T. Gray		Garner H. Tullis
		W. E. Young

Commodore Tessier introduced a number of innovations in an effort to revive the spirit of the members, such as late Sunday afternoon dinner-dances, which had been discontinued. He rearranged the clubhouse's main floor into small private rooms, and brought in a new restaurant steward and chef. The commodore fostered skipperette and junior regattas. His flagship, *Ruth*, was often used as a committee boat.

GOVERNOR HUEY P. LONG VIEWS REGATTA

Although clouds of financial disaster hung over the club, the opening regatta of the 1930 season was well attended by hundreds of guests from New Orleans and points along the Gulf Coast. The racing course was lined with scores of motor vessels, one of them being the Dock Board's yacht *Hugh McCloskey*, which had on board His Honor, Governor Huey P. Long of Louisiana.

Spectators at the regatta were thrilled by the beautiful sight of Garner H. Tullis' *Windjammer* sweeping down the course with all sails set, to win the schooner event. *Balthazar*, owned by DePass and Walker, won in the 21-foot cabin class, defeating *Quakeress III*, owned by Commodore J. M. Kinabrew. *Sparkler II*, with Brennan Cleary and Gilbert Gray, captured the Star Class race over *Blue Star*, owned by Edward "Bud" Jahncke and *Stella*, belonging to Robert J. Kuhn.

During the summer of 1930, with his Star boat *Chico*, Davis S. Wuescher with Gilbert Gray as crew entered the World's Star Class Championship race on Chesapeake Bay. The title escaped Dave in this event, which was won by Adrian Inslee II in *Peggy Wee* of Bayside, Long Island. After his return to the States in 1929, from his long stay of twenty years in the Tropics, Dave Wuescher had invested in the Star *Chico* and was back to championship racing.

Although all clubs in the Gulf Yachting Association were experiencing hard times, this did not prevent the holding of the Sir Thomas J. Lipton cup event in Pensacola the weekend of Labor Day. There was a small number of entries, with only Mobile, St. Petersburg, Biloxi, Pensacola, Sarasota, and Southern yacht clubs appearing on the starting line. In a surprise move, the Lipton Cup was won by the new member in the GYA, the Sarasota Yacht Club from Sarasota, Florida. It had joined the organization in 1927, and after winning the 1930 series of races for the cup, went on to win again in 1931 and 1932.

During the year 1930, SYC members were saddened by the loss of the club's most renowned editor, R. Lee Edwards. After a lengthy illness, he passed away at the early age of fifty-five. Much of the material used in this book was his. Edwards was also a noted civil court reporter for the New Orleans *States* newspaper. Two other prominent members sailed on to their Master in 1930, Mr. John B. Levert and Mr. James R. Behrens.

SIR THOMAS J. LIPTON DIES
AFTER LAST AMERICA'S CUP CHALLENGE

After the defeat of *Shamrock V* by Harold S. Vanderbilt's *Enterprise* in the America's Cup race of 1930, the first to be sailed off Newport, Rhode Island since 1922, Sir Thomas J. Lipton decided that the time had come to retire to Osidge, his estate near London, where he passed away shortly thereafter.

The last race, he stated, had cost him a fortune. He estimated from the time *Shamrock V* was first designed in 1913 until the moment when she was finally defeated in 1930 and he returned to England, the challenge had cost him $2,000,000. A new challenge, it was said, would be more expensive as the cost of materials was 500 percent higher. Wages had risen over 300 percent. Sailors as crewmen used to earn $6.00 weekly but this had risen to $25.00 per week. (All of which has a familiar ring in the 80s.)

Following the 1930 event, a Lipton Loving Cup Fund was established and in that same year the famous humorist, Will Rogers, presented an 18-karat gold cup to Sir Thomas on behalf of the American people for his good sportsmanship.

It was a great shock to the yachting world when the news came in 1931 via the wires of the International News Service that Sir Thomas had abandoned any future challenge for the prestigious America's Cup, saying, "I willna challenge again; I canna win." Not too long after his emotional departure from the America's Cup contest, the "grand old man of yachting" died on October 2, 1931.

One particular misfortune contributing to Sir Thomas Lipton's decision was the sinking of his treasured ship *Erin*, aboard which he had followed the races of his *Shamrocks*. She was lost during the war, going down with all his trophies, a blow that devastated the Yachstman Emeritus. However, upon his return to England, Sir Thomas was softened partially by a membership in the Royal Yacht Squadron, whose officers had once blackballed him because he was "in trade."

New Orleanians were especially saddened by the death of Lipton, who had always been proud to claim New Orleans as his home away from home when he was a young man. Reminiscing on the many visits of Sir Thomas to New Orleans, the news media reported, "On Sir Thomas' last trip to New Orleans in 1928, it was recalled that he remembers the street railway with special fondness known as the tram car company. While earning his way around a large part of the world—before his English groceries became a fad of fortune, he remembered finding lodging with the wife of the car yard foreman. 'I paid $5.00 a week and her pancakes were just like my mother's, now I am paying $5.00 a minute to stay at the St. Charles Hotel'."

It was in 1899 that Sir Thomas J. Lipton of England entered his first yacht, *Shamrock I*, to challenge in the America's Cup races. She was 131 feet long and displaced 260 tons; she was designed by Fife of Scotland and built by John Thorneycraft. *Shamrock I* was defeated by the United States entry *Columbia*, owned by a syndicate headed by J. Pierpont Morgan. Four more *Shamrocks* were built to try for the cup; all were unsuccessful.

When Lipton first sent his *Shamrocks* to the U.S., the Cup boats were all giant sloops from 130 to 145 feet in length, skyscraping sail carriers more than twice the size of today's 12-meter contenders. The rig of the 1903 Cup defender *Reliance* was as high as a fifteen-story building and it flew over 16,000 square feet of sail. The overall length of *Reliance* was 135 feet.

This was an era of professional skippers. (The amateur or Corinthian helmsmen rule followed the success of the *Resolute*, sailed by Charles Francis Adams in 1922.) The boat owners watched their immense chargers race from the comfort of their long steam yachts. (The reigning expert designer of the time was Nathanael Herreshoff.)

Schooners dating from 1851 through 1876 had short rigs with the area of sail spread out fore and aft, rather than high in the air. This put a lot less strain on sails, gear, rigging, spars, and hull. Later schooners were designed with taller rigs, which were more efficient. Eventually, in 1881, a gaff-headed sloop rig appeared in America's Cup competition. From this time through 1920 all Cup contenders used the gaff-headed sloop rig. The last vessel, *Shamrock V*, is still afloat, having been reconditioned to her original J-class specification.

The *Enterprise* of the 1930 challenge was important in the development of yachting. This craft and *Shamrock V* both carried jib-headed rigs, the first in America's Cup racing. The U.S. entry was called a mechanical ship by virtue of the extent to which she used below-deck winches, but an innovation which became the norm was her use of an aluminum alloy mast. Hardly a boat is built today without a light alloy spar.

It was reported in a yachting magazine that "Marine technology like an invisible member of the crew, rides aboard every yacht in an America's Cup contest. As a result, modern preparation for the Cup defense has led to a close collaboration with industry, a relationship that has been compared with that achieved in the U.S. Apollo program."

NATHANAEL C. HERRESHOFF—BOAT DESIGNER

The name Nathanael C. Herreshoff is so prominent in yachting circles all over the world that a brief resume about the man and his boats is pertinent to Southern sailing history. He was born in 1848, a native of Bristol, Rhode Island. Herreshoff lived ninety years, working most of his life as a partner in the Herreshoff Manufacturing Company of Bristol, Rhode Island on Narrangansett Bay. He was the most brilliant of all boat designers from the 1890s to 1920.

The Herreshoff firm built many types of vessels, torpedo boats, steam yachts, and catamarans. But yacht racing was revolutionized when "Captain Nat" returned to monohull sailboats in the 1890s and produced a 71-footer named *Gloriana*. In contrast to the boats of the day, which were usually clipper-bowed, *Gloriana* had a long forward overhang which provided added length on the water when she heeled, resulting in increased speed. She had a cutaway forefoot so that her profile showed an easy sweep from the stem head to the bottom of the keel and what became known as a spoon-shaped bow. This boat began winning races and ushered in "the Herreshoff era," from 1890 to 1920.

Captain Herreshoff achieved his greatest fame as the designer of America's Cup defenders. When the next challenge for the America's Cup (1893) was received from the Royal Yacht Squadron, Herreshoff designed the successful defender, the sloop *Vigilant*. While a keel boat, she also carried a centerboard which worked through a slot in the lead keel.

After the *Vigilant*, Herreshoff designed America's Cup defenders *Defender*, *Columbia*, *Reliance*, and *Resolute* for the races from 1893 to 1922. These were giants, the largest, *Reliance*, being 143 feet long, built of bronze and having a steel mast that supported 16,160 square feet of sail. (Current 12-meter sloops carry 2,000 square feet of sail.)

John Herreshoff, a brother, although handicapped by blindness caused in an accident, was also a successful boat designer—he dictated his designs. The most noted boat designer in the United States before Herreshoff was Edward Burgess in 1885.

The United States Yacht Racing Union's most prestigious award is the Nathanael C. Hereshoff trophy, which is presented to an outstanding individual in all fields of yachting. The Herreshoff trophy was donated to the USYRU in 1957 by the National Marine Manufacturing Association, then NAEBM. Two Southern yachtsmen have received this award, both of them from St. Petersburg, Florida, Commodore Ted Tolson of the St. Petersburg Yacht Club and Roger Brett. In 1957 GYA Commodore J. Gilbert Scheib was a nominee for this trophy.

A much needed injection of life into the SYC membership came when Garner H. Tullis entered the St. Petersburg to Havana race in 1932 for the third long-distance race in this classic and put his 60-foot *Windjammer* over the line to take first place overall and first in Class A. (Winning in Class B was Kent Curtis in *Marlene II*.) The beautiful Machado trophy was presented to Tullis by General Girardo Machado. This was the third time Garner Tullis had sailed in this event. The first year, 1930, he won in Class A; in 1931 he placed second in Class A; in 1932 his ambition was fulfilled by his winning both championships, overall and Class A.

At the supper dance given in his honor by the Southern Yacht Club, Garner H. Tullis displayed the two loving cups he had won—the Machado cup wa awarded to him by the President of Cuba; the other cup was a gift from the city of Havana. Also in recognition of his great sailing achievements, SYC Commodore Charles J. Tessier presented the victor with a large framed photograph of the *Windjammer* entering the Havana harbor.

Of the 1932 opening regatta of the SYC, the *Picayune* reported, "Pretty girls, hardy sailors, speed boats, dark gray Coast Guard cutters- a peeping sun, varicolored Fish Class sloops, veteran cabin sloops, Star boats and a tantalizing five-knot breeze gave color and zest to the 83rd annual regatta on the sporting waters of Lake Pontchartrain."

Robert B. Todd's *Invader* won the 21-foot cabin sloop race with John M. Kinabrew's *Quakeress II* second and the *Circe* with Eugene Aschaffenberg third, with fourth place going to J. Eblen Rau in *Sis*. In the Fish Class race, Robert Hardie won in the "A" Division over Robert Hughes, Jr., Dan Grace, Robert Gaston, Robert Todd, Al Brady, and Charles J. Tessier, Jr. The "B" Class was won by Alfred Tharp over W. Q. Walker, James Bond, A. Clark, and J. Kinabrew.

The Times-Picayune of June 28, 1932 reported on the skipperette regatta:

> Miss Yvonne Phillippi captures skipperette title in SYC race. The order of the day was each skipperette must have two able bodied male crew. When Miss Yvonne Phillippi won she had with her Billy Stewart and Alfred Page. Skillfully handling the tiller to bring her boat up from sixth place to second was Mrs. Garner H. Tullis with her husband Garner as crew and Mickey Richardson. Third place went to Dorothy Johnson with Robert Hughes and Alex Johnson as crew. In fourth place was Margaret Martinez with Jimmy Heaslip and Henry Menge crewmen, followed by Miss Juanita Perrin with D. L. Watson and Richard Menge as crew; Anne Beard assisted by her father Commodore Leslie Beard and Randolph Church; Mrs. Francis Moore with crewmen her husband and Evangel Anagnasti. Also, Ruth Rainold whose crew was her future husband J. Carl Baquie and her friend J. Eblen Rau.

At the dinner-dance following the races, Commodore Charles J. Tessier presented to Miss Phillippi a huge silver punch bowl for winning the skipperette championship.

In the second skipperette regatta held in August 1932, the girls sailed in Star boats. Many had their husbands or fiancees as crewmen. They were:

1. Nan Bryson-Dave Wuescher*
2. Mildred Bond-Jimmy Bond (brother)
3. Bunny Benedict
4. Esther Cleveland Robert Kuhn
5. Rowena Duffy-John Curren*
6. Esther Dupuy-Harry Graham
7. Elizabeth Hughes Freret- Douglas Freret*
8. Eunice Howsman- Robert Tessier
9. Alma Hammett-George Hammett*

10. Dorothy Johnson-
    Robert Hughes*
11. Evelyn Jahncke
12. Barbara Leovy-J. D.
    Miller, Jr.
13. Olive Moore-W. H.
    Hughes, Jr.
14. Mildred Pratt-Miles
    Pratt*
15. Lydia Phillips
16. Ruth Rainold-J. Carl
    Baquie*
17. Sidney Rhodes-Wm.
    Curren
18. Majorie Stair-Maumus
    Claverie
19. Helene Stauffer-J.
    Fornaris, Jr.
20. Earline Taylor-Robt.
    Todd
21. Lou Tharp-Alfred
    Tharp*
22. Malcolm Tullis-Garner
    Tullis (father)
23. Teeta Van Horn-Herbert
    Van Horn*
24. Yvonne Phillippi-Wm.
    Stewart
25. Edna Gray-Gilbert
    Gray*

*Married.

In July of 1932, the Pass Christian Yacht Club celebrated its twenty-fifth annual regatta. Representing the Southern Yacht Club were 21-footers, Stars and catboats. The *Apache*, sailed by Godfrey Schmitt from Biloxi, won the race for working schooners. Eugene Aschaffenberg of Southern won in the 21-foot cabin sloop races in his *Circe*, a champion along the Gulf Coast waters. Dave Wuescher won the Star Class series over Robert Kuhn in a close race; *Tom Cat* of C. A. Sporl took the 16- to 20-foot class trophy. The other catboats were: *Bear Cat*, *Kitty*, *Wampus*, *Krazy Cat*, *Minnie Meow*, and *Black Cat*.

On the return home of the fleet from Pass Christian, only three boats made port following a terrific storm that struck the SYC fleet midway. They ran afoul off Long Point light and St. Joe Pass. Dave Wuescher with his crew, Ike Rea, in their Star boat *Dixie* was the only one to weather the storm under sail. The only other boats that were not towed in were Robert Kuhn's *Stella*, with Al Grevemberg as crew, and the *Circe*, with Abe Leverich and Eugene Aschaffenberg aboard. The SYC patrol boat was ably handled by race committee chairman Auguste Capdevielle, Clarence G. Ferguson, William Johnson, and Owen R. Hutchinson. (The latter was *The Times-Picayune* sports writer who made the trip with the patrol boat. In those days the newspapers of the city generously lent their writers to cover all SYC races on the coast.) Also on board was Ike Kyles, the faithful SYC cook and part-time crew.

Although finances were low with all skippers, the SYC was able to get a team together for a trip to Sarasota, Florida for the 1932 Lipton Regatta. They were C. G. Ferguson, team captain, James Heaslip, Robert Hughes, George Hammett, Robert Gaston, Jr., and John Curren, all skippers. Crews were W. L. Hughes, Jr., Herbert Van Horn, Queley Walker, and William Scott.

The Summer of 1932 was an active one on Lake Pontchartrain for the Star Class skippers vying to be the first to win an Olympic gold medal at the Olympic Games to be held in Los Angeles, California in August 1932. This was the first time that the U. S. Olympic committee had approved sailboat racing as a part of Olympic events. The Star was one of the boats sanctioned. There were two others, the six-meter and eight-meter classes.

Gilbert Gray as skipper, with Andrew Libano, crew, won the eliminations of the New Orleans-Gulf Star Class Fleet on Lake Pontchartrain in Dave Wuescher's *Chico*. After his return home from the tropics, Dave Wuescher had built a new Star, *Dixie*, to enter the Olympics and lent *Chico* to Gray for the sailoff. Gilbert defeated not only Wuescher but other Star sailors Edward B. Jahncke and C. de B. Claiborne, Jr. in *Tempe II*, William Steward and Harry Swain in *Rex*, Robert Kuhn with Al Grevemberg as crew aboard *Stella*, Philip Benedict and Alfred Page on *Moby Dick*, and Brennan Cleary with Denton Wilmot as crew with the famous *Sparkler III*, in which Edrington and Gray had won the Star Class Internationals in 1928. Noticeably missing from the group were Prentice Edrington, Jr. and Earl Blouin.

After winning the finals of the New Orleans-Gulf Coast Star Class eliminations, and representing the Gulf Yachting Association, Gray and Libano had to compete against the representatives of the Texas Yachting Association's team of Rufus Smith, skipper, and H. L. Kemper, crew, of the Houston Yacht Club. In a very close series of races, the SYC-GYA team won over Smith and Kemper by a mere nineteen seconds. Gilbert brought *Chico* to California but changed her name to *Jupiter II*.

The big problem facing the team and the Southern Yacht Club was how the Olympic hopefuls would reach their destination, California. The SYC treasury was depleted. The banks were collecting the daily receipts as the club's obligation toward retiring its debts. So the skipperettes came to the rescue with a "beachcomers" party, which proved to be a big success. Even so, the income from the affair was hardly sufficient, neither were the receipts from the bar, although Prohibition had been repealed. Finally, because of the personal efforts of Commodore Tessier, who volunteered to underwrite the cost of the venture, and with the generosity of the Luckenback steamship line, which offered to ship the Star boat to the coast and back free of charge, the mission was accomplished and the boys were off on the train to California.

The Times-Picayune staff reporter in Los Angeles reported on the first day at the Olympics, August 4, 1932: "The first Star sloop race in the Olympics will be contested here tomorrow. Gilbert Gray and his *Jupiter II* and Andrew Libano, Jr. as crew, representing the Southern Yacht Club of New Orleans and the U.S.A. will race five other boats.

"The boat that Gray has to beat, according to yachting experts is the *Joy* from England, sailed by Colin Ratsey. Ratsey is a member of Lapthorn and Ratsey, famous makers of sails. The skipper of the *Joy* is said to have as many as 18 suits of sails. Another boat that might prove dangerous is the Swedish Star sailed by Gunnar Asher."

The boats that appeared in the Olympic Trials are listed below:

Boat	*Skipper*	*Fleet*
Nomad	F. C. Damon	Honolulu
Mist	Edwin Thorne	Long Island
Jupiter	Gilbert Gray	New Orleans, La.
Zoa	Eddie Fink	Long Beach
Majella I	Ralph Bradley	Great Lakes

GILBERT GRAY AND ANDREW LIBANO WIN 1932 OLYMPICS

In a nose victory over Eddie Fink, sailing *Zoa* from Long Beach, Gilbert Gray and Andrew Libano won the first Olympic trial race after navigating the 10.25-mile course in two hours, thirty-three minutes and forty-one seconds. The *Mist* was second, owned by Langdon K. Thorne of New York and sailed by Edwin Thorne of Long Island Sound, one second ahead of *Majella II*, the Great Lakes' entrant piloted by Ralph Bradley of Peoria, Ill. The *Nomad* from the Pearl Harbor Yacht Club in Honolulu and sailed by F. C. Damon was last.

The celebration of the SYC team's victory was shattered by acts of vandalism during the night while the boat lay in dock in the San Pedro harbor. The vandals (reported by police to have been paid by gamblers, who were very active around sporting events in those days) bent the mast and destroyed the tiller and rudder of *Jupiter II*. Another boat belonging to the Eastern representative, Thorne, had its mast bent. It was necessary to postpone the second day's race of the tryouts so the boats could be put into shape again.

Gray and Libano went on to win two firsts, one second, and one third in the four-race series, and to represent America in the Olympic races for the gold medal.

The Southern Yacht Club's crew and Uncle Sam's proud ambassadors beat the heavy favorite to win the Olympics. Gray outsailed the best skippers of England, Canada, France, Sweden, South Africa, and Holland by winning five out of seven races, to compile a total of forty-six out of a possible forty-nine points.

List of entries:
Jupiter—Gilbert Gray, USA
Windor—H. W. Wylie, Canada
Joy—Colin Ratsey, England
Tramontone—Jean J. Herbulot, France
Holland—Jan Maas, Holland
Swedish Star—Gunnar Asher, Sweden.

Gilbert Gray and Andrew Libano were the winners of the gold medals for their victory in the inaugural entry of Star Class boats in the Olympic sports arena. It was the second Olympic championship in yachting earned by the United States. Owen P. Churchill won the eight-meter crown with *Angelita* when he finished first in the deciding race that defeated Sir Ronald Maitland's Canadian charter, the *Santa Maria*, in a close finish. In the third sailing contest in six-meters, Thomas Holm of Sweden won over U.S. Ted Conant's *Gallant*. The other entries were from Spain, France, Canada, Austria, South Africa, and Italy. In the monotype, Great Britain was the victor.

There to do the honors was none other than the father of the SYC Star Class, Commodore Ernest Lee Jahncke, who was at that time assistant secretary of the Navy under President Herbert Hoover and also a member of the Olympic committee. The commodore presented the gold medals to Gray and Libano in ceremonies at the Olympic stadium in Los Angeles. It was a stellar moment in the history of a time-honored institution. (Commodore Jahncke was also a member of the Olympic committee in 1936 and cast the only dissenting vote against the United States' participation in the event to be held that year in Germany.)

Immediately upon receipt of the great news, SYC's Commodore Tessier reached Gilbert Gray on long distance. On the other end of the phone was absolute euphoria! In a voice filled with emotion,

Commodore Tessier not only thanked the boys on behalf of the entire membership but told them to prepare for a monster reception upon their return to New Orleans.

Gray informed Commodore Tessier that he had been requested to sail in that day's race; it was not necessary, but could lead to an Olympic record and possibly a world's record. He had already cinched the championship and would sail that day only to try to set a record. Victory would give him five out of seven wins. This is exactly what Gray accomplished for the record. This was something never done before in Star Class racing and probably in any yachting series.

When the crack Missouri Pacific *Orleanian* rolled in on the tracks at the Union Station, it was greeted by a noisy crowd of well-wishers. The widely heralded pair, with Mrs. Gray, stepped from the train to the strains of "Anchors Aweigh" and a thunder of applause that resounded through the station. From the station they were taken to the yacht club in a parade of automobiles led by motorcycle police under Capt. Henry Lennie. Several hundred members greeted the winners at the SYC, headed by Commodore Tessier. The New Orleans Public Service band provided the stirring music.

Adler's Canal Street jewelry store displayed the Olympic winners' trophies: the gold medals they had won, a huge electric mantel clock with steering wheel dial for winning the tune-up race after the boat had been damaged by vandals, an engraved plaque showing four sailboats in enamel relief, and the MacDonald trophy for finishing first in the National Olympic Star boat finals of the Long Beach Star fleet. Also on display by Adler's was the prestigious Sir Thomas J. Lipton $5,000 trophy which was presented to the SYC in 1928 for the Star Class fleet, the SYC Gold Challenge cup, and the Commodore Milliken Memorial trophy for 21-footers, which was rededicated to the Star Class.

Gilbert Gray changed from Star boats to Fish Class sloops, where his record of firsts in interclub competition has never been equalled. Sadly, Gilbert's favorite crew, Andrew Libano, met an untimely death a couple of years after his victory. Gray won the Charles J. Tessier plaque for the most outstanding skipper of the year five times. He was the first commander of the SYC's unit of the New Orleans Power Squadron with Eugene Aschaffenberg of the famous *Dolphin*, the Squadron's secretary.

Gilbert Gray was a sailor of the modern school. His knowledge of sail racing was based on the scientific and practical phases of racing tactics as set forth by Dr. Manfired Curry, author of *Aerodynamics of Sails and Racing Tactics*. Gray studied this book intently and he credited his success in part to the pointers he had learned, along with his own ideas gained from many years of sailing.

The hard-fought victory of Gray and Libano acted as a lifesaving transfusion to an institution battling against the Depression. But the SYC had always been a survivor, having come through wars, epidemics, hurricanes, and now the Depression—it is still a great institution.

It was a happy crew that left New Orleans on January 21, 1933 on board the United Fruit Company's SS *Turrialba* bound for Havana, Cuba. With the SYC sailors Edward "Bud" Jahncke, skipper and Charles de B. Claiborne, Jr., crew, were Bud's father, Paul Jahncke, his sister, Evelyn Jahncke, and his fiancee, Zide Benedict, daughter of Commodore Percy Benedict. Also on the ship was their Star boat *Tempe II*.

The event was the eighth annual International Star Class regatta for the Mid-Winter challenge trophy of Cuba donated by the Cuban National Tourist Commission and the Bacardi Cup. "Bud" lost in the 1932 series in a heartbreaker; after leading he fouled out in the last race. He finished fourth in the event, which helped the U.S. team to win over the Cuban entries. This was Jahncke's second attempt at the Star Class championship. His first venture was in 1931, in which event he was leading but lost in the last race by a disqualification.

PRESIDENT ROOSEVELT ORDERS BANKS CLOSED

The very day that Franklin Roosevelt was sworn in as our thirty-second president, he ordered all banks closed. This was the bleak situation that faced Commodore Tessier when he was reelected for a fourth term in 1933. In that year the Great Depression cast its gloomy shadow over the country. The staggering breadlines and hordes of unemployed provided an indicator of the country's economic despair. Bank failures and mortgage foreclosures were commonplace before all banking facilities were ordered closed. The year was marked with change—economic, political, social—and the end of Prohibition.

The club was still struggling to keep afloat. Many suggestions were presented to assist the future stability of the club. One decision was made by the board which reversed the method of allowing more social than sailing memberships adopted in the early '20s when the total membership was 3,000. The pendulum swung back at the 1933 annual meeting, when it was proposed and approved "that the members should consist more of yachtsmen than dancers." In spite of the fact that the present membership included only 250 names, a limit of 600 members was established and the category of life membership, which had been initiated in 1916, was abolished.

When the banks reopened the mood was not entirely grim. The theme song of the Depression, "Brother can you spare a dime?" was gradually being replaced with new music. Tea dances became a sedate form of entertainment.

It was evident from the economic outlook during these Depression times that not too many adults could be found sailing on weekends. Commodore Tessier used the occasion to gather the youth of the club and put to use the twelve club-owned Fish Class boats sitting in the harbor.

The story of the success of the Commodore's junior program is one that will be stressed because it proved to be the lifesaver of the Southern Yacht Club as it spread to the Gulf Coast yacht clubs with interclub competition. For many years the system worked among the juniors and skipperettes. It must have been the type of organization that Commodore John Robinson had in mind when he developed the first SYC Junior Division in 1858.

At the first junior meeting held in 1932, there were 200 young men in attendance. John Curren was elected junior commodore and was successful in getting a junior member appointed to the SYC board of directors. He is also credited with spreading the activity among juniors of the Gulf Coast yacht clubs.

The SYC race committee chairman, Auguste Capdevielle, cooperated by having the big boat owners lend their vessels for the first junior regatta, which was sailed in the summer of 1932 for all juniors under twenty-six years of age. The winners were M. H. Hogan in 21-footers, Alfred Tharp in Stars, Don Chamberlain in Fish boats and Queley Walker in Snipes. In the second annual junior regatta in 1933, the juniors appointed their own race committee and judges. The youngsters skippered in every class of boat in the SYC fleet for the first time. There were as many as twenty-six sail craft. Those juniors and their sailboats are listed below:

>Schooners:
>*Windjammer*—John Curren (owner Garner Tullis)—winner
>*Mallard*—Maumus Claverie
>*Dorothy M*—D. L. Watson, Jr. (owner Louis Rand)
>21-foot cabin sloops:
>*Quakeress III*—Robert Hardy (owner J. M. Kinabrew)—winner
>*Sis*—M. H. Hogan (owner Eblen Rau)
>*Circe*—Jack Kinabrew (owners Eugene Aschaffenberg, A. Leverich)

Invader—Walter C. Keenan, Jr. (owner Robert Todd)

Stars:
Stella—Alfred Tharp, Jr., jr. rear commodore (owner Robert Kuhn)
  —winner
Electra—Al Grevemberg (owner John Longmire)
Dixie—Robert Gaston, Jr., jr. vice-commodore (owner
  Dave Wuescher)
Sparkler II—Chas. de B. Claiborne, Jr. (owner Brennan Cleary)

Snipe:
L. Gagnet
M. P. Heaslip
Wm. Leaumont
A. Pecorara
Robert Zeargain—winner

Fish Class sloops:
Walter Flower—winner
Davis Lee Jahncke
Herbert Jahncke
Thos. C. Kemp
Hartwig Moss
J. W. Smithers, Jr.
George Tessier
Ed. Walker
Caleb Weber, Jr.

The junior race committee appointed Joseph Fornaris, Jr., Jules Humphreys, and Alvin Weinfurter committeemen.

The regatta party after the races was a huge success, with Sidney's Southern Syncopaters entertaining the many dancers until a late hour. The juniors had sponsored other parties during the year. St. Joseph's night had Al Strieman's orchestra, and on Hallowe'en the orchestra of A. J. Peron furnished the music. According to the 1933 junior commodore, M. H. Hogan, the 1933 sailing season was "just great."

Commodore Tessier had also promoted the skipperettes and every Saturday morning during the summer of 1933 could be found the following group of ladies, who later entered into interclub competition with the Gulf Coast skipperettes and brought back many pieces of silverware for the club:

Miss Rowena Duffy	Miss Margie Martinez
Mrs. Gilbert Gray	Miss Yvonne Phillips
Mrs. George Hammett	Miss Sidney Rhodes
Miss Bobby Johnson	Mrs. Herbert Van Horn
Miss Dorothy Johnson	Mrs. Jack Walker
Mrs. Thomas Kemp	Mrs. Dave Wuescher

At the Gulf Yachting Association annual meeting and opening regatta held at Southern in 1933, Commodore Tessier, the genial host, entertained a large group of GYA officials at a luncheon, in addition to the local committeemen for the races.

Owing to the depressed times, only three yacht clubs arrived to participate in the GYA opening regatta. The representatives were Dan Keller, W. L. Parker, R. H. Pringle, and Al Wambagan of the Biloxi Yacht Club; Charles Cottrell of Pensacola; and T. C. Schley and Dudley Selph of the Buccaneer Yacht Club in Mobile.

The GYA regatta held in May 1933 was the last at which Commodore Tessier would serve as SYC's genial host. At the young age of forty-nine, the commodore passed away very suddenly. Members of the SYC felt that the club had lost its rudder and would be floundering for some time. Commodore Tessier's expertise, dedication, and leadership throughout the financially difficult years of the Depression were recognized by the club's board of directors through a resolution adopted and presented to his family, commending him for his many achievements as chief of command during these adverse years.

The Southern Yacht Club not only lost a good member but a very generous benefactor with the passing of Commodore Tessier. He was beloved by all who knew him. Filling his unexpired term until 1934 was Vice-Commodore Leslie P. Beard.

The Lipton Regatta held at the St. Petersburg Yacht Club in 1933 was not without incident. A hurricane came in from the Gulf of Mexico. Although warning had been received, the race was sailed off St. Petersburg's Recreation Pier. The winds blew in hurricane force; all boats were disabled, many capsizing, and crews had to be rescued. Coming through all of it was the veteran skipper from Pensacola, Dave Witherill. He was the only one to finish in the last race of the series. Dave was forever proud of this feat, and to make sure no one else forgot it, he repeated the story many many times at every Lipton Regatta.

CHAPTER XIII

1930-1938

COMMODORES	TERMS
Garner H. Tullis	1934-1936
John Dane	1937-1938

COMMODORE GARNER H. TULLIS—1934-35-36

At the annual meeting of 1934, Garner H. Tullis was elected commodore. He needed no introduction to the members of SYC, having proven himself a valuable administrator in the handling of the club's finances with Commodore Tessier and Crawford Ellis throughout the crucial years of the Depression. Commodore Tullis was a cotton broker and served three terms as president of the New Orleans Cotton Exchange. He was also a member of the New York Yacht Club and the Biloxi, Pass Christian, and St. Petersburg Yacht Clubs. In 1935 he reigned as Rex over the carnival season.

The other flag officers and members of the governing board elected to serve with Commodore Tullis were: John Dane, vice-commodore; O. A. Cotton, rear commodore; L. D. Sampsell, secretary-treasurer; Clarence G. Ferguson, fleet captain; and Dr. Joseph T. Scott, Jr, fleet surgeon. Governing board members were:

Whitney Bouden
Auguste Capdevielle
Stamps Farrar
Charles J. Gambel
J. Monroe Kinabrew

Robert Moore, Jr.
J. Eblen Rau
J. Ben Ravannack
Robert L. Simpson
Bennett Watson
Davis S. Wuescher

Commodore Tullis' active participation in ocean racing events gave him great prestige among yachstmen. He piloted his 58-foot schooner *Windjammer* and 77-foot ketch *Windjammer II* to victories in the St. Petersburg to Havana races, as well as in many other contests. Tullis' other boats included the 21-foot *Circe*, *Mallagar*, and the schooner *Dolphin*, later owned by Eugene A. "Gene" Aschaffenberg.

The opening regatta of 1934 found Lake Pontchartrain crowded with sails, some forty boats of all classes taking part in various events. The *Shellback*, Robert J. Newman's fine schooner recently brought South, made its first official appearance on the lake, competing against the *Windjammer*, Commodore Tullis' slick schooner-yacht. Also participating were the *Dolphin*, owned and sailed by Eugene Aschaffenberg, and Maumus Claverie's *Mallard*, which finished second to the *Windjammer*. Another entry was the *Vagabond*, owned and skippered by Arthur C. Waters.

Other winners were *Robin Hood II* with Beauregard "Bugs" Avegno of SYC at the helm winning over the *Invader*, *Spindrift*, *Circe*, and the *Sis* in the 21-foot cabin class. The *Robin Hood*, skippered by Commodore Edward B. Overton of Mobile, nosed out *Quakeress III*, sailed by Harold Sporl of SYC in the Macaroni-rigged 21-foot class. Dave Wuescher, sailing *Dixie*, won in the Star Class. *Riptide* of R. R. Beasley won in the auxiliary class.

In the catboat class *Mystery*, owned and sailed by Walter C. Keenan, Jr., was the winner. In the Knockabout sloop class *Cinderella*, belonging to John McDonald of Bay St. Louis, won over his neighbor from the Gulfport Yacht Club, Vice-Commodore T. U. Sisson in the yawl class.

THREE YOUNG SAILORS FIGHT
TREACHEROUS LAKE PONTCHARTRAIN

The waters of Lake Pontchartrain can be dangerous to anyone who ventures to cross them. This became evident to three young Southern Yacht Club sailors who set sail from West End to Mandeville—a twenty-four mile journey. Because of its shallow waters, vicious storms quickly erupt on Lake Pontchartrain, and it was during one of these squalls that the three young men in their sloop *Pimpernell* found rough going as the canvas from the cabin was ripped away, forcing them to anchor. The daily *The Times-Picayune* gave this account of the near disaster:

> Night set in, and when they did not return home, their families ob-

tained the services of James R. Wedell, a noted Louisiana flier. After ten trips over the waters in an airplane, the pilot finally located the boys about 12 miles due north of West End—they were just 7 miles off shore headed back to New Orleans when the storm hit. The skipper, Reichard Kahle, with crew George Hopkins and Edward Eustis, were safe but hungry. As told by the skipper, "suddenly the storm hit, the jib and mainsail of our Marconi rigged sloop were ripped loose by the wind before we could lower them so we were forced to drop two anchors and rode out the seas all night. We were pretty hungry, but we had some poor-boy sandwiches along and ate them."

This young skipper, Reichard Kahle, later became a noted New Orleans surgeon. His conquests on the waters of Lake Pontchartrain and the Gulf Coast in his newer yacht, *Corrie*, are too numerous to mention. Dr. Kahle's most important conquest was surviving five heart by-pass operations to live and sail many races thereafter. In 1984 the great Master Skipper called him. His presence in PHRF races is sadly missed by his dedicated crew of many years, who have presented a memorial trophy to the SYC to be sailed for in the PHRF class.

FIRST LONG-DISTANCE RACE FROM BILOXI TO PENSACOLA—1934

Reported *The Times-Picayune*, September 5, 1934: "After the inaugural long distance race from Biloxi to Pensacola got under way on August 30, 1934, the going became pretty rough and the fact that the *Dolphin* was the first and only boat to finish in this race could be attributed to its champion skipper Eugene A. 'Gene' Aschaffenberg and his excellent crew of Robert Hughes, Herbert Van Horn, Sr., Carlos deArmas, Doug Svenson and Eric Hirsch of Memphis, Tenn."

Racing through a terrific storm, "Gene" finished with a "double reefed mainsail and storm jib," ahead of the fleet of six starters: *Shellback* of Robert H. Newman, *Windjammer* of Garner H. Tullis, *Maple Leaf*, belonging to Jack Hyde, *Sea Dream*, owned and sailed by Thomas Burns, and *Silhouette*, owned and skippered by T. Upton Sisson.

The Pensacola News of September 1, 1934 read, "The Dolphin Took It—Like the fish she was named after, battling rough seas, knocked down, she ran like a colt galloping for sheer joy."

The entries in that first long-distance race from Biloxi to Pensacola were:

Dolphin	—	Eugene "Gene" Aschaffenberg, SYC
Windjammer	—	Commodore Garner H. Tullis, SYC
Shellback	—	Robert Newman, SYC
Silhouette	—	T. U. Sisson, vice-commodore, Gulfport Yacht Club
Sea Dream	—	Thomas Burns, Biloxi
Maple Leaf	—	Jack Hyde, Tom and Vic Pringle, Biloxi

At a special meeting held on October 23, 1934, the Southern Yacht Club became incorporated under the title of incorporation by the State of Louisiana.

THE FIRST SUGAR BOWL REGATTA

The first Sugar Bowl Regatta was held in December of 1934, a week before the main attraction of the Sugar Bowl activities, the New Year's Day football game. The winner of this first regatta was SYC's Dave Wuescher, and in 1935 another SYC winner was Alvin Hero.

Commodore Garner H. Tullis was reelected for the year 1935. And for the fifth consecutive year, he entered the St. Petersburg to Havana race but did not win. The commodore's flagship *Windjammer* was also entered in the 1935 long-distance race from Biloxi to Pensacola. From the files of Eugene "Gene" Aschaffenberg, who was also in the race, the following SYC skippers and crews are listed:

Garner H. Tullis—*Windjammer*, crew: Walter Stauffer, Stamps Farrar, Robert Moore, Jr., Malcolm Brown, Franz Hindermann, J. Eblen Rau, Wm. L. Hughes, Jr., John D. Miller

Eugene Aschaffenberg—*Dolphin*, crew: Clarence Elsus, Robert Hughes, Clagget "Tick" Upton, Eric Hirsch of Memphis, Tenn.

Robert J. Newman—*Shellback*, crew: Morris Newman, Larry Larmann, James "Mike" Gibbons, Jay Rauers, Edwin G. Pinac, Walter C. Keenan, Jr., Rage Silverstein, Jeff Steinbardt

The skipperettes were active in 1935, and with their husbands and friends crewing for them, they staged a very successful regatta.

21-foot cabin sloops—Marconi-rigged:
Sorceress II—Miss Cora (Coco) Jahncke—1st
Quakeress III—Miss Alice Anne Kinabrew—2nd
Pimpernel—Miss Laura Fenner—3rd
21-foot cabin sloop—gaff-rigged:

Sia—Catherine Eaves—1st
Robin Hood II—Helen Bastian—2nd
Spendrift—Minna Hopkins—3rd
Invader—Stasia Todd—4th

Stars:
Spray—Mrs. Davis Wuescher—1st
Sparkler II—Mrs. J. B. Cleary—2nd
Jo Jean II—Claire Shadowsky—3rd

Gulf One-Designs:
Chinook—Mrs. Maurice J. Hartson, Jr.—1st
Trade Wind—Laura Lee Martag—2nd
Windflower—Mrs. George Lehleitner—3rd

Fish Class:
Mrs. Herbert Van Horn
Dorothy Dodson
Mrs. Edna Gray
Mrs. Douglas Freret
Edith Harvey
Mrs. Alfred Tharp
Shirley Hollingsworth

Knockabout:
Moonraker—Elizabeth Miller
Eaglet—Elvina Bernard
Willy Nilly—Mrs. P. R. Wheeler

Auxiliary sloops:
Edith—Mrs. Walter Sauer
Cygnet—Mrs. J. C. Baquie
Nepenthe—Mrs. Alvin Hero

Schooners:
Dolphin—Janet Jacobs
Shellback—Aline Elsas

SUGAR BOWL RACE OF CHAMPIONS

A new program was initiated in 1936 when through the efforts of SYC's race committee chairman, Auguste Capdevielle (who was also GYA commodore at the time), an invitation was sent to all GYA yacht clubs to participate in interclub competition in the Sugar Bowl Race of Champions. The entrants consisted of each yacht club's Fish Class champion of the year. This event is the highlight on every yacht club's racing schedule.

The first series in the Race of Champions was won by the Buccaneer Yacht Club of Mobile with skipper Dr. H. J. Walker. Other contestants were the yacht clubs from Biloxi and Gulfport in Mississippi, Fort Worth and Houston in Texas, Southern from New Orleans, and Pensacola and the Pensacola Naval Air Station in Florida. Robert Brodie of Biloxi won in 1937; Dr. H. J. Walker won again in 1938, and the Southern Yacht Club finally had a winner when Carlos J. deArmas sailed in the 1939 challenge. Carlos was also a member of the famous Lipton Cup teams that won for six consecutive years this prestigious trophy.

MANY AMERICA'S CUP SKIPPERS WHO SAILED ON LAKE PONTCHARTRAIN

The Sugar Bowl Regatta has played a prominent part in the sailing world over the years. Many champions, National, International, World, Olympic and of America's Cup fame, have participated with their boats in this annual event as a warm-up for whatever series was to be held either on Lake Pontchartrain or in other parts of the country. (A few sailors of America's Cup fame are Robert N. "Bob" Bavier, Jr., Ted Turner, Emil "Bus" Mosbacher, Jr., John Bertrand, and the coming America's Cup hopeful, John Kolius of Texas.)

Commodore Tullis continued his participation in the annual St. Petersburg to Havana race by entering the 1936 classic—he finished second. There were other competitors in this race from the Southern Yacht Club and Gulf Coast yacht clubs. Eugene Aschaffenberg with his 43-foot schooner *Dolphin*, and Robert J. Newman in his 58-foot schooner, *Shellback* were both from the SYC. H. S. Denniston sailed his 65-foot schooner *Sunshine* from the Mobile Yacht Club; L. M. Harvey of the Pensacola Yacht Club, his 37-foot yawl *Pagan Moon*; and Albert D. Fay of the Houston Yacht Club in Texas, his 44-foot cutter, *Starlight*.

When the *Dolphin* arrived from Havana, the custom agents were eagerly waiting to check the goods abord. According to the manifest covering Gene Aschaffenberg's boat the declared articles were:

Gene Aschaffenberg	—	3 2/5 gal. rum, 25 cigars $17.75
Louis Rand	—	2 cases rum, 25 cigars, perfume 29.00
Arthur Huey	—	4 gals. rum, table cloth, perfume 51.50
W. C. Sinton	—	6 gals. rum, 25 cigars, perfume 33.00
Carlos de Armas	—	6 gals. rum, perfume 54.60

The *Dolphin*'s crew was gratified that the bilge was not checked when the agents looked for rum.

The first yacht to cross the finish line in the 1936 race to win the Mayor of Havana cup was the magnificent *Vamarie* of Vadim Makaroff, the proprietor of the *Vamarie*, who had been an official of the Russian Navy in the time of the Czars, and who was a son of the famour Russian Admiral Makaroff.

The largest yacht taking part in the St. Petersburg to Havana race was the *Azara* of Com. Hugh Matheson. She was one-hundred-twelve feet and came out of Biscayne Bay Yacht Club of Miami. Aboard was Com. L. L. McMasters, organizer of the races in St. Petersburg.

ENTRIES
St. Petersburg–Habana Race
1936

CLASS A

Name	Owner	L.O.A.	Rig	Club
Vamarie	Vadim Makaroff	72'	Staysail Ketch	Oys. Bay
Golacamm	A. Gomez Mena	75'	Schooner	H. Y. C.
Sunshine	H. S. Denniston	65'	Schooner	Mobile
Winsome Too	Harkness Edwards	64'	Staysail Ketch	Long Isl.
Irondequoit	R. G. Jones	61'	Yawl	Chicago
Shellback	Robert J. Newman	58'	Schooner	Southern
Venturer	Ed Spence	58'	Schooner	Clearwtr.
Windjammer	Garner Tullis	57'	Schooner	Southern
Voyager	Arthur Leigh DuPre	54'	Marconi	Jcksnvlle.
San Cristobal	J. W. Pape	52'	Schooner	Ft. Laud.
Water Witch	Leon D. Lewis	49'	Schooner	St. Ptbg.
West Wind	Ken Cowan, Jr.	46'	Ketch	Chicago
Haligonian	L. S. Ruder	45'	Schooner	Clearwtr.

CLASS B

Starlight	Albert D. Fay	44'	Cutter	Houston
Dolphin	Eugene Aschaffenburg	43'	Schooner	Southern
Admate	Theodore Leonard	43'	Schooner	Palmetto
Albatros	Dr. Manuel H. Sordo	42'	Schooner	Habana
Aloha	C. R. Parks	40'	Schooner	Chicago
Artemus	Frank D. Chapman	38'	Yawl	Berlin
Pagan Moon	L. N. Harvey	37'	Schooner	Pensacola
Sea Call	Wm. E. Everitt	34'	Yawl	St. Ptbg.
Duchess	B. C. Davis	32'	Cutter	Tampa
Pieces of 8	Francis C. Bidwell	32'	Sloop	Tampa
Wilma Mae	Henry Phillips	32'	Ketch	St. Ptbg.
Babe	H. M. Matheson	30'	Cutter	Miami

Valarion	Val Kreher	30'	Sloop	Tampa
Game Cock	Wirth Munroe	30'	Cutter	Louisville

In May 1936 the opening regatta of Southern Yacht Club was appropriately described by the *The Times-Picayune* sports writer, Val Flannigan: "A kaleidoscopic panorama showing yachting in all its beauty was present and all its variety in endless shifting patterns was presented on Lake Pontchartrain when the Southern Yacht Club staged its 87th opening regatta.

"The old salts beamed with pleasure as the greatest aggregation of sailing craft ever assembled for an opening day regatta spread their white sails over the windswept waters of the lake off West End. There was evidence aplenty that the sailboat is gaining prestige by leaps and bounds. The competing fleet of 48 boats was viewed by a magnitude of spectators on the club pier and verandas, the seawall and pleasure craft."

THE DEBUT OF THE GULF ONE-DESIGN FLEET

The Gulf One-Design fleet made its appearance on Lake Pontchartrain for its first official race in the opening regatta of 1936. This new class was the first to be adopted by SYC since the Star Class in 1925. It was one of eight classes in the SYC fleet of schooner yachts, 21-foot cabin sloops, International Star Class sloops, Fish Class sloops, Knockabout sloops, Auxiliary sloops and yawls.

The Gulf Ones were not new to local yachtsmen. The first, *Trade Wind*, appeared in 1934, designed by a local naval architect, John A. Prados, brother of SYC skipper, Cliff Prados, who skippered the boat with Al Grevemberg as crew, taking the first prize in the Knockabout sloop class during Biloxi race week in 1936.

When Harold Cornay's *Windward* and Alfred S. Tharp, Jr.'s *Lady Lou*, which was later owned by Gus Lorber, were completed, a movement was started. With four more boats added to the fleet, whose owners were Conrad Berdon and George Lehleitner and co-owners Rear Commodore Davis S. Wuescher, and Maurice J. Hartson, Jr., the Gulf One fleet was approved by the SYC board. Other owners later were Forrest Buchanan and Sandy Davies.

Gulf One-Designs measure 27' 9" overall and 23.6 feet on the waterline. They were designed especially for use in the shallow lake and Gulf waters, carrying spinnakers and balloon jibs. Their cost was $700.

The Olympic winner, Star boat Jupiter II, that brought a gold medal to the Southern Yacht Club.

The Gulf One-Design boats sailed in the first Southern Governors' Race in Biloxi by Governor Hugh White of Mississippi, who won, and Governor Richard W. Leche of Louisiana.

Sailing in the second Southern Governors' Race sponsored by the SYC were seven governors, standing with Admiral Beasley, center, who represented President Roosevelt. From left to right, they are Edward Rivers, Georgia; "Bib" Graves, Alabama; A. B. "Happy" Chandler, Kentucky; Hugh White, Mississippi; Richard W. Leche, Louisiana; Gordon Browning, Tennessee; and James Allred, Texas. Governor White won again.

This class was very popular for thirty-seven years, disbanding in 1973. Each boat carried the name of a type of wind—*Tradewind, Windward, Windflower, Fair Wind, South Wind, East Wind, Windigo, Wind Witch,* and *Whirlwind.*

THE FIRST SOUTHERN GOVERNOR'S SAILBOAT RACE AT BILOXI

The arrival of the fleet of Gulf One-Design boats was timely with the inaugural of the governors' sailboat race on July 4, 1936 during race week on the Gulf Coast and held at the Biloxi Yacht Club. The governors' trophy sailed for by the new Gulf One-Design craft was won in a surprising victory by Ed. Overton of Mobile in the old reliable *Robin Hood IV* over Arthur B. Tipping in *Sorceress II* out of Pass Christian. Overton avenged his defeat in the long-distance race to Biloxi in 1935 when J. Eblen Rau's *Sis* of Southern Yacht Club chalked up an upset victory over the *Robin Hood IV.* There were eighty-five white sails on the waters of Mississippi Sound, which greatly impressed the governor of Mississippi, Hugh White.

At a banquet held in the Elks Club honoring Governor White and visiting yachtsmen, the governor was so impressed that he issued a challenge to the governor of Louisiana, Richard W. Leche, for a match race on the following Labor Day in September 1936. It was suggested that the Gulf One-Design boat be used instead of the club-owned twenty-one-foot Fish Class sloop. And for very good reasons—Governor White was approximately six feet five inches tall and weighed around three hundred pounds, and Governor Leche was approximately six feet four inches tall and weighed around two hundred twenty-five pounds.

For obvious reasons the use of Gulf One-Design boats was approved for the two portly landlubbers. Governor White was the winner of the match race in the *Tradewind* with its owners as crew, Herman Salzar and Cliff Prados of Southern Yacht Club, with Commodore Jack Goodman and Happy Scottswood of the Biloxi Yacht Club to fill the crew list. Governor Leche sailed the *Chinook* with its owners Maurice J. Hartson, Jr. and David S. Wuescher of the Southern Yacht Club, with Commodore Garner H. Tullis and Robert Moore of SYC also assisting as crew. The Mississippian Governor White was the victor in this prestigious first race known as the governors' race.

"Ten thousand spectators watched this gala event from the galleries of the Biloxi Yacht Club as well as from spectator boats and from the shoreline of Mississippi Sound. The crowd was so heavy for the wharfs around the clubhouse that one section fell 15 feet into the water, taking with it Adjutant General John O'Keefe of the Mississippi National Guard in his combination admiral-general uniform. Also, in his Colonel attire, Seymour Weiss, a colonel on the staff of Governor Leche, struck the muddy bottom along with several other men and women in their nautical dress, but after a quick change all were able to be at the starting line," reported a Biloxi newspaper.

This inaugural governors' race was most successful and everyone looked forward to the return race in New Orleans at the Southern Yacht Club, with Governor Richard W. Leche as host and more Southern governors participating.

THE 100th ANNIVERSARY OF THE *PICAYUNE*

The 100th anniversary of the founding of *The Picayune* was celebrated on January 25, 1937. *The Picayune* and its descendant, today's *The Times-Picayune*, is one of the oldest and most outstanding newspaper publications in our country. Its publishers, editors, sports and featurewriters are men and women of high journalistic qualities. Several have been and are members of the Southern Yacht Club and other Gulf Coast yacht clubs—good sailors all. Some have served on the SYC governing board and a few have been made honorary members of the Southern Yacht Club and of the Gulf Yachting Association. All have maintained a high quality of reporting the many sailing events in New Orleans, the Gulf Coast and other parts of the country.

The publicity given by all local news media and those reporters on the Gulf Coast to the various sailing events proved invaluable in revitalizing the sport which had been depressed for so many years. Some of the great sports journalists who covered sailing in the early '20s, '30s, '40s and '50s were Harry Martinez, Wm. McG. Keefe, Val Flannigan, Paul Schrieber, Fred Digby, Clinton Blackwell, Owen Hutchinson, and columnist Hermann P. Deutsch.

DEVELOPMENT OF THE LAKEFRONT

After many storms, West End fell into disrepair. In 1910 a 500-foot seawall was started and completed in 1912 at a cost of $68,255.34. Another contract was awarded the Home Dredging Company in the amount of $45,152 to fill the area some 300 to 400 feet in front of the new seawall by hydraulically dredging 420,000 cubic yards of sand from the lake bed. This project was completed in 1914.

Stretching out into the lake from Robert E. Lee Boulevard, on the east side of the New Basin Canal, were long piers at the end of which were camps. Some of them were well equipped and served as summer homes for New Orleanians. On Saturday nights lively tunes of jazz bands entertaining at parties could be heard floating over the waters of Lake Pontchartrain. The 1915 hurricane destroyed most of these camps. In 1926 the Orleans Levee Board decided to do something about the deplorable condition of these dilapidated structures. Bonds worth some $4,000,000 were issued, which made possible the pumping of the first 36,000,000 cubic yards of hydraulic fill, creating new land from marshes and swamps. This job was completed in 1930.

This was only a part of the major steps taken by the Orleans Levee Board in the early '30s for the protection of the city of New Orleans from the flood waters of Lake Pontchartrain by hurricanes. The most important movement was the building of a seawall which extended for five and a half miles along the lake from West End to the Shushan (New Orleans) airport. The cost was $2,640,000.

This tremendous undertaking required the dredging of the lake bottom, which necessitated the changing of the SYC race course to an outside one and caused the removal of the long pier at the rear of the clubhouse that extended out into the lake. However, the newly created grandstand, the seawall, made it possible for many more spectators to watch the races and to witness the beauty of "red sails in the sunset."

Work on a breakwater was started on the outside of the clubhouse in 1937 by the city and the Works Progress Administration (WPA). Truckload by truckload the old "Silver City" dump was moved to Lake Pontchartrain. With the old dump material the breakwater was shaped to encompass a small-boat pen, about 1200 to 1900 feet north of the Southern Yacht Club. The wall was about 3500 feet. The sides of the wall were riprapped with stone and chunks of concrete, the waste of street rebuilding and demolition. Because the cost of a standard concrete wall would have been prohibitive, this ingenious plan was developed by the chairman of the City Planning Board, Hampton Reynolds. Mr. Reynolds was a reputable engineer with many years experience in levee building. With the cooperation of the Levee Board engineer, Armond Willoz, J. Gilbert Scheib, Orleans Parish Engineer of WPA, and Nat Marks, city engineer, this work was accomplished.

In 1938 the WPA constructed the Municipal Yacht Harbor, which was completed in 1940 and used during World War II for storage of PT boats. (When President John F. Kennedy was serving in the war, he came to New Orleans to pick up the PT boat that was assigned to him.)

One of the main attractions on the lakefront was Pontchartrain Beach, the Coney Island of the South. From 1939 to 1983 Harry Batt, a native New Orleanian, ran this amusement park. It provided many years of fun and laughter with the rides and shows. The writer remembers well many moonlight sailing parties on the lake and remembers watching from the water's edge the extravaganza of firework displays every night. There was also the excitement of seeing daredevil shows, animal acts, acrobats, and "Gamol" the amazing High Diving Horse perform, as well as the beauty pageants, from which groups of girls Miss New Orleans was selected (beautiful Dorothy Lamour of film fame was a product of one such performance). No longer will be heard the shrieking voices as the Zephyr riders zipped up and down and around the curves of one of the largest roller coasters in the country. "The Last Ride" took place on Sunday, September 21, 1983.

COMMODORE JOHN DANE—1937-38

Succeeding Commodore Garner H. Tullis in 1937, after his three-year term in office, was John Dane, a prominent New Orleans businessman well known in yachting circles not only in New Orleans but also on the Gulf Coast. His flagship *Hydro* could be found on the racecourse for every regatta filled with visiting yachtsmen. Commodore and Mrs. Dane were always very hospitable hosts. The commodore owned several fine cabin cruisers in addition to *Hydro*. They were the *Owassa, Chance, Dottie Marie,* and the *Bide-a-Wee*. The last-named boat was the winner of the 1928 West End to Pensacola powerboat race.

During his first year in office, 1937, Commodore Dane was influential in approving the purchase of twelve more Fish Class sloops, to make a total of twenty-four in the SYC fleet. This move increased participation in the club-owned boats so much that each weekend there was a waiting list.

The newly constructed boats were built at the Pullen shipyards in Houma, Louisiana, and towed by the 60-foot yacht of Mr. S. Holloway. My husband and I were invited guests aboard the yacht with Commodore and Mrs. Dane, Leslie P. Beard, SYC secretary-treasurer J. Ben Ravannack, and race committee chairman Auguste and Mrs. Capdevielle.

I remember the trip very well. It was romantic and eventful trailing twelve sloops through the waters of the Intracoastal Canal. The scenery was most picturesque. Passing our boat in his outboard-motored skiff was the mail carrier, delivering the mail to the swampland natives whose homes were on the banks of the canal. Their cheerful waving quickly turned into a warning signal, and when we looked aft we could see a little red light on the last boat wavering hopelessly along the shore a half mile back—six of the boats were adrift. After we captured them, the breakaway recurred a few hours later, making it necessary for us to dock for the night outside the Harvey Canal on the west side of the river. It was too dangerous to enter the swirling eddies of the Mississippi River in the dark.

The night was delightful, with the moon shining overhead, but the gnats and mosquitoes made it a bit uncomfortable. Early the next morning we entered the Mississippi River, apprehensive of the large tugs and ships passing along. We crossed without any mishap into the entrance of the Industrial Canal. After a remarkable display of technology we were lowered by locks to the level of the waters of Lake Pontchartrain. The momentous occasion brought forth photographers from *The Times-Picayune* to take pictures of the event.

RACE WEEK ON THE GULF COAST

A traditional annual event in the history of the Southern Yacht Club and in the Gulf Yachting Association member clubs is race week on the Gulf Coast. This classic was initiated by the SYC race committee chairman, Auguste Capdevielle, in the summer of 1937. All activity begins the weekend of the Fourth of July, and each day of the week there are races held with the Biloxi, Gulfport, Pass Christian and Bay Waveland yacht clubs as competitors on their respective race courses. Most of its popularity was lost in the '70s when the big boats captivated many of the crews for their race from Gulfport to Pensacola.

The exodus to the Mississippi Gulf Coast from New Orleans was phenomenal. The families who did not participate in the long-distance race sailed over in a leisurely fashion or drove. Many remained on their boats for the week; others made reservations at such popular hotels as the Reed in Bay St. Louis, the Miramar at Pass Christian, Edgewater or the Great Southern at Gulfport and at Biloxi, the White House, Biloxi, Tivoli and Riviera Hotels—before motels came along.

The first series of races was always planned at the Biloxi Yacht Club, which is located across from Deer Island and where the Fourth of July was celebrated with a magnificent display of fireworks. On the same night, one could view a panorama of bonfires which lined the beaches of Clermont Harbor, Waveland, Bay St. Louis, then over the old Bay bridge to Henderson Point, Pass Christian, Long Beach, Gulfport, and Biloxi—a dazzling sight.

Preparations for these bonfires were made weeks in advance by children who would gather twigs, branches of trees, and old lumber to assemble a huge Tee-Pee. When the sun set on the beautiful waters of the Sound, the lighted Tee-Pees created a shoreline of flames; around them children held marshmallow and wiener roasts. Another annual sight was that of children holding flares to light their way in ankle-deep water, searching for flounders but careful not to step on a stingaray.

Surprisingly, there were over 100 boats entered during race week in 1937 and over 50 were from Southern. Everyone felt relief from the pressures of life in the city and made this week a true morale-builder.

The debutantes to the fleet were Tom Drennan's *East Wind*, a Gulf-One Design, and George J. Helis' Sound Interclub sloop *Virginia*, to race in the Cutter class. The *Windjammer* was present in all its beauty, and it was reported that there would be a newcomer in the Tullis family—a new boat was on order for the Commodore's daughter Malcolm, "she will name it *Weejammer*," reported *The Times-Picayune*. The foreign entries were:

1. Ed Overton's speedy *Robin Hood* flying the burgees of two clubs, the Buccaneer and Mobile yacht clubs.
2. Dan Ryan's Star class sloop *Dixie* of Houston Yacht Club.
3. Francis Taylor's 32-foot auxiliary sloop *Dixie Girl* of Pensacola Yacht Club.
4. Finley B. "Goat" Hewes in *Maple Leaf* of Gulfport Yacht Club.
5. John McDonald's sloop *Cinderella* of Bay-Waveland Yacht Club.
6. J. C. Wallace's yawl *Manatee* of Pass Christian Yacht Club.

Never a Biloxi Regatta got under way before Finley B. "Goat"

Hewes, commodore and benefactor of the Gulfport Yacht Club, arrived with a dip of the ensign and a three-gun salute. This was a tradition whenever "Goat" was invited to participate in regattas, many of which he won in his beautiful 40-foot sloop *Maple Leaf*.

A familiar picture and beautiful sight on the waters of Lake Pontchartrain and Mississippi Sound during the summer sailing months were the yachts *Betty Ann*, flagship of Commodore Leslie P. Beard, *Hydro*, flagship of Commodore John Dane, *Coo-Coo-Too*, owned by Carl Nussbaum and serving as the official SYC committee boat. Others were the *Cocheco*, Cyprian A. "Junior" Sporl Jr.'s yacht, the *Porte Bonheur* of the Jahncke family with its mother ship *Aunt Dinah*, and the baby boat *Bum boat*. The last three were "hotels on water" for the skippers and crews of several fleets, especially the Star Class. (During the summer months when the Gulfport Yacht Club was washed away by the 1947 hurricane and the Star Class held its Districts, the *Porte Bonheur*, *Cocheco*, *Aunt Dinah*, and *Bum boat* were home for the participants.)

After their return home from the coast in 1937, the SYC skippers engaged the Fort Worth Boat Club of Texas in a team race on Lake Pontchartrain. *The Times-Picayune* reported: "The inland sailors had shown the local tars a thing or two about sailing in last year's races, and they have been smarting over that defeat ever since. So, with SYC's expert sailors, Earl Blouin, Carlos de Armas, Gilbert Gray and William B. Edgar, Jr., after some highly competitive sailing, they defeated the expert team from Texas which consisted of four Georges—George McGowan, George Shoemaker, George Hill and George Armstrong."

The sailing season of 1937 was kept very active with the regattas and parties planned by the juniors and skipperettes. After the Sugar Bowl Regatta, the Carnival Regatta was inaugurated in February, 1937, during the celebration of Mardi Gras in New Orleans. This was a first for the juniors who entered this series of races. Leading the participants were the newly elected officers, Gerald Pratt, jr. commodore; Thomas Avegno, jr. vice-commodore; and George Janvier, jr. rear commodore. The other contestants were:

Philip Benedict	Wm. S. Ferguson
John Capo	Louis B. Graham
James Carbine, Jr.	Robt. Graham
A. P. Claverie	Wm. T. Hardie
David Dabney	C. Ellis Henican

Jules de la Vergne
Thomas B. Denegre
Tommy Earl
Sawyer Labouisse
W. C. Keenan, Jr.
Elmer Kinabrew
Raoul Livaudais
Gus Lorber, Jr.
Chas. Manion
E. L. Marques
J. K. Mayer
Ernest L. McLellan
Sidney L. Menge, Jr.
Robt. Monsted
Geo. P. Hopkins
Ralph Hopkins
Davis Lee Jahncke
J. A. Janin
Dr. H. R. Kahle
Morris Newman
Hugo Phillips
Clif. Prados
E. C. Upton
Geo. Westfeldt
Pat Westfeldt
William Wilkins
J. W. Witherspoon
Samuel Zemurray, Jr.

Following the regatta, the juniors entertained at a supper dance with music by the popular jazz band of "Papa" Celestin.

The skipperettes had a very successful night of entertainment after their 1937 regatta. Hired for their "gay nineties" party was Leslie George and his orchestra. Many accepted the clever invitation sent by the ladies:

> Hustle! Hustle! with top hat and bustle
> To Diamond Jim Brady's big ball. There'll
> Be songs that will charm you, the Floradoras
> Won't harm you,
> Come one, Come many, Come all!

PRESIDENT ROOSEVELT INVITED TO SKIPPER IN GOVERNORS' RACE

Elaborate plans were made for the second Governors' race held on Lake Pontchartrain as part of the Labor Day celebration at Southern Yacht Club in 1937. The event received national publicity because Governor Leche had invited President Roosevelt to participate, in addition to all Southern governors.

With great enthusiasm a committee was appointed composed of Governor Leche, Commodore Garner H. Tullis, and Seymour Weiss, proprietor of the Roosevelt Hotel in New Orleans. Invitations were sent to all Southern governors and a special one was extended to President Franklin Delano Roosevelt.

The president expressed his regrets and stated, "If I did come, it would be as a participant and not as a spectator, as I feel confident I could out-sail any of the 48 governors of these United States." Admiral Charles A. Blakely, a member of the president's cabinet, represented the president, arriving at Shushan Airport the day before the event. The following governors accepted the invitation: A. N. "Happy" Chandler of Kentucky, E. D. Rivers of Georgia, James V. Allred of Texas, Hugh White of Mississippi, Gordon Browning of Tennessee, and Governor "Bib" Graves of Alabama.

Disptaches from Montgomery, Alabama announced that Governor Graves would have as his crew Ed. Overton and Carl Torbert of Mobile and Lieutenant Commander W. O. Baldwin and Colonel W. A. Gayle of Montgomery.

Accompanied by other state officials, Mayor Louis Braun of Biloxi and Commodore George D. Stennis, Jr., of the Biloxi Yacht Club, Governor White arrived at the Southern Yacht Club on board Mississippi's yacht at one o'clock, at which time they were greeted with a twenty-one gun salute from the deck of the U.S. Coast Guard Cutter #302.

Before the regatta, Governor White and his state officials were entertained on board C. A. Sporl's yacht *Cocheco* with Commodore John Dane and other SYC board members, who were the genial hosts for this gala day. The ladies were taken aboard O. A. Cotton's yacht *Ilys*, with Mrs. John Dane and the wives of the SYC board members as hostesses. For viewing the races, all of the wives of the govenors were guests on the Dock Board's yacht *Louisiana*. When all of the governors and their wives reached New Orleans, they were the guests of Governor and Mrs. Leche at a banquet at Antoine's famous French restaurant.

The Times-Picayune reported:

> It was a stirring day on the lakefront and especially in West End Park where band stands were erected for the rest of 500 spectators and distinguished guests. Among them were photographers and newscasters, including the famous sportscaster Ted Husing of the Columbia net-work. There were colorful bands all under the direction of Colonel Castro Carazo, leader of the Louisiana State University band in Baton Rouge, La. They played the National anthem while the American flag was raised on the new flagpole by Admiral Blakely, representing President Roosevelt. [This impressive ceremony was held on the new Southern Yacht Club mole recently made on the landward side of the club.]
>
> Commander Neville Levy of the Naval Reserve acted as liaison officer between the Southern Yacht Club's Patrol boat and the Coast Guard cutters, which were assigned to patrol the race while thousands of spectators watched from boats and from the newly constructed concrete seawall steps along the lakefront. Special speed boats carried newsmen, photographers and broadcasters.

Governor White won the race for the second time, and again in the Gulf One-Design sloop *Tradewind* with the Salzar brothers aboard, Herman and Al. At the banquet held at the Roosevelt Hotel in New Orleans, after the races, in addition to receiving the tin coffee pot as the winner's prize, Governor White was presented with a silver model of the One-Design sloop in which he had sailed. In turn, the Governor presented to Al Salzar the Governor's trophy which he had won in the 1936 Governors' race at Biloxi the previous year.

A tin coffee pot was selected as a permanent trophy for the race to be held in trust for one year by the winning governor, and to be raced for by Governors of the United States every Labor Day. When the trophy was received it was in a velvet-lined case and placed on display in the lobby of the Roosevelt Hotel. Also exhibited was a silver scroll to the winner certifying that one year he had won the tin coffee pot.

Selection of a valueless tin coffee pot as a permanent trophy for one of the most brilliant events in the entire sports calendar was established by the Governors themselves as symbolic of the classical idea of sport for the sake of pure, clean competition, rather than for material awards, just as in the original Olympic Games wherein winners were given wreaths of laurel and bay which had no intrinsic value.

HOUSTON SKIPPERETTE INVADES LIPTON REGATTA

In spite of the financial difficulties that plagued yacht clubs during the post-Depression years, the Lipton regatta continued to be a popular event of the sailing season on Labor Day weekend.

The 1937 Sir Thomas J. Lipton races held at the Mobile Yacht Club were special in that a skipperette appeared on the scene as a member of the Houston Yacht Club Lipton team. "What do we do now?" exclaimed GYA Commodore Auguste Capdevielle and the members of the board. Never had a woman entered the realm of skippers for this prestigious cup. A special meeting was called to decide on the eligibility of a female skipper. Following is the resolution adopted by the board:

> WHEREAS, the Mobile Yacht Club has been informed that the Houston Yacht Club has designated a woman as one of its representatives for the 17th annual Lipton regatta, and
>
> WHEREAS, the Mobile Yacht Club is opposed to women sailing against men, but not against members of their own sex, but,
>
> WHEREAS, the Houston skipperette has travelled hundreds of miles to compete in the present Lipton series,
>
> BE IT RESOLVED further that she be allowed to sail in the present regatta, but,

BE IT RESOLVED that in future regattas for the Lipton Trophy women be barred in the capacities of either helmsmen, crewmen or officials.

It is understood that by the adoption of this resolution a separate skipperette event for women shall not be barred in connection with the regatta.

This incident did not represent an early feminist push. Rather, it concerns the simple story of a teenage girl of 1937 whose sailing skills had measured up to the Lipton team's potential and were acceptable to her yacht club.

It would seem that the Gulf Yachting Association met the unprecedented circumstance with remarkable good humor, hospitality, patience, and self-protection and certainly fair-mindedness. No invasion by women competitors into the Lipton regatta quickly followed, as it was not until the '40s that through the efforts and insight of Gulf Yachting Association's Commodore J. Gilbert Scheib, Mrs. Elizabeth Hughes Freret of SYC won a berth as an alternate on the 1948 Lipton team. The following year Mrs. William H. "Coco" Seemann, Jr. won the right to be a member of the team.

COMMODORE BERNARD "BERNIE" KNOST ALL-GIRL TROPHY

Always an advocate of the so-called weaker sex, who heretofore were permitted occasionally to skipper a boat but needed the masculine sex to crew, Commodore Bernard "Bernie" Knost of the Pass Christian Yacht Club in 1938 (the year he served as commodore) presented a trophy to the Gulf Yachting Association to be sailed for by all-girl crews in interclub competition annually at the Pass Christian Yacht Club. This became a very popular classic and continues to be an annual event.

The first race for the Knost trophy was won by Southern Yacht Club in 1938 with its expert team of skipperettes Mrs. Gilbert T. Gray (Edna), Mrs. J. Carl Baquie (Ruth), and Mrs. Douglas V. Freret (Elizabeth). The other skipperettes were from Gulfport: Yvonne Patrick, Gene Hopkins, Josephine Alfonso, and Marjorie Dee Hopkins. The Pass Christian's top skipperettes were Misses Ann Liversedge, Tut Johnson, and Thelma Demetz.

GERMANY WINS WORLD'S STAR CLASS CHAMPIONSHIP IN SAN DIEGO

A contingent of SYC members attended the 1938 Star Class World championship event in San Diego, California led by Miss Elizabeth Miller and her traveling companion and friend, Miss Mary Virginia Taylor, who was also a professional photographer. In the group were Mr. and Mrs. J. F. A. Lorber, Sr., their son Gus, and the SYC representatives in the series, J. Brennan Cleary, skipper, and his crew, Buddy Cross, with their Star boat *Sparkler III*.

The crew from Germany, Walter von Hutschler, skipper, and Hanse Weise, crew, won the historic World's Star Class championship with the Star boat *Pimm*. Finishing second was Harry Nye of the U.S. with his crew, Barney Lehman, in *Gale*. In the contest, Cleary of SYC placed sixth. This victory by von Hutschler brought the World's Star Class championship event to Europe for the first time in 1939.

THE NEW YORK TRIBUNE SENDS SYC'S ELIZABETH MILLER TO EUROPE

Covering the World's Star Class championship classic in Europe was SYC's Elizabeth Miller. She was sent by *The New York Tribune*. Elizabeth travelled extensively as part journalist, spectator and skipper to all Star Class races. She was a great Star Class enthusiast and the owner of two Star boats in the SYC fleet. With her photographer friend, Mary Virginia Taylor, they made the trip abroad to Kiel, Germany where the 1939 races were held.

Miss Elizabeth Miller was the daughter of a prominent New Orleans surgeon, Dr. C. Jeff Miller. At the age of two, Elizabeth was stricken with polio which left both legs severely crippled. This did not deter her from sailing. She would release her braces, swing her withered legs into the cockpit of her boat and—beware of getting in her way on the starting line!

The following story is about Elizabeth Miller's experience while in Europe, which reflected the trauma of every young man who participated in the races on that fateful day when World War II was declared.

> The big Star Class World's Cup had made its first trip across the Atlantic to be raced for at Kiel, Germany in 1939, as the clouds of war began to gather on the horizon. Once again, it was *Pimm* with von Hutschler as skipper and his crew Hanse Weise the winners of the World's Star

Class Championship Cup. The USA entry was *Wegeforth*, the 1937 champion.

The series was sailed under very trying circumstances. Rumors of war caused a number of entries to withdraw. If it hadn't been for a doubleheader for the last two races, the series never would have finished, as the Holland, British, French and American entries received notices from their consulates to leave for home immediately.

Many stayed to the bitter end. Some of those present were already in uniform. Toasts were drunk with solemn eyes and friends who would in a short time be facing each other on the battle field, parted with unspoken thoughts in their hearts. All foreign Stars reached their home ports safely. The World's championship trophy was salvaged by Walter von Hutshler, otherwise we would never have seen the trophy again.

Miss Miller and Miss Taylor left Germany for New York six hours before the borders were closed, passengers on board the *Bergensfjord* of the Norwegian American Lines. Their ship passed within a few miles of the spot where a day later the *Athenia* was torpedoed and sunk.

Elizabeth and Mary Virginia were assigned a German military escort to cross the German-Danish border. They remained in Copenhagen, Denmark for two days, then boarded a train for Oslo, Norway, and caught a steamer there, leaving just twenty-four hours before England's declaration of war.

FIRST STAR CLASS
SPRING SERIES IN U.S.

Miss Elizabeth Miller had returned from abroad in time to attend the 1939 annual meeting of the International Star Class Association in Havana, Cuba, as a representative of the New Orleans-Gulf Star Class fleet. Rumors had been circulated that because of the dimming interest in the Star Class in Bermuda, where the Spring Series was held in British territory, alternating annually at Nassau, British Bahamas, and at Hamilton, Bermuda, a change to the United States was in the offing.

When the subject matter was brought up for discussion, the "goodwill ambassador of the SYC," Miss Miller, a vivacious, demanding, and aggressive individual, made her usual forceful approach to move the Star Class Spring Series to the United States with the Southern Yacht Club as host, alternating with Nassau each year. Our ambassador won her fight. The event would be held at the SYC on Lake Pontchartrain in March of 1939. (This series continues to be held on alternating basis with the Gulfport Yacht Club, Castro having made it impossible to visit Nassau.)

A reporter for *The New York Tribune*, William H. Taylor, a Pulitzer prizewinner for his articles on the America's Cup races and vice-president and managing editor of *Yachting* magazine, was also there to report on the meeting. Impressed with her salesmanship at the 1939 meeting, he wrote: "Miss Miller has signed Adrian Iselin, Harry Nye, Sam Smith, Bill Picken and Paul Smart of the visiting fleet; Charley de Cardenos, Cuba's outstanding Star skipper, and Commander Miranda who says he is Cuba's youngest (in spirit) Star skipper.

"Also, maybe, Entique Conill of the Paris fleet, and probably others, as she's still on recruiting duty. Just so they can't change their minds once they have agreed to come, she has talked the visitors into giving her their boats as hostages. She will chaperone the fleet back to New Orleans on a steamer, and have them stored in the Southern Yacht Club's boat yard until March 25th when the series starts. If the owners want their boats back, they better go to New Orleans or else." This they did.

Val Flannagan, sports reporter for *The Times-Picayune*, stated in an article on March 12, 1939:

> All eyes are focused on New Orleans and the Southern Yacht Club in anticipation of this historic event—the Spring Series of the Star Class. Heading the list for the championship is Harry Nye's *Gale* of Chicago, the defending champion and last year's 1938 runnerup to the German *Pimm* for the World's Championship at San Diego, California.
>
> Next is Adrian Iselin's *Ace III* from the Western Long Island fleet, twice World's Champion of the Star Class. *Ace* finished on top in the 1934 series in Nassau and in 1935 in Bermuda. Another Western Long Island fleet entry is *Migs* owned by Stanley Turner, Jr., and Paul H. Smart's boat *Melody* from New York, representing the Central Long Island fleet, which just came from winning the 1939 Bacardi Cup in Havana. From Great South Bay, also on Long Island, New York, is coming William Picken, Jr. and his *Fo-Fo*, and Sampson Smith's *Delilah* representing the Lake Otsego Fleet from inland New York. Bill Baxter and crew Lawrence Washburn in *Stormy*, who won the Mid-Winter championship held in San Diego last month, has entered.
>
> Barney Lehman, with crew Jack Streton, in *Solo* is coming. Barney was crowned champion two years straight, 1934 and 1935. Also, he had the honor of having his new boat, which just arrived in New Orleans from Newport, California, christened by a whack of a champagne bottle expertly handled by Miss Elizabeth Miller.
>
> Morris W. Newman, Secretary of the New Orleans-Gulf Star fleet,

announced the Race Committee members for this event: Auguste Capdevielle, Chairman, Garner H. Tullis, J. Gilbert Scheib, Gilbert T. Gray, Leslie P. Beard, J. Eblen Rau, Davis Wuescher, John D. Miller, A. R. "Babe" Roberts, Clarence Ferguson and Edgar Rea. Commodore John Dane is the club's host.

Entries for the Spring Series are expected from Chicago, Long Island, California and all points along the eastern seaboard of North America, South America, Nassau, Cuba and Puerto Rico. The South boasts of fleets from Mobile, which received its charter in 1935, Houston, Florida and New Orleans. The New Orleans fleet has 15 boats and combined with the other entries should equal about 30 participants.

The Spring Series actually consists of two separate events, one a closed affair to two boats from each fleet for the Spring championship, the other is an open series in which all Star Class sloops in the world are eligible to compete. The races are sailed on alternate days.

The Commodore Ernest Lee Jahncke trophy is presented to the winner of the open series. The Spring championship trophy is awarded to the winner of the closed races. The *Windjammer* trophy, which was presented to the Star Class by Commodore Garner H. Tullis in 1941, is awarded to the high point man in both series.

Following is a list of those entries in this historic 1939 International Star Class event:

Boat #	Boat Name	Skipper & Crew	Fleet
254	Spika	George C. Criminale	Mobile Bay
		W. B. Shaw	—
262	Electra	S. W. Labrot, Jr.	N.O.-Gulf
		E. A. Whitehurst	
266	Reverie	Chas. de B. Claiborne	"
		Mrs. Edward B. Jahncke	
423	Tempe III	Edward B. Jahncke	"
		Buddy Cross	
539	Zoa	Elizabeth Miller	"
		Sterling Martin	
562	Rex	Ashton Majeau	"
		Gabe Mouledoux, Jr.	
636	Dixie	Dan Ryan	Houston
		Buster Brown	—
818	Chuckle II	Wm. Rankin, Jr.	N.O.-Gulf
		Sidney Menge, Jr.	
893	Migs	Stanley Turner, Jr.	Western Long
		Robt. Bavier, Jr.	Island
1115	Yankee	Robt. P. Rice	N.O.-Gulf
		Mrs. Robt. P. Rice	
1132	Rebel	Thomas C. Kemp	N.O.-Gulf
		Stewart Mead	

1248	Whistler	Robt. J. Newman E. Aschaffenberg	N.O.-Gulf
1310	Melody	Paul H. Smart Hilary H. Smart	Central Long Island
1459	Sans Souci	Harold D. Sporl Edw. S. Sporl	N.O.-Gulf
1482	Deuce	W. Peck Farley Wm. J. Lee	Lake Ontario American
1488	Maheti	Herbert Van Horn Douglas V. Freret	N.O.-Gulf
1496	Sans Peur	Hartwig Moss II Robert Graham	N.O.-Gulf
1543	Delilah	Sampson Smith Robert W. Brett, Jr.	Lake City
1560	Stormy	C. F. Baxter C. L. Washburn	Newport Harbor
1562	Scout	J. F. A. Lorber, Jr. Edward Leverich	N.O.-Gulf
1563	Gale	Harry G. Nye, Jr. John S. Clifford	Southern Lake Michigan
1670	Nike	Erston Reisch Mrs. Erston Reisch	N.O.-Gulf
1702	Ace II	Adrian Iselin II Major Philip Melville	Western Long Island
1725	Eclair	Earl Blouin Edmond Vallon	N.O.-Gulf
1764	Sparkler III	J. Brennan Cleary Cosby O'Dowd	N.O.-Gulf
1792	Solo	Myron L. Lehman Jack Streeton	Newport Harbor

There were eleven entries from eleven fleets in the Spring Series and twenty-two entries in the Jahncke series. The winner of the Jahncke trophy was C. F. Baxter of Newport Harbor, sailing *Stormy*. In second place was Edward B. "Bud" Jahncke of Southern in *Tempe*. Harry Nye of Chicago in *Gale* placed third.

JAHNCKE WINS STAR CHAMPIONSHIP

The winner of the main event was SYC's own Edward B. "Bud" Jahncke representing the New Orleans-Gulf Star Fleet. With his crew Buddy Cross, "Bud" was the proud winner of the 1939 first Star Class Spring Series championship sailed in the U.S. This great achievement followed a distinguished honor bestowed on "Bud" the previous year, 1938, when he won the Gulf Star Class Lipton Regatta and for his performance merited the Military Order of the World War's Committee for the outstanding seamanship trophy. Rear Admiral R. R. Balknap, USN Retired, made the presentation.

In connection with the Star Class championship races, "Bud" Jahncke was instrumental in getting the ceremonial program off the ground by handling all of the matters concerning the opening procedures. "Bud" was a stickler for protocol; his experience with the flag-raising ceremony is best explained by "Bud" himself:

> It was indeed a matter of protocol to hold flag-raising ceremonies in conjunction with the opening of any great event at the Southern Yacht Club. However, shortly before this series was to take place, a severe storm had blown the flag pole down that had stood before the clubhouse since 1929 when it was presented to the club by Commodore Ernest Lee Jahncke for a similar but more important event, the International Star Class Championship.
>
> There was a mast that had been taken from a ship and placed in the Jahncke Service shipyard. Knowing that it would cost to transfer this mast by barge to the yacht club, I contacted Dick Foster, President of Foster Awing Company, who was in good stead with the Mayor of New Orleans, Robert S. Maestri. A photographer was brought along for good measure and the stage was set for 'His Honor's' picture to be taken presenting a check to the SYC's representative for a flag pole in front of the clubhouse. This brought a check for $500, from the 'good will ambassador' out of the 'Discretionary Fund' of the City.
>
> The sidearms were provided by Captain Neville Levy, President of the Equitable Equipment Company. The stays were secured from Jack Kinabrew, whose father was President of the Southern Supply and Hardware Company, and also the Commodore of Southern Yacht Club. I had gotten Dick Foster to search the attic of his building for flags of all nations and some bunting.
>
> Captain Levy had sent his man to display the flags, then the "Battle of Protocol" began, which was settled in Captain Levy's office with book in hand. It was decided that the burgee of the SYC should fly at the top of the mast and the American flag off the side arm. Finally, the flags of all nations were flown from stays on either side of the mast. The 123-piece Warren Easton High School band played the Star Spangled Banner, and with all hands aboard, the first Star Class Spring Series in New Orleans got under way.
>
> In its usual ceremonious manner, this regatta got off to a flying start by the hoisting of the American flag and the flags of 14 nations, which at that time possessed Star Class fleets; these included Great Britain, France, Germany, Venezuela, Sweden, Italy, Cuba, Japan and China. The speakers for this event were: Ex-Commodore Ernest Lee Jahncke, known as "the Father of the New Orleans-Gulf Star Fleet," the present Commodore John Dane and Thomas C. Kemp, captain of the SYC star fleet.

Mayor Robert S. Maestri, in recognition of his efforts on behalf of the Southern Yacht Club during his years in office, was presented with a parchment scroll and life membership in the Southern Yacht Club by Commodore John Dane, Vice-Commodore Davis S. Wuescher and former Commodore Garner H. Tullis.

CHAPTER XIV

1939-1944

COMMODORES	TERMS
Davis S. Wuescher	1939
Auguste Capdevielle	1940
Garner H. Tullis	1940
Leslie P. Beard	1941-1944

COMMODORE DAVIS S. WUESCHER—1939

At the 1939 SYC annual meeting, Davis S. Wuescher was elected commodore. Dave came into prominence in the early 1900s when he sailed his open sloops *Scamp*, *Sinner*, and *Trouble* to many championships. In 1907 Wuescher represented the SYC in international competition when he piloted the sloop *New Orleans* at Marblehead, Massachusetts, in a contest to represent the U. S. against Germany in the Sonderklasse boats. After winning the first race, Dave lost when his mast broke in the second race, which took him out of the running.

The commodore spent twenty years in the mahogany forests of South and Central America. When he returned to the States in the late '20s he turned to the Star Class. In 1930 he sailed in the Star Class Internationals. He later owned a Lightning, a 21-footer, and won many championship races in the Gulf One-Design class.

Elected with Commodore Wuescher were A. B. Paterson, vice-commodore; Paul F. Jahncke, rear-commodore; Dr. H. R. Kahle, fleet surgeon; C. G. Ferguson, measurer; and W. H. Parham, secretary-treasurer. Board members were: Auguste Capdevielle, William T. Hardie, J. Eblen Rau, Herbert Van Horn, J. Carl Baquie, Garner H. Tullis, John D. Miller, Jr., and John Dane.

The opening regatta of 1939 had a record turn out. The entire fleet of Gulf-One-Designs entered the races:

Cygnet — Carl Baquie
Fairwind — Conrad Berdon
Eastwind — Thomas Brennan
Windward — Harold Cornay
Salt Wind — John Capo
Pepper — Roy Alciatore
Hat — George Sustendal
Tradewind — George H. Sullivan

SECOND LONG-DISTANCE—GULFPORT TO PANAMA CITY, FLA.

The second annual offshore race sponsored by the SYC got off in 1939, starting in Gulfport with the destination the St. Andrews Bay Yacht Club in Panama City, Florida. The grand prize was the handsome $5,000 Peter Lorillard Kent trophy. Also at stake was the Commodore Garner H. Tullis trophy for the cutter class winner. The entries were:

Schooners:
Windjammer—Garner H. Tullis of New Orleans
Stormalong—Wm. Penniman of New Orleans
Sunshine—H. S. Denniston of Mobile, Ala.
Albatross—A. J. Ryan of Chicago, Ill.
Eldes—Mr. Smoot of Biloxi, Miss.
Maple Leaf—Finley B. "Goat" Hewes of Gulfport, Miss.

Cutters:
Salabar—Sylvester W. Labrot of SYC
Pimpernel—Dr. H. Reichard Kahle of SYC
Cygnet—J. Carl Baquie of SYC
Dixie Queen—Jos. Scruggs of Pensacola, Fla.
Dixie Girl—Francis Taylor of Pensacola, Fla.
Banshee—Cyril Pfister and George Groves of Southern

21-foot Cabin Sloop:
Robin Hood—Ed. Overton of Mobile, Ala.

25-foot Auxiliary Sloop:
Patricia—Adele Matthews and George D. Stennis, Jr. of Biloxi, Miss.

FIRST "ROUND THE LAKE" RACE—1939

The first "round the lake" race was held in 1939 and those that won are listed below:

Cutter Class—C. W. McLellan's sloop *Gull*—Sound Interclub.
Schooner Class—ex-Commodore Garner H. Tullis—*Windjammer*
Marconi-rigged 21-foot cabin sloop—William T. Hardie—*Sorceress II*
Gaff-rigged 21 foot cabin sloop—J. Eblen Rau—*Sis*
Star Class sloop—Edward B. Jahncke—*Tempe III*
Gulf One-Design sloop—George Lehleitner—*Windflower*
Fish Class sloop—Charles Manion
Class A. Knockabout—M. Truman Woodward and Dr. Harold Wirth *Eaglet*
Class B. Knockabout—Horace B. Jacob—*Petrel*
Auxiliary sloop—Walter Sauer—*Edith*
Yawl Class—Louis Koerner—*Misognymist*

Another team of champions from the Fort Worth Boat Club in Texas invaded the Southern Yacht Club in 1939, and again the local boys won hands down with their expert crew of Earl Blouin, Gilbert Gray, and Carlos de Armas. The Texas skippers were R. B. Owings, G. Q. McGown, E. P. Walton, George N. Kerby, B. Evans, and Louis and Harris Pruitt.

In 1939 Southern's successful 1938 Lipton team, Earl Blouin, Carlos de Armas, Gilbert Gray and Harry Graham, captained by J. Gilbert Scheib, defended its rights successfully to retain the Lipton Cup for another year. In second place was the St. Petersburg Yacht Club, with the Houston Yacht Club finishing third.

The skipperettes were busy for weeks planning the gala party of the summer months—a premiere showing of the "Star of Hollywood." Henry Dupre, a local professional radio announcer and member of the SYC, announced the celebrities as they arrived and paused before the loudspeaker and bright lights. In costume, flaunting their glittery gowns, with colored feathers adorning their heads and carrying extended cigarette holders were:

Mrs. Carl Baquie	Mrs. Gilbert Gray	Mrs. Robert Newman
Misses Ann and Betty Beard	Miss Shirley Hollingworth	Mrs. Eblen Rau
Misses Dorothy and Rowena Duffy	Mrs. Robert Hughes	Mrs. Robert Rice
	Miss Dorothy Inman	Miss Abbie Ray
Miss Bernice Duncan	Miss Cora Jahncke	Miss Edna Schlegel
Miss Shirley Edgar	Mrs. Ed. Jahncke	Mrs. Herbert Van Horn
Mrs. Douglas Freret	Mrs. Ernest L. Mire	Mrs. Davis Wuescher

After a delicious dinner ($1.35) everyone spent the night dancing to the tune of many popular melodies from the orchestra of Johnny DeDroit.

SYC'S SECOND PATROL BOAT—1939

The second patrol boat was purchased by the SYC in 1939. It was necessary now that the yacht club's pier had been removed. All races were handled from the club's vessel on a course farther into the lake. No more were members and their friends able to watch from the end of the yacht club's pier, where from a small building the race committee sat to start and finish all races.

Toward the end of 1939, the Southern Yacht Club finally got its new boat harbor. The work which had been started in 1937 was now completed and the bulkhead erected around an area of the lake extended from the north end of West End Park out and to the entrance of the New Basin Canal. The cost of the project was estimated at one million dollars. The property owned by the SYC known as the "pen," located behind West End Park where the boats were harbored, was exchanged with the city for space and other property close to the yacht club, where boat slips were provided in the new harbor for SYC owners' vessels and for the SYC patrol boat.

COMMODORE AUGUSTE CAPDEVIELLE—1940

At the annual meeting held in March 1940, Auguste Capdevielle was elected commodore with Edward B. Jahncke, vice-commodore; William T. Hardie, rear commodore; and J. Carl Baquie, secretary-treasurer; Dr. H. Reichard Kahle, fleet surgeon; and Clarence Ferguson, fleet measurer. The governing board members were: Garner H. Tullis, John Dane, George S. Clarke, John D. Miller, Jr., Leslie P. Beard, George W. Healy, Jr., William B. Edgar, and J. Eblen Rau.

Reported *The Times-Picayune* of March 29, 1940: "Capdevielle and Jahncke were very active in yachting here and on the Gulf Coast for many years. The former had been chairman of the SYC Race Committee since 1929, and is at present winding up his three year term as Commodore of the Gulf Yachting Association. Edward B. Jahncke, a prominent Star Class skipper, is captain of the New Orleans-Gulf Star fleet as well as Vice-President of the International Star Class Yacht Racing Association."

In his early days, Capdevielle sailed the well known crafts *Cadillac, Calypso, Susie B.,* and *Olga D.* The latter was named for his spouse, the former Olga Dunbar. He used as his flagship the *Jade*, owned by Charles McLellan, in which the commodore had a part interest. Commodore Capdevielle was the son of New Orleans Mayor Paul Capdevielle, who served as mayor from 1900 to 1904.

After he asumed office, the commodore planned the renewal of the old Southern Marine Marathon. As mentioned before, it was claimed to be the longest power cruiser race held in salt water and the event received acclaim in national yachting journals. The race was conducted annually from West End to Pensacola, Florida, for more than a decade until "honest handicapping became impossible," reported Bill Keefe in the sports news of *The Item*. A revival of this race was inaugurated under the new popular predicted log system.

The commodore selected the following group of active powerboat owners as a committe to handle the revival of these races:

Frank C. Anderson	Dr. Julian Lombard
E. B. Biggs	A. W. McLellan
George J. Delacroix	Charles W. McLellan
Paul Jahncke	A. B. Paterson
Alfred Kaufman	Henry Spang
Stanley M. Lamarie	Dr. William Wagner

Commodore Capdevielle, who had served as the SYC race committee chairman since 1929, was responsible for many innovations. Val Flannigan of *The Times-Picayune* recorded several:

> His first step was to give the skippers more races each year. The SYC was scheduling more races than any other yacht club anywhere. In the early 30s he assigned letters and numbers to the various boats in the racing fleet and made it mandatory that they be displayed on the mainsail, the letter designated the class and the number of the boat.
>
> Another innovation was the adoption of the protest flag. The flag was the means of communication to the race committee that there would be a foul claim made. The Commodore introduced regattas for skipperettes and juniors. He staged the first Mid-Winter regatta ever conducted by the SYC, the Mardi Gras regatta in 1933 and he conceived the "Race of Champions" during the Sugar Bowl regatta in 1936; the Tchefuncte River race and power boat cruise; uniform trophies, simplified race signals and Race Week were also promoted.
>
> When he was Commodore of the Gulf Yachting Association, 1936-1939, Capdevielle recommended suitable prizes be awarded to the individual winners of races in the Lipton series. Previously the winners got no reward other than points toward their team's total. In 1936, the commodore was appointed regional manager of the American Power Boat Association for a seven state territory, Texas, Arkansas, Oklahoma, Louisiana, Mississippi, Alabama and northwest Florida.

A record fleet of 62 boats were on the starting line for the opening regatta of 1940. In charge of the ceremonies were J. Gilbert Scheib and Thomas C. Kemp. The U. S. Coast Guardsmen hoisted the American Ensign, the SYC burgee, followed by colorful long strings of international code signal flags. Stirring martial music was played by Harry Mendelson's band.

COMMODORE CAPDEVIELLE KILLED

A few weeks following the 1940 opening regatta at SYC, came the long-distance race to the Gulf Coast. Over for the big event of race week were Commodore and Mrs. Capdevielle occupying their favorite suite in the Riviera Hotel in Biloxi. The writer had driven Mrs. Capdevielle over while her husband and mine went by water to the coast on the patrol boat.

Commodore Capdevielle was an executive of the Southern Pacific Railroad Line and also a lobbyist for his company. As the Louisiana legislature was in session during the month of July, the commodore's vacation was shortened by having to be in Baton Rouge for Monday morning. On Sunday evening, we were all at the depot to bid farewell to the commodore as he took off by train. Little did we know that this would be our last farewell.

On his trip back home from the capitol city by car, Capdevielle met with a fatal accident just a few miles out of New Orleans on Airline Highway. His injuries caused his death the following day. The driver of the car, Mr. Ray McWilliams, Executive General Agent of the Missouri Lines, was killed instantly, and another passenger was injured.

Although death had robbed "Mr. Cap," as he was often so affectionately called, of directing operations in his most beloved club, the SYC, nevertheless, he was granted his one desire to be commodore of the Southern Yacht Club, if only for six months. His death at the early age of fifty-seven was a shock to everyone at SYC and the yacht clubs along the coast, where he was highly respected.

At a special meeting, Commodore Garner H. Tullis was appointed to succeed the late Commodore Capdevielle for his unexpired term of office. This was Tullis' fourth term as commodore. He had headed the club in 1934, 1935, and 1936.

150th ANNIVERSARY OF
U.S. COAST GUARD REGATTA

The U. S. Coast Guard celebrated its 150th anniversary in 1940. To honor the occasion and in appreciation for the courtesies extended our skippers and for the Coast Guard's watchful eye in times of storms and other emergencies, Commodore Tullis and the SYC board members agreed to hold a regatta to commemorate the founding of this great organization.

A large fleet answered the firing gun for the first half of the regatta; the second half would be the next day for the powerboats. J. Carl Baquie's *Cygnet* won over *Banshee*, sailed by Cyril Pfister, and Dr. H. Reichard Kahle's *Pimpernel*. In the Sound Interclub race, *Intrepid*, sailed by L. A. Girard, won over Rear Commodore William T. Hardie's *Rogue*. In the Star Class, J. F. A. "Gus" Lorber, Jr. in *Scout* got home first over Vice-Commodore Edward B. Jahncke in *Ark* and J. Brennan Cleary's *Sparkler III*.

On the following day, as part of the Coast Guard's anniversary program, the Southern Yacht Club, New Orleans Power Boat Association, and the U. S. Coast Guard Reserve put on a highly successful powerboat regatta. In the thirty-mile race over a course laid out on Lake Pontchartrain, J. M. Porter's motor yacht *Wendy* defeated *Flotil II*, owned by O. J. Litoff, and *Reverie*, owned by R. J. Labrano. Other entrants in this historic race were:

Miss Marion — George Delacroix
Erin IV — E. B. Biggs
Porte Bonheur — Paul Jahncke
Jade — Charles McLellan
Bonne Fortune — A. B. Paterson
Nedra — E. A. Pilsbury

Hasseltine — Henry Dupre
Hussy — Ernest Feinnal
Flomac — T. A. McKinney
Joudee G — J. M. Speed
Shangrila — Dr. William Cain
Marilyn — Dr. William Wagner

Ernest Ziegler's swift racer *Flying Cloud VI* accounted for the free-for-all as well as the twenty-five mile race. Dave Young in *Jitterbug* was best in the 85-horsepower inboards, and *TaTa* with Al Retif at the wheel was first in the 65-horsepower inboards.

The officials were: Henry Spang, S. Y. Hammond, Captain J. Ridcout, George W. Rappelyea, Walter Flower, Norman Hertzer, Commander C. T. Henley, and L. Freeman.

The finest collection of trophies was donated by Dixie Electric Co.,

Auto Parts Corp., Over the Rhine Restaurant, Dixie Machine Welding and Metal Works, Higgins Industries, Bohn Motor Car Co., John M. Walton, Triangle Auto Service, Marcom Boat Works, Acme Radiator Works, Rykoshki, Inc., Marine Oil Co., and N. O. Auto Supply Co.

Commodore Tullis viewed the regatta with many dignitaries and friends on board his new 85-foot motor sailing yacht, *Bonnie Dundee*, which he had recently added to the SYC fleet. This "dream yacht" was one of the most beautifully fitted and modern yachts in the world. Her equipment included fluorescent lighting, air conditioning, oil and gas ranges in the galley, inter-stateroom, ship-to-shore telephone system, and as a cozy touch, a big fireplace in the salon.

The yacht was equipped with electric capstan and winch, including a flexible steel cable to hoist and drop the anchors. The two 165-horsepower auxiliary diesel motors were operated with automatic electric controls. The *Bonnie Dundee* was built to specifications of Clifford D. Mallory of Greenwich, Connecticut, after years of study. The yacht was considered the last word in marine construction of its class. The cost was reported to be upwards of $120,000.

Shortly after the vessel was finished, Commodore Mallory died and Commodore Tullis, after purchasing the *Bonnie Dundee*, sailed down the East Coast from Norfolk around Florida and into the Gulf of Mexico to the SYC harbor. Aboard with the commodore on the trip were Mrs. Tullis, their son, Eli, daughter, Mrs. Laurence Barkley, another daughter, Mrs. Norman Eaves, and Mr. Eaves and Mr. Barkley.

COMMODORE LESLIE P. BEARD—1941-42-43-44

At the annual meeting of 1941 Leslie P. Beard was elected commodore of the Southern Yacht Club, a skipper long familiar to its members as well as those of the yacht clubs on the Gulf Coast. Serving with Beard were: Charles W. McLellan, vie-commodore; Richard G. Jones, rear commodore; and J. Ben Ravannack, secretary-treasurer.

Commodore Beard was a member of the first Lipton Cup team of the SYC in 1920. A born sailor, he knew the waters of Lake Pontchartrain, Mississippi Sound, and the Gulf of Mexico about as well as anyone. He was part-owner with J. Ben Ravannack of the famous *Robin Hood IV*, a 21-footer, which captured more trophies along Southern waters than any boat of her time.

The new commodore was a prominent local attorney. For many years he served as chief counsel of the Gulf Yachting Association and was its president in the years 1942 and 1943. Beard's flagship was a motor yacht, *Betty Ann*, a combination of the names of his two daughters, Betty and Ann. Commodore Beard was slated to serve four successive terms, embracing the awesome war years which followed the blasting of the U. S. fleet by the Japanese at Pearl Harbor on December 7, 1941.

WINDJAMMER TROPHY PRESENTED

At the Spring Series of the Star Class held in New Orleans in 1941, the *Windjammer* trophy was presented by Commodore Garner H. Tullis to be awarded to the high point man in both the Spring Series and the Jahncke Series. This year brought Count Alfred de Marigny of Havana to the event. Harry G. Nye, Jr. of Chicago was the overall winner of both series and thus the first recipient of the *Windjammer* trophy, which was presented by Commodore Tullis personally.

THE FIRST JUNIOR LIPTON CUP REGATTA

The junior program continued to be active since it had been revitalized by John Curren in 1933, and junior regattas became very popular. In 1941 it is reported there were forty boats on the starting line. Curren was a self-appointed ambassador to each yacht club in the GYA. He beat the drums for a regatta no matter where it was staged. Those that did not have a junior program quickly organized one.

Recognizing the increased interest of, and participation by juniors in interclub racing, the Gulf Yachting Association donated in 1941 a beautiful sterling silver bowl and named it the *Junior Lipton Cup* in memory of the "grand old man of yachting," Sir Thomas J. Lipton. (Unlike today, in earlier years only senior members of GYA yacht clubs could participate in the Senior Lipton regattas held on Labor Day weekends.) Now the juniors had a Lipton Cup of their own.

The Buccaneer Yacht Club was selected to host the first Junior Lipton Cup Regatta in 1941. Five clubs participated: Buccaneer, Gulfport, Mobile, Pensacola, and Southern. The Southern Yacht Club won all three races that year with junior skippers William Rudolph, Edward B. Leverich, and Sidney L. Menge, Jr. Southern made a repeat performance in 1942 with skippers Walker Coleman, Charles Justice, Jr., and William Rudolf. After 1942, World War II interrupted this series of races until 1947, with the Biloxi Yacht Club dominating the post-war years.

In addition to the many sailing events, the SYC juniors planned weekly parties and dances to the tempo of the Nickelodeon on "Ye Old College Night," which was every Saturday night, when they could not afford Al Streiman's syncopated jazz dance music. There were also many Badminton tournaments. A special event was put on by the skipperettes and juniors called a "Circus Party"; admission was 55 cents per person.

COMMODORE AUGUSTE CAPDEVIELLE MEMORIAL TROPHY

Another trophy was purchased by the GYA in 1941 named the Commodore Auguste Capdevielle memorial trophy, in memory of Commodore Capdevielle who served the GYA as commodore for six terms. The winning yacht club scoring the highest number of points in scheduled GYA sponsored events over a year's period is the recipient of this trophy.

When the SYC's Lipton Cup team of 1941 sailed at the Houston Yacht Club, it won for the fourth consecutive time, but the victory was accomplished the hard way—a tie. (A rule was later made making it impossible for a series to end in a tie.) The sailoff was with the Mobile Yacht Club, and Gilbert Gray was again the skipper and winner. In addition to Gilbert Gray, the other members of the team were J. Fred Clerc and Carlos de Armas, with crewmen Harry S. Hardin, Jr., William B. Edgar, Jr., James T. Bond, Henry "Hank" Rolling, I. William Ricciuti, and Gilbert's favorite crew, Harry Swain and Alvin J. Weinfurter.

WORLD WAR II DECLARED

Then came the day when the U. S. declared war on Japan, December 7, 1941. As in all previous wars during the club's chronicles, Southern Yacht Club made its personal sacrifice in World War II, its members joining every branch of the military service and several of them giving their lives in defense of their country.

When the war was at its height, the big clubhouse on Lake Pontchartrain was turned over again to the U. S. Government, not as a hospital as in World War I, but as headquarters for both the Navy and the Coast Guard. All motor vessels making up the fleet were placed at the disposal of the Federal Government. (During this period, the Southern Yacht Club had the pleasure of a visit from John F. Kennedy, who came to New Orleans to pick up the PT boat that was later torpedoed while carrying him and landing craft that hit the Normandy beaches on D-day.)

Undaunted by the inconvenience of having no clubhouse, "business as usual" continued with new SYC headquarters set up at 814 Howard Avenue, the office of Jahncke Service Company — the Jahnckes to the rescue again!

The most difficult job within a yacht club is that of the race committee chairman. A casual armchair sailor might be of the uninformed opinion that race committee hassles come with the territory, but, what happens when somebody *moves* the territory? That's what J. Gilbert "Jack" Scheib discovered when he found himself handling the start and finish of the races from the rocks on the edge of the new million-dollar breakwater that had recently been completed.

Code flags were attached to a pole located on the edge of the bulkhead, and large cards were displayed by hand showing the course. It wasn't an easy job, but the races did carry on through the sheer ingenuity of the chairman. After the events, pen in hand, Jack would write the race results and drop them off at *The Times-Picayune* sports desk in downtown New Orleans to meet the nine o'clock deadline for morning news, the war having consumed all sports reporters.

Whenever there was a regatta of consequence, Scheib could rely on many SYC friends, who were most generous with their yachts. His flagship *So-He-Co*, proved invaluable and was in constant use, compliments of its owner, Emmett Smith. The *Coo-Coo-Too*, owned by Carl W. Nussbaum, was the official SYC committee boat for all regattas. Also Edward J. Rowley, Lange W. Allen, and George M. Kellett reponded to many calls by Scheib.

Traveling to the coast by sail or power motor was difficult during the war years and the long-distance races were run with extreme caution. Lights were diminished on shore on the streets and along the docks, while shades were down in homes. The same precaution was taken on the waters. The glow from beacons could be seen no more as the "lighthouse angels" were covered with darkness.

The clubhouse was still in the hands of the Coast Guard in 1942. The regular annual meeting was conducted at 814 Howard Avenue and Leslie P. Beard was reelected commodore with Charles W. McLellan elected vice-commodore, replacing Edward B. Jahncke. Richard G. Jones replaced William T. Hardie as rear commodore and Dr. Henry Macheca took over the duties of Dr. Reichard Kahle as fleet surgeon. Board members were George S. Clarke, Clarence O. Ferguson, Douglas V. Freret, George W. Healy, Jr., Charles J. Tessier, Jr., Lange W. Allen, Conrad Berdon, Stanley Lemarie, and J. Gilbert Scheib.

TRAGEDY STRIKES AT LIPTON CUP REGATTA

With the Navy temporarily housed in the Southern Yacht Club's building during the war years, a sailing event of the magnitude of the Sir Thomas J. Lipton annual regatta required specific organizing by the club's arrangement committees. Therefore, on Labor Day weekend of 1942, it was with sincere gratitude that the SYC accepted permission from the Naval officer in charge to register the race participants in the club's lobby.

It was there that the writer had the pleasure of registering the Mobile Yacht Club Lipton team, which consisted of Commodore Larry Beauvais as skipper and his two sons as crew. They won the first race, which was sailed on Saturday evening, and the Commodore was beaming when he approached me as I extended my hand in congratulations. He stated that he was sorry he would be unable to be at the regatta dance that night as he was too tired from the rigors of the day in the hot sun on Lake Pontchartrain and was returning to the Jung Hotel where he and his two sons were registered.

Because of the occupation by the Navy, the Lipton Regatta party was held in the Tulane Room of the Jung Hotel in downtown New Orleans. While everyone was swinging to the tune of their favorite jazz music, two young men approached my husband and me, inquiring the whereabouts of Commodore Beauvais. We thought they were Mobile yachtsmen and informed them that the commodore was in the Jung Hotel. We will never know if they were the killers of the commodore, who was struck in the head with a glass pitcher and robbed while sleeping in his hotel room about one o'clock the next morning. The mystery is still unsolved.

The usual gaiety that prevails at a Lipton regatta turned into gloom. The Mobile Yacht Club and the Gulf Yachting Association lost a good skipper and a fine gentleman. The remaining part of the regatta was dedicated to Commodore Beauvais. Southern won for the fifth consecutive year. The SYC team consisted of Gilbert Gray, J. Gilbert Scheib, George S. Clarke, and Carlos de Armas.

TRAVELING ON THE ROAD
DURING WORLD WAR II

It was just as difficult to get where you would like to be on the road as it was on the waters of the Gulf during World War II. Saving gasoline stamps for a lengthy trip was the order of the day. If you did travel for pleasure, a sticker on your car's windshield saying, "Is this trip necessary?" helped you to start out with a guilty feeling.

While we were traveling to Pensacola for the Lipton Regatta in 1943, our car had a blow-out. We stopped in Mobile to buy—what else? a second-hand synthetic rubber tire, and we needed a special commercial requisition to get that. Fortunately, we were riding with Carl and Elizabeth Nussbaum. Carl, an electrical contractor, had the necessary voucher; in addition, he always carried with him a set of plans and specifications for a prospective new building somewhere in Florida, in case the law stopped us.

When we reached our destination, the ladies of the Pensacola Yacht Club greeted us with their usual hospitality, coupled with hot coffee and ham sandwiches, which repast was afforded by the generosity of those members who had saved their meat and sugar stamps and sacrificed them for our comfort.

The Southern Yacht Club's 1943 Lipton Cup team won the Lipton trophy for a record-breaking six consecutive years. This record still stands. It was at the Mobile Yacht Club the following year, 1944, that Southern's stronghold on the trophy was broken by the St. Andrews Bay Yacht Club of Panama City, Florida. It was the winner of the four-race series.

Commodore John M. Kinabrew
1926, 1927, 1928, 1929

Commodore Charles A. Tessier
1930, 1931, 1932, 1933

Commodore John Dane
1937, 1938

Commodore Garner H. Tullis
1934, 1935, 1936, 1940

Commodore Davis S. Wuescher
1939

Commodore Auguste Capdevielle
1940

CHAPTER XV

1945–1949

COMMODORES	TERMS
Richard G. Jones	1945–46–47–48
George S. Clark	1949

COMMODORE RICHARD G. JONES— 1945–46–47–48–49

Elected commodore of the Southern Yacht Club for the year 1945 was Richard G. "Dick" Jones. Dick was no stranger to the yachting world. As a skipper he had enjoyed a fine reputation on the Great Lakes before coming to New Orleans from Chicago in 1938 to make his home. Commodore Jones was transferred to the Jackson Brewing Company of New Orleans as the company's vice-president and general manager. He was warmly welcomed and took an active part in business, civic, and social circles in New Orleans.

For eleven years the commodore crewed in annual races to Mackinac Island. He also sailed the 61-foot yawl *Irondequoit* out of Chicago in the 1936 St. Petersburg to Havana race, and he was a member of the Lipton Cup team that raced on Lake Michigan in the sloop *Gossoon*, sailing out of the Chicago Yacht Club.

Elected to serve with Commodore Jones were: Lester F. Alexander, vice-commodore; Leonard K. Nicholson, rear commodore; J. Ben Ravannack, secretary-treasurer; Dr. John B. Gooch, fleet surgeon; Clarence Ferguson, fleet measurer; and Carl W. Nussbaum, fleet captain. The governing committee consisted of men who were a part of the important building committee appointed by the commodore. They were: Lange W. Allen, Leslie P. Beard, F. Evans Farwell, James Gibbons, Stanley Lemarie, Charles McLellan, Thomas F. Regan, and J. Gilbert Scheib.

LIGHTNING CLASS ENTERS SYC FLEET

Despite the disruption wrought by the war to boating activities, the Lightnings arrived in New Orleans as a new class fleet in 1945. J. Eblen Rau and Harold Roberts organized the owners of the craft. The other early owners were Ethan Allen, Joe Meares, Mrs. William Quinn, Harold Bonck, and Ralph Rose.

The Lightning Class Association was founded in 1940. The Lightning sloop was designed by Olin Stephens, one of the finest naval architects, who also designed in collaboration with the Herreshoff family an American Cup defender and other racing and plain yachts. The addition of Lightnings brought many National Lightning Championships to Lake Pontchartrain.

When the SYC ninety-sixth annual regatta was held on July 2, 1945, there were many boats on the starting line and among them were the new Lightnings. They gave to the SYC its second international class fleet, the first being the Star Class added in 1925. In addition to the Lightnings and Stars, the 1945 fleet consisted of Fish Class sloops, 21-footers, Gulf-One Designs and Cutters.

When the ninety-seventh annual regatta was held in 1946, because of the aggressive and constructive leadership of Commodore Jones, the increase in the number of boats participating was most gratifying.

History repeated itself with a refilled prescription for post-war recovery, recreation on the home front. With most of its members back from tours of duty with the armed forces, Southern Yacht Club entered the sailing season prepared to bring the sport of yachtracing back to its former glory on Lake Pontchartrain, where throngs of spectators were treated to an eye-popping afternoon when the opening regatta started.

A splendid spirit of competition developed among club members for places on the team to represent Southern Yacht Club in the annual interclub Fish Class series and for the Sir Thomas J. Lipton trophy. These trials brought out such able skippers as George W. Healy, Jr., James Gibbons, Stanhope Hopkins, Carlos de Armas, Gilbert Gray, Edwin G. Pinac, George S. Clarke, J. Fred Clerc, J. A. Janin, Walker B. Coleman, and Robert Graham.

For the long-distance race from West End to Biloxi in the summer of 1946, Commodore Finley B. "Goat" Hewes of the Gulfport Yacht Club brought his schooner *Maple Leaf* over to the Southern Yacht Club to race with the fleet, particularly to compete against his friend Arthur S. Waters' *Vagabond*. The *Vagabond* won an easy victory. In the Gulf I Class "Rip" Haase in *Chinook* edged Dr. John B. Gooch's *Windflower* to capture the *Tradewind* trophy. Others were Dr. H. Reichard Kahle in *Windsong*, Cliff Prados in *Tradewind*, and Sidney Provensal in *Southwind*. In the Cutter class Dr. John Capo's *Dixie Queen* won over Brooker Duncan II's *Siren II* and David Norman's *Dixie Girl*.

As previously mentioned in the story by Gerald Taylor White, "A Biloxi Regatta," the Star boats sailed in the long-distance races from West End to Biloxi "until they either tore the canvas or spars out of the yachts to reach their objective." After a stormy run to the coast in the 1945 long-distance race, because of hazardous conditions on the waters, the Stars were barred from sailing this long stretch again. Not to be denied, the Stars were trailed over by two very good friends of the fleet, the Jahncke yacht *Porte Bonheur* and J. Paul Treen's *Sweetheart*, so that the boats could participate in the 1946 race week on the coast. The champion in this prestigious event was SYC's Connie Jones, the commodore's daughter, in her Star, *Pagan*. She won over her greatest competitors Richard "Dick" Hadden in *Solo*, and Joseph "Buzzy" Killeen, Jr. in *Urchin*.

The *Sweetheart* was a handsome 60-foot yacht owned by J. Paul Treen, father of Louisiana's Governor Dave Treen. She was built for Past-Commodore Lewis H. Fairchild in 1910 and later bought by A. D. Geoghagen, a SYC member who was the founder of the New Orleans based Wesson Oil Company. The *Sweetheart* was considered one of the most beautiful yachts seen on local waters. Her color was always white and she was a landmark at her dock along the New Basin Canal opposite the New Orleans Country Club on Pontchartrain Blvd.

Mr. Harry Spang, a very active member of the SYC powerboat squadron, was a regular crew on many trips made by Mr. Treen, and he was most helpful in sending me clippings and stories about his experiences on board the *Sweetheart*, one of which I found most interesting. The guests on one of the trips were Peggy Flournoy, a Tulane University great, Ralph Nicholson, owner of *The Item*, Louis Rand, another member of the squadron, Treen's seven-year-old son, Dave, who became the governor of Louisiana in 1980-84, and Roy Alciatore, the proprietor of the famous New Orleans Antoine's restaurant. Because of engine trouble, the crew was delayed for a couple of days, making it necessary for Roy to contact his chef at Antoine's for a new menu to cover the extra days contemplated. From the ship-to-shore 'phone the menu was received, and so all can agree that as fishing trips go, this one had *style!*

At the 1947 annual meeting, friends of the late Lieutenant F. Barlow Duffy of the U.S. Air Corps in World War II presented a trophy to the SYC in memory of their skipper, who had lost his life while serving his country in New Guinea. Duffy owned the *Circe,* and he was very popular in yachting circles. The trophy was dedicated to the 21-foot class. The donors, who had also been Duffy's crew, were Nolfie D. Alfonso, Clarence E. Bonnett, John G. Curren, Walker B. Coleman, Al D. Brady, Jr., David M. Drown, Robert W. Gaston, Jr., Everett J. Molony, Arthur C. Reuter, J. Richard Reuter, and Harry E. Salstrom.

PAN AMERICAN REGATTAS

Commodore Jones' leadership was in keeping with the ideals of the many men who have lead the Southern Yacht Club throughout its history. Yachting has always been a means of assisting materially in the promotion of the true spirit of Pan Americanism, reflecting the friendship we hold for our neighbors to the South. Ever-conscious of New Orleans as a focal trading center to the Latin American nations, the Southern Yacht Club sponsored the Pan American regattas of 1946 and 1947, sharing responsibility with that of the Young Men's Business Club, the American Power Boat Association, and the New Orleans Spring Fiesta.

Swampfire, with Dave Young at the wheel, established a new record in the Class E and D Inboard service runabout race, being timed at 46.643 miles an hour. Another new record was hung up by W. T. S. Critchfield of St. Petersburg, Florida, in the Class E and D racing runabout class when he traveled over Lake Pontchartrain in *Hell's Angel Too* at the rate of 54.979 mph. The regattas were very popular, and each year spectators lined the seawall along Lake Pontchartrain to watch these outstanding events.

The races on Southern's course were won in the Star Class by Cal Hadden, Jr., in *Solo* over Morris Newman's *Cajun* by twenty-two seconds. Gilbert Gray won in the cutter class with *Ibid,* owned by Dr. Eugene Woodward. Cliff Prados at the helm of *Tradewind* was first in the Gulf One-Design fleet. Walter Cooke Keenan sailing *Mystery* took first place in the Lightnings. The cruising event went to *Patricia,* sailed by Clifford Morphy, and the Fish Class winner was James A. Janin.

The Sweetheart, owned by Paul Treen, 1945. Former owners were Commodore Lewis H. Fairchild, 1910, and A. D. Geoghagen, 1938.

This 1938 picture is of the Southern Yacht Club's beautiful clubhouse that was demolished after use by the Navy and Coast Guard during World War II and because of subsidence of the building.

Sir Thomas J. Lipton Trophy, dedicated to the Luder Class in 1946.

In the Pan American Regatta of 1947, all attendance records were shattered by spectators coming out to see the powerboat races held in connection with this regatta. It was estimated that the crowd numbered 25,000 on the first day, with 40,000 spectators lining the shores of Lake Pontchartrain on the second day. (In 1984 all records were shattered again when a crowd estimated at 100,000 witnessed native Al Copeland in his 50-foot Superboat, *Popeye*, break all records at 130.401 mph. Only the great extravaganza of Mardi Gras brings more people into the city of New Orleans.)

ARRIVAL OF THE LUDER CLASS—1946

Growing interest in sailboats was evidenced with the addition of another international class entering the SYC fleet in 1946, the Luders. The first six boats and their owners were:

1. Richard Foster and George Healy, Jr.—*Onda*
2. Harry M. Graham and James "Mike" Gibbons—*Hot Toddy*
3. Boatner Reily, Jr. and John Dicks, Jr.—*Dolphin II*
4. Harold D. Sporl and Edward B. "Bud" Jahncke—*Sybarite*
5. George S. Clarke—*Lagonda*
6. G. Shelby Friedrichs—*Lorelei*

Other owners in the original L-16 fleet included Charles L. Eshleman, Jr., and W. Y. "Gail" deJarnette. In the ninety-eighth opening regatta, the Luders were ready for the starting line. Winning the first race in the new boats was W. Y. "Gail" de Jarnette's *Lagniappe*, with John F. Dicks, Jr.'s *Dolphin II* second and Harold Sporl and Edward B. Jahncke's *Sybarite* third. Later in the year C. A. "Junior" Sporl, Jr. bought into the Luder fleet with his new boat *Ticou*. The winning ways of the two brothers, Harold and "Junior," in the L-16 class in coast regattas won for them a host of trophies.

Before a new fleet is approved by the SYC, as previously mentioned, it must qualify for seaworthiness in the shallow waters of Lake Pontchartrain. In the Luders' first race they were able to give such proof. The regatta got off to a rather slow start as there was not much wind. When the boats rounded the north stake a squall hit the lake. One old-timer on board the committee boat commented, "The old 'sandbagger' skippers would have been in their element with this 55-mile an hour 'breeze.' " Like all squalls, it came with sudden and unexpected fury. Many boats lost their masts and rigging, and motor vessels spent a busy afternoon collecting crews and bringing in capsized boats. The race committee chairman, J. Gilbert Scheib, and his committeemen, Harry Swain, Gordon Gsell and Carl Nussbaum, whose yacht *Coo-Coo-Too* was serving as the committee boat, had their hands full. Throughout all of it, the Luders remained upright, which was the perfect occasion for Chairman Scheib to report to the SYC board that the L-16s were truly seaworthy.

The L-16 Class was most fortunate when the SYC dedicated the recently acquired Sir Thomas J. Lipton trophy to this fleet. By a strange coincidence the Southern Yacht Club had become the owner of a third Lipton trophy in 1944, this one by accident (the other two were personal gifts of Sir Thomas J. Lipton to the SYC and they were sailed for by the Fish Class and the Star Class boats).

It all happened when an SYC member, Milton Adler, was at a New York racetrack and spotted the beautiful Lipton trophy in a case with a saddle, a whip, and a jockey's cap and shirt. After discussing the possibility of buying the cup for the Southern Yacht Club, the track manager agreed to sell it for $500, after arrangements had been made by 'phone with Commodore Leslie P. Beard and J. Gilbert Scheib, who stated they would underwrite the amount. The SYC board approved of the purchase and because the Luders were the latest addition to the SYC fleet, the trophy was dedicated to them.

The juniors, in an effort to return to normal their sailing and partying activities, began the 1947 summer season with a new board. Reactivating the SYC young skippers and skipperettes was Joseph L. "Buzzy" Killeen, who was elected junior commodore, with Herbert Van Horn, vice-commodore; Francis Lejeune, rear commodore; and Miss Connie Jones, secretary-treasurer. G. Shelby Friedrichs, Jr. was made publicity chairman, and George W. Healy, III, chairman of the race committee. (Those were the days when the juniors ran their own races.) The board members were Stewart Morris, Daniel Luke, Lawrence A. Molony, John F. Dicks, and Sellers Meric. There were sufficient monies in Connie's hands to afford the popular "Papa" Celestin and his jazz band with "Sweet Emma" on the piano. (A few years later Connie and Buzzy gave another party—their wedding reception.)

DEMOLITION OF SYC'S 50-YEAR OLD HOME

Commodore Richard G. Jones was reelected in 1948 to serve another term in office. He was faced with the awesome task of ordering the demolition of the Southern Yacht Club's treasured old home. It was during the administration of Commodore Leslie P. Beard in

1947 that the building had been condemned because of subsidence caused by landfill having been placed under the club, which sat on pilings over water. It was not economically feasible to restore this once-beautiful edifice.

No storm, no hurricane, no epidemic, fire, wars, or depressions could equal the 1948 announcement that this monument to the many fine members who had fought hard to save the old building was doomed to fall to the destructive bulldozers. The home that had been erected in 1899 would not be around for its fiftieth birthday in 1949.

The interior of the clubhouse had begun to deteriorate after its use by the Coast Guard and the Navy during World War II. The city's largest and most beautiful dance floor had lost its lustre to the mops of the deckhands. The loveable old porch's screen wire was rusty, ready for some tipsy lad to take a surprise step into low tide.

The building committee appointed by Commodore Jones was composed of many prominent businessmen: Lester Alexander, Cal F. Hadden, Sr., Maurice J. Hartson, Jr., J. Gilbert Scheib, Lange W. Allen, Carl W. Nussbaum, Wallace C. Walker, Carlos de Armas, and J. Benjamin Ravannack. This group of club members spent many long hours diligently studying plans and specifications for the new building, with a very limited budget. They were anxious to have the club ready for the celebration of its one hundredth birthday in 1949.

Orloff Henry was the first architect on the project, and his plans pictured the type of traditional architecture that was hoped for by the members, a design similar to that of the original clubhouse. However, Orloff's bid was rejected and the plans submitted by Freret & Wolf, architects, was accepted—which resulted in the square concrete structure we have today. Haase Construction Company was employed as construction engineers. The cost of the structure was $150,000.

Before the demolition of the clubhouse, the final regatta it would see was held in June of 1948. From the remnants of the old clubhouse porch, the old-time skippers watched with teary eyes the last race they would witness in their favorite cane back rocking chair.

For posterity, the winners of this regatta were Miss Connie Jones, in her Star boat *Pagan*. Bache Whitlock won in the Cutter class with *Salabar*. L. M. Brennan skippered *Eastwind* to victory in the Gulf-One Designs. *Mystery*, with Walter Cooke Keenan, Jr. at the helm, took the Lightning Class trophy. Al Salzar came first in the Knockabout Class sailing *Ellie*, and the Fish Class winner was James

Heaslip, son of ex-commodore Samuel F. Heaslip, a champion of the early 1900s.

There was one bright spot on the horizon—the highlight of the 1948 season—the winning of the St. Petersburg to Havana race by Commodore Garner H. Tullis for the third time. His previous wins were in 1930 and 1932. Again, the commodore sailed in one of his three *Windjammers*.

As the familiar old landmark disappeared, Southern members swapped fond memories of the SYC Saturday night parties, Sunday evening dansants, and buffet suppers. The rugged old clubhouse over open water held memories of lively fraternity rush parties. "Papa" Celestin's great roistering trumpet choruses of "Maryland" had poured out beyond the wave-shaken pier to the vanishing running lights. Lingering hauntingly were the melodious strains of "Stardust" and "Night and Day" as the dancers romanced—the men in their white starched linen suits and the ladies in long evening gowns, white kid gloves and a corsage of sweet scented gardenias.

One freezing cold night a Tulane University dance was held at the old yacht club, the last dance before the club was relinquished to the Navy. The roadway and clubhouse were wrapped in fog, a perpetual wintertime hazard at the lakefront. But inside, giggling co-eds in bare-shouldered formal dresses displayed for each other in the locker room the "pantaloons" they were wearing under several starched petticoats, a trendy fashion comeback during World War II. Not for years would the old walls echo such laughter.

The sentimental old pier was already gone for the construction of a new yacht club harbor. Many a moonlit walk had been taken on her weathered boards, where the high school and college crowd retreated during the intermission of their sorority and fraternity dances and where many a girl maneuvered her date's frat pin.

While the new clubhouse was under construction, a refuge for sailors and their dates for an evening of pleasure, especially after a moonlight sail, was Sail Inn, owned and operated as a lounge by Armond Schroeder, who is the present assistant manager of the SYC. Located just over the bridge that crossed the entrance to the SYC pen on Pontchartrain Boulevard, the lounge was a favorite spot for crews to rendezvous after the Mandeville and the Tchefuncte River races and where protest meetings were held in the back room over many, many glasses of cold Jax beer.

Because of construction work, the annual meeting of 1949 was postponed to late March. However, the members were patient as they wanted to hold this meeting in the new clubhouse.

COMMODORE GEORGE S. CLARKE—1949

Elected as commodore for the anniversary year 1949 was George S. Clarke, another prominent New Orleans businessman. His officers and board members were F. Evans Farwell, vice-commodore; Davis S. Wuescher, rear commodore; J. Ben Ravannack, secretary-treasurer; J. Gilbert Scheib, fleet measurer; and Dr. H. Eugene Woodward, fleet surgeon. The members of the governing committee were: Leslie P. Beard, Harry M. Graham, George H. Ireland, Richard G. Jones, J. M. Kinabrew, Jr., Leonard K. Nicholson, Louis V. Rand, and Herbert W. Van Horn.

Commodore Clarke was a member of seven Lipton Cup teams during the 1940s, winning his race in 1942 and in 1945. He also skippered the cutter *Salabar*, his flagship, in many races and was a charter member of the L-16 Class, owning and sailing *Lagonda* regularly for several seasons.

A vote of thanks was given to Commodore Jones and his building committee members for the excellent work they had performed in having the club ready for the centennial celebration. A large plaque was presented at the meeting, which is displayed at the entrance of the clubhouse honoring those members who so faithfully served on the building committee. The following names are inscribed on it:

SOUTHERN YACHT CLUB
BUILDING COMMITTEE
Ex-Commodore Leslie P. Beard, Chairman
Commodore Richard G. Jones, Ex-Officio Chairman
J. B. Ravannack, Secretary

Lester Alexander	M. J. Hartson, Jr.
Lange W. Allen	C. W. Nussbaum
Carlos de Armas	J. Gilbert Scheib
Cal F. Hadden, Sr.	Wallace C. Walker

The Architects—Freret & Wolf
Haase Construction Co.
1849-1949 100 years

A sentimental gesture was made by several club members who wished to honor the brave SYC skippers who served in World War II. A memorial fund was initiated with the monies dedicated to the building fund for the new clubhouse. The names of the donors are displayed on a plaque in the stairwell of the club. Above the plaque is the following inscription:

> WORLD WAR II MEMORIAL
>
> I know not what course others may take, but for me give me liberty or give me death.
>
> Lieut. Robert S. Hart HSAAF
> Gunnery Sergeant Robert B. Todd USAAF
>
> To those who fought in World War II, we the undersigned have donated a memorial fund to the building of the clubhouse as an eternal memorial to the dead and to the living who came to the aid of their country.

Listed were over a hundred names.

DEDICATION OF THE NEW SYC CLUBHOUSE

In a formal ceremony held on July 21, 1949, one hundred years to the day since the Southern Yacht Club was founded at the Montgomery Hotel in Pass Christian, Mississippi, the newly elected commodore, George S. Clarke, was presented a gold key by Commodore Richard G. Jones with which he opened the glass doors of the new clubhouse. Through them passed many visiting commodores and state and city officials, with hundreds of members and their guests.

Reported *The Times-Picayune*:

> The new club is an imposing building, modern in concept, but designed with maximum attention to the expanse of water and due adherence to that trinity of words "nautical," "social" and "fraternal" holding a haunting memory of those early stalwart sailors' jolly spirits who quaffed many a brimming glass to yachting, the noblest of sports.
>
> Of solid masonry construction, the first floor consists of an entrance lobby, commodious locker rooms and showers for both men and women. The accent was on comfort. An ingenious arrangement enables the second floor, when necessary, to be converted into an auditorium. All space can be screened off, forming a dining room, dance floor and ultramodern bar. An efficient galley serves all areas from this section.
>
> Spacious windows on the second floor of the clubhouse command views in all directions on Lake Pontchartrain, New Basin Canal and the yacht harbor. Concrete sun-breakers, used so successfully in South America, protect rooms from glare by shading glass areas from direct rays of the sun. The sun-breakers, along with an insulated roof and large openings upon all sides, will keep the club rooms airy and cool.
>
> With everything in readiness, all hands standing by, the 100th celebration of the Southern Yacht Club was a notable event in the lives of the

members of this famous organization. As they rejoice and pay homage to those valiant predecessors who banded together at a meeting for the first time at Pass Christian in 1849 and founded the Southern Yacht Club, a feeling of pride comes over them for the great job they have performed over the years—the verdict would be "Well Done."

For posterity, following are the committeemen for the centennial of SYC:

OFFICERS:
George S. Clarke,
 commodore
F. Evans Farwell,
 vice-commodore
Davis S. Wuescher,
 rear commodore
J. Ben Ravannack,
 secretary-treasurer
Dr. John B. Gooch,
 fleet surgeon
G. Shelby Friedrichs,
 fleet measurer

GOVERNING COMM.:
Gilbert T. Gray
Richard G. Jones
J. M. Kinabrew, Jr.
Edwin Pinac
Louis V. Rand
J. Gilbert Scheib
Garner H. Tullis
Arthur Waters

Program Committee
SYC centennial celebration
chairman:
Edward M. Rowley
vice-chairmen:
George W. Healy, Jr.   J. Gilbert Scheib
Joseph L. Killeen, Jr.   Edward J. Thomas, Jr.

Com. Leslie P. Beard
Com. George S. Clark
John M. Cochran
Oliver J. Counce
Carlos J. DeArmas
John F. Dicks, Jr.
Douglas G. Drennan
Charles L. Eshleman, Jr.
F. Evans Farwell
Richard R. Foster
G. Shelby Friedrichs
Charles L. Gambel
James G. Gibbons
Cal F. Hadden
Eldon T. Harvey, Jr.
Arthur L. Herman
Com. Richard G. Jones

J. F. Auguste Lorber, Jr.
Ben A. Martinez
Stewart Maunsell, II
Stewart Morris
Samuel E. Mortimore
Jim T. McMahon, Jr.
Morris W. Newman
Randolph Newman
Herbert O'Donnell, Jr.
Alfred F. Page, Jr.
Thomas A. Parker, II
Sidney W. Provensal, Jr.
Louis Rand
J. Eblen Rau
J. Ben Ravannack
Thomas F. Regan
William B. Reily, Jr.

Walter C. Keenan, Jr.
John M. Kinabrew, Jr.
Com. J. M. Kinabrew, Sr.
Harold G. Legeai, Sr.
Olin Lynn

Dr. Fred L. Reuter
Harold D. Sporl
Com. Garner H. Tullis
Herbert Williams
Barbee Winston

CONTRIBUTORS TO CENTENNIAL BOOK

Adler's
Alcoa Steamship Co.
Alexander Shipyard
American Creosote Works
American Canvas Co.
Avondale Marine Works
Black, Rogers Ins. Co.
Blue Streak Enterprise
Canal Marine Repairs
Canulette Ship Bldg. Co.
Chalmette Laundry
Commander's Palace
Cornay, H. N. Press
D'Antoni, B.S. & Associates
Davis-Wood Lbr. Co.
Delta Line
Donovan Boat Supplies
Elchinger, Chas. F. Co.
Fauria Awning & Shade Co.
Ferran, Chas. & Co.
Fair Grounds Race Track
Gallagher Transfer Co.
George Engine Co.
Great Southern Box Co.
Haase Construction Co.
Harvey Canal Ship Yard
Higgins Industries
D. H. Holmes
Irwin Restaurant,
   2505 Carondelet
Jackson Brewing Co.
Jahncke Service
Labiche's
I. L. Lyons & Co.
Luders Marine Const. Co.
Madison Lbr. Co.
Neeb-Kearney & Co.
Orleans Steel Products Co.
Henri Petetin
Stephens Buick Co.
Standard Supply &
   Hardware Co.
T. Smith & Son Inc.
   Stevedores
Southern Hardware &
   Lbr. Co.
Trade Winds, Inc.
United Fruit Co.
Viking Boat & Cabinet
   Works

    The 1949 L-16 International championship series was awarded to the Southern Yacht Club in conjunction with the centennial jubilee that was to be celebrated during the summer of 1949. The winner was Robert Ziegler of Newport Harbor, California. SYC representative James "Mike" Gibbons was third out of eight competitors. The Chicago Yacht Club had won the Luder championship event in 1948 by one point over SYC.

    Following the L-16 event, the prestigious Sir Thomas J. Lipton Cup regatta was held over the Labor Day weekend. The Gulfport Yacht

Club had won the cup in 1948 but relinquished the holding of these races to the Southern Yacht Club in observance of its centennial jubilee celebration. When the Southern Yacht Club won the Lipton Cup regatta in 1959, it reciprocated and the Gulfport Yacht Club held the races.

"EASTWARD HO!"—1949 CRUISE

One of the finest features of the year 1949 was the "Eastward Ho!" cruise, long in the annals of Gulf Coast yachting and boating an outstanding event for power boatsmen. From a printed program about this cruise, comes this interesting and historical account of a memorable pleasure trip:

> This year's cruise will welcome a fleet of over 100 craft, running from swift 25-footers to majestic and luxurious yachts of the 100-foot type. This year's expectations of over 100 craft will make a record for pleasure cruising not only in the U.S. but in the entire world.
>
> On the eastward swing "port of call" are Biloxi, Gulf Shore, Pensacola, and finally Fort Walton, Florida. Returning to New Orleans, "ports of call" are Pensacola, Fairhope, Alabama, Pascagoula and Gulfport, Mississippi.
>
> There will be evening parties at Gulf Shore, Tower and Silver Beaches, a moonlight cruise on Choctawatchie Bay, fish frys and barbecues in green parks, private estates and selected spots. Fishing contests will be held in unspoiled waters and catches will be measured in terms of hundreds of pounds.
>
> The cruise will be escorted by an 83-foot Coast Guard patrol vessel. The cruise itinerary is planned as: Saturday, depart from West End, moves through Lake Pontchartrain, Lake Borgne and Mississippi Sound to anchor at Biloxi behind Deer Island. Ashore, a shrimp boil and dance will be held at Biloxi Yacht Club. Sunday, through Mississippi Sound, Pass Aud Herons, into and across Mobile Bay entering the Intercoastal Waterway. Cut at Bon Secour and anchoring near Foley Bridge. The Lions Club will then furnish transportation to Alabama Beach (Gulf Shores) where the Guest House will be opened for a dance and beach barbecue. Afternoon and moonlight swimming are featured here.
>
> A late start on Monday moves the boats along the Intracoastal Canal to a rendezvous in Big Lagoon preparatory to sailing into Pensacola Bay in fleet formation and thence to berths in Bayou Chico, one of the Gulf's finest small boat harbors. That evening will be highlighted by a dance, floor show and fish fry on the open beach in front of the Pensacola Yacht Club.
>
> The next morning at nine a short run to rendezvous at Mary Esther and fleet formation to enter the designated docks, moorings and anchorages at Fort Walton, Florida. Fort Waltonians are as fine hosts as

you'll find anywhere. The week's stay includes dances, fishing off the nearby Snapper Banks, swimming in the magnificent surf, steak dinners, watermelon cuttings, surf casts for pompano, fish fries, softball and athletic contests, trolling for mackerel, bonita and ling, angling for snapper, grouper and leatherjack.

A cruise on some of the larger boats to Niceville and Valparaise across beautiful Choctawatchie Bay and return by moonlight, a buffet supper at the Eglin Field Officers Club and an inspection trip to Eglin Air Force Field, where latest designed military aircraft, including jet planes, may be seen in flight, and a demonstration of Guided Missiles with jet fighters in pursuit over the Gulf will be staged.

On the return, Pensacola Yacht Club will be visited again for a dance and the next morning cruise members will take a day's trip on one of the Navy flattops to deep Gulf waters, followed by another dance at the Pensacola Yacht Club.

The following day, the boats cruise through Big Lagoon, Perdido Bay, Wolf Bay and on to the Fairhope Yacht Club on Mobile Bay, where a buffet supper will be served. The next morning early cruising will be across Mobile Bay and into Mississippi Sound to the port of Pascagoula where a dance and shrimp boil will be featured. Access will be had to the famous Ingall's "Longfellow House." Pascagoula is one of the most hospitable places imaginable. It has the "Old South" tradition to a remarkable degree.

An easy cruise down Mississippi Sound brings the boats to Gulfport, where a farewell party will be held on the beach with the members of the Gulfport Yacht Club and their families. The next day's cruise brings the boats of the "Eastward Ho" 1949 cruise home to New Orleans, the participants full of stories and remembrances of two glorious weeks spent along "America's Riviera," the Gulf Coast.

CHAPTER XVI

1950–1955

COMMODORES	TERMS
F. Evans Farwell	1950–1951
G. Shelby Friedrichs	1952–1953
James G. Gibbons	1954–1955

THE FABULOUS FIFTIES

Globally, the fifties were a decade of transition, the progressive strides between World War II and a stable new push-button world. America was preoccupied with space conquest and peacetime creature comforts. If cross-currents were forecasting a generation gap, there was no evidence of it on the shores of Lake Pontchartrain.

The most dramatic gap to be bridged in the fifties was on the Pontchartrain shores, themselves, between a north plaza and a south plaza, with toll booths to collect a dollar for the world's longest bridge over water, the twenty-four mile Lake Pontchartrain Causeway. The erection of this new gateway prevented the continuation of the traditional and very popular Tchefuncte River races.

Southern Yacht Club members were to spend this productive decade in a healthy balance of business and pleasure. The so-called fabulous fifties brought fun and sailing back to a club that had seen its house taken over by the Navy and Coast Guard during World War II and its foundation ruined by man-made fill.

COMMODORE F. EVANS FARWELL—1950–51

For the years 1950 and 1951, the Southern Yacht Club was indeed fortunate to have at the helm F. Evans Farwell as commodore. A member of an old and well-established sugar firm, Milliken & Farwell, Inc., founded in 1857, the new commodore proved to be a forceful and capable leader, fundamentally qualified to handle the difficult problems he faced by inheriting an unfinished building and a very bare treasury. Serving with Commodore Farwell were Arthur C. Waters, vice-commodore; Davis Wuescher, rear commodore; Hampton Gamard, secretary-treasurer; Dr. John B. Gooch, fleet surgeon; and William H. Seemann, Jr., fleet measurer.

Commodore Farwell's flagship was the handsome motor yacht *Pax*. In addition to his promotion of sailboat racing, he was an active member of the SYC Power Boat Division and a director of the Power Boat Association.

Before any programs could be initiated for the pleasure and comfort of the club members, many projects were undertaken. First on the list was a "rock party"—not the swinging kind. The juniors were gathered together under the chairmanship of a governing board member, J. Gilbert Scheib, and presented with shovels, wheelbarrows, and pick axes to dig up the rocks and other debris uncovered when the ground was excavated for the building of the clubhouse. In compensation for their good deed, Commodore Farwell personally distributed sandwiches, Cokes, ribbons, and prizes, which kept the participants busy and smiling in spite of the heat and hard work entailed.

In an effort to revitalize and promote social activities in the club, the gracious and energetic wife of Commodore Farwell, Lynne, organized the first ladies committee of the SYC in 1950, selecting as the first chair-person Mrs. G. Shelby Friedrichs (Virginia).

A "silver tea" gave impetus to plans for decorating the ladies lounge. On the agenda for the SYC governing board meeting was a request that the club grant ten percent of the profits from parties sponsored by the ladies committee. The request was approved and the ladies' lounge reaped the benefits.

The fifties brought many good bands to SYC for its numerous parties. Among the band leaders were Al Strieman, Johnnie DeDroit, and Oscar "Papa" Celestin with "Sweet Emma," the pianist and singer who started with "Papa" in 1923. "Papa" was Oscar Celestin, the trumpeter and venerable New Orleans jazzman who founded the original Tuxedo Brass Band in 1911. One of "Papa's" players was Albert French, who played a tenor banjo which was given to him by Commodore Farwell. French continued the orchestra after "Papa's" death.

On the social calendar were many new ideas. There were "Talent Night," a "Shipwreck party," a "Cruise to the Caribbean" with tropical dances in native costumes "demonstrated by the lovely slim figures of the young daughters of members, Misses Dolly Jordan, Ellen Gambel, Marilyn Bernius, Ginger Friedrichs, Jane Wynne, Elizabeth Hartson, Margaret Robinette, Courtney Gandolfo and Carolyn Gately," reported the monthly newsletter, *Tell-Tale*. Also a "Jitterbug Marathon" was a great success with Suzy Wynne and Jack Scheib out-jitterbugging Pudgy McClure and Molly McArthur for the prize.

Another familiar named band to many New Orleanians is René Louapre's sophisticated orchestra. René was proudly discovered by SYC's entertainment chairman in 1951, J. Gilbert Scheib, when the band was invited to play for the "Welcome Home to the Fleet" party in the summer. Louapre was an instant success and became the favorite for all Sunday thé dansants, Sunday night buffet dances, and the New Year's Eve gala parties. René remains a favorite sophisticated orchestra leader and has a permanent place at the major carnival balls.

The fleet of Fish Class sloops proved to be a lifesaver one more time. It became the financial solution for the club and its members after World War II. Sailboat racing was popular but not many could afford to purchase a boat. With the SYC fleet of twenty-four club owned vessels, many of the skippers took advantage of this opportunity to get the feel of a tiller again. There were long lines of members waiting to obtain one of the sloops for the weekend racing. The problem was solved by the formation of a Fish Class committee, which organized the fleet and proved to be a very successful operation for many years.

The first step taken by the new committee was the formation of three divisions of skippers, "B," "A," and "expert." A beginner was placed in the "B" class and required to win three races to become an "A" skipper. An "A" skipper must win two races to qualify as an "expert." From then on it was every man for himself in the battle to get a berth on the Lipton Cup team.

Only "experts" could qualify for the Lipton team, and the competition was keen against such greats as Earl Blouin, Gilbert Gray, Carlos de Armas, J. A. "Tubby" Janin, Robert Hughes, Ed. Pinac, J. Fred Clerc, Robert Graham, Harry M. Graham, Ferd J. Milhas, Stanhope Hopkins, George Healy, Jr., Cal and Dick Hadden, J. Gilbert Scheib, David Drown, Walker Coleman, with crewmen Harry Swain, Alvin Weinfurter, Wm. "Bill" Ricciuti, Henry "Hank" Rolling, and James T. Bond. This group of hard-nose skippers represented the Southern Yacht Club for over twenty years. Their names are prominent on the many plaques that cover the Sir Thomas J. Lipton wooden shield in the lobby of the yacht club. This masterpiece was designed and built by the late David Drown.

Another problem could have been disruptive to sailing but did not advance that far—the Korean conflict which occurred shortly after Commodore Farwell took office, June 26, 1950. Only a few members were called to duty.

Each yacht club formed a Fish Class Committee and elected its own chairman who automatically became a member of the club's governing board. This position was later dropped and replaced by a Team Captain. There was a Lipton Board of Appeal created of which Leslie P. Beard was chairman for over thirty years. From this committee there was no appeal. This was likewise changed in later years.

Whenever a Lipton Regatta was held, much preparation was made for the event. Everyone had a badge. A huge board was erected by the registration desk on which name badges were pinned with ribbons of every color. Skippers wore red ribbon badges, crews had white, every Commodore carried a light blue while GYA officials wore the royal blue badges. The Chairman of the Board of Appeal was yellow and all of the judges purple. Elaborate programs were distributed, which have been very valuable in my collection of the history of the Southern Yacht Club and the Gulf Yachting Association.

At the annual meeting of 1951 the only change in officers was that of Vice-Commodore Arthur C. Waters. He was replaced by G. Shelby Friedrichs. Waters remained a member of the governing board.

When the yachting season got under way, Commodore Farwell was instrumental in continuing the "Eastward Ho" cruise to Pensacola, Florida, via the intracoastal waterway, which event followed the opening regatta. An account of this cruise was described in the Pensacola News:

> The flotilla of 19 cabin cruisers assembled in full dress in front of the Southern Yacht Club's new swank quarters on Lake Pontchartrain. In command was Harry J. Williams, Jr. of the New Orleans Power Squadron, which sponsored the event.
>
> Escorted by a U. S. Coast Guard cutter, the fleet spent the next few days with other cruisers which joined up at Gulfport, Bay St. Louis, Pass Christian, Fairhope, Biloxi and other points to swell the total to 30.
>
> The cruising yachtsmen were met near the eastern end of Ono Island

in Perdido Bay by Commodore Eugene Taylor of the Pensacola Yacht Club aboard his *Mandalay*, and were escorted to Big Lagoon where other Pensacolians fell in and acted as guard of honor to escort the fleet to the Pensacola Yacht Club.

Members of the cruise were given special privileges by the State Conservation Supervisor, George Vathis, to fish without paying the State's $25.00 non-resident fee.

The skipperettes got into the act during the 1951 sailing season. Every Friday evening the ladies could be found on the lake with an all-girl crew in the club-owned Fish Class sloops competing for their championship. The faithful ones were:

Ruby Billingslea	Flo Mary Scheib
Mrs. Douglas Freret (Elizabeth)	Betty Ann Scheib
	Mrs. John Schilleci (Dottie)
Ginger Friedrichs	Mrs. William Seemann, Jr. (CoCo)
Mrs. Gilbert Gray (Edna)	
Mrs. James Janssen (Dottie)	Harriet Smithers
Florence Jennings	Mrs. Arthur Waters, Jr. (Joy)
Mrs. Thomas Killeen (Alma)	
	Mrs. Davis Wuescher (Nan)

In the Skipperette Regatta, sailing in the various class boats belonging to their husbands, the winners were: Mrs. Ethan Allen (Lydia) in a Lightning, *Lucky*, Mrs. W. E. Hobson, III in Billy Williams' cutter, *Chula*, Mrs. Auguste Lorber, Jr. (Janet), in her Star *Scout*, Miss Elizabeth May in a Luder, *Glendoveer*, Mrs. Sidney Provensal Jr. (Catherine) in a Gulf One-Design, *Southwind*, and Miss Dolores Folse in a Fish Class sloop.

The juniors turned out en masse for their annual 1951 regatta. The winners were: Stars, *Urchin*, sailed by Burt Keenan; Luders, *Standpat*, handled by Danny Killeen; Gulf One-Design, *Southwind*, sailed by Bill Seemann, III; Lightnings, *Chance*, with Charles Gambel, Jr. at the tiller, and in the Fish Class, skipper James Calvert, Jr.

Although the one-sheet SYC newsletters of the early fifties were sketchy, mixed in with the lines of frivolous poetry, card party notices, book reviews, square dancing, juke box Saturday night jamborees, badminton, and other land-lubber entertainment, there was a weathervane predicting future events for Gulf sailors, which chronicled the advent of television to sailboat racing with the report "Commodore Farwell did a splendid job in Video recently with the Sugar Bowl Regatta movies presented by Paul Kalman." Commodore Farwell persuaded Jack Griswold to split the club's newsletter into the *Telltale* and the *Yankee Bo's'n* which he did and performed an excellent job as the *Yankee Bo's'n*. In the early days it was rough trying to keep the newsletters coming owing to the high cost of stamps, paper, and mimeographing, but the publication finally became self-supporting.

Commodore and Mrs. Farwell were great travelers, and on one of their trips the commodore had a bright idea of placing a note in a bottle that someone might find and so notify him if they did. This is what happened to an experiment made by Commodore Farwell after putting over a bottle message from the M. S. *Lindblad Explorer* off the west coast of Nicaragua in May 1976. The bottle was recovered in February 1978 from the beach at Sula, South Island of the Philippines, and his message was returned for a reward. The commodore figured that the bottle travelled approximately 9000 nautical miles in its twenty-two month journey, riding ocean currents south and then west.

At the 1952 annual meeting of the SYC, Commodore Farwell was given a standing ovation for his splendid leadership of a club on a rocky financial foundation, now secure again. His record of increased membership was most rewarding; for the first time the SYC had a waiting list. To the members, the departure of Commodore and Mrs. Farwell left lasting memories of many enjoyable parties not only planned for the club, but also held during race week and during the summer months on the beautifully landscaped grounds of their summer home, "Middlegate," in Pass Christian.

COMMODORE G. SHELBY FRIEDRICHS—
1952–53

Elected commodore of the SYC in 1952 to succeed Commodore Farwell was G. Shelby Friedrichs, (managing) partner of the New Orleans brokerage firm of Howard, Weil, Labouisse, Friedrichs & Company. Serving with the commodore were James "Mike" Gibbons, vice-commodore; William T. Hardie, rear commodore, who was replaced by J. Eblen Rau in 1953; Hampton Gamard, secretary-treasurer; Dr. John B. Gooch, fleet surgeon; and W. Horace Williams, Jr., fleet measurer.

(The Commodore's flagship was a Luder L-16 named *Lorelei*. His second *Lorelei* was an Alden Challenger. Her destruction in 1969 is reminiscent of the tale told about the mythical nymph *Lorelei*. She was a beautiful seductive woman who reclined on a rocky promotory on the Rhine River in Germany and lured boatmen to their doom. In 1969 *Lorelei* met her doom by another vicious woman, *Camille*, the name that was given to the worst hurricane that has hit the Gulf

Coast in this century. In the winds up to 150, some say 200, miles an hour and waves of 20 to 30 feet, *Lorelei* was literally cut into pieces while docked in front of the Levert summer home behind Deer Island in the Biloxi Yacht Club harbor.)

In February 1952 the SYC held the first invitational Mardi Gras Regatta. There were many entries. The most outstanding event was held in the Lightning Class, which was won by Eugene H. "Gene" Walet, III in his Lightning *Spirit II* over the three-time International Lightning Class champion, Walter Swindeman of Toledo, Ohio, and Cliff Prados of Shreveport, Louisiana. Gene was only seventeen years of age. He later became known as the "Whiz Kid" in his rise to the top after winning the Clifford D. Mallory Cup in 1953 for the Men's National Sailing Championship in North America.

ST. PETERSBURG TO HAVANA RACE AND CUBA'S REVOLUTION

An epic event of 1952 was Commodore Garner H. Tullis' *Windjammer II* entry in the nineteenth annual St. Petersburg to Havana race. His attempt at being a four-time winner of this historic race failed when the *Ticonderoga*, a ketch belonging to John Hertz, Jr., of the St. Petersburg Yacht Club, crossed the line in first place.

"A new experience was had in that the majority of the yachts finished during the progress of a revolution in Cuba. General Batista took over the Army, Navy and Police Force, which in turn took over the Presidential Palace and government about 2:00 a.m. on Monday morning," recorded L. L. McMasters, a participant in the race. He continued:

> With the exception of the loss of two police guards, it was a bloodless revolution. However, many soldiers were riding around the city doing a little shooting, mostly in the air. Because of this situation, the committee boat could not fire their usual salute when a yacht crossed the finish line, and our State Department greeted the yachtsmen with the suggestion that they immediately leave Havana, boat, crew and baggage.
>
> The skippers and crews had had enough of the high waves and wind of the Gulf Stream, and preferred to stay right in Havana harbor, tak-

ing their chances on the revolution. Nothing happened, but the party scheduled for Thursday night at the Miramar Yacht Club was cancelled, as was the Bacardi cocktail party on Wednesday. The trophies were given at an informal meeting at the International Yacht Club Tuesday afternoon.

The Coast Guard cutter *Nemesis* and the Air Base did an admirable job of patroling the course until all yachts were accounted for. The *Nemesis* took approximately 50 yachtsmen or friends back to Key West on Monday afternoon at the time when no airplanes were flying. First in fleet was *Carribee* to win the Governor's trophy. Another entry from St. Petersburg Yacht Club was *Malabar XIII*, 2nd in Fleet but 1st in Class "B" for the Commodore Rifley cup.

The following excerpts are taken from a short autobiography of Commodore Garner H. Tullis by Thomas Sancton, journalist, for the SYC *Tell-Tale*. Garner H. Tullis purchased his first beautiful schooner *Windjammer* from a Long Island family and picked up in Norfolk in August 1929. He went on to win the inaugural 1930 St. Petersburg to Havana race in his Class. In 1932 he was the overall champion and returned in 1948 to win this coveted title a third time.

Sancton reported,

> Tullis' scrapbooks and photo albums and his terse log entries are an historical treasure for evoking SYC events and adventures in strange times. How many today remember the rum-runner fleets, the nighttime deliveries along the Gulf Coast beaches and bayous to the men in the cammouflaged trucks and big black limosines. And, the vigilant but futile Coast Guard, the cutters with ominous little one-pounders on deck?
>
> The *Windjammer* was boarded and searched on her first trip out from Norfolk in 1929. And she survived into a period when German subs churned the Gulf like whales, and tankers sank, and oil clogged the beaches, and a warhead exploded in the Mississippi jetties.
>
> Tullis and his crew apparently sighted a torpedo—perhaps underway, or perhaps closely avoided, lying dead in the water; some friends may know, but let us leave it a mystery, as he did. He entered the incident in his log only as "the best torpedo story of the war," and the rest is silence.
>
> But these incidents and the ultimate loan of *Windjammer* and *Southerly* to the military "for the duration," evoke a time in retrospect no less uncanny than the night in 1862 when New Orleans heard Porter and Farragut and thier "bummer" barges blasting the down-river forts with heavy mortar fire.
>
> Reading the *Windjammer* documents, and those of his other yachts is like picking up Robert Louis Stevenson's *Treasure Island* and feeling again the magic of a great story about to begin.

Among the mementoes in the commodore's collection was a 1932 letter from the St. Petersburg Yacht Club that informed Tullis the scheduled race to Havana was still on despite the nationwide closing of banks, but the letter adds dolefully, "Perhaps you'd better load *Windjammer* with cotton bales we can barter in Havana for what we need." Commodore Tullis was a cotton broker and president of the New Orleans Cotton Exchange at that time.

In addition to his *Windjammers* and the *Southerly*, Tullis owned the *Bonnie Doon*, which he had purchased from the estate of NAYRU President and commodore of the New York Yacht Club, Clifford D. Mallory. The *Windjammer III* and the *Southerly* were lent to the military "for the duration" of World War II.

Commodore Tullis was responsible for the founding of the "Tullissippi Cruising Class" which consisted of all those who crewed aboard any of the three *Windjammers*. Each had a burgee, membership card, etc., and only one annual meeting was held at Tullis' estate on the beach in Biloxi. The following invitation was issued by the commodore of this organization, Dr. Charles L. Eshleman, who ordered:

> All members of the "Tullissippi Cruising Club" are hereby ordered by the Commodore to appear at the Club House, 947 East Beach, Biloxi, Mississippi, U. S. A., at 1800 20th July 1957 for a rendezvous of the fleet and members. Refreshments will be served (obviously).
>
> All hands will be called to general quarters at 1900 under the main oak and ceremonies will follow immediately. This is to be followed by dancing, frolicking, tree climbing and what have you. The members who remain standing or sitting, fallen or broken, on the green will be rewarded at 1200 21st. July 1957. At 1400 21st July, the squadron will disband. All members are on their own.
>
> God bless you!

The junior SYC members continued with their infectious enthusiasm. There were many junior boys and skipperette regattas during the 1952 summer sailing season. Those proud juniors who brought home the silver were William H. Seeman, III sailing the Lightning boat *Lucky*; Brian Isaack in *Chinook* took home the Gulf One-Design trophy; J. Gilbert "Jack" Scheib, Jr. won in the Star Class boat *Scout*; Maurice J. "Bubby" Hartson, III won in the Cutter class in *Chula*, and G. Shelby "Buddy" Friedrichs, Jr. was victorious in *Lorelei* in the Luder Class. You will read more about the success of these juniors.

When the skipperettes entered their regatta, as usual, a deluge swamped almost all of the One-Design sloops. "There were many damp curls plastered to streaming faces on that last leg," reported the *Tell-Tale*. Those lucky ones who came through the wind and the rain were, Mrs. Gayle "Gono" de Jarnette in the Star Class; Miss Virginia "Ginger" Friedrichs in the L-16 class; Mrs. William H. Seeman, Jr. (Coco) in a Penguin, and Miss Marilyn Bernius in a

Lightning boat.

At the GYA annual meeting held in Fairhope, Alabama, of paramount interest was the decision of the board to accept other sailing classes in addition to the Fish Class to be sponsored by the Gulf Yachting Association. This action permitted the Lightning, Star, Snipes, and Ravens regattas to be sanctioned GYA events.

This decision altered the limitations on GYA members and numerous other yacht clubs became GYA affiliated, including seven from Texas and possibly Oklahoma. The New Orleans Yacht Club and the Shreveport Yacht Club were admitted as members at the meeting, bringing the total number of yacht clubs on the roster to fourteen.

A beautiful large silver punch bowl was presented to the GYA at the 1952 annual meeting, a gift donated by GYA Commodore Eugene Taylor, commodore of the Pensacola Yacht Club, and dedicated to the popular Lightning Class.

NAYRU PRESIDENT HENRY S. MORGAN
SYC GUEST

Extending the usual hospitality of the Southern Yacht Club to visitors, Commodore Friedrichs welcomed the president of the North American Yacht Racing Union, Henry S. Morgan, who was on a business trip to New Orleans. It was a great pleasure to meet Commodore Morgan when my husband and I were guests on board Commodore Friedrichs' yacht. Mr. Morgan, like his predecessor Commodore Clifford D. Mallory, was responsible for the new approach to sail boat racing rules.

HISTORIES OF NAYRU, MALLORY,
ADAMS AND SEARS TROPHIES

In an effort to stimulate interest in sailboat racing after World War II, the North American Yacht Racing Union, through its President Henry S. Morgan in 1950, proposed a change in the structure of the organization. NAYRU was founded in 1895 and reorganized in 1925 with "the purpose to encourage, promote and unify yachting, racing and rating rules not only in the United States and Canada but throughout the yachting world." These objects and goals have been reached over the years. However, there was a strong need for wider participation in all national championship events.

The members of NAYRU board of directors serving with President

Henry S. Morgan were all prominent yachtsmen of the time: Robert B. F. Barr, J. Amory Jeffries, and Theodore M. Dunlap, vice-presidents; George E. Roosevelt, secretary; Percy Chubb 2nd, treasurer; and Robert N. Bavier, Jr., corresponding secretary, who replaced Commander Ernest Stavey, who also had a major role in the reorganization plans. (Bavier later became president of NAYRU and was also a successful defender in the 1964 America's Cup race.)

A newly reorganized six-man executive committee was formed in 1950. J. Gilbert Scheib, a member of the Southern Yacht Club and also commodore of the Gulf Yachting Association, represented the deep South on this board. The other areas' representatives were Richard Fenton of the Southern California Yachting Association, Stuart Haldorn of the Yacht Racing Association of San Francisco Bay, John R. C. McBeath from Yacht Racing Union of Massachusetts Bay, Robert W. Wayland of Chesapeake Bay Yacht Racing Association, and A. F. Wakefield of the Inter-Lake Yachting Association.

The reorganization plan called for dividing the United States into eight areas. The Gulf Yachting Association was placed in Area 4 with the Texas Yachting Association and the Florida Sailing Association. Commodore Scheib was Area 4's first president; however, he later relinquished this position to Commodore Fred Clark of the Buccaneer Yacht Club in Mobile, Alabama.

At that time there were three NAYRU national championship trophies; the Commodore Clifford D. Mallory Cup for Men; the Mrs. Charles Francis Adams Cup for Women and the Commodore Herbert S. Sears trophy for Juniors. The name of the National Championships of NAYRU was changed by President Morgan to North American Sailing Championships of NAYRU, as Canada was also included. Heretofore, only the East and West Coast yacht clubs had participated in these championship races.

Commodore J. Gilbert Scheib of the executive committee was very vocal about the lack of Southern teams in so-called national championship events. President Morgan was also aware of this problem and steps were taken to change the deed of gifts for the three trophies, making the North American Yacht Racing Union trustee. This was successfully accomplished and the movement revolutionized the One-Design class of boat and promoted wider participation in the sport of sailing in the United States and in Canada for men, women, and juniors.

The Commodore Clifford D. Mallory trophy, a handsome silver soup tureen, carries with it a very interesting story. It was presented to the family of Admiral Lord Nelson by Sultan Selim III, as an expression of his appreciation for the victory of the British fleet over the French at the Battle of the Nile. A symbolic design was placed on the front of the bowl. The ship *San Josef* of eighty guns, captured from the Spanish at St. Vincent, appears on the coat of arms, crest and motto, with a British star on one staff, and on the other side a British lion. The crest is on a wreath over the stern of the *San Josef*. The motto reads: "Palman qui meriut Feratu," meaning "Let him who had deserved the Palm wear it."

When the Mallory Cup was put in competition by NAYRU, the eliminations for this trophy began in local clubs. The winners proceeded to quarter-finals within the association, then on to semi-finals in the association's area, and the finals held in different parts of the U. S. This practice continues today.

The Gulf Yachting Association's representatives in this first event for the Mallory Cup were members of the Buccaneer Yacht Club in Mobile, Alabama: Joe Arns, skipper, Louis Keller and Rudolph Nordman, crew. They made it to the semi-finals but were defeated by the area's team from the Florida Sailing Association which placed third. Florida's fine crew was Edward Nelson, skipper, and Harold Balcom and Charles Morgan, crewmen. The Texas Yachting Association was represented by Commodore Ernest B. Fay of the Texas Corinthian Yacht Club as skipper, with his wife and his brother, Albert B. Fay, as crew. The Florida boys did their best in the finals, which were sailed in Connecticut, but they were not quite the equal of such a skipper as Cornelius "Corny" Shields, who won the first North American Sailing Championship for Men and the Mallory Cup in 1952.

CORNELIUS "CORNY" SHIELDS WINS FIRST MALLORY CUP EVENT

The finals of the first Mallory Cup championship event for men was won by Cornelius "Corny" Shields, with his son Cornelius Shields, Jr. and William LeBoutillier as crew. The races were held on September 6, 1952 off Mystic Seaport, Mystic, Connecticut in Quincy Adams 17s - 26 foot 6 inch keel craft. Commodore Shields was very prominent in yachting circles as a skipper, boat-builder, and author. In 1958 "Corny" was instrumental in winning the America's Cup when he took the helm of *Columbia* in the last stages of the series.

WALET WINS MALLORY CUP EVENT

The finals of the 1953 Mallory Cup event for the Men's North American Sailing Championship took place at the Larchmont Yacht Club in New York. The winner was the "Whiz Kid" from the Southern Yacht Club in New Orleans, Louisiana, Eugene "Gene" H. Walet, III, with his father Eugene H. Walet, Jr., Ralph Christman, and John Ryan as crewmen. Gene was dubbed the "Whiz Kid" because of his quick rise to fame at a very young age by winning local and regional championships. Walet was the youngest skipper ever to win the Mallory Cup—he had turned eighteen, the age limit, just a few days previous to the championship event. His one regret was that he could not compete against the champion, "Corny" Shields, who had failed to make the eliminations in his area.

Not since the winning of the 1932 Olympics by Gilbert Gray and Andrew Libano had the SYC received such exhilarating news as that which came over the 'phone from New York, when voices were heard to say, "We won the National championship!" The sports editor of *The Item*, Wm. "Bill" Keefe, had a headline on his column in the newspaper which read "The South Will Rise Again!"

The champions returned home and received the usual New Orleans welcome. From the New Orleans International airport, their limousine was led by a stream of noisy horn-tooting cars and New Orleans motorcycle policemen. When the motorcade reached Canal Street, a ticker tape parade awaited it.

The victory banquet was held at the Southern Yacht Club. Mayor deLesseps S. Morrison of New Orleans presented the winners honorary citizen certificates and gold keys to the city. SYC Commodore G. Shelby Friedrichs awarded the crew specially designed trophies for their accomplishment. Gene was also given the "Athlete of the Year" award, presented by the New Orleans Athletic Club. This was the first in a long list of championhips to be won by Walet.

Another SYC junior made sailing history in 1953 in Chicago, Illinois when William H. "Bill" Seemann, III, with crew Leonard Isaacks, won the Junior Penguin International championship. Bill placed fourth overall.

The juniors had their election of officers in 1953 and heading their organization were: Allen "Pudgy" McClure, commodore; James L. Smith, vice-commodore, Eugene H. "Gene" Walet III, secretary-treasurer; and completing this brain trust: Wallace Drennan, Roy O'Neil, Mickey Sheehan, James Wadick, Jr., and J. Gilbert Scheib, Jr.

SOUTHERN YACHT CLUB
COMMODORE JAMES G. GIBBONS—1954-55

At the regular annual meeting of 1954, elected to the office of commodore of the SYC was James G. "Mike" Gibbons. Mike was not new to the SYC skippers, as he was a prominent Fish Class skipper and a member of several Lipton SYC teams. He later changed to the Luder Class when it came into being in the SYC fleet, and his flagship was named *Hot Toddy*. The other members of the board were: Clifford D. Morphy, vice-commodore; Charles L. Gambel, rear commodore; Hampton Gamard, secretary-treasurer; Dr. George Sustendal, fleet surgeon, and William H. Seemann, Jr., fleet measurer. A new office was established, fleet captain, and C. A. "Junior" Sporl, Jr. was elected to that position. The governing board members were: Lange W. Allen, Douglas Drennan, G. Shelby Friedrichs, J. Eblen Rau, J. Gilbert Scheib, Bernard S. Shields, Dixon H. Smith, and Wallace C. Walker.

At the annual meeting the members voted to install air conditioning in the club and approved the estimate of $32,000 submitted by Gary Gamble & Associates for a 48-ton unit. Also their blessing was given to the purchase of a television set to be placed in the bar.

MALLORY CUP SERIES HELD ON LAKE PONTCHARTRAIN

The "Whiz Kid," Gene Walet, sailed on to win the 1954 Men's North American Sailing Championship and the Mallory Cup on Lake Pontchartrain in New Orleans. NAYRU selected the SYC to hold the event because of location, plus some persuasion by the SYC member of the NAYRU executive committee, J. Gilbert Scheib, and SYC commodore G. Shelby Friedrichs. There is no defending champion in any of the three national championships. Skippers must qualify each year through eliminations as previously mentioned.

When Walet won the 1954 championship event for the Mallory Cup, he did it with the aid of his very capable crew, which included Allen "Pudgy" McClure, Jr. and Gilbert Frederick, Jr. It was quite a feat to win such a prestigious championship for two consecutive years.

This classic brought the city of New Orleans before the eyes of the nation. The Southern Yacht Club and the city received wide coverage from many newspapers and nautical magazines. The list of visitors to New Orleans for the Mallory Cup event was given in local newspapers. They represented the "Who's Who" of yachting circles:

Robert N. Bavier, Jr., corresponding secretary of NAYRU; Commodore Richard Fenton of Los Angeles, a member of NAYRU's executive committee; the chairman of the Olympic committee of NAYRU, James M. Trenary; William S. Cox of Long Island Sound, New York; Carl Eichenlaub, Jr.; Lowell North of North Sails; William Buchan, Jr. of the Pacific International Yachting Association; and Commodore and Mrs. Karl Smithers of Eggertsville, New York.

Chief judge was J. Gilbert Scheib. His committee consisted of Richard Fenton, Gilbert Gray, and Robert N. Bavier, Jr. Scheib was also general chairman of the regatta with vice-chairman Charles L. Gambel.

Competition was keen in these races, as Gene sailed against the best in the field of champions in North America.

> Yacht Racing Union of Massachusetts Bay
> Yacht Racing Association of Long Island Sound
> Chesapeake Bay Yacht Racing Association
> Lake Yacht Racing Association
> Detroit River Yachting Association
> Yacht Racing Union of Southern California
> Pacific International Yachting Association

Walet's victory was the beginning of a banner year for the SYC sailing teams in 1954.

GYA TEAM ENTERS FIRST ADAMS CUP FINALS

In the inaugural Mrs. Charles Francis Adams Cup event for the North American Women's Sailing Championship in 1954, the team representative of Area 4, the Gulf Yachting Association, and the Southern Yacht Club, consisted of Mrs. William H. Seemann, Jr. (Coco), skipper, Mrs. J. F. A. Lorber, Jr. (Janet), Mrs. J. Fred Clerc (Marion), and Mrs. Louis B. Graham (Dell), crew. To reach the finals, the GYA-SYC skipperettes won the semi-finals hosted by the Houston Yacht Club in Laporte, Texas, where they competed against very strong and capable crews of women from the Texas Yachting Association and the Florida Sailing Association.

The next port of call was the Riverside Yacht Club in Connecticut where the Adams finals were held. The GYA-SYC girls finished a respectable fourth in a field of eight boats. The winner of the first Adams Cup championship was the team from the host club, Riverside: Judy Webb, skipper, Barbara Sheldon, Sandra Gill, and Jill Ayers, crew.

The original women's sailing championship competition was instituted by the Boston Yacht Club in 1924. In 1925 a cup was presented in honor of Mrs. Charles Francis Adams, the daughter of Commodore Clifford D. Mallory, president of NAYRU. The trophy was retired and destroyed in a fire when the American Yacht Club at Rye, New York was burned. It was immediately replaced by Henry S. Morgan, son-in-law of Mrs. Adams, and placed in competition again in 1954 after NAYRU was reorganized.

COMMODORE KNOST TROPHY FOR SOUTHERN WOMEN'S CHAMPIONSHIP

Commodore Bernie Knost of the Pass Christian Yacht Club donated another trophy to skipperettes in 1954 to be known as the Commodore Bernard Knost Trophy for Southern Women's Sailing Championship. It was presented to the first winners who won the semi-finals in the Adams Cup event in Houston in 1954, Mrs. William H. Seeman, Jr., skipper and Mrs. J. G. A. Lorber, Jr., Mrs. J. Fred Clerc, and Mrs. Louis B. Graham, crew.

The new Knost trophy, a beautifully handcrafted silver tureen imported from England, was presented by Commodore Bernie Knost to the GYA commodore, J. Gilbert Scheib, in a special ceremony at the Houston Yacht Club following the Adams Cup event.

Continuing its streak of victories, this same group of skipperettes carried the SYC burgee into the winner's circle at the Pass Christian Yacht Club in 1954 when, after a period of sixteen years, they won the GYA Commodore Bernie Knost all-girl trophy for the most outstanding team in the GYA.

GYA-SYC TEAM ENTERS FIRST JUNIOR-SEARS CUP FINALS

Completing the circle of entries in the three North American Sailing Championship events was another GYA-SYC team of juniors who made it to the finals for the Herbert S. Sears trophy, which represented the championship for juniors in North America. In a hard-fought battle against seven boats in the series, the SYC team of G. Shelby "Buddy" Friedrichs, Jr., with his brother Gore and Jerry McCarthy as crewmen, finished fourth.

SYC IS HOST FOR FIRST PENGUIN INTERNATIONALS

In another first for the Southern Yacht Club in hosting National and International championship events, the Penguin Class Internationals were held on Lake Pontchartrain in 1954. This series was won by SYC junior William H. "Bill" Seemann, III and his crew Robert "Bob" Milling.

In 1951 there were only four Penguins in the SYC harbor. The fleet grew very slowly. It was partly through the efforts of Bill's father, William H. Seemann, Jr. that the Penguin fleet survived. There were many more boats in 1953 and one of the prominent fathers, Walter Flowers, whose son "Chip" was an active Penguin sailor, was elected vice-president of the International Penguin Class. By 1954 there were thirty-three Penguins and things were looking up for the enthusiastic group of young boys and girls at SYC. Along the Gulf Coast the Penguin fleet was becoming popular, which helped interclub competition.

Away from home, Moreland H. "Bill" Hogan's *Tahuna* won the Chicago-Mackinaw race in 1954.

ELIZABETH MILLER ROBIN RECEIVES T. P. LOVING CUP

The SYC's Star Class good-will ambassador, Elizabeth Miller Robin, whose activity in the Star Class was recorded earlier in this book, was also a champion of another cause, the building of the first Children's Hospital in the South.

Conscious of her own plight, having been crippled since childhood by polio, Elizabeth started a program in which she involved several SYC members, to fulfill her life-long ambition to erect a building for the care of invalid children. I was among the several volunteers and was happy to be a part of the three-year struggle to complete such a project. Her dream was realized when the hospital was completed in 1954.

For her unselfish contributions to her fellow men, Elizabeth Miller Robin was recognized and honored in 1954 by her peers and selected as the recipient of the highest civic award given in the city of New Orleans, *The Times-Picayune* Loving Cup. Mrs. Robin passed away in 1962, the victim of cancer, but she will live forever in the memory of those handicapped children who are able to walk today because Elizabeth cared enough to make the first Children's Hospital in the South a reality.

THE FIRST "BARDS OF THE BILGES" BALL

The "fabulous fifties" contributed to the social life of SYC members an annual fling starting in 1955—the "Bards of the Bilge"—which over the years has been set in a diverse collection of interesting waterholes, whatever is pertinent to current events or the imaginative party committee. Costumes and decorations have helped the club's bartenders to transport magically the motley crew to Venetian Canals, mossed-draped bayous, the ancient Nile, a Viking Fjord, the frozen Delaware River, a Tahiti Beach, a dangerous jungle stream, or the polluted New Basin Canal.

With no close second, this very special Mardi Gras Ball, the "Bards of the Bilges," sends the club's most artistic, original invitation of the year to its members. In the interest of history, we now waive a safely guarded secret and enter on the records that the first King Neptune was Commodore James "Mike" Gibbons. (As in the city's other highly respected Carnival organizations, the monarch's identity is not revealed, although instances of jury-rigged costuming and spirited antics of the dukes have been known to unmask His Majesty in mid-tableau.) Neptune's first Queen of the Seven Seas was Miss Virginia "Ginger" Friedrichs. Her maids were Miss Marilyn Bernius, Mrs. Stanley R. Bremermann, Mrs. J. Fred Clerc, Mrs. Oliver Counce, Miss Dollie Jordan, Miss Janice Keller, Miss Arthur Seaver, Jr. and Mrs. Miles Wynne.

The theme of the first ball was "Pirates of the Seven Seas." King Neptune landed by water from the good ship *Patrol*. He was greeted by his loyal subjects who were led by "Papa" Celestin's band, tootin' "When the Saints Go Marching In." Lighting the king's trek with flambeaus across the lawn to the clubhouse was an excited group of pirates called the crew (Krewe), shooting fireworks and exploding aerial bombs, while the guests (only wives and/or girlfriends of members could be guests) looked on from the upper deck in their lovely evening gowns. The ball is always a formal affair for the ladies, while the men costume and mask themselves beyond recognition.

The 1955 crew filed topside and did a rather noisy snake dance. They were followed on the dancefloor by wildly costumed dukes who led the queen and her maids to the throne. There was a conglomeration of pirates, sea captains, old salts, and colonial seamen. There were even three Pensacola Sea Buoys, all lit (electrically and otherwise). One of the best was "Home Stake."

Gene Walet sailing his Lightning Spirit I with crewmen Allen "Pudgy" McClure and Gilbert Frederick, Jr.

The Lipton Tea Company presented this beautiful trophy in memory of its founder, Sir Thomas J. Lipton, to the Gulf Yachting Association in 1953, with the SYC as trustee.

RACE WEEK ON THE GULF COAST IN 1955

In 1955 the long-distance race from New Orleans to Biloxi for race week saw the largest turnout in many years. Robert "Bobby" Normann's *Dixie Girl* led the fleet of thirty-five boats over the finish line in eleven and a half hours to set a new record for the seventy-one nautical miles. The first boat in the Gulf-One Design fleet to win on corrected time was *East Wind*, skippered by Tom Brennan. Second on corrected time was Sidney Provensal's *South Wind*, and third was *Gulf Wind*, with Charles Cary at the tiller. Two other SYC yachts participating in the race were the *Tahuna*, owned and skippered by Moreland H. "Bill" Hogan with his son, Kelly Hogan, Claude Hogan (his brother), George Mattix, Charles L. Eshleman, Jr., G. Arthur Seaver, Jr., and Thomas Parker, II as crew, and the *Vagabond* with its owner, Arthur C. Waters, as skipper and his sons Arthur Waters Jr. and H. Harcourt Waters as crew, with extra muscle-power from George J. and L. Griswold, Stewart Maunsell, II, and Frederich Miller.

After the race to the coast, the next highlight of the holiday week was the annual Gulfport to Pensacola Ocean race, which is the piece de resistance. The usual hospitality was shown by the members of the Pensacola Yacht Club when the boats arrived. There was a shipwreck party for the skippers and their families. Mrs. John Meredith, editor of the Pensacola Yacht Club *Jib Sheet*, reported: "Down for the event were Mr. and Mrs. J. Gilbert Scheib of SYC with their son and skipper Jack, Jr., Warren Whaley, Dolores Folse, William Cahill, Elmo Fischer, Amelia Riers, Braser Finley, Clay Talbot, "Rip" Haase, Bobby Normann, Flo Mary and Betty Ann Scheib with Janice Keller, who proved a favorite with everyone as she swung into a Latin dance with Mr. Ignacia Izaguire, whose papa heads the A. Y. C. Lines in Havana, and who is employed with Jack Merritt."

It was a rip-roaring good time on the coast in the summer of 1955.

LIGHTNING INTERNATIONALS AT SYC

The highlight of events on Lake Pontchartrain in the summer of 1955 was the Lightning International championship and the President's Cup Regatta. The fleet had grown from a handful of boats when the Lightning Class was founded in 1945, to twenty boats in 1955. During those years Gene Walet with his Lightnings, *Spirit I, II,* and *III*, won many championships and was instrumental in bringing the Lightnings Internationals to the Southern Yacht Club.

As usual, the SYC put out the red carpet and proceeded with extensive plans for the entertainment and pleasure of the many hundreds of guests and participants who arrived for a week of sailing.

When *The States* sports editor, Bill Keefe, wrote about the international races, he headed his column, "The Spirit of '55. An All American Field of Lightning champions will be seen on Lake Pontchartrain." The account read, "The General Chairman will be J. Gilbert Scheib, who did such a good job as Chairman of the Mallory Cup last year. He is being ably assisted by the SYC's Entertainment Chairman "Rip" Haase and his committee." The other committeemen were Louis Koerner, Douglas Drennan, Armond Bernius, Ethan Allen, Paul Schreck, and Francis Favalora. Gordon Gsell was race committee chairman.

There were thirty-two entries in the International Lighning Championship event and twenty-five entries for the President's trophy. A fifty-seven boat fleet in two separate races answered the starting gun for the first race of the seventeenth annual Lightning Internationals. The expected Canadian and Hawaiian entries could not make it and the five qualified boats from Argentina were not allowed to come because of the political situation in their country.

The winner in the International Lightning championship series was Tom Allen of Brainbridge, Me., with Ken Warren and Anne Smither as crew. Runner-up was Bobby Adams of Rydal, Pa., then Bob Crane of Darien, Connecticut. SYC's Arthur "Juby" Wynne placed fourth with his crew of J. Gilbert "Jack" Scheib, Jr. and Maurice J. "Bubby" Hartson, III. Charles Dore of Haddenfield, New Jersey was fifth.

SYC's Gene Walet finished seventh in his third straight attempt at the Lightning International title. Another Southerner, Ed. Overton of Fairhope, Alabama was an entry. The only girl in this event was Marge Adams of Rydal, Pennsylvania. Tough luck hit Carl Eichenlaub of San Diego, who was within two points of the leader, Allen, when one of his crew, Eichenlaub's wife, was swept overboard in the fourth race. She was rescued by another boat, but disappointment followed trauma as Eichenlaub was disqualified for finishing without a full crew.

Although Gene Walet's good fortune did not last for the Lightning Internationals, he did win the Western Hemisphere sailing championship when he won the Pan-American Games in the Lightning Class at Buenos Aires, Argentina a few weeks later. Gene defeated nineteen skippers from seven continents for the President Juan Peron Cup, with Daniel Killeen and Carlos Etcheverria as crew.

In the President's Cup series sailmaker Paul Schreck of New Orleans with crew J. Dwight LeBlanc and Julian Richards came from behind in the last race to snatch the cup from Cliff Prados of the Shreveport Yacht Club. Barbara Tolson of the St. Petersburg Yacht Club placed third in the series, with Louis Koerner of SYC placing fourth.

At the banquet held by the SYC in honor of the visiting yachtsmen, the president of the Lightning Class Association, Cliff Prados, honored the SYC general chairman, J. Gilbert Scheib, by presenting him with a gold card of honorary life membership in the Lightning Class Association. He was also given a Resolution, signed by the Lightning District commodore, Charles L. Gambel, and Ethan Allen, secretary, which had been adopted by that organization, thanking Scheib for his cooperation and support of the Lightning Class, in particular for his success in securing the approval of the North American Yacht Racing Union to race Lightnings in the Mallory Cup Finals of 1954.

Mayor de Lesseps Morrison of New Orleans presented honorary citizens certificates and gold keys to the city to twelve skippers honored by the Association. They were: Margaret Teske, Cliff Prados, Ross Allen, Abe Jacobs, Barrows Morley, A. Gordon Adams, Robert Mann, G. W. Rigley, Dick Krauss, Cal Youdos, John McIntosh, and Wayne Brockett.

Reported *The Times-Picayune*: "The dual sailing event drew many out-of-towners from all over the United States. The impressive list of socialites and sporting enthusiasts read like 'New York's 400.' There were numerous cocktail parties and dances honoring skippers and skipperettes who were there to sail in the International Lightning and President's Cup Regattas."

When the publication *Lightning Flashes* appeared in October, the editor, Helen Limbaugh, was most complimentary about the hospitality the SYC had shown its guests and stated, "The people of the Southland treated us with such hospitality that we came back with memories that will last a long time, and, by the way, your author is now a 'bona fide Rebel.'" In this same issue of *Lightning Flashes* the following article was written by one of the participants in the races.

ADVENTURE IN JEFFERSON PARISH
BY YANKEE LIGHTNING SKIPPER

On Wednesday morning, almost an hour before the first race for the Lightnings International for 1955, under the roof of the Deep South Motel in Jefferson Parish outside of New Orleans, could be found three of those Lightning skippers and their crews—meaning those of the yachts *Boom Boom*, *Seductress*, and *Wee Dee 2*; the latter was running behind schedule and left late for the Southern Yacht Club on Lake Pontchartrain (too much Bourbon Street the night before—sometimes called the "Bourbon Street Blues"). Our gracious landlady, who brought us coffee every morning, had told us of a new fast route to the club, which was some ten miles away.

The Buick quivered with all 236 horsepower and we were off. Not for long, though. To the tune of a roaring siren, we were protested off the street. Two men got out of an unmarked noisy green car. The men were unmarked also, except for old slouch hats and big guns (the next size coming on wheels). They took the skipper's license, who just happened to be at the helm, and said, "Boys, follow us." "But we only have an hour or so to make the first race," we pleaded. "What race?" the big one said, "you are all done racing for today—40 miles in a 20 mile zone—don't you --- Yankees know anything?" Three very rejected string-pullers followed the green one at 20 miles an hour for what seemed some 20 miles to the fabulous Jefferson Parish Sheriff's office. Inside the skipper faced the sergeant, "But sir, can't you just give us a ticket and let us go race?" "What race?" (long explanations) "Nope, you have got to get yourself a judge."

The skipper had one bright idea (quota for the day); he called the SYC and screamed about justice—also for help—got much publicity, the P. A. system announcing that the skipper of the *Wee Dee* is in the pokey. Can anyone please help? Yes, one can, God bless him (should be called 'Hawkeye'—him very fast). General Chairman, J. Gilbert Scheib, got the D.A. out of bed and on the phone to the sergeant. Whatever was said on the other end of the line was magic as our sergeant, who with many "Yes Sirs," hung up and said, "you may go now." By the grace of our friends, we did make the first race, but we never will take that breakfast or drive 40 again in the Jefferson Parish of Old New Orleans.

For the third straight year, Gene Walet with his crew of J. Gilbert "Jack" Scheib, Jr. and Allen "Pudgy" McClure won all eliminations to reach the final for the North American Men's championship and the Mallory Cup in 1956 in Toronto, Canada, but victory was not to be. Gene was leading in points until the last race. The morning of that race a heavy fog had set in and the race was postponed. Gene and his crew, while housed near the club, were not notified of the start of the race, and when the fog lifted and they returned to the club, the race had begun. Although he entered late, he finished in fourth place in the series, which was commendable.

CHAPTER XVII

1956-1961

COMMODORES	TERMS
Charles L. Gambel	1956-1957
Hampton A. Gamard	1958-1959
Oliver J. Counce	1960-1961

COMMODORE CHARLES L. GAMBEL—1956-57

The newly elected commodore in 1956 was Charles L. Gambel, a prominent New Orleans businessman. He was very active in the International Lightning Class Association during his early sailing years, serving as commodore of the Southern District of the Lightning Class in 1952. In 1955 the commodore switched from Lightnings to the Luder Fleet. His flagship was an L-16, *Skylark II*. The other elected officials were C. A. Sporl, Jr., vice-commodore; Lange W. Allen, rear commodore; Hampton Gamard, secretary-treasurer; Dr. Russell Monroe, fleet surgeon.

The 1956 social season began, as usual, amidst the city's Mardi Gras festivities. The club celebrated the second year of the "Bards of the Bilges" ball with the lovely Mrs. Charles C. Cary (Ginny) as queen. She was escorted to sit beside Neptune (Commodore Charles L. Gambel). The maids and dukes were: Mrs. Larry Molony (Ann), Miss Rosemary Quinis, Mrs. Lehrue Stevens, Jr. (Betty Ann), Messrs. Walter C. Keenan, Sidney W. Provensal, Jr., A. D. "Juby" Wynne, and Dr. George Sustendal. Climaxing the activities was a sailor's breakfast of grillades and grits, or bacon and eggs and biscuits with much champagne—a royal repast that has become traditional.

Togetherness was a happy by-product of the fifties, and bigger and better racing crews made the scene as skippers trained their wives, sons, and daughters to handle tillers and sheets. Friends and families stayed together for years in racing their boats.

This was evident particularly in the 1956 annual long-distance race from Gulfport to Pensacola, which displayed a large fleet with one of the largest sailing yachts leading the way, *Windjammer II*. The owner, past-Commodore Garner H. Tullis, carried with him a family crew of his son, Eli, daughter-in-law Molly, also Mr. and Mrs. Walter Cooke Keenan, Jr. and Mr. W. Boatner Reily, III. Finishing in second place in the Gulfport to Pensacola race in the cruising class was the *Skylark* sailed by Commodore Charles L. Gambel with his sons as crew, Charles L., Jr., William, Christian, and Peter.

Numbered among the family-crewed sailboats in the long-distance race was the *Vagabond*. "She entertained the family of Arthur Waters for three generations over a period of forty years," reported Cora Payzant in an interview with Harcourt Waters for the *Tell-Tale*. Skippers were Arthur Waters, Sr. and Jr., another son, Harcourt, and Peter, the son of the late Arthur Waters, Jr. This well known "racing schooner," as she was called, did win the West End to Biloxi race in 1946.

The 34-foot schooner *Vagabond* was built in Fairhope, Alabama in 1927. It was found by three young New Orleans fathers, Arthur C. Waters, Barkley Witherspoon, and Wallace O. Westfeldt, and they bought it in October 1931. Among them the three men had many young children, lots of them boys, who worked on keeping the boat in shipshape order. "Although many sailboats are noted for their slick lines and for the number of trophies sitting in a case, the *Vagabond* was noted for the 'nice back porch' on its stern and the many birthday parties held on board," quoted Harcourt Waters.

Following the long-distance race to the coast, the first series of races was held during race week at the Biloxi Yacht Club with only seven yacht club teams participating. They were Southern, Gulfport, Biloxi, Pass Christian, Mobile, Buccaneer, and Pensacola. Southern skippers won the Biloxi series with heir experts Earl Blouin, Gilbert Gray, Carlos de Armas, Oliver V. Baldwin, John E. Koerner, Jr., J. Gilbert Scheib, and James G. "Mike" Gibbons. The SYC skipperettes were also successful when Mrs. Louis B. Graham (Dell) won with a tantalizing crew of J. Gilbert Scheib and Harry Sawin who had her believing she had hit the north stake until she crossed the line and got the winning gun.

During the summer of 1956, another "Whiz Kid," Adriel "Sparky" Graham of SYC at age eleven won the Ladies International Penguin championship sailed at Biloxi, Mississippi. This victory had been denied her in 1954 when at the age of nine "Sparky" was the youngest ever to sail in the finals of the Penguin championship event. She went on to capture the Women's Penguin International championship in 1957 at Chicago, then in Grosse Point, Michigan in 1961, and New York on Long Island Sound in 1962.

It was due to the victory of another junior skipper from SYC, William H. "Bill" Seemann, III, who with his crew James Pinac won the Penguin Internationals in 1955 at Long Beach, California, that the series was sailed in this local area. Bill was second in the 1956 event with his same crew, James Pinac, but first in the Junior Division. The Cardiall trophy was retired by Bill for his three consecutive wins. This trophy was presented to the outstanding junior in the Penguin Internationals by Dr. Charles Glasser in 1953 for the first time.

On the sailing scene in 1956 was the Amphibian fleet, which was very active under the capable leadership of Henry Spang with his boat *Grunner* and others, *Wedger, Republic,* and *See Bee.*

The year 1956 was a banner one for the Pass Christian Yacht Club as its juniors won the Junior Lipton trophy with Gary Terrell, Warren Adams, Jr., and Freddie DeMetz handling the tiller. Successfully defending their club and the Gulf Yachting Association, more PCYC juniors made it to the Finals in the Sears Cup competition for the Junior North American Sailing Championship, where they finished second. The skippers were Warren Adams, Sheila Kerrigan, and Michael Schmidt.

Not to be denied, the skipperettes of the PCYC entered a team in the Adams Cup Semi-Finals held at Savannah, Georgia for the Women's North American Sailing Championship. In a field of eight boats sailed in Cohassett, Massachusetts, they finished second to another Southern group from Texas, Mrs. Glen H. Lattimore of Fort Worth Boat Club with Diane MacFarland, Rose Rector, and Jane Mooney as crew. The GYA-PCYC representatives were: Rosalie Ambler, Lise Kerrigan, Lollette Wittmann, and Elaine Noto.

THE DRAGON FLEET ARRIVES AT SYC

The year 1956 became known as the year of the Dragons. The three original owners of these boats were Dr. George Sustendal, J. W. Clark, and Frank A. Nemec. Although the first boat was launched in New Orleans in 1950, Dragons' first long-distance race was not held until 1956.

The Dragon was a sleek, needle-nosed Marconi-rigged cabin sloop with a fin keel. Originally designed in 1928 by the late John Anker, the Dragon was the winning design in a competition sponsored by the Royal Swedish Yacht Club for the purpose of developing an inexpensive racing and cruising boat that would accommodate two persons.

A Dragon sloop measured 29 feet, 4 inches in length, had a 6-foot beam, and weighed 3,246 pounds. It carried a total of 265 square feet of working sail (mainsail and jib) and flew a parachute spinnaker. The rougher the weather, the better a Dragon sailed.

Paul Odendahl, a Dragon champion, produced a short history of the Dragon Class in 1967. This interesting story follows:

> To the first three: Dr. George Sustendal, Frank A. Nemec and Jay Clark, whose energy and foresight led to our enjoyment of, as Scandinavians endearingly speak of them, "de smaa kloge baade" (the small wise boats).
>
> In 1950 Roland yacht yard of Norway shipped to Houston, Texas for exhibition in a trade fair, a brand new varnished Dragon. After the fair the boat was shipped on consignment to Jim Calvert of New Orleans who sold it to Lange Allen of the SYC for his son. It was not actively used and so was up for sale. In the latter part of 1952, Dr. George Sustendal, thinking back to his earlier days in 21-footers and wanting another sailboat, bought the Dragon and named her *Freebooter*. Its first season out in 1952 she won the championship in the cutter class.
>
> While watching the *Freebooter's* movements in the Sugar Bowl Regatta in December 1953, Jay Clark and his friend Frank A. Nemec, decided this was the boat for them.
>
> The following summer, in May 1954, Jay Clark was leaving for an extended overseas trip that would take him to England. He knew that Dragons were very popular there and would find many for sale. When he arrived he rented a Limousine. With an English colleague and a blank check from Frank Nemec, Clark whizzed along a left-handed path from yacht yard to yacht club to yacht harbor in the south coast of England. One boat was finally found on which he put Frank's name. It was called *Flicka II*. After more driving and inspecting, he decided on a second boat for himself. *Rondinella* was its name.
>
> *Flicka II* was built in 1948 by the Norwegian Bjarne Aas, and *Rondinella* was by Woodnutt (the same yard that built Prince Philip's Dragon *Bluebottle*) in 1947. Jay sent his friend Frank a cable "You are the proud owner of *Flicka Two*." Frank shot back with "What the hell is *Flicka Two*?"
>
> After the new boats arrived, Jay Clark, Frank Nemec and George Sustendal formed a Dragon fleet. George was Fleet Captain and served for 1954 and 1955. Little could they have known that 40 Dragons would

be added to the fleet in the next 13 years.

The first long-distance race of these three Dragons to Biloxi in 1956 with the SYC fleet ended in utter confusion. Sustendal's boat sailed by Gilbert Gray went inshore on the Keesler Air Force field green flasher, thinking it was the Biloxi channel. Nemec later found a lighted-up fishing boat and sailed around it shouting his number, thinking it was the committee boat. And, Clark, believing he was last, approached the Biloxi Yacht Club under spinnaker and mainsail running before a stiff breeze. Wanting to round up and tie up at the club, as he approached, he first dropped his main and later his spinnaker, and coasting toward the clubhouse he heard a cannon; he had won the race with his sails down.

The first new boats that followed were Nathaniel C. "Buster" Curtis' *Sazerac*; Gene Walet's *Spirit III* and Henry Finke's Norwegian Dragon *Frolic*. Many more Dragons were brought in. Harry Tabony's *Wasp*; James Smither took the *Skorve*; Harry Swain the *Enfin* and Edward Hobson the *Banshee* from Norway.

Gene Walet and his crew of Pudgy McClure and Claude Kohler, having sold his Lightning, entered the Dragon fleet with another *Spirit III*, Dragon. He took off for the Pacific Northwest to have a go at the Dragon trials for the fourteenth Olympiad in Port Townsend, Washington in 1956. They never thought they could win the trials, but they did, and the Olympic Committee nominated Gene to represent the U.S. at Melbourne, Australia on the 1956 Olympic team. The SYC boys made a gallant effort. They won four first places but this was not good enough to bring home the gold medal.

Over the years members of the SYC Dragon fleet became very active in national affairs of the class, as well as in sailing. "Buster" Curtis was the technical representative to the Olympic Sub-Committee for Dragons in 1964 and 1965. Henry Finke was made national commodore of the American International Dragon Association (AIDA) from 1965 to 1967. The all-important position of secretary-treasurer of the AIDA was administered by SYC's Ed Hobson from 1963 to 1967.

DAVE GARROWAY'S "TODAY SHOW" FILMS RACE

It was a beautiful day on Lake Pontchartrain during the summer of 1956 when television cameras were turned on the boats as they sailed out of the harbor into the waters of the lake to participate in the Luder Class eliminations for the 1956 Internationals to be held on Lake Pontchartrain in July. The scenes appeared on NBC's "The Today Show," with Dave Garroway the narrator. Charles and Virginia Cary's boat *Gung Ho*, an ocean-going yawl, was lent to carry the television equipment, with John Dickinson from local station WDSU and Paul Schreck.

The prime time show gave New Orleans worldwide recognition as Garroway interviewed SYC Commodore Charles L. Gambel, Gene Walet, and Tom Hicks. Also interviewed was ten-year-old Roy Troendle, Jr., a Pram champion of SYC who had just won the Mobile and Fairhope annual Pram regattas.

The television publicity was a good omen for the SYC representative in the L-16 Internationals, past-Commodore G. Shelby Friedrichs. He not only won the eliminations on the lake that day but he went on to win the championship event. This was a great victory for Friedrichs, who had made three previous attempts, in 1953, 1954, and 1955. Sharing his laurels were his crew and sons, G. Shelby "Buddy" Friedrichs, Jr. and Gore Friedrichs.

The opening of the newly constructed Olympic swimming pool in 1956 was another gala party. A lovely style show celebrated the dedication, titled "Sail into Summer," with many SYC models displaying the newest look in summer togs: Mrs. Callendar S. Hadden, Jr., Mrs. Warren J. Nolan, Mrs. Stanley Bremmermann, Mrs. Russell R. Monroe, Mrs. Miles Pratt Wynn, and Miss Courtney Ann Gandolfo. Also included were summer wearables for the young men modeled by Eugene H. Walet, III, Robert R. Haase, and Eugene Sheehan. The swimming pool was built after much effort was spent selling Class A bonds of $150 each.

After a busy racing season in which the Carys, "Ginny" and Charlie, had used their boat for many of the sailing events held on the lake, "Ginny" closed the year with a cruise she planned for the Girl Scout Mariner troops. SYC members Mrs. I. W. Ricciuti (Dottie) and her husband, "Billy," were very active on the Girl and Boy Scout board of directors in the city. They participated in this grand finale for the year by taking their cruiser *Aweigh*, "Rip" Haase's *Bamsy*, *Tahuna*, belonging to "Bill" Hogan, *Springtime*, owned by John "Pat" Little, and the Carys' *Gung-Ho*; they dug out to sea amid shouts of "anchors aweigh—blast off!"

The result of this cruise was described by "Ginny," who felt that many more lessons were needed as she stated that various major and minor crises arose; for example, one girl was overheard saying, "the cute powder room downstairs in the basement of the boat." Still another young salt told her about her uncle who owned a five-mitre boat. (That's a pretty good capacity, even for SYC waters.) Then an exasperated foredeckhand explained that the heaving line is used to secure seasick passengers.

LAKE PONTCHARTRAIN CAUSEWAY

The year 1957 witnessed one of the engineering marvels of our time, the Lake Pontchartrain Causeway. Not only had the face of the shoreline along the lakefront changed with the development of the many beautiful residential subdivisions, but now the surface of Lake Pontchartrain itself had a "new look," a fascinating miracle to keep racing sailors company, a twenty-four-mile causeway across Lake Pontchartrain.

The Causeway is a concrete double-span highway bridge, and its twenty-four-mile length distinguishes it as the world's longest overwater highway bridge. It was completed in two separate operations. The first span was finished in 1957 at a cost of $27,500,000; a corresponding bridge or twin span was built and completed in 1967 at a cost of $29,900,000. In May 1969 its total completion was celebrated. The project engineers were Davis Volkert and Associates and the builders, Brown & Root, Inc.

This bridge is considered one of the most outstanding accomplishments of the engineering world and has been nominated by some to occupy a position alongside the seven wonders of man's globe.

An interesting footnote to this concrete masterpiece is the fact that the astronauts of Apollo 7 took note of the man-made wonder when from ninety-five nautical miles above the earth they snapped a photograph of southeastern Louisiana, which illustrated the vital connecting role of the span.

Before the construction of Pontchartrain Causeway, there was only one other trestle-bridge, built in the 1930s, which connected the south shore with the north shore of Lake Pontchartrain, called the Watson-Williams bridge and later named the Maestri bridge for the mayor of the city of New Orleans.

The construction of the Causeway brought to an end the race across the lake to Madisonville known as the Tchefuncte River race. Many a wild tale has been told about the "Tchefuncte River Indians" in combat with the sheriff of St. Tammany Parish. This event, the most popular of all long distance races, was replaced by the race to Mandeville, a few miles down along the North Shore of Lake Pontchartrain.

At the 1957 annual meeting, C. A. Sporl, Jr. was replaced by Hampton Gamard as vice-commodore, and Oliver Counce was elected rear commodore over Lange W. Allen. John B. Levert replaced Hampton Gamard as secretary-treasurer.

THE FIRST SEARS CUP SERIES

The Southern Yacht Club was host to yet another North American Yacht Racing Union event in 1957—the Junior North American Sailing Championship for the Sears Cup. Once again through the combined efforts of GYA Commodore J. Gilbert Scheib and ex-Commodore G. Shelby Friedrichs of SYC, with the help of Commodore Charles L. Gamble, who had been appointed the GYA's representative on the Sears Cup committee, the SYC was selected to hold the Junior event in 1957. The efforts of the local committeemen were greatly enhanced by the assistance of Vivyan Hall of Miami, Florida who was a member of the NAYRU Sears Cup Committee, D. Verner Smythe of New York, and John C. Cattus, Bayhead, N.J.

It was a very successful eight-boat series, and great sportsmanship was exhibited throughout the protest-free event. A classic lesson in such sportsmanship was displayed by the representative of the Florida Sailing Association from the St. Petersburg Yacht Club, John Jennings. He had only to sail around the course to win the championship. This he accomplished. However, while he was sailing in a leisurely fashion for the north stake, a passing motorboat's wave wash caused John's boom to hit the buoy. No one witnessed the foul except John. When he approached the judges' boat and did not cross the finish line to take the winner's cannon, everyone on board was curious but soon learned what had happened. The one championship John had struggled to win was denied him. However, he did return and claimed the Sears Cup in 1958. The winner of the event was John Merrifield of Southport, Connecticut, with crewmen Thomas Munnel, Pierce Gerety, and Peter Clark. The score was 51½ to 51 points.

Such outstanding sportsmanship did not go unnoticed. Jennings was awarded a special "good sportsmanship" trophy by the members of the Gulf Yachting Association who co-sponsored the event with the Southern Yacht Club.

LUDER CLASS WORLD SERIES

Many visitors and participants were at the Southern Yacht Club in the summer of 1957 to witness the L-16 Class World Series on Lake Pontchartrain. There were nine boats entered from all parts of the U.S. and Bermuda. Among the crews were an accomplished iceboat skipper, Jack Vilas of Chicago, an Olympic sailor; H. Brownlow Eve of the Royal Bermuda Yacht Club; and a five-time Women's National champion, Lorna Hibberd, who crewed for her brother, Souther Whittelsey.

Jack Vilas was the winner over SYC's Charles Eshleman, Jr. Eshleman had defeated the 1956 champion, SYC's G. Shelby Friedrichs, Sr., who had his sons Buddy and Gore as crew, in Greenwich, Connecticut, to reach the finals. Following is a list of entries:

Yacht	Fleet	Skipper
Glendoveer	Bermuda Sail Boat Club	Cyril Cooper
Lagonda	Lake St. Claire	Ward Detwiler
Skylark II	Southern Yacht Club	Charles L. Eshleman, Jr.
Ticou	Royal Bermuda Yacht Club	Brownlow Eve
Bloody Mary	Los Angeles	Fred Loewy
Lure	Newport Harbor Yacht Club	Bert Sawyer
Alert	Grosse Isle	R. L. Taylor
Lorelei	Chicago Yacht Club	Jack Vilas
Blue Chip	Western Long Island Sound	Joe Weed, Jr.
Sybarite	Indian Harbor Yacht Club	Souther Whittelsey

On the waters away from home, SYC'S Gene Walet, with a crew from Columbus, Ohio, Helen and Jay Limbraugh, won the first Mid-Winter International Lightning Class championship in 1957, hosted in St. Petersburg, Florida by the St. Petersburg Yacht Club. Gene won over eighty-one boats.

During his last year in office, Commodore Gambel was instrumental in renewing the North-South race with the Chicago team. This team race had been inaugurated in 1947 by Commodore Richard G. Jones, who had been a native of Chicago and a member of the Chicago Yacht Club. The race was sailed in L-16s. Commodore Jones presented a trophy and named it the Commodore Richard G. Jones Perpetual Trophy to be sailed for by Southern and Chicago in team racing. The winner was the visiting crew from Chicago, Alfred S. Dowrie, Russ Moore, Ken Korten, and Sam Clarke. Sailing for SYC were Cyprian A. "Junior" Sporl, Jr., Charles L. Eshleman, Jr., ex-Commodore G. Shelby Friedrichs, and ex-Commodore James "Mike" Gibbons.

COMMODORE HAMPTON GAMARD—1958-59

At the annual meeting held in 1958, Hampton A. Gamard, a vice-president of the Whitney National Bank of New Orleans, was elected commodore. Hampton was active in Fish Class sloops and Lightnings. He served as commodore for two terms, 1958 and 1959.

Elected to serve with Commodore Gamard were: Oliver J. Counce, vice-commodore; John B. Levert, rear commodore; Sidney W. Provensal, Jr., secretary-treasurer; Dr. Russ B. Monroe, fleet surgeon; Warren J. Nolan, fleet measurer and James W. Smither, Jr., fleet captain. The board of governors was made up of Ethan Allen, Gorden B. Gsell, Charles L. Gamble, Robert Haase, John Koerner, Jr., John P. Little, J.F.A. Lorber, Jr., and Wallace Walker.

The 1958 "Bards of the Bilges" ball was very unusual. The SYC was contacted by the Alcoa Company and requested that they be permitted to provide the decorations for the party as a part of their advertisement program, to be pictured in *Time* magazine. Permission was granted, and as result the dance floor was elaborately decorated with shimmering and glittering fish suspended from a ceiling illuminated with soft green lighting depicting an underwater setting, and huge sparkling mermaids were situated in the corners of the SYC's ballroom. There were also foil octopuses, whales, seaweed, and coral fashioned from lengths and lengths of aluminum foil. Ten yards of foil were used to make the train worn by the queen of the ball, Mrs. Louis Koerner (Peggy). Her king was Commodore Davis Wuescher, and her maids were Betty Christovich, Mrs. Margaret Hadden, Miss Janie Janssen, Mrs. Russel Monroe (Lillian), Mrs. Warren Nolan (Beede) and Miss Frances Whidden.

CASTRO'S TROOPS TAKE HAVANA— RACE CANCELLED

It was that time of the year in 1958 for the St. Petersburg to Havana race, and many Southern Yacht Club members were down at the St. Petersburg Yacht Club with their yachts and crews eager to participate in the great race. Skippering his handsome 40-foot sloop *Whispering Wind* was Garic Moran, with his able-bodied crew of Frank Anderson out of Houston, Texas, John F. Dicks, Jr., Sheldon Cass, B. Temple Brown, Jr., H. Harcourt Waters, II, Robert Bruce, and Click and Paul Schreck.

Also down for the race was *Tahuna*, formerly owned by Moreland H. "Bill" Hogan and recently bought by Howard S. Cole, an oilman from the Houston Yacht Club, with an SYC crew of Charles Cary, Herbert O'Donnell, Kenny Mitchell, Jerry McCarthy, and Warren Nolan. (When Hurricane Carla hit Texas in 1961, *Tahuna* met a tragic end and sank in the harbor at the Houston Yacht Club.)

As was the custom, many wives and girlfriends would travel to Havana to meet their sailing husbands and boyfriends at the hotel following the big race. However, Fidel Castro's troops were there first in the month of March, 1958, and they were bombing Havana's streets in Castro's effort to overthrow the Batista regime. The gals' favorite hotel was in shambles.

It was not exactly safe to enter the Havana yacht club harbor after Castro's attack, so the race committee quickly changed the plans for the race and a new course was taken around the Florida Keys to Miami, where the lady folk met the crew after changing their airline tickets. Scuttled was the silver anniversary of one of the nation's most colorful yachting classics, the St. Petersburg to Havana race "that has been running since Batista and Castro were in knee-length shorts," reported the news media.

There were twenty-nine boats entered in the 1958 race with the yawl *Criollo* of San Lius Vidana of Havana the winner, with *Tahuna* finishing in third place in Class B, after sailing toward the Government Cut finish line, a hundred miles away.

After much persuasion by Bache Whitlock to change the Gulfport to Pensacola race in 1958 from the week before race week to the weekend after, the Gulf Yachting Association reluctantly agreed to the change. It was feared, and justly so, that too many skippers and crew would abandon a part of race week to make the race to Pensacola. The number of entries in the race increased to eighteen, the largest on record to enter this event. Those that made the trip were:

Tuhuna—Moreland "Bill" Hogan
Psyche—Robt. Rudolf and Maunsell Hickey
Zin Zin—Roy Watson
Dixie Queen—Colles Stowell
Dixie Girl—Robert Normann

Saltwind—Elroy Eckhardt
Picayune—Jerry Nicholson
Salabar—Bache Whitlock
Adonde—Sam Ryniker
Bamsy—Robt. "Rip" Haase
Nimbus—Lanny Chennault
Marie Corneille—John Mayer and Kenneth King
Dockan—Robt. Crongeyer
Vagabond—Arthur C. Waters
Good Times—Harold Cornay
Ibid II—F. C. Feibleman
Aweigh—I. W. Ricciuti
Springtime—John "Pat" Little

COMMODORE KNOST TROPHY CELEBRATES TWENTY YEARS

The GYA all-girl championship regatta at Pass Christian for the Commodore Bernard "Bernie" Knost trophy celebrated its twentieth anniversary in August 1958 with a record twelve yacht clubs participating. For posterity, following are the skipperettes that Commodore Knost paid tribute to with a champagne dinner party after the races and the clubs they represented:

> Bay-Waveland—Joan Cavorac, Ada Wynn, Bay Chamberlain, and Betty Ann Gordon.
> Biloxi—Joyce Fountain, Ann Balter, and Janet Green.
> Fairhope—Sarah Cummings, Rena Hoffman, and Sally Crawford.
> Fort Walton—Barbara Feiblekorn, Leota Feiblekorn, and Virginia Brown
> New Orleans—Audrey Slotness, Margaret Turner, Sammy Reed, and Sue Fisher
> Pass Christian—Rosalie Ambler, Mildred Logan, Sheila Kerrigan, Helen Lafaye, and Thelma Miller
> Pensacola—June Kissinger, Ginger McMillan, and Ann Dunning.
> St. Petersburg—Jane Wray, Nancy Lucas, Bonnie Holloway, and Barbara Tolson.
> Southern—Edna Gray, Susan Miller, Alice Miller, and Frances Whidden.
> St. Andrews Bay—Betty Douglas, Mary Fennel, and Nan Mathis.

The Southern Yacht Club won the series of three races for the trophy. The Mobile Yacht Club team was awarded a good sportsmanship trophy; it brought with it a group of juniors, whose average age was fifteen.

BLUEBOTTLE TROPHY GOES TO DRAGONS

Acting British Consul General George Littler announced that the Lords of the Admiralty had donated a trophy to the Southern Yacht

Club to be used as the prize for the winner in the first annual team race between the Dragon Class fleet of Houston Yacht Club and Southern Yacht Club. Acting Consul Littler donated a marker trophy to Commodore Charles L. Gamble in 1957 in ceremonies at the clubhouse. The trophy was to be called the *Bluebottle* cup. This name was chosen in honor of Prince Philip of Great Britain who owned and sailed a Dragon sloop named *Bluebottle*. The prince and the British government had contributed a great deal toward the rapid growth of the Dragon Class in the U.S. The trophy was made from a part of a silver service recovered from a British warship sunk during World War II.

The first race for the *Bluebottle* trophy was sailed in 1958. The Southern Yacht Club team, composed of Larry Molony, Ed. Hobson, M. O. Delgado, and N. C. "Buster" Curtis, Jr., won the event. Houstonians present for the races were Mr. and Mrs. Reoul Genitempo, Miss Marlene Genitempo, Miss Dolores Aldo, Gaylord Smith, Jack Binion, Daniel, Harold, and Jay Bludworth, Rufus G. Smith, and Duncan Behlett. Missing from the Texas team was a regular contender in the Dragon Class, Robert "Bob" Mosbacher, who was in Newport watching the 1958 America's Cup Trials in which his brother Emil "Bus" Mosbacher, Jr. was skippering *Vim*.

FIRST AMERICA'S CUP RACES SAILED IN 12-METERS

The British had tried fourteen times to win the America's Cup and the Canadians twice. Throughout those years this oldest trophy in international sports has been the subject of fiery controversy. "The Americans cheated," the Earl of Dunhaven had raged in 1895. After his defeat in *Valkyrie III*, he claimed the U.S. boat was carrying extra ballast. He attacked the race officials and forced an inquiry by the New York Yacht Club. He still lost.

After Sir Thomas J. Lipton's *Shamrock V* suffered its fifth defeat, next came from Britain T. O. M. Sopwith, a famed stunt flyer, hydroplane racer, and aircraft builder, and with him the grand era of the J-boats, majestic, 130-foot long monsters with 165-foot masts and clouds of sail, crewed largely by professionals and capable of speeds up to eighteen knots on a close-hauled reach. No faster or prettier ocean racers ever existed—or ever will again.

In 1937, with Europe in turmoil, Commodore Harold Vanderbilt's *Ranger*, designed by naval architect Olin J. Stephen II, represented the U.S. and won four straight races over T. O. M. Sopwith's *Endeavour II*. When Sopwith came back from Rhode Island in defeat, the British press yelped, "Britain rules the waves but America waives the rules." The complaint was that Harold Vanderbilt's *Ranger* had cut off the *Endeavour II* during a tricky maneuver at a turn.

After most of a generation, the America's Cup sat bolted in a trophy case in the New York Yacht Club. Finally, in 1958, came a new challenge from Britain, but not in J-boats, which no one could afford to build. The class now was the International 12-meter sloop, half as big as the Js, half as fast, twice as maneuverable and twice as exciting. The crews of these new boats were gifted amateur one-design small boat sailors. The first United States skipper to defend the Cup since World War II was Briggs S. Cunningham in *Columbia*. He defeated the British boat *Sceptre*.

Away from Lake Pontchartrain, SYC skippers were sailing on the waters of Lake Michigan in 1958, trying to bring home the Commodore Richard G. Jones trophy which the members of the Chicago Yacht Club had won the previous year in New Orleans. The SYC crews were successful in winning this series, and those representing the club were C. A. "Junior" Sporl, Jr., who had participated in all previous series, with his crew Allen "Pudgy" McClure and Thomas Killeen. The other participants were Charles Eshleman, Jr. and his crew of Arthur D. "Juby" Wynne and Edward B. "Bud" Jahncke; and John Dicks, Jr., with crewmen Arthur "Buck" Seaver, Jr., Kent Nelson, and George Ayers.

The last attempt made to carry on the St. Petersburg to Havana race was made in 1959 when Peter Trouchaud, a Sarasota yachtsman, met with Mexican officials and they were successful in getting the St. Petersburg Yacht Club to host the event.

For the first time since Garner H. Tullis and Morris Newman of the SYC sailed the tricky 284-mile run, a schooner entered the race in 1959, the *Salt Wind* skippered by John Blouin. His 45-foot two-masted schooner competed for the largest trophy awarded. The host Havana Yacht Club gives the trophy to the first schooner to cross the finish line on corrected time. John finished fourth, ably assisted by his crew, John Fraser, William H. Ricciuti, Russ Monroe, Robert White, Arthur Lowe, and Rene Valle.

Sailing the SYC Garic Moran's *Whispering Wind*, a 45-foot cutter, was Paul Schreck with crewmen, Juby Wynne, Sheldon Cass, Cal H. Hadden, Jr., Ed. Hobson, Don Organ, Stewart Woody, and Ken

Hamilton. Another SYC entry was the *Glass Slipper* of Moreland H. "Bill" Hogan with his brother Claude, Kenny Mitchell, Herbert O'Donnell, Warren Nolan, Rod Kahr of Chicago, and Bob Love of Martha's Vineyard as crewmen.

Winning the 1959 St. Petersburg to Havana race was the champion of all champions. Emil "Bus" Mosbacher, Jr., (the 1962 and 1967 America's Cup winner). Sailing Jack Brown's 42-foot yawl *Callooh*, Mosbacher was ably assisted by two of his crewmen from the America's Cup Trials, Dick Bertram and Jakob Isbrandtsen. "Bus" did well in all five races, the Lipton Cup, the Miami to Nassau race, the Nassau Cup race, the St. Petersburg to Havana run, and the Havana to Varadero Beach race, which gave him the championship of the Southern Ocean Racing Conference (SORC). Mosbacher also received the Governor's Cup for having the highest number of points in the five-race series. His yacht club was listed as the Storm Trysail Yacht Club out of New York.

In the Havana to Varadero Beach race, the last race of the SORC was won by SYC's Bill Hogan's *Glass Slipper*, winning first place overall and first in Class A. Added to his usual SYC crewmen was an ex-SYC member, Dick Jones, Jr., who was then living and working in Havana.

Another group of SYC travelers in 1959 were the Eshlemans, Charles and Helen, with the Jahnckes, "Bud" and Zide, who set sail for Hamilton, Bermuda, to take part in race week of the Royal Bermuda Yacht Club. They won in team racing between the United States and Bermuda in the Luder Class. The SYC visitors were the guests of Mr. and Mrs. H. Brownlow Eve, whose home was in Hamilton, Bermuda.

In the 1959 Lipton Cup and Miami to Nassau races in Class B, SYC skipper W. Garic Moran with his 44-foot sloop *Whispering Wind* participated with crewmen Sheldon Cass, navigator, John F. Dicks, Jr., B. Temple Brown, William Hayes, Warren Whaley, and Stuart Woody.

The Junior Lipton Cup series of 1959 was won by the Southern Yacht Club's team of its most outstanding group of youngsters the club has trained, time proved this. They were J. Dwight LeBlanc, William H. Seemann, III, Click Schreck, G. Shelby "Buddy" Friedrichs, Jr. and Iljalmar Breit. Although they won the honors, the Lipton Cup was not located by the St. Petersburg Yacht Club's team that won the trophy in 1958.

A few years later, while working on the details for inscriptions on a new Lipton Cup, the GYA Secretary, J. Gilbert Scheib received a phone call stating the lost trophy was found when workers in the clubhouse were renovating a room, after knocking down a wall, behind it was a cabinet in which the Lipton Cup was discovered. An embarrassed commodore of the St. Petersburg Yacht Club immediately returned the prize to the Southern Yacht Club.

COMMODORE OLIVER J. COUNCE—1960-61

Taking over the helm of the SYC in 1960 was Oliver J. Counce, who was elected commodore. Oliver is a prominent businessman, and as a junior sailor at Southern he was a Fish Class skipper for years. He later joined the Luder Class and his flagship was the *Gull*. Serving with Commodore Counce were W. Horace Williams, Jr., vice-commodore; J. F. Auguste Lorber, Jr., rear commodore; Sidney W. Provensal, Jr. secretary-treasurer; Dr. H. Reichard Kahle, fleet surgeon; Warren Nolan, fleet measurer; and William H. Seeman, jr. fleet captain.

Commodore Counce was credited with initiating the across-the-lake race to Mandeville and back to replace the old West End to Tchefuncte River run. Counce was also one of the organizers of the Handicap Class.

By the year 1960 the Penguin fleet was more than fifty strong. The Southern Yacht Club now had the largest racing one-design class in the Gulf area. Many more names were added to the list of owners. These members felt the need to create interest in sailing in the young people, fourteen years of age, and to prepare them better for handling large boats in the future. Older skippers eventually became involved to add to the long list.

Names of some of the active members and skippers of the Penguin fleet, in addition to those mentioned, were: Stella Farwell, G. Shelby "Buddy" Friedrichs, Jr. and his brother Gore, Barton Jahncke, James "Tubby" Janin, Eldon Harvey, Robert Hughes, Louis Koerner, Sr. and Jr., George Sustendal, Roy Troendle Sr. and Jr., and Davis Wuescher and his son Peter. Other juniors who joined this class were: David Cristovich, John Dane, III, Baxie Feitel, Tommy Haslem, Peter Kahle, Robbie Mattox, Nancy Monroe, Linda Scherer, and Bert Keenan.

Both the 1960 Penguin National Championship and the Junior Penguin National Championship were held on Lake Pontchartrain and hosted by the SYC. Co-chairmen for the national championship races were Louis B. Graham and Roy A. Troendle, Sr., with vice-chairman Sam Ryniker, fleet captain, and A. J. Nugon, fleet secretary, assisting. The winner of the National Championship was Gardner Cox of Philadelphia, Pennsylvania. SYC's Peter Wuescher and Roy Troendle, Jr. were third and fourth respectively. Winning the Junior Penguin National Championship was SYC's Roy Troendle, Jr. over SYC junior skippers, Eric Aschaffenberg, Adriel "Sparky" Graham, Reichard Kahle, Jr., John "Jack" Kinabrew, Robert "Bob" Milling, and Peter Wuescher.

Added to the list of sailing events hosted by the Southern Yacht Club in 1960 were the Star Class Spring Series and the Jahncke Series. The winner of the Spring Series was Richard Stearns and crew, Lynn Williams. They took home just about all the silver. The Lake Michigan skipper, sailing *Glider V*, won the Spring Series and the Commodore Ernest Lee Jahncke event, making him the recipient of the *Windjammer* trophy as the high point man in both classics. Second place in the Spring Series went to the local New Orleans-Gulf Star Class representative, Joseph L. "Buzzy" Killeen, Jr., with Robert "Bob" Lippincott of West Jersey in third place.

In the Jahncke series, three boats put up a spectacular finish to a most interesting race from start to finish. Count Alfred de Marigny's *Concubine* of Nassau, Morris W. Newman's *Solo* of SYC, and Harry Nye's *Gale* of Chicago came up to the finish line abreast and it appeared there might be a three-way dead heat for first place. But when the boats were only a few feet away from the finish line, a big rolling wave gave Count de Marigny's craft the impetus it needed to push it over inches ahead of *Solo*, which was judged to be second, while *Gale* placed third. There was only a split second between each of the three boats.

General chairman of the event was Miles Wynn. Eugene H. Walet, III was the fleet captain and J. Gilbert Scheib was chairman of the protest committee (serving with him were Larry Beauvais of Mobile, Alabama and Gordon Gsell, Arthur D. Wynne, and J. F. A. Lorber, Jr. of SYC). The race committee chairman was J. Rollins Murray. His committee consisted of:

Ethan Allen	Walter May
Armand Bernius	Ellis Muther, III
Nathaniel C. Curtis	A. J. Nugon
Douglas Drennan	William Rudolph

Charles Eshleman, Jr.
Walter Flower
G. Shelby Friedrichs
Ed Hobson
James Jones

Mr. and Mrs. Arthur Seaver
Robert Stewart
Roy Troendle, Sr.
Pat Wolfe

A short time after these Star Class races, Commodore Jahncke passed away. He was one of the most outstanding commodores of the Southern Yacht Club and well known for his unabated interest in yachting and for his sailing trips along the South Atlantic and Gulf coasts.

Also a member of the New York Yacht Club, Commodore Jahncke was an avid spectator of America's Cup races. A serious sailor through two wars, Rear Admiral Ernest Lee Jahncke (USN Ret.) was a noted engineer and business executive who had also served as undersecretary of the Navy in 1929 under President Herbert Hoover. In addition to being a member of the 1932 Olympic Committee, Commodore Jahncke was appointed to the 1936 Olympic Committee by President Franklin D. Roosevelt. Jahncke cast the only dissenting vote opposing the sending of a United States team to Germany.

Another exciting event was held on Lake Pontchartrain in 1960, the Mallory Cup Semi-Finals with one of the most interesting finishes ever witnessed between two national champions, Robert "Bob" Mosbacher of Houston, Texas and Ted Turner of Savannah, Georgia (America's Cup winner in 1972). The two skippers began their duel immediately after the start of what proved to be a classic sailing race. They stayed only a boat length apart in the nine-mile course, with Mosbacher slightly in front. As they entered the final windward leg to the finish, Turner sought to cause his rival to make a mistake. Fifty-two times the two boats tacked. Fifty-two times both boats made perfect come abouts. Fifty-two times burned hands and aching backs kept the fast Thistle Class boats almost the same distance apart. At the finish line, Turner on starboard and Mosbacher on port converged to cross for the end of the hectic duel. Mosbacher cleared the line five seconds ahead of Turner in a breathtaking battle. Bob went on to the Finals in Wisconsin, where he finished second to Buddy Melges in Scows.

TULANE UNIVERSITY SAILING CLUB'S FIRST REGATTA

The summer of 1960 witnessed the first Baldwin Wood Regatta

sailed on Lake Pontchartrain. The history of Mr. Baldwin Wood and his boat the *Nydia* was related in a previous chapter. This regatta was started in his memory. Ten Gannet boats were used for the occasion. Past-Commodore Garner H. Tullis had contributed $5,000 toward the $10,000 cost of these 14-foot fiberglass sloops with spinnakers, and Tulane University donated the difference. Thus began the Tulane Sailing Club. The first race was won by SYC's Tulane student, Barton Jahncke. In addition to the local Tulane University, participating were Georgetown University, Ohio State, Mississippi State, Springhill College of Mobile, Alabama, and Louisiana State University of New Orleans.

The achievements of our SYC juniors go on and on. G. Shelby "Buddy" Friedrichs, Jr., with his brother, Gore, and Craig Nelson as crew, won the 1960 Luders International Championship sailed at Indian Harbor Yacht Club on Long Island Sound, in Greenwich, Connecticut. Russ Moon of Chicago was second. The other competitors hailed from Bermuda, Los Angeles, Newport, Indian Harbor, and West Long Island Sound. The senior Friedrichs was also an L-16 champion, having won the internationals in 1958.

Before "Buddy" left to enter the Luders event, he and his teammates from the Southern Yacht Club, Bill Seeman, Hjalmar Breit, and Fred Wirth, won the 1960 Junior Lipton Cup in Pensacola, Florida.

1960 OLYMPIC TRIALS HELD AT SYC

The Southern Yacht Club was host for the 1960 Olympic Trials, which were sailed in Dragon Class boats. Welcoming the many notable guests was SYC's own Frank Nemec, commodore of the American International Dragon Association. James M. Trenary, chairman of the Olympic Yachting Committee, was also in attendance. They were ably assisted by a fine committee:

Burt Cary	J. F. A. Lorber, Jr.
Charles L. Eshleman, Jr.	J. Rollins Murray
Henry Finke	Warren J. Nolan
G. Shelby Friedrichs	J. Gilbert Scheib
Gilbert Gray	Harry Swain
W. E. Hobson, III	Bernard "Pat" Wolfe

The Southern Yacht Club's entries were: J. W. Clark, Nathaniel C. "Buster" Curtis, Jr., Thomas Dreyfus, Henry Finke, Lucien Haase, Edward Hobson, Rene Meric, Frank Nemec, James Smither, II, Dr.

George Sustendal, and Eugene "Gene" Walet, III. The out-of-town skippers were Ralph de Luca, Sharon Johnstone, Charles Kober, Jay Lewis, Charles Lyon, John Moran, Robert Mosbacher, Fred Schenck, Walt Swindeman, and Dr. Glenn Thorpe.

Gene Walet won in a classy fleet of twenty-one boats. Buster Curtis was a close fourth behind two Long Beach, California skippers, Charles Kober and Dr. Glenn Thorpe. This was Walet's second try for the Olympic gold medal (the first attempt was in 1956). Gene's crew was Allen "Pudgy" McClure, Claude Kohler, and Gene's father, Eugene H. Walet, II.

Walet carried the U.S. colors into the 1960 Olympics on the Bay of Naples in Italy, where the seventeenth Olympiad sailing contests were held, with fifty nations entering and about 150 boats competing. Gene's sixth place finish was commendable in such a wide field of champions.

When Gene Walet's boat left New Orleans, free transportation to Italy was provided, courtesy of Lykes Bros. Steamship Company of New Orleans. This was the first time the American team members did not have to pay their own expenses, thanks to the newly formed United States International Sailing Association (USISA). The USISA made it possible, through their funding, for the best U.S. skippers to participate in Olympic and foreign competition and to enable Americans to compete more successfully in International regattas.

Yachting is one of the few sports in the USA still free of professionalism; it is controlled by amateurs. Initially, international sailing was engaged in or supported by only a few wealthy men. The USISA now made it possible for good sailors of modest means to represent the U.S. abroad without resorting to commercial or professional support.

The final long-distance race of the 1960 sailing season was the race to Mandeville and back, which was won by Bill Hogan's *Glass Slipper* in Class A and Art Mahony in *Stranger* in Class B. The fleet captain had made prior arrangements for a six-piece "rock-and-roll" orchestra to play for tea dancing at the harbor pavillion in Mandeville. He was the only one disappointed, for when the fleet arrived, they rushed to Beechac's Restaurant on the beach for food and news of Tulane's and LSU's misfortunes in football.

Closing the sailing season of 1960 was the Mid-Winter Sports Association Sugar Bowl Regatta. In the "race of champions" an SYC junior, William H. "Bill" Seemann, III, won the series with his father,

"Billy" and sister, Suzanne Seemann, as crew. In second and third places were Joe Arns of the Buccaneer Yacht Club and Janet Green of the Biloxi Yacht Club. Twelve boats competed in a hotly contested three-race series.

This was the occasion for the debut of a new fleet, the Knarr Class, captained by Arthur Mahoney, owner of *Stranger*. Mahoney brought the Knarrs to New Orleans—they were built in Norway. The other founders were Dr. Alexander Brock, Bryan Wayne, and Lawrence Heffron. Bryan Wayne won the first race as he posted a one-point victory over Jack Dane, Jr., with A. K. "Buzzy" Northrop in third place.

In the other classes winning Sugar Bowl trophies were: Luders—Arthur D. "Juby" Wynne, with his crew of two SYC juniors, former Lightning champions, Maurice J. "Bubby" Hartson, III and J. Gilbert "Jack" Scheib, Jr. (he had changed to the L-16 class but the name of his boat remained, *Jane's Mink*, a reference to the mink coat that Juby's spouse, Jane, had been promised for Christmas); Cutter Class—Robert "Bob" Nelson over Dr. H. R. Kahle and Tom Trenchard of the New Orleans Yacht Club; Stars—Al Muther over Cal Hadden, Jr. and Richard Nelson; Dragons—M. O. Delgado, Jr. in *Jubilee*, defeating Henry Finke and Walt Swindemann (Walt was a national Dragon class champion from Chicago); Gulf One-Design—Al Salzer; Cruiser Class—William H. Hogan; Thistle class—Paul Schreck of Pensacola; Penguins—Roy Troendle, Jr.; Pram Class (for youngsters aged eight to thirteen)—Jackye Wolfe won over Guste Lorber and Ginny Wynne.

The 1961 social season began with the annual ball of the "Bards of the Bilges." This affair was again filled with riotous freaks and lots of fun. On this occasion, the members were costumed as sea animals and nautical characters, cheering lustily and waving glasses of good cheer as King Neptune (G. Shelby Friedrichs) arrived amidst booming cannon and flaring rockets abord the Royal Yacht SS *Submersible*. The King's court was a group of lovely ladies: Miss Katherine Leach as queen, and Mrs. Nathaniel C. Curtis, Jr. (Francis), Mrs. John Dane (Dot), Miss Robin de Armas, Mrs. William S. Provensal, Jr. (Katherine), Mrs. George Sustendal (Sue) and Mrs. W. Horace Williams Jr. (Harriet) as maids.

In the Lipton Cup ocean race off Miami in 1961, which preceeded the annual Miami to Nassau race, the SYC had two entries, Bache Whitlock's *Bonnie Doon* and John Nixon's *Tabasco*, both Arco 33 fiberglass yawls.

After the 1961 long-distance race to the coast, the annual Gulfport to Pensacola Race was sailed for the first time under the co-sponsorship of the Gulfport and Southern Yacht Clubs and sanctioned by the Gulf Yachting Association. First to finish the Pensacola race was W. Garic Moran's *Whispering Wind*. First in Class A was Bill Hogan's *Glass Slipper* and first in Class B was Bill Cain's *West Indian*. Johnny Dicks' *Pampero* was the overall winner on corrected time.

This was the first year the race was divided into two classes, A and B. Class A boats sailed the 110-mile course from the Gulfport Ship Channel to the sea buoy at the entrance of Pensacola Bay. Class B boats elected to motor out to the Nun buoy off the West end of Ship Island at Gulfport and then hoist sails.

One of the fastest boats to sail in club races was Garic Moran's *Whispering Wind*, a Herreshoff designed 45-foot Fishers Island sloop. This craft finished first in the Gulfport to Pensacola race five times, four of them in a row, and twice won the "race to the coast."

Following the "race to the coast" in 1961, the Fox-Garic Predicted Log race for powerboats got off to its first start in several years. As previously mentioned, this traditional race was first run on July 4, 1912, the course being from New Orleans to Pensacola. The winner was awarded the William M. Garic trophy. This trophy was retired by SYC Vice-Commodore C. Beresford Fox in 1919 after he had won it for three successive years, 1917, 1918, and 1919, with his cruiser *Brenda II*.

In 1957, the Fox family donated the trophy to the Southern Yacht Club, to be known as the Fox-Garic trophy. The first winner was Dr. William Wagner in his yacht *Maryland*. In 1961 Harry J. Williams in *Judylee II* won the trophy, followed by Dr. Charles A. Chambers in *Prowler* in 1962 and by Dr. Clarence Black in *Salty* in 1963.

The Ethan Allen Lightning Crew championship memorial trophy was another beautiful addition to the winners' circle in 1961. It was presented to the SYC by Tommy, the son of Ethan Allen, in memory of his father. The Allen family was a familiar sight on the waters of Lake Pontchartrain in the Lightning Class. Tommy's crew consisted of his father, Ethan, and his mother, Lydia. They sailed as a team for many years, until the death of Ethan. The trophy is a magnificent antique English Binnacle mounted on a large round base.

For the second consecutive year "Buddy" Friedrichs, in a field of twenty boats, was crowned the L-16 International champion in 1961.

His crew was Craig Nelson and Buddy's brother, Gore.

The 1961 sailing season closed with the hotly contested L-16 North-South Team Race on Lake Pontchartrain. The Southern skippers were out to regain the trophy from their Northern friends, who had captured it in 1960, and they succeeded with a championship team consisting of Louis Koerner, Charles Eshleman, Jr., Dan Lehon, and Gus Lorber. The Chicago team consisted of Sam Clarke, Russ Moon, Tom Broeckl, and Art Swift.

Before the 1961 season ended, the juniors, members of TNT (The Nautical Teens) group, held a party at which film stars Gigi Pereau and Virginia Gray looked in on the 250 youngsters who came to dance to the music of the Ivories, a favorite rock-and-roll group in New Orleans. It was at this party that the film star John Gavin presented the Tammy trophy to SYC Commodore Counce.

The year 1961 brought to an end the long life of an SYC honorary member, Capt. Edward "Polly" Polasek, a sailor for 65 years. Captain Polly, as he was affectionately called, was a favorite among the junior sailors of the club. He taught many boys and girls the know-how to win races. After his death, his little friends personally contributed to the cost of a memorial Captain Polly trophy to be sailed for by the Pram Class.

The first winner of the Captain Polly trophy was Frank Livaudais. The other skippers in the race were Cameron Duncan, Fritz Fromherz, John Cerise, Tommy Haslam, George Janssen, and John Dane, III. The following year, Phyllis Fromherz was the winner for participating in all races and good sportsmanship. Another young skipperette, Jackye Wolfe, is the proud owner of one of Polly's treasured trophies which he had won with his boat *Mermaid*. It was given to Jackye to encourage her as one of the first and ever-struggling Pram skipperettes.

Commodore Leslie P. Beard
1933, 1941, 1942, 1943, 1944

Commodore Richard G. Jones
1945, 1946, 1947, 1948

Commodore George S. Clarke
1949

Commodore F. Evans Farwell
1950, 1951

Commodore G. Shelby Friedrichs
1952, 1953

Commodore James G. Gibbons
1954, 1955

CHAPTER XVIII

1962–1965

COMMODORE	TERM
W. Horace Williams, Jr.	1962–1963
J. F. A. Lorber, Jr.	1964–1965

COMMODORE W. HORACE WILLIAMS, JR.—
1962–63

At the SYC 1962 annual meeting, a new commodore was elected, W. Horace Williams, Jr., a member of a New Orleans construction firm W. Horace Williams. Commodore Williams was a very enthusiastic handicap class skipper and the owner of his Evergreen Class sloop *Chula*, which was his flagship. *Chula* compiled an enviable record, winning among others the 1950 long-distance race to Biloxi and the Gulfport to Pensacola race two years in a row. She was one of the outstanding boats in the SYC fleet during the period 1949 through 1951. Williams sailed *Chula* to the Cutter Class fleet championship two years in succession, 1950 and 1951. He participated in every Pensacola race from 1950 through 1965.

Other SYC elected officials were J. F. Auguste Lorber, Jr., vice-commodore, Sidney W. Provensal, Jr., Rear Commodore; Charles L. Eshleman, Jr., secretary-treasurer; Dr. Reichard H. Kahle, fleet surgeon; John Dane, Jr., measurer; and C. A. Sporl, Jr., fleet captain.

One of Williams' first moves as commodore was to revive the annual boat parade and fleet review that had been popular features of opening regattas in the 1890s and early 1900s. He was also responsible for initiating the measurement rule for handicap boats.

For the celebration of the 114th opening regatta of the Southern

Yacht Club in 1962, 105 gayly decorated boats, a combined fleet of power and sail yachts carrying costumed crews and flying their colors, came out of the harbor into the New Basin Canal to enter Lake Pontchartrain. They made a striking and beautiful parade of boats as they passed the spectators lined along the seawall and the officials on board C. A. "Junior" Sporl, Jr.'s yacht *Cocheco*. Just as soon as the protocol was met and the formal air cleared, the sailors hauled down their pennants and flew back to the club to drop off the family members aboard, then head to the starting line, hoping to win in spite of their untried crews, un-tuned rigging, and last year's old trims. (As usual at opening regattas there is organized chaos.) Somehow they arrived in time for the cannon and the start of another busy sailing season.

The 1962 summer sailing months were dramatically successful at the SYC. The old burgee flew far and wide in many outstanding regattas in the U. S. and in Canada.

Numbered among the big sailing events on Lake Pontchartrain and hosted by the Southern Yacht Club was the Star Class Spring series which was won by the old reliable Richard "Dick" Stearns, with his crew Lynn Williams, taking the gun over SYC's champion Star Class skipper, Miles Wynn, with John Shober crew.

Another important classic held by SYC was the Dragon Class North American championship. With twenty-six skippers in five races, it was won by the Chicago representative, Bob Smith, over SYC Nathaniel C. "Buster" Curtis, Jr., who was tied with Smith going into the last race.

In the Davaar Quaich trophy race in Dorval, Quebec, another SYC Dragon Class representative, Albert Crutcher, in a race with thirty-four competitors also had to settle for a second place sailing his Dragon *Bluebonnet*.

Outside of their home waters, the SYC team won the North-South team race against Chicago in L-16s. The team members were B. Temple Brown, Ralph Christman, Morris Newman, and Dr. Elmo Cerise.

Also sailing in Chicago was SYC Commodore Richard G. Jones. The former commodore had returned to his home town and proved that he had not lost his touch at the tiller by sailing a 22-square meter boat on Lake Michigan to conquer the traditional annual "Old Guard" race.

Returning to the windy city Chicago was another team of SYC members for the Luder Class International championship of 1962 sailed on Lake Michigan. The classic was won by Charles L. Eshleman, Jr., with crewmen Craig Nelson and Bobby Delgado. For the third straight year an SYC skipper had won this event. Another skipper from SYC who entered this championship race was Barton Jahncke, who also sailed a fine race.

Remaining on the road in 1962 and sailing in San Francisco, California in the shadow of the Golden Gate bridge was William H. "Bill" Seemann, III. With a second place finish, "Bill" sailed a terrific series for the Finn Zellerbach trophy.

In the Penguin Internationals of 1962 sailed in Sayville, New York, SYC's Adriel "Sparky" Graham was awarded the Women's Israel Perpetual Trophy. She was the first 16-year-old girl to win this coveted trophy.

The junior program was very active in 1962. There were forty-four entries in their Junior Regatta. The winners were: Johnny Williams in the Handicap Class; Reichard Kahle in the Star Class; Bobby Delgado in L-16s; Cort Curtis in a Dragon; Fritz Fromherz in the Lightning Class, and in the Fish Class, Woody Burwell. A new junior commodore was elected for the year 1962: Hjalmer Breit, II replaced Buddy Friedrichs, Jr. Vice-Commodore was Peter Keenan, and secretary was Bobby Delgado.

After a long and gruelling effort by SYC skipperettes Adriel "Sparky" Graham (skipper), Gail Blanchard, Mrs. Henry Finke (Lu), Randy Lorber, and "Sparky's" mother, Mrs. Louis B. Graham (Del) (crew) these brave gals made it to the Adams Cup finals. They survived their club elimination, the quarter-finals and the most difficult of all area sail-offs, the semi-finals. This one sailed in Savannah, Georgia was the toughest, against such competitors as Barbara McIntosh of the South Atlantic Yacht Racing Association, Fredie Cleveland of the Dixie Inland Yachting Association, Nancy Lucas of the Florida Sailing Association, and last but not least the former champion out of the Texas Yachting Association, Glenn Lattimore.

In the 1962 Finals, sailed in Hamilton, Massachusetts at the Manchester Yacht Club, "Sparky" placed fourth of eight entries. They sailed in the 210 class, a large heavy-displacememt sloop. The winner of this event was Mrs. Allegra Knapp Mertz. This was the fourth straight time that "Leggy" Mertz, sister of Arthur Knapp of the 12-meter fame, had won the Mrs. Frances Adams trophy. However, "Sparky" was honored in her home town yacht club when the SYC committee selected her as the first woman in the Southern Yacht

Club's history to have her name placed on the Commodore Charles J. Tessier plaque as the most outstanding skipper in 1962, also honoring for her past accomplishments in the nautical field.

NEW FIBERGLASS BOATS ADDED TO SYC FLEET

The perfection of fiberglass for boat-building provided new fleets on the Lake Pontchartrain. The "Dixie" rotogravure section of *The Times-Picayune* of May 20, 1962 cheered the dawn of spellbinding boat design in an article called "Speed and Luxury":

> The old salts who sailed Lake Pontchartrain in the days of the 21-footers—and even older "machine sloops"—like to talk of making the long-distance races "down the coast" with no more in the way of provisions than a bottle of gin and a watermelon.
>
> But they're casting envious eyes at the modern sailing yachts that now run the same races with benefit of foam rubber bunks, electric refrigeration and all the comforts of home. And in addition to beauty and luxury unknown just a few years ago, the new boats are showing a turn of speed to match the fastest of the windjammers.
>
> Many fine racing-cruising yachts of new design have been brought to the New Orleans area, and interest in sail racing has never been higher. All getting ready for the big events of the season—race to the North shore of Lake Pontchartrain; race to the Mississippi Coast; the annual blue-water race from Gulfport to Pensacola and the leisurely cruise back to the Mississippi Coast through the intracostal waterway then the race back to West End.
>
> One of the finest of the larger new racers is the sleek blue-gulled yacht *Bonnie Doon* recently brought to New Orleans by Bache Whitlock. The 44-foot hull is of molded fiber glass, the spars of aluminum alloy, electric refrigeration, large galley and ample for as many as 7 persons.
>
> The boat was designed by William H. Tripp, Jr., built by Mercer Reinforced Plastics Corp. of Trenton, New York, with a combination keel-centerboard. Working sails total almost 900 square feet and the boat is powered by a 60-horsepower engine.

The many other boats in the harbor were:

Lorelei—a 38 foot Challenger class yawl designed by the American firm of John G. Alden & Co., Inc. She was built in England by Halmatic, Ltd. Her owner was Commodore G. Shelby Friedrichs.

Chiffon Bleau—a Rhodes 19 sloop designed by Philip L. Rhodes and owned by Brooke Helm Duncan, II.

Indigo—a Polaris class fiberglass sloop designed by William H. Tripp, measuring 26 feet 3 inches, owned by Warren Nolan and Herbert

O'Donnell. She arrived November 11, 1961 from Holland after six weeks as deck cargo.

Skylark IV—a 33 foot Malabar cutter designed by John Alden of Boston, Massachusetts and built by Morse, the same as the Tullis' *Windjammer.* Owners of *Skylark IV* were Commodore and Mrs. Charles L. Gambel.

Roulette—a 32-foot Melody yawl designed by Charles Hunt and built by Surfliner Corp. of Lake Wales, Florida, owned by Cal F. Hadden, Jr.

Dos Gris—a 29-foot fiberglass yawl designed by Carl A. Alberg and built by Pearson Corp. of the Stock Triton Class, owned by Mr. and Mrs. Arthur Q. Davis.

Midget—a 22 foot Electra Class sloop. She was a new addition to the Midget Ocean Circuit, designed by Carl A. Alberg of Marblehead, Massachusetts and built by the Pearson Corp. Bristol, Rhode Island. Her owners were Bryan and Noelee Wayne.

Arktoo—a 36-foot Rhodes Whistler Class sloop designed by Philip L. Rhodes. She was owned by Douglas G. Drennan. The main timbers of *Arktoo* were long leaf pine which came out of one of the old cotton presses in New Orleans and were about 100 years old.

Windjammer III was built by Morse and designed by John G. Alden & Co. Her owner was Commodore Garner H. Tullis. She was a clipper bow ship of wood modelled after the small sail ships of Maine during the 1840's, known as "coasters." *Windjammer III* measured 65 feet with a 15½-foot beam, with Ratsey and Lapthorn sails covering 1,846 square feet. Launched in 1959, the beautiful aristocrat was anchored off the pier near the summer home of the Tullis family in Biloxi.

Bug's Bunny was the other new sloop owned by Beauregard "Bugs" and Jacqueline "Quack" Avegno. They sold the *Barcarolo*, an old 33-foot auxiliary sloop designed by Sparkman and Stephens. Of particular interest was her fireplace, which was made of soapstone and brass. The *Bugs Bunny* was a new fiberglass auxiliary cruiser. Tragedy struck on board this new boat when its owner was electrocuted while using an electric drill on a wet deck in the summer of 1964.

"Bugs" was captain of the SYC handicap fleet and very popular in yachting circles in New Orleans and along the Gulf Coast. He sailed and owned over sixty boats. His vivacious manner and sparkling personality will always be remembered. A beautiful memorial trophy was presented to the SYC for competition in the handicap class. It is a large sterling silver punch bowl with a picture of the *Bug's Bunny* engraved on its surface.

A familiar sight on Lake Pontchartrain for many years was the *Elsie M. Reichert*, owned by SYC's fleet captain, William H. Seemann, Jr. and his wife, Coco. She was typical of the Delaware Bay oysterman of the late 19th century. She was built in 1898 by Wm. Rice & Son of Bridgeton, New Jersey, to very heavy specifications, and she spent the early part of her life as an oyster dragger. Converted to pleasure about the early 20's, the *Elsie* was long a familiar sight also in East Coast waters, including the Miami area, and the Bahamas. The Seemanns' son, Bill, and a few of his buddies sailed her down from the Chesapeake in 1958.

The *Elsie* served in the Coast Guard offshore patrol in World War II. She was fifty-four feet long on deck with an eighteen foot beam and drew four feet nine inches with her board up. She weighed about thirty-five tons. She packed close to 2000 square feet of canvas in her four lowers. *Elsie* had retained her original name since her christening date. She is a living member of the Historic American Merchant Marine, and her plans and history are on file with that division of the Smithsonian Institute in Washington. It was difficult for Coco and Billy to surrender their prized possession they had enjoyed with their family and dog for so many years.

In the Handicap Class, the 1963 inaugural championship races on Lake Pontchartrain started off with twenty boats in the different divisions. The two new additions to the fleet were the *Flying Ginny* of the Carys, Virginia "Ginny" and Charlie, she was a new Alberg 35-foot fiberglass sloop. On her shakedown cruise Gene Walet was hired as bartender.

In his new challenger sloop *True Blue* John Dicks entered the annual long-distance race and won the trophy in the Class A division of 1963. As the race carried on from Gulfport to Pensacola, Cal Hadden, Jr. in *Roulette* repeated his 1961 performance by winning in Class A, although A. J. Nugon's *Whistling Wind* was first to finish at the line in Pensacola.

FOUR NEW FLEETS IN SYC HARBOR

A small but active group of interested members banded together to form the Lido Class in 1963. They were Dr. Edward L. Levert and his son Weese, Kathy Bartley, William Droulia, and Eugene H. "Gene" Walet, III. The Lido was a 14-foot fiberglass sloop.

The 5.5 metre class was organized in 1963 by Louis B. Graham. The new boats were an international class 32 foot 5 inch design. The three new 5.5's were owned by Graham, T. J. McMahon, Jr., and John F. Dicks, Jr. In 1964, skippers Dicks and Charles L. Eshleman, Jr., sailed 5.5 meters in the Olympic Trials off Newport, Rhode Island. Other owners were Jerry Touche, Capt. Stephen Jennings, Luis Zerrigon, John Magee, Charles Bohn, and Sam Ryniker.

Also debuting in 1963 was the Rhodes 19 class. The Rhodes is a 19 foot open sloop designed by Philip M. Rhodes, one of the country's leading boat designers. The organizing members and owners of the new boats were Brooke H. Duncan, II in *Chiffon Bleu*, D. Douglas Howard and Henry S. Marshal's *Rinky Dink*, John M. Ellis' *Soupcon*, Charles W. McLellan in *Off Court*, Ben L. Upton's *Dusty*, and Gilbert M. "Gil" Mellin in *Little Ant*.

The fourth new fleet was the Olympic class boat, the Finn Monotype. A Finn is a 14-foot 9-inch fiberglass centerboard dinghy with an unstayed mast that carries a single sail. It is handled by one man and is extemely fast in a breeze. This worldwide class was pioneered in the SYC by Bill Seemann, III, A. J. Nugon, Roy Troendle, Sr., Charles Adams, and Maurice J. "Bubby" Hartson, III. Other owners have been Joseph Young, Drew Whitley, Gary Fritz, Bob Blythe, and Mike Sperry.

The Finn made its debut in a memorable race on Lake Pontchartrain in 1963. At the end of the weather leg, it was Bill Seemann rounding first, followed by Charlie Adams, who tagged the mark at this point, and then Bubby Hartson, who having broke a hiking strap, had gone for a swim. The next two legs were racing and running with no change in places. Bill Seemann crossed the finish line first but was disqualified for not registering, and since Charlie Adams had hit the mark, this gave Bubby Hartson the race, after taking his time, going for a swim and finishing in third place—how lucky can one get!

When the 1963 Finn fleet championship was held at SYC, Maurice J. "Bubby" Hartson, III of SYC was the winner, followed by O. J. Young of the NOYC, Jack Shwartz, Reichard Kahle, Barbara Nelson, and Charlie Adams. In 1964, the Finn Class North American championship was sailed on Lake Pontchartrain with Dan Hurley of Short Hills, New Jersey the winner over O. J. Young of New Orleans Yacht Club in a close race. GYA Commodore J. Gilbert Scheib represented NAYRU as chief judge.

The next championship event to be sailed on Lake Pontchartrain was the Luder International series of 1963. SYC's Charles L. Eshleman, Jr., with his crewman Daniel B. Killeen and Barbee Winston, sailing his Luder *Sybarite* won the L-16 championship for the second straight year. Eshleman was pushed by Roy Troendle of Southern with crew Bubby Hartson and Click Schreck right down to the last race. The Com. Charles A. Tessier trophy for the outstanding skipper of the year was presented to Charles L. Eshleman, Jr. in 1963, making it the third time that Charlie was so honored. He had won this award in 1957 and 1962.

The Lightning Class fleet under the command of Erston Reisch, Jr., fleet captain, and Jules E. Simoneaux, Jr., secretary-treasurer, had a very successful year with many new boats added in 1963. The Eager Beaver contest brought out twenty entries and was won by Bobby Kammer. The new owners were Burt Keenan and his brother, Walter C. "Cookie" Keenan, Jr. The other owners were: Tommy Allen, Armond Bernius, Jack Bertel, A. P. Busch, III, Bob Fabacher, Fabian Fromherz, Palmer Jones, Jack Livaudais, Sr. and Jr., Tommy Moran, James Mullally, Erston Reisch, Sr. and Jr., Jules Simoneaux, Jr., John L. Toye, Luis Verzigon.

The prospects for keen regional and international competition spurred the Lake Pontchartrain Dragon Fleet at SYC to great enthusiasm for the best season they ever had.

One of the Dragon Fleet's most active skippers was Nathaniel C. "Buster" Curtis, Jr., who had traveled to Sao Paulo, Brazil in 1962 to participate in the Pan-American Games. He placed second in the 1962 Dragon North American championship and was in the top bracket in national and international competition for several years.

Lured by the idea of foreign silver, Buster made plans to campaign in Europe the summer of 1963. With his Dragon *Dixie Doodle* he left on his European trip to Copenhagen, Denmark with crewmen Hudson Finke and Timothy Schneidau. Curtis participated in Kiel Week in June, then sailed his new Brites Dragon from Portugal for the Gold Cup in Maarstrand, Sweden and finally to Hanko Week in Hanko, Norway, both in the month of July.

Also holding up the honors for SYC in Europe were Ed. Hobson, Albert Crutcher, Henry Finke, and Paul Odendahl. They competed in Canada for the Davaar Quaich Trophy, the Dulles Trophy, and the North American championship (George E. Craig Trophy) in August. At this time, a team race was scheduled between the Royal

Canadian Yacht Club of Toronto and the Southern Yacht Club, which inaugurated a semi-annual event to be held at each yacht club in turn.

Four new Dragons with familiar Southern names were added to the SYC fleet in 1963. Maurice "Mo" Nauquin and Henry Finke christened their *Mint Julep* with champagne (because it was too early for the mint season). Nathaniel C. "Buster" Curtis, Jr. launched *Sazarac III*, as did John Sharp his new *Rob Roy*, and Stewart Maunsel returned to the fold with *Sugarfoot*. Buster took delivery of *Sazarac II* in Europe during the summer. By the end of the year, others were added by Ed Hobson, Abeking-Rasmussen-built in Germany, and Albert Crutcher bought a new Borreson from Denmark, making a total of twenty-three Dragons.

The SYC Dragons sent a delegation to Houston for their 1963 Mid-Winter Regatta and took all honors in the three-race series. Ed Hobson was first, Albert Crutcher was second, and Henry Finke, third. The Houston Yacht Club had seven boats and was expecting more to be added to their fleet.

The SYC Dragons entered the Olympic Class regatta at the Texas Corinthian Yacht Club in Galveston Bay in 1963 and again won in a highly competitive field of international skippers.

SNOWFALL OF CENTURY
COVERS SUGAR BOWL EVENTS

The headlines on the front page of *The Times-Picayune* January 1, 1964 was: "Snowfall of the century—the heaviest layer of Yankee confetti to cover the city since 1895." The Sugar Bowl football game played that day was witnessed by thousands in the Sugar Bowl stadium. Alabama won over Ole Miss—12 to 7. A few days previously the Sugar Bowl Regatta was held in very cold weather with a record-breaking number of boats on the starting line.

The Sugar Bowl Regatta in New Orleans brought many prominent skippers to Lake Pontchartrain. In the Dragon Class there was a spectacular finish when a visiting yachtman, Robert "Bob" Mosbacher in his Dragon *Puff* out of the Texas Corinthian Yacht Club (located on Galveston Bay, Texas), showed a fleet of twenty other Dragon sailors that the talent in the family was not all up in Newport, where his brother "Bus" of America's Cup fame resides. "Bus" crewed for his brother "Bob" along with George Francisco in winning the race.

Other out-of-towners were Walt Swindeman in *Yankee Doodle* out of Toledo, Ohio, a three time North American Dragon champion. Also competing were Don Genitempo in *Alarm* from Houston Yacht Club, Willis Boyd of Long Beach, California, the present North American Dragon Champion, and others.

Another exciting classic was hosted by the SYC in 1964. A preview for the Tokyo Olympic Trials was the scene on Lake Pontchartrain when the *Windjammer* series was held for Dragon Class sailors from the United States and Canada. Winning the *Windjammer* trophy was Robert "Bob" Mosbacher. He beat eighteen others in a six-race series. Bob had returned to New Orleans where he had left his boat after winning the Sugar Bowl Regatta. The local entries in the races were Albert Crutcher, Edward Hobson, Buster Curtis, and Henry Finke. Crutcher had just returned from Bermuda where he crewed with Bob Mosbacher during the Bermuda race week.

The Dragon Class continued its progress with four new boats owned by Charles Hardy, Robert Boh, Stanhope Hopkins, and Walter Reisch. Another Dragon champion, Paul Odendahl, with his crew of Jack Taylor and Gayle Blanchard, won the 1964 eliminations to represent the SYC Dragon Fleet in the National championship races.

COMMODORE J. F. A. LORBER, JR.—1964–65

Elected to serve the Southern Yacht Club as its commodore for the year 1964 was J. F. A. "Gus" Lorber, Jr. A prominent business executive of the Jackson Brewing Company of New Orleans, Gus was also well known in yachting circles. As a teenager, he began sailing on the Gulf-One design sloop *Lady Lou*.

The commodore later became one of the mainstays of the Star Class Fleet for twenty-five years, and he won many honors with his *Scout*. He was runner-up in the Spring championship and Jahncke trophy Star Class series in 1941. In 1940 Gus was appointed to the race committee for the World's Cup Star Class Championship in San Diego, California. In 1947, he was the recipient of the Commodore Charles J. Tessier Memorial award as the outstanding skipper of the year and for his many sailing accomplishments.

Serving with Commodore Lorber were Sidney W. Provensal, Jr., vice-commodore; Nathaniel C. Curtis, Jr., rear commodore; Charles L. Eshleman, Jr., secretary-treasurer; Dr. Mayo L. Emory, fleet surgeon; Herbert O'Donnell, fleet measurer; and Beauregard Avegno, fleet captain.

The opening regatta of 1964 followed the practice inaugurated by

Commodore Williams and the same program of colorful decorations and costumed crews led the parade of boats, which proceeded along the seawall as far as the Mardi Gras fountain on the lakeshore, where they passed in review before the dignitaries on board C. A. "Junior" Sporl, Jr.'s yacht *Cocheco*.

Prior to the parade, a small ceremony was held at the Penick Dock with Commodore Lorber presenting a memorial plaque to the wife of the late William Penick. Mr. Penick was one of New Orleans' most prominent businessmen and civic leaders; Mrs. Penick deeded over to the Southern Yacht Club that portion of the ground along side the clubhouse, 250 feet of land and 120 feet of pier, to be used as a mooring facility for club members and visiting guests only. During Mr. Penick's forty-six year membership in the SYC he had owned eight yachts.

COMMUTER TRAIN TO GULF COAST DISCONTINUED

The summer months were hampered for those who commuted daily by train to the Gulf Coast with the closing of the railroad line on May 6, 1964, the day on which the L & N railroad ran its last train from New Orleans to the Gulf Coast. No more would the sound of the whistle blowing from the five o'clock train beckon the family to the depot to pick up Dad or hubby. In the heyday of rail travel, wealthy commuters owned their own private cars, luxuriously outfitted with refreshments, porter service, and historic card games that went on for years, morning and afternoon.

The railroad between New Orleans and Mobile had been completed on October 29, 1870. There was continuous commuter service between New Orleans and the Gulf Coast from May 8, 1880 until May 6, 1964. The line originally started at Ocean Springs, but it was later to run only from Pass Christian. (This commuter service was temporarily restored for the World's Fair in 1984.)

SYC CREW WINS MALLORY CUP—1964

The big news of the 1964 sailing season was that SYC "wonder boy" G. Shelby "Buddy" Friedrichs, Jr. won the 1964 Men's North American Sailing championship for the Mallory Cup. His crewmen were Tommy Dreyfus and Roy Troendle, Sr. They sailed at Grosse Point, Michigan, soundly beating his competition with five first place wins, two seconds, and one third place. This was the third time that the GYA and SYC had had a winning team in the Mallory Cup finals. Gene Walet won this trophy for two consecutive years in 1953 and 1954.

On the SYC's home waters, the 1964 International Penguin championship for juniors was held with the hometown skipper Arthur Seaver, Jr. taking a close second to Brazil's winner George Machado.

Team racing is always one of the most interesting of all sailing events. In competition with the New Orleans Yacht Club, the Southern Yacht Club skippers entered the inaugural Commodore J. Gilbert Scheib trophy team race on Lake Pontchartrain in 1964. The NOYC won the series with their top skippers: Don Brennan, Cal Herman, Charlie Erickson, and Billy Ibs. Southern's experts were Buddy Friedrichs, Hjalmar Breit, John Dane, III, Darrell Higgins, Jr., Arthur Seaver, Jr., Larry Taggert, and Roy Troendle.

The 1964 Junior Lipton Cup was won by another SYC team composed of Roy Troendle, Jr., David Blouin, and Bayne Keenan.

In December 1964, a tragic fire occurred on board the *Bonnie Doon*, owned by Bache Whitlock and docked in the SYC pen. The date was Dec. 19. The editor of the SYC *Tell-Tale* wrote: "Two fires on the same day miles apart, severely damaged two establishments well-known to SYC members, Neiman-Marcus' department store in Dallas and the *Bonnie Doon* in the New Orleans Marina. Both fires started the night of December 19th and both did considerable damage. The Levee Board's new rescue fire boat responded quickly and managed to extinguish the blaze before the entire craft was destroyed. Damage to Neiman-Marcus was appraised at approximately 11 million dollars. Damage to the *Bonnie Doon* has been appraised at a lesser figure."

The Sugar Bowl "race of champions" is actually the beginning of the all-around sailing season in the Gulf Yachting Association yacht clubs from Texas to Florida. (The South is blessed; the boats are never kept in moth balls.) This year's "race of champions" was won for the first time by Pass Christian Yacht Club, with Mike Pickich the skipper. He tied with SYC skipper J. Fred Clerc, but Pickich won on horse racing. The previous year, 1963, it was another first for the New Orleans Yacht Club's team with Ben Case at the tiller and his sons Leslie and Billy as crew.

The only change in officers for the year 1965 was that Douglas Drennan replaced Beauregard Avegno as fleet captain.

REGATA AL SOL
(Regatta in the Sun)—1965

One of the biggest events of the decade was the *regata al sol* initiated in 1965. It was at the suggestion of the Mexican National Tourist Council that the Southern Yacht Club was chosen as befitting the challenge of a long-distance ocean race between the Club de Yates of Isla Mujeres and the Southern Yacht Club. The SYC is the second-oldest yacht club in the United States and the Club de Yates holds the same position in Mexico. Both clubs' having yachtsmen of sailing and navigational skills and yachts with offshore capabilities gave impetus to the suggestion.

In cooperation with the Mexican officials, SYC Commodore Lorber welcomed the idea and after several meetings, appointed Richard "Dick" G. Spangenberg to be chairman of the *regata al sol* races. The history of these events over the years from 1965 to date and the gratifying results of Dick's capable leadership are evidence that Commodore Lorber's decision was a wise one.

It was the first race of international character in this area and the *regata al sol* accomplished the additional purpose of cementing friendships with our neighbors to the south, and of increasing tourism to one of the most interesting parts of Mexico. The distance to be covered was 560 miles from New Orleans to Isla Mujeres, Q. R. Mexico, an island off the coast of the Yucatan Peninsula.

The Southern Yacht Club accepted the challenge but was unable to have an entry in the first race because of a conflict of dates with those of the Gulfport to Pensacola race and the Galveston to Gulfport event. The first race started on June 16, 1965 in Mississippi Sound, a few miles south of the Gulfport Yacht Club, and finished off the Isla Mujeres light in Mexico. This is the longest race in the history of the SYC.

Following is a list of boats and their owners entering the 1965 race:

Venus (schooner)	W. J. Broughton of Birmingham, Alabama
Dawn (schooner)	Sam Labouisse of Pass Christian, Mississippi
Marespel (yawl)	Peter Trouchard, Sarasota, Florida
Langosta (schooner)	Don Hazlett, New Orleans, Louisiana

Two Navy Yawls from Pensacola, Florida, one of which was *Tailwind*.

The trophy for the event was awarded to the skipper of the U. S. Navy yawl *Tailwind* 2d Lt. H. F. Wirshing, USMC, by the president of Mexico, Gustavo Diaz Ordaz. It is the "president of Mexico" trophy. A large delegation was guested on the island for the festivities. The Mexican Government had planned a fiesta around the ancient Mayan Ruins of Uxmel, Chichen-Itza, and Kabah, as well as the walled city of Campeche.

There was another inaugural event in 1965, the "race for the case." This classic followed the 1965 long-distance race to the coast from West End, which was won by Bill Droulia sporting his new Vanguard sloop *Lorraine*, which also won the Class B trophy. Winning the Class A trophy and making her debut, was *Gulf Ghost*, co-owned by John "Jack" Dane, Jr. and Oscar McMillan, sailed by McMillan. To prove that his partner's victory was no fluke, Jack Dane won the "race for the case." This is a fun race which was set up by the hospitable Bache Whitlock, whose restored *Bonnie Boon* conveyed the skippers and crews to his Ocean Springs summer home for a shrimp and beer celebration. The very thought of it inspired Jack Dane to win this inaugural race.

The 1965 Gulfport to Pensacola race made history. The race was plagued by light winds and strong tides; however, the big winner of this event was a skipper from the Pensacola Yacht Club, Lewis B. "Buddy" Pollack, Sr., sailing his small Ariel sloop *Brenda* (his first mate's name). It was the fastest Pensacola race on record. Buddy sailed it in a corrected time of seventeen hours and twenty-five minutes after leaving the Gulfport starting line. There were seventy-five boats participating in the race. In this same event, the first boat to finish in Class A was A. J. Nugon's *Whistling Wind*—she also won the 1965 Sugar Bowl Regatta in the Handicap Class.

Along the Gulf Coast, the Biloxi Yacht Club sponsored a Southern Mayor's championship sailboat race. The race was the climax of the annual fifteen state Biloxi Outboard Jubilee sponsored by the port commission. Mayor Vic Schiro of New Orleans was the winner over Mayor R. B. Meadows of Gulfport.

Away from our local waters, there was another ocean race initiated in 1965, a 300-mile race from Pensacola to St. Petersburg, sponsored by the Navy Yacht Club in cooperation with the Pensacola Yacht Club and the St. Petersburg Yacht Club for the "Pensacola Cup" which was donated by the Pensacola Sports Association. The race drew entries from New Orleans, Mobile, Gulfport, Fort Walton, Panama City, Pensacola, and St. Petersburg. Charlie Morgan, race chairman from St. Petersburg, and Lieut. Commander Ken Tracy of the Navy Yacht Club were chairmen of the race.

OLYMPIC COMMITTEE SELECTS DRAGONS

It was good news for the SYC Dragon skippers when the International Yacht Racing Union met in London in 1965 to select the class of boats to be used in the 1968 Olympics. The Dragon Class was one of the five approved. This gave a big boost to those who sailed the twenty-one Dragons in the fleet of SYC.

The Southern Yacht Club was again host for the Dragon championship races in 1965. There were entries from Houston; San Diego, California; Chicago, Illinois; Mt. Clemens, Michigan; Toledo, Ohio; and Toronto, Canada. Returning to New Orleans to defend his title was Bob Mosbacher of the Houston Yacht Club. He sailed the same boat Lowell North won the Olympic bronze medal with in 1964. Winning the 1965 *Windjammer* series was Paul Phelan of Toronto, who had been beaten out of the series in the previous year. Other entries were Don Genitempo and Forbes Wilson of Houston, Judd Goldman of Chicago, Bernard Swindeman of Toledo, and Skip Boston, Bill Greer, Gordon Cheney, and Jan Jonakind of Aalsmeer, Holland.

The American International Dragon Association elected SYC's Henry Finke as commodore for 1965, and another SYC member, Nathaniel C. Curtis, Jr., was elected the Dragon Class representative to the technical sub-committee of the Olympic Yachting Committee.

SYC FORMS OLYMPIC SAILING ASSOCIATION

The Olympic Sailing Association of the SYC was formed in 1965 for the sole purpose of lending assistance to well qualified local yachtsmen in their competition for a position on the U. S. Olympic sailing team and a chance to win a gold medal for the United States of America. Not since 1932 when Commodore Charles J. Tessier and Ernest Lee Jahncke of SYC spearheaded the movement whereby the SYC would have an entry in the 1932 Olympic Games and the necessary funds were raised to send Gilbert Gray, Andrew Libano, and their Star boat *Jupiter* to California, had there been such enthusiasm among yachtsmen in the Southern Yacht Club.

At its first meeting in 1965, the new association elected Nathaniel

C. "Buster" Curtis, Jr. president; Albert B. Crutcher, Jr., vice-president; J. W. "Jay" Clark, treasurer; and Sidney W. Provensal, Jr., secretary. Clark raised the money for the campaign, which was very successful. The following members formed the advisory committee:

Charles G. Cary	Maurice J. Naquin
Capt. Jay W. Clark	A.J. Nugon, Jr.
F. Evans Farwell	J. Gilbert Scheib
Charles L. Gamble	C. A. Sporl, Jr.
James G. Gibbons	Eugene Walet, III
Gilbert T. Gray	Bache McE. Whitlock
J. F. A. Lorber, Jr.	Davis S. Wuescher
Frank A. Nemec	Arthur D. Wynne

The goal of the SYC Olympic committe was to seek funds necessary to purchase a boat and to pay the expenses of a crew to be sent to the Games. This was accomplished through the efforts and dedication of the members of the committe. A Dragon was purchased and named the *Williwaw*. The crew was selected after much deliberation and training over the next three years. Three young men, all in their late twenties, G. Shelby Friedrichs, Jr., a New Orleans stockbroker of Howard, Weil, Labouisse and Friedrichs, Gerald Schreck, a sailmaker of Schreck Sails, Inc., and Barton Jahncke, sales manager for Lykes Bros. Steamship Company. They had their work cut out for them and through the next few years they demonstrated their ability as Olympic champions.

In August 1965, Buddy Friedrichs, with his crew "Click" Schreck and Tommy Dreyfus, won the Dragon North American Sailing Championship held on Lake Erie over Canada's Olympic representative Ed. Botterel by eight and a half points. Twenty-three skippers from all over the country competed in the five-race series.

Before leaving for Canada, Buddy picked up his Star boat *Blitzkrieg* and Barton Jahncke to sail in Mobile, Alabama for the championship of the New Orleans-Gulf Star Class Fleets, which they won. George Brothers of Mobile and his wife, Molly, as crew were second, but they were winners as host at the party for all visiting yachtsmen held at their lovely home on the river.

In this same Star Class event in Mobile, SYC Joseph L. "Buzzy" Killeen, Jr., broke the record winning the Sir Thomas J. Lipton Star Class trophy for the fifth time with his crew, Steve Andre. "Buzzy" also won in 1966 for the sixth straight year.

Following his victory in Canada on Lake Erie, Buddy Friedrichs, with a new crew of his brother Gore and Craig Nelson, travelled over to Montreal for the Royal St. Lawrence Dragon Regatta, which he also won by a slim margin over Bob Mosbacher. Bob had won the 1964 North American Dragon Championship.

Proving that he could win a championship for himself, Buddy Friedrich's crew, Barton Jahncke, an expert skipper in his own right, took the L-16 Internationals in Chicago in 1965 with a big six-point spread. His crew was Arthur "Buck" Seaver Jr. and his son Arthur, III.

SECOND MALLORY CUP EVENT HELD AT SYC

The Southern Yacht Club was selected again by NAYRU to host the Mallory Cup Finals (the first time was in 1954 when Eugene H. "Gene" Walet III was victorious). The 1964 winner of the cup, Buddy Friedrichs, was unable to compete in the 1965 event as he was sailing in other parts of the country preparing for the Olympic Games.

The Mallory Cup Finals proved to be a very exciting series of races. It was sailed in Ensigns, and the winner was Cornelius Shields, Jr. out of the Larchmont Yacht Club in New York, with his crew Dr. George Brazil and Craig Walters. "Corny" Jr. sailed a consistent series as his finish record of 4-4-2-2-3-2-3-3 testifies. Harold Balcom of Tampa, Florida was second; Nicholas Mason of Chatham, Massachusetts, third.

Mixed emotions were displayed at the awards banquet when chairman J. Gilbert Scheib, who was also chief judge, gave the honor of presenting the trophy to the father of the winner, the great yachtsman Cornelius "Corny" Shields, who was the first winner of the Mallory Cup in 1953. With misty eyes "Corny" stated "This is a pleasure I shall never forget," as he shook hands to congratulate his son. One week later, Hurricane Betsy, the worst hurricane to hit New Orleans, did considerable damage to the SYC harbor, where many boats sunk or were wrecked beyond repair. Fortunately, the clubhouse received minimal damage. After the storm abated and telephone lines were restored, the first call at the Scheibs' home was that of "Corny" Shields inquiring as to the wellbeing of his friends at SYC. This was typical of that great gentleman and sportsman who passed away in 1979.

In October 1965 a group of SYC skippers, Arthur Seaver, Jr., Louis Koerner, Jr., Charles Eshleman, Jr., and Barton Jahncke, successfully competed in the two U. S. team races against a Chicago group on Lake Pontchartrain. The Chicago team was made up of Jake Vilas, Nancy Descant, Sam Clark, and John Carlson.

Commodore Charles L. Gambel
1956, 1957

Commodore Hampton Gamard
1958, 1959

Commodore W. Horace
Williams, Jr.
1962, 1963

Commodore Sidney W.
Provensal, Jr.
1966, 1967

Commodore Oliver J. Counce
1960, 1961

Commodore J. F. A. Lorber, Jr.
1964, 1965

CHAPTER XIX

1966-1971

COMMODORES	TERMS
Sidney W. Provensal, Jr.	1966-1967
Nathaniel C. Curtis, Jr.	1968-1969
Charles L. Eshleman, Jr.	1970-1971

COMMODORE SIDNEY W. PROVENSAL, JR.— 1966-67

The 1966 annual meeting and election of officers was held in March for the last time. It was at this meeting that an amendment to the by-laws was adopted, changing to a calendar-year basis and having the annual meetings in December and the semi-annual meetings in June, instead of March and September, respectively.

Elected commodore for the year 1966 was Sidney W. "Billy" Provensal, Jr. A prominent New Orleans lawyer, Billy was also a champion skipper. He had apprenticed under his father aboard the Gulf-One Design sloop *Southwind*. The commodore was active in all classes of boats, starting with Catboats, which he sailed during the summer months in Biloxi. The other types of sailboats were the Fish Class and Gulf-One Design (in which he won the championship three consecutive times, retiring the Commodore Richard G. Jones trophy). He was fleet captain in the SYC Star Class and served on the International Technical Committee of the ISCRA. He held two silver chevrons of the International Star Class Racing Association and won many Star Class championships. Billy held the position of secretary-treasurer for ten years before advancing to commodore.

Serving with Commodore Provensal were Nathaniel C. Curtis, Jr., vice-commodore; Charles L. Eshleman, Jr., rear commodore;

B. Temple Brown, secretary-treasurer; Dr. Edward T. Haslam, fleet surgeon; Herbert O'Donnell, fleet measurer; Cal Hadden, Jr., fleet captain.

THE SECOND *REGATA AL SOL*—1966

The Southern Yacht Club was host in 1966 for a dinner in honor of the winner of the 1965 *regata al sol*, 2nd Lt. H. F. Wirshing, USMC, skipper of the Navy Yawl, and Mexican and United States officials. There were 130 guests greeted by SYC Commodore Lorber and the SYC board members, with chairman of the event, Richard Spangenberg. The honorary guests were Rear Admiral Diego Migica of the Mexican Navy and members of the Mexican Olympic Sailing Committee. Also, Señor Alberto Alverez-Morphy, who was the Secretary of the Club de Yates de Isla Mujeres, Señor Alberto Reyes-Spindola, the Mexican Consul, Señor Jose Lima, representative of the Mexican Tourist Bureau, and Lt. Commander W. Kentwood Tracy, commodore of the Navy Yacht Club in Pensacola, Florida.

As the result of the overwhelming enthusiasm, twenty entries were received for the second annual ocean race from New Orleans to Isla de Mujeres, as compared with six entries in 1965. The race began on May 21, 1966 at the Southern Yacht Club, with the fleet racing a one 66-mile leg to the Broadwater Beach Marina in Biloxi, Mississippi; then on May 28 the fleet sailed the 560-mile second leg from the Marina across the Gulf of Mexico to the Isla de Mujeres.

Cal Hadden of SYC in his Cal-40 sloop *Chandelle* took the lead early in the race. He finished first five days, ten hours, fifty-two minutes, and twenty seconds later at 9:52 P.M. off the island, where the entire town and Mexican officials had gathered to greet the winners. However, *Cal's Gal*, a Cal-30 sloop skippered by Fred Mauldin of Dickinson, Texas, won the race on corrected time, although he finished two hours, two minutes behind Hadden. His lower handicap rating put him one hour and fifty-four minutes ahead on corrected time. *Cal Gal* also carried away the trophy for first boat in Classes A and B. Howard Williams of Houston, Texas, in his Alberg 35 foot yawl *Rebel* was second in the fleet on corrected time. In third place on corrected time was Hadden in *Chandelle*. Another SYC entry, *Silkie*, owned by B. Temple Brown and Maurice J. Hartson, III and sailed by Brown, was second in Class B and fourth in the fleet on corrected time.

The *Silkie* had aboard as crew Arthur Lowe, who navigated,

Maurice J. Hartson, III, Alfred Brown, William Seeman, III, Jack Gooch, John Hammond, and Eduardo Ponce. They survived the calm off the Gulf Coast by fishing for dolphin with great success until the winds came. After an uneventful passage across the Gulf, they reached the tip of the Yucatan only to run smack into the Gulf Stream current. After making six and a half knots for three hours, Arthur located their position off Arrow Smith shoals and renamed the place "Brown's Half Acre." They planned to run closer to Cuba, but got a report of a black pirate boat preying on local fishing boats, so they elected to paint *Silkie* yellow and stay further west.

For four days and nights the *Temptress*, a Cal-50 sloop sailed by Keith Edwards of Houston, followed then broke away trying to beat the *Chandelle* to the finish line, but Perry Joyce had guided Hadden down the west side of the Yucatan channel to avoid the main current of the Gulf Stream by passing too close to Cuba and tried to save time by taking a straight line crossing to the finish. They entered the stream on Wednesday night and began bucking the current with a falling breeze. By Thursday night they picked up the glow of the brightly lit Hotel Yazil-Ha. Here they called for the lights that showed the committee boat and all of the Mexicans prepared to welcome the winner. Although Howard Williams was first on corrected time, as far as the natives were concerned Cal was the winner. Rockets were sent up and the excitement began.

With skipper Hadden at the tremendous reception were crew member Charles Eshleman, Jr., Walter Reich, David Andry, Tommy Coleman, Dr. G. B. Flagg, and Perry Joyce as navigator. As they reached the harbor, local fishing boats came out to meet them. Cal and the crew were escorted onto shore and met by the many officials of the Mexican government and the governor of the island. The local beauty queen, elected for the occasion, placed a necklace around Hadden's neck and welcomed him to Isla de Mujeres. They were taken by auto parade to the hotel and met by a huge group of guitar players, who sang of their victory. A big champagne party was held, commencing what was to be several days of celebration.

A fleet of fifteen boats sailed into Isla de Mujeres harbor in excellent condition. The only mishap occurred when some spinnakers were ripped by fifty-mile winds when a cold front caught up with the leaders on May 31. At the presentation of awards, trophies were presented by a personal representative of the president of Mexico, the governor of Yucatan, and the U.S. Ambassador, Fulton Freeman.

Guests of honor were the governor of the States of Quintana Roo, Campechie, and Yucatan, the three states comprising the Yucatan Peninsula.

Hadden received the trophy of the secretary of the Navy, a silver Spanish Galleon on a plaque. He also received a large silver bowl given by the tourist council for a third-place finish on corrected time. Still another SYC entry, the *Flying Ginny*, sailed by Charles Carey, won the SYC trophy for the best combined time on the first and second legs. Tradition did not change over the years; as Prentice Edrington stated after his return from the Star Class Series in Havana in 1927 "the boys needed wheelbarrows to carry away the prizes."

This is not the end of the story. There is another interesting episode. The most seasoned crew was aboard a SYC boat, the *Girouette*, a Hinkley Bermuda 40 with Herbert O'Donnell at the wheel and as crewmen, Warren Nolan, Claude Hogan, Fabian Fromherz, Tom Bremmermann, Marion Welford, Louis Koerner, and Oliver Counce. The youngest man was forty. Fresh out of their air-conditioned offices, they found the hot calm of two days miserable. Relief came in the form of squalls. When some of the reckless crews of other boats carried full sails through numerous knockdowns, these veterans doused their spinnakers and reefed the main. Although their nights were restless, they enjoyed the good sailing between the squalls and the big schools of porpoise that came to follow their boat every dawn and dusk. But they enjoyed most the sight of land as they reached the island after six days, twenty-four minutes, and thirty seconds at sea. Tom claimed nothing ever looked so good!

Included among the entries in 1966 were the 1965 race winners, the Pensacola Navy crew, and its 44-foot challenger yawl. The entries were:

New Orleans, La.
Calender "Cal" Hadden—40' sloop
Charles Cary—35' sloop
Bache Whitlock—44' yawl
John "Jack" Dane, Jr.—40' sloop
A. Q. Davis & H. O'Donnell—41' yawl
John Blouin—47' schooner
Cyril Laan—43' schooner
Dan Egan—35' sloop
Sidney Jones—41' yawl
Eugene H. "Gene" Walet, III—44' yawl
B. Temple Brown—40' sloop

Osmond "O.J." Young—34' skate

Texas
Houston—Curtis McKallip—41' yawl
Houston—Howard Williams—35' yawl
Baytown—G. L. Smith—35' sloop
Dickinson—Fred Mauldin—36' sloop
Port Neches—D. B. Hatcher—48' yawl

Covington, La.
Fred Blossman—35' yawl

Pass Christian, Miss.
Sam Labouisse—35' sloop

Gulfport, Miss.
G. B. Flagg—37' sloop

Jackson, Miss.
Paul Radewiez—48' ketch

Navy Yacht Club, Pensacola, Fla.
2—44' yawls

Sarasota, Fla.
J. P. Trouchard—35' yawl

Birmingham, Ala.
W. J. Broughton—43' schooner

A large group of New Orleans and Houston yachtsmen and their wives attended the ceremonies and afterwards toured Yucatan.

Another big event was the Southern Ocean Racing Circuit (SORC), which has become popular among the big boat owners. Considered the toughest race was the one from St. Petersburg to Fort Lauderdale. The fleet winner and fourth to finish in this race was the Cal-40 *Vamp*, skippered by Ted Turner of America's Cup fame behind two 70-footers and the 65-foot *Mariden*, with Buddy Friedrichs as alternate helmsman. "Like sailing a 40-foot Star" was Buddy's tribute to the Lapworth-designed hull.

There were many SYC participants in this SORC race. The Columbia 40, *Silkie*, skippered by Maurice J. "Bubby" Hartson, III, finished fourth in Class A and eighth in the fleet against an entry list that read like the "Who's Who" of big boat racing. Serving as crew for Bubby was his co-owner Temple Brown, O. J. Young, Click Schreck, Bill Seeman, III, Albert Lamar, and Elmo Cerise.

The SYC's big boat Handicap Class continued to grow. Harry Kaufman had a new Cal 30, and Fabian Fromherz announced that after finding a "friendly banker," he too would purchase a new boat. Due in town were two Morgan 34s for Nicholas "Nick" Cromwell and Allen Borne, as well as one for Morgan agent William "Bill" Sherar. Ernest Estes' *Triton* and Fred Blossman's new Alberg 35' yawl *Wishing Star* also arrived in the SYC harbor.

SOUTHERN YACHT CLUB WINS DRAGON CHAMPIONSHIP

Two SYC sailors, G. Shelby Friedrichs, Jr. and Nathaniel C. Curtis, Jr., were included in the U.S. entry for the European International championship for Dragons and for the Heriot Trophy (Coupe Virginia Heriot) in Copenhagen, Denmark, sailed on July 26, 1966. The other American entry was Bob Mosbacher of Houston, Texas.

This regatta is limited to three yachts per nation and is one of the premier Dragon events. Over one hundred boats participated. Top Dragon talent from all Europe was there, including His Majesty King Constantine of Greece, who won the Olympic gold medal in 1960 in the Dragon Class, and his brother-in-law, pretender to the throne of Spain at that time, Juan Carlos. He is at present the King of Spain. Also the current Olympic gold medal winner of 1964, Olen Bernstein of Hellerup, Denmark, who won over Lowell North, Simon Tait of England, and the defending champion.

The Heriot Trophy was donated by the Yacht Club de France and is assigned to the International Dragon Class in memory of a famous French yachtswoman and the only woman to win an Olympic gold medal in sailing.

Friedrichs, with his regular crew of Gerald "Click" Schreck and Barton Jahncke, won this prestigious event, which was a giant step on the road to the 1968 Olympics in Mexico. He put together a 1-2-2-3 series to beat some of the greatest Dragon sailors in the world on their home ground. The number two spot was taken by Aage Birch of Denmark, one of Europe's finest. Close behind were Bob Mosbacher of Texas and the Sunderlin brothers of Sweden. The victory shocked all of Europe, as the London *Times* printed the headline, "America Slays European Dragon."

As a result of his capture of the 1966 European Dragon championship, Buddy Friedrichs was "knighted" in the Royal Order of Tuborq Brewery, with approximately 1,000 people in attendance, including King Constantine of Greece, Juan Carlos of Spain, and King Olaf and Prince Harold of Norway. Buddy kneeled, was touched with a sword, and arose as Sir Shelby. King Constantine and Juan Carlos "bummed" a ride with Buddy and his crew back to the boat. As Buddy slipped behind the wheel he announced loudly, "Kings in the front seat, princes in the back." And so, the Southern Yacht Club in addition to its many champions has claim to a new lord—George Sir Shelby Friedrichs, Jr.

At that time, Buddy Friedrichs did not realize that there would be another king in his midst, as Juan Carlos became the King of Spain on July 22, 1969. A champion yachtsman, the King is proud of the many trophies resting on the shelves of his office, representing three world and four European championships.

In 1966, for the fourth time, the Dragon North American Sailing championship was sailed on Lake Pontchartrain. Heading the blue ribbon entry list was Buddy Friedrichs, who had recently returned from winning the European event in Denmark. Buddy had also won the North American Dragon championship in 1965, which was sailed on Lake Erie in Toledo, Ohio.

The 1964 and 1965 winner of the *Windjammer* trophy (and winner of almost everything at one time or another), Bob Mosbacher, shipped his boat to New Orleans from Houston. Adding interest to this series was the fact that the 1967 Dragon World Championship would be held in Toronto, Canada. As this series is limited to three entries per nation, the Dragon Class Association used the North Americans to select the three U. S. representatives.

Also arriving for the championship event was Albert Crutcher's new Borresen *Mary Lee* (his spouse's name) and Buster Curtis' *Dixie Doodle* en route from Denmark, where both skippers had sailed in the Dragon Gold Cup regatta. With W. E. Ed. Hobson, III's new Dragon built by Abeking and Rasmussen in Lomwerden, West Germany, the total number of boats in the SYC fleet was twenty-four, the largest in the U.S.

Again, Buddy Friedrichs, with crew Click Schreck and Barton Jahncke, displayed his uncanny sailing ability in capturing both the Windjammer and the North American Dragon 1966 championship in two series on Lake Pontchartrain. He compiled a 1,2,2,2,7 to win the Windjammer trophy and a fantastic 6,1,1,1,1 to win the North American championship. Bob Mosbacher of Corinthian Yacht Club in Kemah, Texas was second, and Roy Troendle of SYC was third. Nineteen skippers made up the field of Dragons.

After the Dragon championship races were held, the 1966 L-16

National sailing championship took place on Lake Pontchartrain. Another record was made in this event when Rear Commodore Charles L. Eshleman, Jr., wearing his traditional red shorts and carrying as his crew Ralph Christman and B. Temple Brown, kept his head stuck to the rhumb line to win the L-16 championship for a history making third time. He finished nine points ahead of Graham Ross of Chicago, with Arthur Seaver, Jr. of SYC in third place.

The SYC Motor Yacht Association, with its very active captain, Dr. Clarence Black, held its Predicted Log Race to the Coast of 1966 which was won by Roy Mossy in his *Bonnie Blue*. The return trip was won by Dr. Al Chambers on *Prowler*. Missing from the race was the old reliable *Margaret III*, as she had lost her skipper, the genial Harry Booker, in an untimely death.

The juniors were all jubilant over the "Junior Poop-Deck." The grand opening was held on Sunday, June 19, 1966. The invitation announced the clubhouse was complete with "card tables, a bulletin board, telephone with separate lines for the Juniors only, soft drink, candy and sandwiches machines and a Juke Box, and AIR-CONDITIONING!!!!!"

A great shock to the yachting world came in 1966 with the passing of Commodore Garner H. Tullis, the ocean-racing yachtsman extraordinary. Yachting lost a good skipper, and Southern Yacht Club lost a great friend and benefactor. His famous *Windjammers* evoked varied responses from young and old sailors alike.

At the annual meeting held in 1967, Commodore Provensal was reelected. Arthur Seaver, III replaced Cal Hadden, Jr. as fleet captain. The combination of sail and motor yachts parading along the seawall made an impressive show for the many spectators that lined the lakefront. In the parade of boats was the new member of the SYC fleet, *Tiare*, a Cal-48 boat owned by the trio Garic Moran, B. Temple Brown, Jr., and Maurice J. "Bubby" Hartson, III. Her first year of racing was star-studded with firsts. She won her maiden voyage on the New Orleans to Mandeville race, the round-the-lake race, the Frostbite Regatta and the Final Regatta. *Tiare* was the winner of the 1967 Isla Mujeres race. Though her transom bore the name *Tiare*, her competitors, after watching her log knots at a fast clip, nicknamed her *Big Red*.

REGATA AL SOL—1967

The new Cal-48 *Tiare* was the scratch boat in the 1967 Isla Mujeres race. The skippers, veterans of last year's race in their *Silkie*, brought the *Tiare* over the finish line to set a record for the 565-mile course of 116 hours, 16 minutes, and 10 seconds. There were fourteen entries. The largest boat was the 50-foot *Windsong*, owned and sailed by William P. Osterholt. The smallest was the 30-foot *Vagrant*, skippered by Ronald Ripple of New Orleans. The U.S. Navy yawl *Tailwind* was rechristened the *Isla Mujeres* in honor of the Mexican crew that was aboard.

The 1967 entries were:

> *New Orleans, La.*
>
> B. Temple Brown—*Tiare*, 48' sloop
> Cal Hadden—*Chandelle*, 40' sloop
> Henry Finke—*Stardust*, 44' yawl
> Oscar McMillan—*Gulf Ghost*, 40' sloop
> Wm. P. Osterholt—*Windsong*, 50' ketch
> Harold Salmon, Jr.—*Miss Sunbeam*, 36' sloop
> Allen Borne—*Tigress*, 34' sloop
> Ronald Ripple—*Vagrant*, 30' sloop
>
> *Covington, La.*
>
> A. R. Blossman, Jr.—*Wishing Star*, 35' yawl
>
> *Shreveport, La.*
>
> N. W. deBerardinis—*T'en Fais Pas II*, 37' sloop
>
> *Florida*
>
> Lieut. Comdr. R. E. Pearl, Navy—*Tailwind*, 44' yawl (Pensacola)
> J. P. Trouchard—*Maraspel*, 35' yawl (Sarasota)
>
> *Texas*
>
> David Hatcher—*Nimbus*, 48' sloop (Port Neches)
> Dr. G. L. Smith—*The Wanderer*, 32' sloop (Baytown)

In another big race, SYC member Al Gooch participated in the Miami-Jamaica race as crew on board the winning boat *Ticonderoga*. He followed this by sailing as crew on the *Conquistador*, which won the race to Honolulu in 1967.

GYA JUNIOR WINS SEARS CUP FIRST TIME

There were several attempts made by SYC and the GYA to win the Junior North American Sailing championship for the Commodore Herbert Sears trophy, but not until 1967 was this mission accomplished by John Dane, III, with his able-bodied crew of John Cerise and Mark LeBlanc, and alternate William "Billy" Smith, Jr. They sailed in Montreal, Canada, in Shark Class sloops.

For the annual Sunday triangular race on Pensacola Bay in 1967, which was won by *Gulf Ghost* sailed by Oscar McMillan, the host club outdid itself, with engraved trophies for the winners—a far cry from the brass spittoon taken from the men's room by Bache Whitlock when the first such Bay race was scheduled on an early Sunday morning years ago. Regrettably, this year Bache was up East sailing his *Bonnie Doon* in the New York Yacht Club cruise, followed by a view of the 1967 America's Cup trials and challenge by Australia's *Dame Pattie*.

The SYC was invited to a team race with the Seawanhaka Yacht Club in New York in 1967 for the *Kathleen* trophy. It was a first and it was held the same weekend as the Gam at Peacock Point, which featured the new replica of the *America*. The SYC team was composed of Albert Crutcher, Nathaniel C. "Buster" Curtis, Joseph "Buzzy" Killeen, and Miles Wynn as team captain. They won two out of the three races sailed in Shields sloops.

The *Kathleen* trophy is an English-made sextant, which was originally won by the cutter *Kathleen* at the Seawanhaka Corinthian Yacht Club in 1899. The boat was owned and skippered by William Whitlock, whose grandnephew, Bache McE. Whitlock, is a SYC member. The sextant has since passed down into the hands of Bache, who rededicated it to the Seawanhaka Yacht Club with the request that it be sailed for in team racing between Southern and Seawanhaka Yacht Clubs. Needless to say, the South did not let Bache down in its inaugural race. The SYC hosted this event and won again in 1969.

"On the Road with Buddy Friedrichs," reported the *Montreal Star*. Buddy was now in Canada for the World's Dragon Class championship. This is what the *Montreal Star* in Canada had to say in its edition of September 25, 1967:

> Heavily favored European skippers received a 12-day lesson in tactics and logistics during the last two weeks as Buddy Friedrichs of New Orleans captured both the North American and World's Dragon Class sailing championships. Friedrichs went into the five race event with two successive championships to his credit but faced tough opposition from veteran World Champion Ole Bernstein of Helerup, Denmark. Friedrichs not only left Bernstein in 2nd place when the event was cut to four races, but in 7th place in final results of the World championship event.
>
> What impressed most of the European skippers was the manner in which *Williwaw*—the world champion boat sailed by Friedrichs, Barton Jahncke and Click Schreck, could come from far back in the pack and into the lead in only a few minutes.

$350,000 RENOVATION OF CLUBHOUSE

With a resounding crash of metal, the first piling was driven for the Southern Yacht Club's renovation project, with Commodore Provensal standing by to watch the work with his white helmet, compliments of "Rip" Haase. Haase was a partner of the Haase Construction Company employed to do the job, which was started on October 25, 1967. The architects were the firm of Curtis and Davis. The Fromherz Consulting Engineers were also employed. This latter company belongs to the same family of Fromherzs who were the unsuccessful bidders for the erection of this clubhouse in 1899.

The planning committee which had been appointed by Commodore Gus Lorber in 1965 submitted its suggestions and recommendations for extensive renovations needed to provide a more private bar, a newly equipped kitchen, and an enlarged dining room. For financial reasons, the work needed on the lower deck was put on the back burner and only the upper deck was improved.

A contract was let to Haase Construction Company for $227,586, and added to this was the cost of furnishings and equipment, which brought the total to $341,000.00. This expenditure was paid for by funds dedicated for capital improvements, as called for in the by-laws, and by the fund generated from assessments. The interim finances were arranged up to a limit of $250,000 with a very attractive interest rate granted by the Whitney Bank.

In 1967 the SYC attorney Lewis B. Graham was called upon for an opinion clearing the highly suspect title on the lake bottom on which the club was sitting. After enlisting the help of Mayor Moon Landrieu, then a councilman, Buster Curtis was instrumental in having an ordinance passed creating the land in front of the club a park with no construction or mooring permitted. Thus the air was cleared to insure the club an unobstructed view of the lake by prohibiting the extension of boathouses along the breakwater to the entrance of the canal.

Filled with Christmas spirit, the ladies committee of the SYC under the chairmanship of Mrs. Thomas Bremmermann (Gerri), with her committee of Mrs. Alfred Brown (Louisette), Mrs. B. Temple Brown, Jr. (Penny), Mrs. J. Gilbert Scheib (Flo), Mrs. Joseph Killeen, Jr. (Connie), and Mrs. Donald Cousquet (Jean), inaugurated its first Christmas luncheon and boutique in 1967, with all proceeds going to charitable causes. One grateful group of retarded children expressed their appreciation for the piano, playground equipment, and other gifts by dedicating a stained glass window in their chapel to the "Ladies Committee of Southern Yacht Club." Over the years this holiday event has been very popular and several institutions in New Orleans and Louisiana have been the recipients of funds derived from the boutique sales.

COMMODORE NATHANIEL C. CURTIS, JR.—
1968-69

The SYC regular annual meeting was held in December of 1967. Nathaniel C. "Buster" Curtis, Jr. was elected commodore for the year 1968. Serving with Commodore Curtis were Charles L. Eshleman, Jr., vice-commodore; B. Temple Brown, rear commodore; Dr. Elmo Cerise, fleet surgeon; Gilbert Gray, fleet measurer; Edward B. Jahncke, fleet captain.

When Buster Curtis took over as commodore, he inherited an incomplete clubhouse and a lack of finances to do anything about the problems. However, he arranged new financing and personally guaranteed a loan toward the completion of the work started under Commodore Provensal.

The new commodore was instrumental in restoring life to an otherwise dull and cold-looking yacht club. His perseverance and personal financial assistance were responsible for the fresh look Buster created when he purchased plexi-glass cases to house the club's many beautiful and historical trophies. He had placed in a large gold frame the picture of the minutes of the SYC's first meeting on July 21, 1849. He pushed hard to have every commodore's flagship under glass.

Not only were the walls of the clubhouse adorned with historical vignettes, models, old trophies, and original manuscripts, etc., but the commodore also had the cooperation of a terrific staff. One of the finest and most capable managers the club ever had was John Paisant, now the manager of the New Orleans Country Club. Also working with him were the dedicated keeper of the books, Bessie Christoffel, and the wearer of many hats, the ever hospitable executive secretary, Miriam Matthews. A new chef was hired, a move which resulted in good food. The club began to make money and the loan was paid off. As "Buster" put it, "Billy Provensal began it and I finished it."

An architect by profession and a partner of the firm of Curtis & Davis, Architects, Commodore Curtis has made his mark on society as the designer of the Louisiana Superdome in New Orleans. This marvelous engineering feat has been declared the eighth wonder of the world.

"Buster" was an avid sailor since his boyhood days on the shores of the Gulf Coast. He travelled all over the world to represent the SYC and the Dragon Class in international competition and had collected many pieces of silverware to prove his championship ability. The commodore is also an honorary member of the Royal Danish Yacht Club.

Commodore Curtis was vice-president of the International Dragon Class and a past member of the Olympic Yachting Committee as technical representative for the Dragons. He and another SYC Dragon class skipper, Albert Crutcher, concocted the idea of a syndicate to back the most promising young New Orleans sailor available in worldwide competition for Dragon honors, with an Olympic gold medal as the final objective. Thus the SYC Olympic Sailing Association was organized in 1965 for the purpose of purchasing a Dragon, the *Williwaw*, and funding sending a crew to the 1968 Olympics.

The 1968 opening regatta was a spectacular event. Celebrating the 250th anniversary of the founding of the City of New Orleans, the Southern Yacht Club and the New Orleans Yacht Club cosponsored one of the most spectacular parades of boats ever witnessed on Lake Pontchartrain. 250 boats participated.

The new commodore, Buster Curtis, selected as chairman of all water activities former Commodore Oliver J. Counce and Herbert O'Donnell as parade marshalls. Yachtsmen from Florida, Alabama, Mississippi, Texas, and Oklahoma participated in this festive occasion. Patriotic decorations were everywhere. The "dressed" yachts passed in review of the Jahncke flagship *Porte Bonheur*, with Paul Jahncke as host, which was stationed off Pontchartrain Beach.

Reviewing the fleet were Mayor Victor H. Schiro, Admiral Ross P. Bullard USCG, SYC Commodore N. C. Curtis, Jr., New Orleans Yacht Club Commodore E. H. Scott and the flag officers of both clubs. The judge of boats, J. Gilbert Scheib, and his committee selected Ray Sicard's *Gizelle* as the best-dressed yacht. Clyde LeBlanc in his *Hornpipe* with all the thirteen little LeBlancs nattily clad in navy blue and white took second place. Third place was awarded to Warren Campo's *Lela Joice*. Dr. W. H. Kohlman Reed copped the best dressed power-boat prize.

The Power Boat Division of the SYC has been of invaluable service throughout the years. The SYC is indebted to the many skippers for their generosity in using their yachts as spectator boats at all times. There has always been close cooperation with the members of the Motor Yacht Association, which has had as chairmen and officers over the years, Dr. Clarence "Skipper" Black, Dr. Al Chambers, Dr. W. Kohlman Reed, Henry Heyman, Dr. Peter B. Salatich, Jr., Peter Beer, Harry Booker, Carl W. Nussbaum, Edward G. Rowley, C. A. "Junior" Sporl, Jr., A. R. Blossman, J. Rollins "Dutch" Murray, Paul Jahncke, Grant Jahncke, Edward B. Jahncke, Robert "Rip" Haase, James Coleman, and many other generous yachtsmen.

During his reign, Commodore Curtis initiated the flag-raising ceremony at opening regattas and the flag-lowering ceremony at the final regatta.

REGATA AL SOL—1968

The annual *regata al sol* held in 1968 made its destination Cozumel instead of the Isla de Mujeres. The traditional "Mexico Night" was held at the SYC, and the guests from Mexico were Miss Alexandra Alvarez-Morphy of Mexico City, Commodore Anabalde Iturbide of the Isla Mujeres Yacht Club, and Señor Alberto Alvarez-Morphy of Mexico City. Enthusiasm was high among the prospective skippers and crews for the 1968 race.

The fourth *regata al sol* race got off from the Gulfport Yacht Club in June. The "Mexico race" continues to attract a large fleet of boats from all over the Gulf area, primarily because it is the only blue water race in the Central Gulf, and it provides a needed challenge to the sailing skills and navigational ability of all Gulf skippers and crews.

The 1968 regatta was the longest on record. The elapsed time was 155 hours, 19 minutes, and 6 seconds, the corrected time, 142 hours, 48 minutes, and 19 seconds. The *Silkie*, carrying a new owner, George Reynolds, and a new burgee, New Orleans Yacht Club, won the race. The crewmen aboard were F. A. Tupper, navigator, John Drury, Phil Mayeaux, Tom Trenchard, Tommy Dreyfus, and Mac Hill. The SYC yacht *Gulf Ghost*, owned by Jack Dane and Oscar McMillan, crossed the line first with McMillan at the helm, with an elapsed time of 152 hours, 50 minutes, and 5 seconds, making her third in the fleet. *Tiare* or *Big Red* finished fifth but her track record still stands at 116 hours, 16 minutes, and 10 seconds.

O. J. Young of the New Orleans Yacht Club in his yacht *Scarlet O'Hara* won the first Galveston Bay to Gulfport Yacht Club long-distance race in 1968. In return the SYC offered a race to Galveston

Tiara, the winner of the 1967 regata al sol, is shown sailing into the harbor of Isla Mujeres.

The happy crew members of the Tiara with their collection of trophies are, front row: Charles Adams, John Charbonnet, Charles L. Gambel, Jr., Daniel Killeen, Tom Rawlins, Peter Keenan. Second row, John B. Gooch, Jr., Elmo Cerise, M.D., Maurice J. "Bubby" Hartson, Jr., and B. Temple Brown, skipper.

Honored at an SYC banquet were 1968 Olympic gold medal winners Barton Jahncke, crew; G. Shelby Friedrichs, Jr., skipper, and Click Schreck, crew.

in 1970. They joined the Texas boats in the Galveston to Vera Cruz race. Each year thereafter it was planned to alternate between the two starting points.

In 1968 the Rhodes 19 class held its National Championship regatta on Lake Pontchartrain for the first time. It was won by Art Andersen of St. Petersburg Yacht Club with his crew of Jeff Oescher and Ben Case, the latter of New Orleans Yacht Club, in a twenty-boat race.

The newly organized Morgan 34 class became eligible as a fleet in 1968. The six owners were Allen Borne, Nicholas Cromwell, William Sherar, Elroy Eckhardt, Billy Carter, and Dr. Arthur Payzant, fleet captain.

Replacing the Penguin fleet in 1968 was the Windmill Class, under the leadership of J. Dwight LeBlanc, Eric Aschaffenberg, and Roy Troendle, Jr. Other members were Peter Keenan, Bayne and Baldwin Keenan, Billy Williams, H. H. Hillyer, III, Weese Levert, Peter Kahle, Cort Curtis, Mary Lynn Hyde, Celeste Favret, Dickie Walters, Gordon Gsell, and Phi Mayeaux from SYC and Kent Russell and Tom Rawlins from NOYC.

Going into the year 1968, Buddy Friedrichs was the prime contender and the U.S. hope to win the gold medal in the Dragon Class. He had started his campaign three years before and in this period dominated the class by winning three North American championships, three Windjammer series, one European championship, and one world championship. What a record! It was probably the best of any skipper in the world.

Buddy's greatest competitors were in his own club, the other Dragon skippers Ed. Hobson, Albert Crutcher, Jack Taylor, Billy Haase, Bill Balter, Clyde LeBlanc, Roy Troendle, Sr., Paul Odendahl, Buster Curtis, Cort Curtis, and now Tim Schneideau, who had just returned from the Navy.

When the Windjammer series was held in the summer of 1968 on Lake Pontchartrain, all contenders for the Olympic gold medal were on hand. The top Dragon sailors from all over the U. S. and Canada were in attendance. Here for this warm-up event were such National and International champions as Bob Mosbacher and Don Genitempo of Houston, Texas, Paul Phelan and Charles Steinback of Toronto, G. R. Letourneau of Montreal, Chuck Kober and Sid Exley of Long Beach, California, Maurice Rattray and John Buchan of Seattle, Washington, and B. G. Kirkconnell of Jamaica.

The Houston Yacht Club held the North American championship

series in July 1968 and also the Olympic Trials in August. Skipper Friedrichs tells the story:

> The atmosphere for us at the Trials in Houston was one of extreme high tension. The North American championship, a tuneup prior to the Trials added materially to our problems, as we failed to hear our boat recalled at the start of the second race and were subsequently disqualified for starting prematurely. O. J. Young, our sparring partner who had been breathing down our necks all summer, won the series, making the pressure on us going into the Trials almost unbearable.
>
> Believe it or not, the situation worsened. After finishing third behind Mosbacher in the first race of the Olympic Trials, we learned the shocking news of Click Schreck's father's death in New Orleans. Of course, it was necessary for him to go home to be with his family. Fortunately, I was able to get my brother, Gore, to fly in from New York to take Click's place aboard *Williwaw*, and he did a remarkable job, particularly, since he had not been aboard a Dragon since the races in Montreal three years before.
>
> After a second place behind Mosbacher in the second race, *Williwaw* was disqualified in the third race during a rounding maneuver at the weather mark. I owe a great deal of gratitude to the Committee at this point, who rescheduled the lay day for the next day, in order for us to attend Click's father's funeral.
>
> Click was able to return to Houston the day after the lay day for the fourth race. The three of us pulled ourselves together and decided that we had to go out and start winning races. We were somewhat scared but we went out and did just that. We won the Olympic Trials with finishes of 3,2,DSQ,1,1,2,2, leaving only our goal of winning the Olympic Gold Medal ahead.

SYC TEAM WINS OLYMPIC GOLD MEDAL IN 1968

All eyes were turned towards Mexico as the first Olympic flame to travel from Greece to the New World was trotted into the Olympic Stadium in Mexico on October 12, 1968 to open the games of the nineteenth Olympiad. The SYC's crew of Buddy Friedrichs, Click Schreck, and Barton Jahncke was proudly there to represent the United States in the Dragon Class for a gold medal. Joining them was an entourage of New Orleanians headed by Commodore Buster Curtis.

The following are excerpts taken from an interview with the three champions, Buddy, Click, and Barton:

> We arrived in Acapulco on September 29, two weeks early to acclimate ourselves to the area with *Williwaw* completely refinished, sanded and

Williwaw, the Dragon class boat that won the 1968 Olympic sailing event.

The present-day Southern Yacht Club.

compounded to perfection. We had made a new light-to-medium genoa for Acapulco, which we all agreed turned out to be perfect, and later we ended up using it six out of seven races in the Olympics.

We all spent much of our time, prior to opening day, getting the boat and sails measured in. There was a big hassle over the use of glued corner patches and many sails, including some of our own and those of Paul Elstrom, needed minor alterations to separate the layers of cloth at the corners from one another.

The two big questions worrying us were the very publicized heat conditions and the famous Pacific Ocean ground swell, which has plagued so many visitors over the years. We found the heat to be of little consequence, not so unlike our very own conditions on Lake Pontchartrain in New Orleans. The Pacific swell did cause us trouble, but in our pre-opening day trial runs, our speed seemed to improve with every day's outing. We were extremely grateful to Sid Exley who brought his Dragon *Tatsu* all the way from California to help us get tuned up.

Buddy's own narrative of the seven races, his observations on the decisions and traumas, is a cliff-hanger, especially the hair-raising nightmare of losing a pin from the overhaul in the second race. At that moment the crew had to lower the main, refeed the foot of the sail, then rehoist. Thus in the second race they were pushed to a sixth. But by the series' end, they had four firsts and two seconds to nail down the Gold Medal. The treasure was actually theirs before they entered the seventh and last race. Managing to give clear air to the Danish and East German skippers who were battling for a silver medal, an ecstatic Buddy Friedrichs remained composed and had the super satisfaction of crossing the seventh finish line with a first he didn't even need.

After five exciting races, to everyone's amusement the SYC crew crossed first in the sixth amidst guns, horns, etc. "We clinched the GOLD MEDAL," shouted the boys in unison. The Dane placed second, the Frenchman third, followed by the Swede, the West German, and the East German.

"Trying to stay out of the way of the Dane and the East German in the seventh race, we got a good start in front and stayed there all the way around. It was difficult at times to stay in front and still give the Danes and the East Germans clear air, as they were running second and third. We managed to do it, however, and crossed first to our great satisfaction, bringing to a successful climax and end to four years of really hard work for Barton, Click and Buddy."

And they did it sailing against the best in the Dragon world: *Lung Wang* skippered by Hsiu-Hsiung Chen of Taiwan; *White Jewel*, with

Cornet Groot of Holland at the tiller; *Chock*, with Aage Birch of Denmark as skipper; *Calafate*, with Hecton Schenone of Argentina; *Mutafo*, with Paul Borowske of East Germany; *Agoatil*, with Javier Velazquez of Mexico; *Guahahani*, with George Ramsey of the Bahamas; and *Jack Robbie*, with John Cuneo of Australia as skipper.

Following every race via telephone calls from Acapulco where the yachting events took place, members of the SYC were kept in close touch by Commodore Curtis. There was euphoria when the news arrived that our skippers had done what they set out to accomplish, to win the Olympic Gold Medal.

Further commented Buddy, "The day finally arrived and we cannot adequately put into words the emotions experienced during our participation in the Olympic Games in Mexico. Marching shoulder to shoulder with the greatest athletes from all the nations of the world, cheers from thousands of Olympic spectators, witnessing the torch-lighting ceremony, the day-to-day associations with fellow competitors from other nations, the final placement of the Gold Medal around your neck, with the Star Spangled Banner being played in the background—these are experiences that will be carried with us for the rest of our lives.

"The Mexicans knocked themselves out to be sure that everything was right. Yachting events were carried out to perfection."

Greeted by hundreds of well-wishers at the airport, the champions were hurriedly rushed into a limousine, and accompanied by motorcycle escorts and many automobiles they paraded into the city where the Mayor, Vic Schiro, of New Orleans, and city officials greeted them on the steps of City Hall and a program was held in their honor.

A gala affair was held at the Southern Yacht Club to welcome our champions. On the lawn in the front of the clubhouse was perched high and dry in strong spot lights the *Williwaw*, to greet the 400 members who attended the testimonial banquet.

The clubhouse dining room was festively decorated by co-chairmen Mrs. A. Thomas Bremmerman and Mrs. Clay Talbot. Included among the table decorations and spread throughout were gold discs (doubloons) commemorating the occasion—an old New Orleans Carnival custom. The menu was in keeping with the nautical theme: "Buddy cocktail," "Barton salad," "chicken *Williwaw*," "Acapulco rice," and "Click dessert."

The general chairman and master of ceremony was J. Gilbert Scheib. Assisting him were Commodore N. C. Curtis, Jr., former-

Commodore Oliver J. Counce, and Mrs. J. Gilbert Scheib. The invocation was delivered by Fr. Milton Reisch, S.J.

Mayor Victor H. Schiro presented each of the honorees with a plaque bearing a bronze medallion seal of the City of New Orleans in grateful appreciation of the honor brought to this great city by their nautical feat. Albert C. Crutcher, vice-president of the SYC Olympic Sailing Association, on behalf of the Association presented a half model of the *Williwaw* to the Southern Yacht Club.

Substituting for Judge Robert Hughes, commodore of the Gulf Yachting Association, who was ill was former GYA Commodore Larry Sommers. He presented to each honoree a resolution adopted by the GYA.

The piece de resistance was the presentation of the Southern Yacht Club's gifts to the winners. As the champions stood on a miniature platform, emblematic of the Olympic stand, Commodore Curtis awarded each one a sterling silver scroll with the Olympic shield and SYC burgee embedded in the shield, mounted on a walnut plaque, expressings thanks for a "job well done." The handsome scrolls were designed by J. Gilbert Scheib and crafted by the silversmiths of Adler's jewelry store in New Orleans.

Not to be forgotten were the wives of the honorees, the unsung heroines, Suzy Friedrichs, Emily Jahncke, and Judy Schreck. To each of them Commodore Curtis presented a gold charm with the Olympic shield.

When queried about their family life over the past four years and how these brave women yielded their men to that elusive goal of an Olympic gold medal, the champions replied: "We're lucky we are still married," said Schreck; "My dinner was always kept on the back burner," said Friedrichs; "We made it," stated Jahncke.

Many honors were bestowed upon the Olympic winners as the days passed. The highlight of all was the invitation to appear at half-time during the first New Orleans Saints' football game with the Dallas Cowboys at the Tulane Stadium in 1968, before the Superdome.

Headed for Houston and Olympic Trials were other SYC and GYA hopefuls to compete in Stars and Finns, SYC's Cal Hadden and Tommy Haslam in Stars and Drew Whitley in Finns. They qualified for the Olympic Trials in San Diego. Representing the Mobile area Star Fleet were Joe Arns from the Buccaneer Yacht Club and Greg Smith of the Mobile Yacht Club. In 1968 the SYC had the honor of a visit from a very distinguished guest from London, England, Sir

Cedric Charles Dickens, the great-grandson of the British novelist Charles Dickens. Sir Cedric was a sailing enthusiast, being a member of the Royal Thomas Yacht Club and of the Royal Ocean Racing Club, both of London. Former-Commodore Oliver J. Counce welcomed the English dignitary.

When the social calendar for 1968 was issued, heading the list was the inaugural Commodores' Ball. The new Commodore Curtis initiated what became a very popular event in every other year with the changing of the guard. All of the SYC commodores and their wives are honored on this occasion with a very festive dance.

When the Gulf Yachting Association was still in Area F (the USYRU had transferred the GYA to Area F from Area D, where it remained for just a few years), a young skipper out of the Texas Yachting Association won the Junior North American Sailing championship for the Sears Cup in 1968, John Kolius, with his crew of Jay and Dan Williams. Kolius is a prominent name in the 1987 America's Cup circle. He sailed out of the Galveston Bay Cruising Association.

Diplomat that he was, Commodore Curtis resurrected the Press Race in 1968. Yachting news had fallen considerably with the change of hands when Newhouse assumed the reins of *The Times-Picayune* and *The States-Item* papers. No more would the SYC see headlines of regattas. The Nicholsons, the previous owners, were gone; they not only participated in yachting but were responsible for the worldwide publicity the second-oldest and highly reputable yacht club in the nation received.

Wanting his picture on television, John Wilson got just what he wanted by winning the Press Race for his station, WDSU. On board the *Windwitch* with Wilson was Jack de la Vergne. Marie Therese "T.C." Larue, the charming society editor of *The Times-Picayune*, was second. The other three who participated were Bill Wilson of WWL-TV in third place, with Nat Belloni and Buddy Diliberto following. The Gulf-One Design owners were most generous and hospitable as each year they offered their boats for this annual race.

REGATA AL SOL—1969

Cozumel Island was the destination for the fifth sailing of the *regata al sol* in 1969, adding forty-five miles to the race. A newly constructed harbor for small boats on Cozumel and the new Balsa Presidente Hotel awaited the skippers.

For the first time the Galveston Bay Cruising Association participated in this event, which scheduled its Galveston-Gulfport race to finish during the week of June 1, thus making possible several entries in the *regata al sol*. In 1970 and alternate years thereafter, the Southern Yacht Club would sponsor a race to Galveston, timed to provide entries in the Vera-Cruz race, and the *regata al sol* would become biennial. It was hoped that this first cooperation would be expanded in the future into a Central Gulf Ocean Racing Circuit. This *regata al sol* had been a highlight in the history of the SYC and the Galveston and Gulfport Yacht Clubs and without equivocation the most challenging.

The *Tell-Tale* reported: "a motley crew of sailors finished the Cozumel race first." Cal Hadden took first place in Class A on *Chandelle*. His crew was Charles L. Eshleman, Jr., Burt Keenan, and Waldo Otis; also sailing were John Drury of the *Gulf Ghost*, with Robert Ruppel and Terry Joyce, navigator. SYC's Tommy Coleman's *Blaise* took first place in Class B."

The *Tell-Tale* continued:

> Have you ever sailed in a race for six days and 560 miles only to miss the finish line by a few miles? This was the case of the infamous crew of the yacht *Tiare*, with crewmen Bubby Hartson, Frazier Rice, navigator, Alfred Brown, cook, Alfred Lamar, Tom Bremmermann and Kent Russell. Temple Brown was skipper.
>
> Once in Cozumel, the crews of *Tiare* and *Chandelle* were received warmly by the Mexicans. When the trophies were presented at the El Presidente Hotel, Cal Hadden graciously gave Temple Brown, skipper of *Tiare*, the first-to-finish trophy, even though the *Tiare* was disqualified. Cal took home the trophies for winning in Class A and in the Fleet.
>
> The *Tiare* was not the only boat to have navigational misfortunes. The *Allegro*, owned by Harold Roberts eventually wound up in Isla Mujeres, as did the *Tiare*, as they both approached what they thought was Cozumel.

The Galveston Bay Cruising Association ran its annual Galveston-Gulfport race during the week before the race to Mexico. Through the cooperation of Texas boats, the result was a Central Gulf Racing Circuit. In return the SYC had offered a race to Galveston in 1970.

"BARDS OF THE BILGES" BALL—
ABSIT INVIDIE

"A Night in Old Mexico" was the theme for the 1969 ball of the "Bards of the Bilges." King Neptune, J. Gilbert Scheib, arrived on his royal barge, costumed as a Mexican general, wearing a big black sombrero covering a bronze, mustached face and a serape draped over a cortarina vest, to reign over a small village in old Mexico. He welcomed his guests seated with his queen, Mrs. William Sewell (Jane), on a sawed-off tree stump surrounded by barnyard fowl such as live chickens, ducks, etc. Also greeting his audience was a live Abssysian ass, fresh from the Audubon Park Zoo. Ascending and descending the marble steps to the ballroom was no easy task, but the animal made it safely. The maids were dressed in Mexican costume dresses, carrying small corsages of red carnations. They were Mrs. John B. Gooch, Jr., Miss Adriel "Sparky" Graham, Miss Anne Hughes, Mrs. Allen W. McClure, Mrs. J. William Sherar, and Mrs. Jerry Touche. Enjoying the festivities were Commodore and Mrs. Iturbide and Señor Alvarez Morphy from Cozumel, who were guests of the SYC's banquet for members of the Cozumel race and who remained to witness a familiar scene to them, "A Night in Old Mexico."

SOLINGS MAKE DEBUT AT SYC

In the opening regatta of 1969, the Soling Class made its debut. This type of boat had been selected by the Olympic Committee to replace the Dragon class in the 1972 Olympic Games. The decision caused several SYC members to purchase this new 27 foot boat, which carried a minimum weight of 2200 pounds, with visions of another Gold Medal winner for SYC in 1970.

Among the original owners of Solings were John Dane, III, O. J. Young, William "Billy" Ibs, Barton Jahncke, and Kent Russell. A former SYC junior and winner of the 1967 Junior North American Sailing championship for the Sears Cup, John Dane, III, with his teammates Mark LeBlanc and John Cerise, set out to capture the Olympic gold medal.

This young team of juniors won the Southern District Soling championship in 1969 sailed at the Texas Corinthian Yacht Club. From there they travelled to Milwaukee, Wisconsin where they blitzed the North American Soling championship with five firsts and one second. They sailed against some of the top skippers in the country. Dick Stearns was second, followed by Gordon Lindemann, Don Bever, Bob Mosbacher, and Gray O'Day. To prove this was no fluke, John Dane and his crew won the Canadian Soling title with a double blitz—a perfect score of five firsts.

In the Canadian championship series, these three nineteen-year-olds battled for their score in a field of twenty-eight boats, with the runner-up being Han Fogh of Denmark. Called the Cork Regatta, Kingston, the racing classes included Dragons, Flying Dutchmen, Finns, and Solings.

Olympic-like medals were presented to the three places in each class with the crews standing on a platform just like the Olympics, bowing at the waist to have their medals placed around their neck. The beautiful and unique trophy which they won was on display at the SYC.

For Dane, this victory completed an outstanding year which included his selection as high-point skipper in every collegiate regatta sailed throughout the year, in which he represented Tulane University of New Orleans, and his unanimous selection to the All-American Collegiate Sailing Team. Paul H. Smart, regatta race committee chairman and head of the U.S. Olympic Yachting Committee, said, "Dane appears to be the leading young hope for the 1972 American Olympic Sailing Team that will compete in Kiel, Germany."

HURRICANE CAMILLE HITS GULF COAST

In the middle of the 1969 scheduled races on the Gulf Coast, a devastating hurricane hit the area and ravaged the coastline from Waveland to Biloxi and beyond. The South has had its share of hurricanes; the earlier ones had no name, but after names were given, the most vicious has been Camille. It struck on August 17, 1969.

The entire area stripped of beautiful and age-old homes and oak trees resembled bomb-torn villages. Tornadoes spawned off the hurricane, blowing homes and buildings to bits. The dazed survivors counted their dead for weeks and looked down in constant horror at the shambles that twelve feet of water and tidal waves of as high as twenty feet had left their homes. Over 150 lives were lost, many dead were found in trees and along the beach, and thousands of houses were leveled. Included in the shambles were four yacht clubs, Bay-Waveland, Pass Christian, Gulfport, and Biloxi.

It was another disaster for our Southern yacht clubs, but again everyone put together the pieces and rebuilt in record-breaking time. The camaraderie of all yacht club members was heroically demonstrated when a call came for volunteers to man trucks and cars to bring clothes, food, and water to the hurricane victims, who for weeks and even months in some places had nothing.

Hurricanes have never stopped the holding of a Lipton Regatta.

SOUTHERN YACHT CLUB

Just fifteen days following Camille, the commodore of the GYA, Cooper Van Antwerp, announced from his home in Montrose, Alabama that the annual Lipton Cup races would be held as scheduled on Labor Day weekend at the New Orleans Yacht Club. Fortunately, Camille did very little damage to the Southern Yacht Club or to the New Orleans Yacht Club.

The 1969 Lipton regatta was the occasion for the use of the newly selected club-owned boat, the Flying Scot. Strange as it may seem, the Pensacola Yacht Club was the winner of the first Lipton Cup regatta in the new Flying Scots, and it was also the winner of the first Lipton Cup regatta held in the newly constructed Fish Class sloops in 1920.

THE DEMISE OF THE FISH CLASS SLOOPS

The demise of the fifty-year-old 21-foot Fish Class sloops was just another drastic trauma experienced by the GYA yacht clubs in 1969. Time and technology finally took the measure of the venerable old boat and in 1969 it was retired in favor of the more contemporary 19-foot Flying Scot. Featuring fiberglass construction, Marconi rig, spinnaker and centerboard, the Scot was easily trailered and more suited to the mobility required by GYA competition.

An era in gulf coastal yachting now came to an end, one year short of the fiftieth anniversary of the most popular class of sloops in the Gulf Yachting Association and in the South. This unique 21-foot one-design sloop built for local waters in 1919 to be used as a club-owned boat, sailed those fifty years without any significant change in rigging. In early racing, crews used an oar to "wing" the jib on free sheet runs. Later a whisker pole was adopted for the same purpose. In 1949 the GYA allowed a loose-fitting jib to replace the old club-footed jib.

Although built in 1919, the Fish Class boats were not sailed in interclub competition until 1920 when the first Lipton Cup regatta was held with the Southern Yacht Club competing against the Pensacola Yacht Club in a team race won by Pensacola.

The last interclub regatta held in the Fish Class was in the 1970 Mardi Gras Regatta held at the Southern Yacht Club. Bay-Waveland Yacht Club was the winner with its three champion skippers Harry Chapman, William Reeves, and Jack Bell. Because of bad weather only two races were sailed and BWYC had the highest points.

THE SPIRIT OF '69
by Charles Bernard, editor,
Gulf Yachting January 1970

The replacement of the Fish Class sloop by the Flying Scot boat gave rise to speculation that the days of the Gulf Yachting Association as an institution of Gulf sailing were numbered. Opposition to the changeover, plus a growing feeling that interclub competition was being eroded away by preoccupation with individual competition, made it appear that the validity of the GYA was in jeopardy.

For those who attended the Golden Anniversary and annual GYA regatta held at the New Orleans Yacht Club over Labor Day weekend of 1969, this contention was obliterated by a force relative to hurricane Camille herself.

There had been doubts in the minds of those who had come as to just what the reaction would be to the invincible intrusion of Camille upon Gulf yachting, and everything else in its path. Would attendance be intimidated? Would there be mixed emotions? Would the regatta be one of disappointment and guilt of wrong decision? There was no way to anticipating reaction, nor of engineering the situation to provide a satisfactory solution.

None was needed. The determination of the contestants—the determination of the officials—and the determination of all who served and those who witnessed crystallized into a force of spirit and enthusiasm greater than the challenge that spawned it.

Fifty Golden Years culminated in a victory for all that GYA has stood for, and for what it means to the future of Gulf yachting, and that is the invincible spirit of camaraderie among true sailors on the Gulf and everywhere.

No elemental forces—no individual prejudices—no factional ambitions can survive any attack upon the bonds of understanding and sportsmanship among sailors. Camille once again provided a test. New Orleans provided the proving grounds, and GYA laid down the ground rules. And again, the game proved a decisive victory for Gulf Sailors, Gulf Yachting and the Gulf Yachting Association.

"OLD FISH BOATS WILL NEVER DIE"
by MARK ARNOLD

Mark Arnold wrote an article for the *Sailors' Gazette* in the July 1983 issue on the Fish Class Fleet. He referred to these boats as "graceful southern belles." He continued:

> These grand old boats were often discussed like vintage wine, the merits could be defined in a single sentence containing the boatwright's name and the year it was built by local craftsmen.
> The few times I have been fortunate enough to sail on one of these

wood and bronze affairs have been some of the most memorable. The instruction and guidance that I have received from these renaissance sailors and their families have given my sailing a richness that I otherwise would never have known.

These boats quickly became a source of pride and capital investment.... The standard crew of a fish boat consisted of a skipper and two crewmen. The object of the regattas was to pit one entire club against another rather than against individuals.

Due to the lottery system of selecting the crew, each series of races would see as many as 30 different members from each of the clubs actively competing. Add to this the involvement of families and friends and the time ashore was pleasantly spent socializing and picnicking with several hundred people....

The pride and pleasure of these graceful southern belles is being retired and each year sees another "Fish Class" sloop restored to racing trim. Those clubs along the coast that have Fish boat skippers are far richer for having this immediate link with their common past.

As I spoke with an old-timer at the club one day, his comment was, "Old Fish Class boats will never die—they just sail away anywhere there is the two and a half feet of water necessary to float them." Keeping the name alive is the Mobile Yacht Club where the Fish Class World Regatta is held each year on Mobile Bay under the auspices of the Buccaneer Yacht Club. The late GYA Commodore Nolfie Alfonso, an avid fan of this fleet of little wooden boats, was made an honorary member of the newly found organization.

THE "LAFAYETTE SQUARE YACHT CLUB"

There are many stories to be told about the Fish Class fleet and what it has meant to members of yacht clubs along the coast, especially during the lean years in sailing after World War I and II and the lengthy Depression. One story was published in a book written by the late George W. Healy, editor of *The Times-Picayune*, *A Lifetime on Deadline* (published by the Pelican Publishing Company in 1976).

George Healy was a very active member of the Southern Yacht Club, where he served on the board of governors for a number of years and on many committees. He was a Star Class sailor but spent a lot of time sailing Fish Class sloops during the thirties.

A Lifetime on Deadline covered many colorful memoirs. On one occasion, he inveigled his co-workers into the great fun of sailing. Healy arranged to rent the SYC's eight Fish Class boats for contests among the newspaper's off-duty reporters, photographers, copy readers, and other newsroom employees. He referred to them as "the

Lafayette Square Yacht Club," for at that time *The Times-Picayune* was located in a building that faced the Lafayette Square across from City Hall. These pseudo-skippers included sports writer Bill Keefe, photographer Pete Baird, and reporters Thomas Scanton (now Paris correspondent for *Time*), Mortimer Kreeger, and George Vandervort.

The fun didn't end downtown at the newspaper plant. Each helmsman wrote his own story about his race, as did his two crewmen, and these uncensored reports were posted on *The Times-Picayune* bulletin board. Healy recalled that no skipper ever lost through his own fault, but rather through a competitor's dirty trick, an unlucky wind shift, or a defective craft.

Following the 1969 Lipton Regatta, the team race between Southern Yacht Club and the New Orleans Yacht Club for the Commodore J. Gilbert Scheib trophy was won by the Southern Yacht Club for the first time in five years. How could they miss with the team of champions headed by B. Temple Brown as team captain and skippers N. C. "Buster" Curtis, Jr., Maurice "Bubby" Hartson, III, Roy Troendle, Sr., John Dane, III, Herbert O'Donnell, Darrell Higgins, Johnny and Pearson Potts, Mike Sperry, and Arthur D. "Juby" Wynne? Only two races were necessary as Southern won both in a three-race series.

FIRST OLD-TIMERS REGATTA

Completing the SYC sailing season of 1969 was the first Old-Timers Regatta sailed on October 26. The magic age was fifty or over. There were many no-shows—those who were the perennial forty-niners.

At the 1969 annual Banquet of Champions, the SYC honored champions had in their midst the winners of the 1969 Junior North American Sailing championship of NAYRU, John Dane, III, John Cerise, and Mark LeBlanc. There to present the keys to the city was Mayor Victor H. Schiro.

SYC HEROES OF CLUBHOUSE FIRE HONORED

Also at the banquet, special tribute was paid by Commodore Curtis to a group of young SYC heroes who were out late one night and noticed from afar a glow from the window of the upper deck of the clubhouse. "It was not the red glow from the lighthouse nearby, so it must be the clubhouse," thought the boys. They were right. Breaking open the doors, they found the fire extinguishers and used them effectively before the fire engines arrived. However, considerable damage was done to the kitchen area and part of the dining room. Their alertness probably prevented a fourth clubhouse from being erected. These young juniors were Larry Taggart, Tommy Taggart, Fritz Fromherz, Cal Jones, Mark Bradburn, John Charbonnet, Tommy Gordon, George Reviere, and Ricky Fleming.

In December 1969 when the Sugar Bowl Regatta was held, the "Race of Champions" was won by the Southern Yacht Club sailing for the first time in Flying Scots. Maurice J. Hartson, III was the winning skipper and his crewmen were Timmy Brown, John B. Gooch, Jr., Robert LeBlanc, N. Philip Menard, and Nathaniel C. Curtis, Jr.

Another exciting event of the 1969 Sugar Bowl Regatta was the winning of the Penguin Class race by a young nine-year-old, Tom LeBlanc, over defending champion Eileen Eshleman, Cathy Clerc, Adrianne LeBlanc, Charlotte Christman, and Charles Eshleman, III.

A new fleet, the Flying Dutchman, was numbered among the classes sailing in the 1969 Sugar Bowl regatta, and here for the race was Ted Turner of Atlanta (America's Cup 1975 winner) in the out-of-town class.

Although he did not serve two full years as commodore, because of the change in the SYC's by-laws, Nathaniel C. "Buster" Curtis' accomplishments during the period he was in office were astronomical. His greatest reward was witnessing the SYC's skippers win the ultimate in sailboat racing, the Olympic gold medal.

COMMODORE CHARLES L. ESHLEMAN, JR.— 1970-71

The newly elected commodore, Charles L. Eshleman, Jr., took office on January 1, 1970. He was one of a very few who served in all flag officers positions. He held the job of secretary-treasurer for four years before he was made rear commodore, then vice-commodore. Commodore Eshleman is a prominent investment broker for the local firm of Howard, Weil, Labouisse and Friedrichs.

Elected to the SYC board with Commodore Eshleman were Herbert O'Donnell, vice-commodore; B. Temple Brown, rear commodore; Jacques A. Livaudais, secretary-treasurer; Dr. W. Kohlman Reed, fleet surgeon; Gilbert Gray, fleet measurer; and Charles L. Gambel, fleet captain.

Well known in yachting circles, the new commodore had won the

Luder Class national championship three times in 1957, 1962, and 1966. He was selected as the outstanding skipper of the year and the recipient of the Commodore Charles J. Tessier memorial trophy on three occasions. In 1977 Eshleman captained one of the SYC Lipton Cup's team and was a member of the many teams that competed over the years in L-16s with the Chicago Yacht Club in team racing. He also raced in 5.5 and the handicap class.

If the sixties introduced the years of racing, rivalry, and rigging, the decade of the seventies was a saga of rebuilding, rulebeaters, and ratings. What a different complexion these three brought to racing in the deep South!

Up and down the Mississippi Gulf Coast yachtsmen and their families and neighbors were suffering through shock waves into 1970, rising from the incredible debris of hurricane Camille. The loss of boats and private clubs in the tragic face of many deaths and thousands of destroyed homes took a low priority for many, many months. But rebuild they did, straight up from the sand.

By 1970 yachts were built of other material than wood. Glass-reinforced plastic had made its mark some years ago, but now big yachts of sixty to eighty feet were being built on a production line. They were of great strength and durability, able to race and cruise around the world. In this decade, starting in 1957, the latest designs were for speed and seaworthiness, boats of light displacement, great beam, and, of course, cutthroat racing power.

The year 1970 brought to the SYC a new racing class to be called the SYC Portsmouth Class. The organizers were Gilbert "Gil" Mellin and William "Bill" Herbst. Over the years this system, which does not require measuring or weighing, has been very successful. The class is for boats that can be equitably handicapped under the Portsmouth Number System.

In 1970, the Marine Marathon bronze plaque was taken out of retirement, where it had remained since 1922 when C. A. "Junior" Sporl, Jr. had won the trophy in *Quicksilver*. The fleet also still competed in a predicted log contest for the famous Fox-Garic trophy of yesteryear.

Helping to plan the course for the predicted log contests was the jovial and faithful supervisor of the club's motor yacht association, Dr. Clarence E. Black. Their schedule brought the boats to Mandeville, Broadwater in Gulfport, Bayou Lacombe, and other rendezvous.

The elegant yachts continue to furnish spectator, patrol, and press boats for weekend series races and for national events.

THE STORY OF A RUNAWAY BOAT

In the 1970 St. Petersburg to Venice race on the Southern Ocean Race Circuit (SORC), a member of the Southern Yacht Club, J. Fred Clerc, accepted an invitation to crew aboard the *Vanadis* on its ocean-going trip. Following is a story of how a sailboat took a 400-mile ride to nowhere and back. Aboard the vanishing *Vanadis* was Peyson Mayhew, a 65-year-old Chicago owner of the 30-foot sloop. Aboard were Miss Terry Glenn, Ray Howell of Chicago, Jerry Gaudette of Maderia Beach, and Clerc.

The fleet staggered down the Gulf of Mexico, pushed onward by screeching winter winds out of the northwest. North of the southward turning point at Boca Grande sea buoy, a fitting on the end of the spinnaker let go. The big red and white parachute popped out forward and wrapped itself into the well-known hour-glass.

"It was bound real tight in the middle," said Mayhew, an experienced sailor. "I then had two big 'chutes and couldn't puncture them. I really knew I couldn't turn at Boca Grande. The wind was northeast and blowing hard. I tried once to swing the boat but the mast started to shake. It was like a dog playing with a stick. I knew then we were in for a long sleigh ride. I realized the Gulf was long and deep. Besides, it would probably be warmer the farther south we went. But the wind was hitting 40 and 50 in gusts. We were flying." So it was goodbye Boca Grande and hello Dry Tortugas, maybe skirting Cuba and running down to Mexico's Yucatan.

About ten miles away the skipper got the boat around somehow by gybing. Payson and his crew went back to work on how to break the accidental double sail apart. This was finally accomplished by attaching a line to a monkey wrench which was thrown up and over the hour glass bind section. Then, by taking a strain on the line and sawing back and forth, the dacron sailcloth was finally torn through. The spinnaker parted and flapped in the winds, making a flag twenty by forty feet.

Freed of the bonds, Mayhew turned on the engine. He had a full load of fuel. Hour after hour the boat went along until it reached Sarasota, Fla. late Sunday over fifty-five hours from the Friday roll start. At that point, Mayhew figured he had better save the remainder of the fuel. Up went the mainsail and *Vanadis* moved along in the gusty strong southerly winds that came up and overtook her. But she was heading home. Streaming in the night breeze was a torn spinnaker, flapping in protest, the tattered remnants of a 400-mile ride to nowhere and back.

GYA CELEBRATES ITS FIFTIETH ANNIVERSARY

One of the highlights of Commodore Eshleman's first year in office was his acting as host for the celebration of the Gulf Yachting Association's fiftieth anniversary at the Southern Yacht Club. Oddly it was at a West End tavern on Lake Pontchartrain after the first Lipton Regatta of 1920 that the initial meeting promoting the Gulf Yachting Association was held.

Genial Commodore Eshleman welcomed the GYA commodores on this festive occasion. The GYA opening regatta held in conjunction with the annual meeting was won by the Southern Yacht Club team with B. Temple Brown as team captain and skipper. Mike Sperry and John Potts were the other skippers in the three-race series. They were presented with a gold cup symbolic of the GYA's fiftieth anniversary.

Claiming the attention of all Southern sailors and particularly the members of the SYC Olympic Sailing Association, during the summer of 1970, were the accomplishments of a newcomer to seek a berth in the 1972 Olympics with the possibility of another gold medal, John Dane, III with his crew John Cerise and Mark LeBlanc in their new Soling *Quest*.

Their first achievement was to win the British Soling championship. Thereafter they took a close second behind Swedish skipper Stig Wennerstrom in the Soling's Worlds. Our North American champion prevailed over Briton's John Wakley by a comfortable margin, thereby bringing to SYC another international crown to go alongside their Canadian championship of 1969. Although the nineteen-year old Dane had beaten the Swede in five of the six races, under the Olympic scoring system he had to be content with a second in the Worlds.

The defending champion, John Dane III, sailing Roy Troendle's Soling in the 1970 North American Soling championship on Galveston Bay in Texas, placed second to Dave Curtis of Marblehead, Massachusetts in a field of over forty boats. Another entry, O. J. Young who placed seventh in the series, was a member of the New Orleans Yacht Club, the neighbor yacht club to the Southern Yacht Club.

The Olympic hopefuls, John Dane, III, John Cerise, and Mark

LeBlanc, next flew to Germany where they had shipped their Soling *Quest* from England to compete in the pre-Olympics at Kiel. Meanwhile, O. J. Young sold his Soling following the regatta and trailed his Dragon to Cork for the Dragon North American championship in Kingston, Ontario, where another SYC yachtsman G. Shelby "Buddy" Friedrichs, Jr. swept the Dragon Class series competing against twenty-one entries with a spectacular finish of 1-1-1-2-1.

In a very large fleet of sixty-eight Solings from all over the world, only the master, Paul Elvstrom, could beat the SYC crew in the 1970 German Soling championship and pre-Olympics sailed at Kiel, Germany. The SYC team settled for second place. The third place winner was Dave Curtis, who had recently won the 1970 North American championship at Houston, while fourth place went to John Oakley of England.

For Dane, this was the end of a very successful summer in which he won the British championship, was second in the Worlds, fourth in the North American and runner-up in Germany. Special thanks were due Commodore N. C. "Buster" Curtis and the entire SYC Olympic Committee, as well as the USISA Olympic Committee for enabling John and his crew to participate in this International competition with the goal of winning the gold medal in the Olympics in 1972 to be held in Kiel, Germany.

Continuing his sailing activities, John Dane III travelled on to Newport Harbor, California this time as a representative of Tulane University with his classmates "Cop" Perez, Charles Montgomery, and "By" Baldridge as crew. They repeated their win of the previous year to receive the Douglas Cup over the top seven intercollegiate crews in the country. In a Columbia 26, John emerged with a record of seven firsts and no losses to retain the coveted prize for Tulane University, an unprecedented feat in the history of the match-race event.

Southern Yacht Club bid a sad farewell to the Gulf One-Design boats in 1970 when they took their curtain call on Lake Pontchartrain after thirty-six years. The first of these wood sloops had been built in 1934 by naval architect John Prados, brother of SYC skipper Cliff Prados. Prados designed them for shallow Gulf waters. With the centerboard raised, the 28-footers drew only two and a half feet of water, and their cypress boards were resistant to New Orleans' humidity.

The late Tom Brennan raced his *East Wind* for twenty-five years, winning consistently with the Gulf One he and his son, Mike, had built in his back yard. The original plans have been adapted for the popular fiberglass keelboat, the Easterly 30s, thanks to the intervention of Mike. Today the Easterly 30s fleet sails as a one-design; these boats are built by Brennan in his shipyards.

Within the realm of the Gulf Yachting Association, there were other member yacht clubs that boasted champions in the summer of 1970. The Long Beach Yacht Club selection committee appointed Billy Ibs, Jr. of the New Orleans Yacht Club to compete in the sixth annual Congressional Cup match race series held in Columbia 50s in Long Beach, California. Although Billy and his crew finished ninth in the series, they faced very stiff competition. In one race, he was the only skipper to beat the great Argyle Campbell, the series winner. Billy's crew was composed of SYC and NOYC members Bruce Burglass, Cort Curtis, Madden Randle, Robert Ruppel, Phil Mayeaux, and Walter Stinchcomb.

The other GYA yacht club, St. Petersburg, was the winner of the Men's North American Sailing championship for the Mallory Cup. Dr. John Jennings was the skipper and James L. and Barbara Tolson Pardee his crew. They returned to win the championship again in 1973. Jennings also won the 1970 Prince of Wales match race of USYRU.

In between all of its major events, the SYC entertained at a party called a "shipwreck affair." It was held at SYC's West End "desert island" with the upper deck transformed into a tropical paradise of palm trees that grew bananas. The announcement read, "Wear whatever survived your last wreck and dance to René Louapre's band." There were derelict sailors galore, ladies who left their boudoirs in haste, aborigines and even some gray mice. Needless to say it was a big success.

On home waters in 1970, Lake Pontchartrain was host to the Star Class Spring Series and Jahncke trophy race. Commodore Eshleman had the honor of presenting the Spring Series trophy to Lowell North and his crew Bob Andre who finally won this event after several unsuccessful attempts. The Commodore Ernest Lee Jahncke trophy was won by Barton Beek of Los Angeles.

The Lightning North American championship series was sailed in 1970 on Lake Pontchartrain with a star-studded entry list. The event attracted such skippers as Tom Allen, III, who was the winner of the event with the assistance of his wife, Mrs. Allen, and John Halley,

Bill Buckles, Denis Clemence (from as far away as Rio de Janeiro, Brazil), Carl Eichenlaub, Bruce Goldsmith, the Lippincott family represented by Marcy Lippincott, Dr. Louis A. Pocharski, Jr., and Bob Serdelman.

The SYC juniors were also in on the act in 1970, bringing home the coveted Junior Lipton trophy, which they won with a perfect score of three firsts in the regatta held at Pass Christian. The winning skippers were John Potts, Peter Simoneaux, and Corkey Potts.

At the end of the sailing season, the last regatta held was the Windmill Internationals with fifty-five boats on the starting line. John Dane, III with Lee Hughes as crew jumped into a borrowed boat and defeated Denis Fontaine of Lakeland, Florida by four points. Dane won five out of six races.

Many yachts have visited the Southern Yacht Club over the years but few could match *Gillian* for sheer opulence and size. Measuring 120 feet overall and 24 feet abeam, the luxurious *Gillian* was on a visit to New Orleans. Her captain was Jim Sills, with a full-time crew of six. He had been aboard since the yacht's keel was laid at Kaag Island near the Hague and was aboard when she was christened in January 1970. Her owner, Andrew Fuller, who has oil and banking interests in Texas, was a member of the New York Yacht Club, which burgee was flown from the mast. Her replacement value in 1970 was approximately five million dollars.

REGATA AL SOL VI—1971

The *regata al sol* race of 1971 was from Gulfport, Mississippi to Cozumel, Mexico. This was the sixth *regata al sol*, which was first sailed in 1965. With the help and participation of the members of the Galveston Bay Cruising Association, the number and quality of yachts had improved each year.

Skippered by B. Temple Brown, *Tiare* made a clean sweep of the 1971 Cozumel race with a new record time of ninety-seven hours, forty minutes, fifteen seconds. *Big Red*, the Cal 48 *Tiare*, flying the burgee of the SYC, took the President of Mexico trophy, and also won the first-to-finish trophy as well as the first in Class A. Her record time gave her an average speed of six knots for the entire rugged course of 600 miles, almost all of which was on a beat to windward. The record, made by Cal Hadden in 1969, was 142 hours. Second by eleven hours was another SYC skipper, Gene Walet in *Spirit*. Third was George Hanzi's *Heidi*, a new Cal 39. First in Class B was Jerry Smith in *Utopia*, a Cal 40, veteran of several Mexico races. Fred Blossman of SYC in *Kumbaya* was another entry. First in Class C was Dr. Don Neese of Houston, Texas on *Spendrift*, a Cal 36.

Upon arrival, each boat was greeted with fireworks, horns, sirens, and music by local bands, as is the custom. A dinner and trophy presentation was held by the governor of the Territory of Quintana Roo for the large group of friends who were from New Orleans and Houston and their skippers.

In a startling finish was Dr. Arthur Payzant in the 1971 Gulfport to Pensacola race, another winner to be added in the history book. He was skipper of his Morgan 34 *Sacre Bleu*, which won "the big one," with his crew of Chris Alfonso, Pat Dormon, Emmett Fremaux, "Chuck" Hayes, Larry Hoskin, Ken Laborde, George Martin, and J. C. Paciera. At the trophy presentation held at the Pensacola Yacht Club, it took half the crew to carry all the trophies home. Arthur was first in the fleet, first in Class C on corrected time, and first to finish in Class C.

The champions G. Shelby "Buddy" Friedrichs, Jr., with his crew of Click Schreck and Tommy Dreyfus, and John Dane III, with his crew of Mark LeBlanc and John Cerise, were back in the picture during the 1971 sailing season. Buddy dramatically won the Dragon Class North Americans and Windjammer championships sailed on Lake Pontchartrain in a clean sweep placing first in all five races. O. J. Young of New Orleans Yacht Club was second. This was Buddy's fifth Dragon North American championship.

For the second straight year John Dane, III won the John F. Kennedy Memorial Regatta in Annapolis, Maryland for Tulane University. John's crew was Mike Sperry, Chalin Perez, Danny Sullivan, and Charlie Montgomery. They sailed in the U.S. Naval Academy's 44-foot Luder yawls. Mrs. Robert Kennedy presented the trophy to Dane.

John Dane III also won the 1971 Mid-Winter Soling championship over twenty-six rivals. Dane's victory earned him and his crew a second trip to Kiel, Germany, where the previous year he was a runner-up to Paul Elvstrom in the Germany Soling championship. In the 1971 Mid-Winters, Dane built an insurmountable lead by finishing 1,1,1,2,2, to wrap up the championship early. The SYC team was sponsored by the U. S. Soling Association and the United States International Sailing Association (USISA).

In still another event in 1971, John Dane, III was fourth sailing in the Soling World's championship, which was won by the veteran and very popular competitor on Lake Pontchartrain, Bob Mosbacher of Houston, Texas, who had as his crew Tommy Dickey and Thad Hutcheson of Houston.

In 1972, John Dane III's hopes of an Olympic berth were dimmed when he finished fourth again, this time in a star-studded Soling fleet with the winner being a three-time Mallory Cup champion, Buddy Melges from Wisconsin. Thus ended Dane's four years of hard work in his quest to win an Olympic gold medal in his Soling *Quest*, but with a performance to be proud of by all.

CHAPTER XX

1972–1977

COMMODORES	TERMS
Herbert O'Donnell	1972–1973
B. Temple Brown	1974–1975
Arthur D. Wynne	1976–1977

COMMODORE HERBERT O'DONNELL—1972-73

Elected commodore of the Southern Yacht Club for the year 1972 was Herbert O'Donnell, a prominent local general contractor by profession. Serving with the commodore were: B. Temple Brown, Jr., vice-commodore; Arthur D. Wynne, rear commodore; Daniel B. Killeen, secretary-treasurer; Gilbert Gray, fleet measurer; Dr. W. Kohlman Reed, fleet surgeon; and Charles Gambel, fleet captain.

Commodore O'Donnell was a young skipper who had early training in sailing on the Gulf Coast in Skates and later on Fish Class sloops. He sailed and owned many boats in various classes. He crewed aboard the *Tahuna* and *Glass Slipper* in the St. Petersburg to Havana races. The commodore was one of the founders of the Handicap Class in 1960 and the Cruiser/Racer Class in 1976. He was also the chairman and one of the organizers of the social classic of the SYC, the "Bards of the Bilges" annual ball.

RHODES-19 NATIONAL CHAMPIONSHIP

The Southern Yacht Club hosted two national championship events in 1972. The first one was the Rhodes-19 National Championship, which was won by SYC member Al Grevemberg with the aid of his son, Chip, and his friend Chris Clement. For this and other yachting achievements for many years, Al was awarded the Commodore

Charles J. Tessier trophy for the most outstanding skipper of the year 1972. Also participating in the championship classic were SYC's Gil Mellin, Kurt Lange, and Faurie Ferchaud, who used his two daughters, Annie and Marie, to crew for him.

The second event sailed on Lake Pontchartrain was a match race championship for the Prince of Wales trophy sponsored by the USYRU. Winner of the finals was Terry Cronberg of Winchester, Massachusetts, with crewmen Stephen Cucchiaro and Sandy Warrick.

At the 1973 annual meeting, Commodore O'Donnell was returned to office as were all members of the board except Dr. W. Kohlman Reed who was replaced by Dr. Francis E. Lejeune, Jr. as fleet surgeon.

THE *REGATA AL SOL*—1973

The seventh *regata al sol* of 1973 got the gun from A. R. Blossman's yacht *Heavy Moon* off Broadwater Beach Marina in Biloxi on April 28, with destination the Caribbean Island of Cozumel, 600 hard, uphill miles from the starting line.

Wimoweh, a new Erickson 46 skippered by Tommy Coleman of the syndicate of Coleman, B. Temple Brown, and Maurice J. "Bubby" Hartson, III, was the surprise winner and set a course record of 94:30:38 for the 640 mile event. In second place was Fred Blossman's *Kumbaya*. The other local boats were the new Erickson 39 *Banshee* of Oscar McMillan; Jack Valley's *Munequita*, sailed by Click Schreck, and Paul Radzewicz's *Samba*, under the burgee of the Jackson Yacht Club of Jackson, Mississippi.

SYC CREW WINS 1973 SORC ONE-TON CLASSIC

With an unprecedented six firsts out of six races, Click Schreck skippered Jack Valley's new Ranger 37 one-Ton *Munequita* to first in the fleet of the 1973 Southern Ocean Racing Circuit (SORC), which ended with the Nassau Cup sailed in the Bahamas. They won over Ted Turner's Custom S&S *Lightnin*, followed by Ted Hood's own *Robin*. Click's crew members on the *Munequita* were O. J. Young, Jack Valley, John Dane, III, Bill Ibs, Jr., Hjalmar Breit, By Baldridge, and others. They won the most coveted ocean racing trophy in America. The SORC started in 1930 bringing together the best boats, skippers, and crews from the United States, Canada, Ber-

Commodore Nathaniel C. Curtis, Jr.
1968, 1969

Commodore Charles L. Eshleman, Jr.
1970, 1971

Commodore Herbert O'Donnell
1972, 1973

Commodore B. Temple Brown
1976, 1975

Commodore Arthur D. Wynne
1976, 1977

Commodore Daniel B. Killeen
1978, 1979

Commodore Richard D.
Spangenberg
1980, 1981

Commodore Cal F. Hadden, Jr.
1982, 1983

Commodore William C. Gambel
1984, 1985

Commodore Maurice J. Hartson
1986

muda, England, Europe, and even as far away as New Zealand.

In this same race, another outstanding job was done by Buddy Friedrichs and his SYC crew who sailed the new Chance 44 *Jemel* to fourth place in Class B and twenty-first in the fleet, beating handily the two other Chance 44s.

THE GULFPORT-PENSACOLA CLASSIC IN RETROSPECT—1973
by Bache McE. Whitlock

Immediately following World War II, there was but a handful of boats along the Gulf Coast from Texas to Florida capable of making long ocean races. Of those few, about 10 were at the Southern Yacht Club with none at any of the other Coast clubs. SYC did not even possess a Race Committee boat in 1948, so the larger boats were started from an imaginary line between a buoy off the Municipal Yacht Harbor breakwater and a flag pole, turning at the airport beacon, and returning to the starting point. We had no CCA ratings and handicaps were adjusted as the results came in.

Everybody had fun and the races were generally catch-as-catch-can. *Barracuda, Aweigh, Dixie Girl, Dixie Queen, Malihini, Salabar, Pimpernel, Marie Cornielle, Sandpiper* (later the *Picayune*), *Siren, Companero*...these were famous names.

Salabar was the hot boat, being beaten in light airs only by the two *Dixies*. However, this situation didn't last long before newer boats invaded the veteran fleet. As each came and reigned as queen for a few years, her tenure was necessarily short because the fleet was expanding by leaps and bounds. *Chula* was the first of the new boats. She was brought to New Orleans by W. Horace Williams, Jr., and was unbeatable for about five years. Then, in quick succession, came *Whispering Wind, Thunderbolt* (nee *Gray Goose*), *Glass Slipper* and *Tahuna*. And then like bolts from the blue, came the formidable Cal 40s from the same mold that produced *Conquistadore*, winner of the SORC. They held stage center for several years, only to be replaced by a succession of boats so fast that none held the lead more than a year, each new arrival being faster (and more expensive) than the last.

As the aforementioned chronological facts occurred, so did racing interest grow in the big boats. There were, of course, the comparatively tame lake races: Tchefuncte, Mandeville, Bayou Liberty, Round-the-Lake, and the Race to the Coast. But ambitions were restless to try Big Briny, the deep blue Gulf, and although spasmodic races were scheduled now and then, nothing had really jelled, most particularly because all interested parties were from the SYC and it is difficult to persuade some distant yacht club to sit out at the sea buoy and judge the finish for a few boats they have never seen or heard of.

And so, the long distance race, Gulfport to Pensacola's sea buoy and return, was on schedule after many years. Different dates were tried and different starting points experimented with. For several years, we started it out at Ship Island to give the slower boats a better chance. Then it was moved inshore to where it is now in an effort to aid the spectators.

But the grind of the sea buoy and back, silly as it now seems, prevented the race from growing and it was not until the rules were changed to end it at Pensacola that the race grew to the point where it is almost busting its britches.

On the opposite side of the coin, there is nothing more frustrating than to sail a rough 200 miles and find no finish boat, take the time from your own watch, and then argue which was right at the bar after the race. Even after the race was shortened to end at Pensacola, we once endured the experience of having the finish boat evaporate before all the contestants had crossed the line. Lacking a sea-going committee boat, the Pensacola Yacht Club prevailed upon the Navy to provide a tug manned by a crew of civilians employed under civil service. When their normal working day was done, they simply hauled up the anchor and headed for the barn, race or no.

Perhaps a bit of philosophy is in order here. Call it practicality if you will. For whatever it's worth, ocean races are created by "hard noses," the blue water sailors, the do-or-die types who sail in good weather and bad. Filling out this cadre or nucleus are the boats and sailors who constitute the rank-and-file that have increased the fleet to where it is today. These are the cruisers, the folks who dearly love their eight-year-old yachts and hope to win but will not die, or even cry, if they don't. Ironically, many of this latter breed are hard noses of yesteryear who have mellowed with age and frustration in the financial rat race of keeping up with the fast ones.

Both elements are necessary and important in the sport and each deserves consideration in formulating and planning a race such as the Gulfport-Pensacola Classic.

Like the bride, some were old, some were new, some were borrowed, and we all sailed the blue with fun, consideration, and prizes for almost everyone.

The race we enjoy today didn't materialize from any one person's hard-headed scheme. It is based on trials and errors in the past and the collective wishes of the participants themselves. The Gulfport-Pensacola is a race for the many and not for a few. In 1984 there were over 150 contestants.

Making a second but unsuccessful attempt at the Adams Cup for the Women's North American sailing championship was the SYC team of "Sparky" Graham skipper, Peggy Taylor and Karen Furlow as crew in the summer of 1973. They lost the championship in a close race on the waters at Indian Harbor Yacht Club.

COMMODORE B. TEMPLE BROWN—1974-75

The new but well-known sailing commodore of the Southern Yacht Club elected to serve for the year 1974, B. Temple Brown, is the president of an age-old family-oriented New Orleans business, Brown's Velvet Ice Cream Company. Temple made his mark in big boat racing sailing the 48-foot *Tiare* that set a new record of 197 hours and 40 minutes in the 1971 Cozumel race, beating the old record by 5 hours. He sailed *Big Red*, as she was named, to many more victories, as well as his 40-foot *Silkie*. He was captain of the 1976 Lipton Cup team that brought the coveted trophy to the SYC.

Serving with Commodore Brown were: Arthur D. Wynne, vice-commodore; Daniel B. Killeen, rear commodore; Richard Spangenberg, secretary-treasurer; Gilbert Gray, fleet measurer; Dr. Clarence E. Black, fleet surgeon; and M. J. Harton, III, fleet captain.

125th ANNIVERSARY OF FOUNDING OF SYC

Celebrating the 125th anniversary of the founding of the Southern Yacht Club in 1974, the parade of boats and the opening regatta were a colorful spectacle as the more than 200 yachts dressed ship and passed in review along the seawall of Lake Pontchartrain before the dignitaries assembled aboard Fred Blossman's yacht *Heavy Moon*, which was stationed off Bayou St. John.

One of the interesting features of the parade of yachts is competition for the best-decorated yacht, an event with the overtones of Mardi Gras. This year's winner was *Riptide*, owned by Rip Haase, which carried balloons and flags wishing the SYC a happy birthday. Following the parade was the traditional flag-raising ceremony. The festivities began the night before with a formal ball honoring the commodore and the flag officers of SYC.

Celebrating another anniversary in 1974 was the Star Class—its fiftieth year as the New Orleans-Gulf Star Fleet and also the thirty-fifth anniversary of the first Star Class Spring Series held in the United States and won by SYC's Edward B. "Bud" Jahncke in 1939. Many visitors were in New Orleans for the occasion and a record-breaking entry was cause for celebration.

LUDER INTERNATIONALS HELD AT SYC

The SYC was host to another Luder International championship event in 1974, which was won by Bill Fundenberg of Newport Beach

Yacht Club, with crew Bill Symes and Chris Colby. The defending champion of 1973, SYC's Tommy Meric, was sailing his Soling in the North American championship and Canadian Olympic Regatta at Kingston and was unable to enter the L-16 classic.

Eager to play their part in the celebration of the SYC anniversary year, both the Junior and Senior Sir Thomas J. Lipton cup teams won their respective championships. Shawn Killeen, with Chris Christman and Pearson Potts as crew, sailed to a first place finish as SYC took the 1974 Junior Lipton cup regatta at Pensacola. The other member of the team was Gerard Sonnier.

THREE-QUARTER TON WORLD'S CHAMPIONSHIP VICTORY

The year 1974 brought another championship to the South, the three-quarter-ton World's championship. The skipper was O. J. Young, member of the New Orleans and Southern Yacht Clubs. The event was hosted by the Coral Reef Yacht Club in Miami. O. J. was sailing the 34-foot new custom Gary Mull design owned by Young and Jeff Hampton, named *Swampfire*. The crew members, in addition to Young and Hampton, were Dick Deaver, Al Gooch, Mark LeBlanc, Johnny Potts, John Dane, III, By Baldridge, and Dean Schoonmaker. *Swampfire* won three firsts and two seconds.

Runnner-up to Young was SYC skipper Gene Walet, former Mallory champion and twice Olympic skipper, sailing Tampa's Joe Byares' 30-foot *Raven*, which Byares had designed and built in Tampa. By a large margin, Walet won the only race lost by O. J. Young.

The last race of the five, a 200-mile course that crossed the Gulf Stream twice with winds over forty for the entire race, coupled with huge seas, saw only four of the ten entries finish the race. Third was *Bingo* from Britain, a new Bob Miller design sailed by Bob Stewart. Fourth was Lowell North in *Sagitta IV*, designed by Ron Holland.

Continuing her remarkable victories after her victory in Miami, *Swampfire*, later owned by Bill Reese of Hampton Yacht Club but skippered by O. J. Young, won the 1974 North American 3/4-Ton championship hosted by Annapolis Yacht Club with four firsts and a second. Young had previously won the 1/4-Ton championship in 1972 in a Ranger 23, *Dulcinea*. He went on to win the 1976 1/2-Ton championship in a Peterson boat, *Mouth*.

A dazzling new addition to the Lake Pontchartrain fleet in 1974 was the *Southerly* owned by Bert Keenan of the SYC and of the Lake

Arthur Yacht Club located in Lafayette, Louisiana. *Southerly* was a custom-built Sparkman & Stephens aluminum ketch, fifty-five feet long. She won her first race out in record-breaking time, the annual St. Petersburg to Isla Mujeres, Mexico race. The crewmen were Charlie Adams, Peter Keenan, Hjalmer Breit, Jr., Roy Troendle, Jr., Frazer Rice, Barry Fox, and Cyril Laan of the Southern Yacht Club, and Bubba Weatherly of Gulfport and Randy Freret of Lafayette, Louisiana.

The *Southerly* set a new course record of fifty-five hours for the 460 mile St. Petersburg to Isla Mujeres race, to take first in fleet and first in Class A. The previous record had been held by *Ondine*, which had made the course in seventy-two hours. *Southerly* was able to make almost the entire trip under spinnaker or double headsail rig and never had to reef. The race included one other SYC boat, *Impulse*, sailed by Robin Moyer and C. T. Williams.

WIMOWEH CRIES "MAYDAY" IN SORC RACE

Entered in the 1974 Southern Ocean Racing Conference (SORC) annual series of races, was *Wimoweh*, the SYC flagship belonging to Commodore B. Temple Brown, Maurice J. "Bubby" Hartson, III, and Tommy Coleman. During the course of the race tragedy struck when *Wimoweh* hit a rock on the Miami to Nassau leg of the course and went down as a total loss. According to both Brown and Hartson, the impact was "almost like sliding onto a sandbar." There was no great jolt, but they could hear the shearing sound as the rock slashed through the fiberglass hull. If the yacht had struck the rock on her keel, she would have ridden over it as at least three other yachts had done.

A "Mayday" went out on the distress frequency and flares were sent up. The *Osprey*, owned and skippered by M. J. "Mike" Fisher of Muncie Indiana, dropped her sails and stood by under power. When the ship began to founder and to sink, the crew took to the life raft, which was adequate for the eleven-man crew. The transfer was accomplished without any injury, but the crew was able to salvage only what they were wearing at the time.

Before the salvage crew could arrive on the scene, scavengers were there first and managed to strip *Wimoweh* of everything. For some reason the compass had not been taken. The hull was raised and brought to Miami.

The distressed crew members, Al and Jack Gooch, Charlie Gambel, John Charbonnet, Waldo Otis, Tommy Brown, Hjalmar Breit, and Cyril Laan, an outstanding group of yachtsmen, were being detained by customs officials in Mexico when SYC Peter Beer, a New Orleans judge, happened by and succeeded in having the crew released as legitimate survivors of a maritime accident.

The rescue yacht, *Osprey*, which had started out with a crew of seven, resumed the race with a crew of eighteen. Fisher, *Osprey*'s skipper, likened the change of watch to the "act at the circus when all the clowns pour out of a little taxi."

The *America June II* was declared the winner until the time allowance for the *Osprey* provided a dramatic ending to the episode by moving her from eighty-ninth in the fleet to overall winner.

In this same SORC race, O. J. Young sailed his Cal 30 *Nautical* to first in her class.

SYC YACHT *INDRA V* AMERICA'S CUP COMMITTEE BOAT IN TRIALS

The year 1974 was the year of the America's Cup races, which were won by Southern Yacht Club's good friend and favorite guest Robert "Bob" Beavier, Jr. in *Courageous*. There to watch Bob perform were many of his friends from the South and the Southern Yacht Club on board the beautiful *Indra V*, which was owned by Edward B. Benjamin of SYC. He was always an avid spectator at all America's Cup classics. Mr. Benjamin had brought his yacht to Newport and was a genial host to many New Orleanians who viewed the races from his boat.

From an article written for the SYC Tell-Tale, Mr. Benjamin's report follows:

> The scene here is probably the greatest show on earth, nautically speaking. Besides the 12s involved, there are hundreds of spectator boats out for the Trials—some are magnificent, and many of them noteworthy in design.
>
> The Trials between the *Intrepid* and the *Courageous* have been cliff-hangers for the most part. Bob Beavier is still in charge of *Courageous*, but the boat now has Connor handling the wheel at the start with Ted Hood also at the helm part of the time.
>
> In case this is not already generally known, *Intrepid* has been supported by the general public in the Pacific Northwest, through contributions ranging from $1.00 on up. Robert W. McCullough, F. Briggs Dalzell and J. Burr Bartram, Jr. are heading the syndicate on *Courageous*,

all members of the New York Yacht Club, and the donations have been much larger, although some have been a good deal less than contributions made by limited syndicates in the past.

So far *Courageous* has won about two more races than *Intrepid*. However, the New York Yacht Club reserves the right to pick the boat and use their own judgment, rather than adhering completely to the number of wins. The intricacies and the hyper-technical development of the 12-meter hulls compares with the farthest reaches in aerodynamics. Their underbody constructions all vary, and in some instances the hull is wider underbody than on deck or at the waterline.

So far the *Southern Cross*, the new Australian boat, has won all three of its starts against *LaFrance*, except one race that had to be abandoned in thick fog. The Coast Guard boat ranges alongside of my *Indra V* to make sure of direction inasmuch as *Indra* has a radar and this small Coast Guard vessel did not. The second race between the French and the Aussies had to be thrown out, because the rigid rule in the conventions of their match requires that races can take only 5½ hours. This race extended 15 minutes beyond that, with the *Southern Cross* winning by just a few seconds. It looks at this moment as if the *Southern Cross* will be the Challenger, and it also looks as if she is going to be hard to beat by one of our American boats as she has the lowest freeboard of any of the 12s I have seen so far and can really go in either light or heavy airs.

It is estimated that the cost of the Australian challenge will run to about $5 million and the cost of the French $2 million. The *LaFrance* has five masts, the latest of which cost $120,000.

I am an overseas member of the Royal Thames Yacht Club, which is charged with the duty of selecting the Cup Challenger. Commodore Elmer Ellsworth Jones and his wife are living aboard *Indra V* and the boat is being used by the international Jury which consists of Bobby Symonette of Nassau, A.J.S. Forsythe of Vancouver, Canada, Eric Cake of Poole, England—one of the big sailing centers—in fact, Cake is the Commodore of the Poole Yacht Club. *Indra V* has excellent visibility in seated positions from stem to stern and makes an ideal Jury boat.

Little did I think when my father took delivery of the 65-foot *Ogarita* in Boston sixty-five years ago for use in New Orleans after summer cruising in these waters up here that one day I would own a boat that was to be used by the International Jury in selecting a Challenger for America's Cup Races, a boat that would be leading all the spectator fleet in these Challenger match races.

The Jury has allowed Mrs. Benjamin and me to go out on the boat every day with them, but no one else except Commodore Ellsworth Jones and his lovely wife, Eileen, good friends of ours, and it has been great fun because the Jury are the nicest kind of people with Bobby a friend of twenty-five years standing.

Reelected as commodore of the SYC for the year 1975 was B. Temple Brown. With his partners who joined him as a syndicate, Maurice J. "Bubby" Hartson, III and Garic Moran, he ordered a new flagship to replace the *Wimoweh*, which had been lost at sea.

The 53-foot yawl, which carried 1300 square feet of sail, was designed by Vince Lazara and built by Gulf Star in St. Petersburg. Her name, *Itema*, was derived from the former Audubon Park Zoo elephant, Itema, which was purchased back in the 30s by the school children of New Orleans as a result of a drive sponsored by the former *Item*.

1975 NEW ORLEANS TO COZUMEL RACE

As usual, the 1975 annual New Orleans to Cozumel race was handled through dedicated committeemen from Cozumel and the Southern Yacht Club, of which Richard Spangenberg has been the ever-enthusiastic promoter. Robert Kahn of Pensacola Yacht Club in his Carter 3/4-ton *Sirocco IV* took first place in the fleet in a record time race—he was third in elapsed time. First to finish in Class A was the C&C 39-foot *Cajun Queen* sailed by SYC's Gene Walet.

The former course record of 94:30:38 for the 640-mile event set by *Wimoweh* in 1973 was beaten by Walet's time of 86:13:30. Behind him was Fred Blossman in his PJ-40 *Kimbaya* in 88:41. Gene was now among the other greats who had accomplished the triple feat of first to finish, first in the International Ocean Race (IOR), Class A, and first in fleet. At that time, there were only two others in this category, Thomas B. Coleman and B. Temple Brown, Jr., sailing *Wimoweh* in 1973 and *Tiare* in 1971. The third skipper to accomplish this feat was Captain J. W. Clark at the helm of his Erickson 46 *Excalibur* in 1979. The race was sailed in near-hurricane force winds.

Carrying his winning ways up to Chicago, the veteran skipper Gene Walet was successful in the Sheldon Clark Regatta held at the Chicago Yacht Club in 1975, where he sailed the ½-ton Peterson-designed boat *Fair American* accompanied by his crew of Mac Hadden of the Bay-Waveland Yacht Club and Jim Schmidt of Southern, also Doug Samson of Pensacola Yacht Club. The owner of the boat was John Lee of the St. Andrews Bay Yacht Club in Panama City, Florida, who co-skippered. Walet won a decisive victory over a 226 boat fleet with a 1,2,2, series.

The SYC was host to two major events in 1975, the North American Flying Scot championship, which was won by Paul Schreck of Pensacola Yacht Club with crew Eleanor Schreck, his wife, and John Blonski. Second was Marc Eagan of Bay-Waveland Yacht Club. Third was John Levy of Southern. Finishing in fifth place in the series was

Gene Walet.

The second classic was the 1975 Finals of the Men's North American Sailing championship for the Clifford D. Mallory cup, which was won by Christopher W. Pollack of Long Island Sound, with Lisa Hamm and William Ehrhorn as crew.

PENSACOLA WINS 420 CHAMPIONSHIP

Away from home, representing the Gulf Yachting Association, Bob and Tom Whitehurst of the Pensacola Yacht Club swept the 1975 420's World Championship in Holland. They flew from Holland to Largs, Scotland to sail in the World's Youth Championship in 420s. Bob, age eighteen, and Tom, age seventeen, won the Youth championship hands down. This event was sponsored by the U.S. International Sailing Association.

LOUISIANA SUPERDOME OPENS IN 1975

The year 1975 will always be a memorable one for Louisianians. The Superdome Stadium was opened on Sunday, August 3, 1975. This magnificent structure, declared by some to be the eighth wonder of the world, is twenty-seven stories high, contains a seating capacity of 90,000, and has 9000 tons of computerized air conditioning and heating equipment. Its cost 163 million dollars. It is a tribute to the masterful architects who designed the Dome, and the Southern Yacht Club is proud to claim them as members, Commodore Nathaniel C. Curtis and Arthur Q. Davis.

COMMODORE ARTHUR D. WYNNE—1976-77

The year 1976 celebrated the 200th birthday of our country, America. Great plans were made by the new flag officers and board members. Elected commodore was Arthur D. "Juby" Wynne, who was a well-known businessman in New Orleans and president of Arthur D. Wynne Co., office supplies and equipment. Juby was a highly competitive skipper in the Lightning Class and was champion many times of the fleet. He was also a Luder Class helmsman and in retirement selected a cruiser-type boat, still carrying on the transom the name *Jane's Mink*.

The other flag officers and board members serving in this bicentennial year were: Richard B. Spangenberg, vice-commodore; John Y. Taylor, rear commodore; G. Joseph Sullivan, secretary-treasurer; Dr.

Elmo J. Cerise, fleet surgeon; Gilbert Gray, fleet measurer; and Eugene H. Walet, III, fleet captain.

SYC CELEBRATES 200th BICENTENNIAL—
1976

Maybe it was the beautiful weather and the ever-present awareness that 1976 was the Bicentennial year worthy of parades, bright color, and gaiety...but whatever the reason, the events of the opening regatta of the SYC were really super with boats decorated with red, white and blue minute men aboard yachts oozing with the spirit of colors of the day.

The racing part of the day was fun too, until the wind died and the finish line looked like a sale table located in Macy's bargain basement.

As the parade of boats passed in review of the SYC officials and other dignitaries standing at attention in full dress uniform aboard the yacht *Porte Bonheur*, it was memorable to watch the parade marshall, Robert "Rip" Haase's beautiful sailing sloop *Riptide* leading the parade.

The 1976 "Bards of the Bilges" party also had patriotic overtones with the theme enhanced by the arrival of Neptune costumed like George Washington on board his raft, having made it across the 17th Street Canal together with his rowdy troops to the "Revoltin' Ball." The troops (K-Crews) arriving with the Delaware River Rowing Club had adequate medicinal potions, and the club reeked with bicentennial decorations. "Ole George" was represented by "Ole Bud," Edward B. "Bud" Jahncke, and his pretty Martha was Mrs. George V. Talbott (Pamela). Her maids were Mrs. John Dane, III (Susan), Mrs. Lawrence R. deMarcay, Jr., Mrs. William C. Gambel (Carol), Miss E. Maurer Ingraham, Mrs. Robert W. Nugon (Peggy), and Miss Susan Anne Potts.

Also celebrating the bicentennial year were Cal Hadden and his wife Nancy with Fabian and Carol Fromherz, who joined the Tall Ship bicentennial fleet in a chartered boat for the last leg of their journey from Newport, Rhode Island, to New York harbor. On July 4, 1976 they experienced an emotional spectacle of patriotism, a celebration they will always remember.

The Senior Sir Thomas J. Lipton trophy was won by the 1976 team consisting of Commodore B. Temple Brown, Jr., team captain, John Dane, III, Hjalmar Breit, Robert Schimek, Jr., Arthur Seaver, III,

Larry Taggart, Jr., and Eugene H. "Gene" Walet, III. The *Itema*, Commodore Brown's flagship, a Gulfstar 53, provided a floating hotel for dozens of spectators on Lake Pontchartrain.

The juniors decided to get their act together again in 1976 by reorganizing and electing a slate of officers. Kenneth Moran was commodore, vice-commodore was Donald Kuebel, rear commodore was Shawn Killeen, and secretary-treasurer was Ellen Eagan. In addition to social parties, a car-wash was planned with the profits going to redecorating the Junior Yacht Club.

It was years ago that the club had sponsored a teen-age dance for those under eighteen. At their 1976 party, 200 kids of extremely various ages danced from eight to midnight to the music of Deacon John and the sounds were really neat—the chaperons were strangely afflicted with sudden cases of deafness.

SKIPPERETTE REGATTA FOR CHAMPIONS' WIVES

Closing the 1976 sailing season was a spectacular Skipperette Regatta. "It looked like a 'WHO'S WHO IN AMERICAN YACHTING'" said *Tell-Tale* reporter Anne Hughes,

> as Flying Scots were carrying aboard the sailing super jocks of the South to aid the skipperettes. There were Olympic Gold Medalists, a Mallory representative and crew, Bay-Waveland Yacht Club's best female sailor, Amy Chapman, a Commodore and other local talent to vie for the Scot Skipperette silver.
>
> The battle proved close to the end as each skipperette had a moment in the lead. All six boats finished the one round race within two minutes of each other. It went 'down to the wire' as positions changed throughout the moderate air race. No one knew who would be winner until the final seconds. Boats crossed each other frequently on the windward leg until it was Joan Hartson in front at the first mark. Issuing commands right and left to her "novice" crewmen, Temple Brown and Uncle Roy Troendle, Joannie popped her chute first and took off!
>
> The last leg downwind saw the wives of our recent Olympic Champs fighting it out for the lead. Carol Schreck and Suzy Friedrichs jibed back and forth trying to out pace the other. Both gals were able to keep their husband crews cool and calm (?@?↙*??#) in the tight situation. Karen Baltar, 1975 Lipton team member, with Bobby Schimek and Beau LeBlanc aboard, challenged the leaders, gaining each time Carol and Suzy jibed, leaving it anyone's race. Meanwhile, while most of the fleet was sailing up, up, up, Amy Chapman used some sensible tactics and sailed right through to the finishing mark. Amy, the youngest Scot skipperette participating, crossed the line first just seconds ahead of Carol

Schreck and Suzy Friedrichs. Close behind were Karen Baltar, Anne Hughes, Joan Hartson, and Bonnie Rawlins.

PEP TALK TO SKIPPERETTES
by *Tell-Tale* editor

Before this featured event took place at the Southern Yacht Club, it was thought advisable to prepare those skipperettes who were unaccustomed to sailing with expert male skippers aboard, and so the following pep talk was given:

Most sail boat skippers have to battle the elements and each other. Skipperettes have to battle the elements, each other, and the owner of the boat. He can be the captain any other Sunday, but in a Skipperette race, you're the admiral, and make him ask permission to ask permission! Sieze authority as soon as he puts the sail up and hollers for the crew to throw the "bag" below. Right then, you say "No! the 'bag' is going to reef the sail."

And remember there's nothing to steering a boat. You just have to do everything backwards. It isn't like a car where you're never supposed to smash the fenders. On a boat, you'd better smash the fenders and not the boat, or he becomes unreasonable. In a car the gear is one simple knob that comes up from the floor and does all the work. On a boat, the gear is wall-to-wall junk, and it never works. It would give Ralph Nader mal-de-mer. That's French for you-can't-take-it-with-you.

But don't knock the old man's gear, because throughout the whole race he'll stand behind you and tell you where to go. When you get home, you can tell him where to go. Let him know he's a responsible member of your crew. Whatever you do wrong, he's responsible!

From there on, it's a simple matter of your interpreting his instructions. If he says "Watch your beam!" he's not getting personal. If he talks about the boat's shrouds or wake, he's not getting morbid. If he mentions the sheets, he's not propositioning someone else. If he's hollering about tackle, don't jump overboard. And, if he exclaims, "Watch that broad reach!" you just harrumph: "I *do* beg your *pardon*!"

I've prepared an alphabetical list of nautical terms to review, so we don't disgrace ourselves, girls. The letter "A" is prefixed to everything a sailor says. If he's winding a winch and mumbles: abaft, abeam, adrift, afore, alee, aloft, amidships—he's just grunting—it only means if the boat's got wind, he doesn't. (Uh-beam! Uh-drift!.)

Moving on to the letter "B": Backstays: Well, for sailing you probably won't be wearing any stays.... Bunk: At the party following the Skipperette race, it'll be our turn to swap lies about what a great race we sailed, then you'll know the definition of the word "bunk".... Deck: It would be a good idea to bring a deck on your boat, if the wind dies. Bring two decks if you prefer canasta.... Downhall: The new commotion about hauling beer cans down below instead of throwing them in the lake like we did before the Sierra Club crackdown....

Granny Knot: Now I know that's derogatory, because grannies are

The Southern Yacht Club wins the 1976 Lipton Regatta. Skippers and crews circle the coveted Sir Thomas J. Lipton trophy.

Winners of the Women's North American Sailing Championship for the Mrs. Charles Frances Adams trophy in 1977 were these skipperettes from the Bay-Waveland Yacht Club in Bay St. Louis, Mississippi: Judy Reeves; Cindy Stieffel, skipper; and Amy Chapman.

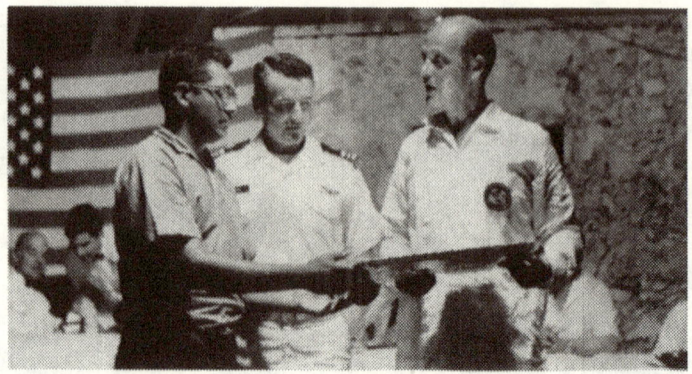

Cal Hadden of the SYC, right, is presented the winners' trophy by representatives of the Mexican government in the regata al sol race to Isla Mujeres.

The SYC Olympic gold medal winners were honored at a New Orleans Saints football game at Tulane Stadium in 1968. Standing with the crew, second from left, is SYC Commodore Nathaniel C. Curtis, Jr.

Gulf Yachting Association Commodore J. Gilbert Scheib, right, presents the gold cup trophy to the winner of the GYA's 50th anniversary annual regatta, B. Temple Brown of the SYC, center. SYC Commodore Charles L. Eshleman, Jr., is at left. Not shown are crewmen Johnny Potts and Mike Sperry.

square to start with.... Head: In every boat there's a little boy's room and a little girl's room with a picture on the door.... Heel: A playboy sailor who brings a different gal on board every weekend while his wife waits at home.... Leech: A dingbat who just won't stay ashore.... List: The memorandum of things you were supposed to bring on board.... Mayday: Only at McGehee's school is "Mayday" the first Friday in May. Nautically, Mayday presents the fascinating prospect of talking to real live sailors. Only, in signalling the Coast Guard, a good first impression is important, like a wicker chair in a nudist colony. In other words, if you call "Mayday, mayday—This is the *Racquel Welch!*"—Vrooom! They arrive in their fastest speed-boat! But, if you call "Mayday, mayday—This is the *Lydia E. Pinkham!*" forget it....Spreaders: I think this refers to the oleo commercial where the sailors compare sandwiches....Stern: A wealthy family in Metairie who own everything but a boat....

I forgot to define Bow: If you don't collide with anything on the starting line, and this includes the committee boat, don't stand on the edge of the dock to take your bow....Tack: In a skipperette race you must realize some women have tack and some don't....Winches: Ancient term referring to the skipperettes of Shakespeare's day....And my last definition is Luff, not in alphabetical order, because it's the most important for you to remember. Luff is going into a protest meeting, and never having to say you're sorry!

SYC HOSTS FINNS NORTH AMERICAN CHAMPIONSHIP—1976

The Southern Yacht Club hosted the 1976 Finn North American championship with sixty-two boats registered. Sailors came from all over to participate, since the top ten would qualify for the Finn Olympic Trials to be held during the summer of 1976 at Association Island. Winning the event was John Bertrand of Chelsea, Australia (1983 America's Cup winner). He wrapped up another major sailing triumph, having won this classic in 1975. SYC's John Dane, III made the cut and he and Bertrand were the top two to qualify to sail in the Finn European championship in April and May.

ASSOCIATION PLANS FOR 1976 OLYMPICS

When the Olympic Sailing Association of the Southern Yacht Club was organized in 1965, it was the first such local association formed to help Olympic aspirants. Immediately following the 1972 Olympics and under the capable and enthusiastic leadership of its president, Edward B. Benjamin, a group of the association's members composed of Commodore Herbert O'Donnell and A. J. Nugon, Jack Dane,

Joseph L. Killeen, Jr., and President Benjamin went to Cork to meet the NAYRU officials there.

Chairman of the Olympic Committee of NAYRU, Dick Stearns, was an old friend of SYC members. While they were in Cork, steps were initiated so that SYC could be considered as one of the hosts for the regional pre-Olympic regattas, commencing in 1973. With the full support of the SYC board, the SYC was selected for this event in the spring of 1973. This gave an opportunity for our local skippers to compete against some of the top sailors in the country.

After careful scrutiny, three SYC crews were sent to contests all over the nation in their quest, first to qualify for the Olympic Trials to be held at Association Island in 1976 and then to make the Olympic team for the Games to be sailed at Kingston, Canada in July, 1976.

The crews finally selected to represent the SYC in the 1976 trials were Tommy Meric in the 470 Class, a former L-16 International champion, with crewman Robert Brennan. In the Finn Class was past Intercollegiate All-American, Junior North American Sailing Champion for the Sears Cup and Soling Champion, John Dane, III. In the Flying Dutchman Class, also representing Southern, were two Tulane students, Augie Diaz of the Coral Reef Yacht Club in Miami and Marshal Duane of Florida. Augie was an Intercollegiate All-American, past Snipe Champion as well as a past International Youth Champion.

An excellent effort was made on the part of all contestants. Augie Diaz, whose crew, Marshal Duane was ill, barely missed representing the country in the last race. John Dane, III came within a half point of being second against the best sailors in the United States. Tommy Meric placed sixth among the outstanding skippers in that class.

Not one country dominated in the six classes sailing in the 1976 Olympics, with the possible exception of Great Britain in the Tornado class. Europeans did win gold in all classes. The U.S. garnered two silvers, in Soling and Tornado classes, and one bronze in the Tempest class.

Missing from the 1976 Olympic Games for the first time since 1932 when sailing was sanctioned as a sport in the Olympics were the Star boats. The Dragons were eliminated in favor of the Tornado; International 470 Dinghy, Soling, Tempest, Flying Dutchman and Finn classes were the other entries.

INDRA V VIP BOAT AT OLYMPICS

Indra V, Edward B. Benjamin's impressive motor sailor, was chosen by the Olympic protocol officers as VIP spectator boat for the duration of the yachting races. In ideal weather, the *Indra* was permitted a position near the starting line, and the New Orleanians aboard, Mr. and Mrs. Jack Dane, Jr., Commodore and Mrs. Herbert O'Donnell, Mr. and Mrs. T. Sellers Meric, Mr. and Mrs. William C. Gambel, and Mr. and Mrs. John Duane of Delray Beach, Florida had a beautiful view of the seven races.

The Benjamins also played host to the team captains of the Olympic sailing teams—United States, Great Britain, New Zealand, Austria, Japan, Sweden, Switzerland, Norway, Greece, and Italy. Prince Bertel of Sweden and Prince Albert, son of Prince Rainier and Princess Grace of Monaco, were aboard as well as Lord Killanin, International Olympic Committee president, accompanied by the president and board members of the International Yacht Racing Union (IYRU).

On these royal occasions, extra security men were placed on the *Indra*, with police boats following closely astern. She was certainly Southern Yacht Club's most prestigious boat of the era, for before the 1976 Olympics she had participated as flagship for the Royal Thames Yacht Club, of which Mr. Benjamin was a member, at the America's Cup Trials races of 1976.

Mr. and Mrs. Benjamin returned to Newport, Rhode Island for the race again in 1977, one of the *Indra V*'s last voyages before being donated before Mr. Benjamin's death to the Smithsonian Institution as a research vessel by Tropical Research operating from Panama.

The Southern Yacht Club honored Mr. Benjamin at the 1976 banquet. A scroll was presented to him in appreciation of his unlimited efforts in behalf of the Olympic Sailing Association, from which he was retiring as president. Former Commodore Herbert O'Donnell was elected the new president with Jack Dane vice-president.

REGATA AL SOL—1977

Reelected to office in 1977, Commodore Arthur D. Wynne was host to another banquet honoring the participants in the Mexico race—the *regata al sol* of 1977, from Gulfport to Cozumel. The overall winner was Allen Borne of SYC, owner and skipper of the Heritage One-Ton *Samurai*. She was first on corrected time and first in Class B. Another SYC entry a Cal 48, *Tiare*, was sailed by Tom Coleman.

Owners with Tom were B. Temple Brown and Maurice J. Hartson, III. *Tiare* was first to finish. First in Class A was *Cajun Queen*, a C&C 39, sailed by Jim Bates of the New Orleans Yacht Club. First in Class C was Bill Roth's *Gundagar*.

The Mexico race this year was a comedy and near-tragedy of errors for a group of Jackson Yacht Club sailors. It began with a false start, was interrupted when a crew member had a heart attack, and ended with some of the crew finishing the race in a bus after Mexican authorities impounded the boat.

The Jackson crew was aboard a Pearson 10-meter, 33-foot yacht *Antares*, owned by Dr. W.A. "Gus" Neely, with crewmen Harry Shaw, Robert Pendelton, Bill Beemer, Jack Harding, Ed Wennerland, and Jack Callahan. Four days out Ed. Wennerland suffered a heart attack and after thirty hours of frantic distress messages sent out to the Coast Guard in Miami, which responded but never arrived, the sailors changed their course to reach the closest port of Progresso, where they were met by a Mexican naval ambulance. After two hours of red tape Wennerland was admitted to the hospital in Merida, Mexico. He did recover and was home within a few days.

When the crew returned to the boat, Mexican custom officers had boarded the *Antares* and confiscated all weapons. A political battle followed and the weapons were finally returned. When they reached the Cozumel Yacht Club, they attended the dinner Saturday night. The commodore had invited too many guests and so instructed the *Antares* crew to leave rather than set up more tables. However, they did have a wonderful evening of entertainment provided by Crescencio Rivero Flores and Alfredo Ferrer, two of the finest hosts in Mexico.

The 1977 GORC champion was Allen Borne sailing *Samarai* with crewmen H. Hampton and G. Melancon. They were winners of the newly presented trophy to the SYC, the Capt. Wilfred A. Grusich Sr. perpetual memorial trophy given by his son.

1977—THE YEAR OF THE SYC JUNIORS

The year 1977 was the year of the Juniors. Under the capable leadership of the junior activity chairman of the SYC, William Gambel, the juniors captured all GYA junior titles, the Sears, Smythe and Bemis national USYRU regional championships. Southern's representative, Shawn Killeen, went on to capture the Area F title to enter the finals of the Sears National Junior championship. The SYC won the National Junior Flying Scot championship and also the

Junior Liptons.

Another SYC junior achievement was the winning of the 1977 National Sea Explorer Sailing championship at the Alamitos Bay Yacht Club in California by Chris Friend and his crew, Rich Ashman. To be eligible competitors they had to be Sea Explorers and had to qualify by winning local and regional eliminations. Chris was also a junior at Yale University and a member of Ship 23 which belonged to a local group of Sea Explorers to which SYC Larry and Tom Taggart served as advisors. The Southern Yacht Club hosted the Sea Explorer Scouts' national championship in 1976 which was won by Skip Koury of Newport Beach, California.

The greatest spectacle of the decade was the thrill of watching the Southern Yacht Club's well-trained juniors grow up and win, week after week, some of the most treasured trophies in sailboat racing. And then having done so, the young skippers cop the club's own coveted Commodore Charles J. Tessier most outstanding skipper award richly deserved and proudly presented.

SKIPPERETTES ENTER 100 BOATS

The most successful SYC skipperette regatta was staged by Edna Gray, who had 100 boats registered and on the starting line for the 1977 skipperette regatta. The amazing part was there were no protests! At the flag raising ceremony an innovation was introduced in the rather curvacious form of SYC's "First Mate," our skipperette insignia, compliments of Jean Bousquet and Janet Lorber. The races were successfully run by Joel Barnett and Butsie Ingraham. For another trip down memory lane, the winners in the eleven classes of boats are listed:

Carol Gambel—L-16	Burdette Bremmermann—Rainbow
Nina Killeen—Star	
Susan Drennan—Flying Scot	Miranne LeBlanc—Pram
Julie Ann Gooch—Cal-25	Anne Penn Graham—5.5
Sharon Davis—Gulf-One	Leslie Higgins—Dragon
	Karen Balter—Soling
	Pat Grevemberg—Rhodes 19

In the handicap classes Shelia Walet, Janet Caspers, Nancy Sullivan, and Melody Jacobs were winners.

SOUTHERN YACHT CLUB

BAY-WAVELAND SKIPPERETTES WIN ADAMS CUP

After many unsuccessful attempts by GYA member yacht clubs to win the Women's North American Sailing Championship, in 1977 the young skipperettes of the Bay-Waveland Yacht Club finally won the prestigious Mrs. Charles Frances Adams trophy in Newport, sailing Shields' boats. They set an amazing sailing championship record in the history of USYRU finals by winning seven out of eight races and one second place—this record has never been equalled to date.

The winning team consisted of Cindy Stieffel, skipper, Amy Chapman and Judy Reeves crew with Ellen Eagan as alternate. Cindy's mother, Mrs. Ray Stieffel (Ann) was a second alternate. At the GYA annual meeting in 1978, these young ladies were presented scrolls honoring their achievements and were given gold charms. The Gulf Yachting Association finally had reached its goal. No one was happier than "Mr. G.Y.A.," J. Gilbert Scheib, who struggled from the fifties to have the South and particularly the GYA achieve the three national championships for men, women and juniors by winning the Mallory, Adams and Sears trophies. At last this was accomplished.

Because of her outstanding achievement in the sailing world, Cindy Stieffel was extended an invitation from the editor of *Yacht Racing/Cruising* magazine, Major Hall, to compete in the first *Yacht Racing/Cruising* Women's International Invitational Regatta in 1977 against nineteen of the best women sailors in the world from the U.S., Canada, England, and Europe. It was to be held at the Yale Corinthian Yacht Club in Branford, Connecticut in 420s. Cindy was unable to accept because of other commitments.

CHAPTER XXI

1978–1981

COMMODORES	TERMS
Daniel B. Killeen	1978–1979
Richard D. Spangenberg	1980–1981

COMMODORE DANIEL B. KILLEEN—1978-79

Another SYC junior to rise from the ranks to become commodore of the Southern Yacht Club in 1978 was Dr. Daniel B. "Danny" Killeen. He was a professor of computer science at Tulane University. An avid sailor, Danny was very active in senior and junior Lipton cup teams and raced in several L-16 events against the Chicago Yacht Club. He was also a crew for Gene Walet in his unsuccessful attempt to win the Olympic gold medal in 1972.

Serving with Commodore Killeen were Richard G. Spangenberg, vice-commodore; John Y. Taylor, rear commodore; G. Joseph Sullivan, secretary-treasurer; Dr. Elmo Cerise, fleet surgeon; Gilbert Gray, fleet measurer; and Gene Walet, fleet captain.

It was through the efforts of Commodore Killeen, who was Area D representative of USYRU, that the United States Yacht Racing Union's annual meeting was held at the Southern Yacht Club in January 1978. This was the first time that such a meeting was held in this area of the South.

During Killeen's reign, the SYC won many championships. Under his leadership the L-16 fleet hosted the North-South team race with the Chicago Yacht Club. After being dormant since 1975, this event was rejuvenated in 1978 and sailed on Lake Pontchartrain.

With Confederate and American flags flying off the sterns, designating the team boats, four light hulls and four dark hulls got off at 10 a.m. Southern won two out of three races and was declared the champion. Team and fleet captain Greg Gambel presented everyone with a red shirt to commemorate the occasion and after trophy presentation all enjoyed a beer party on the upper deck of the clubhouse.

The twelve Chicago sailors competed against a strong SYC team composed of Commodore Killeen, past Commodore Charles Eshleman, Jr., Tommy Taggart, and Peter Wuescher.

At the 1978 Gulf Yachting Association's annual meeting and opening regatta, the SYC team won the series of races and received the Commodore J. Gilbert Scheib trophy which had been presented to the GYA in 1977 for the yacht club of the GYA winning the opening regatta. The New Orleans Yacht Club was the first winner in 1977.

When the SYC junior Lipton team won the 1978 Junior Lipton trophy, Commodore Killeen was privileged to present the award to the group of juniors of which his son was one of the skippers. It was reminiscent of the commodore's early days as a member of the junior team that represented the SYC in 1952 with Jack Scheib, Jr. as captain, and Gene Walet, III and Pudgy McClure the other team mates. The 1978 junior Lipton members were J. Dwight LeBlanc, III, team captain, Shawn Killeen, T. Garic Moran, Daniel B. Killeen, Jr., and Robbie Young. Danny, Jr. was the recipient of the Roy Troendle Sr. trophy for winning the last race.

Five SYC junior skippers were invited to participate in the U.S. Youth championship in 1978 which was conducted by USYRU at the U. S. Naval academy in Annapolis, Maryland. The winner would then advance to represent the U. S. at the World Youth championship scheduled for Perth, Australia. Those juniors were Robert Killeen, Jr., J. Dwight LeBlanc, III, Dan Keller, Kenneth Moran, Shawn Killeen, Greg Christman, T. Garic Moran, and Robbie Young.

Another plus for the Bay-Waveland Yacht Club, whose sailing program has produced many champions for the GYA in the past few years, was the winning of the 1978 North American Flying Scot Junior championship by Marc Eagan with crewman Ed. Turnipseed and Ted Trash. The event was sailed on Long Island Sound.

At the end of a sailing season trophies are presented and awards made. One such tribute was paid to a longtime friend of many SYC members and particularly their children, Lester Collins, who was retiring in 1978 after twenty-eight years of loyal service as SYC's renowned bartender. Many of the well-wishers were those who had sipped their first brew under Lester's winking but watchful eye—

he was fond of our youngsters. Lester continued to serve the club after his retirement on special occasions until his death in 1983.

The 1978 SYC Testimonial Banquet paid honor to Burt Keenan and his crew on the *Acadia* for their many victories during the year. *Acadia* was a beautiful 51 foot long racer designed for Burt by the leading designer of Grand Prix ocean racers, German Frers. Her mast height was seventy-one feet with triple spreaders, extensive hydraulic systems and winches, 3100 pound displacement and 17,000 pound ballast. Her cost was $400,000. Keenan's racing record for 1978 included the St. Petersburg to Isla Mujeres race in which *Acadia* made a clean sweep of first to finish, first in class and first overall on corrected time.

Burt Keenan's 51-foot yawl *Acadia* lost no time in making herself a contender in blue water races. In the spring of 1978 *Acadia* won the Class A, Division II cup in the SORC, regarded as the World Series of yacht racing. After a break-down in the first race, *Acadia* came back to finish first in her class in each of the five subsequent series races. A few weeks later, Keenan's yacht captured the trophy in the 456-mile race from St. Petersburg to Isla Mujeres, Mexico, in both Class A. and overall fleet. It was the third time Keenan had won this race across the Gulf of Mexico, he having previously done it in 1974 and 1975 with his 53-foot yawl *Southerly*. Another feather in Keenan's cap came when he won the IOR division in the Newport-Bermuda race in 1978.

At the annual meeting held in December, Commodore Danny Killeen was re-elected for the year 1979. He was applauded for his accomplishments during the year in furthering the juniors of SYC and congratulated on his appointment to the Yacht Racing Council of the United States Yacht Racing Union (USYRU).

Danny literally sailed into his second term when he won the 1979 "race of champions" in the Sugar Bowl Regatta. His crew consisted of his son Danny, Jr. and J. Dwight LeBlanc, III. He won his races in spite of having had a busy night closing the bar and kitchen following the New Year's Eve party which is always associated with the Sugar Bowl Regatta.

REGATA AL SOL—1979

The *regata al sol* celebrated its tenth year in 1979. A review of those ten successful years was made in the *Tell-Tale* by the chairman of the regatta, Richard Spangenberg. The *regata al sol* got its start back in 1965 when the SYC Commodore Auguste Lorber, Jr. was approached by the Mexican tourist council, which suggested a race. Commodore Lorber appointed Richard Spangenberg chairman of a committee to check such a possibility, knowing that Dick had all the expertise necessary for the success of such an enterprise. A prominent Mexican businessmen's group headed by former President Miguel Aleman met with Richard Spangenberg and with the endorsement of Commodore Lorber plans for the first race were concluded.

When Dick Spangenberg reviewed the ten years of the race, he failed to state that he had shouldered the enormous task of planning and coordinating this race for the past eleven years. The complexity of details is magnified a hundredfold because of working long-distance with a foreign country in a foreign language. Dick's counterparts resided in Mexico City.

The bright spot in the Mexican organizational process was the redoubtable Alberto Alvarez Morphy, who like Dick had spearheaded the regatta since its inception. The time Dick took out of his life and the money out of his pocket has been well worth it to all of us at the SYC and we shall be forever grateful to him and his helpful mate, Nicole, a lady of many languages. Her Spanish-speaking talents and hospitality were boundless.

The 1979 *regata al sol* proved to be an endurance contest with stormy weather and gale force winds at the outset, followed by fair and then dying breezes later in the race. It started on Saturday and by Monday more than half the fleet had withdrawn owing to human or gear failure. The winner, Captain J. W. Clark of SYC at the helm of his Erickson 46 *Excalabur*, swept the field finishing in 110 hours, 54 minutes to give him first in IOR, Class A and first in fleet.

R. H. Kahn of Pensacola skippering *Sirocco IV* finished first in IOR, Class B and second in fleet. Third in fleet and second in IOR Class B was William Roth of Houston, Texas in *Gundagar*, a Peterson 34. In the PHRF Class, W. P. Farr of Jackson, Mississippi sailed *Toulouse*, an Erickson 35, across the line to take first place.

Following the Mexican race was the Ocean Triangle in the 1979 Southern Ocean Racing Circuit (SORC) which was won by the *Acadia*, which had sailed in 1978, and by the same skipper, Burt Keenan. This race in the SORC is recorded not only for the outstanding work performed by Burt and his crew, but to relate the story of how one of his crew "dropped in" on the race.

THE "DREYFUS CAPER" IN THE
SORC OCEAN RACE—1979
Written for the *Tell-Tale*

French history tells an exciting story of the "Dreyfus Affair," a soldier framed on espionage charges and exiled to Devil's Island. The SYC has its own "Dreyfus Affair" anecdote with the hero escaping one peril after another, only to land in the middle of the ocean like his predecessor at the turn of the century.

Burt Keenan flew from New Orleans to Miami for the race. Tommy Dreyfus, a crew member, missed the flight, but ticketed himself to arrive eight hours before the race. Then, with THAT flight cancelled, Tommy hopped another that would just barely get him aboard in time. Only THIS one was the target of hi-jacking. Once the hi-jacker was subdued and tied in the plane's lavatory, the flight had to land in Orlando to meet federal authorities.

When Dreyfus finally streaked through the Miami Airport an hour before the race started, he noticed another rushing passenger wearing topsiders. His luck did a flip. The man was a *Sports Illustrated* photographer heading for a helicopter at the blimp base. The resourceful Dreyfus cut a quick deal, agreeing to let the photographer snap him jumping the 65-feet from the chopper to the *Acadia's* side.

Keenan's jaw sagged a bit as he dropped sail and collected Tommy and his bag from the water. Then he quipped, "Nice of you to drop in for the race, Tommy."

ACADIA SETS NEW RECORD—1979
by "Sparky" Graham Arceneaux

In winning the Southern Ocean Racing Circuit, Ted Turner may have out-distanced the Aussies at Newport, but he was totally outclassed by an SYC-bred crew led by skipper Burt Keenan aboard *Acadia*. Turner's six-year old *Tenacious* was the pre-series pick to take the circuit with a crew consisting of America's Cup defenders including tactician Gary Jobson.

But, Burt's crew of 12 locals including "Buddy" Friedrichs, the Olympic gold medal winner, John Dane, III, Sears and Soling National champion, Tommy Dreyfus, Al Gooch, Cyril Laan, Peter Waters, Billy Smith, Charlie Adams, Jack Rettig, Dan Lehon, and Mark LeBlanc drove the new German Frers design to the Class "A" title and the mythical crown "King of the Circuit." Ted Turner was quoted as saying his crew "used to be the best in the world." *The New York Times* correspondent, William N. Wallace, reported, "The big sail area combined with extreme light weight—only 31,000 pounds and 17,000 of that in the ballast—has made *Acadia* an extremely fast boat and one that Ted Turner admits he cannot catch."

The *Acadia* also won the Bermuda race—I. O. R. Overall and the

Onion Patch Team—U. S. A. The Onion Patch Team race in an international team race series is held before and in conjunction with the Newport to Bermuda race. England, South America, Bermuda and the U. S. were this year's international competition. Each participating nation was represented by a three-boat team. It is a long-distance race from Oyster Bay to Newport, two Olympic-course races in Newport on the America's Cup course and the Bermuda race. *Acadia* was high-point boat for the series and led the U. S. team to first place.

After the Bermuda race, *Acadia* was shipped by the Aga Khan to the Mediterranean for a special regatta to suit his pleasure. She was one of three boats on the U. S. team which finished second.

THE FORTIETH ANNIVERSARY OF THE STAR CLASS

The fortieth anniversary of the Star Class Spring Series and Jahncke Series, which events were inaugurated in 1939 by the New Orleans-Gulf Star Fleet at the Southern Yacht Club, was celebrated in the spring of 1979 with eighty entries in this historic Star Class classic. The list of participants was star-studded, with such SYC stalwarts as Gold Medal Olympic winner G. Shelby "Buddy" Friedrichs, Jr. and his crew of Barton Jahncke, plus John Dane III, Joseph L. "Buzzy" Killeen, Jr., and Tommy Meric. From out-of-town the list continued to read like a "Who's Who," with 1979 Worlds' winners Dennis Connor and Tom Blackhaller (overtones of the 1983 America's Cup team), Ding Schoonmaker, Bill Buchan, Peter Wright, and Buddy Megles, to name a few.

It was a repeat performance for the winner of this event, Edward "Bud" Jahncke, who amassed enough points by winning the Star Class Spring Series and the Commodore Ernest Lee Jahncke Series to take home the *Windjammer* trophy, as Bud had won the first event held in 1939.

It was in June 1939 that the New Orleans-Gulf Star Fleet petitioned the International Star Class Yacht Racing Association (ISCYRA) to take the Spring championship series away from Bermuda, which held it in alternate years with Nassau, and give it to New Orleans. After much promotional travelling on the part of Mrs. Ernest Robin (nee Elizabeth Miller), which story is related in an earlier section of this book, plus much letter writing and long-distance phone calls by Edward B. "Bud" Jahncke, permission was granted. However, careful consideration had been given this request before

SYC held the races, and it was granted only after the president of ISCYRA, George W. Elder, demanded and received a record of the wind, weather, and sailing conditions in March and April for the past twenty-five years. When President Elder received the report, he exclaimed that "Lake Pontchartrain must be the paradise of yacht racing" and awarded the series to New Orleans.

Suffice it to say that in the inaugural 1939 Spring championship series, the weather was anything but what the record of the prior twenty-five years would indicate. In one race there were hailstones as big as chicken eggs. In another, there were cyclone winds which drove the boat of the Star Class champion, Adrien Iselin, into the bridge, breaking her masts. The last race was sailed by skippers who had stayed out too late the night before in the French Quarter and imbibed too heavily to enjoy the calm and heat of the Sunday morning hot sun. The SYC skipper, Edward B. "Bud" Jahncke, sailing Gus Lorber's Star *Scout* on his home waters, was the only one to catch a fresh Southerly breeze. He scudded past the entire fleet to win the only race and the Spring Series as well.

The year 1979 was the first time that the South had the honor of holding the finals of the Adams cup. Many letters of commendation were received for a "job well done" and for a great time had by all from the USYRU committees headed by Helen Ingerson, chairman of the Adams Cup committee, Mrs. Faye Bennet of Beach Haven, New Jersey, and Mrs. Glen Lattimore of Fort Worth, Texas, a past Adams cup winner. The officials were Commodore John A. S. Brown, chief judge, Robert A. "Bob" Schimek, Jr. of SYC, Commodore Marshal J. Brown of Fort Walton Yacht Club, and past Commodore J. A. Auguste Lorber, Jr. Mrs. James C. Arceneaux, III ("Sparky") of SYC, a past finalist in the Adams Cup event, was general chairman.

THE TRAGIC FASTNET RACE—1979

Southern sailing in the sixties had faded into history on the tragic mid-August scene of hurricane *Camille*. So also did the sailing world reel from the shocking impact of its Fastnet disaster ten years later on August 13 and 14, 1979. It was a shattering finale to a decade of dynamic sailboat action. The totally unpredicted force 10-to-11 storm swept the fleet racing in the Royal Ocean Racing Club's biennial classic in the 180-mile Irish Sea stretch between Land's End and Fastnet Rock. Fifteen crewmen died in more than 300 yachts, 24 of which were abandoned.

In the forty to forty-four-foot waves, nearly half the fleet reported knockdowns, many horizontal, with a third of the fleet enduring inversions and 360-degree rolls. Twenty-two percent reported that one or more crew members were washed overboard at least once. Dedicated helicopter pilots and skippers of seventy rescue vessels brought about a rescue bigger than World War II's Dunkirk.

The USYRU swung into an immediate, extensive, productive examination of safety equipment, weather forecasts, boat stability, and vitally important design technicalities. The officials based a complete report on its computer analysis of 235 inquiries out of 303 participating boats.

Out of the roaring blackness among the 2500 people smashed for 20 hours by 40-foot waves, was O. J. Young of the New Orleans Yacht Club. His is a simple story. Young was one of the lucky ones. Ted Turner, also survived to win the race.

COMMODORE RICHARD G. SPANGENBERG—
1980-81

After serving two very fruitful and rewarding years as commodore, Danny Killeen was succeeded by Richard B. "Dick" Spangenberg at the SYC annual meeting on December 6, 1980. Dick's election culminated ten years of dedicated service on the board of governors and as a flag officer. He was first elected to the board in 1970 and served as regatta chairman, house and finance committee chairman, three years as secretary-treasurer, then rear commodore, vice-commodore and now commodore. Dick was well known not only at SYC but also along the Gulf and Mexican coastlines. He served as chairman of the Mexico Race for eleven years and was the founder and first fleet captain of the SYC Cruiser/Racer Class.

Serving with Commodore Spangenberg were: John Y. Taylor, vice-commodore; Cal F. Hadden, Jr., rear commodore; J. Fred Clerc, secretary-treasurer; Earl J. Sonnier, M. D., fleet surgeon; J. F. A. Lorber, Jr.; fleet measurer; and Stewart R. Barnett, Jr., fleet captain.

SYC's Burt Keenan, unsuccessful in three previous attempts, won the 1980 Southern Ocean Racing Circuit (SORC) in his new *Acadia*. Years ago Burt had campaigned in his 56 foot *Southerly*, which was a fine cruising boat racing against the machine. He then had German Frers design the 51-foot *Acadia*, which made her debut in the SORC in 1979; he ended up second in the fleet to *Williwaw*, sailed by Dennis Connor.

After sailing in the Fastnet race in 1979 and thereby winning the World Ocean Racing championship, Burt sold the 51-footer to a Swede, who renamed her *Bla Carat*. The new *Acadia* was a Doug Peterson 43, built locally at his New Orleans Marina. She won in the 1980 Sugar Bowl Regatta in her class and then headed for Florida. *Acadia* maintained her lead throughout the series of races to emerge first in class and fleet. Her crew consisted of Tommy Dreyfus, John Kolius, Butch Ulmer, Fred Baggerman, Neil Harvey, Mark LeBlanc, Billy Smith, Peter Keenan, Bruce Kirby, Ed Matthews, George Sustendal, and John Dane, III.

In the oldest long-distance race in existence, West End to the Mississippi Gulf Coast, a second all-female crew sailed in the summer of 1980. The first was in 1928 when Doris Zemurray and her all-girl crew sailed to a close second-place finish. SYC skipperette Anne Salzar captained an Easterly 30 assisted by crewettes and clubmates Anne Hughes, Mary Salzar, and Gerri Nicholson and Gulfport Yacht Club's Ellen Andre. They finished in the middle of the fleet after battling strong winds and rough seas.

In the Rhodes 19 National championship series sailed in 1980 on Lake Pontchartrain, SYC's "Chip" Grevemberg with Johnny Potts and Wayne Gsell won a second place to the champion Bob Jenien of Chicago.

The decade of the '80s began with juniors and former juniors of the SYC winning many championships. It started when Joe Blouin, a former junior, won the North American championship in the Sunfish Class beating 134 contestants at the Gulfport Yacht Club. Danny Killeen, Jr., a junior, won the North American Flying Scot sailing championship sailed at the Pensacola Yacht Club against a fleet of sixty-six boats.

Through the assistance of junior SYC's John Lovell, a fleet of twenty International Optimist Dinghies was introduced to the Southern Yacht Club in 1980. This was the largest International Yacht Racing Union (IYRU) one-design class in the world at that time. Ted Turner and Mary Helen Edgecomb had picked up ten of the boats for the Fort Worth Boat Club out of thirty Optimists which had arrived from Denmark.

In the U. S. Olympic sailing trials of 1980 held at new Fort Adams Sailing Center in Newport, Rhode Island, over 200 of the nation's top sailors competed. Representing Southern Yacht Club were Shawn Killeen, and Conrad Kuebel, Jr., crew. They took a third place in the Star Class and first in the Free World Olympics at Kiel, Germany. Another Southerner, Marshall Duane of Delray Beach, Florida, won the Flying Dutchman Class and the right to go to the Olympics.

BAY-WAVELAND YACHT CLUB WINS ADAMS CUP

The Women's National Sailing championship of North America for the Mrs. Charles Francis Adams trophy was sailed for the first time in the South and the Southern Yacht Club hosted the event in 1980. Again, the Bay-Waveland Yacht Club's team was the winner. Judy Reeves McKinney was the skipper with Amy Chapman, winner of the Adams Cup in 1977, as crew and Charlotte Gordon. They sailed a beautiful series.

Many letters of commendation were received for a very successful event from the USYRU committees headed by Helen Ingerson, chairman of the Adams Cup committee of USYRU, Mrs. Faye Bennet of Beach Haven, New Jersey, and Mrs. Glen Lattimore of Fort Worth, Texas, a past Adams Cup winner.

The other officials were chief judge, Commodore John A. S. Brown and serving with him were Robert A "Bob" Schimek, Jr. of SYC, Commodore Marshall Brown of the Fort Walton Yacht Club in Florida, past commodore of SYC J. F. A. Lorber, Jr., and Mrs. James C. "Sparky" Arceneaux, III of SYC, who was general chairman. "Sparky" was a finalist in the Adams Cup on three occasions.

MOBILE YACHT CLUB CELEBRATES 50 YEARS OF STARS

In 1980 the Star Class fleet of Mobile Yacht Club celebrated its fiftieth anniversary. Chairman of the event was Commodore George Criminale, a veteran skipper for forty-eight of those fifty years. George had sailed in the first Star Class championship series held in 1939 on Lake Pontchartrain, and he has entered every event since that time. Far away from home, SYC Cal Hadden represented the New Orleans-Gulf Star fleet on the race committee of the 1980 International Star Class World's championship series.

At the 1980 Gulf Yachting Association's annual meeting, GYA Commodore Mike Johnson presented to Frank Pericola, Editor emeritus of the Panama City *News Herald*, a resolution adopted by the GYA expressing appreciation for his dedication to yachting over the years. His coverage of sailing events carried back to 1920 the year of the first Lipton Regatta. Mr. Pericola was the second member of the press to be so honored by the Gulf Yachting Association. In 1971 Harry

Martinez, sports editor of *The States-Item*, was made an honorary commodore of the GYA.

SYC KYLE SMITH IS CREW IN 1980 AMERICA'S CUP RACES

Kyle Smith was a crew for Dennis Connors in his victory on the 12-meter *Freedom* in the 1980 America's Cup races at Newport. Kyle was chosen over more than 100 top sailors in the country to be part of the 11-man crew in the summer Trials. Connors had won against the tough competition of Ted Turner, who sailed *Courageous* in the Trials.

At the banquet of champions in 1980, Joe Blouin and Daniel B. Killeen, Jr. were awarded the Commodore Charles J. Tessier memorial trophy in a tie for the most outstanding skipper of the year. Kyle Smith was presented with the Mariner's crew trophy awarded each year to the most outstanding crewman.

The year 1980 saw the passing into that great harbor in the sky four prominent SYC members, SYC Commodore Charles L. Gambel, GYA Commodore J. Gilbert Scheib, Dr. John B. Gooch, and Edward B. Benjamin.

Commodore Gambel was very active in the yacht club's history. He was one of the first owners of a Luder and competed in that class for many years. Charlie served on the SYC board in numerous capacities and was the USYRU Area D junior Chairman. He was chief judge in the Sears Cup Finals sailed at SYC in 1957. He was beloved by all who knew him. A jovial personality and fine sportsmanship were his finest qualities.

Shortly after the passing of Commodore Gambel, J. Gilbert Scheib died just one week before the Gulf Yachting Association's annual meeting, which was held at the Southern Yacht Club. Jack was to return as GYA secretary-treasurer in May, 1980. He was known as "Mr. G.Y.A.," having served this organization as its commodore, vice-commodore and secretary-treasurer.

Scheib was elected to the NAYRU (USYRU) executive committee in 1952. He served in this capacity for eleven years, and was instrumental in bringing the three national championships for the Mallory, Adams and Sears cups to the South. Jack was chief judge for many national events. His proudest moments were when he captained the SYC Lipton Cup teams for six straight victories—a record never equalled in the GYA. He was also a Fish Class skipper and sailed other class boats as well.

Jack Scheib was a member of the SYC board of governors for several years and served as race committee chairman for six consecutive years, during those trying years of the second World War. He was elected an honorary life member of the SYC in 1964 and was also a life member of the New Orleans, Buccaneer and Jackson Yacht Clubs.

Edward B. Benjamin was highly respected in all yachting circles and was a sponsor and financial backer of many movements in the SYC. He was the first president of the SYC Olympic Sailing Association. His yachts *Indra I, II, III, IV* and *V* were used in Olympic Trials and America's Cup events. The Southern Yacht Club lost a loyal, valuable, and dedicated member.

Commodore Richard G. Spangenberg was reelected to serve a second term in office in 1981. Vice-Commodore John Y. Taylor, owing to illness, was forced to resign. Cal H. Hadden Jr. was then made vice-commodore and William C. Gambel was elected rear commodore. J. Fred Sonnier as fleet surgeon, J. F. A. Lorber, Jr. and Stewart R. Barnett, Jr. remained as fleet measurer and fleet captain respectively.

REGATA AL SOL—1981 FIRE ON BOARD *TIARE*

"FIRE IN THE GALLEY: WE'RE IN TROUBLE." Early on the morning of May 12, 1981, the *Tiare* and her New Orleans crew had left for Cozumel on May 9 in the biennial *regata al sol*. If the weather held, the crew would be sipping margueritas in a day and a half, celebrating *Tiare's* third overall win in the race.

Thirty-six hours later, *Tiare* was out of the race. The boat's cabin was charred. Two crewmen were in the hospital. And the other ten crew members were in a numbed state of disbelief. FIRE. No other word in the dictionary commands more respect from sailors. At sea there is no escape, no fire department to call.

The prudent skipper reads all he can about fire prevention. He outfits his boat with an approved fire extinguisher. He conducts fire drills with his passengers. Still, tragedies and near tragedies occur. Not even seasoned sailors are immune from the painful lessons that a fire on board can teach, like the one that took place on May 12, leaving an ugly imprint on two experienced New Orleans sailors.

Maurice "Bubby" Hartson III and Danny Killeen, Jr. were in the galley that day, preparing a 7 a.m. breakfast for the rest of the crew. Hartson remembers all too vividly what happened next. "We were changing a cylinder in the propane stove to heat coffee," he said. "We also had an alcohol stove on. We could hear the cylinder hissing. I told Danny, 'We're in trouble.' Suddenly there was just one big ball of fire. The cylinder erupted, filling the cabin with propane gas. The flame from the alcohol stove ignited it." Hartson and Killeen scrambled to get out of the cabin, now a floating gas chamber. Killeen went out the forward hatch, Hartson out the back. "I was in such a panic to get out I ran over the navigator and sprained his ankle," said Hartson. "I don't even remember doing it. The people on deck said they saw big balls of fire coming out of the hatches and felt the heat. I started to go into shock. I felt faint, nauseated." The fire—or more correctly, the flash—was extinguished by the crew.

Luck was riding with Hartson and Killeen. *Tiare's* owner, Jack Valley, had included a physician, Dr. Gus Lott, among the boat's crew. Lot administered a painkiller to the sailors, scrubbed them, pulled the burned skin off, and bandaged the burns. A decision had to be made. Lott was running out of bandages and Killeen and Hartson needed hospitalization. Cozumel had the closest facilities, but Mexico is not renowned for its medical care.

Trailing the seventeen-boat fleet was *Acushnet*, a Coast Guard cutter. *Tiare* made radio contact and decided to abandon the race and to rendezvous with the cutter. On board the cutter, Hartson and Killeen were rebandaged and treated by a medic. A helicopter ferried them to Key West where they were hospitalized a day and a half after the fire. Two days later they returned to New Orleans.

After meeting the cutter, *Tiare* motored to Cozumel, the nearest port. But the crew was no longer in a partying mood. Hartson had second-degree burns over ten percent of his body. Killeen suffered second-degree burns over twenty-seven percent of his body. Hartson admitted that they were handling the propane cannister improperly, that it shouldn't have been done around another stove. There were no instructions on the cannister and if the whole thing had leaked out it would have blown the boat apart. "Frankly," said Hartson, "I wouldn't have one on my boat." Propane stoves are prohibited by the Coast Guard on boats carrying passengers for hire. "They are terribly hazardous. Just about anything sets them off," said a Coast Guard spokesman.

Although Hartson had made ten Cozumel races, this one was the first for Killeen. He said, "I really wanted to go to Cozumel and I almost made it." A lot of credit and thanks must be given to Commodore Brown, who acted immediately and calmly in extinguishing the fire within seconds, thus reducing any further injury to the men or boat.

Commodore Brown commended the officers and men of the Coast Guard cutter *Acushnet* for the dispatch with which they handled the search and rescue mission of *Tiare's* burn victims. Also gratifying was the support group and flight crew of the U. S. Navy helicopter.

In the 1981 *regata al sol Evangeline* finished first overall; in second place was SYC's *Esprit* and in third place was *Lord Jim*.

PRESS RACE ON SQUALLY LAKE PONTCHARTRAIN

On a sunny Saturday afternoon in June 1981, the Southern Yacht Club had as its guests sportswriters and sportscasters of local newspaper, radio and TV stations. They were invited for a sail on Lake Pontchartrain. Great effort was put forth by Chairman Sandy Davies, and his co-chairman Dr. Joseph Kuebel, who selected a fleet of Easterlys, manned with the club's champion skippers and crews, plus a delicious lunch.

Bob Roesler, executive sports editor of the *Times-Picayune*, undoubtedly expressed the reaction of a landlubber for the first time at the tiller of a boat better than anything I have read.

> The sun was smiling through a gentle westerly breeze as the sleek *Linda II* cleared the yacht harbor and made her way onto Lake Pontchartrain. One of her sails started to fill, skipper Al Gooch cut the engine, then the winds became our fuel as we gently took on a port tilt.
>
> "Head toward the committee boat and get the feel of the boat," Gooch said. His crew, Mike and Buzzy Brennan, Gaylord Wilson and Harry Colomb, busied themselves with sails, ropes and other gadgets. Gooch, a sailmaker and veteran of countless races, calmly explained the nautical rules of the road. Who had the right of way, who didn't.
>
> Suddenly, another Easterly appeared to starboard moving at a fast clip. 'Relax' Gooch said. 'He'll clear us with plenty to spare.' I fought the urge to pull the tiller hard toward me. If ever I thought there was a need for a sharp left turn (to port, as any good sailor knows) it was now. But Gooch calmed my fears, and I held to my dead-ahead course. The skipper was correct. The other Easterly zipped across the bow with lots to spare—like 100 feet.
>
> 'We're in good position for the start,' Mike Brennan said through a pleasant grin. A cannon boomed in the distance, sending its message across the water. It was nothing like an Indy 500 start. No neat rows of sails. I scanned the lake looking for the competition. I don't know why, because I don't know an Easterly from a Luder.
>
> 'Don't look around like that,' Gooch suggested diplomatically. 'Just keep your eyes on the squirrels and keep looking ahead!' Squirrels? What are they doing aboard a sailboat? Then I remembered, Squirrels are those strips attached to the sails that tell the helmsman if he is using the wind properly. Officially, I believe they're called telltales. Anyhow,

we settled down on our chase up the race's first leg. Our boat was third, then fourth, going into the first turn. It was a piece of cake.

This was fun, and I was secretly thanking the SYC for putting on this race for the press. On the second leg, my handling of the tiller cost us some ground, uh, water. But things were going along well enough to slake one's thirst. Suddenly, I became competitive. How far ahead were the leaders? Was there a chance that we could win? 'Sure, we're still in the hunt,' Gooch assured me. 'We've got good position.'

Our spirits soared when an Easterly ahead of us hit the marker turning for home. That meant she had to go around the marker again. Suddenly, bad weather moved in from the west. The skies turned an angry black, and sheets of rain swept into the fleet. *Linda II's* crew went into action. Down came the spinnaker. Ropes were tightened or loosened as we heeled hard to port. The crew scrambled to the starboard side and leaned far overboard in an attempt to balance the craft.

Mike Brennan must have read the panic on my face. "We'll be okay" he yelled. "This isn't real bad weather. Just keep her pointed at that boat ahead." Aren't we going to tip over? "No," Brennan yelled. "Not if you do exactly what Al tells you. Stay calm." I wanted to believe Mike. After all he designed and built the boat. He should know what *Linda II* can stand. "We're doing just fine," Gooch said, sounding like a father trying to calm the fears of his young son. Still, I didn't know. The winds were whistling at a 30 mph clip, and the rain was blinding. As quickly as the squall had hit us, it was gone, bound for the Rigolets. The committee boat, the finish line was dead ahead. "Aim for the committee boat's stern," Gooch commanded. I did the best I could. The sun again was smiling as *Linda II* streaked past the finish line in third place.

"How 'bout a beer?" Harvey Colomb asked. The best I could do was nod in the affirmative. Sipping the suds, I remembered that long ago a wise journalist wrote that sailing was about as exciting as watching grass grow. Believe me, that is a lot of baloney! Sailing into and surviving a squall like that is one helluva experience, as exciting a one as I'll want to go through. Watching grass growing it ain't.

Sailors like Gooch, Colomb, Wilson and the Brennans are athletes. Good ones, too. And thank goodness, without their expert sailing, I would have had to swim back to the SYC from an overturned *Linda II*.

The winners in the 1981 Press race were Al Massar of Radio Station WTIX, having as his crew Frank Davies and Shawn Killeen. In second place was Ron Swoboda of Channel 8 TV, with Mary and Steve Salzar and Roy Troendle as crew. Bob Roesler of *The Times-Picayune/The States-Item* was third, with Al Gooch, Mike and Buzzy Brennan, Gaylord Wilson and Harry Colomb. In fourth place was Buddy Diliberto of Channel 6 TV with Frank Peragino and Bubby Hartson as crew. The master of ceremonies at the luncheon was Joseph "Buzzy" Killeen, who showed many interesting films of yesteryear when yachting made the headlines every weekend.

In July 1981, Skipper J. Dwight LeBlanc, III, his brother Beau

LeBlanc and Robbie Young of the SYC participated in the invitational Governors' Cup regatta in Newport Beach, California. They finished fourth at the Balboa Yacht Club event.

September 10, 1981 was another sad day in the history of SYC, as Edward B. "Bud" Jahncke, who had become an institution, passed away. His jovial personality was superseded only by his super hospitality. He was an avid Star Class skipper and promoter, always claiming his greatest achievement was winning the first Star Class Spring Series in the U. S. raced on Lake Pontchartrain in 1939. Bud was vice-commodore for the years 1940-41. Regattas have never been the same without Bud and his *Bumboat* and *Zide*, his last boat. He was always available for visitors and spectators at all races.

At the annual 1981 meeting, outgoing Commodore Richard G. Spangenberg was congratulated on his capable leadership, and for his outstanding accomplishments throughout his two years in office, especially as chairman of the *regata al sol's* many races.

CHAPTER XXII

1982–1986

COMMODORES	TERMS
Callender F. Hadden, Jr.	1982–1983
William H. Gambel	1984–1985
Maurice J. Hartson, III	1986

COMMODORE CAL F. HADDEN, JR.—1982-83

In the change of command, Cal F. Hadden, Jr. was elected commodore for the year 1982. His father, Cal F. Hadden, Sr., was a very prominent member of the SYC in the days when the club was prosperous and boasted 3,000 members and a full treasury. Mr. Hadden was also present when the tide changed and the membership dwindled to 250 with the till empty. He was one of the few loyal members whose leadership and personal finances helped to pull the club through those days of the Depression so that the members today continue to enjoy the privileges of not only a beautiful clubhouse but one that is sound. Mr. Hadden was rear commodore in 1934.

Those elected to serve with Commodore Hadden were: William H. Gambel, vice-commodore; Maurice J. Hartson III, rear commodore; J. Fred Clerc, secretary-treasurer; Fabian G. Fromherz, fleet captain; Dr. Elmo J. Cerise, fleet surgeon; and J. F. A. Lorber, fleet measurer.

Commodore Hadden was another one of the Southern Yacht Club's juniors and with his brothers Richard and William sailed on Lake Pontchartrain and the Gulf Coast in Fish Class sloops and Star boats.

Cal sailed in every conceivable corner of the country, in Batista's Havana and Venezuela and Nassau. Later he switched to big boats and won many championships in races to Nassau and Mackinac, and his adventures in the Mexico races have been related in previous chapters. When he wasn't sailing on the lake over weekends, the commodore was performing in his plane flying over the Star Class fleet. At that time, he was interested in aerobatic flying.

In the 1982 opening regatta, even the ominous raingod Jupiter Pluvius cooperated. A record-breaking number of boats colorfully decorated was led in a parade along the seawall of Lake Pontchartrain by the parade marshall "Rip" Haase sailing his 50-foot *Riptide* and passing in review of the officials and dignitaries aboard the *Heavy Moon*, the beautiful yacht of A. R. Blossman, who is always generous in using his boat for special occasions. On board to bless the fleet was the ordained deacon of St. Paul's Episcopal Church, Ross Allen, and his lovely wife, Mary Ellen, who were both active Lightning sailors. Ross was appointed the official chaplain of the Southern Yacht Club in 1982.

THE TRICENTENNIAL OCEAN RACE FROM FRANCE

The big feature of the 1982 season was the historic La Rochelle, France to New Orleans Transatlantic Yacht Race, which served as a primary event in a series of functions commemmorating the tricentennial of the French discovery of the Territory of Louisiana. The race was a highlight of events commemorating the 300th anniversary of French explorer La Salle's claiming of the Louisiana Territory for King Louis XIV of France in 1682.

Plans for this historical race got under way in 1979 when the French consul general in New Orleans, Gilbert Bochet, Dr. Pierre Chambonnet, president of the La Rochelle Yacht Club, and Richard Spangenberg, commodore of the Southern Yacht Club met at Commander's Palace restaurant in New Orleans to announce the international race.

The contest was sponsored by the L'Epreuve Transatlantic La Rochelle/New Orleans, la Société des Regates Rochelaise, the Southern Yacht Club, the Gulfport Yacht Club, Translouisiane and L'Union Nationale pour la Course au Large. J. Edward Barr was general chairman.

In La Rochelle to represent Louisiana and the Southern Yacht Club was a delegation headed by Governor Dave Treen and SYC members Commodore Cal and Nancy Hadden, Jr., Fabian and Carol Fromherz, Hugh Williams, Arthur and Mary Davies, Henry and Kitty Barnett, and Bill and Mary Jane Thompson. They were all there in La Rochelle when the starting gun boomed just offshore from the ancient seaport where Robert Cavelier de La Salle set sail prior to discovering the Mississippi Delta in 1682 and naming Louisiana for King Louis XIV of France. The ceremonies were held on May 15, 1982.

The yacht harbor of La Rochelle, France is one of the most famous ports in France, which has been a center of sail commerce since before the time of La Salle.

Covering the race for the *Times-Picayune*, Darrell Higgins, Jr., reported in an article of March 27, 1982

> Besides an obviously insatiable appetite for adventure and the thrill of maneuvering a 35 to 85-foot ocean going yacht through open water, the lure for the more than 60 crews of blue-water yachtsmen, including two all-women French teams, is the $50,000 prize offered to the first elapsed time finisher.
>
> "In 50 days a dream will become a reality," commented race organizer Michel Etevenon. This dream, which came into being a few days before Christmas in 1979, will be part of world news. For the first time an open yacht race allowing every type of yacht one can imagine will encourage men to go faster by sail and only sail.
>
> The best men in the sport will start from France, aiming to cross the Atlantic in a minimum of time, while rounding Puerto Rico and Jamaica before arriving on the shores of the Mississippi Gulf Coast. I am sure you will like these crazy sailors in their funny machines.
>
> In races of this kind with 5200 nautical miles to cover on one, two or three hulls at nearly incredible speeds, the leaders will make an average of 260 miles per day. Usually the forerunners are not multihulls. Multihulls, boats having more than one hull, are traditionally faster in the straight run while reaching or running before the wind. However, if the wind direction slaps the boats on the nose, forcing them to beat or tack upwind, the monohulls could have a marked advantage. Also the weighted keel monohulls are virtually impossible to right in the open sea. This route was taken so that competitors would avoid the Azores (doldrums) and the Bermuda Triangle.
>
> "From New Orleans to La Rochelle all the great designs have entered," continued Etevenon. "Among these are two famous catamarans. *Elf Aquitaine*, 62-feet long with a beam of 36-feet, manned by a past world vintage champion, and silver Olympic medalist, Marc Pajot and his competent crew. This is the same French crew that smashed the North Atlantic crossing record under sail last July, breaking the 76-year-old record of Charlie Barr of the New York Yacht Club earned about his schooner *Atlantic* with a crew of 14 hands. A minimum crew of three people is required for the La Rochelle race.
>
> "The other catamaran is British," explained the race's founder. The 70-foot long, 33-foot wide *Sea Falcon* which in 1981 covered 318 nautical miles in 24 hours on its crossing of the Atlantic Ocean.

The warm-up race, representing the cream of Europe's, England's and America's long-distance ocean racers, also attracted two all-women crews in 60-foot yachts and a team of journalists skippered by Eric Loiseau. The smallest boat in the fleet measured 36 feet while the biggest was an 80-footer. The majority were 60 feet and upwards.

A total of thirty-three boats started the race in La Rochelle but four dropped out for various reasons. The remaining twenty-three catamarans and six monohulls sailed the 5,800-mile course on a southward on northeast trade winds to Puerto Rico up the Caribbean Sea and Gulf of Mexico to the Mississippi Coast with virtually no problems except a scare from tropical storm *Alberto*, which simply helped the lead boats to go faster.

Of the thirty-three entered craft, twenty-nine had French skippers, two had Swiss, one Italian and one Canadian. Among those vying for first place were two all-women French teams, *Charles Heidsieck III* skippered by Claire Marty and the *Kriter IX*, commanded by Sylvie Vaneck.

Stiff Mississippi River currents and one hull with a draft close to eleven feet encouraged regatta officials to terminate the heat at a buoy off Ship Island in the Mississippi Sound, where Iberville anchored his fleet almost three centuries ago.

The race was monitored by the Argos satellite system, which electronically reported the sailors' positions and immediately signal a capsized craft. Transponders, "black boxes," placed aboard every hull continuously transmitted the position of each yacht via satellite to race officials in New Orleans and in La Rochelle, who would update the course charts daily. An electronic tracking board was located in the lobby of the International Trade Mart building at the foot of Canal Street in New Orleans.

Early Tuesday morning, co-skipper Jean-Francois Fountaine radioed race officials in Gulfport that the *Charante-Maritime* was expected to reach Ship Island about noon. Members of the press scrambled aboard two powerboats to intercept *Charante-Maritime* as soon as she entered the ship channel.

Already on the scene when the winner, *Charente Maritime*, passed the sea buoy were a Coast Guard cutter, a big powerboat carrying Gulfport Yacht Club's Commodore Walter Vic and former SYC Commodore Richard G. Spangenberg, and the Gulfport club's committee boat, *Weather Leg*.

Larry Molony's trawler *Last Resort*, with son Tim at the helm, accommodated the American reporters, photographers, and TV cameramen, while Tommy Coleman's *Gem V* did the same for more than a dozen French journalists. It was the consensus that the sexiest feature of the event was the arrival of the two female boats *Kriter IV* and *Charles Heidsieck III*. The wide-eyed crewmen on board the *Last Resort* and *Gem V* awaited the topless French gals as they went below to dress for the welcoming ceremonies.

The twelve women aboard the 58-foot monohull *Kriter IV*, which finished sixteenth in the race, became the first all-female crew to finish a transatlantic sailboat race, said their captain, Sylvie Vanek, a veteran long-distance racer and mother of two. The women ranged in age from twenty-one to thirty-three. They became close friends while battling the elements during the thirty-three day crossing. Vanek had sailed around the world twice with men. The Parisian housewife said it was more difficult with girls putting up sails as they were not as strong as men.

About 2 p.m. a zephyr came out of the southwest to push the big cat *Charente Maritime* over the line in first place at an approximate speed of seven knots in the Gulfport harbor at 3:03 p.m. on Tuesday, June 8, 1982, to finish first in the 5,800-mile race from La Rochelle, France. The gun boomed from the end of the pier on the east side of Gulfport's ship harbor, prompting *Charante Maritime's* crew to douse the spinnaker and run a big Confederate flag up to the top of her 78-foot mast. She was then towed to the Gulfport Yacht Club's harbor by *Weather Leg* to the accompaniment of deafening horns and sirens.

Charente-Maritime, sailed by a crew of four professionals, was a sleek 65-foot catamaran named for the province where she was built. She was not only the fastest boat in the race but the handsomest. Built from molded fiberglass, she appeared to be moving even when tied to the dock and was considerably better-looking than the aluminum *Elf Aquataine* whom she bested by more than 600 miles. She won the tricentennial trophy and $100,000 cash. The *Charente Maritime* was built in La Rochelle especially for this race and was skippered by a citizen of that town, Jean-Francois Fountaine.

All the boats were stripped out expressly for racing. Aboard *Charente Maritime*, the crew's accommodations were crammed inside a tiny pod slung from the spreaders between the twin hulls. A navigator's table was approximately twice the size of the V-berth where the two off-duty crew slept. In addition to Loran and other customary electronics, there was an alcohol-fueled hotplate to make coffee and tea. All other meals were eaten cold and were mostly "space food" packed in disposable containers like toothpaste. Asked to show where the head is located, Jean-Francois Fountaine pointed overboard.

Charente-Maritime was steered by a wheel, but most of the other catamarans used tillers which were remarkably well-balanced. The rigging on all boats resembled something out of *Star Wars*. One particularly unusual boat, a "proa," has only one hull, one outrigger, and two masts of identical size. The masts are stayed only on the side of the hull. To come about, the booms are jibed completely about in a half circle so the bow becomes the stern and vice versa. There are rudders at either end of the hull so one can be retracted while the other is lowered. The resultant effort by the crew looks like a Chinese fire drill.

Because of their draft, the boats were compelled to anchor in the Gulfport ship harbor rather than moor at the yacht club. The race officially ended at the Ship Island sea buoy off Gulfport where a large flotilla of local and Gulf Coast-based yachts welcomed the fleet. The Gulfport Yacht Club's Commodore Walter Vic, assisted by Donald Sutter, Bache Whitlock, and Stanford Morse handled the actual finishing of the yachts near the yacht club. They also handled the technical aspect of the race.

Standing nearby were Southern Yacht Club's representatives Commodores Cal Hadden and Richard Spangenberg, who joined the Gulfport Yacht Club's crew to be the first to welcome the victorious champions whom they toasted with champagne, the Frenchmen's first cold drink in twenty-four days.

Elf Aquataine pulled into Gulfport shortly before midnight on Friday, almost two and a half days behind *Charante-Maritime*. However, she set a new speed record of 387 nautical miles in 24 hours and was the early favorite to take top honors. *Lestra Sport* trailed just twenty-three miles astern and took third place.

This race marked the first transatlantic regatta staged between the United States and France, a no-handicap race lasting three to five weeks before the first and last boats crossed the finish line at Gulfport.

Some of the multihull sailboats in the race and their famous skippers were the 60-foot trimaran *Gautier III* and Jean-Yves Terlain; the French trimaran *Kriter VIII* and Martin Matininovsky, also Olivier de Kersauson.

The crews, members of their families, supporters, and race officials were feted at a round of parties in New Orleans where the winners were honored at a reception in Jackson Square on June 19.

Louisiana's governor Dave Treen and New Orleans mayor Dutch Morial had gathered to accept replicas of the eleven and a half foot cross of the eight-foot wooden post used by La Salle to claim Louisiana for France. They are on display at the old U. S. Mint, which building was completely restored in 1983.

Charente-Maritime sailed to New York where a new crew would attempt to break the modern-day speed record set by *Elf Aquataine*. Most of the smaller boats were sent home by ship, while the bigger ones returned under sail. *Elf Aquataine* came briefly to the SYC's junior dock, but left after two days when her skipper could not locate a shipyard capable of unstepping her towering mast. At seventy-eight feet in length and thirty-five feet abeam, she also was difficult to maneuver in the narrow confines of most marina.

After the big show was over, SYC Commodore Hadden had these comments to make concerning any yacht clubs participating in future such events:

> Now that it's over, we will all be a little wiser for the experience. The SYC decided not to be an official sponsor of the race but agreed to help with the finish line and to give one reception for the participants and dignitaries involved.
>
> We did not want to jeopardize our USYRU amateur status, and we did not want to get involved, except superficially, in local, national or international politics. I feel that we struck a pretty fair balance. There were many pluses in this race, one being that we all got the chance to see and inspect some of the most ultramodern ocean-going sailing machines that man has ever invented.
>
> The big 25- and 30-knot catamarans and trimarans were straight out of *Star Wars*, not to mention the big, magnificient monohulls that made the trip. There were also some negatives involved. Apparently, whenever you participate in a form of any sport that has professional overtones, then everything is different. The promoters are in it to make a profit. The sponsors and participants are in it for the publicity and advertising advantages, and everybody expects to be given things that legitimate amateur yachtsmen are accustomed to paying for.
>
> The Frenchmen on the boats had been led to believe by the promoters that they would probably finish in New Orleans on the Mississippi River at the foot of Canal Street, that the entire town would turn into one big Mardi Gras to welcome them, and there would be wine, women, and song lavished on them gratis. They were a little disappointed when these things didn't materialize. The plan to bring the first six winning boats to New Orleans for display in the Mississippi River at the Spanish Plaza was abandoned when the race promoters were unable to obtain proper insurance coverage.
>
> Another negative is that apparently when a private amateur club becomes involved in real life politics of any kind, the people concerned are speaking two entirely different languages (no pun intended because of the French-English translations.) Anyone in politics at any level is subjected to completely different types of forces and pressures than those existing in a private club milieu. Everyone involved tries to do his best to make everything come out right, but politicians look upon clubs, and club people, as sort of a Disney Land where everything is make-believe.

Club people assume that politicians are acting to achieve an entirely different set of goals than merely the advancement of the amateur sport (in our case yacht racing.) All things said, the La Rochelle to New Orleans Tricentennial Race was a great success and the SYC participation was worth-while. This emerging philosophy of professionally sponsored sailboat racing will become more prevalent, and our education acquired this time will help the next time we are asked to participate in something of this nature.

GULFPORT TO PENSACOLA RACE IN FRENCH BOAT

The 1982 Gulfport to Pensacola race was unique in that *Disque D'or 3*, a Bruce Farr design built in France which had just completed the Southern Ocean, the world's largest race course, was one of the entries in the record-breaking race of 170 boats. The yacht clubs participating were: SYC, sixty-three, Pontchartrain twenty-three, Pensacola twenty, and New Orleans eighteen in nine classes.

Gauntlet, a Kaufman 45, owned by G. Shelby Friedrichs, Jr. and Ray Fretz of SYC was sailed by Friedrichs netting first in Class A and first in fleet. IOR results show *Gauntlet* first, Cal Hadden in *Disque D'or 3* in second place, Dave Dunham with *Masquerade* third, and Dr. Reichard Kahle's *Corrie*, a C&C 39, fourth.

First to finish the race was Cal Hadden in the French boat *Disque D'Or 3*. Tim Molony tells the story for *Tell-Tale* as a crew on board this unique craft:

> Sitting quietly at anchor in the Gulfport ship harbor, she looked more like an oversized quarter tonner than one of the world's foremost racing yachts. With her raked transom, fractional rig, and hull graphics, she was easily discernable among the yachts that had made the Southern Ocean the world's largest race course.
>
> Closer inspection revealed a deck bristling with winches, cockpits, instruments, sheetstoppers, and a tandem pair of elk-skin covered destroyer wheels. It was apparent that *Disque D'or 3* was well equipped to fulfill her owner's intention, that of surfing at over 20 knots in the Roaring Forties to win the Whitbread Round the World Race. Finishing third, she was an unsuccessful but well respected contender in yachting's most grueling contest.
>
> She had now made her way to Gulfport as part of the fleet in the La Rochelle to New Orleans race. I had been asked to be part of her 14 man crew to race her in the annual Gulfport to Pensacola Ocean Race.
>
> To a composite crew of the SYC yachts *Susan* and *Wild Thang*, skipper Cal Hadden had made known his three wishes: to break *Tiare's* 10 year-old record, to finish first and to win on corrected time.
>
> A Bruce Farr design built in France, the 58-foot light weight aluminum ocean racer appeared to be the perfect weapon to achieve our

goals. *Disque D'or 3* is owned by a Swiss syndicate whose director Commodore Hadden had befriended at the start of the transatlantic race. We were to furnish the crew and provisions and cover the costs of the Pensacola race. He was to supply *Disque D'or 3* and two of her most experienced sailors to show us the ropes.

Boarding on Friday morning of the race was the first time most of us in the crew had ever seen the boat. After meeting the crew that would accompany us, Dominique and Rogi, we made a tour of the exterior and interior. From her flush deck painted aircraft carrier style with her racing number 20 to her Star Wars navigation room she projected a sole purpose, high speed on the world's oceans.

Her fractionally rigged mast was over 85-feet tall, she was very broad aft (18 feet), and she drew over nine feet of water. Equipped with 23 winches and over 40 sheetstoppers, she had tandem wheels, spinnaker poles and crew cockpit. Below from aft to forward were her sail bins, heated sleeping cabins, navigator's cabin to port, and head to starboard. Amidships was her galley main salon with gimballed table and seats. Forward was her open bow compartment housing the engine and gimballed diesel generator.

Her navigation equipment included Sat Nav, SSB, weatherfax received, RDF, complete instrument repeaters with dead reckoning, and tactical computers. Other below-deck features included hot and cold running water, two desalinators, holding plate refrigeration, three-burner stove, central heat and a stereo system in the salon with Sony Walkman stereos in the sleeping cabins. With a usual crew of nine, she was equipped with seven gimballed berths. She also was completely finished in teak and sound insulated.

After our familiarization tour, we loaded provisions and with the help of our Swiss crew, identified and relabeled every sheetstopper and winch previously marked in French. With a light southerly wind, we cast off and donned our official yellow and white race shirts.

With our cameras snapping like a bunch of tourists, we made our way out the channel. Under the direction of Dominique, we hoisted her immense mainsail and light number one genoa. After a number of practice tacks, we noted the crew's emphasis on setting up the main and bendy fractional rig.

My official duty was to tension the starboard running backstay and play the starboard traveler control. On this boat, there was plenty for the 14 of us to do when short tacking up the sound.

After an inauspicious start, we slowly got the feel of the boat. It soon became apparent that a beamy, fractionally rigged ocean racer designed for high speed racing was not at her best in light air and a short chop. As we approached Ship Island Pass, one boat had managed to stay ahead of us, Buddy Friedrichs' and Ray Fretz's *Gauntlet*.

As we came abeam the island, I took my turn at the wheels. With a large rudder and wire drive, she was very easy and precise to steer. Making our way into the Gulf, *Disque D'or 3* began to stretch her legs. The boats astern were falling back and we were closing on the smaller but well sailed *Gauntlet*.

We got our first break in the race as the wind veered 45 degrees and built to 15 to 18 knots in a small squall. With started sheets and a straight shot to the sea buoy, *Disque D'or 3* drew abeam and to leeward of *Gauntlet* and then ahead. Clocking well over eight knots, we rounded, set one of her powerful spinnakers, and roared off towards Pensacola.

Now making close to 10 knots, *Disque D'or 3* was truly in her element. With the crew lining her broad transom and weather rail, we broke out the refreshments and grinned at each other. This was what we had come to see. The fleet was disappearing astern and the Gulf's horizon was bare except for an occasional shrimper.

Our exhilaration was short lived. As the sun went down, so did the wind and our masthead rigged and lighter competitors slowly ground down our lead. We were soon back on the wind, straining to lay the Mobile sea buoy on starboard tack. *Gauntlet* was tenaciously closing the gap. Our second break occured a few hours later when the wind again veered and built. The entire horizon ahead was alternately darkened and lightened by numerous squalls and flashes of lightning.

Disque D'or 3 came to life and, as the wind built, she felt more like a locomotive than a sailboat. With the Sat Nav spitting out positions, hot hors d'oeuvres appearing from the galley, and sheets straining, we raced through the darkness with a phosphorescent wave spraying the foredeck. We soon picked up the lights of Perdido Key to leeward and, with sounds of thunder on the horizon, the roar of the boat's bow wave was occasionally interrupted by the thump of the forefoot splitting the sea.

We were now close reaching and with her sails set, it became a simple three-man job to race the boat. With some of the other crew, I made our way down below to the salon where we found Dominique brewing French coffee and telling stories of sailing *Disque D'or 3* off the top of 25-foot seas at 27-knots. Tales full of standing jibes, exploding spinnakers, and broken booms captured our attention.

The question came up: would they race around the world again? The answer, yes, but on their new boat a 90-foot version of *Disque D'or 3*. Currently in the planning stage, *Disque D'or 4* is to be an ultralight Bruce Farr designed maxi boat.

An hour later, *Patrol II* was spotted and, at 2:41 a.m., the finishing cannon fired. No record but a good run. It was now up to our competitors to establish our handicap finish as the clock continued for another 20 minutes to determine our corrected time. Less than an hour later, *Gauntlet* finished to win class and fleet.

As we made our way up the Pensacola channel, our resident mixologist passed out the requisite Gazoomees. We hadn't set a record or won on corrected time but we did have a great sail. The thought occurred isn't there another La Rochelle race in 1985? What if *Disque D'or 4* were to sail?

SYC HOSTS USYRU TEAM RACE

The SYC was selected to host the second annual USYRU Team Race

Championship of 1982 for the George R. Hinman trophy. Team racing, a seemingly new aspect for the sport sailing actually had been in existence for quite some time around local waters. Among the many series are the annual Commodore J. Gilbert Scheib series between Southern and its neighbor New Orleans Yacht Club, the Mississippi Coast club's Chapman Regatta, and for many years the North-South team races between SYC and Chicago Yacht Clubs. Fort Worth and Savannah Yacht Clubs have also participated with Southern in team racing. Intercollegiate sailing consists of team races. Now, in 1982 team racing joined the ranks of other national championships sponsored by USYRU, such as the Adams, Mallory, Sears, etc.

The rules governing this type of sailing are very complex. The event involved all eight areas in the USYRU using the Flying Scots which were divided into four fleets, three boats to a fleet. The technical aspects of the event were meticulously handled by SYC's very capable Larry Taggart. The overall winning team represented Area B with nine wins and one loss.

The winning team members of Area B were Steve Benjamin and John Clard, David Dellenbaugh and Paul Murphy, Peter Isler and Curt Oetking. The SYC crew finished second; they were John Dane, III, Joe Blouin and Danny Killeen, Jr. and Beau LeBlanc, Tommy Meric, and Greg Sonnier, all from Area D. The *Lacosta*, a 56-foot house yacht of Commodore B. Temple Brown and Bubby Hartson was an ideal boat for the event and was volunteered for all thirty races sailed.

Several SYC skippers took the road for the 1982 L-16 Internationals held in Bermuda. Dave Summer was the winner with SYC Peter Wuescher in second place. Peter had as his crew his son Allen and Richard Ehrlicher. In third place was the 1981 champion SYC Tony Smythe, with his crew of Jerry Blouin and George Janssen.

In California a crew from the SYC did an outstanding job when skipper Eldon Harvey, III with crew Keith Andrews won the 1982 USYRU Bemis trophy for the U. S. Junior Doublehanded sailing championship, hosted by the Richmond Yacht Club of California. This outstanding accomplishment won for Eldon Harvey the SYC outstanding skipper of the year award and the Tessier trophy, while Keith Andrews was presented the outstanding crew trophy for 1982.

Southern Yacht Club's Christian Gambel was crowned the new 1982 Flying Scot Junior North American champion in a series of five races out of the Corinthian Yacht Club in Buzzard's Bay, Massachusetts. Gambel, along with crewmen Patrick Gambel and Storey Charbonnet, sailed to a fourth and four aces.

The SYC juniors had another victory when they won the Junior Lipton Cup Regatta of 1982 on Lake Pontchartrain. Flurry Normann and Christian Gambel won both races to take the series.

The SYC juniors had a banner year. They made a great showing in Dallas, Texas where they participated in the trials for the Optimist nationals team selection. Johnny Lovell, his brother Andy Lovell, and Graham Arceneaux won in their respective age groups. Other participants were Flurry Normann, Cam Mitchell, and Douglas Gambel.

The top ten finishers travelled to Clearwater, Florida to vie for the right to represent the U. S. in the World Optimist championship in July in Italy. Flurry, accompanied by her mother and father, Gloria and Robert Normann, were among those who travelled to Ireland for the Optimist World regatta where Flurry finished fourth. In the Laser II Nationals sailed at Newport Beach, California in 1982, Flurry finished a close third.

SYC ENTERS OPTIMIST WORLD CHAMPIONSHIP

The following was written by John Lovell, Sr. for the *Tell-Tale*:

> They arrived in Rome on July 13, 1982 for the Optimist World championship. The regatta site was on the Mediterranean Sea. The coach, Clyde Wright, required the boys to be in bed by 9:30 p.m., so that the World Championship team's pillow fights were sometimes shortened.
>
> The boys drove to Pisa one day and visited the Tower of Pisa, which was fun. On their way back, they drove up to the surrounding hills and were amazed at the extent of the wine-growing activities. In several of the small towns, the USSR flags were flying (maybe the Red Brigade). So, they did not stop and were happy to arrive back in Follonica.
>
> In all, twelve races were completed. We were proud of the U. S. sailors. The results were: Team racing—there were five races; the U. S. finished seventh. Individual championship racing—there were five races; SYC team members K. Davids and J. Lovell were fifth and eighth respectively. In the Miami Herald Race Johnny Lovell finished first. There was one race in the Prins Bertils race in which SYC's J. Lovell placed third. The sailors were Johnny Lovell, Joe Logan, Keith Davids, Jim Weber, and Robin Vanderkreeke. In summary we had a great experience sailing with 130 to 160 boats on the starting line and making friends with sailors from around the world. Everyone should try to make the U. S. team in the future. It is a rewarding experience. John Lovell's father was of great assistance.

The Soling national championship was another series held by the SYC in 1982. There were twenty-nine entries from Southern California to Seattle, St. Petersburg to Montreal and many points in between. The winners were Han Fogh of the Bauleward Yacht Club, Bill Abbott of the Samia Yacht Club, Ed. Baird of the St. Petersburg Yacht Club, Donald Cohan of the Vineyard Haven Yacht Club, Peter Hall of the Royal St. Lawrence Yacht Club, Dave Perry of the Pequot Yacht Club and Terry McMahan of the Milwaukee Yacht Club.

The success of this regatta was due to the efforts of Tony Smythe, chairman. On the water the marker boats were manned by Dr. Arthur Payzant, Pat McCurnin, Dr. Reichard Kahle, John Borders, Leonard Tubbs, Franklin Jones, Bob Koch, Johnny Dicks, and Roy Troendle, Jr. all of whom did a terrific job.

Another important event was sailed on Lake Pontchartrain and sponsored by the SYC in 1982 was the Sunfish Mid-Winters. There were fifty boats from the South and Mid-West. SYC Eldon Harvey, III won over a field of seventeen in the junior division. Christian Gambel of SYC was fourth. In the senior division SYC Joe Blouin was second.

In 1982 Paul Tipton, S. J. of Mobile Chairman of GORC reported at the semi-annual GYA meeting on the GORC series sailed under PHRF rating. It drew forty-two yachts, of which thirty-six finished the series. An IOR Associaton for GYA has been established and PHRF registrations within the GYA now total 800 boats. Tipton gave credit to John Oerting of Pensacola for work on the handicapping over the past two years. (Paul Tipton S. J. is the president of Springhill College in Mobile, Alabama, where he has initiated a very active and successful sailing program.)

The high-light of the 1982 Awards Banquet at SYC was the presentation of the coveted Star Class Sir Thomas J. Lipton trophy to Shawn Killeen for his winning of the Star Class Gulf championship. See the photograph showing Shawn with his father and mother, Mr. and Mrs. Joseph L. Killeen, Jr., "Buzzy" and "Connie," who also were winners of this cup, "Buzzy" for a record six consecutive years, 1964-1969, and "Connie" in 1971. For the first time in the history of this trophy, which was donated by Sir Thomas J. Lipton in 1928, the names of a complete family are inscribed as winners.

The Sugar Bowl Regatta was held the Sunday after Christmas of 1982. Competing in the Sugar Bowl Regatta handicap class was Commodore Hadden in his flagship *Wild Thang*, which won its race in Class C. The commodore had a unique crew; they were two midshipmen from aboard the HMS *Fearless*, a British amphibious assault ship that participated in the Falklands misunderstanding. The ship was visiting New Orleans for Mardi Gras. The two sailors were Iain

Graham and Stuart McQuaker.

Winning the "race of champions" in the Sugar Bowl Regatta was the Bay-Waveland Yacht Club's skipper Dennis Stieffel, with crew Corky Hadden and Edgar Santa Cruz. Second place went to the Southern Yacht Club with skipper Preston Christman and crew Paul Christman and Christian Gambel. In third place was the Gulfport Yacht Club's skipper Sam Hopkins and crew Gail Galloway and William Westerly. Other teams participating were from Biloxi, Buccaneer, Fort Walton, New Orleans, Pontchartrain, and Singing River of Pascagoula, Mississippi. All participants were presented the usual complimentary tickets for the New Year's Day Sugar Bowl football classic and special commemorative T-shirts.

When the new year 1983 began, Commodore Hadden was returned to office, and again the *Tell-Tale* issues would be brightened with the messages and bits of nostalgia that the commodore was so good at preparing for the "Commodore's Corner." The January issue brought back the good old days when the "Pen" always had enough room and enough slips for all of the boats that existed.

> You didn't need the "right connections" nor an excess of money with which to acquire a mooring spot. Everyone was happy. There was an abundance of friendliness, courtesy and mutual respect.
>
> Many remember cranking a Star boat out of the water and then pushing it around on the dollies and railroad tracks outside the back door of "Sail Inn," [previously described as the favorite "hang out" for yachtsmen back in the Forties when the club was under repair and Armond Schroeder was the owner]. Afterwards, you could walk on the wharf past Bill Johnson's big shed, where many a boat was built, and past Oscar Lamar's "ways" on which at any given moment one of the fine old classics like *Pimpernell*, the Norwegian doublender might be in for a new paint job. There were some boat houses then, not many and not very elaborate like today. Most seemed to have the owner's name proudly displayed on little mahogany and gold leaf signs.
>
> Those who were fortunate enough to go through some formative years in the old "Pen" can recall sitting on the deck of some treasured boat listening to the strains of music from the "Owls" band playing on the West End Roof Garden across the way, or Louis Prima's jazz tunes. Those golden days in the old "Pen" are gone forever but their memories will live forever.

One of the first socials of the year is the ever-popular ball of the "Bards of the Bilges." Approximately 300 loyal subjects heeded the dictum for the 1983 annual ball. The theme was "Moses in the Roseauxs," with James Janssen as King Neptune XXVII (Moses) and

Cynthia "Cindy" Bailey, one of the entourage of maids who drew the lucky bracelet that elevated her to the rank of queen to reign over the mock carnival ball. The maids were Betsy Blouin, Ann Bruce, Matt Dymond, Mina Meric, and Janie Wynne. They wore identical Egyptian costumes.

With all the burnooses and other Middle East headgear worn by the members, the ball could have passed for a meeting of OPEC nation oil ministers. The Ten Commandments of Sailing created on a plywood "tablet" were designed by the king:

I. Thou shalt have no interests before sailing.
II. Thou shalt not make any changes to falsify your boat's rating.
III. Thou shalt not take the name of the Lord in vain asking to win if you haven't cleaned thy bottom.
IV. Remember the Sabbath to keep it open for sailing.
V. Honor thy Commodore and thy Governing Board that thy days may be long in the club.
VI. Thou shalt not barge the line.
VII. Thou shalt not commit a foul coming about in front of a starboard tack boat.
VIII. Thou shalt not steal thy competitor's foredeck man.
IX. Thou shalt not bear false witness in protest committee hearings.
X. Thou shalt not covet thy neighbor's boat, nor his slip, nor his crew.

"MEXICO NIGHT" GRAND PARTY

More than 300 members and guests attended a gala "Mexico Night" at the SYC, a very festive party that will be remembered most as a grand festival of margaritas, daiquiris, enchiladas, tacos, and all other ingredients that make for a successful evening of yarnspinning, gourmet dining, and dancing to various Latin tunes (after four margaritas, everything seemed Latin).

The reason for all the over-indulgence, if there has to be a reason, was a discussion of plans for the forthcoming 1983 twelfth *regata al sol*. The biennial classic was sponsored by Southern Yacht Club, Club de Yates de Cozumel, and Consejo Nacional de Turismo. Chairman of the regatta, Jack Gordon of the SYC, affectionately referred to as "El Supremo" by his "El Segundos," Commodores Richard Spangenberg and D. Temple Brown, delivered his version of their visit to Mexico City and Cozumel the week prior to work out details.

The club representatives were warmly received by our friends from

Mexico, Don Anibal de Iturbide and his son, Anibal, and his beautiful wife, Mercedes, Don Alberto Alvarez Morphy, Consejo Nacional de Turismo, Hector Mestre, and Pacho Rangel, all of whom since the inception of the regatta have played vital roles in making this event a grand success.

The headquarters for the fleet on the island was the Sol Caribe, and 125 rooms were reserved. (This brings back fond memories of the days when families and friends who attended Lipton regattas on Labor Day weekends would fill up three and four floors of the hotels along the Gulf Coast down to Sarasota, Florida.)

REGATA AL SOL XII—1983

In the 1983 Cozumel race, a record thirty boat entries left the Gulfport Yacht Club with Jack Gordon of the SYC as general chairman of this the twelfth *regata al sol*. The biggest yacht was Jim Bates' 65-foot *Runaway*. Only four entries were carrying the SYC burgee, *Tiare*, skippered by Hjalmar Breit, *Sun Witch*, sailed by Roger Barielle, Dr. Victor Oliver's *Esprit*, and *Sovereign*, entered by Al Gooch and Ed Boos.

Winning the Mexico race was *Sinbad*, a new Morgan-45 owned by Terry Rhodes and sailed by Benz Faget of New Orleans Yacht Club, navigated by Phil Lambke and Steve Terrell. They won the Gulfport to Cozumel race in the elapsed time of 110 hours and 27 minutes. *Sinbad* was first in fleet and first in Class A. She was followed in the fleet by *Esprit*, owned by Vic Oliver from SYC and sailed by Henry Tillman out of Singing River Yacht Club.

With Class A honors going to *Sinbad*, with *Esprit* second, in third place was *Sovereign*, sailed by Al Gooch and Ed Boos from SYC. Winner of Class B was *H. Dirigo*, sailed by John Carr of Pensacola; second was *Sugar Cookie*, sailed by Scott Gregory from St. Andrews Bay.

In Class C, first was *Sandpebble*, sailed by Bob Krievel of Pensacola Yacht Club, and second was Joe Angelini, sailing the *K. H. Tibblets* of Fort Walton Yacht Club.

Paul Kalman, editor of *Tell-Tale*, wrote:

> According to skippers and crews of the front runners, their strategy was based on a keen pre-race analysis of all meteorological and oceanographic data. Their hindsight ability to analyze these factors increased in direct proportion to the rumor of margaritas consumed once on the island.

When asked to comment on the winner's postmortem remarks, the skipper of *Patricia*, the last boat to finish with an elapsed time of 175 hours, said *@!@‡!.

With over 400 skippers, crews and friendly fans there were few dull moments. The festivities included a pool-side party at the Sol Caribe, a beach party at the Plaza Azul and the trophy presentation hosted by the Governor of Quintana Roo around the pool at El Presidente Hotel.

The highlight of the Governor's party was a short soliloquy in Spanish delivered by Commodore Temple Brown. It was well received but little understood by those of both countries.

In the 1983 GORC race a twenty-year-old Tulane University student, Nelson Roltsch, who had impeccable sailing credentials during his nine-year racing career, was lost overboard. Nelson was wearing a safety harness; the harness was reportedly not hooked on.

As the result of this incident, stricter guidelines have been added to the USYRU and Gulf Yachting Association's "Safety-at-Sea" rules. "Survival techniques are not awarded at the trophy presentation, but at least the sailors are there to race another. But, all the safety procedures will not replace a life or the commom sense decision that face one who goes to sea. In offshore sailing the bottom line is up to you," reported John Weber, editor of *Sailors' Gazette* in an editorial on this event.

According to the statistics of 1983, it was noted that the one-quarter of the year's fatalities on water were attributed to falls overboard. However, they also showed a decrease in deaths on water down to 7.9 per 100,000 boats while a decade ago this ratio was 16 per 100,000 boats.

In the 1983 Gulfport-Pensacola race for the Offshore Challenge Cup, there were 167 entries and 154 starters. Host clubs were Southern, Gulfport and Pensacola Yacht Clubs. *Gauntlet*, the Kaufman 45-footer sailed by Buddy Friedrichs and John Meade of SYC, was first to finish and first in the Performance Handicap Rating Fleet (PHRF). This was a repeat performance as *Gauntlet* had also won in 1982. F. Keller Riess, also of SYC, sailed *Spirit*, a Newport 41-footer to first overall in the Cruiser/Racer division. During the 1983 season the PHRF group served 1,000 boats.

SYC's skipper Prieur Leary decided after race week at Antigua, for the second year in a row, to bring his magnificent Swan 57 *Gone With The Wind* some 2,000 miles back to Lake Pontchartrain to sail in the race to the coast and the Gulfport-Pensacola Race. The first part was a success, as Prieur was first to finish, first in class, and first in fleet in the race that started in Lake Borgne, rounded buoy 52 in the Gulfport Ship Channel and finished at the Gulfport Yacht Club.

Gone With The Wind recorded a sixty-minute elapsed time victory, as well as a fourteen-minute corrected time margin in her 1983 re-debut "back home." However, in the second part, for the second year in a row, the mighty *Gauntlet* humbled the 150-plus boat fleet in the thirty-fifth annual Gulfport-Pensacola race. Sailing *Gauntlet* were co-skippers Buddy Friedrichs and Ray Fretz. They finished first, first in Class A, and first in fleet on corrected time.

The SYC 1983 opening regatta was held in April with the usual boat parade in which a record-breaking number of boats headed by the SYC parade marshal Larry Molony. The yacht *Hello Dolly V*, owned by Denver Gray, was used as the flagship of the SYC for the occasion. Mr. and Mrs. Gray were lovely hosts and graciously received on board Commodore and Mrs. Cal Hadden with the board of governors and their wives, past commodores with their spouses, and Coast Guard dignitaries. SYC Chaplain Ross Allen blessed the fleet as it passed in review.

The flag-raising ceremony was held on the front lawn of the clubhouse, with the opening invocation delivered by Chaplain Allen. Music was furnished by the melodious sounds of the U. S. Navy Steel Band. An unknown bagpiper appeared to render his piping sounds.

The summer of 1983 found Lake Pontchartrain sprinkled with the white sails of the thoroughbreds of sailboats, the Stars. Again the Southern Yacht Club played host to the Spring Series of the Star Class. John Fraser served as regatta chairman, Stewart Barnett as race committee chairman, with Gene Walet of SYC and Roger Brett of St. Petersburg as judges. Roger had also sailed in the first 1939 first Spring Series on Lake Pontchartrain.

As, usual, this Star Class event was star-studded with many champions. Buddy Melges, the American sailor who won an Olympic gold medal in a Soling in 1972, Durward Knowles, a past World's champion from Nassau, and Tut Greening from Springfield with his son.

The oldest participant was thirty-two year-old Gordon Bell, who sailed as crew for Dr. Frank Shoemaker. Mr. Bell sailed in the first Spring Series and has not missed a series in ensuing years. Another old-timer was Commodore George Criminale of Mobile, star skipper emeritus of the Gulf South. He has skippered in every series from the first held in 1939.

When Criminale was introduced by Commodore Cal Hadden of SYC at the trophy presentation, Cal said, "When I first met George in 1939, I will never forget the tremendous impression he made on me as an 'Iron Man of the Sea.' He had a set of running lights permanently secured to the forward deck of his Star boat. George had just sailed into the SYC pen. His purpose in the trip was to turn around and sail in a race from New Orleans to Mobile. As the kids now say, I thought that was 'cool.' "

The local participants were John Dane, III, John Lovell, Tommy Meric, Shawn Killeen, and Eldon Harvey, III. Peter Wright of Chicago with Todd Cozzens won the Spring Series and the fifty-boat Jahncke Series for the overall winner. In second place was Alex Smigelsky of Lake Heateons, New Jersey. Third place went to SYC John Dane, with crew Fred May in *Quest*. Maryland skipper Andrew Menkart and crew James Kayle, recent winners of the Bacardi Star Series in Miami, were fourth.

With the 1984 Olympics on the horizon, most of the top Star crews were sailing in a maximum number of important series to earn qualification for the North American and World championships and pre-Olympics to be sailed in California in the fall.

John Dane, III had ordered a new Star from Buddy Melges for delivery in Miami on the provision that John crew for Buddy in the series. In his new Star *Quest* John planned to campaign again for the Olympics to be held in October 1984. Those who trailed their boats to the Bacardi series in Miami were Conrad Kuebel, Shawn Killeen, Chris Christman, Eldon Harvey, and Walter Keenan, Jr. The winner was Yankee Andrew Menkart and crew Jim Kayle. Second among eighty Stars was the Melges-Dane team.

DIETICIAN ENTERS PRE-OLYMPIC PROGRAM

At a meeting called by Sam Merrick, chairman of the 1983 U. S. Olympic Yachting Committee, at the Coral Reef Yacht Club in Miami, it was reported by Marilyn Mower of the *Sailors' Gazette* that "In addition to talking about rules and selections, Merrick trotted out dietician Jane Kent to give the sailors some nutrition tips—sure-to-be-followed tips such as 'don't drink before dinner, don't eat lunch out on the water.' The 'yes ma'ams' must have been deafening!"

At another meeting called on the fourth day of the races for the Bacardi Cup, ten sailors were counted as Olympic contenders. The list included Vince Brun, Peter Wright, John Dane III, Augie Diaz, and Andrew Menkart. It was pointed out three American 12-meter skippers, all America's Cup contenders, have spent considerable time driving Stars—Dennis Connor, Tom Blackaller, and Ted Turner.

"Star boating is not a class where middle age is fatal," commented Marilyn Mower. "White-haired Barton Beck is still racing. The Lippincott boys were winning while in their 40s and Sam Merrick believes he did his best sailing 10 years ago when he was 58."

John Dane, III of Southern Yacht Club was best of six Southern boats in the '83 Star Worlds at Los Angeles. Dane won the Vanderveer trophy for series leader after three races, and went on to take a sixth in the light-air series. Augie Diaz of Miami was eleventh, Shawn Killeen of SYC was twenty-second, with Stig Wennerstrom and Ding Schoonmaker, both of Miami, in thirty-four and forty-fourth place, respectively. Harry Walker of Vero Beach was sixty-third. The title was won by defending champ Antonio Gorostegui of Spain.

Leslie Weatherly of the Gulfport Yacht Club, a two-time winner of the Women's Sunfish championship in 1980 and 1981, had an easy time of winning the 1983 Women's Sunfish North America title in August at Laporte, Texas. She won all five heats in the thirty-nine boat field. Earlier in 1983 Weatherly ranked as the top woman sailor in the South. Also out of the Gulfport Yacht Club Andy Pimental won the Laser 1983 Mid-Winters.

LASER WORLD CHAMPIONSHIP AT GULFPORT YACHT CLUB

Foreigners may have taken the top spots in the 1983 Chrysler Laser World championship but the officials of the Gulfport Yacht Club figured they got the big prize—they sponsored the event.

It was the first time the world class regatta has ever been held in the United States and Gulfport members were still stunned over their good fortune in landing the event, which was sailed October 13-29, 1983 in the Gulf just offshore from the club. They had been competing with many more prestigious clubs around the country for the honor, but won out after having run a successful mid-winter regatta earlier in the year.

About 147 sailors from 25 countries made it to the competition. Oscar Paulich, age twenty-five, of Holland won the eight race series. Per Arne Nelson of Norway finished in second place. You had to look all the way down to sixth place before finding a North American, Andy Roy of Canada, who finished sixth overall.

The Fort Walton Yacht Club was host for the warm-up races preceeding both the Mid-Winters and North American Flying Scot championships. The Mid-Winter event was held in April 1983 at the St. Andrews Bay Yacht Club in Panama City, Florida. Wind, oysters, rain, cocktails, sailmakers—each of these was a notable part (just about that order) of the 1983 Flying Scot Regatta. Fifty-five Scot skippers from as far away as Michigan and Massachusetts gathered for this six-race with one throw-out event. The champions were:
1. Andy Fox, Larry Klein, Jamie Guerdan of Orlando, Florida
2. Bubby Eagan, Corky Hadden, Chris Merrifield, Bay-Waveland
3. Marc Eagan, John Aras, Patty Fisher, Bay-Waveland
4. Ken Kleinschrodt, Tom Dabney, Jennifer Ollinger, Buccaneer, Mobile, Alabama
5. Larry Taggart, Elizabeth Merrifield, Peter Merrifield, SYC

The Bay-Waveland Yacht Club hosted the 1983 Flying Scot Senior North American championship in July, which was won by Bay-Waveland's Bubby Eagan, who also won the Mid-Winters, with his brother Marc Eagan as crew. (Marc was twice a winner of the Flying Scot North American championship.) Second place was won by Andy Fox, with Larry Klein and Kathy Allen from Orlando, Florida. They failed in their attempt to be the first ever to win three consecutive Flying Scot North American championshiops. In third place was SYC's Larry Taggart with Julie Anne Gooch and Peter Merrifield as crew. Fourth place was taken by another Bay-Waveland skipper, Dennis Stieffel, with Janet Gordon and Liz Merrifield as crew.

The weekend before the Flying Scot North American races, the ever-cordial Bay-Waveland Yacht Club members welcomed the Junior Flying Scot North American championship of 1983. Although GYA clubs did not win this event, they placed second, third, fourth and fifth. It was Brian Koivu, skipper, and Aimes Schmidt and Michael Casano from Orlando, Florida who took the honors. In second place was SYC's John Lovell, skipper, and crewmen Arthur Wynne and Barton Jahncke, Jr. Third place was taken by Bay-Waveland's Peter Merrifield, with Mike White and Chip Peterson. In fourth place was SYC's Christian Gamble, with Storey Charbonnet and Kam Mitchell. Fifth place went to Pass Christian Yacht Club's Watt Duffy, Susie Christensen, and Jed Duffy.

The SYC summer camp celebrated its twenty-fifth anniversary in 1983. This pilot program was initiated in the summer of 1958 by Janet Lorber and Flo Scheib who recognized the need for a sailing program for the youth of SYC.

The project ran for six long and hot weeks during the months of July and August. We secured the service of some junior skippers, who were instructors at $2.00 per hour. They were Jimmie Smithers, Dabby Wuescher, Buddy Friedrichs and his brother Gore, William Murray, Bert and Cookie Keenan, Roy O'Neil, Bubby Hartson, Mickey Sheenan, Merrill True, Jack Scheib, Jr., J. Dwight LeBlanc, Louis Koerner, Jr. and others. All were young and handsome, thus the boats overcrowded with young skipperettes.

This sailing camp became an ongoing project and proved to be the spawning grounds for future sailing champions. Today the program is under the supervision of a sailing director and is very successful.

SYC JUNIOR TEAM WINS CALIFORNIA GOVERNOR'S CUP RACE

The SYC juniors Scott Sonnier and Johnny Lovell with crewmen Keith Andrews and Flurry Normann were off to sail in California for the Governor's Cup of California. This event is similar to the Congressional Cup except that it is limited to juniors. The SYC crews won in a highly competitive series that had fifteen eliminations sailed in match-race format. The series was extended an additional five races when Johnny and Scott found themselves tied for the lead, out of the six participants at the conclusion of the series. The best three out of five in the sail-off was won by Scott Sonnier and his crew of Keith Andrews and Flurry Norman.

The 1983 GYA Junior Lipton Cup Regatta was a tremendous success in all aspects again this year. There was a record turnout of over a hundred participants, with fifteen boats crossing the starting line on Lake Pontchartrain. The SYC had the winning team. The first race was won by SYC Flurry Normann, with crew Storey Charbonnet and Johnny Lovell. Bay-Waveland's Tom Allen won the second race. Other members of the SYC team were Christian Gambel, Arthur Wynne, Barton Jahncke, Douglas Gambel, Eldon Harvey, III, Kam Mitchell, Robert Normann, and Philip Rawlins. The Uncle Roy trophy was won by SYC Johnny Lovell for winning the last race.

The SYC's juniors did it again at the Gulfport Yacht Club, when John Lovell with crew Bruce Levey won the Junior Laser II Mid-Winter National championship with eight boats entered. They converged on the yacht club from all parts of the United States and

Canada, plus some from England, France, and Trinidad.

1983 PRESS RACE

The Southern Yacht Club held its annual Press Race in 1983, with co-chairman Dr. Joseph Kuebel and Sandy Davies (Sandy was the founder of this event). With an organized group of top skippers to assist the various newscasters and reporters, ten Easterly boats, which were so generously lent by their owners, got under way. The winner was Liz Curren of Channel 6 in *Y-Knot II*, while her stationmate Buddy Diliberto, a previous winner, could only get a ninth place out of the ten boats entered. Ron Swoboda of Channel 8 took second place on *Blue Mist* to keep the whole series from going to the ladies, as Andrea Kingsmill of *The Times-Picayune* took third place. Other press participants were Ed Clancy and Richard Anderson of Channel 8.

A fine luncheon for the skippers, their spouses and other notables preceeded the race (an extra bribe), with Buzzy Killeen showing films of bygone days when a National or International sailing champion would receive front page coverage. Large bold black headlines would be given annual regattas on Lake Pontchartrain and the Gulf Coast.

There were ten participants in the L-16 Internationals sailed on Lake Pontchartrain in 1983. SYC's Greg Cambel, with crew of Tommy Harris and Elaine Buchtel, won the event and is now listed with four other SYC champions of the Luder championship. In second place was Arthur Mears of SYC; Tommy Meric of SYC placed third, and in fourth place was another SYC skipper, Danny Killeen, Jr. The crews for this event in addition to Harris and Buchtel were Chuck Lapeyre, Tommy Taggart, Tony Smythe, and Peter Wuescher.

The 1983 Sir Thomas J. Lipton Cup Regatta was held at the Bay-Waveland Yacht Club with a record breaking attendance of twenty-one Gulf Yachting Association yacht clubs out of twenty-five. This put approximately 500 skippers and crews on the waters of Bay St. Louis for the four races, and approximately 1,000 spectators in over a hundred boats. The Bay-Waveland Yacht Club won the Lipton Regatta for the ninth time in the yacht club's history.

Sadly missed from this Lipton Regatta was the presence of SYC past Commodore Arthur D. "Juby" Wynne, who passed away a few months before the event. Jane and Juby's summer home on Pass Christian Isle was the usual rendezvous for all SYC members and crews. Juby sailed into his heavenly harbor leaving a record of good sportsmanship in his many sailing activities.

Also in the SYC news was the rise to "captain" by Lou and Henry Finke. Now they are qualified to captain any boat, having merited their certificates by spending thousands of hours before the mast during the more than two decades they have been cruising all over the world. This adventurous couple live aboard their *Star Dust II* in the Virgin Islands, and members of SYC are proud of the first SYC couple captains.

AMERICA LOSES "AMERICA'S CUP"

The New York Yacht Club was the domain of the prestigious America's Cup until that memorable day of September 27, 1983, when the Cup was surrendered for the first time in its 132-year history to Australia, the winner with the boat *Australia II* skippered by John Bertrand; Ben Lexcen was the designer. The Australians won four out of seven races against the United States representative, *Liberty*, with Dennis Conner the helmsman, who was the celebrated winner of the trophy in 1980 on board *Freedom*.

The 1983 America's Cup event was not without action, as heated controversy raged over the America's Cup challenger *Australia II's* radical winged-keel, about which the members of the New York Yacht Club asked the International Yacht Racing Union (IYRU) for a ruling as to whether it was larger than a 12-meter boat. The ruling of the IYRU was that it was properly measured and designed and the races were held on schedule. However, the winged-keel permitted the boat to turn faster on the all-important windward legs. The bone-white *Australia II* was 3½ tons lighter in displacement than the Ruby-hulled *Liberty*.

During the victory celebration, the Aussies dropped the plastic sheets that had covered the bottom of the boat and ended months of suspense over what the keel looked like. The keel's appearance lived up to expectations, with a large ball of weight at the front sweeping back into a winglike design. The water-blue wings, however, were angled downward, instead of horizontal as many thought.

The beautiful ornate bottomless silver pitcher, called the America's Cup, with the long bolt that held it in place at the New York Yacht Club was released from its inner sanctum and handed over by Commodore Robert Stone of the NYYC to the Australian syndicate, saying it was a day "many of us hoped would never come." Peter Dalziell of the Royal Perth Yacht Club accepted the trophy. Alan

Bond, head of the syndicate that spent 16 million dollars over ten years to win the Cup, said, "This is the greatest thing that you could do for our country, Australia. This great competition between our country enables us to say, 'We're close friends with the American nation.'" Commodore Stone replied, "After the effort the Australians have put into this for years, there's no country we'd rather see get it than Australia."

President Reagan expressed the same sentiment in a telegram to the Aussies' prime minister, Robert Hawke, "I am delighted that its home will be Australia," Reagan said, adding "at least until the next race." (Each of the four new American boats constructed for the 1983 event cost over $300,000—the cost of the sails was estimated at more than $500,000.)

1983 marked the twenty-fifth time that the *America's Cup* had been placed in competition, nation against nation. The United States has been the victor in all twenty-four other attempts. The summer of 1983 witnessed nine teams from six different countries, Australia, Britain, Canada, France, Italy, and the United States sailing their 12-meter yachts on the bluewater of Newport, after two years of rigid practice by the crews.

The America's Cup had its beginning in 1851 when the United States was invited by the British to participate in the race around the Isle of Wight. The race was won by the *America*, skippered by Commodore John C. Stevens of the New York Yacht Club. The "100 Guinea" Cup was the reward. The *America* was owned by a syndicate which presented the cup to the New York Yacht Club. Henceforth, it became known as the *America's Cup*, and is the oldest regularly contested trophy in the world of sports.

INTERVIEW WITH KYLE SMITH, CREW IN AMERICA'S CUP RACES OF 1983

Kyle Smith, a six-foot five, twenty-eight-year-old member of the Southern Yacht Club, was one of 277 sailors trying for spots on the America's Cup defender *Liberty*, and he was selected to be on the eleven-man crew. Kyle was a veteran crewman on board *Freedom*, sailed by Dennis Conner, when she won the last America's Cup in 1980.

An article of June 28, 1983 in *The Times-Picayune* was written by Marty Mule, covering an interview with Kyle Smith before he departed for Newport, Rhode Island. Mule stated, "Kyle Smith is feeling pressure John Cox Stevens couldn't. There's no winning streak like this winning streak. One hundred and thirty-two years separated Smith from Stevens. And the America's Cup from the rest of the world. The difference is Stevens won the first race aboard the schooner *America* in 1851 when the trophy was called the "Guinea Cup" and the race was sailed around the Isle of Wight in England."

"When you're 24-0, 24-1 can look cataclysmic. 'Losing the America's Cup is not a pleasant thing' said Kyle, 'and what if we were the crew that lost the America's Cup? What would we do? I suppose we would have to keep sailing to somewhere where nobody knew us.'"

They did lose, but there was no need to sail some place where nobody knew them. All America is proud of this team. They lost to the Australians in a hard-fought battle down to the last leg of the course when the perfect record of 132 years was marred by 41 seconds. Dennis Conner and his crew have the distinction of being the last to win the America's Cup and the first to lose it.

Kyle Smith was honored by the Southern Yacht Club at the Banquet of Champions and was the recipient of the outstanding crew award of 1983 for the Mariner's trophy. Kyle had also received this trophy in 1980 when he crewed on board *Freedom*.

COMMODORE WILLIAM C. GAMBEL—1984-85

At the annual meeting of the SYC held on December 1, 1983, William C. "Bill" Gambel was elected commodore. His father, Charles L. Gambel, was also a commodore of the SYC in 1956 and 1957. This was a first in the 136-year history of the Southern Yacht Club that a father and son held the position of commodore. The new commodore is a prominent New Orleans attorney. His flagship is his late father's *Grand Banks*, on which Bill crewed.

Serving with Commodore Gambel were the following: Maurice J. Hartson, III, vice-commodore; John C. Levert, Jr., rear commodore; J. Fred Clerc, secretary-treasurer; Dr. Earl J. Sonnier, fleet surgeon; J. F. A. Lorber, Jr., fleet measurer; and Jack Dane, fleet captain.

Southern Yacht Club's Tommy Meric, one of the top one-design and handicap skippers in the South, was named to lead an SYC team to California to sail in the inaugural Yacht Club Challenge Cup to be hosted by Newport Harbor Yacht Club in April 1984. The invitation was extended by Newport's Commodore John S. Griffith, Jr. to

Southern because of SYC's reputation in sailing over the years. It was an elite field of yacht racers who attended the invitation-only contest at the Newport Beach Yacht Club, Balboa, California. Others among those listed were the New York and the St. Petersburg Yacht Clubs.

Meric's crew was Bobby Schimek, Billy Smith, Peter Lowe, Tim Molony, Peter Kahle, Jay Kuebel, and Greg Gambel. The New York Yacht Club won the series.

The opening regatta of the 1984 season began with the parade of boats along the seawall of Lake Pontchartrain and passing in review of the official yacht *Hello Dolly* of the Denver Grays. The 100-boat fleet was led by the parade marshall, Barton Jahncke, who was costumed as George Washington. Bill Wright's *Moon Pic* won the prize for the best-decorated craft.

At the flag-raising ceremony held on the lawn of the clubhouse, appearing on the scene were Mickey and Minnie Mouse and Donald Duck from Disney World. They were in New Orleans as part of the 1984 World's Fair.

Visiting New Orleans for the World's Fair was the presidential yacht *Sequoia* on her first major cruise since she was auctioned in 1977. She was anchored in the harbor of the Southern Yacht Club. This distinguished guest had served eight presidents for a period of forty-four years.

When the Memorial Day Regatta was held at the SYC, it was dedicated in honor of SYC's John G. "Jack" Weinman, the U. S. commander general of the Louisiana World's Exposition of 1984. G. Shelby Friedrichs, Jr. was the regatta chairman. The *Sequoia* was used as a spectator boat for the occasion. Among those on board and attending a dock-side party after the races were the hosts, Commodore and Mrs. Gambel, the vice-admiral, F. G. A. Fitch, and Capt. G. F. Walwyn, who came to town aboard another visiting yacht, HMS *Bristol*.

A fleet of fifty-one sailboats, ranging in length from twenty-five to fifty feet, embarked on the annual sixty-two-mile pilgrimage from the south shores of Lake Pontchartrain to Gulfport in the 1984 race to the coast. Because of repairs to the Rigolets bridge, the boats had started their race from Lake Borgne for the past two years. This year the usual route was restored and the boats departed from the buoy in front of the clubhouse. The small number of entries was due to bad weather.

Buddy Friedrichs and John Mead raced their 45-foot Kaufman, *Gauntlet*, through a blustery thunderstorm to capture first in fleet (PHRF). The crew was Barton Jahncke, Bobby Schimek, Philip James, Beau LeBlanc, Bill Keller, Jr., and Ronnie Lanasa. The *Gauntlet*, sailed by Friedrichs and Meade, also won in Class C in the Nassau Cup race, the sixth and final race of the GORC. Lowell North sailing *Secret Love* was a close second.

The SYC again hosted the 1984 Rhodes 19 National championship races in which twelve boats were entered. Eight skippers represented the Southern Yacht Club. The remaining participants came from Chicago, Alabama, and Marblehead, Massachusetts. Barrett Normann of Marblehead skippered the winning boat with two local SYC crewmen, J. Dwight LeBlanc Jr. and Keith Andrews.

Away from home, SYC had many representatives in the 1984 Optimist National Sailing championship at the Naval Academy in Annapolis, Maryland. Michael Demarcy, age fourteen, and Charles Meade, age eleven, won in their age division. Demarcy not only won the Red Division but placed second in the overall competition, in which seventy-two Optimist skippers from the U. S. participated. The winner of this event was Mark Mendelblatt of the St. Petersburg Yacht Club. In the other divisions, the SYC competitors were:

Nick Cromwell	Dorothy Manard
Dolly Hightower	John Alden
Michael Jones	Rosalind Meade
Jennifer Lovell	Robert Normann
	Douglas White

The Southern Yacht Club's Olympic Sailing Association has served the skippers and crews well over the years. In their first Olympic effort and with the aid of personal contributions and some help from the SYC Olympic Sailing Association, a team from the Bay-Waveland Yacht Club in Bay St. Louis, Mississippi—Dennis Stieffel, skipper, his brother Rod and Randy Santa Cruz as crewmen in their Soling *Spirit of Bay St. Louis*—sailed out of the Balboa Yacht Club in the summer of 1984, after participating in several series of races in order to reach the Soling trials.

Among the thirty boats entered, Stieffel ranked as high as fourth in the ten-race series. He finished ninth in the trials, which were won by Robbie Haines of California. Joining the Bay-Waveland crew in the Soling trials was George C. Francisco IV of Houston, Texas, a twenty-year old Tulane University student and junior member of the

Southern Yacht Club. (His father sailed on Lake Pontchartrain many times.)

Other local entries were in the Star Class: John Dane, III and crew Fred May; John Lovell with John Greening; Eldon Harvey IV and Shawn Killeen. Out of Mobile, Alabama was George Brothers. Dane finished fourth in the trials, which were won by Bill Buchan of Washington. He went on to capture the Olympic gold medal in the Star Class.

The Bay-Waveland Yacht Club had won the Lipton Cup for two consecutive years, 1982 and 1983, and for this reason it could not hold the Lipton Regatta of 1984, according to the GYA rule. Having been in second place in the 1983 event, the Pensacola Yacht Club was host. This did not prevent the Bay from taking the cup again for the third straight year. It was the first time in history of the Lipton regattas that all GYA yacht clubs owning club-owned Flying Scots, of which there were twenty, participated in this annual series of races.

The Men's North American Sailing championship for the Clifford D. Mallory Cup was won by another group from the Bay-Waveland Yacht Club in Bay St. Louis, Mississippi. The skipper, Marc Eagan, was ably assisted by expert crewmen Beau LeBlanc of SYC and Corky Hadden of Bay-Waveland. The victory was won over Jack Slattery of Boston. They sailed in keel boats, Holder 20s, at Bay Head, New Jersey. Previous GYA winners of the Mallory Cup were Buddy Friedrichs in 1964 and Gene Walet in 1954 and 1955.

A great group of Southern sailors coming from the Southern Yacht Club won another Mallory Cup, emblematic of the Interscholastic Yacht Racing Association 1984 National Championship Youth Regatta held at the U. S. Naval Academy. They were John Lovell, Richardson Farnsworth, Andy Lovell, Thomas Keating, Gore Friedrichs, and Prieur Leary.

Olympic gold medal winner, G. Shelby "Buddy" Friedrichs, Jr., was elected to the Intercollegiate Hall of Fame in Annapolis, Maryland in 1984.

Another championship for the South: Brodie Cobb of the Pass Christian Yacht Club in Mississippi prevailed over a tough field of twenty-three competitors in USYRU's singlehanded sailing championship, to win the George O'Day trophy. Larchmont Yacht Club hosted the regatta, sailed on Long Island Sound in August 1984 in Lasers supplied by Laser International. In second place was Geoff Moore of East Greenwich, Rhode Island, and Henry Filter of Montgomery,

Ohio was third. Participants represented the eight USYRU areas, the Intercollegiate Yacht Racing Association and the U. S. Women's and Youth singlehanded events.

Luis Tonizzo's 345-foot *City of Slidell* was the first monohull in Class IV to finish the Observer/Europe Singlehanded Trans-Atlantic race in 1984 ahead of fifteen other boats in his class. It took twenty days, seven hours and forty minutes to sail from Newport, Rhode Island to Plymouth, England. Tonizzo is a member of the Tammany Yacht Club in Slidell, Louisiana on Lake Pontchartrain.

THE HANDICAP CLASS

The Handicap Class is one of the largest in the SYC fleet. As the name implies, it is racing with handicap (time allowance).

The class comprises the larger boats designed for offshore racing. At first, the class was known as the Handicap Cruising Class. Later, the word cruising was dropped. During its first few years of racing, all boats used the Cruising Club of America (CCA) ratings. Then most boats sailed with the International Offshore Rule (IOR) ratings because they were more acceptable throughout the world. The IOR became less popular with those boat owners other than those owning the latest designs. The IOR became the rule for "Grand Prix."

Increased enthusiasm among club members for deep water racing brought about organization of this class. It got started in 1959 with a push from Commodore Oliver Counce and soon thereafter had mushroomed to more than 100 boats.

Formation and growth of the Handicap Class was largely due to the work by such ardent sailors as Charles Cary, Herbert O'Donnell, Warren Nolan, Jack Dane, Moreland Hogan, William Ricciuti, Robert Nelson, Oliver Counce, and W. Horace Williams, Jr., who was responsible for the new measurement rule. This group, all of whom were boat owners, worked closely to promote more racing and cruising as one class but they recruited new members and worked with them in bringing new boats to New Orleans.

The Handicap Class probably is the most active class within the SYC. They generally start more boats in regattas than any other class and sail each season as many or more races than the other classes.

The intense rivalry in this class is reminiscent of the old days of the big cabin sloops when members regularly brought in new craft to challenge *Susie B.* and *Seawanhaka*. The Handicap Class is one of the few classes in which SYC owned craft are likely to find capable competition from other GYA clubs along the coast, particularly Pensacola, Gulfport, and Biloxi.

In the more popular Performance Handicap Rule Fleet (PHRF) class there were two divisions. In Class A and in fleet the winner was *Patricia*, the C&C 34 sailed by Pensacola's Dr. Lindsay Riddle and his son, Hunter. Second in Class A was the C&C 35 *Defiance* sailed by Gulfport's Tisdale and Collins. Third in A went to the new S2, *Rooma Zoom Zoom*, owned by Pontchartrain Yacht Club's Joe Bishop. In the PHRF fleet, the Class A boats dominated. The first five were *Patricia, Defiance, Rooma Zoom Zoom, Impetuous*, a Tartan 37 sailed by Pontchartrain's Jim Lane, and *Stella Maris*.

In an interview with one of SYC's old timers, Julian Richards, an avid SYC skipper in offshore racing, sports reporter for *The Times-Picayune/The States-Item* Andrea Kingsmill had this to say about the skipper of *Detente*:

> It was Richards' competitive nature, along with his keen foresight, to assemble a topnotch crew, that won *Detente* four trophies in the 1984 SORC "Battle of Champions" in February 1984. Richards' modified version of a Peterson 43, a proven winner, finished first in its class and tenth in a fleet of 82 high-tech production racing yachts. The official record was 1-5-4-6-1-3.
>
> The boats sailed from Florida's Gulf Coast to Atlantic Coast, then on to the Bahamas during chilly weather that didn't let up until the sailors headed east. Quoting Richards, "In no other race, with the exception of the America's Cup, can you find such intense competition and first-rate sailors. The SORC is the Super Bowl of Sailing. You compete against only the best.
>
> And the best to Richards was *Detente* and its crew of outstanding sailors. Richards had every reason to be awed by his crew. They are, by any measure, truly awesome—the best in the field, a team that can race and win the big race.
>
> Making up the formidable crew were skippers Tom Blackaller of San Francisco, California, a former defender helmsman in the America's Cup; John Dane III of Southern Yacht Club in New Orleans, a Soling national champion; and Buddy Melges of Zenda, Wisconsin, a two-time Star boat champion and an Olympic gold medal winner. Other ex-America's Cup sailors included navigator Peter Stalkus, Newport, R. I., Hank Stuart, New York City; and Kyle Smith, a member of the crew of *Freedom* and *Courageous*. Also aboard was Tommy Dreyfus of New Orleans, the boat builder who built *Detente*—the price $200,000.

Other members of Richards' crew who were involved in some of his racing were New Orleanians Al Gooch, Mark LeBlanc, and Hjalmer Breit, Jim Kinsey of Fort Myers, Florida, David Hulse from

San Francisco, California, and Tony O'Brien from Detroit, Michigan.

Southern Yacht Club's Prieur Leary, Jr. finished second overall and second in class A in the 1984 Rolex Swan World Cup in Sardinia, Italy. Leary and his crew of New Orleanians Douglas Black, Tommy Coleman, Bob Edmondson, Bill Everett, Al Gooch, and Rick McMillan raced *Medeis*, a Swan 46 designed by the noted naval architect German Frers.

In 1984 the Southern Yacht Club cosponsored the inaugural Key West race with the Singing River Yacht Club of Pascagoula, Mississippi. *Heavy Metal* won the Pascagoula to Key West race, a distance of 520 miles. In a fleet of nineteen boats, George Rogers' *Creekmore*, a 60-footer, won Class A and fleet. John Levert's F&C 44-footer *Evangeline* took the Class B honor, and V. J. Kurgweb's Gulfstar 44-footer *More Kayos* took first in Cruising Class. *Heavy Metal* also took IOR Class A in a near-perfect trade wind breeze.

The '84 Gulf Ocean Racing Circuit was sailed in beautiful weather, unlike the '83 series. This year the fleet was divided into an Offshore Division, sailed under IOR, and the Inshore Division, sailed inside the barrier islands under the PHRF rule.

In the eight-boat IOR the winner was the Chance-designed 40-footer, *Masquerade*. She was sailed by Dave and Jo Dunham of the Southern Yacht Club to consistent finishes of 2-1-2-2. They received the Sir Thomas J. Lipton Memorial trophy at a festive awards presentation at the host Gulfport Yacht Club. Runner-up was *Gauntlet*, a 45-foot Kaufman design, sailed by Buddy Friedrichs and John Meade, also of SYC. Third place went to Pensacola's Joe Kennicott with his Hood One-Ton, *Hubbub*.

In 1984 the Southern Yacht Club played host to the Mid-Winter Sports Association's fiftieth anniversary. Winning the "race of champions" in this historic Sugar Bowl Regatta was the team from the Pensacola Yacht Club—Chuck Barnes, skipper, with Steve Bellows and Jack Crane navigating the 19-foot Flying Scot through layers of light fog. In a tie-breaker between the Pontchartrain Yacht Club (Greg Reardon, skipper, and crewmen Thomas Baker and Brian Farrell) and Bay-Waveland Yacht Club (Bubby Eagan, skipper, and crewmen Corky Hadden and Liz Merrifield), Bay-Waveland won second place, having defeated Pontchartrain in two out of three races.

There were many close calls at the finish lines which were ably handled with the cooperation of the New Orleans Yacht Club race committeemen. In the record-breaking entry, there were eight handicap classes and seventeen one-design fleets sailed on the weekend after a week of intercollegiate races. It was estimated that over 500 sailors were on the race courses of Lake Pontchartrain. One of the finishes was a heartthrob for me as my son, Jack Scheib, Jr., barely won his first Sugar Bowl trophy after thirty years of sailing. He skippered a Pearson 26 owned by George Durant, who crewed for Jack with another George, George Hill.

At the Banquet of Champions, Flurry Normann received the Janet Lorber Memorial trophy as the outstanding skipperette in 1984. Johnny Lovell won the McCloskey Junior trophy as the outstanding junior, and Beau LeBlanc got the Mariner Trophy as the outstanding crew in 1984.

The Janet Lorber Memorial Trophy is awarded each year to the most outstanding skipperette in the SYC. The first winner was Peggy Taylor; she was followed by Karen Furlow, Nathalie James, and Flurry Norman. Janet, who passed away in 1980, was the wife of Commodore J. F. A. "Gus" Lorber, Jr. She was an outstanding skipperette and above all a super person and my good friend. The trophy is a mounted ship's wheel. It was a gift from Janet's father, the late Commodore Richard G. Jones, to the Gulf One-Design Class of the SYC.

The year 1984 brought to a close the life of Commodore Sidney W. "Billy" Provensal, Jr. in an untimely and sudden death. He was a valued longtime member, serving a total of twelve years on the governing committee, and he was largely responsible for the extensive renovations to the club facilities during his regime. Billy was an active Gulf-One sailor and retired the Commodore Richard Jones trophy by winning the championship in 1953, 1954, and 1956. He rededicated the cup to the Star Class for the Provensal series, having changed to Star boats in later years.

At the 1985 annual meeting, with the exception of one elected official, all officers were returned to office. His term having expired, J. Fred Clerc, secretary-treasurer, was replaced by G. Arthur Seaver, Jr.

The summer of 1985 was particularly rewarding. A North American and two national champions were added to the SYC Hall of Fame. Flurry Normann and crew Sidney Charbonnet won the Laser II national championship in Dallas, Texas. Al and Jack Gooch captured the Cal-25 nationals sailed on Lake Pontchartrain and a 470 title was added to the list with Johnny Lovell and Bruce Levy's victory on the waters of San Francisco.

The race to the coast—New Orleans to Gulfport—with an entry of only fifty boats because of bad weather, was won by SYC Tommy and Larry Taggart as the overall fleet winners. In the PHRF Division A, *Acadia*, with SYC's Bert Keenan at the helm, won the trophy. Division B was won by Tom Trenchard of the New Orleans Yacht Club in *Avanti*. Division C was won by SYC George Janvier in *Overdraft II*. Tommy and Larry Taggart in their Easterly 30 *Sibony* won in the Cruiser/Racer class. In the Easterly 30s Class Sandy Davies, the invincible champion in his *Windigo II*, was the winner. Arthur Wynne, Jr. captured the trophy in the non-spinnaker class.

In the 1985 Gulfport to Pensacola ocean race *Gauntlet*, skippered by owners Buddy Friedrichs and John Meade, accomplished the unbelievable feat of winning for the fourth straight year. *Gauntlet* won Class A and fleet honors each beginning in 1982. In second place were Gene Walet and David Gyer out of the Gulfport Yacht Club sailing the *Big J*, a J-35. Earl J. Sonnier of SYC was third, sailing *Bolt*, a Carter One-Ton.

In the IOR results, an old-time skipper's name appeared, Morris Newman, still going strong sailing his Ranger 29, *Schuss*. Morris had sailed in the first long-distance race fifty-one years before.

When the Cal-25 national event, hosted by Southern Yacht Club, was sailed on Lake Pontchartrain in 1985, co-skippers Jack and Al Gooch held off assaults from five other local sailors and four crews from the East and West coasts to win the championship. Other local skippers were, Arthur Seaver, Jr. who finished fourth, Fred Dymond, fifth, Jack Gordon, sixth, Stan Chiocchio tenth, and David Morgan from the New Orleans Yacht Club, who finished ninth.

Another group of many skippers won the Junior Lipton regatta for the SYC, sailing out of the New Orleans Yacht Club, also on Lake Pontchartrain. They were Andy Lovell, Robert Normann, Philip Rawlins, skippers, and crewmen Sid Choe, Michael James, and Barton Jahncke, Jr. Biloxi Yacht Club was second with Mobile Yacht Club third.

The Southern Yacht Club won the coveted Sir Thomas J. Lipton trophy when it was victorious in the 1985 Lipton regatta held at the Bay-Waveland Yacht Club, where the usual enthusiasts from all GYA yacht clubs were gathered to boost their club in this annual championship event, and where the usual hospitality was extended by Commodore Frank Allen, Vice-Commodore Basil Kennedy, and their terrific committeemen and women.

The team representing the SYC was composed of J. Dwight LeBlanc, III, Daniel B. Killeen, Jr., Scotty Sonnier, and Keith Crum, all skippers, and crewmen Beau LeBlanc, Greg and Preston Christman, and Steve McNair. Bay-Waveland Yacht Club was second with the Pontchartrain Yacht Club third and Gulfport Yacht Club fourth among twenty-one boats out of the twenty-six GYA yacht clubs participating. Bay-Waveland's top skippers, Marc and Bubby Eagan, had just returned from Riverside, Connecticut, where they won the championship division of both the Junior and Senior Flying Scot North American championships.

The 1985 Lipton Regatta was sailed in spite of the approaching Hurricane Elena, which did considerable damage to the Gulf Coast, completely destroying the Singing River Yacht Club at Pascagoula, Mississippi. Once again, these yachtsmen, survivors all, will be called to task for the rebuilding process.

Another survivor of another hurricane which approached the coast line a few weeks prior to Elena was Brody Cobb of the SYC, a student at the University of Texas in Austin, who won the O'Day trophy for the USYRU men's single-handed championship. The series was sailed in the Sunfish Class. He won over Paul Jon Patin by one half point. Patin was from the Sayville Yacht Club in New York. Scott Harrison of the U. S. Naval Academy in Annapolis, Maryland was third.

The Southern Yacht Club was the scene of yacht racing events of the National Sports Festival on June 21-29, 1985, an off-year event sponsored by the U. S. Olympic Committee. Sixteen teams were invited. The yachting contingent included thirty-two sailors aboard four boats from the 1984 470 Class Olympic Trials, four from the 1985 Intercollegiate championship which took place in early June, four from the 1985 Women's championship, and four from the U. S. Youth's championship. The Southern Yacht Club was represented by Keith Andrews, Sidney Charbonnet, and Flurry Normann. SYC committeemen were Doug Weber, Natalie James, Richard Kammer, Harry Chapman, and Byron Gorman.

The Olympic Torch, which symbolizes the spirit that prevails during the famous games, was brought to the SYC immediately prior to the opening of the National Sports Festival's yachting regatta in June 1985. Receiving the Torch were Flurry Normann and her crew Sidney Charbonnet. The SYC hosts for the regatta were Byron

Gorman, former Commodore Herbert O'Donnell, president of the SYC Olympic Committee, and Harry Chapman.

The Women's Division in the 470 class has been added to the Olympic program and here to campaign for the '88 Olympics were the best in the field. Also, the best youths were on Lake Pontchartrain.

The gold medalists were Meredith Adams and Amy Wardell of Newport, Rhode Island. Winning the silver medals were Bill Draheim of Austin, Texas and Keith Andrews of SYC. Heather Gregg of South Harwich, Massachusetts and Julie Starkweather of Riverside, Connecticut, won the bronze medals. Presenting the awards was SYC's Shelby Friedrichs, Jr., the 1968 Olympic gold medalist skipper in the Dragon Class.

The National Sports Festival VI held in 1985 at Baton Rouge, Louisiana was the last U. S. competition under that name. Beginning with the 1986 event in Houston, Texas, the meet will be known as the U. S. Olympic Festival. "This is a special event," said U. S. Olympic President Robert H. Helmick of the thirty-four-sports, twelve-day amateur extravaganza, "and we want to recognize it as such." The festival is held in each of the three years between Olympic Games for the athletes seeking berths on the U. S. Olympic and Pan-American teams. Helmick said, "It keeps alive the Olympic flame in the U. S. in the years between the Games."

Members of the SYC and the friends of Beau LeBlanc are breathlessly waiting for the verdict as to whether Beau will be accepted as a crew member of the 1987 America's Cup entry in Australia, where that beautiful trophy is resting, having been removed from the New York Yacht Club in 1983. Commodore of the New York Yacht Club, Emil "Bus" Mosbacher, Jr., and the other members of his team, Chuck Kirsch, chairman, Richard DeVos, Walter Cronkite, and John Kolius, skipper, are making an all-out effort to bring back the America's Cup.

The members of the new *America II* march are anxious to return this prized possession from Perth, Australia to its former resting place in the New York Yacht Club. It is estimated that twelve million dollars will be spent in training, technology, and research to bring back this valued trophy—formerly raced for 10,000 guineas, that figure being the equivalent of $500,000 today. Sparkman and Stephen, which had designed a record-breaking six defenders of the *America's Cup*, has been hired to design *America II* with which the New York Yacht Club will challenge the defending champion.

The winner of the 1985 Pascagoula, Mississippi to Key West, Florida race, for the second time in so many years, was *Heavy Metal*. This handsome yacht is the "brainchild" of George Rogers, III, a young Mobile, Alabama business executive. She was designed by Lee Creekmore of Miami with an elevating keel and rudder, a unique feature that allows the boat to sail in shallow water.

Named for her steel hull and keel, and not the rock band, *Heavy Metal* is the largest offshore yacht between New Orleans and Pensacola, Florida. She is the same length as some 12-meter yachts in the 60-64-foot range that are sailed in the America's Cup competition.

In an interview by *The Times-Picayune/The States Item* sports staff reporter, Andrea Kingsmill, George Rogers, III stated that "he enjoyed sailing in the races of the SORC" (Southern Offshore Racing Circuit) and said "of course I always race to win, but I'm not going to eat peanut butter sandwiches for five straight days to do it. I like to have fun when I am racing." In March 1986, Rogers competed in a race from Miami to Montego Bay, Jamaica.

COMMODORE MAURICE J. HARTSON III—1986

At the annual meeting held in December 1985, another junior skipper rose from the ranks to be elected commodore of the Southern Yacht Club, Maurice J. "Bubby" Hartson, III. Bubby's sailing career began as a crew for his uncle and former commodore of the SYC, Arthur "Juby" Wynne in the Lightning Class. With the other crew member, J. Gilbert "Jack" Scheib, Jr., this threesome won many Lightning Class titles. The commodore was also co-owner of the celebrated *Tiara* that won the famous Isla de Mujeres ocean race in 1965 and many other handicap races. Serving with him were John B. Levert, vice-commodore; G. Arthur Sevar, III, rear commodore; and Lawrence Taggart, secretary-treasurer.

CONCLUSION

Throughout the pages of this book it is evident that yachting has always been a family-oriented sport. It knows no age limit and the minimal cost of small boats makes sailboat racing a favorite pastime for many families.

The time-honored record of yachting is an unbroken chronicle of sportsmanship in the truest sense, seldom targeted by gamblers, an invasion fortunately prohibited by the rules enforced by individual yacht clubs as well as by the "watchdog" of the sport, the United States Yacht Racing Union (USYRU).

The USYRU is an organization composed of capable leaders and knowledgeable yachtsmen who have been successful, so far, in defending sailboat racing against its two most deadly enemies—commercialism and professionalism. It is hoped that this institution will continue in its efforts to uphold the tradition for which the founders dedicated their lives and fortunes.

We are grateful for another prestigious organization which has been the epitome of yachting since it was founded in 1844, the New York Yacht Club, the patriarch of yacht clubs in the U. S. Its commitment to yachting traditions is the same today as it was in 1844. It has survived vicious criticism and many vicissitudes to maintain the traditions of integrity, dignity, and good sportsmanship to keep yachting the "noblest of sports." When Clifford D. Mallory, commodore of the New York Yacht Club, was a visitor to the Southern Yacht Club in 1926, he promoted the sport of sailboat racing after the decline caused by World War I. "We must create and nurse our 'junior yachtsmen,' teach them the science of the sailrace sport, and nurture them. You and I know how we hungered, when we were little lads, for recognition from the sailors we worshipped. We'd have, in our ignorance, and ambition, spent a whole day in trying to bail out the centerboard case, if they'd have set us to do it, and never have complained, even if our backs were breaking and our arms aching."

There is one aspect on the national yachting scene which is disturbing, the de-emphasis of the long-standing tradition of "Corinthianism" in sailing competition. This is particularly evident in yachting magazines, which are increasingly becoming trade magazines for the industry. In reporting a major race, it was always traditional to give the name of the boat, the owner, and the owner's yacht club. Today, the name of the boat receives due credit, but the owner is casually mentioned and the yacht club very seldom, although, every major yachting event is still sponsored and conducted by a yacht club and every participant (registered) must be a member of a recognized yacht club. Never missing from these reports, however, is the name of the designer, the manufacturer, the sailmaker, the number of so and so's winches on board, and which semi-pros comprise the crew.

Today our commitment to yacht racing is no less strong than that of our ancestors. Our heritage is rich. It consists of able-bodied skippers and crews, both men and women, with thousands of miles of saltwater sailing under hundreds of keels. It dates back to the "skimmering dishes" of the 1850s, and comes down from the "sandbaggers" to the fiberglass hulls of today, with glorious years between spent in sailing Biloxi cats, cabin sloops, schooners, sharpies, and craft of every design.

There are names to remember, such as *Undine, Eliza Riddle, Coralie* and *Pilgrim*, winners of regattas in 1849; *Metawee*, most famous of the early 21-footers, the days of the *Cadillac, Calypso, Cricket* and the *Invader*, followed by *Robin Hood IV, Maid Marion, Sis*, and *Circe*. Then there were the graceful highmasted schooners *Windjammer, Mallard, Bonnie Doon* and *Shellback*.

There will be many others whose names will be fondly recalled years from now. There will be new hands on the tiller and new names on the transom, new and possibly better. Let us hope that they will take pride in the lengthy tradition of the Southern Yacht Club and carry it on to new and greater heights.

The Southern Yacht Club is proud of its own recorded achievements and prouder of the individual contributions made by generations of yachtsmen. Perhaps some of these are less perceptible, but the hands of all participants have shaped events that keep our heritage and cement a common bond of friendship and fellowship with yachtsmen of other clubs. It is the substance of Southern sailors. In it we take great pride.

I would like to take from context an article which appeared in the seventy-fifth anniversary of the SYC souvenir program in 1924, written by one of the old-time sailors Emile Baumgarden:

> To the "old guard," those whose misty memories go back to the golden days of *Silence, Nepenthe* and *Susie B*, it will give more than one nostalgic moment. Little imagination will be required on their part to recreate the stirring scenes of long, long ago. For the skippers and crews of ghostly craft resting these many years in Davy Jones' locker, will surely return and hover for a moment over the historic waters of old Pontchartrain.
>
> And, as they rejoice and pay homage to a never-to-be-forgotten past, cheered by the thought that they have helped carry the torch through seventy-five glorious years, the successors of that valiant band meeting for the first time at Pass Christian in 1849, may well feel proud of their work. They have not failed. Nay, the verdict of their revered predecessors would be "Well done!"

And now that the sails are furled away and the long race from 1924 to 1986 is over, there is no doubt that the verdict of those revered predecessors would be the same, "Well done!" However, let it be our hope that the years contained in this log are but a prelude to bigger and better years of the great sport of yachting.

IN MEMORIAM

In memory of the many men and women who have devoted their time and energy to keep yachting the "noblest of sports":

>Some time at eve when the tide is low,
>   I shall slip my mooring and sail away,
>   With no response to the friendly hail
>   Of kindred craft in the busy day,
>   In the silent hush of the Twilight pale,
>When the night stoops down to embrace the day,
>   And the voices call in the waters' flow -
>   Some time at eve when the tide is low,
>   I shall slip my mooring and sail away.
>
>Through the purpling shadows that darkly trail
>   O'er the ebbing tide of the Unknown Sea
>   I shall fare me away, with a dip of sail
>   And a ripple of waters to tell the tale
>   Of a lonely voyager, sailing away
>   To the Mystic Isles where at anchor lay
>   The crafts of those who have sailed before
>   O'er the Unknown Sea to the Unseen Shore.
>
>   A few who have watched me sail away
>   Will miss my craft from the busy day;
>   Some friendly barks that were anchored near,
>   Some loving souls that my heart held dear,
>   In moorings sheltered from storm or gale,
>   And greeted the friends who have sailed before
>   O'er the Unknown Sea to the Unseen Shore.

Elizabeth Clark Hardy

CHAPTER XXIII

Yacht Clubs of Alabama

THE BUCCANEER YACHT CLUB

The Buccaneer Yacht Club is made up of men who dream dreams and then set about to make them come true. Three young Mobilians had a dream while sailing in their new boat, *Buccaneer*, on Mobile Bay in the summer of 1928, to organize sailing and erect a yacht club. Through determination and hard work their dream was realized.

On June 2, 1928, amid the cheers of the enthusiasts who had answered the neatly engraved invitation to the proposed launching of the good ship *Buccaneer* at the Acme Boat Works on the River of Mobile, Norman Nelson, acting as toastmaster for the occasion, gave the toast as Old Glory was raised and the thirty-foot cabin sloop, gaff rigged and carrying two jib sails, slipped quietly down into the waters of the river. The proud owners in the syndicate were Leon Delaplaine, Foster Pfleger, and Ben Mayfield. The three skippers joined with four other yachtsmen, Norman Nelson, Barthold Nodop, Sledge Hoffman, and John E. Mandeville to hold a meeting at the home of Ben Mayfield. A constitution and by-laws were adopted. A chairman presiding at the meeting called for the election of officers. Leon Delaplaine was elected commodore, Norman Nelson, vice-commodore, Foster Pfleger, treasurer, and John E. Mandeville, secretary. Their motto, "One for all and all for one," was chosen, the skull and crossbones being decided as the club emblem. The club colors were black and white; the name selected was "Buccaneer."

The membership grew from seven to twenty-five in a short time. About December 1, 1928 the club rooms on Dauphin Street were abandoned and an entire two-story house leased at 57 South Joachim Street. Up until this time the club had no house on the Bay of Mobile. Activities were on the par, however, races being held off Arlington Pier with the small fleet. On December 15 a boat building campaign was begun, the purpose of this campaign being to raise money to begin the construction of three new Fish Class boats.

The Buccaneers, seeing a clear path ahead of them for making a big yacht club, began looking for a permanent clubhouse site on Mobile Bay. At that time Mr. W. J. Barrett was constructing a summer resort at Alba Beach, about a quarter of a mile from the mouth of Dog River. He offered a site to the club, which was accepted, and construction of the clubhouse was begun immediately by him.

The new yacht club was built over the water. It was a two-story building at the end of a one thousand-foot wharf, with wide galleries all the way around on both floors. The first floor was used as an assembly hall with ladies' lounge in the south end. Adjoining this was the ladies' dressing room. In the north end was the place where the boys "resail" the races. Adjoining this was the office. The second floor was the dormitory.

The night of May 16, 1929 the members of the Buccaneer Yacht Club and their friends gathered at the Country Club to trip the light fantastic and celebrate the launching of the three new Fish Class boats. This event took place on May 18 at the Altice Marine Ways amid another big celebration. The sloops were christened *Silver Fish*, *Flying Fish*, and *Sail Fish*, all names of fish found in local waters.

At the beginning of the 1929 sailing season the Mobile Athletic Association offered the club a loving cup to be presented to the skipper winning the highest number of points during the season.

The first annual election of officers was held on May 30, 1929. This election resulted in placing S. Springertam at the helm of the yacht club as commodore and Ben Mayfield as vice-commodore. The other officers, Pfleger and Mandeville, were reelected. At this meeting there was also elected a new officer, fleet captain, whose duty it was to care for the club's fleet.

Mr. Springertam was reelected commodore for 1930. He had done extensive sailing and racing in waters from Pensacola, Florida to New Orleans, Louisiana. Mr. J. O. Delaplaine was elected vice-commodore for the year. The name Delaplaine has been among the list of officers since the club's organization, "Mr. Jake" being the father of Leon, the first commodore and organizer of the Buccaneer Yacht Club. Mr. Claborne Schley was elected secretary and treasurer.

The *Resolute*, with an overall length of 390 feet and a beam of 55 feet, constructed of Oregon fir to carry her approximately 45,000 square feet of sails, with four king-sized solid fir, 150 foot masts, was ordered to Mobile in 1929 by her New York agents to pick up a cargo. When she arrived the cargo was not waiting and shortly afterwards the *Resolute* was ordered to the Industrial Canal in New Orleans to be decommissioned. The Buccaneer Yacht Club decided to purchase the *Resolute*.

After acquiring the ship, the Buccaneer Yacht Club converted her into a clubhouse. Club members armed with brushes and buckets turned to below decks and gave the *Resolute* a fore-to-aft scrubbing and painting, then with a heave-a-ho and nary a bottle of rum, the Buccaneers took turns walking the capstan, taking in some 120 fathoms of heavy anchor chain. The *Resolute* was towed down river and tied up alongside Arlington Pier. A dredge had dug a slip at the end of Arlington Pier and with the ballast removed and at mean high tide the ship was humped into the slip and made fast. The *Resolute* officially became the Buccaneer Yacht Clubhouse in May 1930.

Some time later, the *Resolute* began to leak badly and a special slip was dredged at the end of Arlington Beach into which she was moved. Shortly thereafter a disastrous fire broke out, which badly damaged most of the after quarters in the ship and destroyed the club's records, ship's log, and all the club's trophies. Undaunted by the tragedy, the club's members made the necessary repairs to overcome the effects of fire and leakage, the main deck was completely decked over, and activities grew.

Social events aboard the *Resolute* during the 1930s were numerous, owing mainly to the progressive spirit of the club. Every year at the time of the opening regatta, a formal ball was held, which became one of the highlights of Mobile's social calendar. Dances were held on deck under the stars throughout the summer months, usually each Saturday night nearest to a full moon; these dances became a very popular event of the club. The writer experienced one of these moonlit nights at a black-tie Saturday night event, which was most enjoyable. The party was given in conjunction with the Gulf Yachting Association's annual meeting and opening regatta. Other social events included afternoon dances, "Slack Party," "Shipwreck Party," "Pirates Costume Ball," and many others.

The Buccaneer Yacht Club joined the Gulf Yachting Association in 1932 and in 1934 was the proud winner of the prestigious trophy, the Sir Thomas J. Lipton Cup, in a series of races at the Pensacola Yacht Club. The yacht club prospered and in 1935 owned the clubhouse and appurtenances outright, along with a total of six Fish Class sloops and a motor tender. In the years following, the yacht club developed into one of the most outstanding yacht clubs on the Gulf Coast.

Along came World War II and the building of Brookley Air Force Base in Mobile. For a time the members of the Buccaneer Yacht Club were granted special passes to visit their clubhouse, but by 1942 she became a warehouse in which supplies were stored. Shortly afterwards the government took over the *Resolute*. The members of the Buccaneer Yacht Club were forced to vacate and a room was rented on St. Francis Street in 1943, which served as a meeting and club room. During this very trying period the Mobile Yacht Club and the Fairhope Yacht Club, both located on Mobile Bay, very kindly assisted the BYC. They made their facilities available by docking the Buccaneer's Fish Class boats and helping in running the racing events.

After World War II, in May 1945, negotiations were started to purchase the Foster property for a clubhouse. In May of 1946, the Buccaneer Yacht Club members entered their three Fish Class sloops in a race at Fairhope Yacht Club, the first since 1943. However, the membership continued to be active and in November of 1947, with a total of 241 names on the roster, the board voted to authorize the purchase of the Foster property and the new clubhouse got under construction.

With everything running smoothly, in the meeting of September 1948 four new Fish Class sloops with sails were purchased, at a cost of $1,575 each. In this same month, which is hurricane season in the South, a vicious storm wrecked the wharf and sailing facilities. Afterwards, it was thought that digging a channel would be the most practical thing to do, but it was not the most economical and so the wharf was repaired.

The Buccaneer Yacht Club celebrated its twentieth anniversary in October 1948 with a highly spirited and well-attended dance. The members continued to struggle to keep their club alive, despite the many adversities.

In 1958 the club chartered a bus to take the Lipton Cup team and its many followers down to the St. Petersburg Yacht Club, where the races for the Sir Thomas J. Lipton trophy were being held. In 1959 the first annual long-distance race to Dauphine Isle was initiated. It continues to be a popular event on the race schedule. In 1960 the club held its first "Old Timers'" Regatta. The clubhouse renovations were completed in 1966, after the swimming pool was installed in 1957, at a cost of $6,000. The bar and lounge were added in 1960, and the channel and harbor construction improvements were finished in 1966. With everything in shipshape order, the Buccaneer Yacht Club anxiously and proudly hosted the 1966 opening regatta and annual meeting of the Gulf Yachting Association, which was a huge success.

Pioneer members of BYC are:

Charles J. Barter, Jr.	B. F. Mangold
Brad Bowron	P. O. McAllister
Fred Clarke	Thomas P. McArdle
C. Gibson	W. P. Rees
Joe Hall	Phil Sargent
Henry Izard	Paul Schmohl
Bruce Johnson	Roy L. Sellers
Johnnie Lynch	L. H. Thietje
	Tom Wall

Three Buccaneer Yacht Club members have been honored by the Gulf Yachting Association with the distinction of being elected commodore of the organization: Commodores Fred Clarke (1950), Foster P. Pfleger (1966), and Roy L. Sellers (1981).

Much of the history of the Buccaneer Yacht Club was submitted by John E. Mandeville.

FAIRHOPE YACHT CLUB

The area in which the Fairhope Yacht Club is located is considered one of the most historical in the history of yachting in the South. As early as 1852 a long-distance race is recorded in the minutes of the Southern Yacht Club as having started from Lake Pontchartrain and ended at Battles Wharf on Mobile Bay, just a short distance from where the present-day Fairhope Yacht Club is situated at the foot of the bluffs overlooking Mobile Bay. A more picturesque scene cannot be found any place in the South. In addition to the race, also mentioned is the regatta dance that followed at the nearby Grand Hotel, on the lawn of which was fought a bloodless duel between a New Orleanian and a Mobilian over the hand of a fair lady.

Mobilians were very prominent in racing circles and the names of many famous yachts and yachtsmen appear in the schedule of early racing on the Gulf Coast. Next to New Orleans, Mobile had one of the most social sets in the South. The names of socialites from this area were always listed among those present at the Mardi Gras balls held in New Orleans. Likewise, the debutantes of New Orleans were in attendance at the Mobile balls. It is also a matter of record that Mobile held Mardi Gras parades before they were held in New Orleans.

There were three yacht clubs built on Mobile Bay over the years. The Mobile Yacht Club organized in 1847 was the first. It became extinct after several years, although the yachtsmen continued to sail in races. Then the Eastern Shore Yacht Club was organized in 1920. It was later dissolved and the Mobile Yacht Club was reactivated. The Buccaneer Yacht Club originated in 1928. There remains today the two, Mobile and Buccaneer Yacht Clubs.

The Fairhope Yacht Club of Fairhope, Alabama, was organized in October 1939. The meetings were held in a small clubhouse, ten by twelve feet, located on the present yacht club site. The membership increased and activities grew, until a fine clubhouse was built, which is considered one of the best on the Gulf Coast. The club's founders were: Otto Wadewitz, first commodore; Herbert Forster, vice-commodore; Marvin Berglin, secretary; Robert Faulkenburg and Dr. C. J. Godard, treasurers. The governing board consisted of Walter Forster, John Greggs, R. Roy Meyers, L. W. Schnitzer, Rudolph E. Tuveson, and Homer Vincent.

The Fairhope Yacht Club joined the Gulf Yachting Association the same year it was originated, in 1939. With a fleet of six Fish Class sloops, the members were very active in interclub racing and have entered every Lipton Regatta since the club was founded. Two members of the FYC have been commodores of the Gulf Yachting Association: Jack W. Bonnell in 1956 and T. Cooper Van Antwerp in 1969.

The Fairhope Yacht Club has been host to many national events. The USYRU Finals for the Women's North American Sailing Championship for the Adams trophy were sailed at the Fairhope Yacht Club, with one of its members "Buzzy" Van Antwerp, wife of Commodore Van Antwerp, as chairman of the event. "Buzzy" was the Area D Adams Cup representative of USYRU. She is an expert skipper herself, having won many championships in the Rhodes 19 Class, and is still going strong.

Another champion of the Fairhope Yacht Club among many was Commodore Ed Overton. Ed's sailing days began when he and a few other Mobilians organized the Eastern Shore Yacht Club. As commodore of the ESYC, he invited the yachtsmen of the first Sir Thomas J. Lipton Cup race sailed on Lake Pontchartrain to Mobile for the inaugural meeting of the Gulf Yachting Association. Overton was elected commodore of the Gulf Yachting Association in 1926.

Having purchased the famous *Robin Hood IV* from the owners, J. Ben Ravannack and Leslie P. Beard of the Southern Yacht Club, Ed went on to win many more races, although the *Robin Hood IV*, when bought in 1935, had become almost obsolete after winning fifty-one of fifty-four races. Overton was also a participant in a St. Petersburg to Havana race.

When the 21-footers were no longer a class in which to contend, Ed Overton turned to the Lightning Class, where his accomplishments were many. He served as vice-president and also treasurer of the Lightning Class Association. He participated in every Lightning regatta until he became disabled.

The Fairhope Yacht Club had its first National champion in 1965 when Jack Glover won the Rhodes 19 National championship on Long Island Sound. In 1966 Tom Torbert won this championship. In 1967 Dr. Bob Stine, with his wife, Mary, and son Chip as crew, won the Rhodes 19 National championship sailing in Chicago. The Fairhope Yacht Club had a large fleet of Rhodes 19s.

THE MOBILE YACHT CLUB

The waters of Mobile Bay have been and still are the home waters of a number of yacht clubs. As early as January 1, 1839 a boat race was reported in the files of *The Mobile Register*; "New Year's Boat Race—The Wave and Savage have made up a race to take place this afternoon in front of the city—the prize, a silver pitcher to cost $100. A well contested race may be expected."

The first Mobile Yacht Club was organized in 1847. The first of the club's races took place the year the group organized. Sailing was intermingled with pigeon shoots in those days. Added to the pleasures of sailing was the launch run from the mainland to the island where the first clubhouse was located across the Mobile River opposite the foot of St. Francis Street.

In the archives at Oakleigh there is a silver pitcher made by J. Conning and won by the sloop *Joseph Forsythe*, sailed by C. Davidson and James Allen. It was a first prize in a Mobile regatta held at Howard's on July 30, 1849.

Regattas seemed to be the rage during the time of the first yacht club, and visitors came from all along the Gulf Coast to see them. One young lady whose name was Kate wrote a letter to Miss Rebecca Robinson on August 22, 1849, expressing her delight at a regatta, stating, "The regatta was rather exciting. The *Oriole* came over perfectly laden to see the sailing, but not many stayed for the dance as Mr. C. did not announce there was to be a ball. Fortunately we all dressed a little more in case there would be one."

The balance of her letter was quite amusing: "The prizes for the races were to be given that evening, which was the best part of the entertainment. Mr M. behaved badly. He was quite intoxicated and went up to the speaker, bowing backwards and sideways. When he reached him he said, 'Ladies and Gentlemen, you perceive I have a slit in my coat, but no difference.' Then instead of receiving the little pitcher that was presented to him he reached for the $150 one and waited. It was taken from him. It struck us the more because the other gentleman who came up for his prize received it in so gentlemanly a manner. The Brig boat, *Undine*, was so superior to the rest that the others would not sail with her. She will be changed, she will be repainted and run at the different watering places as regattas are all the rage."

The first yacht club lasted twelve years, the Civil War intervening. After the War between the States, the Magnolia Yacht Club was organized, but the Reconstruction period made it too difficult to continue and the club, which had been started on Mobile River by twenty Confederate veterans, lasted only five years. At that time all races were held on Pole Cat Bay and Mobile Bay. In 1882 a second Mobile Yacht Club was formed and in 1891 a "Constitution and Sailing Instructions of the Mobile Yacht Club" was adopted. The flag approved was triangular, with colors divided blue, white and red.

A 1903 publication by the Southern Gulf Coast Yachting Association reported:

The Mobile Yacht Club is an ornate two-story building with a pavilion at Monroe Park. It is a very neat and commodious structure and is very comfortably furnished. The walls are decorated with pictures of many of the celebrated crack yachts of the past and cup defenders. For years its membership rolls list the leading citizens of Mobile.

The club owns its own power launch, which is used in carrying the members across the river to and from the club. The annual regattas of the MYC are held off Point Clear, and are largely attended by citizens of the interior of Alabama and Mississippi, as well as those who reside along the Gulf Coast.

An addition last season to the MYC fleet was the fast cup defender, the *M.Y.C.*, which took part in all the regattas along the Gulf Coast. In addition to yachting a special feature of this club is trap shooting. There has just been completed new grounds for both blue rocks and live birds. The club gives a semi-weekly shoot; a great many of the members who take an enthusiastic interest in this sport have become splendid shots.

When the Southern Gulf Coast Yachting Association was organized in 1901, the Mobile Yacht Club was a charter member with Biloxi, Pass Christian, Bay-Waveland, and Southern Yacht Clubs—Gulfport entered a few months later.

In 1902, T. G. Bush was elected commodore of the Mobile Yacht Club. He was one of the South's leading yachtsmen and also a leading businessman, being the president of the Bush-Hall Shoe Co. He was a huntsman who had the finest horses and dogs and the finest guns and tackle. Commodore Bush owned the sloop *El Heirie*, at one time the champion half-rater of this country, formerly owned by Crane, the noted yacht designer. He was also the principal owner of the open sloop *M.Y.C.*, which was built to represent the Mobile Yacht Club in the championship races of the Southern Gulf Coast Yachting Association. His flagship was the large cabin sloop *Annie*. He later replaced her with a more modern seventy-three-foot designed boat, the *Falcon*. The designer was one of the best of the North, B. B. Crowninshield, second only to Herreshoff in reputation as a designer, and thought by some to be a more experienced man on smaller yachts. The commodore owned this boat with his brother, J. C. Bush, Jr.

Captain W. B. Curran, one of the organizers of the Mobile Yacht Club, had served as commodore, vice-commodore and secretary. He was owner of the *Zephine*, a thirty-foot fast cabin sloop, which was a sister boat to the old Southern Yacht Club's boat *Zoe*. During the summer, Captain Curran was the Commander of the *Heroine*, the steamboat that operated up and down Mobile Bay. In the *Barometer*, we find this report:

> Le Baron Lyons, the owner of the handsome naphtha launch *Venetta*, serves on the Regatta Committee of MYC. He is the President and General Manager of the Alabama Corn Mills and Vice-President and Director of the Bienville Brewing Co., also Director of the City Delivery Co. He takes a prominent part in Mobile's mystic organizations.
>
> Charles DeBriere is one of the most enthusiastic members of the MYC. He is the owner of the *Mallard*, the finest two-horse power launch. At one time he owned the finest private shooting grounds in this section. He is the proprietor of the popular restaurante on Royal Street known as "Festorazzi's Coffee Saloon."
>
> Rolf Seeberg is also a leading member of the MYC and a Director of the City Bank & Trust Co., President of the Commercial Steamship Co. and a member of the Manasses Club and also of the Biloxi Yacht Club.
>
> A. L. Mangold, the present owner of a handsome cabin launch *Madame*, has been established in the ship chandlery business at Mobile since 1887. He was at one time a boat builder.
>
> H. V. Bachelder, Chairman of the Governing Committee of the MYC, owns the naphtha launch *Syble*, and is a prominent member of the Elks, Masons, the Odd Fellows and the Commercial Club.
>
> T. H. Chamberlain, the owner of the half-rater *Vesper*, stands high in Elks circles. He is the City of Mobile's Electrician.
>
> In 1903, when J. C. Bush, Jr. was Commodore of the Mobile Yacht Club, he was also elected President of the Southern Gulf Coast Yachting Association in that same year. His flagship was the *Falcon*.
>
> D. R. Burgess is one of the owners of the 50-foot power boat *Encore*. He is the senior member of the big cotton firm of D. R. Burgess & Co., and Vice-President of the Cotton Exchange, also a member of the Chamber of Commerce, the Manasses & Athelston Clubs.
>
> E. Dorgan Ledyard, an active yachtsman, owned the *Siren*, the fast cabin sloop. He is a Director of the Cotton Exchange and a member of the well-known cotton firm of D. R. Huger & Co. Also, a member of the Athelston and Hunting and Fishing Clubs.
>
> Another active member, Captain Tom St. John, is the owner of the cat boat *Cokonocus*, the *Bertha*, the *Muscatt* and the *Este Jay*, which is a torpedo shape power boat. He is the Secretary-Treasurer and General Manager of the Eclipse Milling Co., and a member of the Chamber of Commerce, the Athelston and the Gulf Hunting and Fishing Clubs.
>
> Col. D. E. Huger, another active member, is the President of the Mobile Cotton Exchange and also a member of the New Orleans Cotton Exchange, the Liverpool Cotton Brokers Association and one of the most prominent men of the Mobile Yacht Club. For nine years he was a member of the Board of Aldermen. He was a member of the Manasses and Athelston Clubs and President of the Gulf Hunting and Fishing

Club.

Thomas L. Cook, who had charge of the construction of their club's defender the *M.Y.C.*, is one of the owners of the steam yacht *Veneta*. Cook is serving his third term as Vice-Commodore of the Mobile Yacht Club and was the club's representative to the Southern Gulf Coast Yachting Association meeting in Biloxi last year and took an active part in the framing of the racing rules. He is a member of many prominent organizations.

Frank E. Overall, the President of the Yacht Club Corporation, is one of the leading yachtsmen of Mobile and the owner of the *Scimitar* and the *Cymbal*, which he uses as a tender to the *Scimitar*. He is President of the Bay Shell Road Co., a leading real estate man and a member of the Commercial Club, Chamber of Commerce and the Athelston Club.

The following gentlemen elected to serve with Commodore Bush for the year 1903 were T. L. Cook, Vice-Commodore, L. C. Dorgan, Secretary-Treasurer, M. J. Parker, Measurer. The Directors were Messrs. H. V. Bachelder, T. G. Bush and W. H. Bryant.

The boats were few but the sailors were many. The Mobile Yacht Club was predominantly a man's club. A pinnacle was reached of lavish social elegance. However, the beautiful clubhouse was hit by the 1916 hurricane and this era of magnificence was ended. The restoration of the club was delayed until the end of World War I, when it was moved to the Eastern Shore across the bay. Reorganized by a group of twenty-six young men and named the Eastern Shore Yacht Club, the club traced its succession from the original club which had had its foundation in 1847. The remoteness of the club lent itself to romance but this was terminated with the building of the Cochran Bridge in 1927.

After the formation of the Gulf Yachting Association in 1920, the Eastern Shore Yacht Club purchased three Fish Class boats in order to participate in the big annual event, the Sir Thomas J. Lipton Regatta, and other interclub races. The Eastern Shore Yacht Club, headed by Commodore Ed. Overton won the Lipton Cup in 1921, the second year of this event. In 1926, the club tied with St. Petersburg Yacht Club for the trophy. It was in this same year that Commodore Overton of the Eastern Shore Yacht Club was elected commodore of the Gulf Yachting Association. As papers of incorporation had been obtained under the designation of the original name, the Mobile Yacht Club, in 1928, it was under that name that the Lipton Cup regatta of 1928 was won. The name Eastern Shore Yacht Club ceased. Noted Fish Class skippers in addition to Commodore Overton were Shaw

Freeman, John Shinners, J. C. Henry, Mallory Blanton, and Warren Harris. (In 1956 the Mobile Yacht Club again won the prestigious Sir Thomas J. Lipton trophy.)

In 1934 the Mobile Yacht Club moved to the western shore of Mobile Bay under the regime of Commodore Eugene Malone. The move was decided upon because the location was more accessible—the club could be reached in a fifteen-minute automobile drive from the city. The clubhouse was built out over the water and the wharf connected directly to the building. The second floor was a naturally air-conditioned dormitory for visiting yachtsmen—"no ladies allowed, just men, booze and an occasional crap game," stated the club's rule. (For many years there was a screened porch on the east face of the club until 1969, when Hurricane Camille hit, doing extensive damage to the club, and depositing the screen porch and most of the wharf and furniture in George and Millie Brothers' front yard.)

With the club now within easy reach, the membership showed an increase in activity. In addition to an active sailing program, many social affairs were held—Mobile is noted for its social functions. Among the annual events were the Christmas Ball and the masquerade party. Eddie Beauvais as a child bride and Sam Bauer as "Betty Boop" won the prizes at the 1937 masquerade party.

During the years 1935 to 1937 Commodore William J. Wall's leadership and that of his fine board members, Larry Beauvais, Jr., vice-commodore; Jerome Van Liew, secretary; Carl Torbert, treasurer; and governing board members Joe Hunt, Jack Lamey, and Sam Bauer with other committeemen, Eddie Beau, Winston Groom, Dr. Haas Zieman, Beverly Christy, John Luis Marty, Carl Kling, and E. W. Bobby Hankins, brought the club out of the red and marked the end of the depression years through which so many clubs along the coast had suffered.

On Christmas Eve in 1945 a tornado hit Mobile and the yacht club. The Star boats suffered severely as there were only two Stars left in the fleet; the owners were George Criminale and Marvin Bergman.

Late in 1929, N. Price Oliver, John E. Mandeville, Berney Sheridan, W. B. Patterson and L. W. Nobile bought three Jahncke-built Stars in New Orleans. In early February 1930 they sailed two of these boats from New Orleans 175 miles to Mobile (there were no trailers). The Mobile Bay Fleet was born on February 26, 1930 when the third boat was brought over as deck cargo on a ship.

In 1948 George Brothers bought a Star and in that same year the

Mobile Bay Star Class Fleet joined the New Orleans-Gulf Star Fleet—the charter was dated 1948. The Mobile Bay Cruising Association was organized in 1959 and in 1967 the Mobile Bay Dauphin Island Racing Association was formed with Dr. Jack R. Hays chairman. The largest races on the Gulf Coast are handled by these associations.

George Criminale is the oldest member of the Mobile Star Class Fleet. Before joining the Stars, George had been a champion Fish Class skipper from 1930 to 1933, when he bought his first Star boat, and he has been sailing with the fleet continuously to date. He holds the record for his time in sailing the longest race in the Star Class world, having sailed from the Southern Yacht Club in New Orleans to Buccaneer Yacht Club on Mobile Bay, a distance of 175 miles in thirty-three hours.

George Criminale was one of the entries in the first Star Class Mid-Winter championship sailed on Lake Pontchartrain in 1939. He sailed in four Star Class World championships. Running George Criminale a close second is another George, George Brothers, who has also remained with the fleet since 1948 and has won many championships with his faithful crew, his wife, Molly.

In 1954, George Criminale won the Turkey Creek Yacht Club Regatta in Gulfport, Mississippi and the Sportsmanship award as the best sportsman on the Gulf Coast. He was commodore of the Mobile Yacht Club in 1955 and 1956 and again in 1966 and 1967.

In 1980 the Mobile Yacht Club celebrated its fiftieth anniversary with George Criminale chairman of the evnt. Throughout the years the members of MYC have been real troopers and survivors of many disasters. The last one happened in 1979 when Hurricane Frederic devastated the yacht club; a new one was dedicated in 1980. For the opening a gala affair was held with many New Orleanians and Gulf Coast yachtsmen present.

The MYC members honored by the Gulf Yachting Association as commodores of the GYA date back to the original organization, the Southern Gulf Coast Yachting Association founded in 1901. Following is a list of their names: J. C. Bush (1902), E. B. Overton (1926), Thos. P. Kroutter (1947), Larry Beauvais, Jr. (1958), Cal Weiss (1951), and George C. Criminale (1976).

Shawn Killeen, left, winner of the Lipton Star Class trophy in the 1982 Star Class championship of the New Orleans-Gulf Star fleet, stands with his mother, Connie, and his father, Joseph L. "Buzzy" Killeen, Jr. Each of the three has won this trophy. "Buzzy" has won it thirteen times, including five consecutive years.

CHAPTER XXIV

Yacht Clubs of Florida

THE FORT WALTON YACHT CLUB

The Fort Walton Yacht Club (FWYC) in Florida is located in the heart of a resort area called Fort Walton Beach or the Miracle Strip—a 125 mile slice of the Gulf of Mexico shoreline where the dark blue waters lap onto a shore of clear sand that is almost all pure white.

The Fort Walton Yacht Club was organized in July of 1951 by a small group of local businessmen and sailing enthusiasts. Several meetings were held during early summer of '51 at the Magnolia Club, and later at the Shalimar Club, in order to organize the club on a sound basis. Probably two of the club's most enthusiastic, hardworking members were among its original founders, namely, Donald K. Kimbrell and E. W. Sudduth. However, these are just two among many.

The club's first constitution was approved on September 12, 1951 and an election of officers was held with the following results: Clifford H. Meigs, commodore; Dr. Henry Clay White, vice commodore; W. E. Duggan, rear commodore; Harry Vandergriff, fleet captain; Mrs. C. J. Yarbrough, secretary; T. J. Yarbrough, treasurer. The members of the board of directors were: Thomas E. Brooks, French Brown, Sr., Roger Clary, Robert Frazier, A. M. Hyer, Donald K. Kimbrell, Dr. R. P. Maxon, and E. W. Sudduth.

At the December 1951 annual meeting of the FWYC the original slate of officers and directors was reelected for the 1952 term of office. And in December 1952 they were reelected again for 1953. The standing committees appointed included the regatta, house, budget and auditing, finance, junior sponsor, membership, entertainment, obstruction to navigation, rules, water, sports, publicity, investigating, and electoral committees.

Six classes of membership were formed and a membership drive initiated. All active members were also required to purchase or subscribe to a $100 certificate of membership, in addition to the usual fees and yearly dues. By January 9, 1952, there were forty-two paid members and one honorary member, Mr. E. W. Sudduth.

In June 1952 the very popular Eastward Ho (Power Squadron) from New Orleans extended their cruise from Pensacola to Fort Walton Beach, where they were enthusiastically received by members of Fort Walton Beach and a group from the newly organized yacht club. The visitors were entertained with a cocktail party and buffet supper at the Miramar Hotel.

Although enthusiasm was high, the early days of the yacht club were hectic because of numerous problems and a shortage of money. Problems of any young club are numerous and the Fort Walton Yacht Club was no exception—there were the problems of securing land, roads, drainage, landscaping, boathouses, chit books, barbecue pit, and bingo, the problem of slot machines, and many others.

One of the early social events in the club's history was the Shep Fields Dance held November 8, 1951. Other events included cocktail hours, Thanksgiving Day dance, Christmas party, Ladies Day, Family Supper Night, and many other gatherings in order to keep the members active.

Realizing that it was formed as a yacht club and not a social club, members of the FWYC made concrete plans for a clubhouse, docks, sailboats, etc. early in its history. The original donation of land for the clubhouse was made in October 1951. It was located on Cinco Bayou. Later, at the request of the club, it was changed to the Smack Point overlooking Choctawhatchee Bay, on land generously donated by E. W. Sudduth.

At the July 23, 1952, meeting a resolution was presented to construct a clubhouse at an estimated cost of $20,000 and to issue bonds to cover the cost of construction. Mr. Anker K. Hansen of Memphis, Tennessee volunteered to draw plans for the clubhouse without charge. At this same meeting the board approved the organization of the FWYC Ladies Auxiliary, which was very helpful in entertaining the next group of Eastward Ho cruisers, who had arrived from

Pensacola, Florida, at the Miramar Hotel.

The next few months were full of activity. Through the efforts of Rear Commodore W. E. Duggan, chairman of the building committee, a road was constructed to the clubhouse site, and by February 1953 the work of filling in the yacht club property was completed. However, many of these days looked very dark. The membership drive was far short of the anticipated 150 members, and bond sales moved rather slowly. The problem of adequate financing still remained.

It was decided at this time that January 1, 1954, would be the cut-off date for charter membership in the club. It was voted to secure a plaque and have the names of the original seventy-three charter members of the Fort Walton Yacht Club inscribed on it as a permanent record, and this plaque now hangs on the walls of the yacht club.

The charter members are:

Mrs. George Adams	R. T. Frazier	W. D. Partin
Colonel W.N. Amis	Dr. T. D. Griffin	Steve Powell
John B. Ames	Anker F. Hansen	T. Carl Ratliff
Joseph R. Anderson	W. B. Harbeson	Paul Roberts
Page Bacon	B. T. Hinson	C. W. Ruckel, Jr.
Frank E. Bass	A. M. Hyer Brownlow	Roy L. Scarborough
E. P. Beaudoin	Jackson, Jr.	Mrs. J. G. Scherf
H. J. Benkert	Claude J. Kendrick	Sidney Schulder
Colonel Wm. L. Boyd	Jim Kendrick	Harry O. Seymour
T. E. Brooks	D. K. Kimbrell	General F. C. Sibert
H. French Brown	Gary E. Lee	J. Frazer Smith
John F. Campbell	F. M. Lyon	W. C. Stacy
Luther Clary	Ross Marler	Jas. G. Stahlman
Roger Clary	Dr. R. P. Maxon	Hillary T. Stewart
Moultrie Clement	Clifford M. Meigs	E. W. Sudduth
A. N. Dawson	Clyde D. Meigs	Eugene Taylor
J. Lee Drake	Jas. W. Middleton	Nathan Taylor
John W. Drennan	P. W. Miller	J. J. Tringas
W. E. Duggan	Dale C. Moon	Harry Vandergriff
Harry Ellinor	Mrs. Martha McBrayer	Dr. H. C. White
Mrs. Byron Ellinor	R. P. McCreary	W. B. Williams
H. R. Falkenberg	Howard McGee	Dr. J. C. Wilson
Dr. H. C. Forsythe	E. E. Pair	O. B. Wilson
J. C. Foster, Jr.	Wayne W. Patton	T. J. Yarbrough

After much planning, effort, sweat, blood, and tears, the Fort

Walton Yacht Club moved into its new clubhouse, and the official opening was held on January 1, 1954. Mr. Pratt was appointed the first manager of the club.

The 1954 yachting season was very active. A Power Squadron was formed with thirteen members. They became very active in the Eastward Ho cruising races and in the summer of 1954 entertained the group of cruisers from the New Orleans Southern Yacht Club. The club was in good financial condition and voted to purchase three used Fish Class sloops from the Pensacola Yacht Club, which was the minimum requirement for membership in the Gulf Yachting Association, which it joined in 1954.

The boats were sailed over from Pensacola in freezing February weather, a chore well remembered by one of the courageous yacht club members, Marshall Brown. Competitive achievement came slowly, but year after year of trying paid off with a race win here and a regatta victory there. Brown also recalled the first major achievement came when Jerry Black, Mike Brown, and Billy Bigelow, all fifteen years old, and Richard Beaudoin, thirteen, traveling by Greyhound bus to St. Petersburg and won the 1962 Junior Lipton Regatta at St. Petersburg Yacht Club.

The original three Fish Class sloops had been reduced to one by a hurricane named Florence in 1956. By 1961, a member-built fleet of seven new Fish Class boats was completed. It was in this same year that Commodore Marshall Brown, who was commodore of the FWYC in 1958, became the commodore of the Gulf Yachting Association, which brought the opening regatta and annual GYA meeting to the Fort Walton Yacht Club.

A major yearly event was brought to the club when the members initiated the Meigs Regatta. Clifford H. Meigs was the first commodore of the Fort Walton Yacht Club.

The conversion to the Flying Scot sloops from the club-owned Fish Class boats in 1969 only served to heighten the interest, with many of the members owning private Scots and joining the Flying Scot Sailing Association. In 1979 present secretary-treasurer of the GYA Michael Johnson crossed the line in first place in his Flying Scot on St. Andrews Bay, Florida, as photographed by Al Audleman for the June 1979 issue of *Scots n'water*.

The growth of the club was steady over the years, with major physical growth in 1956, 1960, and 1981, as reported by Commodore Brown. He states that this growth and the current active membership of 300 is due to the club's outstanding commodore-yachtsmen.

GRAND LAGOON YACHT CLUB

The Grand Lagoon Yacht Club, located in Pensacola, Florida on Big Lagoon, was formed in April, 1967. Making it possible was Roland E. Weatherhead, who offered to sell the property which he owned to the yacht club members and to construct the building, parking lot, pier, etc. In appreciation for his help in giving the Grand Lagoon Yacht Club its firm foundation, Roland E. Weatherhead was honored by the club, which made him "first skipper" and "charter commodore."

There were 130 members enrolled that first year of 1967 and the following members were elected to office: Roland E. Weatherhead, commodore; Frank Hubbard, vice-commodore; Lucille Hubbard, secretary; Katherine Paschke, treasurer; Jack Humberstone, fleet captain (sails); and Rusty Paschke, fleet captain (power).

During its first year the junior sailing club was initiated, with Bill Blair, commodore; Steve Symons, vice-commodore; Bobby Humbesh, fleet captain (sails); and Melody Blair, secretary-treasurer.

The following year, 1968, the Gulf Yachting Association approved the application for membership of the Grand Lagoon Yacht Club, and their skippers have been active participants in all interclub regattas each year since its founding.

THE PENSACOLA YACHT CLUB

The Pensacola Yacht Club (PYC) was organized in 1908 under the name the Pensacola Yacht and Motor Boat Club. The fifteen charter members were motor craft owners and enthusiasts. It had been reported that "from the immediate years after the Civil War Pensacola maintained one of the three recognized yacht clubs in the United States and that many of its regattas were attended by devotees, notably the one in 1888 with prizes for fortunate winners totaling $5,000."

The first meeting was held in 1908 in an office on De Luna Street. Mr. George T. Morgan, then city comptroller, was elected the first commodore; James C. Watson, vice-commodore; C. M. Jones, rear commodore; D. H. Sheppard, secretary; and Robert B. Hargis, treasurer. Commodore Morgan retired after serving three months. He was succeeded by J. C. Watson, who served the unexpired term. Watson was reelected commodore in 1909.

During the administration of Commodore C. M. Jones in 1910, the club was officially chartered the Pensacola Yacht Club under the laws of the State of Florida. Other charter members were Dave

Witherill, Hobart Cross, Oscar Sheppard, Charlie Cottrell, Willie Walters, and W. L. Mitchell.

The Pensacola Yacht Club moved often during its early history. Its first clubhouse was aboard a government-owned boat named *Clarence Hutchinson*, purchased from the government and docked on the beach of Bayou Chico. It later moved to a building on Palafox Street. Under the administration of Commodore C. E. Hute, the U. S. Army transport *General Wilson* was purchased from the U. S. and used as a clubhouse until it was destroyed by fire in 1925. Then the club moved back to Palafox Street until 1948 when Commodore James T. Warthen negotiated for the 1870 mansion on Bayou Chico, the estate of J. M. Muldon. Under the administration of Commodore John Pace, the new clubhouse was converted into a comfortable, convenient, and luxurious home. The twelve acres of ground were beautifully landscaped with moss-covered oak trees.

The first Lipton Cup race was sailed in October of 1920 on Lake Pontchartrain in New Orleans with the Pensacola Yacht Club racing against Southern Yacht Club. The three-race series was won by Pensacola, with "Willie" Walthers winning all three races. The Pensacola team consisted of Walthers, Capt. Dave Witherill, Capt. Dan Sheppard, W. A. Curtiss, Peter Altrink, W. L. Mitchell, Oscar Sheppard, and Thomas H. Johnson. The SYC crew was made up of Leslie P. Beard, Edward H. Keep, A. R. "Babe" Roberts, William Porteous, Jr., Finley Mitchell, Reginald H. Carter, and William B. Edgar, Jr. Immediately following the races, the Pensacola Yacht Club commodore purchased three of the original six Fish boats from the SYC before returning home.

In 1921 the flag officers of PYC were J. H. Cross, commodore; Dr. Clasen, vice-commodore; E. Hutchinson, vice-commodore; Capt. Dan Sheppard, Rear Commodore; Capt. J. C. Watson, fleet captain; Capt. H. Ketchum, fleet lieutenant, and W. C. Frederic, secretary-treasurer.

The first skipperette regatta was held in 1921 in the recently acquired Fish Class sloops. The wife of Dave Witherill, Ruth, won with the wife of Dan Sheppard placing second. Mrs. Witherill travelled with her husband to every regatta until her death in 1978. She was proud of her trophy, a silver charm replica of a Fish boat. Mrs. Sheppard won a framed verse, *Good Luck*:

When the Ship
   of Good Luck
With its sails
   all furled
Comes wandering round
   To your part
Of the world
   I hope you'll discover
Amidst the gay din
   It's the port
Of your life
   That it's anchored in.

Mrs. Sheppard remarked that Mrs. Witherill claimed to be an expert skipper but she did not know the stem from the stern, and as no one but the skipper could touch the tiller, her husband pulled her sweater in the direction she was to steer the boat. Another expert skipperette was Mrs. Angus McMillan. In 1952 the first skipperette to make the Lipton team was Marge Rotureau.

In 1937 three classes of membership were enrolled, namely, senior, intermediate (70), junior (35) and the women's or skipperettes' division (35), which had Mrs. John L. Burda as commodore.

The same Lipton team that won the 1936 Lipton Cup participated in the 1937 event. The members were Joseph Marques, Tom Bingham, Raelou Witherill, who promised to carry on the Witherill tradition, W. S. "Bill" Lurton, Jr., and Bill Wells. The balance of the team consisted of the commodore, Henry Hilton-Green, Thomas H. Johnson, chairman of the Fish Class committee, John H. Cross, chairman of the Fish Class board of appeal, Dan H. Sheppard, judge, and Edgar Langford, timer.

The Pensacola to Fort Walton Beach long-distance race held in June is always a popular event. The first Pensacola Cup race, on March 20, 1965, was a 300-mile race from Pensacola to St. Petersburg. The Navy Yacht club in cooperation with the Pensacola Yacht Club and St. Petersburg Yacht Club scheduled the first annual Navy Ocean Race that has been termed "the longest off-shore race ever planned for this area." The race drew entries from New Orleans, Mobile, Gulfport, Fort Walton, Panama City, St. Petersburg, and Pensacola. In 1967 Dr. Chuck Smith in his New Islander 27 *Sangaree* won the first annual Pensacola to Panama City ocean race.

A few of the outstanding members of the PYC in the days of the Fish Class and other classes were:

Martin Anderson	Howard Mitchell
Max L. Bear	Peter Noonan
Charles Cottrell	John C. Pace
Rox Cowley	R. G. Patterson
R. M. Crongeyer	Nat Rotureau
J. D. Cross	Schrecks, Paul Sr., Jr., and Gerald
Henry Hilton-Green, Sr. & Jr.	Lee Sharp
Bill Harvey	D. H. Sheppard
Ashton Hayward	O. N. Sheppard
W. M. Horigan	Eugene Taylor
Edgar Langfor	James T. Warthen
Wm. Lurton, Sr.	J. C. Watson
J. J. Marien	D. M. Witherill
J. F. Marques, Jr.	Ray Witherill
	Joe Youd

One of the most outstanding events of the sailing season is the Five Flags Regatta. During the War between the States, Pensacola flew the flag of the Confederacy. Because of the kaleidoscopic changes in the colors that flew from the military masts of the town and harbor, Pensacola has been known as the City of Five Flags.

In 1969 when the Fish Class boats were replaced by the Flying Scot as a GYA club-owned sloop, members of the Pensacola Yacht Club placed one of its Fish Class boats on a pedestal on the front lawn of the yacht club with a plaque resting on it saying, "Pity not the Fish boat for, like a great statesman, it has performed with a nobility that can never be erased from the annals of history, and bred a race of skippers of whom we will always be proud."

In 1971 the Pensacola Yacht Club skipperettes won the Commodore Bernard Knost trophy in Pass Christian. The PYC team was made up of Mrs. Paul Schoen, Carol Fae Youd, Lucy Sheppard, and Dale Scott.

Members of the Pensacola Yacht Club who have served as commodores of the Gulf Yachting Association are:

1920—J. H. Cross
1923—E. G. Quina
1940-41—H. Hilton-Green, Sr.
1952—Eugene Taylor
1965—Alan Sheppard
1978—Lewis B. Pollak
1983—Robert Boyle

ST. ANDREWS BAY YACHT CLUB

First steps to organize a yacht club in Panama City were taken in August 1933, when seventeen enthusiastic men with a common vision met and laid plans for the formation of a club on St. Andrews Bay. After a short time, the membership had increased to the extent that the building of a clubhouse became possible. Before the completion of the clubhouse, meetings were held in the Dixie Sherman Hotel.

The site upon which the building stands was donated to the club by H. L. Sudduth, and additional property to the east and west was acquired, mainly through the efforts of W. C. Sherman and E. N. Pagelson.

The charter members are:

Charles O. Bingham	Dr. W. C. Roberts
J. C. Cogburn	A. R. Rogers
Burnis Coleman	Philip A. Roll
J. W. Crews	B. J. Russell
M. J. Daffin	Harry Ryder
Sidney A. Daffin, Jr.	Douglas B. Sale
M. H. Edwards, Jr.	Thomas Sale
Harry G. Fannin	J. A. Smith
Paul Lindsay	Ernest R. Spiva
Robert Muthis, Jr.	W. E. Spiva
Will D. Muse	H. L. Sudduth
Malcolm Parker	Dell E. Wood
	Major F. B. Wood

The first meeting in the clubhouse was held on May 27, 1937. However, the first officers were elected in 1933 and served through 1934. They were Major F. B. Wood, commodore; Philip A. Roll, vice-commodore; Charles O. Bingham, rear-commodore; and Robert Mathis, Jr., secretary-treasurer. The first honorary members were H. L. Sudduth, E. N. Pagelson, and Asa G. Candler.

The St. Andrews Bay Yacht Club is a non-profit corporation owned by its membership. It is located on beautiful St. Andrews Bay in the midst of one of Panama City's finest residential sections, and has a frontage of 350 feet on a cove in the bay.

Before the opening of the 1935 sailing season, five Fish Class sloops were under construction, and in May of the same year, 1935, the St. Andrews Bay Yacht Club became a member of the Gulf Yachting Association.

St. Andrew's Bay Yacht Club staged its inaugural interclub regatta in November, 1935, with four clubs participating. Pensacola was the winner and was awarded the Erling Riis Trophy. It was at this regatta that plans were completed for the Candler race in 1936, and May 30 was set as the date.

An active branch of the yacht club was the power boat division, consisting of a fleet of some twenty-five power-driven yachts. General club cruises were held from time to time.

The Ladies Auxiliary and the Skipperettes, formed in 1933, are organizations that have been of outstanding value to the progress of this club. A very active junior program brought the Junior Lipton Cup to the club in 1950 when the juniors won the event in St. Petersburg.

The Daily Herald of August 25, 1937 reporting on the dedication of the harbor in Gulfport, Mississippi, noted that the officers of the St. Andrew's Bay Yacht Club in 1937 were A. M. Lewis, commodore; H. B. Everett, Jr., vice-commodore; P. Lorrillard Kent, rear commodore; Major F. B. Wood, chairman of the board of governors; Dr. W. C. Robert, secretary; and W. J. Oenslager, treasurer. P. A. Roll was fleet captain.

The outstanding skippers for many years in Fish Class boats were:

Julian Bennet	H. A. Heim
Isaac W. Byrd	Dayton Logue
W. J. Cook, Jr.	George McLaughlin
George Cowgill, Jr.	Hugh Nelson
Idus Darby	Carmel Roberts
Floyd Davis	John W. Sherman
Allen Douglas	Harold Steadman
Wilton Duncan	Bud Weaver

Commodores of the Gulf Yachting Association from the St. Andrews Bay Yacht Club are Major Frank B. Wood (1944-45), Commodore Wilton Duncan (1955), and Commodore Allen M. Douglas (1972).

ST. PETERSBURG YACHT CLUB

The St. Petersburg Yacht Club (SPYC) was organized on the night of October 29, 1909 at a meeting held in the store of the Marine Supply Co. by a group of civic-minded yachtsmen who may have foreseen that at some time in the future St. Petersburg on Tampa Bay would become the yachting capital of the South. At this initial session the officers elected were Dr. M. H. Axline, commodore; W. R. Jones, vice-commodore; W. L. Straub, secretary; Tracy Lewis, treasurer; and George Presstman, measurer. Directors named, in addition to the flag officers were Ed. T. Lewis, Walter Robertson Howard, George Waller, and W. H. English.

The club held its first outing on December 26, 1909 with twenty boats carrying approximately one hundred members and guests to Blind Pass. The first regular cruise was held March 6-7, 1910 with eleven boats making the trip to Bradenton and back. However, the lack of a yacht basin discouraged activities in boating, and the club was more or less inactive until 1916 when waterfront developments were well under way.

It was A. T. Roberts, a newspaper man who had been city editor of *The St. Petersburg Times*, and Lew B. Brown who called for a meeting on the evening of May 30, 1916. Seven men heeded the call: W. L. Straub, Ed. T. Lewis, C. W. Soringstead, Arthur L. Johnson, Frank C. Carley, Roberts, and Brown. A finance committee was chosen, a membership drive staged, and a re-organization meeting held June 23, 1916. On this date, the St. Petersburg Yacht Club was reborn. Articles of Incorporation were drawn up and filed with the Circuit Court of Pinellas County, Florida on June 23, 1916. The founders were:

Lew W. Brown	George S. Gandy
D. W. Budd	G. W. Greene
Abbott G. Butler	Roy S. Hanna
F. C. Carley	John D. Harris
Robt. S. Carroll	Arthur L. Johnson
T. A. Chanceller	Ed. T. Lewis
Wm. M. Davis	A. T. Roberts
J. G. Foley	C. M. Roser
H. Walter Faller	W. L. Straub

The following officers were duly elected: Frank C. Carley, commodore; A. G. Butler, vice-commodore; D. W. Budd, rear commodore; A. T. Roberts, secretary, and John D. Harris, treasurer.

All officers were reelected in 1917, and a new clubhouse was formally opened on June 15, 1917. At this ceremony, Commodore Carley presented the club with a beautiful silver "commodore's cup" on which were to appear from time to time the names of the club's commodores.

The club grew so fast that it became evident a larger building was needed. Plans were made for a new clubhouse, which opened formally on December 21, 1922. The ballroom in the new building was the scene of many brilliant social events, and in general the club came into its own as the social center for St. Petersburg. Many internationally famous figures who visited the city aboard their yachts were entertained by the members of the St. Petersburg Yacht Club.

During 1923 the club became affiliated with the Gulf Yachting Association and acquired a fleet of the G.Y.A. club-owned Fish Class sloops. There is a model of this gaff-rigged keelboat in the lounge. It was built and donated to the club by Bruce Watters, Jr.

In 1925 A. L. Gandy was elected GYA commodore, and through his efforts other clubs on Florida's West Coast joined the GYA. The following year, 1926, a team of club sailors tied with the Eastern Shore Yacht Club of Mobile for the Sir Thomas J. Lipton trophy and the GYA championship. The St. Petersburg Yacht Club won the Lipton Cup in 1946, 1951, and 1957. Members who were prominent in GYA team-racing events included Babe Fogarty, George Rifley, who became GYA commodore in 1949, Dr. Howard Rees, who was elected GYA Commodore in 1964, Lou Schowe, Jane Wray, Tom Ellis, Halsey Ford, and others.

The club grew and prospered during the twenties, but during the Great Depression of the thirties it fell upon hard times and at one period almost failed to survive. Fortunately, it was saved by Al D. Strum, who enlisted new members from the Junior Chamber of Commerce at a $25.00 per year membership fee. Through his efforts and those of other dedicated members including Eugene Bennett, A. L. and Gidge Gandy, Leon D. Lewis, L. L. McMasters, Paul V. Reese, E. C. Robinson, Tom Pierce, and Shirley Gracy the club was saved and has become the world-famous institution it is today.

Despite those early trying years the club managed to inaugurate two major events which were destined to be of national stature. First was the St. Petersburg-Havana ocean yacht race in 1930. From a rather humble beginning with five starters, this event grew to become an important international yacht race which attracted entries from many clubs and eventually became a part of the Southern ocean-racing circuit. The other event became known as the Southland Sweepstakes for power racing boats.

Gidge Gandy, better known to his friends as "Admiral," originated the idea of a St. Petersburg-Havana race. The first five boats to answer the call were *Sunshine* from Mobile, *Windjammer* from Southern in New Orleans, *Haligonian* of Tampa, *Wawatam* and *Marelen* from St. Petersburg. *Haligonian* owned by Houston Wall was first in Class A and the *Windjammer* of Garner H. Tullis was first in Class B.

There was a large contingent of enthusiastic power racing members in the Southland Sweepstakes event. Those who became famous for setting new speed records and winning national championships were Jim Appley, Sherman Critchfield, Sammy Crooks, Bert and Ed Davidson, Tom D'Eath, Frank Foulke, Norman Bradford, Ray Gassner, Marty Howard, Guy Lombardo, J. D. "Pop" McIntyre, Al Strum, and Les Trafton. Les Trafton and Sherman Critchfield are in the Gulf

Marine Hall of Fame and Frank Foulke and Ray Gassner are in the A. P. B. A. Honor Squadron. In 1979 Kell Hennessy was the recipient of an award for services rendered in power cruising in the U. S.

World War II interrupted most yachting activities including the race to Havana. However, just after the close of the war, the St. Petersburg Yacht Club turned to One-design classes and new fleets were formed in the Rhodes, Bantam, Thistle, and Windmill classes. A group of club members decided that the club should be represented in a national class with a fleet of privately owned sailboats. It was decided that the Lightning Class would be best suited to sailing conditions on Tampa Bay. In November of 1946 the first four Lightning Class boats were purchased. In 1948 the Midwinter Championship Regatta of the Lightning class was initiated and this event became and remains a very successful and popular annual event of a three-race winter circuit for the International Lightning Class Association.

The ladies of the St. Petersburg Yacht Club were very much a part of the yachting scene as champion skipperettes and committeemen. At the urging of Rear Commodore Bill Jennings in 1951, the wives of the club sailors organized a sailing group. They called themselves "Salty Sisters." Their successors became so widely known that neighboring yacht clubs formed their own organizations. All of which developed into an active program of individual and team sailing competition among the West Coast yacht clubs.

The nineteenth annual St. Petersburg-Havana race got under way on March 8, 1952 with a record breaking fleet of twenty-nine yachts sailing the 284-mile course. Seven boats were flying the St. Petersburg colors. Class A had John Hertz, Jr's. *Ticonderoga*, R. M. Demere of Savannah in *Ocean Queen V.*, also Dudley Sharp's *Gulf Stream* and Garner Tullis of Southern Yacht Club in *Windjammer II* (the latter two were former winners of this race). The winner was Carleton Mitchell's *Caribbee*, with a corrected time of thirty hours, thirty-seven minutes and twenty-eight seconds. This 58-foot Rhodes-designed yawl was the only boat ever to win the Miami-Nassau and St. Petersburg-Havana races in the same year.

In 1952 the St. Petersburg Yacht Club's Lipton team won the Lipton trophy at Panama City with its expert sailors, Louis Schowe, Jane Wray, Fred Deuel, Homer Allen, skippers and John Sandy, Eddie Adair, Commodore George W. Rifley, Paul Williams, Al Strum, Alex Corbett, crewmen. Heading the team were Fish Class committee chairman Dr. Howard Rees, with committeemen Tom Ellis, Jane Wray, Lee Brooks, Richard Tucker, Homer Allen, and Bill Cobler. Team captain was Richard Tucker.

The first member to win a One-Design Class national championship was Barbara Tolson with her father, Ted Tolson, as crew. This was in 1956 in the Rhodes Bantam Class. Two years later in 1958 John Jennings won the Thistle Class National championship. Both of these members were trained in the junior sailing program.

From 1964 on, every time a British Royal Navy vessel visited St. Petersburg, its sailing team would challenge the "Salty Sisters" to race. While this became a great social event for the British sailors, it has never demonstrated their superiority. During 1973, Ardith Rutland coordinated an interclub committee and thus the Florida Women's Sailing Association was born. In 1966 the SPYC sold its fleet of Fish Class boats in favor of fleets of Flying Juniors and Rhodes-19 keelboats. When the Gulf Yachting Association adopted the Flying Scot Class as its association boat in 1969, the St. Petersburg Yacht Club terminated its GYA membership in 1972. It returned to the fold in 1981.

From the ranks of the very active Junior Training program of SPYC came John Jennings, who won the Mallory Cup in 1970 and 1973 for the USYRU Men's National Sailing Championship, with James Pardee and Barbara Tolson Pardee as crew. Ed Sherman, Jr. won the Mallory Cup in 1972, with Harvey Ford and Hubert Rutland, III as crew. In 1970 Jennings also won the U. S. Inter-Club Match Racing championship for the Prince of Wales Bowl, and he repeated this victory in 1979 with his crew, Harvey Ford and Hubert Rutland, III.

Many other national and international championships have been won by members of the St. Petersburg Yacht Club. Several junior sailors have travelled to Australia, France, Ireland, Portugal, and Thailand to compete in world championships.

Numerous men and women have dedicated their time and effort to further yachting in all its phases. In 1979 Commodore Ted Tolson was awarded the prestigious Nathaniel G. Herreshoff trophy by the United States Yacht Racing Union "for his contributions and services to yacht racing" in the U. S.

Over the years sailors of larger boats created a series of races on Tampa Bay and along the west coast of Florida. Mainly through the efforts of L. L. McMasters and Bobby Davis of the Davis Island Y. C. in Tampa, these sailors and their clubs formed the Florida Ocean Racing Association organized to hold a series of annual races.

CHAPTER XXV

Yacht Clubs of Louisiana

CYPREMORT YACHT CLUB

In the year 1968 a new yacht club joined the circle of yachting in the South, the Cypremort Yacht Club on Vermilion Bay in New Iberia, Louisiana. The boat owners in this Southern town, the home of Avery Island, where the famous Tabasco sauce is made, desired to be a part of the great movement sweeping the South. Many new yacht clubs have been added to the Gulf Yachting Association in the past few years. The charter members of the Cypremont Yacht Club were: Rene Broussard, Michael DeBlanc, Tom Delcambre, Lambert Duhe, Richard McMahon, Dan Regard, and Bill Ryan.

As is the custom when a new yacht club has made application for membership in the Gulf Yachting Association, a committee is sent to check on the prospective member. A constant companion and advisor on these missions with GYA secretary-treasurer Commodore J. Gilbert Scheib was Gilbert Gray, the Olympic gold medal winner. At the invitation of the club's most enthusiastic and energetic member, Richard Mire, Jr., the modest one-room new clubhouse was inspected, as was the location for racing on the Bay. After some fine crawfish bisque at a nearby restaurant in this Cajun country, the writer, who was along for the trip, and her escorts returned to New Orleans well pleased with the prospects of a well-planned yacht club.

The Cypremort Yacht Club became a member of USYRU and also

joined the Gulf Yachting Association in 1978. Throughout the '70s and into the '80s the club has been very active and has held many invitational regattas.

In 1983 the board approved the acquisition of two or more acres of land at the southeasternmost part of Cypremort Point facing Vermilion and Cote Bay, to build a new clubhouse and facility. A completely new marina has been constructed for 250 or more boats. It will be bulkheaded with concrete walls for durability and beauty.

An appropriation of $300,000 was allocated for the clubhouse facility and for eighteen slips and a ramp that will belong to the Cypremort Yacht Club. Things are looking up for these enthusiastic yachtsmen who are planning wider participation in GYA and NAYRU events.

THE LAKE ARTHUR (BOAT) YACHT CLUB

From the records found in the Southern Yacht Club's archives we learn that after World War I, in 1922 "A committee of Southern Yacht Club yachtsmen visited a Calcasieu city in the western section of Lafayette in an effort to re-awaken yachting fervor. One of the most recent clubs formed was Lake Arthur Boat Club of Lake Arthur, Louisiana, which had recently joined the Mississippi Valley Power Boat Association. It was anticipated that with the prospective organization of the Lake Charles Yacht Club a great series of regattas could result." It is possible that these two clubs continued until 1929 when the stock market crashed and most yacht clubs in the South disbanded.

According to a brief history of the Lake Arthur Yacht Club submitted by Commodore Al Rees, 1968 was the year that a group of prominent businessmen from the area of Lafayette and Lake Arthur, Louisiana, who were also enthusiastic yachtsmen, gathered together to organize a yacht club. The Lake Arthur Yacht Club was the name selected and the club burgee was designed by Randy Freret.

The yacht club was chartered in 1968 by the State of Louisiana as a not-for-profit social and athletic club. The principal organizers from Lafayette were Richard Byler, Charles Conner, and his son, Edward Conner. From the town of Lake Arthur were Carroll Cronchet, Randy Freret, Ken Jones, Alfred Lamson, Bert Keenan, Randy Newman (the latter two are also members of the Southern Yacht Club in New Orleans), and others.

The first permanent resident of the yacht harbor was the *Pussy Cat*, a Cape Cod catboat owned by Bert Keenan, who is well known in racing circles along the Gulf Coast. He has been a participant in many ocean-going races. His notoriety began in the St. Petersburg to Bermuda race of 1980, which he won but was disqualified from by the ruling of a NAYRU race committee which acted as judge and jury.

Another famous but foreign member, a native of the State of Georgia, was Edward Lormand who sailed the Atlantic singlehanded from Florida to Britain. The only national champion of the Lake Arthur Yacht Club has been Fred Brunt, who in 1979 was the best in the Harpoon 5.2 class.

The first One-Design fleets at LAYC were the Lido 14s and the Day Sailors. The Sunfish fleet was spawned because of the interclub competition for the Louisiana Governor Edwin Edwards Cup. Fleets of Balboa 26s and Flying Scots were also added.

In 1980 the Lake Arthur Yacht Club joined the United States Yacht Racing Union and in 1981 was elected to membership in the Gulf Yachting Association, where the yacht club's team of expert skippers has been very active in interclub regattas and is a real contender for the Sir Thomas J. Lipton Trophy.

The popular annual regattas are the Crawfish Regatta in April, the Lake Arthur Junior Championship Regatta in September and the Gumbo Regatta in October. The perpetual trophy awards by the club are the Commodore Charles Conner Cup for the Day Sailors competition and the Jenny Jones trophy for the outstanding junior. With the yacht clubs located in surrounding areas, Cypremort, Lake Charles, and Pelican in Baton Rouge, the competition for the Governor Edwin Edwards trophy is very keen and is the outstanding regatta of the year.

THE LAKE CHARLES YACHT CLUB

In a campaign to re-awaken the sport of sailing around the South, after World War I, a group of enthusiastic yachtsmen from the Southern Yacht Club set out in the vicinity of Calcasieu Parish to the west of New Orleans, where they visited members of the Lake Charles Association of Commerce and the *Daily American Press*.

"Lake Charles was a hustling town at that time working for the advancement of things to do with making a bigger and better Lake Charles," reported the SYC *Barometer*. "There were several boat owners in the town and interest was beginning to take shape for a yacht club." Those boat owners were: Paul Barbe, R. L. Cline, J. W. Gardiner, Henry Gray, E. R. Henry, J. L. Hennings, Robert Leake,

Edgar Miller, C. O. Noble, Edward E. Richards, Charles A. Richardson, Hugo See, Harry Shutts, A. D. Spooner, and others.

The future looked bright for a yacht club and interclub events with the sister city Lake Arthur just a few miles to the south, where the Lake Arthur Yacht Club had organized. But as happened with so many yacht clubs during the twenties, it is possible that these yacht clubs disbanded with the stock market crash of 1929.

Another group of enthusiastic yachtsmen got together and formed the Cal Lake Yacht Club of Lake Charles on March 1, 1965. There were six members and three boats. By 1967, forty-four members and thirty-five boats appeared on the roster. In 1970 the first clubhouse, located on the lake at North Beach, was dedicated.

NEW ORLEANS YACHT CLUB

The New Orleans Yacht Club is located in New Orleans, Louisiana on the shoreline of beautiful Lake Pontchartrain, close by its neighboring Southern Yacht Club.

During the late summer of 1948, there were several persons with boats of various design and size docked in the municipal harbor of New Orleans. These skippers had a burning desire but no opportunity to enter into the sport of sailing on a competitive basis. In the April 1948 issue of *Yachting* was an article titled "Launching a Yacht Club," giving detailed organizational information. The magazine was passed around for the group to read in order that they contemplate forming a yacht club.

On the night of March 19, 1949, a group of five persons met at a small restaurant on Elysian Fields Avenue. At this meeting the New Orleans Yacht Club was formed and dues set at $15.00 per annum. Other basic rules were made and a resolution was adopted to set up a set of by-laws.

S. H. Crochet was elected acting commodore and Arthur Fleitas acting secretary, with instructions to proceed with incorporation. The organization met weekly immediately thereafter and in short order had set up articles of incorporation, a constitution and by-laws. Thirty-two persons appeared for the signing of the charter on April 10, 1949, and two weeks later on April 24, 1949, by-laws were formally adopted and the first officers and board of directors elected as follows: S. H. "Sy" Crochet, commodore; A. A. "Slim" Bryant, vice-commodore; Jerry Rees, rear commodore; Arthur Fleitas, secretary-treasurer. The board at large consisted of B. J. Lawrence, Sr., and V. J. Sheldon, Sr. and Jr.

On June 3, 1949, with great enthusiasm, the members at a gala get-together party, marked the first social function and launching of the first season of activity. At this point, the membership fleet consisted of seven-odd sailing craft and five power craft. Under the guidance of race committee chairman V. J. "Pee Wee" Sheldon, Sr., the first racing season was very successful.

Before headquarters were set up in a rented small frame structure built during the war years on top of the Municipal Yacht Harbor building, meetings were held in various places including the cabin cruiser *Lucille L*, the flagship of the 1950 elected commodore, B. U. Lawrence.

Through the cooperation of Mr. Felix Lorino, harbormaster, in the early part of June 1950, this small building, which was later enlarged, became the official New Orleans Yacht Club's home. The clubhouse was furnished through the courtesy of its members, Mr. Raymond Bassich being most generous with his gifts of furnishings and photomurals which presently adorn the club interior.

It was in the late summer of 1951, through the efforts of "Slim" Bryant and Nolfie Alfonso, Sr. that Gulfport Yacht Club sold four of its somewhat weathered Fish Class sloops to the NOYC. Through untiring efforts of newly elected Rear Commodore Ernest Loeb, III, and many others, membership bonds were sold and the necessary loan made to enable the purchase of these craft. They were put in racing condition by a group of hard workers, Elmer Bush, N. Alfonso, Mrs. Alfonso, Larry Thonn, Joe Young, and others.

The NOYC from its inception has always received the wholehearted cooperation of the Southern Yacht Club, its hundred-year-old neighbor, and with the acquisition of a requisite Fish Class fleet, the SYC saw fit to sponsor the club in the Gulf Yachting Association. Acceptance was granted in May of 1952 and the members of the NOYC enthusiastically entered into GYA activities immediately. To date it has been only on rare occasions that the NOYC has not been represented at GYA events.

The NOYC has always had the younger boating enthusiasts and their welfare as one of its prime considerations. Among the early members were several scouting masters with close ties to the Sea Scout trainingship *Viking* for several years. It was quite fitting, therefore, for the club to accept the invitation tendered it in the early months of 1955 to sponsor the Sears Cup trophy eliminations for juniors. This was the first major regatta and was sailed on Lake Pontchartrain July 30-31, 1955, under the guiding hand of Commodore Nolfie Alfonso, who was at the helm of the club in that year.

SOUTHERN YACHT CLUB

CHARTER MEMBERS

Raymond Bassich
Luto J. Broussard
Preston W. Brown, Jr.
A. A. Bryant
Stanley Cohen
S. H. Crochet
John C. DeCorte
Norton Joseph Druilhet
Arthur M. Fleitas
Roy N. Gaston

Fred Geissler
Stephen Grilletta
Carl N. Hazelwood
Gene Honore
Ralph R. Hopkins
E. J. Johnson
L. J. Johnson
B. J. Lawrence, Sr.
Clarence Martin
Julius F. Martin
Earl H. Rees

Jerry Rees
Jack Rich
William E. Richardson, Jr.
Willard E. Robertson
H. C. Sale, Sr.
E. H. Scott
V. J. Sheldon
V. J. Sheldon, Jr.
William W. Wales
Thomas J. Williams, Jr.

The NOYC won its first Sir Thomas J. Lipton trophy in 1968 with Commodore Nolfie Alfonso as captain. Nolfie was elected commodore of the Gulf Yachting Association in 1962, and another NOYC commodore, Larry Sommers, was also elected commodore of the GYA in 1971.

In 1969 O. J. Young won the three quarter and half-ton World championship. In 1970 Bill Ibbs conquered the coveted Congressional Cup. Benz Faget was the 1979 and 1980 Lindenberg 22 North American champion and also the winner of the 1983 New Orleans to Cozumel, Mexico race.

TAMMANY YACHT CLUB

The Tammany Yacht Club is located on the north shore of beautiful Lake Pontchartrain in Slidell, Louisiana. It was granted a charter on July 25, 1980. Within a year this fledgling had been welcomed into the Gulf Yachting Association and had moved into a quaint bungalow near the banks of meandering Bayou Liberty.

The first commodore, Guy C. Geller, was aided in this initial endeavor by Charles J. Fleming, vice-commodore; H. G. Hagoort, Jr., rear commodore; Harry B. Grant, Jr., secretary; and Ronald Vaughan, treasurer. Board members were Edwin Randle, Roland Decrevel, and David Barnes.

In 1981 the club's first regatta was conducted under the performance handicap rule. Charles Erickson of New Orleans in *Voo Doo* finished in first place.

The club's first foray into endurance racing was in 1981 with the establishment of the annual single-handed "Round the Lake (Pontchartrain) Race." First in fleet for the inaugural event was Al Gooch of the Southern Yacht Club sailing *Scampi,* a Cal 25.

Series racing was introduced in 1982 and the first two years were dominated by Robert E. "Bobby" Boos in a red-hot Cal 25, *Country Mama.*

The Tammany Yacht Club became a member of the Gulf Yachting Association in 1981, and in order for it to enter the 1982 Lipton Cup event, the rule of the GYA that in order to participate in any GYA sponsored regattas, a club must own at least three club-owned Flying Scots, was suspended. Tammany was given permission to charter its neighboring yacht club, Pontchartrain's, Flying Scot to sail in this prestigious race. The TYC sailors who travelled to Pensacola Yacht Club for the Lipton Regatta were Dr. U. J. "Joe" Arretteig, Robert "Bob" Boos, Harry Grant, and Thomas "Tom" Kane, with commodore Guy Geller and William "Bill" Yauger as alternates. "Wives and kids are going along to crew," reported the TYC *Spyglass.*

Tammany skippers accepted the challenge of the Gulf Yachting Association's Offshore Challenge Cup races in 1983 and were rewarded with a third place finish.

The club's first experience with international competition was gathered by Mr. Luis Tonizzo and Mr. Jim Bates in Class IV of the 1984 *Observer*/Europe Single-Handed Transatlantic Race, a prestigious five-class yachting event which draws racing sailors from all over the world. Luis piloted his *City of Slidell* to first in its class, with Jim and *Big Shot* following in fourth place.

This is a very hazardous solo race over icy waters off Newfoundland. "There were a lot of icebergs and much dense fog, but I guess none of those icebergs had my name on them," said Tonizzo, who sailed into the harbor at Newport, Rhode Island after piloting his 35-foot, 10,300-pound monohull, a custom Norton/Marek design built in New Orleans shipyards, but outfitted with special care by Tonizzo. The cost of all this? More than $100,000 most of which was Luis' savings. It was his second attempt and Bates' first to conquer foreign waters.

Under the watchful eye of Bruce Jackson, the junior chairperson at Tammany Yacht Club, the nine juniors of the club took to the lake in five Lasers in the first ever race for the youthful sailors on Sunday August 8, 1982. Group A consisted of Rob Decrevel, Chris Grant, Mike Grant, Brian Stanford, and Doug Stanford. Doug Stanford was the winner in his group. Group B juniors were Ashley Jeffery, Glen Merrell, Jamie Randle, and Greg Stanford. There was a tie for first place between Jamie Randle and Greg Stanford.

CHAPTER XXVI

Yacht Clubs of Mississippi

BAY-WAVELAND YACHT CLUB

The name Bay-Waveland is a combination of Bay St. Louis and the adjoining town of Waveland in Mississippi, both lying on the beautiful shore of the Bay of St. Louis, described by *The Picayune* as "That little aquamarine jewel framed in pine trees in the sunset over Wolf River near DeLisle, Mississippi."

On the beach between Waveland and the Bay was the family home of SYC Commodore Emile J. O'Brien, the "father of the Southern Yacht Club." Another SYC commodore, Lewis H. Fairchild, resided in Waveland, where he served as mayor of the town.

In a *Picayune* "Flashback 8/1/1891" it was reported that "Bay St. Louis residents announce a regatta to be held at Martin's Wharf on August 7th. It has been arranged under the rules of the Southern Yacht Club except as to classifications of boats by lengths. Prizes range from $200 to $75.00. Yacht owners from Mobile, Southern in New Orleans and the Gulf Coast are invited." This was the first annual regatta held and there were many entries. "The flower of Southern womanhood was well represented. Ladies of New Orleans and Mobile as well as the belles of the Coast were adorned with flying colors of their favorite and the day of the race was a gala one at the Bay, after which followed champagne suppers on board the yachts and a grand ball at the hotel, during which the prizes were presented to the winners amid the greatest enthusiasm and cheers, refreshments were served and dancing kept up to a late hour."

From a publication issued in 1903 by the Southern Gulf Coast Yachting Association, the following information is recorded:

> In 1892 there was formed a Bay St. Louis and Waveland Regatta Association. At a regular monthly meeting, the Mayor and aldermen at Waveland adopted a resolution 'that the privilege be granted to the Gulf Coast Southern Yacht Club to build in front of Nicholson or Coleman Avenue, a building with the necessary adjustments for a clubhouse, said privilege to be granted for 99 years and the club be exempt from any corporate taxes. The shares will be $25.00 each for full membership. Therefore, 200 shares will make $5,000 sufficient to give a final building with all the needed equipment. The object of the club is not only to give annual regattas but to have a fine band of music with a concert at least once or twice a week, with grand balls, etc. In fact the rules of the Southern Yacht Club of New Orleans will be adopted.'
>
> One of the gentlemen agitating this question has just returned from a long trip and was in Canada during last week's great regatta and says the people of Waveland and the Bay have no idea how extensively these regattas advertise this section, and of how much interest is taken in them all over the United States.
>
> It is thought every property holder at Waveland will subscribe, which will at once bring forward the desired amount and will also be the means of raising the value of real estate on account of the inducements for summer pleasures.

In 1893 there is mention of a measuring committee created by an SYC member W. A. Gordon for schooners. The boats entered in this regatta were 22-foot sloops owned by Peter Labouisse, H. P. Lanphier, Judge O'Donnell, and Samuel Heaslip all of Southern, D. Penrose of Biloxi, H. dePass of Ocean Springs, and Rathborne deBuys from Mississippi City.

In 1898 the Bay-Waveland Yacht Club obtained a charter and provided to build a clubhouse located out in the water of Mississippi Sound, near the center of the town of Bay St. Louis at the foot of Washington Street, which was connected to the shore by an 1100-foot wharf. "It was the handsomest equipped and prettiest of club houses in the South," said *The Picayune*.

It was reported that the yacht club had 560 members in 1901 (membership was limited to 600). The club had a new $10,000 clubhouse and funds for improvement of pen and club anchorage. Club dues were $6.00 per year.

The members of the Bay-Waveland Yacht Club in 1903 were E. J. Bowers, commodore; L. H. Fairchild, vice-commodore; J. B. Dunbar, rear commodore; Emile J. O'Brien, secretary; Richard Mendez, treasurer; John A. Rawlins, fleet captain; and Dr. R. J.

Turner, fleet surgeon. The regatta committee consisted of T. J. Lanaux and E. L. Pinac. E. L. Pinac was an active member of the Southern Yacht Club and lived in New Orleans. Another organizer of the yacht club was "L. A. deMontluzin who has been a resident of Bay St. Louis since 1874, is a graduate of the University of France. Mr. deMontluzin is a stockholder in the Hancock County Bank and is the leading druggist of Bay St. Louis."

The Bay-Waveland Yacht Club continued to thrive until 1915 when the original clubhouse was destroyed by a "West Indian Hurricane." However, meetings were held in various homes and operation of their regattas was managed from an old steamship landing known as "Stokies Pier."

Around 1916, because there was no clubhouse, the sailing club gradually lapsed into inactivity, but the more avid sailors operated periodically, holding their own sailing races but without collecting dues.

According to the minutes of the Southern Yacht Club of August 1921, a committee of two, Commodore Percy Benedict and G. H. Chapman, was appointed to represent the Southern Yacht Club in the formation of the Bay-Waveland Yacht Club. On December 6, 1921, a group of Bay-Waveland sailing enthusiasts, namely Messrs E. J. Leonard, P. V. Lacoste, H. S. Renshaw, John Osoinach, Charles Breath, and G. R. Rea, henceforth, met, and moved and seconded that this corporation was to be known henceforth as the Bay-Waveland Yacht and Athletic Club. They purchased property located at Front and Washington Streets, now the Star Theatre. Officers elected were E. J. Leonard, commodore; Carl Marshall, vice-commodore; R. W. Sistrunk, treasurer; and Hugh Bourgeois, secretary.

In 1922, the year of the first regatta of the newly reorganized Bay-Waveland Yacht Club, the officers were Earnest J. Leonard, commodore; Edgar M. Rea, vice-commodore; E. V. Richards, rear commodore; Clem Penrose, fleet captain; Dr. C. L. Horton, fleet surgeon. Board members were W. W. Chapman, Charles A. Breath, J. Osoinach, W. Patridge, and B. C. Shields. A familiar sight on the waters of the bay was Commodore Leonard's flagship *Winnifred* with many guests.

At the annual meeting of the Gulf Yachting Association held at the Houston Yacht Club in Texas in 1922, the Bay-Waveland Yacht Club was elected to membership in the Association. The Bay-Waveland Yacht Club had been a charter member of the predecessor of the GYA, the Southern Gulf Coast Yachting Association, organized in 1901.

The club struggled through several years until the Depression, when it became inactive and remained so until 1948, which was the year of the expiration of the original fifty years charter issued in 1898. The men of Bay St. Louis realized there was a great need for a yacht club. No other place offered such natural facilities, and although numerous suggestions were made by various groups, nothing definite developed until one year later.

A group of citizens, spearheaded and inspired by the dynamic John Bell of Bay St. Louis, held a meeting on February 21, 1949 at the home of Mr. Bell to discuss the proposal of a new yacht club. From the seventy-five interested persons who attended the meeting a new committee was formed, with Mr. Bell as temporary chairman, who was to select his own committee. Shortly thereafter, Mr. Bell appointed the following to assist him: Charles Breath, Ed. Brignac, N. L. Carter, Lucien Gex, John McDonald, Leo Seal, E. N. Spence and J. J. Kelleher. They then set out to secure the necessary funds to finance the property. Largely because of the untiring energy and efforts of Mr. Bell, more than $40,000 had been pledged.

On March 19, 1949, a meeting was held in the Bay High School and owing to the enthusiastic developments, all pledgers were called on to form a permanent organization—about 135 interested persons attended the meeting. Twelve persons were selected at this meeting to form the board of governors. This was done by secret ballot and the following comprised the first board of governors of the newly reorganized club: John Bell, Charles Breath, Jr., Robert Camors, N. L. Carter, Lucien Gex, J. J. Kelleher, Howard LeTissier, John McDonald, L. Nicholson, E. N. Spence, Dr. Marion Wolfe, and E. Brignac.

Immediately after the election, the committee elected the following officers to govern for the following year: John Bell, commodore; Charles Breath, Jr., vice-commodore; Robert Camors, rear-commodore; J. J. Kelleher, secretary; and John McDonald, treasurer. Trustees were selected to handle the finances of the club, and the Bay-Waveland Yacht Club was in business. It was briefly called Yacht Clubs, Inc., but this name lasted only a short while and was changed to the Bay-Waveland Yacht Club.

The property selected for the site of the first yacht club was the property owned by a canning factory at the intersection of North Beach Boulevard and North Second Street, with approximately 180 feet of beach frontage. Bids were called for the erection of a clubhouse and construction was started on May 11, 1949. During construction, there was a tropical storm which washed away some of the construction lumber, but the building was completed on schedule and the official opening of the new club was held on December 31, 1949, with approximately 600 members and guests attending.

The club received four Fish Class sloops during the first year of operation making it eligible for competition in the Gulf Yachting Association's interclub races. Later the club owned six of these sloops of plywood construction, the same as those of Biloxi and Gulfport yacht clubs, making a fleet of eighteen boats in all the Mississippi Coast Yachting Association, an organization born in 1950.

In 1950 the flag officers of the four Mississippi Coast yacht clubs, Biloxi, Gulfport, Pass Christian and Bay-Waveland, conceived the idea of forming the Mississippi Coast Yachting Association (MCYA) so that better coordination and liaison could be accomplished by the coast yacht clubs in their sailing activities, particularly during the annual Fourth of July race festival.

One of the prime movers in establishing this new association was Henry B. Chapman, who twice served as commodore of the Bay-Waveland Yacht Club and as president of the MCYA. He was later made commodore of the GYA. Henry's brother, Wallace Chapman, was the other instigator who contributed to the formation of the new association. Wallace was a past commodore of the Biloxi Yacht Club and also a commodore of the GYA. The two Chapmans donated in 1960 the Chapman Trophy in memory of their father and brothers, all past yachtsmen.

Their father "Will" Chapman, an old time coast yachtsman and a charter member of the old Bay-Waveland Yacht Club organized in 1898, first sailed an old split sail skiff and later the renowned racing vessel *Virginia*. Brother "Will" also built and sailed the 18-foot open sloop *Coquille*, which went undefeated in one summer of racing. Brother Alfred built and raced the Biloxi Cat *Hindu* after World War I.

Commodore Bell was largely responsible for the new fleet of Lightnings in the harbor of the Bay-Waveland Yacht Club in the early fifties. In the years 1952-53 and 1954 the Lightning Association held its Southern Districts at the club. It had the most active fleet in this area.

In 1954 the ladies auxiliary of the club became very active under the leadership of Mrs. Charles Lozano. A wading pool was constructed for the children and it became so popular that the members and Mr. Hardin raised funds by voluntary contributions for a swimming pier and summerhouse. Before these projects were completed they went further and obtained complete playground equipment.

As of 1955 the club had 750 members. Piers were gradually added to hold berths for sixty-five boats, and modern facilities such as an electric boat hoist, a small boat ramp, a gas pump, etc. were added.

By 1956 J. W. Terrell of Pass Christian Yacht Club, Tommy Kemp with Dr. Eldon Bolton of Biloxi Yacht Club, and Leo Seal, Jr. of Bay-Waveland began a campaign to extend th MCYA championship regattas which now included all the Gulf Coast yacht clubs sailing their entire fleet.

1957 marked the first year that twenty-four skippers from Biloxi, Gulfport, Pass Christian, and Bay-Waveland with two crewmen on each boat, making a total of eighteen persons in each race from the four clubs, sailed in this event. Commodore Carl Alfonso of the Gulfport Yacht Club, who was also president of the MCYA, and his committee, along with Commodore J. E. Erwin and Leo Seal, Jr. of the Bay, planned the successful regatta for both participants and spectators.

In 1969 Hurricane Camille destroyed the rear of the Bay-Waveland clubhouse; however, the yacht club remained standing on pilings in the same location. After much fund raising the members were back in business within the year.

The seventies and the eighties brought many national and international champions to the Bay-Waveland Yacht Club. The families of these prominent young men and women were the Henry Chapmans, Ray Stieffel, Maurice and Fritz Eagan, Richard Hadden, and Clifford Gaudin. These are household names among the champions of the Gulf Yachting Association. In 1980, the Bay-Waveland hosted the finals of the North American Men's sailing championship for the Mallory Cup.

The Bay-Waveland committeemen of 1903 were:

D. C. Bacon	T. L. Evans	Leonard Nicholson
N. E. Bailey, Jr.	Edmond Fairchild	Yorke Nicholson
Dr. J. C. Beard	John A. Fell	W. E. Norris
Lloyd Blake	James Garvey	R. F. O'Brien
W. W. Boullemet	J. W. Glenny	Lawrence O'Donnell
E. J. Bower	W. B. Gillican	John Olsen
Charles Breath	W. J. Hannon	E. A. O'Sullivan
J. A. Breath	A. R. Hart	Henry Peters
H. L. Burton	Henry Heber	A. W. Powell
C. A. Butler	L. J. Henderson	Judge H. H. Price
Edmond Cabiro	John M. Huger	George R. Rea
A. F. Cameron	W. W. Jenks	James Rea
J. F. Cazenave	George Mallard	
George Clay	B. F. Markey	

Paul Conrad
H. P. Dart
J. M. Demarest
W. J. Demarest
Rene de
 Montluzin
Capt. W. A. Dill
John K. Edwards

J. Mazerat
John Menge
J. Edmond Merilh
John T. Michel
N. H. Moody
Charles G.
 Moreau
Dennis Lenauc

E. H. Roberts
Dr. A. R.
 Robertson
John C. Shansy
B. C. Shields
Dr. J. M. B.
 Spence
L. N. C. Spotorno
C. A. Thiel, Sr.
S. T. White

THE BILOXI YACHT CLUB

Excerpts from the condensed history of the Biloxi Yacht Club compiled by Gerald J. Quave of Biloxi, have been taken and form a major part of the background for this book.

In the late 1800s, sailboat racing on Biloxi waters was one of the most popular sports of the time. The first races on record were sailed in catboats in the year 1870, but it is believed sailboat racing was prominent before the Civil War. Reported the *Picayune* of August 23, 1870: "A regatta at Biloxi was declared a complete success. Interest centered on the race between the jaunty and beautiful rig rivals the *Limnas* and the *Protos*. At one time the *Limnas* led by eighteen seconds but the *Protos* came in first by twenty-four seconds. The victory was attributed to 'the famous sailing master of the *Protos*, Clements.' "

Stories about how these races began have been handed down from generation to generation. The most logical explanation is the story about two boat captains who became involved in a heated argument as to which one of their boats was the faster. This argument continued for several weeks until finally it was decided to mark off a measured distance in the Mississippi Sound. The two catboats were to start at the same time in front of the Biloxi small craft harbor. The first boat to traverse the designated course and return across the starting line would be declared the faster.

The date and time for the race were announced. Two boat captains, their crews and their relatives spent many days preparing the two boats for the race. News of this race spread throughout the town, and on the day of the race hundreds of people gathered on the beach to witness the first organized sailboat race in Biloxi.

Owing to the abundance of seafood in the Gulf waters, seafood-packing plants were built in order to process the seafood for shipping out of state. Biloxi was the largest shrimp and oyster-packing center in the world. The high demand for processed seafood brought about the design and construction of a much larger sailing craft than the catboat, which measured sixteen to twenty-four feet in length, with centerboards and large shallow draft rudders to maneuver in shallow water. These new boats were of the schooner class and were forty to sixty feet in length, with shallow draft and two masts. When under full sail, they carried a total of seven sails.

During the latter part of the nineteenth century, more and more of these mariners who made their living on the water started also to enjoy it as a means of pleasant relaxation. The Biloxi schooner quickly replaced the catboat at the many regattas held each year on the Gulf Coast.

In 1900, a group of men organized to get a "big-time" regatta in Biloxi with the participation of the Southern Yacht Club fleet. The organizers of this event were T. P. Dulion, who owned several yachts, and many other prominent businessmen of Biloxi, John Carraway, H. F. Sawford, A. O. Bourdon, George W. Wilkes, L. Lopez, Sr., W. K. M. Dukate, and W. L. Via. Shortly after the regatta, the New Orleans *Picayune* reported, "It is the present plan to construct a building which will be large, with great galleries surrounding it, with quarters for dozens of yachtsmen. The proposed building will face the sea, and directly in front of the home will be sailed all of the races of the club."

Work on the clubhouse was begun in July 1901. *The Herald* reported on July 2, 1901, "The roofing on the new yacht clubhouse set in 10 feet of water from the beach in front of the Hotel de Montrose is now actively under way."

The Herald continued, "Interest in this regatta was so great that leading citizens discussed the possibility of erecting a clubhouse on the beach in connection with aquatic sports. The city sprung into sudden prominence in the annual regattas and the handsome new clubhouse was the culmination of their labors." Biloxi soon became the chief yachting center between Point Clear, Alabama and New Orleans, Louisiana. Vacationers and natives alike would gather at the beaches by the thousands to watch these colorful races.

At the first meeting, the Biloxi Yacht Club adopted a very pretty design for their club burgee, the colors being white and blue, the same colors as the Southern Yacht Club's flag. The letters 'BYC' and a star in blue are in a white field," reported *The Herald*.

The Biloxi Yacht Club held a state charter as an organized stock company of 150 shares at $25 per share. The first commodore was elected in 1901, T. P. Dulion, a prominent Biloxian. In 1902 Dr. D. A. Nash was made the commodore with J. J. Kennedy, president.

In 1903 J. J. Kennedy was elected commodore; the same year he was elected president of the Southern Gulf Coast Yachting Association.

"In 1902, May 11, the Cup Committee of the Southern Gulf Coast Yachting Association (SGYCA) held a meeting in Biloxi with Commodore J. C. Bush of Mobile Yacht Club as President of the Association. Present: Dr. R. A. Robertson, Pass Christian, Dr. D. A. Nash, Biloxi. Com. E. J. O'Brien of Southern and Com. Walter Gautier of Pascagoula were unavoidably delayed. The Com. T. P. Dulion and Sec. H. F. Sawford of Biloxi were thanked. Sawford is proprietor of the Montrose Hotel. Commodore Baldwin of Southern will give the Commodore Cup just like is done in the North. A new boat, Edward Schleeder's new motor launch built by Johnson at Back Bay, Biloxi for Santa Oteri was added to the Biloxi fleet," reported the SGCYA monthly publication of 1903.

On July 15, 1904, *The Herald* read,

> the Biloxi Yacht Club will disband and cancel its charter on the 30th of this month. This decision was reached at a meeting of the stockholders last night at which 82 of the 113 shares of stock were represented either by person or by proxy. The club stock has largely fallen into the hands of persons who did not pay dues or did not participate in the work for which the club was organized, and there was a considerable indebtedness which had to be liquidated. A committee composed of President I. Heidenheim, Dr. E. R. Bragg, J. B. Lemon and W. J. Grant was appointed and instructed to sell the assets of the club as soon as they could do so for enough to pay the club debts. Another Yacht and Social club will be organized which will be composed largely of members of the old club.
>
> The lease on the property on which the building stands has still 22 years to run and the clubhouse is an ideal place for the headquarters of such a club as is contemplated.

Another article in *The Herald* on August 13, 1904, read, "The new yachting, athletic and social club met last night at the old Yacht Club rooms. More than 50 men have signed the list of members and it is the intention of the promoters of the new club to increase this number to 75 or 80 before going into permanent organization."

On June 16, 1905, officers elected were I. Heidenheim, reelected president; Martin Haas, reelected vice-president; W. H. Buck, treasurer; Edward Suter, reelected secretary; E. Desporte, commodore; V. J. Tucie, vice-commodore; E. Desporte, official measurer; and Dr. E. R. Bragg, fleet surgeon. It was also decided at this meeting to set the membership dues at fifty cents per month.

The Picayune reported in July 1906, "The big harbor was crowded with craft of all description from the big revenue cutter *Winona* to the smallest power dink, all decorated from stem to stern with bunting. About 20 boats, 60 feet overall, schooners, light draft, powerful vessels with long clean lines. In their summer rigs, they carry enormous club topsails and staysails in addition to the working canvas. They finished amid a tremendous din of whistles, fog horns and guns."

Many interesting stories are told in the SYC *Barometer* of famous races sailed over the Biloxi race course during those early days between two SYC crafts, the *Susie B* and the *Picayune*. The *Picayune* was built for the Nicholson brothers, Leonard and Yorke, of the New Orleans newspaper, in the Biloxi shipyard of Wm. N. Johnson.

"The hurricane of 1915 completely destroyed the clubhouse and plans were immediately formulated for rebuilding along the same specifications. When all arrangements were completed, a cost estimate was authorized in the amount of $3,500. The new club would be built south of Elmer Flats, just East of the old location. The contract for construction of the pilings and wharves was awarded to Chris Thompson," reported Quave.

With construction underway on the pilings and wharves, another hurricane struck in July 1916. However, the only loss was loose lumber and tools amounting to about $250. The new clubhouse was opened on January 1, 1917 and its first commodore was Douglas Watson. In 1921 it was reported that the condition of the club both financially and socially was found to be the best in its history. At the time of the twenty-fifth annual regatta, held on July 9 and 10, 1924, the races were conducted under the auspices and classification of the Gulf Yachting Association. The Biloxi Yacht Club had purchased three Fish Class sloops and joined the GYA in 1922. The classes entered were Fish Class Sloops, Cabin Sloops, Knockabout Sloops, Open Sloops, catboats, Marconi-cats (Toppan Tot Class), sailing skiffs, motor boats, auto speed boats, express cruisers and schooners. It was noted on the instructions, "Schooners to race with working sails and no black lead or grease of any kind allowed."

On July 10 and 11, 1929 the thirtieth annual regatta of the Biloxi Yacht Club was held and from a souvenir program it is clear that new types of craft were added to the race schedule. They were: 21-foot Marconi-sloops, 21-foot Gaff sloops, Marconi-cats and the Star Class boats.

In 1936, the Biloxi Yacht Club received a shot in the arm when they held the first governors' race. It was a two boat event featuring the governor of Mississippi Hugh White against the governor of Louisiana, Richard W. Leche. Thousands of spectators witnessed the governor of Mississippi win by fifty-eight seconds over the governor of Louisiana in a classic battle. Seeking revenge, Governor Leche challenged Governor White to a repeat performance on his home waters on Lake Pontchartrain in New Orleans, Louisiana. This was an invitational race to which all Southern governors were invited. Seven governors were on the starting line in 1937; again, Governor White was the victor.

The year 1937 was a banner period in the history of the Biloxi Yacht Club. Struggling to rebound from the weary years of the Depression, the members of the club, who numbered 135, made every effort to bring the sailing spirit back. Through the determination of the race committee chairman, Dan Keller, the skipperettes, of which there were twenty-four, were organized by Mrs. W. L. Parks (Mercedes), chairman; Mrs. B. B. O'Mara (Lydia), vice-chairman; and Mrs. W. P. Kennedy (Beatrice), treasurer. They had a busy schedule and entered forty-five regattas both within their area and outside as well.

Not to be outdone by their counterparts, the Biloxi Yacht Club skippers continued to win their share of sailing events. For the fourth time since race week was inaugurated in 1934, the Biloxi Yacht Club had won this regatta. This feature of the racing season in Biloxi, race week, attracts up to 100 craft, ranging from small dinghies to schooner yachts, and marks the opening of the mid-summer regatta season on the Mississippi Coast.

"Assisting in making Race Week probably the most outstanding regatta along the Gulf is the presence of sailing vessels from the Southern Yacht Club fleet of New Orleans," reported Clinton C. Blackwell of *The Daily Herald* of Biloxi, "which always precede this event with a long-distance race from the Crescent city to Biloxi." In the junior races, they won five out of the seven events.

There was absolute euphoria within the halls of the Biloxi Yacht Club when the expert skippers of the Fish Class won the prestigious Sir Thomas J. Lipton trophy for the first time in their many years of trying. The outstanding skippers of 1937 were Bob Brodie, Bill Kennedy, Jr., Alf Dantzler, John Joyce, Dr. Eldon Bolton, John Holland, and Walter Seymour.

The members of the board for the year 1937 were George R. Stannus, commodore; Earl W. Sadler, vice-commodore; Dr. Eldon Bolton, rear commodore; Wallace Chapman, secretary-treasurer; W. L. (Bill) Parks, fleet captain; and Dr. J. F. Detweiler, fleet surgeon. The governing board members were A. F. Dantzler, Jr., Robert H. Pringle, William P. Kennedy, G. J. Wiltz, P. T. Kettering, F. C. (Jack)

Goodman, Dan Keller, Finley B. Hewes, Jr. and G. E. Moore.

The Biloxi Yacht Club teams, both skippers and skipperettes, were great competitors for many, many years. The Biloxi Yacht Club was one of the few yacht clubs whose skippers classified as experts were considered as such by ability alone and not by their sex. The skipperettes battled for and were rewarded with berths on many Lipton Cup teams. For several years, the Biloxi Yacht Club team monopolized the Commodore Knost Trophy all-girl regattas, carrying home most of the beautiful silver trophies which were a trademark of this event. Some of the well-known skipperettes were Joyce Fountain, Janet Green, Mrs. William Kennedy, Jr. (Bea), Mrs. Alf Dantzler (Val), and many others. The Biloxi Yacht Club's Lipton Cup teams went on to win this historic trophy of Sir Thomas J. Lipton in 1952, 1953, 1954, 1955, 1958, 1961, 1966, and 1967.

In 1938, after a lapse of several years, the schooner races were started again. It was recalled by one of the old-time skippers that the feature of this regatta was at one time the famous Fisherman's Schooner Race. "Old-timers remember the keen rivalry between such champion schooners as the *Queen of the Fleet*, the *Henry M*, the *American Girl*, the *Mary Margaret*, and the *H. E. Gumbel*," reported *The Herald*.

Over the Fourth of July weekend in the summer of 1938, the third Carnival Regatta and also the twenty-ninth annual regatta were held. Reported *The Times-Picayune*, "This is always a spectacular event as on the Fourth there is a brilliant display of fireworks, bursting flares of rockets along the waterfront which is visible for several miles."

After the 1941 season, the Biloxi Yacht Club became inactive for the period of World War II. Keesler Air Force Base used the clubhouse during this period as a base of operations for its rescue boats. Keesler was training bomber pilots and using the Gulf waters as a bombing range. Occasionally a plane would have to "ditch" in the Gulf and these rescue craft would be sent out to pick up survivors. During this same period, the federal government imposed certain restrictions on water craft. The Coast Guard patrolled the Mississippi Sound, enforcing a law that prohibited any private vessel from venturing more than three miles out from the shoreline because of the mines. After this short span of inactivity and restrictions, the club reopened in 1946 with renewed interest, and it began growing at a prosperous pace.

The four club-owned Fish Class sloops, cypress-hulled boats, were sold in 1945 and construction was started on ten new mahogany marine plywood Fish Class craft. Six of the new sloops were for the Biloxi Yacht Club and the other four were for the Pass Christian Yacht Club. These boats were completed and raced in the September 1946 regatta, which was the first regatta since 1942, also the first GYA regatta in which plywood-constructed boats were used.

Then in 1947 a hurricane destroyed the bottom deck of the clubhouse and carried away all of the docks. Wind speeds were clocked at 97 m.p.h. and tides were 12 to 15 feet above normal. The docks were rebuilt and the damaged building repaired. Several years later in 1965, Hurricane Betsy made a glancing blow to the Mississippi Sound and the club was damaged again.

In the fifties the National Penguin and the District Lightning championship series were held at the Biloxi Yacht Club. In the late sixties, with a very active and large membership, it was felt that there was a need to enlarge and remodel the entire club facilities. The dock area, the lounge and bar areas were expanded, new furniture and fixtures were purchased, a modern electric kitchen was installed and the ladies powder room was air conditioned.

The renovation began in 1968, and by August 16, 1969, (the exact date will never be forgotten) Commodore Jay Lopez and several other members of his committee were completing the installation of the last recessed lighting fixtures in the ceiling of the upper deck. Meanwhile Keith Fountain and other members were removing pictures, trophies, and documents from their newly made cases, in preparation for Hurricane Camille, the most destructive hurricane of the century. It struck the next day, August 17, with all its fury, winds were clocked at 200 m.p.h. with 20-foot waves. The entire renovation of the club had cost approximately $35,000 and within twenty-four hours after completion all that remained was a cluster of broken and split pilings.

This beautiful yacht club stood majestically over water at the terminus of the 28-mile long, 300-feet wide sand beach in Biloxi, Mississippi, the longest man-made beach in the world. This beach replaced the large public-type piers that extended into the water in front of the homes from Henderson Point to Biloxi on Mississippi Sound. It was no more.

To some members, this seemed like the end of the Biloxi Yacht Club. However, like those of the Southern Yacht Club, Biloxi Yacht Club yachtsmen are true survivors. After many long meetings and a lot of legwork, in October 1971 the Biloxi Yacht Club completed the purchase of the El Capitan Lounge, the Trade Winds Hotel swimming pool, and the marina and sand beach south of Highway 90.

Today there stands a very fine yacht club with full accommodations and a marina with eighteen boat slips; there are plans to increase this number in the near future. This edifice is dedicated to those courageous men and women who over the many years gave unselfishly of their time and money to maintain an age-old tradition that began in 1870 when two captains decided to see whose boat was the faster and so began the first race on these same waters in the small boat harbor of Biloxi.

Despite the many disasters which befell the Biloxi Yacht Club, its members remained undaunted and they continued to rebuild. Biloxi was a special place for visiting yachtsmen and the many followers of the races. It was the place to be during Race Week.

Many fond memories this writer holds of viewing races from the large open-air gallery of the old Biloxi Yacht Club, which was always crowded with spectators, many sitting in the large cane-backed rocking chairs, breathlessly awaiting the booming sound of the cannon as it fired for the start or the finish of the race. The line was but a pebble throw from the clubhouse.

THE GULFPORT YACHT CLUB

The Gulfport Yacht Club is listed as one of the "ports of call" along the racing circuit in 1903 of the Southern Gulf Coast Yachting Association, the predecessor of the present day Gulf Yachting Association.

With the completion of one of the most magnificent and expensive resort hotels in the South, the Great Southern, which cost when finished $300,000, predictions were made that Gulfport was destined to become famous as a summer and winter pleasure resort.

In 1902 a call had been issued by some of the local businessmen for a meeting of those interested in the formation of a yacht club. Said the notice, "The club will take in members from all points between Gulfport and Jackson and from the Gulf Coast towns. The purpose will be to build an up-to-date clubhouse devoted to the interests of boating and fishing. The subject is being agitated by Mr. John J. Kennedy of Gulfport. His efforts are being met with the enthusiastic approval of Gulfport's best citizens."

And so the Gulfport Yacht Club was born on April 2, 1902. In 1903 the club joined the newly formed Southern Gulf Coast Yachting Association (SGCYA) and became an active participant in the SGCYA racing circuit, which had as its most popular event the races of club-owned boats. Southern Yacht Club owned the *Red Skin*; Bay-Waveland, the *Irma*; Pass Christian, *Gladiola*; Gulfport, *Joker*; Biloxi, *Urania*; Mobile, *Vesper Belle*; and E. Pascagoula, *Moki*.

At the first meeting of the Gulfport Yacht Club in 1903, the following were elected to office and to committees: Joseph T. Jones, commodore; John C. Kennedy, vice-commodore; J. R. Pratt, rear commodore; R. W. Shipp, secretary; George P. Hewes, treasurer; A. J. Catchot, fleet captain; Thomas Favre, measurer; Dr. J. B. Kilgore, fleet surgeon.

The Picayune reported:

> To its first meeting, the Gulfport Yacht Club invited Emile J. O'Brien and H. L. Burton of the Southern Yacht Club to assist them by their advice in carrying out their programme. The experience of these two well-known yachtsmen will help considerably to make the regatta a success.
>
> The Reception Committee for the first regatta consisted of the following members:

J. W. Bozeman	E. C. Lucas
A. J. Cachot	L. Martin
Frank Foster	A. McAlpin
S. S. Henry	S. P. Mooreman
W. Haddow	G. E. Northrop
F. B. Hewes	F. V. Osborne
H. Hewes	W. T. Steward
H. A. Jackson	J. T. Stopp
J. B. Kilgore	Frank Taylor
	J. T. Walker

> These Southern gentlemen, dressed in their yachting attire, warmly welcomed their first Southern Gulf Yachting Association regatta's guests in July 1903.

In a description of the Great Southern Hotel, it was noted that for the amusement of the guests a pavilion enclosed in solid glass was erected over a mile out on the Sound at the extreme end of the pier, to which electric trolley cars ran every few minutes, and to which a pleasant promenade could be had if desired; shaded resting places provided with seats were erected at short intervals along a substantial plank walk running parallel with the car track. From this pier a line of passenger and excursion boats would run for general service of the entire Gulf, also a line of naphtha launches to local and nearby islands, on which all conveniences for surf bathing would be provided second to no other pleasure resort in America. It was at the end of this pier that the yacht club was built as an annex to the hotel.

The Picayune of July 31, 1903 reported on the first Gulfport regatta and meeting.

> The programme of the first regatta of the Gulfport Yacht Club was

sailed under the rules of the Southern Gulf Coast Yachting Association. Each of the clubs was represented by a special boat in the feature race. Schooners, catboats, cabin and open sloops, racing machine and launches had many entries.

Great interest was shown in the regatta as many spectators were present. The steam yacht *Semper Idem* from the Southern Yacht Club, belonging to SYC Commodore Albert Baldwin, was here with a party. Harry Howard sent from Biloxi his houseboat in tow of his launch *Sea Toy* and SYC Walter Glenny's power yacht *Chewink III* with a party of friends aboard was also a visitor. Commodore Jones of the Gulfport Yacht Club, the multimillionaire "daddy of Gulfport" sent his speedy power launch, the natty "Grace" to take part in the motor launch race with Captain A. J. Catchot in charge of *Grace*. [Captain Joseph T. Jones was the builder of the Gulf and Ship Island Railroad and founder of the city of Gulfport.]

The presence of these fine yachts, with the Louisiana Naval Reserve ship *Stranger* laying off the pier, added an attraction to the scene. The spacious galleries and reception rooms of the headquarters of the yachtsmen, the magnificent new Great Southern Hotel, were thronged with fair visitors, many of whom wore the colors or badges of their favorite craft.

There is no doubt that the sensation of the yachting season is the speedy open sloop *Gladiola* brought down from the North by Commodore Samuel F. Heaslip of the Southern Yacht Club.

This, the 4th regatta in the series of six like events of the racing and cruising circuit of the Southern Gulf Coast Yachting Association along this coast this summer was one of more than usual moment because it marks the entrance into the Association of the 7th club enrolled in the first three years of the organization. The SGCYA was originally created for a one-design class. All yacht clubs belonging to the Association were well represented especially a large group from the newly formed Gulfport Yacht Club who were particulary noticeable from the fact that every one of its members was in full yacht club uniform.

The prizes were: for schooners 45 ft. and over $35.00, under 45 ft. $30.00, barges, one class $10.00, cabin sloops 30 ft. and over $60.00, under 30 ft. $40.00. Open sloops 22 ft. and over $35.00, under 22 ft. $25.00. Catboats, model 20 ft. and over $25.00, model under 20 ft. $15.00. Racing machines 18 ft. and over $30.00, under 18 ft. $15.00, launches, one class $10.00.

The 1905 season was cancelled owing to a yellow fever epidemic in Pass Christian. The years following were not very good ones for sailing. A depression, then World War I brought disaster to the One-Design sport.

After the war, in 1919, the Fish Class One-Design sloops were born at the Southern Yacht Club and soon all the yacht clubs on the Gulf Coast had a fleet of these newly designed boats, which became the official club-owned boat of the Gulf Yachting Association.

In 1932, the Gulfport Yacht Club was reactivated and here to tell the story of its new beginning is C. Blackwell, sports editor of *The Daily Herald* of Gulfport. It was related in his article of August 25, 1937, when the Gulfport Yacht Club celebrated the opening of its new home.

Years after the original yacht club was destroyed by fire and yachting faded out with those burned embers, a handful of sailing enthusiasts assembled at Captain Manzey's wharf on West Pier in 1932 and held some match races with their five catboats, all under seventeen feet. Racing rules were simple in those days; first, the contestant was required to sail a triangular course; second, the first boat finishing the course was declared the winner. There were no handicaps and no right-away boats.

From the start, yachting captured the interest of Mayor Joseph W. Milner, and practically every Sunday afternoon he had his yacht *Seawind* available for the yachtsmen to start their races from. In the early days, the club did not own a cannon and the members used a small pistol for the preparatory and starting gun.

Then came 1933 when a group of young men formed a club that was called the Gulfport Yacht Club. The first members were: James Todd as commodore, Ashton Hardy, Nathan Alfonso, G. B. Flagg, Arvah S. Hopkins, Sr., Vincent Alfonso, Tut Alfonso and Felton Ladner. Probably there were a few others.

The first race after the organization of the club was sailed among three catboats, Vincent Alfonso's *Revenge*, G. B. Flagg's *Carolyn*, Ashton Hardy's *Star Wind*, and Arvah S. Hopkins' sloop *What-Not*. The race was held off a clubowned pier some 700 feet south of Captain Manzey's wharf on West Pier. The sinking of this pier owing to overcrowding by spectators was recalled by many.

Almost immediately, the efforts of those few who reorganized the yacht club for the primary purpose of reviving sailboat racing began to pay dividends, and by 1934 the membership in the club had grown to approximately 200.

The season of 1934 marked the first step for the club as an up-and-coming institution. The catboat fleet increased; interest about town generated with a greater velocity; the first regatta was held; and climaxing it all the Gulfport Yacht Club was admitted to membership in the Gulf Yachting Association—even without having the required two-club Fish Class sloops. Arvah S. Hopkins was elected commodore, and under him the club was incorporated. Upton Sisson served as vice-commodore; Gus Alfonso, rear commodore; and Leonard Hardy, secretary-treasurer. With nominal membership dues, the club expanded almost at once.

Among the catboats joining the fleet that season were Upton Sisson's *Barbara Jane*, the Philip Schilling-Bob Heath-Dick Gay syndicate-owned *Alibi*, Tut Alfonso's *Krazy Kat*, Nathan Alfonso's *Amberjack*, James Todd's *Mebitable*, Arvah Hopkins Jr.'s *Betty Jean*, G. B. Flagg's *Skimp Jack* and possibly others. Commodore Hopkins also launched his machine sloop *Mystery* late that summer.

In August 1934 the club was granted full active membership and participated in the Lipton Cup regatta, which was held in Pensacola. It did not make a good record as it was the first time the Gulfport representatives had had a hand on the tiller of a fish craft.

The first annual Gulfport Yacht Club regatta held in mid-summer of 1934 was sailed on a course offshore on the west side of the steamship basin. A stand was erected several hundred feet inland and this was used as the starting pavilion of the races. Despite these handicaps, the regatta attracted an entry of some thirty-five craft, and the event was declared a great success in view of the fact it was the club's first undertaking.

The minutes of the Gulfport Yacht Club's meeting of August 15, 1934 show that the vote carried in favor of the name of the Gulfport Yacht Club being changed to the Gulfport Yacht Racing Association. Also a motion was made and adopted to have the Gulfport Yacht Racing Association incorporated, which was done in accordance with the club's application.

Those members whose names appeared on the charter signed by A. S. Hopkins, president, and L. D. Hardy, secretary, were:

A. Alfonso
G. Alfonso
N. Alfonso
Randolph Batson
Joe Bolton
Floyd Brown
Bill Dauphin
G. B. Flagg
Marvin Fortner
Dick Gay
L. D. Hardy
A. S. Hopkins
A. M. Hopkins
Philip Schilling
Robert Shearin

In 1935 the club functioned on a still larger scale. Funds were raised for the construction of two club-owned Fish Class sloops, one of which was launched that season. The catboat fleet continued to grow and the club membership was again around 200. Mr. Hopkins was reelected commodore, and other flag officers included Nathan Alfonso, vice-commodore; G. B. Flagg, Sr., rear commodore; Philip Schilling, secretary; and Andy Alfonso, treasurer. Jack Jordan served as secretary during the latter part of the year following the resignation of Schilling.

Gulfport Yacht Club's third annual regatta in 1935 was still larger than those of 1933 and 1934, with sixty-five boats taking part. The races were started from a club-built pier off the west steamship docks. All the while the club was campaigning for a home, a clubhouse.

The honor of winning the first opening regatta trophy in 1936 went to Commodore Hopkins and Nathan Alfonso. This interclub event was held in the early summer of 1936. They finished with high point laurels.

The 1936 flag officers were Ava S. Hopkins, who was reelected for his third term, commodore; Upton Sisson, vice-commodore; Marvin Fortner, rear commodore; Joe Bolton, secretary; and Andy Alfonso, treasurer.

In that it created sailing enthusiasm among the youngsters, the designing and construction of the Alfonso racer, a small catboat, by Vincent Alfonso in 1936 was another great step forward for the club. The little boats immediately became a hit and before the season closed eight were taking part in regular weekend races, and also the various regattas along the Mississippi Coast.

In 1936 the Gulfport Yacht Club really began putting on steam. Three Fish Class boats were put over to increase its fleet to four; the skipperette club was organized; the Alfonso racers were introduced; larger catboats and sloops joined the fleet; the club won its first trophies in interclub Fish Class competition; and climaxing the season, it tied the Biloxi Yacht Club for second place in the seventeenth annual Lipton Cup regatta sailed in Panama City.

The Gulfport skipperettes were an important and hard-working group in the club and immediately became a power in their division in the Gulf Yachting Association. They won the Biloxi Yacht Club Race Week trophy and also captured honors in the Gulfport regatta. Regular intraclub Fish Class skipperette races began expanding and as a result the club was one of the largest skipperette organizations in the association.

Then came the recreational and yacht harbor project. The Gulfport Yacht Club took an active part in the campaign for this recreational facility. The proposed project met with the approval of the citizens of the municipality and today the Gulfport Yacht Club has a home, probably one of the most elaborate on the Gulf Coast.

The year 1937 was a banner year from the start for the club. In view of the new facilities and harbor that were being constructed, the Pensacola Yacht Club surrendered its right as host club for the 1937 Lipton regatta in favor of Gulfport. And Biloxi, which had tied

Gulfport for runner-up place in the 1936 Lipton cup regatta, also stepped aside in cooperation with her sister city.

"In some respects, it all is something in the nature of a dream being host to the Lipton Regatta, moving into a beautiful new home, which is part of the recently completed Joseph T. Jones recreational park and the Bert Jones yacht harbor, and boasting a club membership of nearly 500," reported Mr. Blackwell.

Commodore Hopkins served a fourth term at the helm of the club in 1937. Other flag officers were G. B. Flagg, vice-commodore; Finley B. "Goat" Hewes Sr., rear commodore; Joe Bolton, secretary; Andy Alfonso, treasurer; Gus Alfonso, fleet captain; Dr. Archie Hewes, fleet surgeon; Donald Suter succeeding Upton Sisson, who resigned, chairman of the race committee; Harry Kane, chairman of the entertainment committee and the special Lipton Cup committee; Oscar Cassibry, Sr., chairman of the housing committee; and G. B. Flagg, chairman of the membership committee. Board members in addition to the above were, Harry Larson, N. E. Gaston, Jack Jordan, Nathan Alfonso, Owen Palmer, Sr., and Mayor Joseph W. Milner.

The club had another new fleet of boats, the International Snipe Class, and additional catboats and Alfonso racers came out. The club also purchased two more Fish Class sloops and now had a fleet of six. The Fourth of July annual regatta exceeded the expectations of the club members. A total of eighty-two boats entered, ranging upwards from the small Alfonso racers to the large schooners of the Southern Yacht Club fleet. The inner harbor was filled with sail craft and pleasure yachts—it was a colorful pageant.

Then came another war, World War II, and the Coast Guard, Navy and Army used the clubhouse in various capacities such as coast patrol, air-sea rescue and training units. It was returned to the members of the Gulfport Yacht Club in May 1946.

Another disaster struck when the 1947 hurricane, which devastated the Gulf Coast, washed away the Gulfport Yacht Club. The only remaining part was the foundation and the flag pole. Soon afterwards, a building was purchased and moved under the flag pole to be used as a temporary clubhouse until the city could rebuild on the old foundation.

Before the storm hit the club, the Gulfport Yacht Club was chartered by the International Star Class Association as a member within the New Orleans-Gulf Coast Star Class Fleet charter given to the Southern Yacht Club in 1926. Charter members of the new fleet were Nathan Alfonso, Donald Suter, Roy Halter, Elizabeth Robin, and Bob Milner in 1947.

Undaunted by the many vicissitudes, in the summer of 1948 Fish Class racing was again under way with eight new boats built by Grenade Boat Works of Mobile, Alabama. This was also the year that Commodore George P. Hopkins, Jr. was elected commodore of the Gulf Yachting Association and the clubhouse was packed with GYA members and their guests for the annual meeting and opening regatta of the GYA.

The year 1948 marked the first time that the Lipton trophy was won by the Gulfport Yacht Club. A great effort would have been to host the Lipton Regatta in 1949 despite the club's limitations, but in good neighborly fashion the hosting of the Lipton Regatta in 1949 was surrendered to the Southern Yacht Club, which was celebrating its one-hundredth anniversary. The provision was made, however, that when the Southern Yacht Club won its next Lipton Trophy it would return the favor to the Gulfport Yacht Club. This was done in 1956.

In 1955 the Biloxi Yacht Club won the Lipton Cup for the fourth consecutive year. According to GYA rules, no club may hold a Lipton Regatta in two consecutive years, thereby permitting the second place club to host the next year's event. In this case it was the Southern Yacht Club. Now was the time to "return the favor" to the Gulfport Yacht Club, which it did. With the members in their new home, in 1956 everything was GO for the second Lipton Cup Regatta ever held by the Gulfport Yacht Club.

In 1961 the Gulfport Yacht Club hosted the Mississippi Coast Yachting Association's regatta during Race Week. In 1963 it was likewise host to the fifteenth annual Ocean Race circuit. In 1968, the Gulfport Yacht Club hosted the twentieth annual sailboat race from Gulfport to Pensacola. There to fire a cannon from the deck of the *Mapleleaf* to start the race was "Goat" Hewes. Finley B. "Goat" Hewes was well known along the Mississippi Coast yachting world. Four times commodore of the Gulfport Yacht Club and also commodore of the Gulf Yachting Association in 1959, Commodore Hewes was instrumental in securing the necessary piling and filling for the new clubhouse. He sold $22,000 of the $70,000 in bonds to finance the new club. For this Commodore Hewes was awarded a life membership in the yacht club.

In the thirty-fifth annual Sugar Bowl Regatta held on Lake Pontchartrain in 1969, the "Race of Champions" was won by Gulfport Yacht Club skipper Donald Sutter. William Davis of the Buccaneer Yacht Club was second and Nolfie Alfonso, sailing for the New Orleans Yacht Club, was third. In fourth place was SYC David Blouin, Jerry

Ellis from Biloxi was fifth, with Pat E. Baroco of Fairhope in sixth place. It was encouraging to see ageing skippers (and skipperettes) still winning—Sutter was fifty-seven and Alfonso, sixty-eight.

Still another catastrophe for the members of the Gulfport Yacht Club happened in 1969 when the worst hurricane in history, *Camille*, struck the Gulf Coast, killing 250 people and devastating the entire shoreline from one end of the twenty-five-mile-long beach to the other. Included in the destruction was the Gulfport Yacht Club again. But troupers that they are, the yachtsmen spent the next two years replacing the building that housed their club. In that hurricane the *Mapleleaf* of Commodore Hewes was also destroyed. It happened when he was out of town; he arrived too late to save his pride and joy.

The first annual GYA 200-mile New Orleans Lightship Ocean race got under way from the Gulfport Yacht Club harbor in 1970 with a large turnout of about fifty boats. In 1976 the National championship of the Half-Ton and the Cougar Cat National championship events were held by the Gulfport Yacht Club.

The '80s brought to the Gulfport Yacht Club a real champion who came up from the junior ranks, Leslie Weatherly, who was the junior champion in her club. At twenty-three years of age, Leslie won her third consecutive Sunfish Women's North American title in Houston, Texas in August 1983. By virtue of her victory, she qualified for the 1984 Sunfish World championships in Colombia and was the top woman finisher. She also was the top woman finisher in the 1981 Sunfish World Championships in Sardinia, Italy, when she took tenth place in a field of eighty boats, and the winner in 1982.

In October 1984 the Gulfport Yacht Club held the Chrysler Laser World championships.

One of the most distinguished trophies in the Gulfport Yacht Club is the Commodore Arvah S. Hopkins memorial trophy. The commodore was a prominent physician in Gulfport. He was most influential in the founding of the first Gulfport Yacht Club and was indefatigable in his efforts to secure the municipal harbor of Gulfport for safe anchorage of small boats.

Members of the Alfonso family of Gulfport became very prominent in the yachting world along the Gulf Coast, where they had sailed since they were knee-high boys. The Alfonso racer was the brainchild of Vincent Alfonso. This fleet of small boats was a stimulus to junior racing in the club. Five of the Alfonso brothers Tut, Joe, Nathan, Andy, and Gus, were all top-notch skippers and dedicated workers of the Gulfport Yacht Club. The sixth brother, Nolfie, was a champion skipper in the New Orleans Yacht Club, as he was a businessman in the city. Two of the brothers, Nolfie and Joe, were commodores of the Gulf Yachting Association, Nolfie in 1962 and Joe in 1977.

THE JACKSON YACHT CLUB

The Jackson Yacht Club (JYC) was originally chartered on August 18, 1958 by three Jackson residents, George Porter, Richard Porter, and Robert Fulton Thompson. As planning of the Pearl Reservoir progressed, greater interest was shown in the sport of yachting, and on the evening of July 28, 1960 a group of fifty-five people, including two of the original club incorporators, gathered at the Capital City Club to discuss the advisability of proceeding with formal establishment of such a club, in anticipation of the resources which would be provided on completion of the reservoir.

On September 28, 1960 the steering committee's report on recommendations for a constitution, fees and dues, and an initial fleet of Class sailing boats was favorably acted upon and the Jackson Yacht Club came into being, aided by the transfer by the original incorporators of the Jackson Yacht Club charter to the newly formed group. All formalities required for transfer of that charter establishing the Jackson Yacht Club as a non-profit corporation were completed. Following are the original officers: William T. Phelps, commodore; Harry D. Owen, vice-commodore; Joseph A. Blythe, Jr., rear commodore; Thomas J. Biggs, secretary-treasurer; and William A. Gill, fleet measurer. The board of governors consisted of Oscar Cassibry, Negley England, Robert Gordin, George Porter, and Vaughn Watkins.

At the November, 1961 annual meeting, the planning and finance committee recommended a series of plans for the future establishment of a clubhouse on the Pearl River Reservoir in the latter part of 1964 and means for financing an adequate facility at that location.

The nominating committee submitted the following members to serve for the year 1962:

> commodore—Negley England, Oscar Cassibry
> vice-commodore—Joe Blythe, Forrest North
> rear commodore—Bing Witty, Sam Oldham
> secretary-treasurer—Dr. Arthur Guyton, Joe Fountain
> fleet measurer—Bob Gordin

The members elected were England, Blythe, Oldham, Guyton and Gordin. The board of governors was made up of William Young, Steve Burwell, Milton Everett, Homer Porter, and William Suddath.

For temporary headquarters, in October 1961, an A-frame clubhouse was erected at Shore Station #1 on Lake Hico by the Mid-State Construction Company for the sum of $1,700, exclusive of heating and painting. Financing arrangements were made for this amount plus $300 for furnishings and equipment, or a total of $2000. The Blue Jay Fleet was used as collateral to secure this loan.

With the completion of the temporary clubhouse, great plans were made for the sailing season of 1962. The first invitational regatta was held on April 22 and 23, 1962, with Bingham Witty as chairman and a group of enthusiastic committeemen consisting of Commodore Negley England, Homer Porter, Sam Oldham, Tom Biggs, Bill Phelps, Bob Gordon, Bill Cole, Don Blythe, Joe Blythe, Robert Field, Bill Suddath, and Bob Tyson.

The Coast Guard furnished a safety patrol and provided powerboats to assist in the race. Reported *The Clarion Ledger, Jackson Daily News* of April 22, 1962: "Sails flapping, skippers commanding and crews hiking will be the scene at Lake Hico on April 26-29 as the Jackson Yacht Club holds its first invitational regatta.

"At least 25 sail boats are expected. Visiting boats from Memphis, Tennessee, Columbus and Charleston in Mississippi, Baton Rouge, Louisiana, New Orleans, Louisiana, Bay St. Louis, Mississippi, Florence and Sheffield, Alabama will complete with Jacksonians. Classes of sail boat scheduled to race are Thistles, Day Sailors, Blue Jays, Lido-14 and Penguins. Skippers to represent the host club are: Tom Biggs, Don Blythe, Bill Cole, Negley England, Bob Gordon, Mrs. Harvey Mitchell, Forrest North, Sam Oldham, Bill Phelps, Homer Porter and Bingham Witty."

The juniors had an excellent turnout, with Don Blythe winning the first junior sailing championship of the Jackson Yacht Club. The skipperettes also made a good showing.

Behind every successful regatta lies that ever-loyal and dedicated group known as the Ladies Committee. These charming individuals were chaired by Mrs. Joe Blythe and Mrs. Sam Oldham. Each member of the committee acted as hostess for visiting couples.

With limited space owing to the A-shaped building, luncheon accommodations could be handled only on long picnic tables and benches, which were situated on the newly mud-filled ground surrounding the building. As usually happens on such occasions, the weather was most uncooperative and the rain poured most of the day. The picnic baskets filled with fried chicken, potato salad, and cookies were salvaged and served with cold drinks under a canvas-topped porch, but the fun and excitement of this first regatta has lingered in the memory of those die-hard yachting enthusiasts. It makes for good story telling now that the members are located in their beautiful and luxurious clubhouse as their guests crowd the grassy point from which the yacht club overlooks the waters of the Ross Barnett Reservoir.

The opening of the new club facility was celebrated in 1966. This beautiful new clubhouse was built on a bluff overlooking the waters of the Ross Barnett Reservoir. The 35,000-acre reservoir was completed in 1965 through damming of the Pearl River.

I remember the day, October 22, 1966, very well, as a group from New Orleans arrived at the club early Saturday morning just ahead of the moving van carrying the chairs and sofas for the lounge. It was hectic but lots of fun and we were proud to be a part of this memorable occasion. Taking spade in hand, many of the ladies supervised the planting of azaleas and rose bushes around the flag staff in front of the club.

The dream of fifty-five yachtsmen who gathered that night of July 28, 1960 to promote a yacht club was realized far beyond their expectations. One might say the same of the dream of the members of the first budget committee, who approved the sum of $3,087 for operations costs the initial year. And the finished clubhouse was far above the hopes of the first commodore William T. Phelps, and architect Thomas Biggs, who met with GYA Commodore J. Gilbert Scheib in a private dining room at a downtown hotel to discuss whether the dues should be $10.00 or $50.00 a month. Helping to get the Jackson Yacht Club under way, Scheib insisted on $50.00.

Tempus fugit, and the Jackson Yacht Club's opening regatta, which is known as the Hospitality Regatta, has become one of the most popular events in the South. Each year it draws from Illinois to Texas.

The juniors of Jackson Yacht Club were the first to win the GYA Commodore Leslie P. Beard trophy for the most outstanding junior program in the Gulf Yachting Association. The presentation was made in 1968 by GYA Commodore J. Gilbert Scheib at the clubhouse. The recipients were Jan Wennerlund, commodore of the junior group, and Amy Everett immediate past commodore. Proudly watching their youngsters were Commodore Henry Lampe, Dr. Ben Douglas, Miss Barbara Anderson, and Robert Field, junior advisors.

By the year 1970 the Jackson Yacht Club, it was estimated, represented an investment of $360,000, which included the clubhouse, land, and club-owned boats. It had proudly served with distinction as host for two championship regattas, the National Flying Dutchman championship and the 1970 International championship for the

Lido-14 class.

A JYC skipperette team won the Dixie Inland Yacht Racing Association's eliminations and went to the semi-finals for the Adams Cup, the top national trophy for women. Also, a JYC crew represented the Dixie Inland Yacht Racing Association at the Prince of Wales club-match races at Los Angeles, in 1970.

When the Sears Cup finals for the National Junior sailing championship were sailed at the Jackson Yacht Club in 1972, the winners, Clark Thompson, skipper, with Paul Thompson and Buddy Brown as crew, were all presented with scholarships to the University of Hawaii, where they would become members of the University of Hawaii sailing team.

In 1974, the Jackson Yacht Club hosted the GYA annual meeting and opening regatta, at which event Commodore Henry Lampe of the JYC was formally installed as commodore of the Gulf Yachting Association.

In 1977 Dick Durgin of JYC won the fifth National Catalina 22 championship, with daughter Nancy and Guyer Buzhardt as crew.

In the Gulfport to Cozumel, Mexico ninth Regatta al Sol ocean race, a happy and spirited crew of Jacksonians boarded Dr. W. A. "Gus" Neely's yacht *Antares*. They were, in addition to Neely, Harry Shaw, Robert Pendleton, Bill Beemer, Jack Harding, Ed Wennerland, and Jack Callahan. The *Antares* was a Pearson 10-meter and was the smallest boat to participate in the race.

The start of the 700-mile race was called at 11:00 A.M. on Saturday, April 16, 1977. All went very well that day. Sunday was spent riding twenty-foot seas and gales as a front moved through the Gulf. The electric and manual bulge pumps took care of the water problems. On Monday morale was high, the weather was good, and the sea a beautiful deep clear blue.

Tragedy struck on Tuesday when Ed Wennerland suffered a heart attack around noon. Almost immediately distress messages were sent out. Their position was slightly past the half-way mark, in the middle of the Gulf. In about two hours word was received that the U. S. Coast Guard in Miami had gotten their message and that help was on the way, but it never arrived.

Finally about thirty hours after Ed's heart attack, the *Antares* crew arrived at Progresso and was met by a Mexican naval ambulance. After much red tape, Ed was in the hospital in Merida, Mexico—he remained there for a couple of weeks before returning home.

Since the race was abandoned, the *Antares* crew decided to see some of the interior of Yucatan and then work their way to Cozumel by land, but not before more hard luck. On Thursday morning Mexican customs officers boarded the *Antares* and confiscated all weapons aboard. A political battle then followed, which finally led to the return of the unjustly seized weapons. During this episode, a fellow Jacksonian, Wesley Lutken, came by to give the crew a morale boost. Wesley was in Mexico on a fishing trip.

A two-day 300-mile trip to Cozumel began on Friday morning and ended on Saturday morning after more disappointments and transportation problems when the crew finally made it to the ferry for the island of Cozumel.

Disappointment for the crew was not over yet. Upon arriving at the yacht club dinner on Saturday night and visiting the crews they had not seen in seven days, they were met with insults and discourtesies from the host, the commodore of the Cozumel Yacht Club. Fortunately, the evening was saved by two of the finest hosts in Mexico, Alfred Ferrer and Crescencio Rivero Flores, who provided them with an entertaining time.

The crews flew home on Sunday leaving Ed in the hospital. The *Antares* made its way back to Gulfport two weeks later.

The above story was related in the JYC monthly publication *Main Sheet*, in the August 1977 issue.

PASS CHRISTIAN YACHT CLUB

Regattas in the deep South, as we know them today, had their origin in Pass Christian, Mississippi on Mississippi Sound. Reporting on this section of the Gulf Coast, *The Times-Democrat* in 1904 called it "The Riviera of America" and Pass Christian "The Newport of the South, where the very air is a narcotic."

Before trains and bridges, the only way one could get to the Coast from New Orleans was by boat or steamer. When trains did arrive, families that spent the summer at the Pass would ship their horses, carriages, barouches, and later their automobiles by train. Two trains with fifteen coaches each ran daily.

Long piers extended 100 to 150 feet out into the water from the shell roads in front of the cottages and bungalows. These roads were maintained by dumping loads of oyster shells upon the ground and allowing the hoofs of the horses and the wheels of the vehicles to crush them. Later, with the advent of trolley cars and electric lights, conditions were no longer primitive at the Pass.

There was a large number of hotels and boarding houses along the coast, but the Montgomery Hotel at the Pass was the most famous for its many notable winter visitors from the North. The number of residents was around 2,000 until the visitors arrived to change that figure to 8,000.

It was at the Montgomery Hotel in 1849 that the Southern Yacht Club was organized on July 21, 1849 with a distinguished group of gentlemen and yachting enthusiasts summering on the coast from New Orleans and as far as Mobile, Alabama. All regatta races were started from the long wharf of the Montgomery Hotel. It was noted that this hotel had all modern conveniences such as electric bells, gas, steam heat, etc.

Research into the history of the Pass Christian Yacht Club (PCYC) revealed that this club was not organized until 1896, as far as records could be found. Although the Southern Yacht Club was founded at Pass Christian, there was no yacht clubhouse there.

The following article appeared in a publication issued by the Southern Gulf Coast Yachting Association in 1903: "Pass Christian Yacht Club is a member of the Southern Gulf Coast Yachting Association and has been in existence about nine years. The membership, which is very flattering, is greatly augmented during the summer months by the large number of wealthy society people of New Orleans summering at Pass Christian.

"This club especially prides itself on its reputation for presenting the finest of prizes on the coast. There is a movement on foot to erect a handsome club-house. At present all of the regatta races are started from the long wharf of the Mexican Gulf Hotel. The officials are: Joseph A. Menge, Commodore, N. E. Bailey, Jr., Vice-Commodore, J. H. Morey, Rear Commodore and Dr. A. R. Robertson, Secretary-Treasurer."

The Times-Democrat of 1903 reported, "It was to the amazement of everyone that with all the wealth at the Pass, there were no promoters for the building of a yacht club." Further reference to the founding of the Pass Christian Yacht Club was made in *The Daily Herald* by the sports editor, Clinton C. Blackwell, in a publication dated August 27, 1937. "The first Pass Christian Yacht Club was formed around such prominent yachting enthusiasts as the Blakes, Brensters, Harrises, Leroys, Martins, and the Paynes."

The first commodore of record of the Pass Christian Yacht Club was Joseph A. Menge in 1903. Serving the club for the next years and until World War I, were: J. Walton Glenny, ex-commodore of SYC, Samuel Heaslip, ex-commodore of SYC, Peter Labouisse of SYC, Richard Chotard, Nicholas Holly, Dennis Amile, Gage Clark, and Dr. A. R. Robertson.

The original Pass Christian Yacht Club faded out with the entrance of the U. S. into World War I, but after the war the club was reorganized in 1919. Following are those commodores who kept the PCYC active until 1929: Bernard Chotard, Guy Northrop, Luther Barksdale, Leo McDermott, and Henry Roux.

The stock market crash of 1929, the banks closing, and the Depression of the early thirties brought yachting to a halt for the second time. Through the perseverance and dedication of the PCYC die-hards and the active part taken by the Pass Christian Rotary Club in the revival of sailing interest in the city, an organizational meeting was held at the old red school-house on Hiern Avenue and Scenic Drive in October 1936, at which time the PCYC was incorporated. At the Gulf Yachting Association's semi-annual meeting held in September 1936, the Pass Christian Yacht Club was introduced by Commodore Arvah H. Hopkins of the Gulfport Yacht Club and accepted for membership.

When the 1937 PCYC annual meeting was held, Bernard "Bernie" Knost, who had taken a very active part in the reorganization of the club, was elected commodore. Serving with him were J. M. "Rip" Terrell, vice-commodore; Henry Roux, rear commodore; Cary Spence, secretary-treasurer; Elwood Abbley, fleet captain; and Dr. Wesley Lake, fleet surgeon. Board members were Donald Sutter, chairman, Bidwell Adam, Max Connett, E. A. Lang, Leo McDermott, Dr. Donald G. Rafferty, Walter Reed, G. A. Schmidt, Fred Sutter, Wolters Terrell (Fish Class chairman).

With 145 members enrolled, 70 active skippers and 75 skipperettes, enthusiasm returned and the starting line of the 1937 annual regatta found 68 boats waiting for the gun. Several craft came from New Orleans and Ed Overton brought his *Robin Hood* over from Mobile, Alabama for the race.

In the following year, 1938, Commodore Knost was reelected to serve another term. He had worked tirelessly to develop a ladies sailing program. His dream came true in the summer of 1938 when the first Gulf Coast interclub all-girl regatta was held at the PCYC. Three GYA clubs participated: Southern, Gulfport, and Pass Christian, with the SYC skipperettes the winners.

Commodore Knost was the donor of two beautiful trophies for skipperettes. The original Knost trophy was presented in 1938 to the Gulf Yachting Association. It represented the winning GYA yacht club's skipperette team for the GYA skipperette championship. This event has remained popular throughout the years. In the early days, "Bernie" purchased many beautiful silver trophies for all of the girls;

one needed a wheelbarrow to carry them home. Several of these prizes were from England, where John Curren, who was also a great advocate of all-girl racing, purchased many sterling silver candelabras and pitchers for the commodore.

The second Knost trophy, a magnificent silver soup tureen, also brought over from England, represented the winner of the Southern Women's Sailing championship, which would be the team that won the semi-finals elimination in the Southern area and which would go on to the finals for the Mrs. Charles Francis Adams trophy and the North American Women's Sailing championship. Commodore Knost presented this trophy to Commodore J. Gilbert Scheib of the Gulf Yachting Association at the Houston Yacht Club where the semi-finals were sailed. The winners were from the Southern Yacht Club, Mrs. William H. Seemann, Jr. (Coco), Mrs. J. F. Auguste Lorber Jr. (Janet), Mrs. J. Fred Clerc (Marion), and Mrs. Leslie B. Graham (Dell). They finished fourth in the Adams cup finals.

During the second and third years of the new club, through the efforts of Commodore Fred Sutter and Vice-Commodore E. A. Lang, a skipperette division was organized with Miss Peggy Guest, commodore; Mrs. Robert Allen, vice-commodore; Mrs. Effie Terrell, rear commodore; and Myrtle McDermott, secretary-treasurer. The club owned four boats, two Snipe and two Fish Class sloops. The skipperettes sailed the two Snipe and also sailed in the Fish Class division.

In 1941 the junior division of the PCYC was organized under the direction of the popular J. W. "Rip" Terrell, chairman of the senior race committee and junior adviser. But then World War II came along and sailing was put on the back burner until 1948, when the board approved the purchase of six Fish Class sloops and the sport of sailing was continued as before.

Immediately after hostilities ceased, the PCYC membership again banded together under the leadership of Commodore Jack Kerrigan. In 1953, at the end of the Pass Christian's long revetment, an immense Quonset hut had been transformed into one of the neatest yacht clubs along the Gulf Coast. The hut replaced a factory that was located in that spot. Chairman Charles Merrick of the building committee, who was also an ex-commodore of PCYC, the present commodore, Jack Kerrigan, Warren Adams, Wm. Perry Brown, Lynn Cook, John Curren of New Orleans, Richard Hammet, Bernard Knost, John M. Parker, Shannon Pickich, J. W. Terrell, Arthur Tipping, and Frank Wittmann, plus many others, kept plugging and finally achieved their goal, a clubhouse.

Just when the PCYC appeared to be well organized and well on its way to many championships, two of the yacht club's greatest sponsors met very untimely deaths—Commodore Charles B. Merrick and Jack Kerrigan, to whom a memorial dock was erected in 1961 in memory of these two fine young yachtsmen.

The new clubhouse remained just a few short years, until a new state road survey showed that the highway road to be expanded would pass right through the middle of the Quonset hut. The property was sold to the state and temporary headquarters were set up in a very attractive white bungalow located on the boulevard.

Another clubhouse was built only to be destroyed by Hurricane Camille, which destroyed not only the yacht club but many beautiful homes and landmarks, as well as much of the town of Pass Christian. All that was left after the hurricane was the club's flagpole to mark the spot where the PCYC was located. Survivors of many storms and financial woes, the interested citizens of the Pass and enthusiastic yachtsmen erected a much more attractive yacht club in 1978, which is the present day clubhouse.

Throughout the club's hectic life, trying to survive all the elements that threatened its very being, the fun and gaiety of a yacht club could not be denied. On December 1, 1962 the PCYC held the inaugural Commodores' Ball. The young debutantes of the Pass were honored at the Commodores' Ball as "The American Beauties." These young ladies and their escorts for the first ball were:

> Miss Mary Helen Allen, escort Thomas Esward Netto
> Miss Joy Lee Blackburn, escort Andrew Wallace Wilkie
> Miss Pat Boyd, escort John J. Housey
> Miss Linda Braun, escort Robert L. Sockett
> Miss Violet Benedict Collins, escort Charles Stair Mitchell
> Miss Patricia Marshall Dugan, escort Maynard V. Hacker, Jr.
> Miss Janet French, escort Bert R. Wittman
> Miss Judith Ann Gamard, escort Robert R. Regalbuto
> Miss Ann Homes, escort Tom Ash, Jr.
> Miss Laurie Katliff, escort W. Robert Ellis
> Miss Mary Jean Sokaloski, escort Lynn E. Cook, Jr.

Music was furnished by Al Ballanco and his orchestra.

The honor of presenting the first "American Beauty" was the commodore of the Gulf Yachting Association, J. Gilbert Scheib. The ball committee chairmen were Commodores William Perry Brown and John M. Parker, and reception committee chairmen were Mrs. Gordon

Bishop, Mrs. Ogden Lafaye, and Mrs. Charles D. Taylor, Sr.

There is a large enrollment of members and continued activity on the water. Among the most popular sailing events are the Commodore Bernard Knost All-Girl GYA Championship regatta, the Frostbite Regatta for the N. T. "Buddy" Beyer Memorial trophy and the Commodore Wm. Perry Brown Pram trophy. The PCYC is very active in the affairs of the Mississippi Coast Yachting Association and the Gulf Yachting Association.

Pass Christian Commodores elected as GYA Commodores are: Arthur B. Tipping (1954); J. W. "Rip" Terrell (Posthumously, 1967); and William Perry Brown (1970).

CHAPTER XXVII

Yacht Clubs of Texas

HOUSTON YACHT CLUB

From *The Houston Chronicle* of August 2, 1964 the following excerpts are taken from an article by reporter Edward C. "Chap" Hutcheson, Jr.:

> "THE HOUSTON YACHT CLUB—A 67-Year-Old Monarch of Galveston Bay. The Houston Yacht Club has a past as colorful as its pink walls and filled with more romance than *Gone With the Wind*. It is a legend of Galveston Bay.
>
> In 1897 some ambitious outdoorsmen formed the Houston Aquatics Club at the old Rice Oyster House on Main Street near Buffalo Bayou. Boats were anchored in the muddy water of the bayou and towed to the bay for weekend sailing. In the early days, sail boats had to be poled along the bayou to and from Houston, as auxiliaries were then very rare.

As far back as 1889 *The Yachtsman* magazine reported a race in Galveston, Texas. In 1906, the minutes of the Southern Yacht Club state that an invitation was received from the Houston Yacht Club (HYC) for an interstate race. Probably one of the earliest names in sailboat racing on Galveston Bay was Dr. John Beazley who owned the *Country Girl*. The original *Country Girl* was destroyed in the 1900 hurricane that took 6,000 lives in its wake and almost wiped out the island of Galveston. Beazley then had *Country Girl II* built.

A great name among boats was the *Augusta* owned by C. G. Pilot. It was a steamboat and the pride of the early yacht club. It was considered the biggest boat west of the Mississippi. It was designed by Herreshoff.

There were sailboats that sailed on Galveston Bay at the turn of the century, of the 25- to 30-foot class. Their booms were low, extended aft of the transom a few feet and swept the deck. They were mostly centerboarders and many of these had sandbags for ballast. The crew, some twelve to thirteen of them, had to be strong and athletic as they must each shift two fifty-pound bags of sand (sixty pounds when wet) to the high side before the tack.

Some of the familiar names were Herreshoff-designed. In addition to *Country Girl* the *Augusta* and *Bo Peep*, Congressman Joe H. Eagle owned the *Mary Jane* and *Irma* and usually lent them to other skippers to race. One of these skippers was the then-young Roland Bradley who competed against John Bludworth's *Novice* from Rockport.

The last great race of these ships was probably in 1913. There followed the 1915 storm, which demolished everything in sight, then World War I, and sailing was at a lull.

Back in the year 1908 a small group of enthusiastic boatsmen and lovers of the water organized the Houston Launch Club. Their clubhouse at Harrisburg was built, and this was their home until the completion of the present clubhouse at Shore Acres in 1925.

Following are excerpts taken from an article written by Jack T. McCully for *The Daily Herald* of Gulfport, Mississippi of August 25, 1937:

> About the time the new clubhouse was built, very large yachts were also constructed. The club was able to boast a considerable flotilla of power and sail boats.
>
> Houston grew into a port in later years and local yachting underwent numerous changes. At one time, when canoes were quite popular, the club organized a Canoe Division with nearly fifty canoes. In the Power racing division, the prominent men were Frank H. Robertson, L. A. Layne, L. G. "Shorty" Walker, Doc Selman, Jim Glass and Commodore Henry Falk. These men took the Houston Yacht Club burgee to various sections of the country and carried off many top honors.
>
> Several men have been the Houston Yacht Club's leaders: Past Commodore W. E. Hamilton, who served as Commodore for several years; Dr. E. T. Fox; Past Commodore J. S. "Uncle Johnny" Bonner; Sam Streetman, Sr.; and Steve LaPeyce.

In the year 1920, at the first meeting of the Gulf Yachting Association held in Mobile, Alabama, the Houston Launch Club was invited to join and became one of the five charter members of the GYA with Southern, Pensacola, Eastern Shore, and Biloxi Yacht Clubs.

Six Fish Class one-design sloops, which had been designated as the GYA approved club-owned boat, were purchased from the Southern Yacht Club. Said Hutcheson,

> "The boats were owned by the club and rented for $1.50 per race. Many of the old skippers can recall driving from Houston for the weekend, paying for an inexpensive bed in the wooden dormitory, and drawing for the boats just before starting time. The crossed fingers and held breaths were always present as each sailor hoped someone else would come up with the number seven, the black sheep.
>
> When everything was finally organized, one of the boats would pick up Gus Schulenburg and take him out to the old judge's stand where he would preside with iron-hand authority over the handful of racers. The same triangular course was always sailed, and more than once a nimble crewman could be spotted leaping onto a boat's keep to prevent it from going all the way over in a strong puff.
>
> This was the class that had its own breed of sailors. Ray Girasty, Don Townsend, John Bynum, Charlie Nathan, Bill Moody, Bates Thomas, David Red, the Hutcheson brothers, and the club's leading skipperette, Fairfax Moody, could be found on the fish boat docks.

Other known skippers in those days were Sam and Boyd Streetman, Billy and George Humphreyville, W. R. Hamilton, Ray Davis, Johnny Green, and Herbie Burgard, who ruled the Bay.

The Houston Launch Club participated in the second Lipton Regatta held in 1921 at the Pensacola Yacht Club, and in 1922 the Houston Launch Club Commodore H. Falk was elected the third commodore of the Gulf Yachting Association.

As sailing came back into prominence during the ensuing years, the motor-boaters were pushed aside and a new clubhouse built on the present location at Shore Acres, the north end of Galveston Bay at Laporte, Texas in 1925. It was known as the "Pink Palace." A treaty was finally reached between lovers of sails and motors, and in 1926 the two merged into the once-used name of Houston Yacht Club.

Hutcheson reported:

> In 1929 the Houston Yacht Club was thrilled by the chance to hold the Gulf Yachting Association's Lipton Cup races. The best sailors from clubs up and down the coast raced in Fish Class sloops. Perhaps the key to the Houston Yacht Club's history came in these boats. A far cry from today's modern racing machines, the Fish Class sloops were heavy 20-foot, gaff-rigged boats with shallow V-shape bottoms. The cockpit was surrounded by a seven-inch combing, and when the stiff winds blew,

sailors found themselves scrapping to get over the windward rail.

When the Lipton races got under way, it was unique in that colors on the peak of mainsails were used to designate the clubs. Biloxi, Lavendar, Mobile, Orange, Houston, Green, Pensacola, Red, St. Petersburg, White, Southern, Blue and Sarasota, Red and White. The Pensacola Yacht Club was the winner of the Sir Thomas J. Lipton trophy.

At the GYA semi-annual meeting held in conjunction with the Lipton Regatta, HYC's Commodore J. S. Bonner, who served as commodore of the GYA in 1928, was reelected for the year 1929.

The Lipton Cup program of 1929 revealed the fact that "Houston's world record holding hydroplanes, and the yacht club's active participation in internationally famous water events, both power and sail, have brought world wide publicity to the city of Houston.

"All of the 600 members of the Houston Yacht Club may enjoy the following privileges:

A round of golf on the Shoreacres course
A swim or fishing trip, starting from the club harbor
A sail in one of the club-owned Fish Class sloops
An excellent meal and comfortable sleeping quarters for
    a week-end visit to the bay
A well-protected harbor for private-owned boats
An affiliation with more than a hundred other yacht clubs
    in various parts of the U. S., whose privileges
    are extended to the Houston Yacht Club members."

In addition to the club-owned boats were the several cabin sloops that sailed out of HYC during the '30s. Harry Tillichet, Jr. raced his black R boat *Pirate* against Bill Hilliard's *Anita*. Tommy Lee sailed his Six Meter, and four Victory sloops were raced by Paul Richmond, Walter Sterling, the Lee twins and others. A final addition to the fleet was Albert and Ernie Fay's Louisiana lake sailor *Sorceress*.

In 1932, Rufus "Bud" Smith of the Houston Yacht Club arrived in New Orleans to challenge Gilbert Gray of SYC for the Southern distict eliminations in the final Olympic trials in Stars, which Gray won by only nineteen seconds to go on to win the Olympic Gold Medal in sailing in 1932. Also prominent Star skippers of HYC were Ray Crasty and Don Townsend.

At the 1936 Lipton Regatta held in Mobile, Alabama, HYC skipperette Fairfax Moody appeared as a member of the Houston Yacht Club Lipton team. This shocking incident called for a special session of the officers of the Mobile Yacht Club, against whose rules it was for ladies to be members of the Lipton team. The following resolution of the GYA board of governors was adopted:

> WHEREAS, the Mobile Yacht Club has been informed that the Houston Yacht Club has designated a woman as one of its representatives for the 17th annual Lipton regatta, and
>
> WHEREAS, the Mobile Yacht Club is opposed to women sailing against men, but not against members of their own sex, but
>
> WHEREAS, the Houston skipperette has travelled hundreds of miles to compete in the present Lipton series,
>
> BE IT RESOLVED that in future regattas for the Lipton trophy women be barred in the capacities of either helmsmen, crewmen or officials.

In *The Times-Picayune* of 1938, an article appeared by sports writer Val Flannigan which stated that "T. P. Lee of Houston Texas has been invited to enter his schooner *Shellback* in the SYC 2nd annual Gulfport to St. Andrews Bay race on June 9, 1938."

The 21-foot Corinthian came into being just prior to World War II when the Fay brothers, Al and Ernie, had Sparkman and Stephens design a one-design boat for a three-man keelboat with spinnakers, which was built at Platzer shipyard in Houston and later by the Fay brothers at their newly built Seabrook Shipyard. The Corinthian replaced the Fish Class sloop and they were used by both the Houston and the Corinthian Yacht Club. This new spinnaker-type boat, and the hurricane that struck during the war years and demolished most of the fleet of Fish Class sloops, saw the end of the Fish Class reign.

In the '40s and '50s other clubs sprang up around the bay, and the Houston Yacht Club found itself in the middle of a sailing explosion. More classes were added, and the club was twice remodeled to keep up with the demands of hundreds of weekend water-lovers.

The Cruising Class boats became popular in the '50s. The Galveston Bay Cruising Association (G.B.C.A.) was founded in 1947. Its real game is racing, from the Rabbit races to the 630-mile Galveston to Vera Cruz ocean race. As it was not a formal organization in the beginning, its unofficial commodore was Rufus "Bud" Smith. In 1943 the club did organize and its first commodore was

Clyde Gamble, its vice-commodore, Don Genitempo, and its secretary-treasurer, Rufus Smith.

In the early 1950s, HYC member Rufus "Bud" Smith was one of the founding fathers of the Texas Yachting Association. He was its secretary for ten years. This was the beginning of the HYC's participation in the North American Yacht Racing Union's national events for the Mallory, Adams, and Sears Cups.

Hurricane Carla in 1961 destroyed many boats. If it had not been for the generosity of powerboat owners, the Houston Yacht Club might not have been able to rebuild its harbor after Carla, the killer storm of 1961. This group guaranteed the loan of funds necessary to rebuild the harbor after it was destroyed.

It was in 1961 that the HYC developed a $350,000 expansion program. The annual regatta had been initiated and a wonderful junior program came into being. The club's official publication was the *Windjammer*.

The GBCA grew in leaps and bounds. Because of its many ocean races, the Texas Ocean Racing Circuit was inaugurated in 1963. G. C. Francisco won the first trophy in *Patti*. In 1965, the first Galveston to Biloxi race was held. The Regata de Amigos was inaugurated in 1968.

Many other classes were added to the Houston Yacht Club's fleet in the mid-sixties. They were Stars, Ensigns, Thistles, Geary 18s, Sunfish, and Dragons. The Houston Yacht Club was host to the 1968 U. S. Dragon Olympic Trials. The winner of this event was G. Shelby Friedrichs, Jr. of the Southern Yacht Club, with crewmen Barton Jahncke and Click Schreck. They went on to win the Gold Medal in the Dragon Class in the nineteenth Olympiad Games in Acapulco, Mexico, in 1968.

The junior program of the Houston Yacht Club, The Ragnot, founded by Roger Toler, was very active, and one of its juniors, John Kolius, came up through the ranks to win the first Junior North American Sailing championship for the Sears Cup in 1969. Two years later, Kolius added the Men's North American Sailing championship for the Mallory Cup in 1971 to his many victories. After winning many other championship events, John Kolius is listed in *Who's Who In Sailing*. "A name familiar to virtually every sailing enthusiast in the nation," said the commodore of the New York Yacht Club, Emil Mosbacher, Jr., as he announced John Kolius the U. S. representative in the *America II* challenge to recover the America's Cup.

In 1970 another Houston Yacht Club junior from The Ragnot, Danny William, won the Junior North American Sailing Championship for the Sears Cup. He was a crew for John Kolius when he won the Sears Cup in 1969. Then came Clark Thompson, Jr., who crewed for Williams in the Sears Cup event, to win this junior championship in 1972 with the aid of his brothers, Paul and Glenn Thompson, and "Buddy" Brown, Jr.

When it became known that the Soling class would be the coming Olympic choice boat for the 1972 Olympics, Solings were purchased by the HYC skippers, which ended the era of the Corinthians.

In August 1976, the Galveston Bay Cruising Association sponsored with the club de Yates de Vera Cruz the Galveston to Vera Cruz 700-mile ocean race of four days. The entire event included three regattas and lasted two weeks. First to finish was *Mirage*, beating the old record set in 1968 by *Temptress* by seven hours, thirty-one minutes and two seconds. At trophy presentation, all yachts that participated received beautiful certificates and traditional dolls for the skippers' ladies. The visitors were presented keys to the city by Mayor Juan P. Maldonado.

The Houston Yacht Club has hosted many outstanding events throughout its years, among which were the North American championship races for Stars, Flying Dutchmen, Dragons and Flying Scots.

Appendix

Southern Yacht Club

PRESIDENTS   **YEAR**

James W. Behan	1849
T. L. Dabney	1850-51
Harry R. Hill	1852 (died in office)
W. E. Leverich	1852-53

COMMODORES

Thomas Kershaw	1854-55
Sidney Story	1856-57
John G. Robinson	1858
Richard Milliken	1859
Ignatius Szymanske	1860
War Between the States and Reconstruction	1861-1877
Emile J. O'Brien	1878-80
Ambrose A. Maginnis	1881-83
Charles T. Howard	1884 (resigned)
Emile J. O'Brien	1884-87
Robert S. Day	1888-91
W. A. Gordon	1892
Thomas Sully	1893-94
Lawrence O'Donnell	1895-96
J. Walton Glenny	1897-98
Albert Baldwin	1899-1909
L. H. Fairchild	1910-11
Samuel F. Heaslip	1912-13
Ernest Lee Jahncke	1914-16
Chandler C. Luzenberg	1917
Percy S. Benedict	1918-20
Harry T. Howard	1921-23
W. Milton Miller, M.D.	1924-25
John M. Kinabrew	1926-29
Charles A. Tessier	1930-33
Leslie P. Beard	1933

Garner H. Tullis 1934-36
John Dane 1937-38
Davis S. Wuescher 1939
Auguste Capdevielle .... 1940 (died in office)
Garner H. Tullis 1940
Leslie P. Beard 1941-44
Richard G. Jones 1945-47
George S. Clark 1948-49
F. Evans Farwell 1950-51
G. Shelby Friedrichs 1952-53
James G. Gibbons 1954-55
Charles L. Gambel 1956-57
Hampton A. Gamard 1958-59
Oliver H. Counce 1960-61
W. Horace Williams, Jr. 1962-63
J. F. Auguste Lorber, Jr. 1964-65
Sidney W. Provensal, Jr. 1966-67
Nathaniel C. Curtis, Jr. 1968-69
Charles L. Eshleman, Jr. 1970-71
Herbert O'Donnell 1972-73
B. Temple Brown 1974-75
Arthur D. Wynne 1976-77
Daniel B. Killeen 1978-79
Richard G. Spangenberg 1980-81
Cal F. Hadden, Jr. 1982-83
William C. Gambel 1984-85
Maurice J. Hartson, III 1986

SIR THOMAS J. LIPTON
CHALLENGE TROPHY WINNERS

1920—Pensacola Yacht Club
1921—Eastern Shore Yacht Club
1922—Southern Yacht Club tied with Pensacola Yacht Club
1923—Pensacola Yacht Club
1924—Pensacola Yacht Club
1925—Southern Yacht Club
1926—Eastern Shore Yacht Club tied with St. Petersburg Yacht Club
1927—Pensacola Yacht Club tied with Southern Yacht Club
1928—Mobile Yacht Club

1929—Pensacola Yacht Club
1930—Sarasota Yacht Club
1931—Sarasota Yacht Club
1932—Sarasota Yacht Club
1933—Pensacola Yacht Club
1934—Buccaneer Yacht Club
1935—Pensacola Yacht Club
1936—Pensacola Yacht Club
1937—Biloxi Yacht Club
1938—Southern Yacht Club
1939—Southern Yacht Club
1940—Southern Yacht Club
1941—Southern Yacht Club won in sailoff w/Mobile
1942—Southern Yacht Club
1943—Southern Yacht Club
1944—St. Andrews Bay Yacht Club
1945—St. Andrews Bay Yacht Club won in sailoff with Southern
1946—St. Petersburg Yacht Club
1947—St. Andrews Bay Yacht Club
1948—Gulfport Yacht Club
1949—Pensacola Yacht Club
1950—St. Andrews Bay Yacht Club
1951—St. Petersburg Yacht Club
1952—Biloxi Yacht Club
1953—Biloxi Yacht Club
1954—Biloxi Yacht Club
1955—Biloxi Yacht Club
1956—Mobile Yacht Club
1957—St. Petersburg Yacht Club
1958—Biloxi Yacht Club
1959—Southern Yacht Club
1960—Southern Yacht Club
1961—Biloxi Yacht Club
1962—Southern Yacht Club
1963—Bay-Waveland Yahct Club
1964—St. Andrews Bay Yacht Club
1965—St. Andrews Bay Yacht Club
1966—Biloxi Yacht Club
1967—Biloxi Yacht Club
1968—New Orleans Yacht Club
1969—Pensacola Yacht Club
1970—Pensacola Yacht Club
1971—Bay-Waveland Yacht Club
1972—Bay-Waveland Yacht Club
1973—Bay-Waveland Yacht Club
1974—Southern Yacht Club
1975—New Orleans Yacht Club
1976—Southern Yacht Club
1977—Bay-Waveland Yacht Club
1978—Bay-Waveland Yacht Club
1979—Southern Yacht Club
1980—Bay-Waveland Yacht Club
1981—Pensacola Yacht Club
1982—Bay-Waveland Yacht Club
1983—Bay-Waveland Yacht Club
1984—Bay-Waveland Yacht Club
1985—Southern Yacht Club

JUNIOR LIPTON CHAMPIONSHIP TROPHY

1941—Southern Yacht Club
1942—Southern Yacht Club
1943-1946—World War II
1947—Biloxi Yacht Club
1948—Biloxi Yacht Club
1949—Biloxi Yacht Club
1950—St. Andrews Bay Yacht Club
1951—Fairhope Yacht Club
1952—Fairhope Yacht Club
1953—Fairhope Yacht Club
1954—Mobile Yacht Club
1955—St. Petersburg Yacht Club
1956—Pass Christian Yacht Club
1957—St. Petersburg Yacht Club
1958—St. Petersburg Yacht Club
1959—Southern Yacht Club
1960—Southern Yacht Club
1961—Southern Yacht Club
1962—Fort Walton Yacht Club
1963—Bay-Waveland Yacht Club
1964—Southern Yacht Club
1965—Southern Yacht Club
1966—Southern Yacht Club
1967—New Orleans Yacht Club
1968—St. Andrews Bay Yacht Club
1969—Pass Christian Yacht Club
1970—Southern Yacht Club
1971—Bay-Waveland Yacht Club
1972—Southern Yacht Club
1973—Pensacola Yacht Club
1974—Southern Yacht Club
1975—Pensacola Yacht Club
1976—Pontchartrain Yacht Club
1977—Southern Yacht Club
1978—Southern Yacht Club
1979—Bay-Waveland Yacht Club
1980—Bay-Waveland Yacht Club
1981—Southern Yacht Club
1982—Southern Yacht Club
1983—Southern Yacht Club
1984—Southern Yacht Club
1985—Southern Yacht Club

COMMODORES
GULF YACHTING ASSOCIATION
(Formerly Southern Gulf Coast Yachting Association)

Joseph Alfonso	Gulfport	George P. Hopkins	Gulfport
Nolfie D. Alfonso	New Orleans	Judge Robert G. Hughes	
Albert Baldwin	Southern		Southern

Leslie P. Beard	Southern
Larry Beauvais, Jr.	Mobile
*Thomas D. Beery, Jr.	Singing River
Dr. Eldon Bolton	Biloxi
Jack Bonnell	Fairhope
J. S. Bonner	Houston
E. J. Bowers	Bay-Waveland
Robert K. Boyle	Pensacola
Marshall Brown	Fort Walton
Wm. Perry Brown	Pass Christian
J. C. Bush	Mobile
Auguste Capdevielle	Southern
Henry Chapman	Bay-Waveland
Harry Chapman	Bay-Waveland
Wallace Chapman	Biloxi
A. Clark	Sarasota
Fred Clark	Buccaneer
George Criminale	Mobile
J. H. Cross	Pensacola
Allen W. Douglas	St. Andrews Bay
Wilson Duncan	St. Andrews Bay
Jerry J. Ellis	Biloxi
Wm. M. Ellis	Southern
Byrd Enochs	Biloxi
H. Falk	Houston
A. L. Gandy	St. Petersburg
H. Hilton Green, Sr.	Pensacola
Finley B. Hewes	Gulfport
Michael S. Johnson	Fort Walton
J. J. Kennedy	Biloxi
Daniel B. Killeen	Southern
J. M. Kinabrew, Sr.	Southern
Thomas P. Kroutter	Mobile
Henry E. Lampe	Jackson
Dr. Eugene Liddy	Sarasota
Dr. W. M. Miller	Southern
J. P. Moore	Biloxi
Edward B. Overton	Eastern Shore
R. G. Patterson	Pensacola
Foster P. Pfleger	Buccaneer
Lewis B. Pollak	Pensacola
E. G. Quina	Pensacola
Dr. Howard F. Rees	St. Petersburg
George W. Rifley	St. Petersburg
J. Gilbert Scheib	Southern
Roy Sellers, Jr.	Buccaneer
Walter Seymour	Biloxi
Alan Sheppard	Pensacola
Lawrence C. Sommers	New Orleans
Eugene Taylor	Pensacola
Arthur B. Tipping	Pass Christian
T. Cooper Van Antwerp	Fairhope
J. Alvin Weinfurter	Bay-Waveland
Cal Weiss	Mobile
Frank Wood	St. Andrews Bay

*Resigned

Harry Martinez-Honorary Commodore

J. W. Terrell-Honorary Commodore

SOUTHERN YACHT CLUB
GULF YACHTING ASSOCIATION
MEMBER YACHT CLUBS

Club	Year
Bay-Waveland–Bay St. Louis, Ms.	1901
Biloxi–Biloxi, Ms.	1901
Buccaneer–Mobile, Ala.	1933
Cypremort–New Iberia, La.	1978
*D'Arbonne–Monroe, La.	1968
*Davis Island–Tampa, Fl.	1954
*East Pascagoula–Pascagoula, Ms.	1901
*Eastern Shore–Fairhope, Al.	1920
Fairhope–Fairhope, Al.	1944
Fort Walton–Fort Walton Beach, Fl.	1955
Grand Lagoon–Pensacola, Fl.	1968
Gulfport–Gulfport, Ms.	1903
*Houston–Laporte, Tx.	1920
Jackson–Jackson, Ms.	1960
Lake Arthur–Lafayette, La.	1981
*Lake Charles–Lake Charles, La.	1973
Lake Forest–Daphne, Al.	1980
*Lake Polurde–Morgan City, La.	1973
Long Beach–Long Beach, Ms.	1982
Mobile–Mobile, Al.	1901
Navy Air Station—Pensacola, Fl.	1932
New Orleans—New Orleans, La.	1953
Ocean Springs–Ocean Springs, Ms.	1971
Pass Christian–Pass Christian, Ms.	1901
Pelican–Baton Rouge, La.	1963
Pensacola–Pensacola, Fl.	1920
Pensacola Beach–Pensacola, Fl.	1983
Pontchartrain–Mandeville, La.	1968
*Port Lagoon–Panama City, Fl.	1976
St. Andrews Bay–St. Andrews Bay, Fl.	1935
St. Petersburg–St. Petersburg, Fl.	1981
*Sarasota–Sarasota, Fl.	1927
Singing River–Pascagoula, Ms.	1971
Southern–New Orleans, La.	1901
Shreveport–Shreveport, La.	1957
Tammany–Slidell, La.	1981
*Tampa Yacht Country Club, Tampa, Fl.	1934
*Tarpon Springs–Tarpon Springs, Fl.	1927
U.S. Navy of Corpus Christi, Tx.	1941

*Resigned

Affiliate Members

Bluewater Bay Sailing Club
Niceville, Fl. 1984

Grand Maumelle Sailing Club
Little Rock, Ar. 1984

Index

Abunza, G., 106
Acadia, 371, 373-74
Adair, Eddie, 451
Adams, Charles, 301, 355
Adams, Charles Francis, 90, 143
Adams, Mrs. Charles Francis, Cup, 259; 1954, 263-64; 1962, 297; 1973, 352; 1977, 368; 1979, 375; 1980, 378. *See also* Women's North American Sailing Championship
Adams, Warren, Jr., 273
Adler, Milton, 240
Alciatore, Roy, 237
Alden, John, 171
Alfonso, Andy, 482
Alfonso, Gus, 482
Alfonso, Joe, 482, 483
Alfonso, Nathan, 479, 482
Alfonso, Nolfie, 338, 457, 482
Alfonso, Tut, 482
Alfonso, Vincent, 482
Algerine Club, 13
All-girl crew, first, 175
All-girl regatta, first interclub, 489
Allen, Homer, 451
Allen, James, 432
Allen, Lydia, 253
Allen, Ross, 386
Allen, Tom, 268
Allen, Tom, III, 345
Allen, Tommy, 292
Allen, Wm. B., 179
Allen, Ethan, Lightning Crew championship memorial trophy, 292
Altrink, Peter, 444
American International Dragon Association, 275, 309

America's Cup, x, 99, 181-82, 183-84; 1895, 53-54; 1922, 143; 1958, 283-84; 1974, 356-57; 1983, 408-09; 1988, 420
Amile, Dennis, 488
Amphibian fleet, 273
Anderssen, Art, 327
Andre, Bob, 344
André, Steve, 310
Andrews, Keith, 395, 406, 419
Anniversaries of SYC: 70th, 114-16; diamond jubilee, 152-54; 100th, 244-46; 125th, 353
Annual regatta of SYC: first (1849), 6-9; 1878, 26; 1899, 58; 1901, 70; 1902, 70; 1903, 70; 1904, 81; 1905, 87; 1907, 91; 1945, 236; 1946, 236
Arceneaux, Graham, 396
Armstrong, Duval, 66
Aschaffenberg, Coralie, 115
Aschaffenberg, Eric, 327
Aschaffenberg, Eugene A., 186, 197, 200
Ashman, Rich, 367
Association Cup, 66; 1903, 75, 80; 1904, 83
Aunt Dinah, 103
Avegno, Beauregard, 196, 299
Avegno, Henry J., 158
Avenger, 147
Awards banquet, 397
Axline, M.H., 448
Ayers, George, 284
Ayers, Jill, 263

Bacardi series, 403
Bailey, N.R., 59

Bailey, Cynthia, 399
Baldridge, By, 350, 354
Baldwin, Albert, 57, 59, 63, 67, 92
Baldwin, Oliver V., 272
Balter, Karen, 361, 367
Banquet of Champions, 339
"Bards of the Bilges" Ball: first (1955), 266; 1956, 271; 1958, 280; 1961, 291; 1969, 333; 1976, 360; 1983, 398-99
Barksdale, Luther, 489
Barnes, Chuck, 416
Barr, J. Edward, 386
Barrett, W. J., 426
Bartley, Kathy, 300
Baquie, J. Carl, 226-27
Baquie, Ruth, 213
Bates, Jim, 366, 459
Batt, Harry, 206
Battle House, 125
Baumgarden, N. Emile, 51, 59, 64, 111-12, 423
Baxter, C. F., 218
Bay St. Louis and Waveland Regatta Association, 56
Bay-Waveland Yacht Club, 56, 81, 407, 461-67; and Adams Cup, 368, 378; and Flying Scot championships, 370, 405; and Olympic Games, 412
Bayou St. John, 138
Bayou St. John Rowing Club, 137
Beard, Leslie P., 85, 120, 124, 150, 158, 228, 231, 240, 252
Beard, Commodore Leslie P., trophy, 485
Beasley, R. R., 196
Beaudoin, Richard, 442

508   SOUTHERN YACHT CLUB

Beauvais, Larry, 232
Beavier, Robert, Jr., 356
Beavier, Robert N., 171
Beek, Barton, 345
Behan, James W., 5
Behrens, J., 59
Behrman, Martin, 116
Bell, Jack, 336
Bell, John, 464
Bellows, Steve, 416
Bemis trophy, 395
Benedict, Percy S., 108, 114, 119, 122, 124, 130, 131, 463
Benjamin, Edward B., 356-57, 363, 365, 379, 380
Benjamin, Steve, 395
Bernius, Marilyn, 257
Bertrand, John, 363
Beyer, N. T., Memorial trophy, 492
Bigelow, Billy, 442
Biloxi Fishing Schooner Championship races, 167-68
"Biloxi regatta, A," 168-69
Biloxi to Pensacola race: 1934, 197-98; 1935, 198
Biloxi Yacht Club, 107, 168, 272, 308, 467-74
Biscayne Bay Yacht Club, 56
Black, Clarence, 292, 341
Black, Jerry, 442
Blake, Lloyd, 81
Blonski, John, 358
Blouin, David, 306
Blouin, Earl, 157, 169, 175, 223, 272
Blouin, Joe, 377, 379, 395
Bluebottle Cup, 282-83
Blythe, Don, 484
Boat builders, 44
Boat parade and fleet review: 1962, 295-96; 1964, 305; 1967, 320; 1968, 325; 1974, 353; 1976, 360; 1982, 386; 1983, 402; 1984, 411
Bond, James T., 230
Bonner, J. S., 494, 496
Bonnie Doon, 298, 306

Bonnie Dundee, 228
Boos, Robert E., 459
Borne, Allen, 327, 365, 366
Bouden, Mable, 118
Bowers, E. J., 67, 462
Breath, J. A., 169
Breit, Hjalmar, 285, 289, 297, 350, 355, 360
Bremmerman, Burdette, 367
Brennan, L. M., 241
Brennan, Robert, 364
Brennan, Tom, 86, 267
Brett, Roger, 184
Brewster, Alex, 35, 39, 46, 59
Brewster Cup, 46
Brock, Alexander, 291
Brodie, Robert, 200
Brothers, George, 437
Brown, B. Temple, 296, 320, 339, 343, 346, 353, 357, 360
Brown, Buddy, Jr., 486, 499
Brown, Marshall, 442
Brown, Mike, 442
Brown, Commodore Wm. Perry, Pram trophy, 492
Brunt, Fred, 455
Buccaneer Yacht Club, 338, 425-429
Buchtel, Elaine, 407
Building committee of SYC, 235, 241, 243
Burgee of SYC, 29, 54; pin, 64
Burton, H. L., 475
Burwell, Woody, 297
Bush, J. C., Jr., 67, 434
Bush, T. G., 433
Button for SYC, 50
Byrne, Thomas, 7, 16

Cadillac, 69, 87-89, 91, 95
Cain, Bill, 292
Cal Lake Yacht Club, 456
Cal-25 National Championship, 418
Calvert, James, Jr., 253
Calypso, 69, 70, 75, 83, 87-88, 91
Cambel, Greg, 407

Campbell, Jack, 81
Candler Race, 448
Cannon of SYC, 32
Capdevielle, Auguste, 199, 207, 224-26
Capdevielle, Commodore Auguste, Memorial trophy, 230
Capo, John, 237
Cardiall trophy, 273
Carley, Frank C., 449
Carnival regatta, 209
Carter, Billy, 327
Carter, Reginald H., 124
Cary, Charles, 316
Cary, Virginia, 271, 276
Case, Ben, 306
Caspers, Janet, 367
Catamarans, 45
Causeway. *See* Lake Pontchartrain Causeway
Cerise, Elmo, 296
Cerise, John, 321, 334, 339, 343-44, 347
Chamberlain, Don, 192
Chamberlain, Margaret Gillican, 146
Chambers, Charles A., 292
Champers, Al, 320
Chapman, G. H., 463
Chapman, Amy, 361, 368, 378
Chapman, Harry, 336
Chapman, Henry B., 465
Chapman, Wallace, 465
Chapman trophy, 465
Charante Maritime, 388-91
Charbonnet, Storey, 406
Charbonnet, Sidney, 419
Charter of SYC, 38-39
Chewink III, 69, 70, 75, 83, 87
Chicago Yacht Club. *See* North-South team race
Choe, Sid, 418
Chotard, Bernard, 489
Chotard, Richard, 488
Christman, Chris, 354
Christman, Greg, 370, 419
Christman, Preston, 419
Christman, Ralph, 261, 296, 320
Cinderella, 149. *See also*

Princess; Robin Hood IV
Civil War, 20-21
Claiborne, Charles deB., 140
Clard, John, 395
Clarence Hutchinson, 444
Clark, J. W., 273, 372
Clark, Gage, 488
Clark, Sheldon, 142
Clark, Sheldon, regatta, 358
Clarke, George S., 232, 243
Cleary, Brennan, 180
Clement, Chris, 349
Clerc, J. Fred, 230, 342-43
Clerc, Marion, 263, 264, 490
Closing regatta of SYC, 1912, 97
Club-owned boats, 34, 72
Clubhouse of SYC: first, 25, 29, 54, 57; second, 58-59, 63, 64, 109, 122, 130-34, 154, 240-42; third, 244, 323
Coast Guard regatta, 227
Cobb, Brody, 413, 419
Coleman, Tom, 333, 350, 365
Coleman, Walker, 229
Collins, Lester, 370-71
Commodores' Ball, 332
Congressional Cup match race series, 345
Conner, Commodore Charles, cup, 455
Constitution of SYC, 10
Cooke, A. M., 59, 68, 88, 91, 95
Copeland, Alvin, 128, 239
Corbett, Alex, 451
"Corinthianism," 422
Cornay, John, 35
Counce, Oliver J., 286
Crane, Jack, 416
Crawfish regatta, 455
Creole Club, 13
Cricket, 69, 70, 87, 91
Criminale, George, 378, 437
Critchfield, W. T. S., 238
Crochet, S. H., 456
Cromwell, Nicholas, 327
Cross, J. H., 444
Cruise to the coast, 47-48

Cronberg, Terry, 350
Crum, Keith, 418
Crutcher, Albert, 322
Cunningham, Briggs S., 284
Curran, W. B., 433
Curren, Liz, 407
Curren, John, 192, 490
Curtis, Cort, 297
Curtis, Nathaniel C., Jr., 275, 283, 302, 309, 318, 322, 324, 332, 339, 359
Curtiss, W. A., 444
Cypremort Yacht Club, 453

D'Antoni, Blaise S., 140, 149, 163
Dabney, T. L., 11, 15
Dances. *See* Subscription dances; Parties at SYC
Dane, Jack, 308, 365
Dane, John, 175, 206
Dane, John, III, 321, 334-35, 339, 343-44, 346, 347-48, 350, 354, 360, 363, 364, 395, 403-04
Davidson, C., 432
Davies, Sandy, 382, 418
Davis, Arthur Q., 359
Davis, Sharon, 367
Day, Robert Slack, 41
de Armas, Carlos J., 200, 223, 230, 232, 272
de Buys, J. Rathbone, 119, 120
Deaver, Dick, 354
Defender, 54
de Jarnette, W. Y., 239
de Jarnette, Gayle, 257
del Corral, J. F., 85
Delaplaine, Leon, 425
Delgado, Bobby, 297
Delgado, M. O., 283, 291
Dellenbaugh, David, 395
Demarcey, Michael, 412
DeMetz, Freddie, 273
Denegre, Henry, 36
Denniston, H. S., 179
Depression, the, 177, 178, 179, 180, 191-92
Deuel, Fred, 451
Deutsch, Eberhardt P., 157
Diamond Jubilee of SYC. *See*

Index 509

Anniversaries of SYC
Diaz, Augie, 364
Dicks, John F., Jr., 284, 301
Dicks, Johnny, 292
Disque D'or 3, 392-94
Donnes, Pierre F., Jr., 162
Douglas Cup, 344
Dragon Class, 273-74, 282-83, 289, 302-04, 309; American International Association, 275, 309; European International championship, (1966) 318; North American championship, (1962) 296, (1965) 310, (1966) 319, (1968) 327, (1970) 344, (1971) 347; World's championship, 322. *See also* Royal St. Lawrence Dragon regatta
Drennan, Susan, 367
Dreyfus, Tommy, 305, 310, 347, 373
Droulia, William, 300, 308
Duane, Marshal, 364
Ducourge, Alfred, 85
Duffy, E. Barlow, 238
Dulion, T. P., 67, 468
Duncan, Brooke H., II, 301
Dunham, Dave, 416
Dunham, Jo, 416
Dunn, Hattie, 89
Dunn, John, 81
Dupre, Henry, 223
Durgin, Dick, 486

Eagan, Bubby, 405
Eagan, Ellen, 368
Eagan, Marc, 370, 413
Eager Beaver contest, 302
Eastern Shore Yacht Club, 124, 139
"Eastward Ho!" Cruise, 246-48, 252-53, 440
Eastward Ho Power Squadron, 442
Eckhardt, Elroy, 327
Edgar, William B., Jr., 124, 141, 158, 230
Edrington, Prentice, Jr., 161, 169-71, 173, 174,

175, 177, 178
Edwards, R. Lee, 112-13, 181
Edwards, Governor Edwin, trophy, 455
Edwin Forrest Club, 13
Elaine, 50
Ellis, John M., 301
Elmasada II, 114
Elsie M. Reichert, 300
Elvstrom, Paul, 344
England, Negley, 483
Enterprise, 183
Eshleman, Charles L., 257
Eshleman, Charles L., Jr., 280, 284, 293, 297, 301, 302, 311, 320, 340-41, 370
Eustis, Edward, 197
Everett, Amy, 485

Faget, Benz, 400, 458
Fairchild, Louis H., 95
Fairhope Yacht Club, 429-31
Falk, H., 495
Farnsworth, Richardson, 413
Farwell, F. Evans, 249-50, 254
Farwell, Lynne, 250
Feingold, Rose, 175
Fetterly, Billy, 106
Fiberglass boats, 298-99
Fin-keel sloops, 45
Finke, Henry, 275, 309, 408
Finke, Lou, 408
Finn Class, 301; North American championship, (1964) 301, (1976) 363
Fish Class, 119-20, 123-24, 153, 172, 206, 251, 336-38; and skipperettes, 138, 253; committee, 251, 252; interclub series (1946), 236; World regatta, 338
Fisher, 355-56
Five Flags regatta, 446
5.5 Metre Class, 301
Florida Ocean Racing Association, 452
Florida Women's Sailing Association, 452

Flowers, Walter, 265
Flying Dutchman fleet, 340
Flying Scot, 336; North American championship, (1975) 358, (1980) 377; North American Junior championship, (1977) 366, (1978) 370, (1982) 395, (1983) 405
Foch, Ferdinand, 140
Foley, Thomas I., Jr., 110
Folse, Dolores, 253
Force, W. T., 68
Ford, Harvey, 452
Fort Walton Yacht Club, 439-42
Fort Worth Boat Club, 209, 223, 273
Fox, Barry, 355
Fox, C. Beresford, 292
Fox, E. T., 494
Fox-Garic Predicted Log race, 292
Fox-Garic trophy, 292
Foxley, Fred J., 145
Francisco, G. C., 498
Frederick, Gilbert, Jr., 262
Freret, Elizabeth Hughes, 213, 214
Freret, Randy, 355
Fretz, Ray, 402
Friedrichs, G. Shelby, 166, 254-55, 276, 278, 280, 291
Friedrichs, G. Shelby, Jr., 166, 257, 285, 289, 292, 305, 311, 318, 319, 322, 327-331, 344, 347, 351, 392, 401, 402, 412, 413, 418, 498
Friedrichs, Gore, 276, 289, 293, 311, 413
Friedrichs, Suzy, 361
Friedrichs, Virginia, 250, 257, 266
Friend, Chris, 367
Fromherz, Fritz, 297
Fromherz, Phyllis, 293
Frostbite regatta, 492
Fry, Josephine, 175
Fundenberg, Bill, 353
Furlow, Karen, 352, 417
Furr, C. C., 106

Galveston Bay Cruising Association, 497
Galveston Bay to Gulfport Yacht Club race, 326
Galveston Yacht Club, 56
Gamard, Hampton A., 280
Gambel, Carol, 367
Gambel, Charles, Jr., 253
Gambel, Charles L., 271, 278, 279, 379
Gambel, Christian, 395
Gambel, William C., 410
Gamble, Clyde, 498
Gambling, 10, 62, 188
Gandy, A. L., 450
Gandy, Gidge, 450
Garic, William, 117
Garic, William, trophy, 107, 292
Gaston, Robert W., 159-61
Gauthier, Sam, 35, 66
Gautier, Walter, 67
Geller, Guy C., 458
Gelpi Cup, 70, 80
General Wilson, 144, 444
Gibbons, James G., 262, 266, 272, 280
Gibbons, Mrs. George L., 117
Gill, Sandra, 263
Gillian, 346
Gillican, Walter Boyer, 146-47
Girard, L. A., 227
Gladiola, 72, 75, 80
Glasser, Charles, 273
Glenny, J. Walton, 55, 69, 90, 488
Gloriana, 183
Glover, Jack, 431
Gold Challenge Cup (for sailboats), 85-86
Gold Challenge Cup (for powerboats), 127
Gold Cup race, 138
Gooch, Al, 321, 354, 418, 459
Gooch, Jack, 418
Gooch, John B., 379, 380
Gooch, Julie Ann, 367
Gordon, Charlotte, 378
Gordon, Jack, 399-400
Gordon, W. A., 42, 90

Governor's Cup of California, 406
Governor's race, 203-04, 210-11, 470-71
Gragard, Thomas A., 110
Graham, Adriel, 272-73, 297, 352
Graham, Anne Penn, 367
Graham, Dell, 263, 264, 272, 490
Graham, Harry, 223
Graham, Louis B., 301
Grand Lagoon Yacht Club, 443
Grant, Ulysses S., 31
Gray, Edna, 213
Gray, Gilbert T., 173, 175, 177, 180, 181, 187-91, 223, 230, 232, 238, 272, 496
Grevemberg, Al, 349
Grevemberg, Chip, 349
Grevemberg, Pat, 367
Griswold, Jack, 253
Grunewald, Theodore, 138, 141
Grunewald Cup, 95
Grusich, Captain Wilfred A., Sr., perpetual memorial trophy, 366
Guest, Peggy, 490
Gulf Ocean Racing Circuit, 416
Gulf One-Design fleet, 202, 221-22, 344-45
Gulf Yachting Association, 124-126, 166, 257-58, 337, 343; and Bay-Waveland Yacht Club, 463; and Buccaneer Yacht Club, 428; and Cypremort Yacht Club, 453; and Fairhope Yacht Club, 430; and Fort Walton Yacht Club, 442; and Grand Lagoon Yacht Club, 443; and Gulfport Yacht Club, 477; and Lake Arthur Yacht Club, 455; and New Orleans Yacht Club, 457; and Pass Christian Yacht Club, 489; and St. Andrews Bay Yacht Club, 447; and St. Petersburg Yacht Club, 449; and Tammany Yacht Club, 459

Gulfport to Panama City race, 222
Gulfport to Pensacola race, 351-52; 1955, 267; 1956, 272; 1958, 281; 1961, 292; 1963, 300; 1965, 308; 1971, 347; 1982, 392-94; 1983, 401; 1985, 418
Gulfport Yacht Club, 75-77, 404, 474-83
Gumbo regatta, 455

Haase, Rip, 237, 353
Hadden, Cal F., 120, 123, 141
Hadden, Cal F., Jr., 238, 300, 314, 331, 333, 378, 385-86, 391, 397-98, 402
Hadden, Cal, trophy, 175
Hadden, Corky, 413
Half Moon, 146
Hamilton, W. E., 494
Hamilton, Will R., 130
Hampton, Jeff, 354
Handicap Class, 300, 317, 414-15
Harbor of SYC, 224
Hardie, William T., 223
Hardin, Harry S., Jr., 230
Hardy, Robert, 185
Harmsworth trophy, 127-28
Harris, Tommy, 407
Hartson, Joan, 362
Hartson, Maurice J., III, 257, 301, 320, 339, 340, 380-81, 421
Harvey, Eldon, III, 395, 397
Haslam, Tommy, 331
Havana to Varadero Beach race, 285
Hayward, James D., 158
Hayward, James D., Jr., 162
Healy, George W., 337-38
Heaslip, James, 241-42
Heaslip, Samuel F., 39, 69, 72, 88, 90, 91, 96, 100, 488

Heavy Metal, 421
Heffron, Lawrence, 291
Heidenheim, I., 469
Herbst, William, 341
Heriot trophy, 318
Herndon, G. O., 59
Hero, Alvin, 198
Herreshoff, Nathanael, 45, 183-84, 494
Herreshoff, Nathanael G., trophy, 184, 452
Hertz, John, Jr., 255
Hewes, Finley B., 208-09, 236, 481
Hickok, Dan, 11, 12, 13
Higgins, Darrell, 339
Higgins, Leslie, 367
Hill, Harry W., 14
Hinderman, Franz, 158
Hinmann, George R., trophy, 395
Hobson, Ed, 275, 283, 303
Hobson, Mrs. W. E., III, 253
Hoefeld, Julia, 175
Hoefeld, Maude, 175
Hogan, Bill, 285, 292
Hogan, M. H., 192
Hogan, Moreland H., 265
Hogan, William H., 291
Holly, Nicholas, 488
Hopkins, A. S., 478, 479, 480
Hopkins, George, 197
Hopkins, George P., Jr., 481
Hopkins, Commodore Arvah S., memorial trophy, 482
Hotel Pitcher, 7
Houston Yacht Club, 92, 283, 493-99. See also Ragnot, the
Howard, Charles T., 35, 37
Howard, Charles T., Challenge Cup, 35, 40
Howard, D. Douglas, 301
Howard, Harry L., 101-02
Howard, Harry T., 129, 145
Hughes, Ann, 361-62
Hughes, Lee, 346
Humphreys, W. O., 109, 170, 171
Hurley, Dan, 301

SOUTHERN YACHT CLUB

Hurricanes: 1893, 48-49; 1906, 91; 1915, 100; 1916, 101-02; Betsy, 311, 473; Carla, 281, 498; Camille, 254-55, 335-36, 466, 473, 482, 491; Elena, 419
Hute, C. E., 444

Ibs, Bill, Jr., 345, 350
Ibs, William, 334
Ida Q, 158-60
Indra V, 356-57, 365
Industrial Canal, 145
Intercollegiate Hall of Fame, 413
Interstate regatta, 33-34
Invader, 69, 70, 83
Isaack, Brian, 257
Isaacks, Leonard, 261
Islen, Adrien, III, 158
Isler, Peter, 395

Jackson Yacht Club, 483-87
Jacksonville Yacht Club, 56
Jacob, Horace B., 223
Jacobs, Melody, 367
Jahncke, Adele Townsend, 145
Jahncke, Barton, 289, 311, 318, 319, 322, 328-331, 334, 498
Jahncke, Barton, Jr., 418
Jahncke, Edward B., 218-19, 223, 224, 284, 360, 374, 384
Jahncke, Ernest Lee, 90, 91, 98, 100, 101, 102, 111, 120, 148, 149, 154, 156, 165, 169, 189, 288
Jahncke, Ernest Lee, trophy, 217; 1939, 218; 1970, 345
Jahncke, Fritz, 57, 136
Jahncke, Paul, Jr., 169
Jahncke, Stanton, 85, 148, 156
Jahncke series: 1960, 286-87; 1979, 374; 1983, 403
James, Michael, 418

James, Nathalie, 417
Janin, James A., 238
Janssen, James, 398
Janvier, George, 418
Jazz, 108, 111, 135. *See also* Six and seven-eighths band
Jennings, John, 278, 345, 452
Johnson, Thomas H., 444
Jones, C. M., 443
Jones, Connie, 237, 241
Jones, Jenny, trophy, 455
Jones, Joseph T., 475
Jones, Richard G., 235, 240, 279, 296
Jones, Commodore Richard G., perpetual trophy, 279, 284, 313
Journalists. *See* Reporters
Jubilee (at Mobile Bay), 74
Junior championships: U.S. Doublehanded, 395. *See also* Flying Scot Junior North American Championship; Governor's Cup of California; Junior Lipton Cup; Junior North American Sailing Championship; Laser II Class Junior Mid-Winter National Championship; McCloskey Junior trophy; National Sea Explorer Sailing Championship; Penguin Class International Championship for Juniors; Penguin Class Junior National Championship; Sears, Commodore Herbert S., Cup; Youth, U.S., Championship; Youth, World's Championship
Junior Division of SYC, 19, 192, 229, 288-89, 293, 320; in 1937, 209; in 1947, 240; in 1952, 257; in 1953, 261; in 1962, 297; in 1976, 361; in 1977, 366; in 1982, 396; in 1983, 406. *See also* Junior championships;

Junior Lipton Cup; Junior regattas
Junior Lipton Cup, 229; 1941, 229; 1942, 229; 1950, 448; 1956, 273; 1959, 285; 1960, 289; 1962, 442; 1964, 306; 1970, 346; 1974, 354; 1977, 367; 1978, 370; 1982, 396; 1983, 406; 1985, 418
Junior North American Sailing Championship, 264; 1967, 321; 1969, 339. *See also* Sears, Commodore Herbert S., Cup
Junior regattas, 229; 1932, 192; 1933, 192-93; 1951, 253; 1962, 297
Justice, Charles, Jr., 229

Kahle, Reichard, 197, 297
Kahn, Robert, 358, 372
Kammer, Bobby, 302
Kathleen trophy, 322
Keating, Thomas, 413
Keep, Edward H., 92, 98, 124
Keefe, Wm. B., 130
Keenan, Bayne, 306
Keenan, Burt, 253, 371, 372-73, 376, 418, 454
Keenan, Peter, 355
Keenan, Walter C., Jr., 196, 238, 241
Keller, Dan, 370
Kennedy, J. J., 468
Kennedy, John F., 231
Kennedy, John F., Memorial Regatta, 347
Kent, Peter Lorillard, trophy, 222
Kerner, Louis, 292
Kerrigan, Jack, 490
Kershaw, Thomas, 17
Killeen, Daniel B., 253, 302, 369, 370, 371
Killeen, Daniel B., Jr., 370, 377, 379, 380-81, 395, 419
Killeen, Joseph L., Jr., 240, 310, 322

Index 513

Killeen, Nora, 377
Killeen, Robert, Jr., 370
Killeen, Shawn, 354, 366, 370, 377-78, 397
Killeen, Thomas, 284
Kimbrell, Donald K., 439
Kinabrew, John M., 163, 175, 176, 180
Kitsey, 114
Knarr Class, 291
Knickerbocker Club, 13
Knost, Bernard, 264, 489-90
Knost, Commodore Bernard, trophy: 489-90, 492; 1938, 213; 1958, 282; 1971, 446
Knost, Commodore Bernard, and Southern Women's Championship, 264, 489-90
Koerner, John E., Jr., 272
Koerner, Louis, 223, 293
Koerner, Louis, Jr., 311
Koerner, Peggy, 280
Kohler, Claude, 275, 290
Kolius, John, 498
Krievel, Bob, 400
Kuebel, Conrad, Jr., 377-78
Kuebel, Joseph, 382

La Rochelle to New Orleans Tricentennial race, 386-91
Laan, Cyril, 355
Labouisse, Peter, 81, 83, 488
Ladies committee of SYC, 250, 323
Ladies' Day luncheons, 106, 117
Ladies of Pass Christian trophy, 9-10
Lady Emma, 51, 113
Lady of the Lyon Boat Club, 13
"Lafayette Square Yacht Club," 337-38
Lake Arthur Boat Club, 139-40
Lake Arthur Junior Championship regatta, 455
Lake Arthur Yacht Club, 454-55

Lake Charles Yacht Club, 139-40, 455-56
Lake Pontchartrain, 2, 13-15; regattas on, 11, 39, 107
Lake Pontchartrain Causeway, 249, 277
Lampe, Henry, 486
Landry, Alfred F., 85
LaPeyce, Steve, 494
Laser Class: Mid-Winter championship, 404; World championship, 404
Laser II: Junior Mid-Winter National championship, 406; National championship, 417
Lawrence, B. U., 457
Lazara, Vince, 358
Leach, Katherine, 291
Leary, Prieur, 401, 413, 416
LeBlanc, Beau, 395, 412, 417, 419
LeBlanc, J. Dwight, 269, 285, 327
LeBlanc, J. Dwight, III, 370, 419
LeBlanc, Mark, 321, 334, 339, 343-44, 347, 354
LeBlanc, Miranne, 367
LeBlanc, Tom, 340
LeBoutillier, William, 260
Leche, Richard W., 203, 210
Lehleitner, George, 223
Lehon, Dan, 293
Leonard, Earnest J., 463
Leverich, Edward B., 229
Leverich, W. E., 15
Levert, Edward L., 300
Levert, Weese, 300
Levey, Bruce, 406, 417
Lewis, A. M., 448
Libano, Andrew, 189-91
Lido Class, 300
Lightning Class, 236, 302; Association, 236; International championship, 267-69; Midwinter Championship regatta, (1948) 451, (1957) 279; North American Championship series, 345-46
Lillian C, 73

Limbraugh, Jay, 279
Limbraugh, Helen, 279
Lipton Board of Appeal, 252
Lipton, Sir Thomas J., 116, 121, 122-23, 138-39, 143, 173-74, 181-82
Lipton, Sir Thomas J., Cup Regatta, 252; 1920, 124, 444; 1921, 139; 1922, 143; 1925, 158; 1926, 172, 450; 1929, 176; 1930, 181; 1932, 187; 1933, 194; 1934, 428; 1936, 496-97; 1937, 212, 445, 471; 1938, 223; 1941, 230; 1942, 232; 1943, 233; 1944, 233; 1946, 236; 1948, 481; 1949, 246; 1952, 451; 1955, 481; 1959, 285; 1965, 310; 1966, 310; 1969, 336, 339; 1974, 354; 1976, 360; 1982, 397; 1983, 407; 1984, 413; 1985, 418-19. See also Junior Lipton Cup
Lipton, Sir Thomas J., trophy, 122-23, 174, 240
Livaudais, Frank, 293
Locofoco Club, 13
Long, Huey P., 180
Lopez, Jay, 473
Lorber, Gus, 293
Lorber, J. F. A., Jr., 227, 304
Lorber, Janet, 253, 263, 264, 405, 490
Lorber, Janet, memorial trophy, 417
Lorelei, 254-55
Lormand, Edward, 455
Lott, Gus, 381
Lovell, Andy, 396, 413, 418
Lovell, Johnny, 396, 413, 417
Luder (L-16) Class, 239-40, 275; International championship, (1960) 289, (1962) 296-97, (1963) 302, (1965) 311, (1974) 353, (1982) 395, (1983) 407; National championship

(1966), 319; World series (1957), 278-79
Luzenberg, Chandler C., 105, 106

Machado, George, 306
Maestri, Robert S., 220
Maginnis, Arthur A., 35, 36
Magnolia Yacht Club, 431
Mahoney, Art, 291
Makaroff, Vadim, 201
Maid Marion Cup, 148
Mallory, Clifford D., 164-66, 422
Mallory, Clifford D., Cup, 259-60; 1952, 260; 1953, 260-61; 1954, 261-62; 1960, 288; 1964, 305, 311; 1971, 498; 1975, 359; 1984, 413. See also Men's North American Sailing Championship
Malone, Eugene, 436
Manchester, 91. See also *Seawanhaka*
Mandeville Yacht Club, 56
Manion, Charles, 223
Mardi Gras regatta: 1952, 255; 1970, 336
Marine Marathon bronze plaque, 341
Mariner's trophy: 1980, 379; 1982, 395; 1983, 410; 1984, 417
Marshal, Henry S., 301
Martinez, Harry, 378-79
Massachusetts, 91-92
Mauldin, Fred, 314
May, Elizabeth, 253
Mayhew, Peyson, 342-43
McClellan, A. W., 141
McClellan, C. W., 223
McClellan, Charles W., 301
McCloskey Junior trophy, 417
McClure, Allen, Jr., 261, 262, 270, 275, 284, 290
McClure, Robert C., 106
McDermott, Leo, 489
McDonald, John, 196
McKinney, Judy Reeves, 378

McMasters, L. L., 255-56
McMillan, Oscar, 308, 322
McNair, Steve, 419
Meade, Charles, 412
Meade, John, 401, 412, 418
Medical manual for skippers, 27
Meigs, Clifford H., 439
Meigs regatta, 442
Melges, Buddy, 348
Mellin, Gilbert M., 301, 341
Memorial Day regatta at SYC, 411
Menge, J. H., Jr., 67, 488
Menge, Sidney L., Jr., 229
Men's North American Sailing Championship, 260-61; 1953, 260-61; 1954, 262-63; 1964, 305; 1970, 345; 1975, 359; 1984, 413. See also Mallory, Clifford D., Cup
Meric, Tommy, 364, 395, 410
Merrick, Charles, 490
Merrifield, John, 278
Meteor, 50
Miami to Nassau race, 285
Mid-Winter Sports Association, 416-17
Miller, Elizabeth, 214-16. See also Robin, Elizabeth Miller
Miller, W. Milton, 114, 147, 158
Milliken, Richard, 19
Milling, Robert, 265
Mire, Richard, Jr., 453
Miss New Orleans, 127
Mississippi Coast Yachting Association, 465
Mississippi Valley Power Boat Association, 142
Mitchell, Finley, 124
Mitchell, W. L., 444
Mobile Bay Cruising Association, 437
Mobile Bay Dauphin Island Racing Association, 437
Mobile Yacht Club, 56, 338, 378, 431-47
Molony, Larry, 283

Molony, Tim, 392-94
Montauk, 40, 59
Montgomery Hotel, 3
Moody, Fairfax, 496
Moorman, M., 59
Moran, Kenneth, 361, 370
Moran, W. Garic, 292, 320, 370
Morencovitch, J., 39
Morgan, George T., 443
Morgan, Henry S., 258
Morgan 34 Class, 327
Morphy, Clifford, 238
Morphy, Regina, 93
Mosbacher, Emil, Jr., 285
Mosbacher, Robert, 288, 304, 319
Mossy, Roy, 320
Motor boat cruises, 118-19
Motor Yacht Association, 320, 326
Murphy, Paul, 395
Muther, Al, 291

Naphtha-powered boats, 46, 55
Nash, D. A., 66, 468
National Sea Explorer Sailing Championship, 367
National Sports Festival, 419
Neese, Don, 347
Nelson, Craig, 289, 293, 297, 311
Nelson, Kent, 284
Nelson, Robert, 291
Nemec, Frank, 273, 289
Nepenthe, 40, 43-44, 50
Nereus, 43
New Basin Canal, 14, 135-37
Newman, Morris, 296, 418
Newman, Randy, 454
New Orleans, 63
New Orleans, 90
New Orleans to Biloxi race, 266
New Orleans Yacht Club, 258, 306, 456-58
Newsletters of SYC, 253-54
New York Yacht Club, 2, 422

Index 515

Nicholson, Leonard, 69-70, 96
Nicholson, Yorke, 69-70
Normann, Barrett, 412
Normann, Flurry, 396, 406, 417, 419
Normann, Robert, 418
North American Yacht Racing Union, 164-66, 258-60
North, Lowell, 345
North-South race, 279; 1961, 293; 1962, 296; 1978, 369-70
Northrop, Guy, 489
Nugon, A. J., 300, 301, 308
Nydia, 55, 59, 62, 71
Nye, Harry G., Jr., 229

O'Brien, Emile J., 25, 27, 29, 34, 38, 39, 41, 66, 67, 75, 83, 90, 475
Observer/Europe Single-Handed Transatlantic Race, 413, 459
O'Day, George, trophy: 1984, 413; 1985, 419
Odendahl, Paul, 274, 304
Odenheimer, Elizabeth S., 175
O'Donnell, Herbert, 339, 348, 350, 365
O'Donnell, Lawrence, 53, 54, 90, 176
Oetking, Curt, 395
Offshore Challenge Cup, 401
Ogden, R. G., 26
Old Timers regatta, 339
Olsen, T. Hoffman, 129
Olympic Class regatta, 303
Olympic Games, 186-90; 1956, 275; 1960, 289-90; 1968, 309, 327-331; 1976, 363-64; 1980, 377-78; 1984, 412
Olympic Sailing Association of SYC, 309, 363
Opening regatta of SYC: 1881, 35; 1882, 36; 1888, 41; 1903, 73; 1912, 96; 1914, 99; 1917, 106; 1918, 108; 1919, 111;

1923, 145; 1926, 163; 1928, 174; 1930, 180; 1932, 185; 1934, 196; 1936, 202; 1939, 221-22; 1940, 226; 1946, 239; 1962, 295-96; 1964, 304; 1968, 325; 1969, 334; 1974, 353; 1976, 360; 1982, 386; 1983, 402; 1984, 411
Optimist: National Sailing championship, 411; World championship, 396
Osprey, 355-56
Overton, Ed, 125, 139, 196, 203, 431
Overton, Marion, 144

Pagelson, E. N., 447
Paisant, John, 324
Pan-American Games, 268
Pan-American regatta, 238-39
Parade of boats. *See* Boat parade and fleet review
Pardee, Barbara Tolson, 345. *See also* Tolson, Barbara
Pardee, James L., 345, 452
Parham, W. H., 139
Parker, John M., 99
Parties at SYC, 8, 129, 134-35, 172, 242, 345; junior division, 230, 293; "Mexico Night," 399; "rock party," 250-51; "Stars of Hollywood," 223. *See also* "Bards of the Bilges" Ball; Ladies Day luncheons; Subscription dances
Pascagoula to Key West race: 1984, 416; 1985, 421
Pass Christian, 2-3
Pass Christian, Ladies of, trophy, 8-9
Pass Christian Yacht Club, 77-79, 186, 273, 306, 487-92
Patrol boat of SYC, 224
Payzant, Arthur, 327, 347
"Pen," the, 81, 205, 224, 398

Penguin Class, 265, 286, 340; International championship, (1954) 264, (1955) 273, (1962) 297; International Junior championship, (1953) 261, (1960) 286, (1964) 306; International Ladies championship, (1956) 272-73; National championship, (1960) 286
Penick, William, 305
Pensacola Cup, 308
Pensacola to St. Petersburg race, 308
Pensacola Yacht Club, 56, 124, 144, 443-46
Pericola, Frank, 378
Pershing, John J., 116
Phelan, Paul, 309
Phelps, William T., 483
Phillippi, Yvonne, 185
Picayune (boat), 69-70
Picayune, The (newspaper), 204
Pickich, Mike, 306
Pimental, Andy, 404
Pinac, Edward, 138
Pinac, Edwin G., 85, 158
Pinac, James, 273
Polasek, Edward, 293
Pollak, Christopher W., 359
Pollak, Lewis B., Sr., 308
Polly, Captain, trophy, 293
Pontchartrain Beach, 205-06
Pontchartrain Rowing Club, 137
Poole, Mildred, 138
Porteous, Douglas, 163
Porteous, William A., Jr., 124, 158
Porter, George, 483
Porter, J. M., 227
Porter, Richard, 483
Portsmouth Class, 341
Potts, Corkey, 346
Potts, Johnny, 339, 346, 354
Potts, Pearson, 339, 354
Powerboats, 44, 111, 114, 126-28, 230, 442; regatta, (1940) 227. *See also* "Eastward Ho!" cruise;

Fox-Garic Predicted Log race; Motor boat cruises; Southern Marine Marathon; Southern Power Boat Association; Southland Sweepstakes; Speedboats
Power Boat Division of SYC, 335
Prados, Cliff, 202, 238
Pratt, Gerald, Jr., 209
"President of Mexico" trophy, 308, 346
President's Cup regatta, 267-69
Press Race: 1968, 332; 1981, 382-84; 1983, 407
Press reporters. *See* Reporters
Prince of Wales trophy, 350
Princess, 149. *See also Cinderella; Robin Hood IV*
Provensal, Catherine, 253
Provensal, Sidney W., Jr., 313, 320

Race for the case, 308
Race of Champions: 1936, 1937, 1938, 1939, 199; 1960, 290; 1963, 1964, 306; 1969, 340; 1979, 371; 1982, 398; 1984, 416
Race to Mandeville, 290
Race to Pensacola, 101-02
"Race to the Coast": 1850, 12-13; 1904, 81; 1928, 174; 1965, 308; 1985, 418
Race Week: 207-08; 1946, 237; 1955, 266-67
Races. *See* names of races
Ragnot, The, 498
Rareshide, H., 6
Rau, J. Eblen, 157, 169, 203, 223, 236
Ravannack, J. Ben, 85, 137, 138, 150, 174
Ravannack, Walle, 150
Rawlins, Bonnie, 361
Rawlins, John A., 59, 83, 87, 129
Rawlins, Mrs. John A., 89

Rawlins, Philip, 418
Rea, James, 164
Rees, Al, 454
Reeves, Judy, 368
Reeves, William, 336
Regata al sol: 1965, 307-08; 1966, 314-17; 1967, 320-21; 1968, 326; 1969, 332-33; 1971, 346-47; 1973, 350; 1975, 358; 1977, 365-66; 1979, 371-72; 1981, 380-82; 1983, 399-401
Regata de Amigos, 498
Regattas, 2, 12, 20, 114, 241; of Gulfport Yacht Club, 75; of Mobile Yacht Club, 432. *See also* names of regattas
Regulations, 164-66
Reine, Mrs. C. E., 89
Reporters, 130, 204, 378-79. *See also* Press Race
Resolute, 426-27
Retif, Al, 227
Reynolds, George, 326
Reynolds, Hampton, 205
Rhodes 19 Class, 301; National championship, (1965, 1966, 1967) 431, (1968) 327, (1972) 349-50, (1980) 377, (1984) 412
Ricciuti, William, 230
Rice, Frazier, 355
Richards, Julian, 269, 415
Riess, F. Keller, 401
Rifley, George W., 451
Riis, Erling, trophy, 448
Roberts, A. R., 124
Roberts, Harold, 236
Robertson, A. R., 488
Robin, Elizabeth Miller, 265. *See also* Miller, Elizabeth
Robin Hood IV, 150. *See also Cinderella; Princess*
Robinson, J. G., 10, 18, 25
"Rocking Chair Fleet," 64-65, 84
Roesler, Bob, 382-83
Rogers, George, III, 421
Rolex Swan World Cup, 416

Rolling, Henry, 230
Roosevelt Cup, 89-90
Roosevelt, Franklin D., 210
Roosevelt, Theodore, 99
Roth, Bill, 366
Rotureau, Marge, 445
"Round the Lake" race, 222-23, 458-59
Roux, Henry, 489
Rowing, 137
Royal Canadian Yacht Club, 302
Royal St. Lawrence Dragon regatta, 311
Rudolf, William, 229
Rules. *See* Regulations
Russell, Kent, 334
Rutland, Hubert, III, 452
Ryan, John, 261

St. Andrews Bay Yacht Club, 447-48
St. Augustine Yacht Club, 56
St. Charles Hotel, 12
St. Petersburg to Fort Lauderdale race, 317
St. Petersburg to Havana race, 178-79; 1930, 176, 450; 1931, 179; 1932, 184; 1936, 200-01; 1948, 242; 1952, 255-56, 451; 1958, 280-81; 1959, 284
St. Petersburg to Venice race, 342-43
St. Petersburg Yacht Club, 448-52
Salzar, Al, 241, 291
"Salty Sisters," 452
Sampsell, L. D., 3, 56, 66, 67
Sanchez, Albert, 158
"Sandbaggers," 33-34, 46
Santa Cruz, Randy, 412
Sandy, John, 451
Sauer, Walter, 223
Saunders, A. L., 9
Scamp, 61-62
Scheib, Commodore J. Gilbert trophy; 1964, 306; 1969, 339; 1978, 370
Scheib, Flo, 405

Index

Scheib, J. Gilbert, 70, 166, 184, 223, 231, 232, 240, 250, 259, 269, 272, 278, 333, 379-80, 485
Scheib, J. Gilbert, Jr., 257, 270, 417
Schimek, Robert, Jr., 360
Schiro, Vic, 308
Schmitt, Godfrey, 186
Schneidau, Baron von, 66
Schoen, Mrs. Paul, 446
Schoonmaker, Dean, 354
Schowe, Louis, 451
Schreck, Carol, 361
Schreck, Eleanor, 358
Schreck, Gerald, 285, 310, 318, 319, 322, 328-31, 347, 350, 498
Schreck, Paul, 268, 291, 358
Schroeder, Armond, 242
Scooler, M., 56
Scooler Cup, 55
Scott, Dale, 446
Sears, Commodore Herbert S., Cup, 259; 1954, 264; 1957, 278; 1967, 321; 1969, 499; 1970, 499; 1972, 486, 499; 1977, 366. *See also* Junior North American Sailing Championship
Seaver, Arthur, Jr., 284, 311
Seaver, Arthur, III, 311, 360
Seawanhaka, 91-92, 98. *See also Manchester*
Seawanhaka International Challenge Cup, 91
Seawanhaka Yacht Club, 322
Seemann, Coco, 213, 257, 263, 264, 490
Seemann, William, III, 253, 257, 261, 265, 273, 285, 288, 290, 301
Sewell, Jane, 334
Shaughnessy, Clark, 137
Sheldon, Barbara, 263
Shelton, Mrs. Kenneth, 16
Sheppard, Dan, 444
Sheppard, Lucy, 446
Sheppard, Oscar, 444

Sherar, William, 327
Sherman, W. C., 447
Sherman, Ed, Jr., 452
Shields, Cornelius, 260, 311
Shields, Cornelius, Jr., 260, 311
Shreveport Yacht Club, 258
Simoneaux, Peter, 346
"Six and seven-eighths" band, 111
Skates, 81
Skipperettes, 138, 144, 193, 212, 223, 253; regattas of SYC, (1932) 185-86, (1935) 198-99, (1937) 209-10, (1951) 253, (1952) 257, (1976) 361-63, (1977) 367; regattas of Pensacola Yacht Club, 444. *See also* Knost, Commodore Bernard, trophy; Lorber, Janet, memorial trophy; Women
Smith, Bob, 296
Smith, Chuck, 445
Smith, Jerry, 346-47
Smith, Kyle, 379, 409
Smith, Rufus, 497
Smith, Willliam, Jr., 321
Smythe, Tony, 397
Soling Class, 334-35; National championship, (1969) 334, (1982) 396; Southern District championship, (1969) 334
Sommers, Larry, 458
Soniat, G. Leon, 110
Sonnier, Gerard, 354
Sonnier, Greg, 395
Sonnier, Scott, 406, 419
Sorceress, 149
Sorceress II, 150
Souchon, Edmond, 110
Southerly, 354-55
Southern Gulf Coast Yachting Association, 66-67, 433; annual meetings, (1902) 72, (1903) 74, (1904) 82; and Gulfport Yacht Club, 474; summer circuit, (1902) 73
Southern Marine Marathon,

97, 130, 141-42, 225
Southern Mayors' championship sailboat race, 308
Southern Ocean Racing Circuit: 1966, 317; 1973, 350; 1974, 355-56; 1979, 372-73; 1980, 376
Southern Power Boat Association, 158
Southern Yacht Club: adoption of name, 4; first meeting, 3-4; founders, 3-4; incorporation, 198; objectives, 4; summer camp, 405
Southern Yacht Club Gold Challenge Cup, 10
Southern Yacht Club Motor Yacht Association, 319-20
Southern Yacht Club *Waltz, the*, 93
Southland Sweepstakes, 450
Spang, Henry, 237, 273
Spangenberg, Richard G., 307, 371-72, 376, 380
Speedboats, 96. *See also* Powerboats
Sperry, Mike, 339
Sporl, Cyprian A., 141, 186
Sporl, Cyprian A., Jr., 239, 280, 284
Sporl, Harold, 239
Springertam, S., 426
Stannus, George R., 471
Star Class, 154-57, 171, 186-90, 237, 310, 353, 378, 436; International Association, 155; International championship, (1925) 154-57, (1926) 169-71, (1928) 175, (1929) 177-78; Lipton Cup, 173; Mid-Winter series, (1926) 161, (1927) 173, (1933) 191; Spring series, (1939) 215-20, (1960) 286-87, (1962) 296, (1970) 345, (1974) 353, (1979) 374-75, (1983) 402-03; World championship, (1930) 181, (1938) 214, (1983) 404

Stearns, Richard, 287, 296
Stieffel, Cindy, 368
Stieffel, Dennis, 398, 412
Stieffel, Rod, 412
Stine, Bob, 431
Story, Sidney, 18
Streetman, Sam, Sr., 494
Strum, Al D., 450, 451
Subscription dances, 107
Sudduth, E. W., 439
Sudduth, H. L., 447
Sugar Bowl Race of Champions. See Race of Champions
Sugar Bowl Regatta, 200; 1934, 198; 1935, 198; 1960, 290-91; 1964, 303; 1969, 340, 481-82; 1979, 371; 1982, 397-98; 1984, 416
Sullivan, Nancy, 367
Sully, Thomas, 45, 50, 59
Sully Cup, 46, 55, 141
Sunfish Class: Mid-Winter championship, (1982) 397; North American championship, (1980) 377; Women's North American championship, (1983) 404
Susie B., 40, 41, 59, 61, 67-68, 70, 80, 82
Sustendal, George, 273
Sutter, Donald, 481
Sutter, Fred, 490
Swain, Harry, 230
Szymanske, Ignatius, 19

Taggart, Larry, Jr., 361, 395, 418
Taggart, Tommy, 370, 418
Talbott, Pamela, 360
Tamm, Emma, 144
Tammany Yacht Club, 458-59
Tawanta, 54
Taylor, Eugene, 258
Taylor, Peggy, 352, 417
Taylor, Mary Virginia, 214, 215
Tchefuncte River race, 277
Team racing, 395. See also Fort Worth Boat Club; North-South race; Scheib, Commodore J. Gilbert, trophy; Seawanhaka Yacht Club; USYRU team racing championship
Tell-Tale, 253
Terrell, Gary, 273
Terrell, J. W., 490
Tessier, Charles A., 179-80, 191-92, 193, 194
Tessier, Commodore Charles J., plaque, 297
Tessier, Commodore Charles A., trophy, (1963) 302, (1972) 349, (1980) 379, (1982) 395
Testimonial Banquet of SYC, 371
Texas Yachting Association, 498
Tharpe, Alfred, 175, 185, 192
Thompson, Clark, Jr., 486, 499
Thompson, Glenn, 499
Thompson, Paul, 486, 499
Thompson, Robert Fulton, 483
Three-quarter-ton World's championship, 354
Tiare, 320, 346, 380-82
Times-Picayune, The. See *Picayune, The*
Todd, James, 477
Todd, Robert B., 86, 185
Toler, Roger, 498
Tolson, Barbara, 452. See also Pardee, Barbara Tolson
Tolson, Ted, 184, 452
Tonizzo, Luis, 414, 459
Torbert, Tom, 431
Tormentor, 51
Toutsy, 33
Tradewind trophy, 237
Tranchina-Oliviera Cup, 55
Treen, J. Paul, 237
Trenchard, Tom, 418
Troendle, Roy, Jr., 276, 287, 291, 306, 327, 355
Troendle, Roy, Sr., 301, 305, 339
Troendle, Roy, Sr., trophy, 370
Trophies. See names of trophies
Tulane Sailing Club, 289
Tulane University, 71, 289
Tullis, Garner H., 9, 164, 176, 178, 180, 184-85, 195, 198, 217, 223, 226, 227-28, 242, 256-57, 272, 289, 320
Tullis, Garner H., trophy, 222
"Tullissippi Cruising Class," 257
Turner, Ted, 288, 317
21-footers, 148-51

Uncle Roy trophy, 406
United States International Sailing Association, 290
United States Yacht Racing Union (USYRU), 422; Men's Single-handed championship, 419; Team Racing championship, 394
Uniforms, 28
Universal Rule. See Regulations
Upton, Ben L., 301
Urania, 75, 83

Vagabond, 272
Valley, Jack, 350
Vanadis, 342-43
Vanderveer trophy, 404
von Hutschler, Walter, 214, 215

Wadewitz, Otto, 430
Wagner, William, 292
Walet, Eugene H., Jr., 261
Walet, Eugene H., III, 255, 260-61, 262, 267, 268, 270, 275, 279, 290, 300, 354, 358, 361
Walet, Sheila, 367
Walker, H. J., 199

Walker, Joseph A., 46
Walker Cup, 46
Walker, Queley, 192
Wall, William J., 436
Walthers, William, 124, 444
Washington Club, 13
Waters, Arthur S., 236
Watson, Douglas, 470
Watson, J. C., 443
Wave Boat Club, 13
Wayne, Bryan, 291
Weatherhead, Roland E., 443
Weatherly, Bubba, 355
Weatherly, Leslie, 404, 482
Webb, Judy, 263
Weinfurter, Alvin J., 230
Weise, Hanse, 214
Wennerlund, Jan, 485
West End, 30-31, 204-06
West End to Biloxi race, 236-37
West End to the Mississippi Gulf Coast race, 377
Wharton-Davies, E. H., 85
White, Hugh, 203, 211
White, Gerald Taylor, 167-69
Whitehurst, Bob, 359
Whitley, Drew, 331
Whitlock, Bache, 241, 281, 308, 322, 351-52
William, Danny, 499
Williams, Johnny, 297
Williams, Lynn, 287, 296
Williams, Paul, 451
Williams, W. Horace, Jr., 295
Williwaw, 310, 322
Wilson, John, 332
Wilson, Woodrow, 98
Wimoweh, 355
Windjammer, The (publication), 498

Windjammer trophy, 217, 229, (1960) 286, (1964) 304, (1966) 319, (1968) 327, (1971) 347, (1979) 374
Windmill Class, 327; International championship, 346
Winston, Barbee, 302
Wirth, Fred, 289
Wirth, Harold, 223
Witherill, Dave, 194, 444
Witherill, Ruth, 444
Wolfe, Jackye, 291, 293
Women, 41, 43-44, 84, 213, 377, 389, 471-72, 489-90. *See also* Adams, Mrs. Charles Francis, Cup; All-girl crew; All-girl regatta; Knost, Commodore Bernard, trophy; Florida Women's Sailing Association; Penguin International Ladies Championship; Skipperettes; Sunfish Women's North American championship; Women's Israel perpetual trophy; Women's North American Sailing Championship
Women's Israel perpetual trophy, 297
Women's North American Sailing Championship: 1956, 273; 1973, 352; 1980, 378. *See also* Adams, Mrs. Charles Francis, Cup
Wood, A. Baldwin, 71
Wood, Baldwin, regatta, 288
Wood, F. B., 447
Woodward, M. Truman, 223

World War I, 105, 108-9, 110-11, 115-16, 142
World War II: and SYC, 230-33, 243; and Buccaneer Yacht Club, 428; and Biloxi Yacht Club, 472; and Gulfport Yacht Club, 480
Wray, Jane, 451
Wright, Peter, 403
Wuescher, Carrie, 84
Wuescher, Davis, 62, 90, 93, 181, 186, 196, 198, 221, 280
Wuescher, Peter, 370
Wynne, Arthur D., 284, 291, 339, 359, 365, 407
Wynne, Arthur, Jr., 418
Wynn, Miles, 322

Xiphias, 93

Yacht Club Challenge Cup, 410
Yankee Bos'n, 253
Yellow fever, 16, 89
Youd, Carol Fae, 446
Young, Dave, 227, 238
Young, O. J., 326, 334, 350, 354, 356, 376, 458
Young, Robbie, 370
Youth, Interscholastic Yacht Racing Association National championship, regatta, 413; U.S., championship, 370; World's championship in 420s, 358-359

Zemurray, Doris, 175
Ziegler, Ernest, 227
Ziegler, Robert, 246

www.ingramcontent.com/pod-product-compliance
Lightning Source LLC
Chambersburg PA
CBHW030328240426
43661CB00052B/1567